T0281499

Lecture Notes in Computer Science   14394

The series Lecture Notes in Computer Science (LNCS), including its subseries Lecture Notes in Artificial Intelligence (LNAI) and Lecture Notes in Bioinformatics (LNBI), has established itself as a medium for the publication of new developments in computer science and information technology research, teaching, and education.

LNCS enjoys close cooperation with the computer science R & D community, the series counts many renowned academics among its volume editors and paper authors, and collaborates with prestigious societies. Its mission is to serve this international community by providing an invaluable service, mainly focused on the publication of conference and workshop proceedings and postproceedings. LNCS commenced publication in 1973.

Jonghye Woo · Alessa Hering · Wilson Silva ·
Xiang Li · Huazhu Fu et al.
Editors

Medical Image Computing and Computer Assisted Intervention – MICCAI 2023 Workshops

MTSAIL 2023, LEAF 2023, AI4Treat 2023, MMMI 2023
REMIA 2023, Held in Conjunction with MICCAI 2023
Vancouver, BC, Canada, October 8–12, 2023
Proceedings

 Springer

Editors
Jonghye Woo
Harvard Medical School
Massachusetts General Hospital
Boston, MA, USA

Alessa Hering
Radboud University Nijmegen Medical Center
Nijmegen, The Netherlands

Wilson Silva (iD)
The Netherlands Cancer Institute
Amsterdam, The Netherlands

Xiang Li (iD)
Harvard Medical School
Massachusetts General Hospital
Boston, MA, USA

Huazhu Fu (iD)
A*STAR
Institute of High Performance Computing
Singapore, Singapore

Additional Workshop Editors *see next page*

ISSN 0302-9743   ISSN 1611-3349 (electronic)
Lecture Notes in Computer Science
ISBN 978-3-031-47424-8   ISBN 978-3-031-47425-5 (eBook)
https://doi.org/10.1007/978-3-031-47425-5

Workshop Editors

Xiaofeng Liu (iD)
Harvard Medical School
Massachusetts General Hospital
Boston, MA, USA

Fangxu Xing
Harvard Medical School
Massachusetts General Hospital
Boston, MA, USA

Sanjay Purushotham
University of Maryland Baltimore County
Baltimore, MD, USA

Tejas S. Mathai
National Institutes of Health
Bethesda, MD, USA

Pritam Mukherjee
National Institutes of Health
Bethesda, MD, USA

Max De Grauw
Radboud University Nijmegen Medical Center
Nijmegen, The Netherlands

Regina Beets Tan
The Netherlands Cancer Institute
Amsterdam, The Netherlands

Valentina Corbetta
The Netherlands Cancer Institute
Amsterdam, The Netherlands

Elmar Kotter
University Hospital Freiburg
Freiburg, Germany

Mauricio Reyes (iD)
University of Bern
Bern, Switzerland

Christian F. Baumgartner (iD)
University of Tübingen
Tübingen, Germany

Quanzheng Li (iD)
Harvard Medical School
Massachusetts General Hospital
Boston, MA, USA

Richard Leahy (iD)
University of Southern California
Los Angeles, CA, USA

Bin Dong
Peking University
Beijing, China

Hao Chen (iD)
Hong Kong University of Science and Technology
Kowloon, Hong Kong

Yuankai Huo (iD)
Vanderbilt University
Nashville, TN, USA

Jinglei Lv (iD)
University of Sydney
Camperdown, NSW, Australia

Xinxing Xu (iD)
Institute of High Performance Computing
Singapore, Singapore

Xiaomeng Li (iD)
Hong Kong University of Science and Technology
Hong Kong, China

Dwarikanath Mahapatra (iD)
Inception Institute of Artificial Intelligence
Abu Dhabi, United Arab Emirates

Li Cheng
ECE
University of Alberta
Edmonton, AB, Canada

Caroline Petitjean (iD)
LITIS
University of Rouen
Rouen, France

Benoît Presles
ImViA Laboratory
University of Burgundy
Dijon, France

MTSAIL 2023 Preface

The 1st MICCAI Workshop on Time-Series Data Analytics and Learning (MTSAIL 2023) was held at the Vancouver Convention Centre, Vancouver, British Columbia, Canada on October 8–12, 2023, in conjunction with the 26th International Conference on Medical Image Computing and Computer-Assisted Intervention.

Recent advances in imaging and data acquisition have led to an increase in both the temporal resolution and dimensional complexity of available datasets, making time-series data analysis more challenging. Dynamic data acquisition and sequential image analysis have seen significant growth in healthcare and related fields, and have been applied to a range of applications including real-time imaging, cardiac motion analysis, speech motion analysis, respiratory motion analysis, and the analysis of physiological processes and brain activation using a variety of imaging/measurement techniques. Time-series data, which is collected through continuous monitoring and recording of a subject over time, requires specialized methods for extracting and connecting related datasets through the analysis of temporal information. These methods are essential for effectively studying time-series data and gaining insights from it.

The study of time-series data and related methods has long been a focus of research, but it has gained increased importance in recent years due to the proliferation of dynamic data acquisition frameworks that often produce high-dimensional datasets. This trend underscores the need for effective methods for analyzing and interpreting time-series data. The analysis of time-series data also presents a number of algorithmic challenges, including insufficient data structure, irregular sampling, inaccurate motion tracking, spatiotemporal misalignment, and multimodality data synthesis. These issues can make it difficult to extract meaningful insights from time-series datasets and highlight the need for robust methods for addressing them.

This workshop served as a venue to facilitate advancements and knowledge dissemination in the field of temporal data processing and analysis algorithms, as well as application areas. It incorporated algorithmic, theoretical, and statistical approaches and aimed to bring together methods from various imaging disciplines that involve video and motion data tracking/processing.

Authors were asked to submit full-length manuscripts for double-blind peer review. A total of 8 submissions were received (1 desk reject), and with a Program Committee of 8 experts in the field, reviewed by at least 2 reviewers. Based on the feedback and critiques, 5 of the best papers (62.5%) were selected for oral presentation at the workshop, and were included in the LNCS volume published by Springer.

We thank the authors for submitting their excellent work, our reviewers for their timely and detailed reviews, our invited speakers, and all our attendees. We sincerely hope that the efforts coming together to make this workshop possible will help shape the direction of future research in this field.

October 2023

Xiaofeng Liu
Fangxu Xing
Sanjay Purushotham
Jonghye Woo

MTSAIL 2023 Organization

Proceedings Chair

M. Emre Celebi   University of Central Arkansas, USA

Steering Committee

Jerry L. Prince   Johns Hopkins University, USA

Workshop Chairs

Xiaofeng Liu   MGH and Harvard Medical School, USA
Fangxu Xing   MGH and Harvard Medical School, USA
Sanjay Purushotham   University of Maryland, Baltimore County, USA
Jonghye Woo   MGH and Harvard Medical School, USA

Program Committee

Jiachen Zhuo   University of Maryland, USA
Jewon Kang   Ewha Womans University, Korea
Jaeyoun Hwang   DGIST, Korea
Harry Yang   AlphaSense
Junghoon Lee   Johns Hopkins University, USA
Taehoon Shin   Ewha Womans University, Korea
Andreas Maier   Friedrich Alexander Universität, Germany
Jinah Park   KAIST, Korea

LEAF 2023 Preface

The first MICCAI Workshop on Lesion Evaluation and Assessment with Follow-up (LEAF) was held at the Vancouver Convention Centre, Vancouver, British Columbia, Canada on October 8, 2023, in conjunction with the 26th International Conference on Medical Image Computing and Computer-Assisted Intervention.

The measurement of structures that are suspicious for malignancy in longitudinal radiologic imaging studies are crucial for charting the course of therapy in patients with cancer. As many of these suspicious structures can also be incidentally found during a routine scanning procedure, various standardized guidelines exist for the evaluation and follow-up of patients based on imaging.

Manual assessment is significantly burdensome for radiologists in terms of both time and effort. As the incidence of cancer increases primarily driven by an aging population, the number of imaging studies per patient continues to rise due to modern follow-up protocols and better access to healthcare.

Recent developments in AI and machine learning have shown promising results in assisting radiologists or even automatizing parts of the reporting process. Limited to single organs and single scans, some of the published methods have demonstrated near-human performance in detecting, segmenting and classifying lesions or other abnormalities, and can aid radiologists with automated measurements, diagnosis and prognosis. Despite these advances, many challenges remain including universal lesion/abnormality detection across multiple organs or anatomical structures, identification and detection of other structures related to cancer staging, effective incorporation of longitudinal information from multiple studies, fusion of information from multi-modal imaging and reporting data, and the performance robustness to heterogeneous.

This workshop served as a venue to facilitate advancements and knowledge dissemination in the field and provided a platform to connect researchers working on different subproblems.

Authors were asked to submit full-length manuscripts for double-blind peer review. A total of 5 submissions were received and were reviewed by at least 2 experts of the field and meta-reviewed by 1 member of the Program Committee. Based on the feedback and critiques, 4 of the best papers (80%) were selected for oral presentation at the workshop and included in the LNCS volume published by Springer.

We thank the authors for submitting their excellent work, our reviewers for their timely and detailed reviews, our invited speakers, and all our attendees. We sincerely hope that the efforts coming together to make this workshop possible will help shape the direction of future research in this field.

October 2023

Alessa Hering
Tejas S. Mathai
Pritam Mukherjee
Max De Grauw

LEAF 2023 Organization

Proceedings Chair

M. Emre Celebi   University of Central Arkansas, USA

Steering Committee

Jerry L. Prince   Johns Hopkins University, USA

Workshop Chairs

Alessa Hering   Radboudumc, The Netherlands
Tejas S. Mathai   National Institutes of Health (NIH), USA
Pritam Mukherjee   National Institutes of Health (NIH), USA
Max De Grauw   Radboudumc, The Netherlands

Reviewers

Jan H. Moltz   Boah Kim
Benjamin Hou   Liangchen Liu
Sayantan Bhadra   Bikash Santra
Ricardo Bigolin Lanfredi   Lena Philipp
Sven Kuckertz   Heather Selby

AI4Treat 2023 Preface

The AI for Treatment Response Assessment and Prediction (AI4Treat) Workshop was held at the Vancouver Convention Centre, Vancouver, British Columbia, Canada on October 12, 2023, in conjunction with the 26th International Conference on Medical Image Computing and Computer-Assisted Intervention (MICCAI).

The path towards improving oncological outcomes and quality of life while reducing costs in cancer care is directly linked to personalized medicine. Since some imaging-relevant features are not discernible to the human eye, machine learning (ML) systems are the last resort to identify prognostic and predictive features, allowing clinicians to select the best treatment for a particular patient and oncological characteristics. However, current ML systems have considerable limitations. Simple radiomics approaches might require manual segmentations, depend on hand-crafted features, and risk missing clinically-relevant information. On the other hand, more complex deep learning approaches overcome the previous limitations by performing task-related representation learning, but have difficulties generalizing to new datasets and lack interpretability. For many years, the MICCAI community has provided novel diagnosis algorithms to help radiologists improve their decision-making and optimize their workflows. However, little has been done and explored in the context of treatment outcome prediction, currently a main focus of the radiology and radiation oncology communities.

This workshop, a joint effort between the European Society of Radiology (ESR) and MICCAI, aimed at calling the attention of the MICCAI community, fostering discussions and the presentation of ideas to tackle the many challenges and identifying opportunities related to the topic of treatment response assessment and prediction based on imaging data by means of machine learning techniques. Invited speakers included prominent figures in ML for treatment outcome prediction and medical imaging, and authors of accepted papers.

Authors were asked to submit full-length manuscripts for double-blind peer review. A total of 2 submissions were received, and with a Program Committee composed of 4 experts in the field, reviewed by at least 2 reviewers. Based on the feedback and critiques, both submitted works were considered excellent contributions and were accepted for presentation at the workshop, and included in the LNCS volume published by Springer.

We are grateful to all Program Committee members for reviewing the submissions and giving constructive comments. We also thank all the authors and attendees for making the workshop very fruitful and successful.

October 2023

Wilson Silva
Regina Beets-Tan
Valentina Corbetta
Elmar Kotter
Mauricio Reyes
C. F. Baumgartner

AI4Treat 2023 Organization

Proceedings Chair

M. Emre Celebi — University of Central Arkansas, USA

Workshop Chairs

Wilson Silva — The Netherlands Cancer Institute, The Netherlands

Regina Beets-Tan — The Netherlands Cancer Institute, The Netherlands

Valentina Corbetta — The Netherlands Cancer Institute, The Netherlands

Elmar Kotter — University Hospital Freiburg, Germany

Mauricio Reyes — University of Bern, Switzerland

Christian F. Baumgartner — University of Tübingen, Germany

Program Committee

Valentina Corbetta — The Netherlands Cancer Institute, The Netherlands

Tiago Gonçalves — FEUP and INESC TEC, Portugal

Kevin Groot Lipman — The Netherlands Cancer Institute, The Netherlands

Eduardo Pais Pooch — The Netherlands Cancer Institute, The Netherlands

MMMI 2023 Preface

On behalf of the organizing committee, we welcome you to the proceedings of the 4th International Workshop on Multiscale Multimodal Medical Imaging (MMMI 2023), held in conjunction with the International Conference on Medical Image Computing and Computer-Assisted Intervention (MICCAI 2023) in Vancouver, Canada. The workshop was organized by the combined efforts of the Massachusetts General Hospital and Harvard Medical School, the University of Southern California, Peking University, Vanderbilt University, the University of Sydney, and the Hong Kong University of Science and Technology.

This series of MMMI workshops aims at tackling the critical challenge of acquiring and analyzing medical images acquired at multiple scales and/or from multiple modalities, which has been increasingly applied in research studies and clinical practice. This workshop offers an opportunity to present : (1) techniques involving multi-modal image acquisition and reconstruction or imaging across multi-scales; (2) novel methodologies and insights of multiscale multimodal medical images analysis, including image fusing, multimodal augmentation, and joint inference; and (3) empirical studies involving the application of multiscale multimodal imaging for clinical use and medical research.

This year, the MMMI workshop received a total of 27 submissions. All submissions underwent a double-blinded peer-review process, each being reviewed by at least 2 independent reviewers and one Program Committee (PC) member. Finally, 17 submissions were accepted for presentation at the workshop, which will be included in the workshop proceeding based on the review scores and comments from PC. Time and efforts from all the PC and reviewers are highly appreciated, which ensured that the MMMI workshop would feature high-quality and valuable works in the field.

With the increasing application of multi-modal, multi-scale imaging in medical research studies and clinical practice, we envision that the MMMI workshop will continue to serve as an international platform for presenting novel works, discussing essential challenges, and promoting collaborations within the community. We would like to thank everyone for their hard work. See you in Vancouver!

October 2023   MMMI 2023 Workshop Chairs

MMMI 2023 Organization

Proceedings Chair

M. Emre Celebi   University of Central Arkansas, USA

Workshop Chairs

Xiang Li   Massachusetts General Hospital, USA
Jinglei Lv   University of Sydney, Australia
Yuankai Huo   Vanderbilt University, USA
Hao Chen   Hong Kong University of Science and
                                    Technology, China
Bin Dong   Peking University, China
Richard M. Leahy   University of Southern California, USA
Quanzheng Li   Massachusetts General Hospital, USA

Program Committee

Hui Ren   Massachusetts General Hospital and Harvard
                                    Medical School, USA
Jiang Hu   Massachusetts General Hospital and Harvard
                                    Medical School, USA
Jerome Charton   Massachusetts General Hospital and Harvard
                                    Medical School, USA
Cheng Chen   Massachusetts General Hospital and Harvard
                                    Medical School, USA
Shunxing Bao   Vanderbilt University, USA
Mariano Cabezas   The University of Sydney, Australia
Ye Wu   Nanjing University of Science and Technology,
                                    China
Luyang Luo   Hong Kong University of Science and
                                    Technology, China
Yingxue Xu   Hong Kong University of Science and
                                    Technology, China
Lu Zhang   University of Texas at Arlington, USA
Abder-Rahman Ali   Massachusetts General Hospital and Harvard
                                    Medical School, USA

Peng Guo	Massachusetts General Hospital and Harvard Medical School, USA
Sekeun Kim	Massachusetts General Hospital and Harvard Medical School, USA
Ho Hin Lee	Microsoft, USA

REMIA 2023 Preface

The 2nd International Workshop on Resource-Efficient Medical Image Analysis (REMIA) was held on October 12th 2022, in conjunction with the 26th International Conference on Medical Image Computing and Computer-Assisted Intervention (MICCAI).

Deep learning methods have shown remarkable success in many medical imaging tasks over the past few years. However, there exists a challenge that current deep learning models are usually data-hungry, requiring massive amounts of high-quality annotated datasets to produce high performance. Firstly, collecting large scale medical imaging datasets are expensive and time-consuming, and the regulatory and governance also raise additional challenges for large scale datasets for healthcare applications. Second, the data annotations are even more challenge as the experienced and knowledgeable clinicians are required to have high quality annotations. The annotation will become more challenging when it comes to the segmentation tasks. It is infeasible to adapt data-hungry deep learning models to achieve various medical tasks within a low-resource situation. However, the vanilla deep learning models usually have the limited ability of learning from limited training samples. Consequently, to enable efficient and practical deep learning models for medical imaging, there is a need for research methods that can handle limited number of training data, limited labels and limited hardware constraints when deploying the model.

This workshop focused on the issues for practical applications of the most medical imaging systems with data, label and hardware limitations. It brought together AI scientists, clinicians and students from different disciplines and areas for medical image analysis to discuss the related advancements in the field. A total of 9 full-length papers were submitted to the workshop in response to the call for papers. All submissions were double-blind peer-reviewed by at least three members of the program committee. Paper selection was based on methodological innovation, technical merit, results, validation, and application potential. Finally, 5 papers were accepted at the workshop and chosen to be included in this Springer LNCS volume.

We are grateful to the Program Committee for reviewing the submitted papers and giving constructive comments and critiques, to the authors for submitting high-quality papers, to the presenters for excellent presentations, and to all the REMIA attendees from all around the world.

October 2023

Xinxing Xu
Xiaomeng Li
Dwarikanath Mahapatra
Li Cheng
Caroline Petitjean
Benoît Presles
Huazhu Fu

REMIA 2023 Organization

Proceedings Chair

M. Emre Celebi   University of Central Arkansas, USA

Program Committee

Xinxing Xu	Agency for Science, Technology and Research, Singapore
Xiaomeng Li	The Hong Kong University of Science and Technology, Hong Kong, China
Dwarikanath Mahapatra	Inception Institute of Artificial Intelligence, Abu Dhabi, UAE
Li Cheng	University of Alberta, Canada
Caroline Petitjean	LITIS, University of Rouen, France
Benoît Presles	University of Burgundy, Dijon, France
Huazhu Fu	Agency for Science, Technology and Research, Singapore

Contents

**Proceeding of the Second International Workshop on
Resource-Efficient Medical Image Analysis (REMIA 2023)**

Proceedings of the First MICCAI Workshop on Time-Series Data Analytics and Learning (MTSAIL 2023)

Learning Dynamic MRI Reconstruction with Convolutional Network Assisted Reconstruction Swin Transformer

Di Xu[1]($\boxtimes$), Hengjie Liu[2], Dan Ruan[2], and Ke Sheng[1]

[1] Radiation Oncoloy, University of California, San Francisco, USA
{di.xu,ke.sheng}@ucsf.edu
[2] Radiation Oncology, University of California, Los Angeles, USA

Abstract. Dynamic magnetic resonance imaging (DMRI) is an effective imaging tool for diagnosis tasks that require motion tracking of a certain anatomy. To speed up DMRI acquisition, k-space measurements are commonly under-sampled along spatial or spatial-temporal domains. The difficulty of recovering useful information increases with increasing under-sampling ratios. Compress sensing was invented for this purpose and has become the most popular method until deep learning (DL) based DMRI reconstruction methods emerged in the past decade. Nevertheless, existing DL networks are still limited in long-range sequential dependency understanding and computational efficiency and are not fully automated. Considering the success of Transformer's positional embedding and "swin window" self-attention mechanism in the vision community, especially natural video understanding, we hereby propose a novel architecture named Reconstruction Swin Transformer (RST) for 4D MRI. RST inherits the backbone design of the Video Swin Transformer with a novel reconstruction head introduced to restore pixel-wise intensity. A convolution network called SADXNet is used for rapid initialization of 2D MR frames before RST learning to effectively reduce the model complexity, GPU hardware demand, and training time. Experimental results in the cardiac 4D MR dataset further substantiate the superiority of RST, achieving the lowest RMSE of 0.0286 ± 0.0199 and 1-SSIM of 0.0872 ± 0.0783 on 9 times accelerated (9x) validation sequences.

Keywords: Transformer · Dynamic MRI · Reconstruction · Deep Learning

1 Introduction

Tracking dynamic processes using time-resolved magnetic resonance imaging (MRI) can reveal anatomical and physiological anomalies that evade detection based on static images [1]. Theoretically, a dynamic target can be acquired frame-wise under the assumption that motion in each frame at the time of acquisition is within the chosen pixel size. However, the assumption of which requires extremely high spatial-temporal (ST) resolutions and thus is often violated due to slow data acquisition speed [2].

To speed up the process of dynamic MRI (DMRI) acquisition, a wide range of approaches have been proposed. Advanced fast imaging sequences [3] and modern

© The Author(s), under exclusive license to Springer Nature Switzerland AG 2023
J. Woo et al. (Eds.): MICCAI 2023 Workshops, LNCS 14394, pp. 3–13, 2023.
https://doi.org/10.1007/978-3-031-47425-5_1

gradient system allow efficient data sampling in k-space. Supported by massive coil arrays [4], parallel imaging [5, 6] has increased scanning speed by 2–4 folds in clinical practice. Followed by that, further acceleration has been achieved through reducing temporal [7, 8] or spatiotemporal [9, 10] redundancy in dynamic images, enabled through the design of special k-space under-sampling trajectories (e.g. variable density Cartesian, radial, spiral and etc.). Those methods heavily rely on effective reconstruction to recover artifact-controlled images [11].

Among them, Compressed sensing (CS) [12, 13] has demonstrated its potential in MRI acceleration. CS methods were developed by solving a constrained optimization problem, including priors as regularization to stabilize the solution [2, 14–16]. Pertinent to the dynamic MRI problem, for cohesion in T axis, several studies combined motion estimation/compensation (ME/MC) in a unified reconstruction framework for more effective acceleration [1, 17]. More recently, Zhao et al. proposed to integrate an intensity-based optical flow prior into the optimization so that motion is compensated through the optical flow estimated motion field [1]. Many studies show that properly implemented CS methods can reconstruct artifacts-free images with k-space data not meeting the Nyquist condition. On the other hand, CS methods share two common weaknesses. First, being iterative methods, they tend to be slow. Second, the results depend on heuristic hyperparameter (HP) tuning. Because of these limitations, CS is often incompatible with the clinical needs for an efficient, automated, and generalizable solution [18].

Recently, research has pivoted to a new direction using deep learning (DL) models for DMRI restoration. In specific, Schlemper et al. extended a 2D convolutional neural network (CNN) based MR reconstruction framework into 3D and then introduced a data-sharing layer derived from K nearest neighbor (KNN) to regularize the temporal correlation among frames [19]. Their CNN model can recover information on individual 2D frames, but the KNN data-sharing layer is insufficient to robustly and efficiently estimate the dynamic relationship among frames. Nonparametric algorithms, including KNN, are more likely to suffer from overfitting, sensitive to HP tuning, and are computationally expensive [20]. To better conduct ME/MC in DL-based DMRI reconstruction, researchers have started investigating the potentiality of recurrent neural networks (RNNs) for temporal pattern modeling. For DMRI reconstruction, Qin et al. deployed the conventional iterative reconstruction scheme with an RNN, with recurrent hidden connections capturing the iterative reconstruction and bidirectional hidden connections characterizing spatial-temporal dependencies [21]. Huang et al. introduced a motion-guided network using ConvGRU to reconstruct initial images I in ST space and then U-FlowNet to perform MC to I through learning optical flow [22]. Yet, RNN models suffer from practical failure in learning long dependencies and bi-directional information that are undesirable in the modern concept of large-scale parallel training. Moreover, RNNs perform sequential learning, assuming each state to be dependent only on the previously seen states, which mandates the sequences to be processed frame by frame and limits encoding of a specific frame to the next few evolutions.

Transformer was introduced to overcome these drawbacks in machine translation, aiming to avoid recursion, allow parallel computation, and reduce performance drops due to long sequential dependencies [23]. Subsequently, the vision community has seen a modeling shift from CNNs to Transformers which have attained top accuracy in numerous video processing benchmarks [24]. Apart from the preeminence in positional embedding, Video Swin Transformer (VST), one of the frameworks benefitting video understanding, uses a novel hierarchical shifted window mechanism, which performs efficient self-attention in the ST domain using non-overlapping local windows and cross-window connection [25]. Since DMRI can be considered a form of video data, we propose extending VST to the DMRI reconstruction task.

To this end, we developed a novel Reconstruction Swin Transformer (RST) network for four-dimensional (4D) MR recovery. To accelerate the training speed and reduce the complexity of RST, we employed a CNN-based 2D reconstruction network named SADXNet [26], for rapid recovery of MR frames prior to feeding into RST. To our knowledge, this is the first work that introduces self-attention and positional embedding to DMRI reconstruction. Experiments on a cardiac dataset have demonstrated the superiority of our proposed architecture over several baseline approaches.

2 Materials and Methods

2.1 SADXNet Assisted Reconstruction Swin Transformer

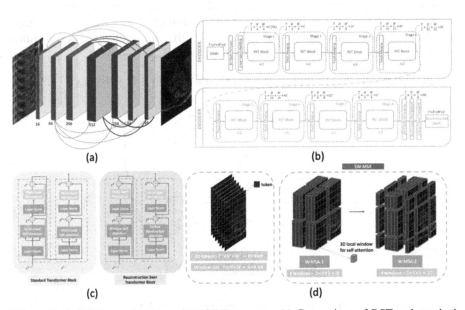

Fig. 1. (a) SADXNet architecture. (b) RST-T structure. (c) Comparison of RST and standard Transformer blocks. (d) An instance of the SW-MSA layer.

Our framework consists of two stages. 1) Initial 2D frame-wise reconstruction using SADXNet [26]. 2) 4D tensor learning in the ST domain with RST. Theoretically, RST can yield comparable performance without SADXNet initialization conditioned upon unlimited network parameters, training time, and GPU capacity. Nevertheless, numerous studies showed that training on high-resolution 4D tensors requires significantly more parameters to fully generalize the feature representation, which takes overly long training time to converge, deviates from the clinical aim of sub-second prediction, and is beyond most of the current commercial GPU memories [27, 28]. Thus, we proposed to use SADXNet for spatial information recovery, followed by a comparable lighter-weighted RST for collective spatial-temporal data reconstruction. We elaborate on the structures of SADXNet and RST as follows.

SADXNet. SADXNet was originally introduced as an image-denoising network in [26] for chest x-ray rib suppression. Noting that the tasks of image denoising and reconstruction fundamentally work on pixel-level recovery, we applied SADXNet to reconstruct MR frames. SADXNet is designed to be fully convolutional and densely connected, as shown in Fig. 1 (a). Firstly, it has seven densely connected layers designed to be channel-wise concatenated, where feature maps produced from a specific layer and all its preceding layers are concatenated in the channel dimension and fed into all its subsequent layers. Secondly, three consecutive operations are conducted for each convolution layer, including batch normalization (BN), rectified linear unit (ReLU), and convolution with a filter size of 3×3. Thirdly, no up- or down-sampling is implemented to preserve the spatial dimension of feature maps through the forward flow. Fourthly, the convolution kernels in the seven layers are organized with an increased-to-decreased number of channels. Lastly, the cost function for SADXNet is formulated as a combination of negative peak signal-to-noise ratio (PSNR), muti-scale structure similarity index measure (MS-SSIM), and L_1 deviation measurement as shown in Eqs. (1–4) [29].

$$L = -\alpha \cdot L_{PSNR} + (1 - \alpha) \left[\beta \cdot (1 - L_{MS-SSIM}) + (1 - \beta) \cdot L_1 \right] \qquad (1)$$

$$L_{PSNR} = log_{10} \left(\frac{MAX_X^2}{1/mn \cdot \sum_{j=0}^{m-1} \sum_{i=0}^{n-1} [x_{ij} - y_{ij}]^2} \right) \qquad (2)$$

$$L_{MS-SSIM} = \frac{(2\mu_x\mu_y + c_1)}{(\mu_x^2\mu_y + c_1)} \cdot \prod_{j=1}^{M} \frac{(2\sigma_{x_jy_j} + c_2)}{(\sigma 2_{x_j}^2 + \sigma_{y_j}^2 + c_2)} \qquad (3)$$

$$L_1 = \frac{1}{mn} \cdot \sum_{j=0}^{m-1} \sum_{i=0}^{n-1} \left\| x_{ij} - y_{ij} \right\|_1 \qquad (4)$$

where α and β, set as 0.5 and 0.5 respectively, are tunable HPs, x and y are input and supervision, MAX_x is the maximum possible input value, S is the dynamic range of the pixel values, (k_1, k_2) are two constants, and $\|\cdot\|_1$ is the l_1 norm.

Reconstruction Swin Transformer. RST strictly follows the hierarchical design of the VST backbone. We introduce a novel reconstruction head in the RST decoder stage to fulfill the goal of pixel-wise information recovery. As a variant of VST, RST also has four architectures with distinct model complexities. 1) RST-T: $C = 96$, block numbers

$= \{2, 2, 6, 2, 2, 6, 2, 2\};$; 2) RST-S: $C = 96$, block numbers $= \{2, 2, 18, 2, 2, 18, 2, 2\};$; 3) RST-B: $C = 128$, block numbers $= \{2, 2, 18, 2, 2, 18, 2, 2\};$; 4) RST-L: $C = 192$, block numbers $= \{2, 2, 18, 2, 2, 18, 2, 2\}$, where C represents the channel number of the first RST block [25].

We illustrate the architecture of RST-T in Fig. 1(b). First, the backbone of RST consists of four stages and performs $2\times$ down-sampling solely in each block's spatial dimension of the patch merging layer [25]. The RST blocks within the backbone and head are symmetrically parameterized, except that all the patch merging layers in the reconstruction head perform $2\times$ spatial up-sampling. Second, for an input 4D tensor of dimension $T \times H \times W \times Z$, we define each patch of size $2 \times 4 \times 4 \times Z$ as a 3D token, where the Z-axis of DMRI is considered as the color channel in natural images. Thus, after processing through the initial 3D patch partition layer, we obtain $\frac{T}{2} \times \frac{H}{2} \times \frac{W}{2} \times Z$ 3D tokens. Third, a linear embedding layer is applied right after 3D patch partition to project the channel dimension from Z to pre-specified C with respect to the destined RST variant, which is 96 in RST-T.

The critical component of the "swin window" mechanism lies in the RST block, which replaces the multi-head self-attention (MSA) layer in the block of the standard Transformer with 3D shifted window-based MSA (SW-MSA) and keeps the rest sub-components unaltered (see Fig. 1 (c)) [25]. The design of SW-MSA introduces a locality inductive bias in its self-attention module to accommodate additional temporal information intake. SW-MSA scheme is realized with two consecutive W-MSA modules. In the first W-MSA, given an initial input composed of $T' \times H' \times W'$ 3D tokens and a window of size $P \times M \times M$, windows are arranged in a manner that can non-overlappingly partition the input tokens. Next, a 3D-shifted window is introduced immediately following the W-MSA layer to establish cross-connections among various windows. Given the $\frac{T'}{P} \times \frac{H'}{M} \times \frac{W'}{M}$ windows obtained from the first W-MSA having size of $P \times M \times M$, the partition configuration of the second W-MSA will shift the windows along the ST axis by $\frac{P}{2} \times \frac{M}{2} \times \frac{M}{2}$ tokens from the partition coordinates in the first W-MSA. In Fig. 1 (d), given $8 \times 8 \times 8$ tokens and a window of size $4 \times 4 \times 4$, W-MSA-1 will partition the tokens into $\frac{T'}{P} \times \frac{H'}{M} \times \frac{W'}{M} = 2 \times 2 \times 2 = 8$ windows. Next, the windows are shifted by $\frac{P}{2} \times \frac{M}{2} \times \frac{M}{2} = 2 \times 2 \times 2$ tokens, resulting in $3 \times 3 \times 3 = 27$ windows in W-MSA-2.

The cost function of RST is designed to be identical to that of SADXNet in Eqs. (1–4), which is a combination of PSNR, MS-SSIM, and L_1 deviation.

Experimental Setup and Baseline Algorithms. Both SADXNet and RST were implemented in Pytorch, and the training was performed on a GPU cluster with $4 \times RTXA6000$. For the training of SADXNet, data augmentation, including random rotation, resizing, cropping, and Gaussian blurring, was implemented. Adam optimizer with an initial learning rate (LR) of 0.001, an epoch of 1000, and a batch size of 2×4 was applied during learning. RST-S without SADXNet initialization was trained, and vice versa for RST-T. Data augmentation was implemented for all RST training, including random cropping, resizing, and flipping. Adam optimizer with an initial LR of 0.001 and batch size of 1 × 4 was applied.

We compared with four state-of-the-art approaches, including k-t SLR [2], k-t FOCUSS + ME/MC [30], DC-CNN (3D) [19], and MODRN (e2e) [22]. The first two are conventional CS-based methods, where k-t FOCUSS + ME/MC includes ME/MC procedures. The latter two are DL methods where DC-CNN (3D) explores ST information using 3D convolution and MODRN (e2e) includes ME/MC into their RNNs. Three quantitative metrics are used for evaluation: rooted mean squared error (RMSE), PSNR, and SSIM.

2.2 Data Cohort

The open-access cardiovascular Magnetic resonance (OCMR) dataset provides multi-coil Cartesian-sampled k-space data from 53 fully sampled and 212 prospectively under-sampled cardiac cine series with both short-axis (SAX) and long-axis (LAX) views. The fully sampled scans have average frames of 18, and the under-sampled scans each have 65 frames. The dataset was collected on three Siemens MAGNETOM scanners - Prisma (3T), Avanto (1.5T), and Sola (1.5T) – with a 34-channel receiver coil array, using bSSFP sequence with FOV=800 × 300 mm, acquisition matrix 384 × 144, slice thickness = 8 mm, and TR/TE = 38.4/1.05 ms. The fully sampled data was collected with ECG gating and breath-holding. The under-sampled data with an acceleration rate (AR) of 9× was collected under the free-breathing condition in real-time. More details can be found in [31]. We prepared 3 subsets, including training, validation, and test sets to assess our framework. The training and validation sets were split from the 53 fully sampled sequences with balanced long/short-axis views and scanner types at the ratio of training/validation = 40/13, whereas the 212 prospectively under-sampled data was used for testing. Variable-density incoherent spatial-temporal acquisition (VISTA) [32] was used to retrospectively under-sample the training/validation sequences.

3 Results

For the OCMR dataset, performance comparison was made among SADXNet initialized RST-T, solely RST-S, and the selected benchmark algorithms - k-t-SLR, k-t-FOCUSS-ME/MC, DC-CNN, and MODRN (e2e). We respectively trained SADXNet + RST-T and RST-S for around 2000 and 8000 epochs till observing training convergence.

Quantitative results and visualization of the validation set are reported in Table 1 and Fig. 2 (a). Solely visualization on the prospective test set of OCMR is reported in Fig. 2 (b-c) since the GTs of the test set are not available. Overall, statistical results in Table 1 and visual outcomes in Fig. 2 (a-b) consistently show that DL models, including DC-CNN, MODRN (e2e), RST-S, and RST-T, significantly outperform CS methods (k-t-SLR and k-t-FOCUSS + ME/MC). In addition to the promising performance illustrated by the quantitative metrics in Table 1, we can also observe that the DL predictions in Fig. 2 have fewer residuals and streaking artifacts, sharper edge delineation, detailed morphology (arrows pointed), and better concentration of optical flow estimated motion on the cardiac region of interest (ROI) than the ones made by CS methods. Those imply that DL methods have better dynamic motion understanding than the selected CS baselines. Meanwhile, all the DL approaches take considerably less time to reconstruct incoming dynamic imaging than CS algorithms, as seen in Table 1.

Within the two CS-based methods, the predictions from k-t-FOCUSS + ME/ME are marginally better than those from k-t-SLR. Among all listed neural networks, the performance ranking can be summarized as SADXNet initialized RST-T > RST-S > MODRN (e2e) > DC-CNN with SADXNet + RST-T, RST-S, and DC-CNN able to make a subsecond prediction. Additionally, though trained significantly longer for 8000 epochs, RST-S still has difficulty capturing finer morphologies and subtle dynamic movements compared with SADXNet + RST-T, which further substantiates the importance of CNN 2D frame initialization prior to RST training in practice. Finally, we observe that predicted frames from SADXNet + RST are consistent and steady along the T axis in Fig. 2 (c), where the robustness of our proposed framework is demonstrated.

Table 1. Results of OCMR validation sets. Mean values and standard deviation are reported. Results from the best performer are bolded, whereas those from the underperformer are underlined. The time reported is the averaged prediction time for each validation sequence.

Algorithm	RMSE ↓	PSNR ↑	1-SSIM ↓	Time (s)	Device
k-t SLR	0.132 ± 0.105	19.792 ± 5.274	0.327 ± 0.276	200.731	CPU
k-t FOCUSS + MC/ME	0.0873 ± 0.0572	21.245 ± 6.143	0.201 ± 0.243	256.874	CPU
DC-CNN	0.0552 ± 0.0431	25.796 ± 4.342	0.145 ± 0.0872	0.543	GPU
MODRN (e2e)	0.0392 ± 0.0311	29.341 ± 3.776	0.121 ± 0.0788	5.736	GPU
RST-S	0.0323 ± 0.0353	30.868 ±3.104	0.114 ± 0.0996	**0.337**	GPU
SADXNet + RST-T	**0.0286 ± 0.0199**	**33.587 ± 2.991**	**0.0872 ± 0.0783**	0.681	GPU

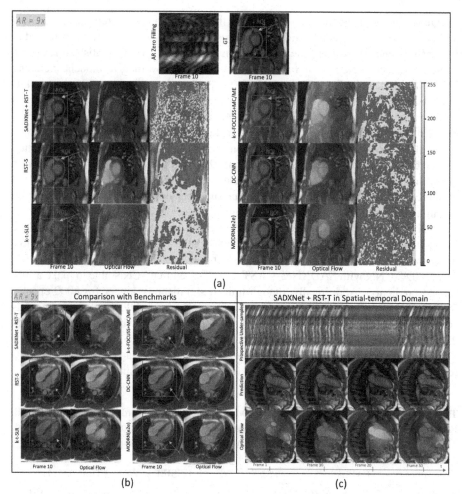

Fig. 2. (a) Visualization of reconstruction results on a SAX sequence in the validation set. (b) The reconstruction results on a LAX four-chamber-view sequence in the test set (AR = 9x). In both (a) and (b), outcomes were visualized having each panel consisting of predictions with and without optical flow overlayed on the 10th frame. ROIs are bounded out in red with arrows pointing out the comparison of artifact and morphology. (c) Visualization of frames 1–30 from a LAX two-chamber view sequence predicted by SADXNet + RST-T.

4 Discussion

The current study presents a novel RST architecture adapted from VST for DMRI reconstruction. RST inherits the backbone of VST and introduces a novel reconstruction head to fulfill the demand for pixel-wise intensity prediction. Compared with existing DL-based reconstruction approaches [19, 22], RST markedly improved efficiency and efficacy. The efficiency stems from the positional embedding scheme of the Transformer, which enables fully distributable processing in the spatial and temporal domains, resulting in enormously reduced training and prediction time. The efficacy is boosted via SW-MSA, which conducts self-attention learning in both spatial and temporal dimensions. Additionally, the SADXNet for the initial restoration of 2D MR frames substantially reduced the training burden, model parameters, and GPU momory footprint. RST-based algorithms outperformed the comparison state-of-the-art CS and DL reconstruction methods by a large margin in the experiments reconstructing the unsampled OCMR dataset. Compared to training RST-S on raw under-sampled images, SADXNet-initiated RST-T delivered an additional performance boost in statistical and visual outcomes while significantly reducing training and model complexity. The results thus support the importance of 2D frame initialization prior to official training from the 4D domain.

Our method is not without room for improvement. SADXNet was introduced to reduce the computation demand of RST, but the current framework still requires substantial GPU memory restricted to higher-end non-consumer grade hardware. As SADXNet demonstrates the promise of RST parameter reduction with spatial domain initialization, we will explore temporal domain initialization before conducting joint 4D ST dimensional learning in future studies.

5 Conclusion

A dynamic MR reconstruction framework, SADXNet-assisted RST, is proposed with accuracy enabled through the "swin window" mechanism and efficiency guaranteed from Transformer positional embedding and CNN spatial initialization. Validation from the OCMR dataset substantiates the superior performance of SADXNet + RST to state-of-the-art CS and DL methods.

References

1. Zhao, N., O'Connor, D., Basarab, A., et al.: Motion compensated dynamic MRI reconstruction with local affine optical flow estimation. IEEE Trans. Biomed. Eng. **66**, 3050–3059 (2019). https://doi.org/10.1109/TBME.2019.2900037
2. Lingala, S.G., Hu, Y., DiBella, E., Jacob, M.: Accelerated dynamic MRI exploiting sparsity and low-rank structure: k-t SLR. IEEE Trans. Med. Imaging **30**, 1042–1054 (2011). https://doi.org/10.1109/TMI.2010.2100850
3. Tsao, J.: Ultrafast imaging: principles, pitfalls, solutions, and applications. J. Magn. Reson. ImagingMagn. Reson. Imaging **32**, 252–266 (2010). https://doi.org/10.1002/jmri.22239
4. Buehrer, M., Pruessmann, K.P., Boesiger, P., Kozerke, S.: Array compression for MRI with large coil arrays. Magn. Reson. Med.. Reson. Med. **57**, 1131–1139 (2007). https://doi.org/10.1002/mrm.21237
5. Griswold, M.A., Jakob, P.M., Heidemann, R.M., et al.: Generalized autocalibrating partially parallel acquisitions (GRAPPA). Magn. Reson. Med.. Reson. Med. **47**, 1202–1210 (2002). https://doi.org/10.1002/mrm.10171
6. Sodickson, D.K., Manning, W.J.: Simultaneous acquisition of spatial harmonics (SMASH): fast imaging with radiofrequency coil arrays. Magn. Reson. Med.. Reson. Med. **38**, 591–603 (1997). https://doi.org/10.1002/mrm.1910380414

7. Van Vaals, J.J., Brummer, M.E., Thomas Dixon, W., et al.: "Keyhole" method for accelerating imaging of contrast agent uptake. J. Magn. Reson. ImagingMagn. Reson. Imaging **3**, 671–675 (1993). https://doi.org/10.1002/jmri.1880030419
8. Parrish, T., Hu, X.: Continuous update with random encoding (CURE): a new strategy for dynamic imaging. Magn. Reson. Med.. Reson. Med. **33**, 326–336 (1995). https://doi.org/10.1002/mrm.1910330307
9. Madore, B., Glover, G.H., Pelc, N.J.: Unaliasing by fourier-encoding the overlaps using the temporal dimension (UNFOLD), applied to cardiac imaging and fMRI. Magn. Reson. Med.. Reson. Med. **42**, 813–828 (1999). https://doi.org/10.1002/(sici)1522-2594
10. Hansen, M.S., Baltes, C., Tsao, J., et al.: Accelerated dynamic Fourier velocity encoding by exploiting velocity-spatio-temporal correlations. Magn Reson Mater Phys **17**, 86–94 (2004). https://doi.org/10.1007/s10334-004-0062-8
11. Tsao, J., Kozerke, S.: MRI temporal acceleration techniques. J. Magn. Reson. ImagingMagn. Reson. Imaging **36**, 543–560 (2012). https://doi.org/10.1002/jmri.23640
12. Donoho, D.L.: Compressed sensing. IEEE Trans. Inf. Theory **52**(4), 1289–1306 (2006). https://doi.org/10.1109/TIT.2006.871582
13. Lustig, M., Donoho, D., Pauly, J.M.: Sparse MRI: the application of compressed sensing for rapid MR imaging. Magn. Reson. Med.. Reson. Med. **58**, 1182–1195 (2007). https://doi.org/10.1002/mrm.21391
14. Miao, X., Lingala, S.G., Guo, Y., et al.: Accelerated cardiac cine MRI using locally low rank and finite difference constraints. Magn. Reson. Imaging. Reson. Imaging **34**, 707–714 (2016). https://doi.org/10.1016/j.mri.2016.03.007
15. Jung, H., Sung, K., Nayak, K.S., et al.: K-t FOCUSS: a general compressed sensing framework for high resolution dynamic MRI. Magn. Reson. Med.. Reson. Med. **61**, 103–116 (2009). https://doi.org/10.1002/mrm.21757
16. Knoll, F., Clason, C., Bredies, K., et al.: Parallel imaging with nonlinear reconstruction using variational penalties. Magn. Reson. Med.. Reson. Med. **67**, 34–41 (2012). https://doi.org/10.1002/mrm.22964
17. Usman, M., Atkinson, D., Odille, F., et al.: Motion corrected compressed sensing for free-breathing dynamic cardiac MRI. Magn. Reson. Med.. Reson. Med. **70**, 504–516 (2013). https://doi.org/10.1002/mrm.24463
18. Majumdar, A.: Advances In Online Dynamic MRI Reconstruction. In: Chen, C.H. (ed.) Frontiers of Medical Imaging, pp. 41–61. WORLD SCIENTIFIC (2014). https://doi.org/10.1142/9789814611107_0003
19. Schlemper, J., Caballero, J., Hajnal, J.V., et al.: A deep cascade of convolutional neural networks for dynamic MR image reconstruction. IEEE Trans. Med. Imaging **37**, 491–503 (2018). https://doi.org/10.1109/TMI.2017.2760978
20. Asmare, E., Begashaw, A.: Review on parametric and nonparametric methods of efficiency analysis. Biostat. Bioinforma **2**, 1–7 (2018)
21. Qin, C., Schlemper, J., Caballero, J., et al.: Convolutional recurrent neural networks for dynamic MR image reconstruction. IEEE Trans. Med. Imaging **38**, 280–290 (2019). https://doi.org/10.1109/TMI.2018.2863670
22. Huang, Q., Xian, Y., Yang, D., et al.: Dynamic MRI reconstruction with end-to-end motion-guided network. Med. Image Anal. **68**, 101901 (2021)
23. Vaswani, A., Shazeer, N., Parmar, N., et al.: Attention Is All You Need (2017)
24. Han, K., Wang, Y., Chen, H., et al.: A survey on vision transformer. IEEE Trans. Pattern Anal. Mach. Intell.Intell. **45**, 87–110 (2022). https://doi.org/10.1109/TPAMI.2022.3152247
25. Liu, Z., Ning, J., Cao, Y., et al.: Video swin transformer (2021). https://doi.org/10.48550/ARXIV.2106.13230

26. Xu, D., Xu, Q., Nhieu, K., et al.: An efficient and robust method for chest x-ray rib suppression that improves pulmonary abnormality diagnosis. Diagnostics **13**, 1652 (2023). https://doi.org/10.3390/diagnostics13091652
27. Fu, Y., Lei, Y., Wang, T., et al.: An unsupervised deep learning approach for 4DCT lung deformable image registration. In: Landman, B.A., Išgum, I. (eds.) Medical Imaging 2020: Image Processing, p. 100. SPIE, Houston (2020)
28. Oh, S.W., Lee, J.-Y., Xu, N., Kim, S.J.: Video Object Segmentation using Space-Time Memory Networks (2019). https://doi.org/10.48550/ARXIV.1904.00607
29. Xu, D., Xu, Q., Nhieu, K., et al.: An Efficient and Robust Method for Chest X-Ray Rib Suppression that Improves Pulmonary Abnormality Diagnosis (2023). https://doi.org/10.48550/ARXIV.2302.09696
30. Jung, H., Park, J., Yoo, J., Ye, J.C.: Radial k-t FOCUSS for high-resolution cardiac cine MRI. Magn. Reson. Med.. Reson. Med. **63**, 68–78 (2010). https://doi.org/10.1002/mrm.22172
31. Chen, C., Liu, Y., Schniter, P., et al.: OCMR (v1.0)--Open-Access Multi-Coil k-Space Dataset for Cardiovascular Magnetic Resonance Imaging (2020). https://doi.org/10.48550/ARXIV.2008.03410
32. Ahmad, R., Xue, H., Giri, S., et al.: Variable density incoherent spatiotemporal acquisition (VISTA) for highly accelerated cardiac MRI: VISTA for highly accelerated cardiac MRI. Magn. Reson. Med.. Reson. Med. **74**, 1266–1278 (2015). https://doi.org/10.1002/mrm.25507

A Groupwise Method for the Reconstruction of Hypergraph Representation of Resting-State Functional Networks

Mingyang Xia[1,2] and Yonggang Shi[1,2(✉)]

[1] Stevens Neuroimaging and Informatics Institute, Keck School of Medicine, University of Southern California (USC), Los Angeles, CA 90033, USA
yonggans@usc.edu
[2] Ming Hsieh Department of Electrical and Computer Engineering, Viterbi School of Engineering, University of Southern California (USC), Los Angeles, CA 90089, USA

Abstract. Functional MRI (fMRI) is an important modality for exploring the brain state and characterizing connectivity across brain regions, but the application of fMRI for disease diagnosis remains limited in clinical practice. To enhance the reliability in modeling functional brain connectivity, we propose a novel method to construct a hypergraph representation of brain networks from resting-state fMRI. Each edge in a hypergraph can connect an arbitrary number of brain regions instead of just two regions as in conventional graph-based networks, allowing for measuring high-order relationships between multiple regions. Existing hypergraph reconstruction methods in fMRI studies typically have a central node in each hyperedge, which limits the edge set by the number of brain regions. However, this hypergraph still needs a high-dimensional space to represent. In addition, only positive weights were previously allowed for the hypergraph incident matrix. In our proposed method, we remove those constraints and develop a novel computational framework to reconstruct general hypergraph representations from resting-state fMRI with consistent topology across groups. In our proposed method, the number of hyperedges does not need to be the same as the number of regions, which decreases the feature dimension space. To validate our method, we classify the brain state using hypergraph-based features and demonstrate superior performance over competing methods on two datasets.

Keywords: Hypergraph · Functional connectivity · Groupwise

This work is supported by the National Institute of Health (NIH) under grants R01EB022744, RF1AG077578, RF1AG056573, RF1AG064584, R21AG064776, U19AG078109, and P41EB015922.

Supplementary Information The online version contains supplementary material available at https://doi.org/10.1007/978-3-031-47425-5_2.

1   Introduction

Functional MRI (fMRI) enables the analysis of brain connectivity by measuring the co-activation of fMRI signals across different brain regions. To explore brain networks using fMRI signals, various methods have been developed, including (1) Seed-based methods, (2) Independent component analysis (ICA) methods [1], and (3) Graph-based methods. Graph-based representation seems to be the most popular among these methods because, using graph theory tools, the brain network's properties can be evaluated. However, because multiple brain regions work cooperatively, it may not be enough to use a simple graph to represent the brain network. Hence, a hypergraph may be a better choice to represent the brain relationships because each hyperedge can join any number of nodes instead of two. In hypergraphs, each hyperedge can connect any number of nodes, in contrast to the two-node limitation of graph-based networks. Recent studies [2] have developed several methods to construct hypergraphs and use features derived from hypergraphs to classify brain states. However, most fMRI-based hypergraphs are constructed by defining a center vertex in each hyperedge, which might limit their representation power to explore the sophisticated relations among brain regions and limit the number of hyperedges. It needs a high-dimensional feature space to represent the hypergraph. Furthermore, most hypergraph methods only consider positive relationships and ignore negative relationships.

To address the above issue, we propose a novel hypergraph construction method. Firstly, we construct the hypergraph without including a central node in each hyperedge. Hence, the number of hyperedges does not need to be equal to the number of brain regions. We demonstrate that using fewer hyperedges can more effectively represent the brain network and achieve better performance in classification tasks. Secondly, we propose a simple way to measure the signal variation when the hypergraph incident matrix contains both positive and negative values. Thirdly, we demonstrate that better performance can be achieved with our hypergraph-based features in classifying brain states. Lastly, we utilize hypergraph features to illustrate underlying differences between brain states.

2   Method

2.1   Hypergraph

In mathematics, a hypergraph is an extended definition of a simple graph. In a hypergraph, each edge, referred to as a hyperedge, can connect multiple vertices, unlike a simple graph where edges connect only two vertices. Hence, hypergraphs could measure more complex relationships than simple graphs, better representing the brain network.

Formally, an undirected hypergraph H can be defined as $H = (V, E)$, where V is a set of elements called nodes or vertices, and E is a set of non-empty subsets of V called hyperedges. Assume $V = \{v_1, v_2, ..., v_{|V|}\}$, $E = \{e_1, e_2, ..., e_{|E|}\}$, with $\bigcup_{i=1}^{|E|} e_i = V$. The hypergraph can be denoted as an incident structure.

$$H_{ij} = \begin{cases} c, c \neq 0 & \text{if } v_i \in e_j \\ 0, & \text{otherwise.} \end{cases} \tag{1}$$

2.2 Hypergraph Construction

Let fMRI data be represented by the spatial-temporal data, X. $X = R^{n_1 * T}$, where n_1 is the number of the segmented regions, and T is the number of time points. Each region's signal could be viewed as a combination of source signal and noise. For region i, we have $X_i = H_i * S + \epsilon$, S is source signal, $S \in R^{n_2 * T}$, where n_2 is the number of separate source signals, ϵ is the noise. For all brain regions, we have $X = H * S + \varepsilon$. Then a hypergraph H can be constructed by making each hyperedge represents one of the source signals and each coefficient of the incident matrix $H_{i,j}$ represents the weight of source signal j contributing to the average signal in the region i.

After preprocessing, we assume the source signal should have zero means. This assumption allows us to reconstruct the source signal based on the hypergraph structure. Suppose hypergraph has incident matrix H, where $H = [h_{e_1}^T, h_{e_2}^T, ..., h_{e_{|E|}}^T]$ and $h_{ej} = [h_{1,ej}, h_{2,ej}, ..., h_{|V|,ej}]$. Each coefficient $h_{i,ej}$ represents the contribution to the average signal in the i_{th} region from the j_{th} source signal. Let $X_i = \sum_{j=1}^{|E|} H_{i,j} * S_j$, thence, we can estimate the source signal S_j by the following equation:

$$S_j \approx \frac{\sum_{i=1}^{|V|} (h_{i,j} * X_i)}{\sum_{i=1}^{|V|} (h_{i,j}^2)} \tag{2}$$

Based on the above equation, a hypergraph incident matrix should satisfy the equation

$$S \approx (I \oslash (H^T * H)) * H^T * X = K * H^T * X, \text{ where } K = I \oslash (H^T * H) \tag{3}$$

$\oslash$ is dot division. I is the identity matrix, where only diagonal entries are one, and the other are 0. Then Eq. (4) can be established,

$$X = H * S \approx H * K * H^T * X \tag{4}$$

To find out the hypergraph incident matrix H, we could construct the reconstruction term

$$\min_{H} \|X - H * K * H^T * X\|_2 \tag{5}$$

To prevent the incident matrix from converging to identity matrix I, we add a matrix $\bar{I}$ to Eq. (5), which has zero values on the diagonal entries, and other entries have value 1. The new equation can be written as:

$$\min_{H} \|X - \bar{I} \odot (H * K * H^T * X)\|_2 \tag{6}$$

where $\odot$ represents dot products, which calculates element-wise corresponding product.

We define that the hypergraph H possesses the following features: (1) the signal on the hypergraph should be smooth and have relatively small variation (2): Each observed signal should be a combination of a limited number of the source signals and noise instead of all source signals.

The vertex degree and hyperedge degree on the hypergraph H could be defined as follows:

$$d(v_i) = \sum_{j=1}^{|E|}(abs(H_{i,j})), \ and \ d(e_j) = \sum_{i=1}^{|V|}(abs(H_{i,j})) \tag{7}$$

Accordingly, define vertex degree matrix and hyperedge degree matrix D_v and D_e respectively. $D_V = diag(d(v_1), d(v_2), ..., d(v_i), ..., d(v_{|V|}))$ and $D_E = diag(d(e_1), d(e_2), ..., d(e_j), ..., d(e_{|E|}))$. Unlike other papers [2], we treat each hyperedge equally important; hence, the weights of every hyperedge are equal to 1. Then, we could define the similarity matrix Sim, as:

$$Sim = HD_E^{-1}H^T, \ where \ Sim_{m,n} = \sum_{e_k \in E} \frac{H_{m,k} * H_{n,k}}{d(e_k)} \tag{8}$$

This can be viewed as the proportional weights of all the hyperedges connecting vertex i and vertex j. Based on the similarity matrix, we can define the Laplacian matrix directly:

$$L = D_v - Sim \tag{9}$$

Let $f = (f_1, f_2, ..., f_{|V|}) \in R^N$ be an arbitrary signal defined on the hypergraph nodes. The variation of the signal could be written as:

$$f^T L f = \frac{1}{2} * \sum_{e_j \in E, v_m, v_n \in V, H_{m,k}*H_{n,k} \geq 0} (\frac{|H_{m,k} * H_{n,k}|}{d(e_k)} * (f_m - f_n)^2) +$$
$$\frac{1}{2} * \sum_{e_j \in E, v_m, v_n \in V, H_{m,k}*H_{n,k} \leq 0} (\frac{|H_{m,k} * H_{n,k}|}{d(e_k)} * (f_m + f_n)^2) \tag{10}$$

This equation reflects the higher-order relation between vertices. Furthermore, suppose the regions' average signal has a high negative correlation, the time series will have opposite directions. In that case, the graph signals on the vertex should be similar in absolute value but have different signs. We use $(f_m + f_n)$ to measure their absolute value difference if they have a negative correlation.

We obtain the hypergraph incident matrix using the following equation:

$$\begin{aligned} \underset{H}{argmin}(\|X - \overline{I} * H * K * H^T * X\|_2 \\ + \alpha * \frac{1}{|T|} * \sum_{t=1}^{|T|} *x_t^T * L * x_t + \lambda * |H|_1) \end{aligned} \tag{11}$$

where the first term is to reconstruct the signal. The second term is a regularization term that constrains the smoothness of the graph signal for the reason that

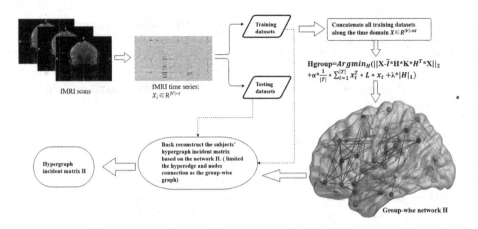

Fig. 1. The diagram shows the pipeline of group-wise and individual hypergraph construction.

the signal on an appropriate hypergraph should be smooth and have a slight variation. The third term is sparse regularization, which constrains sparseness. Each hyperedge should not contain all the nodes, and each region's signal should not consist of all the source signals.

2.3   Individual Hypergraph Incident Matrix

To obtain the individual subject's incident matrix, we first concatenate all fMRI time series along the time domain. We initialize the incident matrix based on our K-Means method using $d = 1 - |P|$ as the distance metric, as shown in Algorithm 1. Then we apply gradient descent to obtain the incident matrix $HGroup$ based on the Eq. (11). After obtaining the group-wise hypergraph incident matrix, we calculate the individual subject's hypergraph incident matrix. We limit each individual subject's hypergraph incident matrix to have the same hypergraph structure, which means that if $HGroup_{i,j} = 0$, we limit the k-th subject's incident matrix $Hk_{i,j} = 0$. Based on the above limitation, we use the $HGroup$ matrix to initialize the individual subject's incident matrix based on Eq. (11). The workflow is illustrated in Fig. 1.

Algorithm 1. Initialization: K-Means for Hypergraph

1: Random choose $|E|$ centroids $C = c_0, c_1, ..., c_{|E|}$.
2: Compute the distance between centroids and each x_i, each x_i belongs to the centroids with the minimum distance $d = 1 - |p|$, p is the Pearson correlation.
3: Compute new centroids, n_j is the number of samples(x_i) belongs to c_j.

$$c_j = \sum_{x_i \in c_j} \frac{p_{i,j}}{|p_{i,j}| * n_j} * x_i \qquad (12)$$

4: Repeat 2,3 until every centroid c_j does not change.
5: Calculate initialization incident matrix H $H_{i,j} = p_{i,j}$.

3 Results

3.1 Datasets

ECEO Datasets (Eyes Closed and Eyes Opened Datasets). In resting fMRI studies, many experiments have proven that brain shows different states between eyes opened and eyes closed state during scanning [3]. The ECEO dataset collected data from 48 college students, with one eyes closed study and one eyes opened study for each student. [4]. One subject is excluded because of the incomplete data. The data are preprocessed by the software DPABI [5] using conventional preprocessing pipeline.

OASIS3 Dataset (Open Access Series of Imaging Studies Dataset). Oasis3 [6] dataset is an open access retrospective compilation of dataset which collects 1378 data over 30 years, which have 2842 sessions. However, not all MR session contains resting-state fMRI bold scanning. Because many subjects have been scanned multiple times, to prevent data leak, we choose the most recent scan. We selected 102 Alzheimer subjects and 120 normal controls. The mean age of AD subjects is 76.96 and the mean age of normal control is 73.17. We use AFNI (Analysis of Functional NeuroImages) [7] to preprocess the resting fMRI images and register the images to CerebrA [8] template, which is divided into 102 brain regions.

3.2 Competing Methods

We compared our method with following methods: (1) PC (Pearson correlation method); (2) SR (Sparse representation method); (3) WSGR (Weighted Sparse group representation method) [9]; (4) Single-Paradigm HL method [2] (Hypergraph Learning Based Method for Functional Connectivity Network Construction Using Single-Paradigm fMRI Data), which is a representative hypergraph construction method based on fMRI.

To compare the different methods, we tuned the hyper-parameters to be consistent with the original papers' setting. We used a linear SVM (Support Vector Machine) to perform classification in the following section. In our proposed method, we used hypergraph incident matrix coefficients as the input to classify brain states.

3.3 Classification Results

We employed leave-one-out cross-validation to classify the brain states of two datasets. This involves leaving one subject as the test set during each epoch and utilizing the remaining subjects as the training set (Tables 1 and 2).

Table 1. ECEO classification results.

	Accuracy	Sensitivity	Specificity
PC	71.28%	72.34%	71.21%
SR	43.62%	42.55%	44.68%
WSGR	79.79%	82.98%	76.60%
Single-paradigm HL	56.38%	55.31%	57.44%
Proposed method	88.29%	91.48%	85.10%

Table 2. OASIS3 classification results.

	Accuracy	Sensitivity	Specificity
PC	60.47%	57.31%	63.15%
SR	64.26%	56.80%	70.57%
WSGR	67.11%	63.73%	71.67%
Single-Paradigm HL	66.22%	60.78%	70.83%
Proposed method	76.57%	74.50%	78.33%

We found that the proposed method outperforms the other four methods in both of the two datasets. In this experiment, we set 10 hyperedges to represent the brain network, which is fewer than the other methods. In comparison to graph-based methods and other center-node hypergraph-based methods, our proposed method only requires 10% of the dimensions to represent the brain network. Both SGR and our method achieve high accuracy because the fMRI signal is unstable, which needs to consider groupwise patterns. We provide the performance curve under different hyperparameter settings in the supplementary material.

3.4 Statistical Significance of Results

As shown in Fig. 2(a), we compared the hypergraph incident matrix generated by the proposed method and the single-paradigm method. We used PCA (principal component analysis) to reduce the dimension to show the distribution of the hypergraph representation of both eyes closed and eyes opened fMRI scans.

We found that our method can better divide the two groups of fMRI scans. In contrast to alternative approaches, our approach imposes limitations on the range of representation by considering group-wise structure, thereby mitigating the potential emergence of outliers within the dataset.

We conducted further examinations of the t-test scores between eyes closed and eyes opened subjects' incident matrices by the proposed method. We selected p-value threshold of smaller than 0.001. Our findings revealed significant differences in some regions, including the lingual gyrus, superior parietal gyrus, inferior occipital lobe, supramarginal gyrus, and superior temporal gyrus. We visualized the results using BrainNet Viewer [10]. Specifically, we chose two regions (lingual gyrus and inferior occipital gyrus) to show their hypergraph vertex degrees. As shown in Fig. 2, the orange columns represent the eyes closed state, while the blue columns represent the eyes opened state. We observed that both regions exhibited higher hypergraph vertex degrees in the eyes opened state, indicating increased activity compared to the eyes closed state.

In our proposed method, we observed that there are 24 incident matrix coefficients with a p-value smaller than 0.001 between the two groups, and 18 of them belong to the same hyperedge. The regions belonging to the second hyperedge are shown in the lower right corner of Fig. 2. The regions, including the lingual gyrus, parts of the occipital lobe, and postcentral gyrus, have significant differences between two groups in this hyperedge, which reveals that these regions have a different effect on visual network and sensorimotor network in two brain states. When compared to center-based hypergraph models, where distinct regions are distributed across various hyperedges, the direct revelation of their relationship might be limited. However, the proposed methods could more effectively demonstrate higher-order relationships directly.

For the OASIS datasets, we also identified regions with significant differences. The regions with distinction include the left lingual gyrus, both sides superior frontal gyrus in the media part, the left hippocampus, and the left posterior cingulate. As shown in Fig. 3, we can find that in the normal control group, both the hippocampus and the superior frontal regions have higher vertex degrees. This shows that some brain regions associated with memory in Alzheimer's disease patients show less activity, which may decrease the connectivity between these regions and other regions.

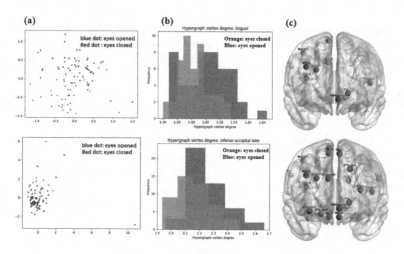

Fig. 2. This figure shows the statistical results of ECEO datasets. (a): Hypergraph representation distribution by PCA (Upper fig is generated by the proposed method and the lower fig is generated by the Single-Paradigm HL method); (b): hypergraph vertex degree distribution; (c): Upper fig shows parts of discriminative ROI between two groups in 2nd hyperedges and lower fig shows parts of ROI in 2nd hyperedges

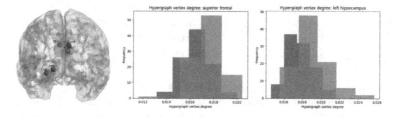

Fig. 3. This figure shows the statistical results of OASIS datasets. The left fig shows discriminative regions between groups; The middle to the right fig shows the hypergraph vertices degree distribution, (middle: superior frontal; right: hippocampus; Blue column represents AD patients and orange column represents normal control) (Color figure online)

4   Conclusion

In summary, our proposed method is effective in constructing hypergraphs for brain network representation that considers both positive and negative correlations in fMRI signals. Experimental results show that our method can use fewer hyperedges to better represent the brain network and extract important features. Our results demonstrate the superior performance of our method in classifying brain states and identifying important brain regions, highlighting the potential for this method to advance the field of neuroimaging. By making use of hypergraph features, the proposed method has the capability to unveil the underlying distinctions between different brain states.

References

1. Calhoun, V.D., Liu, J., Adal, T.: A review of group ICA for fMRI data and ICA for joint inference of imaging, genetic, and ERP data. Neuroimage **45**(1), S163–S172 (2009)
2. Xiao, L., et al.: Multi-hypergraph learning-based brain functional connectivity analysis in fMRI data. IEEE Trans. Med. Imaging **39**(5), 1746–1758 (2019)
3. Liang, B., et al.: Brain spontaneous fluctuations in sensorimotor regions were directly related to eyes open and eyes closed: evidences from a machine learning approach. Front. Hum. Neurosci. **8**, 645 (2014)
4. Liu, D., Dong, Z., Zuo, X., Wang, J., Zang, Y.: Eyes-open/eyes-closed dataset sharing for reproducibility evaluation of resting state fMRI data analysis methods. Neuroinformatics **11**, 469–476 (2013)
5. Yan, C.G., Wang, X.D., Zuo, X.N., Zang, Y.F.: DPABI: data processing and analysis for (resting-state) brain imaging. Neuroinformatics **14**, 339–351 (2016)
6. LaMontagne, P.J., et al.: OASIS-3: longitudinal neuroimaging, clinical, and cognitive dataset for normal aging and Alzheimer disease. MedRxiv, pp. 2019 (2019)
7. Cox, R.W.: AFNI: software for analysis and visualization of functional magnetic resonance neuroimages. Comput. Biomed. Res. **29**(3), 162–173 (1996)
8. Manera, A.L., Dadar, M., Fonov, V., Collins, D.L.: CerebrA, registration and manual label correction of Mindboggle-101 atlas for MNI-ICBM152 template. Sci. Data **7**(1), 237 (2020)
9. Yu, R., Zhang, H., An, L., Chen, X., Wei, Z., Shen, D.: Connectivity strength weighted sparse group representation based brain network construction for M CI classification. Hum. Brain Mapp. **38**(5), 2370–2383 (2017)
10. Xia, M., Wang, J., He, Y.: BrainNet Viewer: a network visualization tool for human brain connectomics. PLoS ONE **8**(7), e68910 (2013)

MomentaMorph: Unsupervised Spatial-Temporal Registration with Momenta, Shooting, and Correction

Zhangxing Bian[1]([✉]) [iD], Shuwen Wei[1] [iD], Yihao Liu[1], Junyu Chen[2],
Jiachen Zhuo[4], Fangxu Xing[3], Jonghye Woo[3], Aaron Carass[1] [iD],
and Jerry L. Prince[1] [iD]

[1] Johns Hopkins University, Baltimore, MD, USA
{zbian4,swei14,yliu236,aaron_carass,prince}@jhu.edu
[2] Johns Hopkins School of Medicine, Baltimore, MD, USA
jchen245@jhmi.edu
[3] Massachusetts General Hospital and Harvard Medical School, Boston, MA, USA
{fxing1,jwoo}@mgh.harvard.edu
[4] University of Maryland School of Medicine, Baltimore, MD, USA
jzhuo@umm.edu

Abstract. Tagged magnetic resonance imaging (tMRI) has been employed for decades to measure the motion of tissue undergoing deformation. However, registration-based motion estimation from tMRI is difficult due to the periodic patterns in these images, particularly when the motion is large. With a larger motion the registration approach gets trapped in a local optima, leading to motion estimation errors. We introduce a novel "momenta, shooting, and correction" framework for Lagrangian motion estimation in the presence of repetitive patterns and large motion. This framework, grounded in Lie algebra and Lie group principles, accumulates momenta in the tangent vector space and employs exponential mapping in the diffeomorphic space for rapid approximation towards true optima, circumventing local optima. A subsequent correction step ensures convergence to true optima. The results on a 2D synthetic dataset and a real 3D tMRI dataset demonstrate our method's efficiency in estimating accurate, dense, and diffeomorphic 2D/3D motion fields amidst large motion and repetitive patterns.

Keywords: Temporal registration · Tagged MRI · Motion estimation

1 Introduction

Tagging magnetic resonance imaging (tMRI) [2,3] is an important imaging technique, enabling precise measurements and visualizations of tissue move-

Supplementary Information The online version contains supplementary material available at https://doi.org/10.1007/978-3-031-47425-5_3.

J. Woo et al. (Eds.): MICCAI 2023 Workshops, LNCS 14394, pp. 24–34, 2023.
https://doi.org/10.1007/978-3-031-47425-5_3

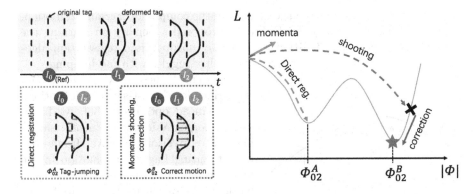

Fig. 1. Conceptual illustration of tag-jumping in unsupervised registration. The left panel demonstrates two strategies for estimating motion between the reference time-frame I_0 and the moving timeframe I_2: Method A (Φ_{02}^A) directly registers I_0 and I_2, while Method B (Φ_{02}^B) utilizes the temporal information from I_0 *thru* I_2 for registration. The right panel visualizes the loss landscape (L on y-axis) in optimization, highlighting local optima caused by image periodicity in Φ space.

ment and deformation. However, the tagged periodic patterns present considerable challenges in estimating Lagrangian motion. Lagrangian motion traces tissues from their resting state and is especially suited for strain computation [18,22,28]. Existing approaches typically employ raw tagged [34] or harmonic phase [8,26,33] images which *all* have periodic patterns as inputs to unsupervised registration algorithms [5,25], to estimate the Lagrangian motion. However, when the deformation between the registration pair exceeds half of the tagging period, these methods risk falling into local optima, leading to substantial errors—a phenomenon known as "tag-jumping"—as illustrated in Fig. 1.

Several strategies have been proposed to address this issue. For instance, Shortest Path Refinement [23] incorporates a static region assumption into a region growing alrithm to correct the motion estimation. This approach requires strong assumptions and human intervention. Phase unwrapping [29,32], another strategy, unwraps the periodic patterns before registration. Yet, it is often susceptible to image noise and artifacts [19,32]. Deep learning-based pattern unwrapping methods, though demonstrating better accuracy, are mostly trained on synthetic images, raising questions about their generalizability to real data. While many methods primarily utilize pair frames, it is possible to leverage the entire sequence. Yu *et al.* [35] utilize traditional iterative registration [33], proposing to initialize the registration with composition of motion between every successive pair of frames. However, this approach incurs high computational costs due to its iterative nature and on-the-fly optimization.

Unsupervised deep learning-based registration methods have recently shown promise, offering good registration accuracy, fast inference speed [8,12,14,16, 24,34]. Ye *et al.* [34] propose to estimate Lagrangian motion from raw tMRI by composing small Eulerian motions. However, this can lead to drifting issues, where small errors in each step accumulate in the composed Lagrangian motion, leading to inferior accuracy. DRIMET [8] proposed a penalty on learning the incompressible motion in tMRI, yet like many unsupervised registration algorithms that focus on registering frame pairs, it struggles with tag-jumping.

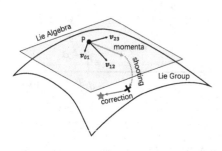

Fig. 2. A high-level overview of "momenta, shooting, and correction".

Inspired by these previous works and the principle of "fast-slow optimization" in look-ahead optimizers [36], we introduce "MomentaMorph: momenta, shooting, and correction", a novel framework for estimating Lagrangian motion in the presence of repetitive patterns and large motions. As shown in Fig. 2, this framework operates under Lie algebra and Lie group principles, where momenta accumulate in the tangent vector space (Lie algebra) and shooting occurs in the diffeomorphic space (Lie group) through exponential mapping, serving as the "fast" step in "fast-slow" optimization. This process "shoots" towards an approximation near the true optima, avoiding the local optima presented by large motions in repetitive patterns. A subsequent correction step ensures convergence to the true optima, thereby enhancing accuracy and acting as the "slow" step.

While MomentaMorph shares similarity in nomenclature with LDDMM [31], there are differences. LDDMM estimates an initial momentum field that, when "shot" forward via a geodesic path within the context of a diffeomorphism, deforms one image to align with another. However, it does not exploit temporal information from multiple frames and carries the risk of falling into local optima during the "shooting" process. It also requires a precise initial estimate of the momentum and can be computationally intensive due to the necessity of solving a partial differential equation at each iteration. In contrast, MomentaMorph exploits temporal information from multiple frames and is an amortized learning-based approach, enabling rapid inference once trained. Our context also differs from optical flow [7,17,21,30] in computer vision, which typically have less emphasis on incompressibility, diffeomorphisms, or Lagrangian motion.

Our contribution is that we introduce a novel framework MomentaMorph for motion tracking using unsupervised registration techniques. MomentaMorph can estimate accurate, diffeomorphic, and incompressible Lagrangian motion. MomentaMorph is validated using both a 2D synthetic motion dataset and a real 3D tMRI dataset capturing tongue motion, demonstrating its broad applicability. Broadly speaking, this work also offers a promising solution for harnessing the temporal information inherent in biological dynamic imaging modalities.

2   Method

Drawing on previous research [1,6,13,14], we define the deformation field via an ordinary differential equation (ODE) $\frac{\partial \phi^{(\tau)}}{\partial \tau} = \boldsymbol{v} \circ \phi^{(\tau)}$, where $\phi^{(0)}$ represents the identity transformation and v is a stationary velocity field (SVF). One can integrate v over $\tau = [0,1]$ to obtain the final registration field $\phi^{(1)}$. In the context of group theory, v belongs to the Lie algebra and yields a member of the Lie group through the exponential map $\phi = \exp(v)$.

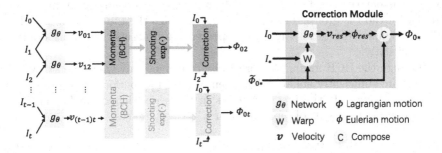

Fig. 3. The architecture of MomentaMorph. The input is a sequence of images $\{I_0, I_1, I_2, \dots\}$, and the output is the Lagrangian motion between the reference frame and others. A detailed view of the correction module is shown on the right.

Consider $\{I_0, I_1, I_2, \dots\}$ as a sequence of 3D images, such as a tMRI sequence. By convention, I_0 is selected as our reference frame. The motion field between consecutive frames t and $t+1$ is referred to as Eulerian motion, denoted as $\phi_{t(t+1)}$, while the motion field between the reference frame I_0 and any other frame I_t is referred to as Lagrangian motion, denoted as Φ_{0t}. We propose an unsupervised framework to estimate the 3D dense diffeomorphic Lagrangian motion fields given the sequence $\{I_0, I_1, I_2, \dots\}$.

For frames I_t and I_{t+1}, $v_{t(t+1)} = g_\theta(I_t, I_{t+1})$ estimates the SVF, where g is a convolutional neural network with learnable parameters θ. We assume that there is no tag-jumping problems between successive frames when imaging settings are appropriately configured. To obtain Lagrangian motion, one might consider composing the Eulerian motions. However, such an approach can lead to drifting issues, resulting in inaccurate motion. Instead, we introduce the momenta, shooting, and correction framework, as shown in Fig. 3.

2.1 Momenta, Shooting, Correction

Momenta. The Lagrangian motion can be expressed in terms of velocity fields, for $t \geq 1$, as follows:

$$\log\left(\Phi_{0t}\right) = v_{0t} = \log\left(\phi_{(t-1)t} \circ \Phi_{0(t-1)}\right) \tag{1a}$$

$$= \log\left(\exp\left(v_{(t-1)t}\right) \circ \exp\left(v_{0(t-1)}\right)\right) \tag{1b}$$

$$= v_{(t-1)t} + v_{0(t-1)} + \frac{1}{2}\left[v_{(t-1)t}, v_{0(t-1)}\right] + \cdots \tag{1c}$$

with $\log\left(\Phi_{00}\right) = v_{00} = \mathbf{0}$.

Equations (1a)–(1b) represents a recursive formula, valid for $t \geq 1$, indicating that each Φ_{0t} can be expressed as a composition involving the preceding term $\Phi_{0(t-1)}$ and a new term $\phi_{(t-1)t}$, and thus can be expressed with elements in Lie algebras. Equation (1c) applies the Baker-Campbell-Hausdorff (BCH) formula [4,11,15], which establishes a connection between the product of exponentials and associative algebras. Specifically, $\circ$ represents a composition map associated with the Lie group. The operator $[\cdot, \cdot]$ denotes the Lie bracket. The dots indicate higher-order terms involving repeated Lie brackets, which are omitted for simplicity.

Although the BCH formula theoretically converges only when the two velocity fields are sufficiently small, it has been observed to perform well in broader situations. Using only the first few terms in the series defined in Eq. (1c), we form two approximations of momenta (for $t \geq 1$), as follows:

$$[\text{Mmorph-1}] \quad \boldsymbol{p}_{0t}^1 := \boldsymbol{v}_{(t-1)t} + \boldsymbol{p}_{0(t-1)}^1 \tag{2a}$$

$$[\text{Mmorph-2}] \quad \boldsymbol{p}_{0t}^2 := \boldsymbol{v}_{(t-1)t} + \boldsymbol{p}_{0(t-1)}^2 + \frac{1}{2}\left(J_{\boldsymbol{p}_{0(t-1)}^2}\boldsymbol{v}_{(t-1)t} - J_{\boldsymbol{v}_{(t-1)t}}\boldsymbol{p}_{0(t-1)}^2\right) \tag{2b}$$

$$\text{with } \boldsymbol{p}_{00}^1 = \boldsymbol{p}_{00}^2 = \boldsymbol{0},$$

where $J_{\boldsymbol{v}}$ is the 3×3 Jacobian matrix of vector field $\boldsymbol{v}$.

Shooting. From either (2a) or (2b), we use the scaling and squaring [1] to compute the exponential mapping $\widetilde{\Phi}_{0t} = \exp(\boldsymbol{p}_{0t})$. This shoots solutions to an approximate location near the true deformation on the manifold. The approximation arise from two sources: the omitted high-order terms in Eq. (1c), and the interpolation during the scaling and squaring on the discretized image grid.

Correction. We refine the Lagrangian estimate by first estimating the residual motion $\phi_{\text{res}} = \exp(\boldsymbol{v}_{\text{res}})$ where $\boldsymbol{v}_{\text{res}} = g_\theta(I_0, I_t \circ \widetilde{\Phi}_{0t})$, and then composing with $\widetilde{\Phi}_{0t}$ to obtain the final result $\Phi_{0t} = \widetilde{\Phi}_{0t} \circ \phi_{\text{res}}$.

2.2   Learning

Our overall training objective is $\mathcal{L} = \mathcal{L}_{\text{eul}} + \gamma \mathcal{L}_{\text{lag}}$ which involves both Eulerian motion, Eq. (3), and Lagrangian motion, Eq. (4), where

$$\mathcal{L}_{\text{eul}} = \sum_{t=0}^{T} \mathcal{L}_{\text{sim}}(I_t, I_{t+1} \circ \phi_{t(t+1)}) + \alpha \mathcal{L}_{\text{smooth}}(\phi_{t(t+1)}) + \beta \mathcal{L}_{\text{inc}}(\phi_{t(t+1)}) \tag{3}$$

$$\mathcal{L}_{\text{lag}} = \sum_{t=1}^{T} \mathcal{L}_{\text{sim}}(I_0, I_t \circ \Phi_{0t}) + \alpha \mathcal{L}_{\text{smooth}}(\Phi_{0t}) + \beta \mathcal{L}_{\text{inc}}(\Phi_{0t}). \tag{4}$$

In the above equations, γ, α's, and β's are hyper-parameters, determined by grid search. $\mathcal{L}_{\text{sim}}$, $\mathcal{L}_{\text{smooth}}$, and $\mathcal{L}_{\text{inc}}$ denote similarity loss, smoothness loss, and incompressibility loss, respectively. During training, we employ mean squared error (MSE) as our similarity loss. We encourage the spatial smoothness of the

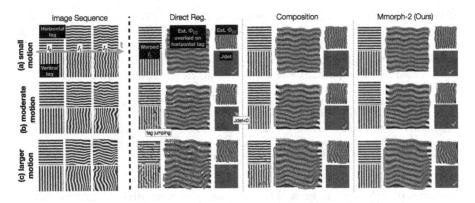

Fig. 4. Qualitative results on synthetic data. The first column displays the input image sequence, while the other columns correspond to the results of different approaches. Row (a) to (c) demonstrate an increasing amount of motion. The red areas on the Jacobian determinant map highlight the locations where foldings occur, and the symbol ✓ represents a pure diffeomorphism. We have omitted the results of Mmorph-1 as they are visually similar to those of Mmorph-2. (Color figure online)

displacement u, with the smoothness loss defined as $\mathcal{L}_{\text{smooth}} = \sum_x |\nabla u(x)|^2$. Incompressibility is a crucial characteristic for image registration in moving biological tissues, such as myocardium muscles, the tongue, and the brain. The Jacobian determinant of a deformation, representing the ratio of volume change, is frequently utilized to quantify growth or shrinkage in biological tissue [9,10,27]. We adopt the determinant-based penalty proposed by DRIMET [8] $\mathcal{L}_{\text{inc}} = \sum_x |\log \max (|J_\phi(x)|, \epsilon)| - \sum_x \min (|J_\phi(x)|, 0)$, where $|J_\phi(x)|$ is the Jacobian determinant of ϕ at x. The $\mathcal{L}_{\text{inc}}$ pushes the Jacobian determinant toward unity, encouraging incompressibility in the deformation field.

The training process is end-to-end, leveraging the differentiability of Eq. (2a) and (2b), exponential mapping, and composition with respect to the velocity field estimated by our network. The $\mathcal{L}_{\text{eul}}$ guides the network to learn effective deformation fields for neighboring frames. Simultaneously, $\mathcal{L}_{\text{lag}}$ encourages the network to predict a temporally-consistent Lagrangian motion field that can match the reference timeframe with any other timeframes, while promoting diffeomorphism and incompressible characteristics.

3   Experiments

3.1   Synthetic Elastic 2D Data

Materials. We synthesized a dataset of 10,000 "movies", where each movie is composed of three sequential images with dimensions 96×96. These images undergo elastic deformation. We ensure that the maximum deformation between consecutive frames does not exceed the theoretical critical point for tag-jumping $(P/2)$. Those deformation fields are subsequently used to deform simulated sinusoidal images (both horizontal and vertical patterns), resulting in a

Table 1. Performance comparison on synthetic 2D data. Wilcoxon signed-rank tests was conducted between "Mmorph-2" and the other methods. The p-values are adjusted by Bonferroni correction (×3). The symbol ** indicates a statistically significant improvement (**: p-value < 0.001; *: p-value < 0.01). **T** indicates how many timeframes is used by each approach. "Mmorph" stands for MomentaMorph.

	T	RMSE ↓			EPE (pix) ↓			NegDet (%) ↓		Time(s) ↓
		Mean ± Std	Median	p	Mean ± Std	Median	p	Mean ± Std	p	Mean
Composition	3	0.073 ± 0.025	0.064	**	1.315 ± 0.587	1.149	*	0.108 ± 0.384	**	0.05
Mmorph-1	3	0.031 ± 0.012	0.027	**	1.304 ± 0.610	1.136	2.76	0.073 ± 0.192	**	0.07
Mmorph-2	3	**0.031 ± 0.014**	**0.025**	–	**1.303 ± 0.610**	**1.130**	–	**0.002 ± 0.012**	–	0.07

time-series of deformed images. The data samples were divided into training, validation, and test datasets in a 6:2:2 ratio.[1]

Evaluation. We assess registration accuracy using two metrics: root mean square error (RMSE) and end point error (EPE). RMSE measures the intensity match between the reference image and the warped moving image, while EPE quantifies the discrepancy between the estimated motion and the motion utilized to generate synthetic moving images. The diffeomorphism of the deformation field is assessed by calculating the percentage of negative determinants (NegDet).

Results. Table 1 offers a comparative analysis of our proposed methods (Mmorph-1,2) against two alternative strategies: Direct Registration (Direct Reg) and Composition. The Direct Reg method serves as a baseline, where we directly estimate the Lagrangian between the reference frame ($t = 0$) and last timeframe ($t = 2$), without utilizing the temporal information within. Its high RMSE and EPE values suggest that the predicted motion significantly deviates due to the tag-jumping issue caused by the periodicity in the images. The Composition approach mitigates the tag-jumping issue by simply composing the Eulerian motion to obtain the Lagrangian motion. However, it is less robust on complicated motion and has a higher percentage of negative determinants. Our proposed "momenta, shooting, and correction" framework (Mmorph-1,2) outperforms the others in terms of registration accuracy and a lower percentage of negative determinants. Interestingly, Mmorph-2, which employs a more accurate approximation of the BCH formula, achieves similar registration accuracy as Mmorph-1 but significantly reduces the percentage of negative determinants in the field, all while maintaining competitive computation time. Figure 4 provides a qualitative comparison of the different strategies on small, moderate, and large motion (Table 2).[2]

3.2 Tongue 3D tMRI Data

Materials. We further validate MomentaMorph using a real 3D MR dataset that includes 25 unique subject-phrase pairs. Participants spoke specific phrases

---

[1] See Appendix ?? for more details on simulation and training.
[2] See Appendix ?? for additional visual results.

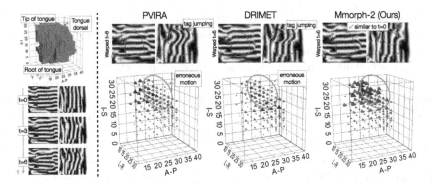

Fig. 5. Qualitative Results on 3D tMRI. The left panel depicts the 3D tongue shape and the sagittal slice with horizontal and vertical patterns. The right panel presents the results of three methods: PVIRA [33], DRIMET [8], and Mmorph-2 (our approach). The results of Mmorph-1 and the composition method have been omitted due to their visual similarity to Mmorph-2.

Table 2. Performance comparison on real 3D tMRI. The notation $\mathbf{T}$ = "a" signifies that the method employs all neighboring pairs between the reference and moving frames for analysis. The p-values are adjusted by Bonferroni correction ($\times 5$).

	$\mathbf{T}$	RMSE ↓ Mean ± Std	Median	p	DetAUC ↑ Mean ± Std	Median	p	NegDet (%) ↓ Mean ± Std	Time(s) ↓ Mean
PVIRA [33]	2	0.211 ± 0.090	0.209	**	$\mathbf{0.915 \pm 0.030}$	0.917	0.55	$2e^{-5} \pm 6e^{-3}$	50.03
DRIMET [8]	2	0.191 ± 0.075	0.185	*	0.910 ± 0.058	0.919	*	$8e^{-6} \pm 1e^{-7}$	0.15
Composition	"a"	0.192 ± 0.074	0.186	**	0.912 ± 0.057	0.923	3.5	$3e^{-4} \pm 1e^{-3}$	0.29
Composition	3	0.190 ± 0.074	0.184	**	0.912 ± 0.055	0.923	4.45	$5e^{-5} \pm 2e^{-4}$	0.24
Mmorph-1	3	0.188 ± 0.073	0.183	2.9	0.913 ± 0.053	0.920	2.95	0 ± 0	0.25
Mmorph-2	3	$\mathbf{0.188 \pm 0.073}$	$\mathbf{0.182}$	–	0.913 ± 0.058	$\mathbf{0.924}$	–	0 ± 0	0.26

during tMRI scans, enabling tongue motion tracking. Each phrase lasts 1 s, during which 26 timeframes were acquired. The data was split subject-phrase-wise into training, validation, and test datasets in a 6:2:2 ratio.

Training Details. We applied a sinusoidal transformation [8] to the harmonic phase images [26] as a preprocessing step. We adopted a similar hyperparameter tuning strategy as in our synthetic experiments. Notably, T timeframes were randomly selected from speech sequences during training. We find $T = 3$ effectively captures large tongue motion while preventing tag jumping.

Evaluation. We do not employ end-point error (EPE) due to the lack of true motion. We use the determinant of the area under the curve (DetAUC) [8] to quantify the incompressibility. This measures how closely the Jacobian of the deformation approaches unity at each location. The motion between the reference frame (i.e., $t = 0$) and all subsequent frames (i.e., $t = 1, 2, \ldots, 26$) is estimated for evaluation. It is important to note that for multi-frame approaches (including ours and the composition approach) that utilize $T \geq 3$ frames, additional $(T-2)$ intermediate frames are evenly sampled from the sequence.

Results. Figure 5 illustrates a case where the tongue initiates from a neutral position ($t = 0$) and subsequently undergoes rapid backward and downward movements, as seen from the bent patterns at ($t = 6$). Both PIVRA and DRIMET are challenged by substantial deformation, resulting in tag jumping. Interestingly, when compared between the composition strategies, composing fewer frames (T = 3) demonstrated a slight advantage over composing every neighboring frame (T = "a"), which could be attributed to the drifting issue caused by successive interpolation. MomentaMorph achieves the best RMSE. In terms of incompressibility, MomentaMorph exhibits performance on par with the others. Consistent with the synthetic experiments, MomentaMorph had a lower percentage negative determinant than the composition strategy.

4   Conclusion and Discussion

In this work, we proposed a "momentum, shooting, and correction" framework that operates within the construct of Lie groups and Lie algebras, which provide a sound theoretical background, to estimate an accurate and biologically plausible Lagrangian motion field. The approach is validated through a 2D simulated dataset with elastic motion and a real 3D tMRI dataset. We believe that our approach is applicable beyond tMRI to general dynamic imaging. As future work, we plan to validate the approach on cardiac imaging during heartbeat cycles and 4D lung CT scans during respiration, where substantial motion is often present.

References

1. Arsigny, V., Commowick, O., Pennec, X., Ayache, N.: A log-Euclidean framework for statistics on diffeomorphisms. In: Larsen, R., Nielsen, M., Sporring, J. (eds.) MICCAI 2006. LNCS, vol. 4190, pp. 924–931. Springer, Heidelberg (2006). https://doi.org/10.1007/11866565_113
2. Axel, L., Dougherty, L.: Heart wall motion: improved method of spatial modulation of magnetization for MR imaging. Radiology **172**(2), 349–350 (1989)
3. Axel, L., Dougherty, L.: MR imaging of motion with spatial modulation of magnetization. Radiology **171**(3), 841–845 (1989)
4. Baker, H.F.: Abel's Theorem and the Allied Theory: Including the Theory of the Theta Functions. University Press (1897)
5. Balakrishnan, G., Zhao, A., Sabuncu, M.R., Guttag, J., Dalca, A.V.: Voxelmorph: a learning framework for deformable medical image registration. IEEE TMI **38**(8), 1788–1800 (2019)
6. Beg, M.F., Miller, M.I., Trouvé, A., Younes, L.: Computing large deformation metric mappings via geodesic flows of diffeomorphisms. IJCV **61**, 139–157 (2005)
7. Bian, Z., Jabri, A., Efros, A.A., Owens, A.: Learning pixel trajectories with multiscale contrastive random walks. In: CVPR, pp. 6508–6519 (2022)
8. Bian, Z., et al.: Drimet: deep registration for 3d incompressible motion estimation in tagged-MRI with application to the tongue. arXiv preprint arXiv:2301.07234 (2023)

9. Bian, Z., Zhong, J., Hatt, C.R., Burris, N.S.: A deformable image registration based method to assess directionality of thoracic aortic aneurysm growth. In: Medical Imaging 2021: Image Processing, vol. 11596, pp. 724–731. SPIE (2021)

10. Burris, N.S., et al.: Vascular deformation mapping for CT surveillance of thoracic aortic aneurysm growth. Radiology **302**(1), 218–225 (2022)

11. Campbell, J.E.: A Course of Differential Geometry. Clarendon Press (1926)

12. Chen, J., et al.: A survey on deep learning in medical image registration: new technologies, uncertainty, evaluation metrics, and beyond. arXiv preprint arXiv:2307.15615 (2023)

13. Christensen, G.E., Rabbitt, R.D., Miller, M.I.: Deformable templates using large deformation kinematics. IEEE TMI **5**(10), 1435–1447 (1996)

14. Dalca, A.V., Balakrishnan, G., Guttag, J., Sabuncu, M.R.: Unsupervised learning for fast probabilistic diffeomorphic registration. In: Frangi, A.F., Schnabel, J.A., Davatzikos, C., Alberola-López, C., Fichtinger, G. (eds.) MICCAI 2018. LNCS, vol. 11070, pp. 729–738. Springer, Cham (2018). https://doi.org/10.1007/978-3-030-00928-1_82

15. Hall, B.C.: Lie groups, lie algebras, and representations. In: Quantum Theory for Mathematicians. GTM, vol. 267, pp. 333–366. Springer, New York (2013). https://doi.org/10.1007/978-1-4614-7116-5_16

16. Hering, A., Häger, S., Moltz, J., Lessmann, N., Heldmann, S., van Ginneken, B.: CNN-based lung CT registration with multiple anatomical constraints. Med. Image Anal. **72**, 102139 (2021)

17. Horn, B.K., Schunck, B.G.: Determining optical flow. Artif. Intell. **17**(1–3), 185–203 (1981)

18. Ibrahim, E.S.H.: Myocardial tagging by cardiovascular magnetic resonance: evolution of techniques-pulse sequences, analysis algorithms, and applications. J. Cardiovasc. Magn. Reson. **13**(1), 1–40 (2011)

19. Jenkinson, M.: Fast, automated. N-dimensional phase-unwrapping algorithm. Mag. Reson. Med. **49**(1), 193–197 (2003)

20. Jia, X., Bartlett, J., Zhang, T., Lu, W., Qiu, Z., Duan, J.: U-net vs transformer: is U-net outdated in medical image registration? In: Lian, C., Cao, X., Rekik, I., Xu, X., Cui, Z. (eds.) MICCAI 2022, pp. 151–160. Springer, Cham (2022). https://doi.org/10.1007/978-3-031-21014-3_16

21. Jonschkowski, R., Stone, A., Barron, J.T., Gordon, A., Konolige, K., Angelova, A.: What matters in unsupervised optical flow. In: Vedaldi, A., Bischof, H., Brox, T., Frahm, J.-M. (eds.) ECCV 2020. LNCS, vol. 12347, pp. 557–572. Springer, Cham (2020). https://doi.org/10.1007/978-3-030-58536-5_33

22. Knutsen, A.K., et al.: Improved measurement of brain deformation during mild head acceleration using a novel tagged MRI sequence. J. Biomech. **47**(14), 3475–3481 (2014)

23. Liu, X., Prince, J.L.: Shortest path refinement for motion estimation from tagged MR images. IEEE TMI **29**(8), 1560–1572 (2010)

24. Liu, Y., Zuo, L., Han, S., Xue, Y., Prince, J.L., Carass, A.: Coordinate translator for learning deformable medical image registration. In: Li, X., Lv, J., Huo, Y., Dong, B., Leahy, R.M., Li, Q. (eds.) Multiscale Multimodal Medical Imaging: Third International Workshop, MMMI 2022, Held in Conjunction with MICCAI 2022, pp. 98–109. Springer, Cham (2022). https://doi.org/10.1007/978-3-031-18814-5_10

25. Mansi, T., Pennec, X., Sermesant, M., Delingette, H., Ayache, N.: iLogDemons: a demons-based registration algorithm for tracking incompressible elastic biological tissues. Int. J. Comput. Vision **92**(1), 92–111 (2011)

26. Osman, N.F., Kerwin, W.S., McVeigh, E.R., Prince, J.L.: Cardiac motion tracking using CINE harmonic phase (HARP) magnetic resonance imaging. Mag. Reson. Med. **42**(6), 1048–1060 (1999)
27. Rohlfing, T., Maurer, C.R., Bluemke, D.A., Jacobs, M.A.: Volume-preserving non-rigid registration of MR breast images using free-form deformation with an incompressibility constraint. IEEE TMI **22**(6), 730–741 (2003)
28. Shao, M., et al.: Analysis of tongue muscle strain during speech from multimodal magnetic resonance imaging. J. Speech Lang. Hear. Res. **66**(2), 513–526 (2023)
29. Spoorthi, G., Gorthi, S., Gorthi, R.K.S.S.: Phasenet: a deep convolutional neural network for two-dimensional phase unwrapping. IEEE Signal Process. Lett. **26**(1), 54–58 (2018)
30. Stone, A., Maurer, D., Ayvaci, A., Angelova, A., Jonschkowski, R.: Smurf: self-teaching multi-frame unsupervised raft with full-image warping. In: CVPR, pp. 3887–3896 (2021)
31. Vialard, F.X., Risser, L., Rueckert, D., Cotter, C.J.: Diffeomorphic 3d image registration via geodesic shooting using an efficient adjoint calculation. Int. J. Comput. Vision **97**, 229–241 (2012)
32. Wang, K., Kemao, Q., Di, J., Zhao, J.: Deep learning spatial phase unwrapping: a comparative review. Adv. Photon. Nexus **1**(1), 014001 (2022)
33. Xing, F., et al.: Phase vector incompressible registration algorithm for motion estimation from tagged magnetic resonance images. IEEE TMI **36**(10), 2116–2128 (2017)
34. Ye, M., et al.: Deeptag: an unsupervised deep learning method for motion tracking on cardiac tagging magnetic resonance images. In: CVPR, pp. 7261–7271 (2021)
35. Yu, J., et al.: New starting point registration method for tagged MRI tongue motion estimation. In: Medical Imaging 2023: Image Processing. SPIE (2023)
36. Zhang, M., Lucas, J., Ba, J., Hinton, G.E.: Lookahead optimizer: k steps forward, 1 step back. Adv. Neural Inf. Process. Syst. **32** (2019)

FusionNet: A Frame Interpolation Network for 4D Heart Models

Chujie Chang[1], Shoko Miyauchi[1(✉)], Ken'ichi Morooka[2], Ryo Kurazume[1], and Oscar Martinez Mozos[3]

[1] Kyushu University, Fukuoka 819-0395, Japan
`miyauchi@ait.kyushu-u.ac.jp`
[2] Okayama University, Okayama 700-8530, Japan
[3] Örebro University, Örebro 701-82, Sweden

Abstract. Cardiac magnetic resonance (CMR) imaging is widely used to visualise cardiac motion and diagnose heart disease. However, standard CMR imaging requires patients to lie still in a confined space inside a loud machine for 40–60 min, which increases patient discomfort. In addition, shorter scan times decrease either or both the temporal and spatial resolutions of cardiac motion, and thus, the diagnostic accuracy of the procedure. Of these, we focus on reduced temporal resolution and propose a neural network called FusionNet to obtain four-dimensional (4D) cardiac motion with high temporal resolution from CMR images captured in a short period of time. The model estimates intermediate 3D heart shapes based on adjacent shapes. The results of an experimental evaluation of the proposed FusionNet model showed that it achieved a performance of over 0.897 in terms of the Dice coefficient, confirming that it can recover shapes more precisely than existing methods. This code is available at: https://github.com/smiyauchi199/FusionNet.git.

Keywords: Frame interpolation · 4D heart model · Generative model

1 Introduction

Cardiac magnetic resonance (CMR) imaging provides non-invasive 4D (i.e. 3D space + time) visualisation (cine images in Fig. 1) of a beating heart over a cardiac cycle. The cardiac cycle consists of two periods: diastole, during which the heart muscle relaxes, and systole, during which the heart contracts. By observing the cardiac motion during this cycle, physicians can diagnose diseases and cardiac defects [10]. However, CMR scans are time-consuming and require patients to lie still in a confined space inside a loud machine for 40–60 min, which increases patient discomfort. Moreover, reducing the acquisition time lowers either or both the temporal and spatial resolutions of the resultant cardiac images, which reduces their usefulness to physicians in accurately diagnosing heart disease.

To reduce CMR scanning times while maintaining spatial and temporal resolutions, various studies [8,14] have been conducted on the application of neural

© The Author(s), under exclusive license to Springer Nature Switzerland AG 2023
J. Woo et al. (Eds.): MICCAI 2023 Workshops, LNCS 14394, pp. 35–44, 2023.
https://doi.org/10.1007/978-3-031-47425-5_4

network models. By contrast, in studies on the temporal resolution of CMR images, Lyu et al. [9] proposed a recurrent neural network (RNN) with a bi-directional convolutional long short-term memory (ConvLSTM) architecture to reduce motion artifacts and perform frame interpolation tasks. However, their method assumed that only one frame of the CMR image was missing from a sequence and did not consider the overall improvement in temporal resolution. In addition, the inputs for their method were 3D (i.e. 2D space + time) CMR images. Kalluri et al. [6] proposed a frame-interpolation network designed to utilise spatiotemporal convolutions to predict the intermediate frames of a video. However, this method is intended for 3D (i.e. 2D space + time) media, and was not designed for application to 4D media, such as 4D CMR images. The frame interpolation results for 4D CRM images can be obtained by stacking the out-put of each slice obtained using these methods. However, in this case, smooth interpolation between slices is difficult because the interpolation of each slice is performed independently.

Therefore, to recover 4D high-frame-rate heart motion from 4D low-frame-rate heart motion generated from CMR images simultaneously, we propose a new frame interpolation network called FusionNet. Furthermore, the results of an experimental evaluation of the performance of the proposed FusionNet confirmed its effectiveness compared with existing methods.

2   Dataset

In this study, we represent one cardiac cycle as a set of 3D voxel models covering the one cardiac cycle in time, called a 4D heart model. Each 3D voxel model represents a 3D heart shape at one specific frame. Among CMR images, 4D cine images from the UK Biobank Resource under Application No. 42239 were used to generate 3D heart models, each corresponding to a single cardiac cycle. The details of the cine images can be found in the UK Biobank [1]. The original cine image dataset contains 50 frames to represent each cardiac cycle. To reduce the complexity of the problem, we only use 10 frames that were subsampled every 5 frames from the original 50 frames. We sampled equally because we want to keep one full cardiac cycle.

In the generation of the 4D heart models, to segment the myocardial region of the left ventricle in each frame, a joint learning model [11] is first applied to a sequence (a set of ten frames) of cine images. Subsequently, a voxel model consisting of $80 \times 80 \times 80$ voxels representing the 3D shape of the segmented myocardial region is generated for the sequence in a similar way to [3]. In the voxel model, myocardial regions are represented by 1 and other regions by 0. This set of ten voxel models is called a high-frame-rate (HFR) heart model X_h ($= 80 \times 80 \times 80 \times 10$ voxels) which is used as the ground truth. In all heart models, the first frame corresponds to the end-diastole of the cardiac cycle. In addition, the heart models are spatially aligned based on the 3D shape of the end-diastole. The HFR set is subsampled at different intervals (lower frequencies) to form a low-frame-rate (LFR) heart model. In our experiments, the subsampling frame interval was set to one, resulting in a subset of five voxel models corresponding to the odd-numbered frames used as the LFR heart model X_l ($= 80 \times 80 \times 80 \times 5$ voxels).

3 FusionNet Architecture

The input to FusionNet is the LFR heart model X_l, and the output is its corresponding HFR heart model X_h. Various diagnostic support systems [3] treat as input only the segmentation results and the volume changes in the heart region calculated from them, not the original MR images. Therefore, FusionNet outputs directly the set of voxel models generated from the segmentation results instead of the original MR images.

As shown in Fig. 1, the architecture of the proposed FusionNet is constructed by adding skip connections, residual blocks [5], and spatiotemporal encoders [6] to a baseline. The baseline is constructed using a generative model [3] which uses the 4D heart models as the input and generates the 4D heart models for visualisation of the shape features that contributed to a classification. Similar to the generative model, our study also aims to build a network with the heart models as the input and output. Therefore, we employed the generative model as the baseline of our network.

The generative model [3] is an explainable classification network for hypertrophic cardiomyopathy. It is composed of a spatial convolutional autoencoder, a three-layer ladder variational autoencoder (LVAE), and a multilayer perceptron (MLP). The input of the network is the 4D heart model containing two-frame voxel models, and the output is also the heart model containing two-frame voxel models restored by LVAE and the classification result obtained by MLP. To achieve frame interpolation from the LFR to the HFR heart model, we modified the baseline network by removing the MLP and changing the number of input and output frames in a 3D convolutional autoencoder. Based on the results of the preliminary experiments, we set the latent variables for each layer of the LVAE to 64, 48, and 32 dimensions.

FusionNet comprises three additional elements compared to the baseline. The first is the addition of skip connections to the spatial encoder and decoder layers of the baseline to prevent the loss of pixel details in the generated image.

The second is the addition of residual blocks [5] to the spatial encoder to solve the degradation problem, which commonly affects deep networks. The residual block consists of two paths: main and skip connection paths. In our network, the main path comprises two convolution blocks, each of which has a $3 \times 3 \times 3$ kernel, whereas the skip connection path has one convolution block of the same kernel size.

The third is the addition of spatiotemporal encoders [6] to extract the features of changes in the heart shape over time. In the baseline spatial encoder, 3D convolution is performed for the 3D space of the heart model. However, the spatial encoder does not consider convolution for temporal shape changes. By contrast, the spatiotemporal encoder performs 3D convolution in 2D space and

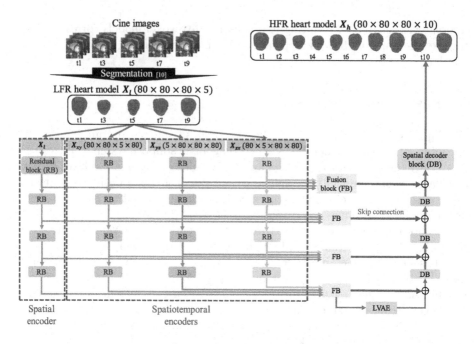

Fig. 1. Overview of our FusionNet.

time. Therefore, it extracts features while considering the temporal 2D shape changes. Given that the heart model contains three-dimensional spatial information, three types of spatiotemporal encoders are trained by transposing the axes of X_l: $X_{xy} = 80 \times 80 \times 5 \times 80$, $X_{yz} = 5 \times 80 \times 80 \times 80$, $X_{zx} = 80 \times 5 \times 80 \times 80$. This changes the combination of 2D spaces to be convolved for each spatiotemporal encoder. To achieve 4D convolution, we combined a spatial encoder and three types of spatiotemporal encoders. The spatial encoder and three spatiotemporal encoders have the same structure. Each encoder consists of four residual blocks, and the output feature from each residual block is fed into the fusion block.

In our network, a fusion block is constructed based on a gated information fusion (GIF) block [7]. The GIF block can adaptively fuse different feature maps obtained from multimodal inputs by learning different weights for each feature map. As shown in Fig. 1, in our fusion block, the four feature maps obtained from the four encoders are concatenated as a feature map. Next, a convolution block with a $3 \times 3 \times 3$ kernel is applied to the concatenated feature map, and a sigmoid function is applied to produce a weight map. Finally, the weight map is multiplied by the concatenated feature map, and a convolution block with a $3 \times 3 \times 1$ kernel is applied to the multiplication result.

In the FusionNet inference, as shown in Fig. 1, an LFR heart model is input to each encoder which consists of four residual blocks. The output of the residual block at a given depth of each encoder is input to the fusion block at that depth to obtain a fused feature of the four encoders. Using skip connections, the fused feature of the deepest fusion block is input to the encoder of the LVAE, whereas the other fused features are input to the corresponding spatial decoding block of the spatial decoder. The output of the LVAE decoder is then input into the spatial decoder. At each spatial decoding block of the spatial decoder, the input is concatenated with the corresponding fused feature. Finally, the spatial decoder outputs the HFR heart model.

The loss function of FusionNet comprises the following four terms: 1) A Dice loss term DL is used to evaluate the degree of similarity between the generated heart model and the ground truth. 2) Three Kullback-Leibler divergence terms KL_i ($i = 1, 2, 3$) are used to penalise the deviations between the prior and posterior distributions at each level of the three-layer LVAE. As the prior distribution for the highest level, we set the standard Gaussian $\mathcal{N}(0, 1)$. Therefore, the loss function L_{system} can be expressed as follows: $L_{system} = DL + \alpha \sum_{i=1}^{3} \beta_i KL_i$, where α and β_i are the weighting factors for each term. In this study, α, β_1, β_2, and β_3 were set to 1.0, 0.001, 0.001, and 0.01, respectively.

FusionNet is trained to minimise L_{system}. The batch size and number of epochs were set to 10 and 500 in our experiments. Early stopping was introduced, and the Adam optimiser was used. The learning rate was set to $1 \times e^{-3}$ and multiplied by 0.5 for each set of 30 epochs.

4 Experiment and Discussion

To evaluate the effectiveness of FusionNet, its accuracy was compared with that of existing methods. We then conducted an ablation study on different components of the FusionNet architecture to evaluate their specific contributions. In the experiments, we simulated frame interpolation over a cardiac cycle (from 1 to 10 frames) to generate an HFR heart model composed of ten voxel models from an LFR heart model composed of five voxel models in odd-numbered frames (1, 3, 5, 7, and 9). The FusionNet was trained from scratch. In the experiments, statistical significance was tested using the t-test.

Each HFR model was divided into two subsets using subsampling. The first subset (input) comprised odd-numbered frames (1, 3, 5, 7, and 9) and corresponded to the input LFR set. The second set (estimated) comprised of even-numbered frames (2, 4, 6, 8, and 10). The estimated set was used as the ground truth. In our experiments, we used FusionNet to estimate frames 2, 4, 6, 8, and 10 using LFR frames 1, 3, 5, 7, and 9 as inputs.

Because it is generally unknown whether a subject is healthy or diseased at the time of scanning, experiments were conducted on datasets that included healthy and diseased subjects without distinction. The original dataset comprised CMR images obtained from 210 subjects (100 patients with ischemic heart disease and 110 healthy subjects). First, 210 heart models were generated from CMR images, as described in Sect. 2. Then, to perform 7-fold cross-validation, the heart models were repeatedly divided into 150 samples as a training dataset, 30 samples as a validation dataset, and 30 samples as a testing dataset while

Table 1. Comparison with previous methods using the average Dice coefficient from 7-fold cross validation.

	Frame 2	Frame 4	Frame 6	Frame 8	Frame 10	Average
FusionNet	**.897 ± .005**	**.879 ± .006**	**.877 ± .007**	**.928 ± .003**	**.905 ± .006**	**.897 ± .019**
ConvLSTM [9]	.884 ± .003	.867 ± .005	.854 ± .006	.912 ± .003	.892 ± .007	.881 ± .020
U-Net [12]	.892 ± .004	.875 ± .004	.871 ± .007	.922 ± .003	.899 ± .008	.892 ± .018
Bilinear [4]	.821 ± .008	.831 ± .008	.813 ± .008	.915 ± .004	.890 ± .005	.854 ± .041

varying the subjects included in the validation and testing datasets. In addition, we performed data augmentation by shifting and rotating the heart models in the training dataset, increasing the number of heart models in the training dataset from 150 to 1200.

To measure the accuracy of our approach, we calculated the Dice similarity coefficient [13] between each generated heart 3D voxel model and the corresponding ground-truth 3D voxel model.

4.1   Comparison with Existing Methods

There are various methods based on neural networks for interpolating the frames of 3D (2D space and time) images. Among them, in this experiment, we compared FusionNet with three existing methods: a ConvLSTM-based method [9], a U-Net-based method, and a bilinear interpolation.

The ConvLSTM-based method is a state-of-the-art frame interpolation method for 3D (2D space and time) cine images. In the method, the voxel model of the estimated frame is obtained using voxel models of multiple adjacent frames centred on the missing frame. In our experiments, the number of input adjacent voxel models was set to four. For example, if we aim to estimate frame number 4, we put two voxel models for frames 1 and 3 into the forward ConvLSTM branch and used two voxel models for frames 5 and 7 in the backward ConvLSTM. Using a separately trained network for each target frame number, we obtained an HFR heart model from the corresponding LFR heart model.

U-Net [12] is frequently used in medical image processing. In this study, the U-Net-based method was constructed by replacing the autoencoder of the U-Net with a 3D convolutional autoencoder for 3D space. The input and output of the U-Net-based method were the same as those of FusionNet; that is, given an LFR heart model as the input, the HFR heart model was the output in a single inference.

The bilinear interpolation is a simple traditional method that does not use neural networks. In the interpolation, a voxel model of the estimated frame is calculated using the voxel models of two adjacent frames. When a simple linear interpolation was applied, the interpolation accuracy was low. To improve the accuracy, for each target voxel, we calculated the target voxel value by considering neighboring voxel values based on the idea of a traditional bilinear interpolation [4].

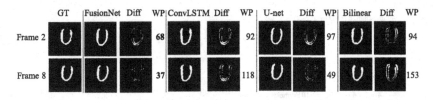

Fig. 2. Cross-section of the generated voxel model corresponding to the estimated frame (e.g. frames 2 and 8) and the difference image between the model and the ground truth. The last column, WP, indicates the number of white pixels in the difference image. The results of our FusionNet contain the lower values.

Table 1 presents the results of the 7-fold cross-validation. Each value in the table shows the average Dice coefficient of FusionNet for the estimated frames of the testing dataset compared with that of the existing methods. FusionNet performed better than the three existing methods for all the frames. For the average Dice coefficient, FusionNet performed better, with a statistical significance level of 0.05. In addition, the first column in Fig. 2 shows the cross-section of the voxel model corresponding to the ground truth. The following columns show the pixel differences from the models estimated using the four approaches. The final column lists the number of different pixels. Our FusionNet achieved a lower pixel difference. Overall, these results show that the proposed FusionNet can generate HFR heart models with higher accuracy than the existing methods.

Table 1 shows that frames 2, 4, and 6 exhibit the lowest accuracies. Figure 3(a) shows the average volume change of the voxel models in each frame, which was calculated from all ground truth 3D voxel models by counting the number of voxels corresponding to the heart region within the model. It can be observed in this figure that frames 2, 4, and 6, which have low accuracy, correspond to frames with drastic volume changes around the end-systole. Even in such cases, the proposed FusionNet outperformed the existing methods in all frames.

Here, a left ventricular (LV) myocardium is treated as the heart region in this study. Dice coefficients for manual LV myocardium segmentation results between different observers were reported to be 0.87–0.88 [2]. In all frames, the Dice coefficients of the proposed FusionNet are equal to or exceed this inter-individual difference. These results show that FusionNet provides stable shape estimation regardless of the frame.

4.2 Ablation Study

We then conducted 7-fold cross-validation by comparing our complete Fusion-Net architecture with the following configurations: FusionNet without skip connections (FusionNet-SC), FusionNet without residual blocks (FusionNet-RB), FusionNet without spatiotemporal encoders (FusionNet-TE), and the baseline described in Sect. 3. The average Dice coefficients for each configuration were **0.897 ± 0.019** (FusionNet), 0.810 ± 0.015 (FusionNet-SC), 0.891 ± 0.019 (FusionNet-RB), 0.892 ± 0.018 (FusionNet-TE), and 0.806 ± 0.016 (baseline).

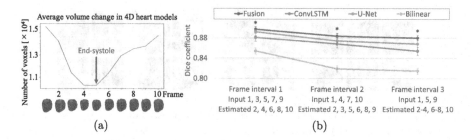

Fig. 3. (a) Average volume change in ground truth 4D cardiac models. (b) Relationship between the average Dice coefficients and the input frame interval for FusionNet and the three existing methods (* p < .05).

Based on the average Dice coefficients, FusionNet exhibited the highest accuracy among the five configurations. This improvement was statistically significant at a significance level of 0.005. The results showed that the addition of each element had a positive effect on FusionNet.

4.3   Robustness to Changes in Frame Intervals

To evaluate the robustness of FusionNet to changes in the frame interval, 7-fold cross-validations were performed for the LFR heart models generated using three different frame intervals for the input: input frame interval 1 (input frames 1, 3, 5, 7, 9, and estimated frames 2, 4, 6, 8, and 10), input frame interval 2 (input frames 1, 4, 7, 10, and estimated frames 2, 3, 5, 6, 8, and 9), and input frame interval 3 (input frames 1, 5, 9, and estimated frames 2, 3, 4, 6, 7, 8, and 10).

Figure 3(b) shows the generation accuracy for different networks using different frame intervals, indicating that FusionNet is statistically better at a significance level of 0.05. Furthermore, FusionNet exhibits a slower decrease in accuracy with increasing frame intervals than the methods based on ConvLSTM and U-Net. These results show that FusionNet, which introduces spatiotemporal convolution into a generative model, is more robust to changes in the frame interval than conventional RNN models or U-Net-based methods which only consider spatial convolution.

5   Conclusion

In this study, we propose FusionNet to estimate a HFR heart model from the corresponding LFR heart model. The experimental results confirmed that FusionNet with spatiotemporal convolution was more accurate and robust to changes in the frame interval than conventional methods using RNNs or spatial convolution alone.

In future work, we can increase the sampling frequency but always need to keep the full cardiac cycle. Also, to further improve the accuracy of frame interpolation, we plan to use not only a 4D heart model but also CMR images as inputs for FusionNet. In addition, by applying FusionNet, we aim to develop a diagnostic support system for heart diseases that can provide highly accurate results, even from low-frame-rate CMR images.

Acknowledgements. This work was supported by JSPS KAKENHI Grant Number 20K19924, the Wallenberg AI, Autonomous Systems and Software Program (WASP), Sweden funded by the Knut and Alice Wallenberg Foundation, Sweden, and used the UK Biobank Resource under application no. 42239.

References

1. Cardiac MRI Procedures in UK Biobank. https://biobank.ndph.ox.ac.uk/showcase/refer.cgi?id=349
2. Bai, W., et al.: Automated cardiovascular magnetic resonance image analysis with fully convolutional networks. J. Cardiovasc. Magn. Reson. **20**(1), 1–12 (2018)
3. Biffi, C., et al.: Explainable anatomical shape analysis through deep hierarchical generative models. IEEE Trans. Med. Imaging **39**(6), 2088–2099 (2020)
4. Bovik, A.C.: Basic gray level image processing. In: Bovik, A. (ed.) The Essential Guide to Image Processing, Chapter 3, pp. 43–68. Academic Press, Boston (2009). https://doi.org/10.1016/B978-0-12-374457-9.00003-2
5. He, K., Zhang, X., Ren, S., Sun, J.: Deep residual learning for image recognition. In: Proceedings of the IEEE Conference on Computer Vision and Pattern Recognition, pp. 770–778 (2016)
6. Kalluri, T., Pathak, D., Chandraker, M., Tran, D.: Flavr: flow-agnostic video representations for fast frame interpolation. In: Proceedings of the IEEE/CVF Winter Conference on Applications of Computer Vision, pp. 2071–2082 (2023)
7. Kim, J., Koh, J., Kim, Y., Choi, J., Hwang, Y., Choi, J.W.: Robust deep multimodal learning based on gated information fusion network. In: Jawahar, C.V., Li, H., Mori, G., Schindler, K. (eds.) ACCV 2018. LNCS, vol. 11364, pp. 90–106. Springer, Cham (2019). https://doi.org/10.1007/978-3-030-20870-7_6
8. Lin, J.-Y., Chang, Y.-C., Hsu, W.H.: Efficient and phase-aware video superresolution for cardiac MRI. In: Martel, A.L., et al. (eds.) MICCAI 2020. LNCS, vol. 12264, pp. 66–76. Springer, Cham (2020). https://doi.org/10.1007/978-3-030-59719-1_7
9. Lyu, Q., et al.: Cine cardiac MRI motion artifact reduction using a recurrent neural network. IEEE Trans. Med. Imaging **40**(8), 2170–2181 (2021)
10. Motwani, M., Kidambi, A., Herzog, B.A., Uddin, A., Greenwood, J.P., Plein, S.: MR imaging of cardiac tumors and masses: a review of methods and clinical applications. Radiology **268**(1), 26–43 (2013)
11. Qin, C., et al.: Joint learning of motion etimation and segmentation for cardiac MR image sequences. In: Frangi, A.F., Schnabel, J.A., Davatzikos, C., Alberola-López, C., Fichtinger, G. (eds.) MICCAI 2018. LNCS, vol. 11071, pp. 472–480. Springer, Cham (2018). https://doi.org/10.1007/978-3-030-00934-2_53
12. Ronneberger, O., Fischer, P., Brox, T.: U-net: convolutional networks for biomedical image segmentation. In: Navab, N., Hornegger, J., Wells, W.M., Frangi, A.F. (eds.) MICCAI 2015. LNCS, vol. 9351, pp. 234–241. Springer, Cham (2015). https://doi.org/10.1007/978-3-319-24574-4_28

13. Sorensen, T.A.: A method of establishing groups of equal amplitude in plant sociology based on similarity of species content and its application to analyses of the vegetation on danish commons. Biol. Skar. **5**, 1–34 (1948)
14. Xia, Y., Ravikumar, N., Greenwood, J.P., Neubauer, S., Petersen, S.E., Frangi, A.F.: Super-resolution of cardiac MR cine imaging using conditional gans and unsupervised transfer learning. Med. Image Anal. **71**, 102037 (2021)

A New Large-Scale Video Dataset of the Eyelid Opening Degree for Deep Regression-Based PERCLOS Estimation

Ko Taniguchi$^{(\boxtimes)}$, Takahiro Noguchi, Satoshi Iizuka, Hiroyasu Ando, Takashi Abe, and Kazuhiro Fukui

University of Tsukuba, Tsukuba, Japan
kotaniguchi@cvlab.cs.tsukuba.ac.jp

Abstract. In this study, we focus on PERcent time of slow eyelid CLO-Sures (PERCLOS), a measure of drowsiness based on physiological indicators. Our main contribution is to design and construct a large-scale dataset for training regression-based models to estimate PERCLOS directly. PERCLOS is known to be highly correlated with decreased vigilance in humans, and its calculation requires the estimation of the Eyelid Opening Degree (EOD). Two approaches can be used to estimate EOD: segmentation-based and regression-based. Although the regression-based approach shows promise, constructing regression models is challenging due to the limited availability of training datasets with assigned EOD. The segmentation-based approach does not require training data with annotated EOD. However, when considering a real-world scenario, it may not be easy to accurately estimate subtle eye-opening levels from the segmentations in low-resolution images. To address the above problems, we constructed a new EOD dataset using a non-contact eye tracker FX3 to acquire EOD and video data simultaneously. Our dataset assigns EOD at the frame level for temporal images near the subject's iris. Furthermore, we used our dataset to train several deep regression models to estimate the EOD from input images directly. Comparison experiments on the dataset confirm that regression outperforms the segmentation baseline, leading to a practical high-performance result.

Keywords: Vigilance Level Estimation · PERCLOS · Eyelid Opening Degree · Dataset Construction · Regression Model

1 Introduction

In modern society, it is necessary to constantly pay attention and maintain sustained concentration while driving to prevent drowsy driving and sudden steering maneuvers. Sleep loss and circadian misalignment can lead to decreased vigilance, resulting in decreased attention [2]. If vigilance declines, it poses a risk of life-threatening situations, such as traffic accidents. The National Highway Traffic Safety Administration

---

K. Taniguchi and T. Noguchi—The authors assert equal contribution and joint first authorship.

Supplementary Information The online version contains supplementary material available at https://doi.org/10.1007/978-3-031-47425-5_5.

J. Woo et al. (Eds.): MICCAI 2023 Workshops, LNCS 14394, pp. 45–55, 2023.
https://doi.org/10.1007/978-3-031-47425-5_5

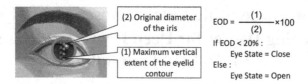

Fig. 1. Definition of the Eyelid Opening Degree (EOD) based on Dinges et al.'s study [1].

(NHTSA) reports that 2.1% to 2.5% of fatal accidents in the United States are attributed to drowsy driving [3]. Subjective sleepiness is more likely to be underestimated compared to objective decreased alertness. Therefore, it is difficult for individuals to notice signs of decreased alertness, and they often find themselves in a dangerous state when they are unaware of their sleepiness [4]. Therefore, it is important for a third party to recognize the decrease in alertness and provide information to the individual.

There are various methods by acquiring and estimating physiological information, such as eye state, facial expressions, heart rate, and brainwaves, to detect vigilance [5,6]. In particular, eye information can be easily obtained using cameras, which can then be used to measure PERcent time of slow eyelid CLOSures (PERCLOS) [7,8]. This metric indicates the percentage of time the eyes are closed during a certain period and has been shown in many studies to have a strong correlation with decreased vigilance [9]. The calculation of PERCLOS requires a measurement known as the Eyelid Opening Degree (EOD) [9] (Fig. 1). EOD is defined as the ratio between the maximum vertical extent of the eyelid contour and the original diameter of the iris. If this ratio is less than 20%, it is considered as closed-eye, and otherwise, it is considered as open-eye. This metric was defined in a study by Dinges et al. [1], which demonstrated the effectiveness of PERCLOS in the field of sleep science for the first time. Many studies have estimated PERCLOS in a non-contact and automatic manner. However, to the best of our knowledge, there are no studies that calculate PERCLOS based on the definition by Dinges et al., and most studies rely on simpler measures, such as Eye Aspect Ratio (EAR) or presence of pupils [10–13].

There are two approaches to estimating EOD based on the definition by Dinges et al.: segmentation-based and regression-based. In the segmentation-based approach, deep learning models are used to extract eyelid contours [14] and perform iris segmentation [15], enabling automated estimation of EOD from facial images. However, these deep learning models assume well-lit, high-resolution images, and there are challenges in robustness and generalization performance when dealing with low-resolution images. In real-world usage scenarios, such as driving environments with constraints, there are issues with cameras and computational resources, and acquiring low-quality images is expected as the focus is on the area near the iris. Therefore, iris segmentation becomes difficult for blink detection and estimating subtle eye-opening states. Meanwhile, the regression-based approach requires labeled ground truths for all images during training. Additionally, during the validation of both approaches, a large amount of paired data consisting of input person images and their corresponding EOD is needed. However, there is currently no dataset available that provides EOD based on the definition by Dinges et al., and the existing datasets that have attempted to annotate eye opening information using their own criteria [16,17] may also suffer from subjectivity and biases, leading to the possibility inaccurate assignment of eye opening information. Therefore, both segmentation-based and regression-based approaches for EOD estimation have limitations and constraints. To achieve accurate and generalizable EOD estimation in low-resolution settings, a new large-scale dataset is required.

In this study, we propose a large-scale image dataset that includes EOD based on the definition by Dinges et al. for temporal person image data. Furthermore, we aim to build a highly accurate and fast EOD estimation model using this dataset. To create such a dataset, we conducted a Vigilance Test [18] using a web camera and the FX3 non-contact eye tracker, equipped with an infrared sensor. In this experiment, videos are recorded using the web camera, and the FX3 captures information such as EOD, pupil diameter, and gaze point location of the subjects. This allows us to acquire a large amount of data consisting of person images with corresponding EOD without the need for manual annotation. We conducted the experiment with 97 participants and obtained approximately 24,000 images per participant, resulting in a total of 2,328,000 person images with EOD. Such data can be considered as paired data, where the person images serve as input, and the corresponding EODs act as the ground truth labels. With this dataset, it becomes possible to train a deep regression model that directly estimates EOD from individual person images captured by a common web camera. Web cameras are affordable and widely accessible, contributing to the proliferation of this technology. When attempting to estimate EOD directly from person images, there is a risk of instability due to the inclusion of unnecessary information, such as background or other facial features besides the eyes. To avoid this, our proposed framework first employs a technique called Blaze Face [19] to extract a rectangular region around the iris. Then, based on the extracted image region near the iris, we construct a regression-based model that outputs the corresponding EOD. This model utilizes popular image classification model, such as VGG19 [20], ResNet [21], EfficientNet [22], and Swin Transformer [23], where the feature extraction and output layers are optimized to accurately estimate EOD from low-resolution images. By training these models using the proposed dataset, it becomes possible to directly estimate EOD from images near the iris without the need for segmentation or other intermediate steps. Validation experiments using test data demonstrate that the regression-based models outperform the segmentation-based models by a significant margin. Furthermore, unlike the segmentation-based models, the regression-based models can directly estimate EOD, enabling fast computation. This research demonstrates the feasibility of a non-contact, sleep science-based approach for estimating vigilance with higher reliability. Our trained model will be made publicly available. Additionally, our dataset will be made publicly available to proven entities upon request and verification.

2   Proposed Dataset

In this study, we constructed a large-scale image dataset that includes EOD based on the definition by Dinges et al. for temporal person image data. To achieve this, we conducted a Vigilance Test [18] using a web camera and non-contact eye tracker.

48   K. Taniguchi et al.

2.1 Experimental Procedure

The experiment involved 97 healthy participants (44 males, 53 females) with an average age of 32.0 ± 13.2 years. The experiment was conducted in an environment with
adequate soundproofing, and the lighting conditions were set to a frontal illuminance of
300 lx. The distance between the display and
participants' eyes was set to 60 cm, and the
angle between the display and line of sight
was set to 30°. The total duration of the experiment was 2 h. During the first 30 min, subjects received an explanation of the experiment and provided their consent to participate.
After calibrating the eye tracking device, they
performed a 3-minute Vigilance Test as a practice. The start time of the 40-minute Vigilance
Test was adjusted to be at 9:00, 11:00, 13:00,
15:00, and 17:00. The experimental setup is
shown in Fig. 2. We used the FX3, a non-
contact eye tracker with an infrared sensor,
developed by Eye Tracking Inc. This device
utilizes infrared technology to measure EOD,

Fig. 2. Experimental environment setup.
The webcam is placed on top of the display. The FX3 is positioned below the display.

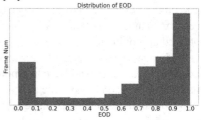

Fig. 3. Distribution of EOD. The x-axis
represents EOD, and the y-axis represents
the number of frames.

pupil diameter, gaze point location, and other metrics at a rate of 61.6 Hz, while simultaneously recording a 10 fps video of the participant. For EOD, if both eyes can be measured, the average value of the left and right eye's EOD is outputted. In the case of measuring only one eye, the EOD of that eye is outputted. In this experiment, we assumed
that the EOD is equal in both eyes because there is virtually no condition in which
only one eye is closed and the degree of vigilance is low. The performance of FX3 is
as follows: Gaze Accuracy: 0.78°/mean, 0.59°/standard deviation; Gaze Field of View:
±30°/horizontal, +30 to −15°/vertical; Field of View: 26°/horizontal, 32°/vertical; and
Relative Distance between FX3 and subjects: 40 to 80cm. The experiment was conducted with the approval of the ethics committee of the affiliated institution. Through
this experiment, a total of 2,328,000 person images with associated EOD information
were obtained. However, the data were imbalanced, as there were fewer images capturing blinks or subtle open-eye states compared to images with eyes fully open. The
distribution of EOD in the proposed dataset is shown in Fig. 3.

2.2 Time Series Data Analysis

Due to the overwhelming majority of open-eye images compared to closed-eye images
obtained from the FX3, there is a possibility that the estimation accuracy for blinks
or subtle open-eye states may decrease if all images are used for training. Therefore,
in this study, we limited the number of open-eye images used for training and validation to three times the number of closed-eye images. For the entire dataset of 97
participants, we used 77 participants' data for training/validation and the remaining 20

participants' data for testing. After data preprocessing, the training/validation dataset consisted of approximately 1,600 images per participant on average, resulting in a total of 161,240 images. Among these, 128,992 images were used for training and 32,248 images for validation. The test dataset consisted of 480,000 images from the 20 participants. For PERCLOS, which indicates the percentage of time with closed eyes within a certain time period, blink events are not included. Therefore, it is necessary to determine whether each sequential image of a person contains blinking or not. To achieve this, the EOD obtained from the FX3 was used to calculate the start and end points of eye closure. Intervals with closed eyes that are less than 500 ms in duration are considered as blink events [4]. Detailed information about blink detection will be provided in the supplemental items.

3   Proposed Approach

As there is no existing method for estimating EOD based on the definition by Dinges et al., we build a baseline model. In this section, we explain two approaches: segmentation-based models, which can be constructed without using the proposed dataset, and regression-based models, which can be trained using the proposed dataset.

Segmentation-Based Model. We construct a framework combining face mesh and iris segmentation (Fig. 4). First, Blaze Face [19], an architecture for face detection and keypoint estimation, is used to quickly estimate the position of the face and facial keypoints in the temporal image sequence. From this, a cropped image near the iris is obtained. For the keypoints representing the eyelids, a quadratic curve approximation is applied to represent the eyelid contour. Then, the maximum visible vertical height in the eye region is calculated from the eyelid contour. Next, the cropped image near the iris is input into the segmentation model to perform iris segmentation. An approximate circle is fitted to the segmentation result to represent the original shape of the iris. The diameter of the fitted circle is equivalent to the diameter of the original iris, and the EOD (Fig. 1) is calculated from these values. As the segmentation architecture, we adopt U-Net [24], and use a total of six models as the encoder: ResNet18 (RN18) [21], ResNet50 (RN50) [21], EfficientNet-b1 (EffNet) [22], Timm-EfficientNet-b4 (timm-EffNet) [22], Mix Vision Transformer-b1 (mit-b1) [25], and Mix Vision Transformer-b4 (mit-b4) [25]. These models are pre-trained on ImageNet [26]. The UBIRIS Periocular dataset [27] is used for training. This dataset includes cropped images covering a large portion of the eye region and masks for the eyebrow, iris, and sclera.

Regression-Based Model. We construct a framework to directly estimate EOD from the cropped images near the iris using the proposed dataset (Fig. 5). Similar to the segmentation-based framework, we first use the Blaze Face architecture to obtain cropped images near the iris from the temporal image sequence. Then, we pass the cropped images to the EOD estimation network to directly estimate the EOD. For the baseline models, we adopt VGG19 [20], ResNet50 (RN50) [21], EfficientNet (EffNet) [22], and Swin Transformer (Swin) [23]. We replace only the output layer to output a 1-dimensional EOD. These models are pre-trained on ImageNet [26], except for the

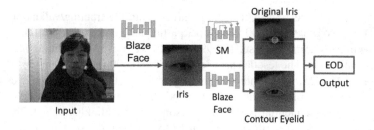

Fig. 4. Framework of the Segmentation-based Models (SM). First, the cropped image near the iris is obtained from the input image using Blaze Face, which also provides keypoints for further processing. Second, a quadratic curve approximation is applied to the keypoints representing the eyelid. Then, the cropped image near the iris is input to the segmentation model to perform iris segmentation. An approximate circle is fitted to the segmentation result to represent the original shape of the iris. Finally, the EOD is calculated from these values.

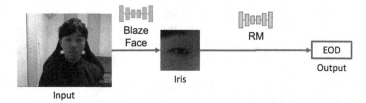

Fig. 5. Framework of the Regression-based Models (RM). First, the cropped image near the iris is cropped from the input image using Blaze Face. Then, the cropped image near the iris is input into the regression model to estimate the EOD.

last fully connected layer. The proposed models enable faster processing compared to the segmentation-based approach as they directly estimate EOD. We train these models using the proposed dataset.

4 Experiments and Analysis

4.1 Implementation Details

Data augmentation is performed in the following steps. The image size is randomly adjusted within the range of 64 to 90 pixels, based on the smaller dimension of the image edges. The image is randomly rotated within the range of -30 to $30°$. A region of size 64×64 pixels is cropped from the center of the image. The image is horizontally flipped with a probability of 0.5, with the vertical axis as the mirror. For the training of the networks, we use the Adam optimizer [28] with an epoch count of 50 and batch size of 8. The learning rate is set to 0.0001, and the Mean Squared Error (MSE) loss function is employed. In this experiment, the evaluation is performed with a focus on the right eye. When calculating PERCLOS, blink detection is performed on the estimated EOD, and the segments corresponding to blinks are removed before the calculation. All experiments are conducted on an NVIDIA GeForce RTX 4090 GPU and Intel(R) Core(TM) i9-12900 CPU.

Table 1. Comparison of MSE, ICC, F-score, and FPS performance for an average of 20 subjects in the Segmentation-based Models (SM) and the Regression-based Models (RM). The best values are shown in bold, and the second best values are underlined.

Method		MSE ↓		ICC ↑		F-score ↑	FPS ↑
		EOD	PERCLOS	EOD	PERCLOS		
SM	EffNet [22]	0.1565	0.1382	0.2006	0.1884	0.1333	26.187
	timm-EffNet [22]	0.1609	0.1628	0.1798	0.1622	0.1319	26.582
	RN18 [21]	0.1377	0.1375	0.19	0.1827	0.1391	53.165
	RN50 [21]	0.1529	0.14	0.1968	0.1843	0.1281	45.684
	mit-b1 [25]	0.1562	0.141	0.1969	0.1828	0.1289	43.303
	mit-b4 [25]	0.1579	0.1363	0.1819	0.169	0.1439	18.177
RM	VGG19 [20]	**0.1002**	<u>0.0785</u>	0.2841	**0.8447**	<u>0.3396</u>	**74.145**
	EffNet [22]	0.1021	0.0846	<u>0.3039</u>	0.8268	0.3214	41.514
	RN50 [21]	0.1121	0.1042	0.2756	0.7889	0.2704	<u>69.817</u>
	Swin [23]	<u>0.1038</u>	**0.0713**	**0.3121**	<u>0.8377</u>	**0.3442**	36.84

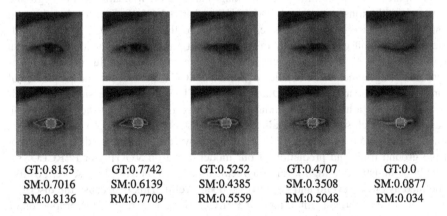

GT:0.8153   GT:0.7742   GT:0.5252   GT:0.4707   GT:0.0
SM:0.7016   SM:0.6139   SM:0.4385   SM:0.3508   SM:0.0877
RM:0.8136   RM:0.7709   RM:0.5559   RM:0.5048   RM:0.034

Fig. 6. The top row represents original images near the iris region. The bottom row depicts the contour of the eyelids and the original shape of the iris, along with the segmentation results of the iris. GT indicates ground truth EOD computed by non-contact type eye tracker FX3 with an infrared sensor. SM represents output EOD of the segmentation-based model using ResNet18. RM represents output EOD of our regression-based model using VGG19.

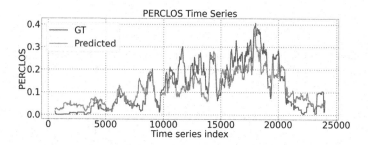

Fig. 7. Time-series PERCLOS data of Ground Truth (GT) and Predicted values of our method. The x-axis represents time series index, and the y-axis represents PERCLOS values. GT indicates PERCLOS for non-contact type eye tracker FX3 with an infrared sensor. Predicted represents predicted PERCLOS using our regression-based model based on VGG19.

4.2 Experimental Results

We quantitatively evaluated the baseline segmentation-based models and our regression-based models. The performances of EOD and PERCLOS at the frame level, in terms of MSE and Intraclass Correlation Coefficients (ICC) [29], were compared for an average of 20 test subjects (Table 1). Additionally, the performance was compared in terms of F-score and FPS. MSE-EOD represents the average squared error in the overall EOD. In cases where the data mainly consists of open eyelid states, the accuracy may be high even if the estimation of EOD for closed eyelid portions is not accurate. Therefore, it is necessary to consider the values of MSE-PERCLOS and F-score. Figure 6 shows the time series of images around the iris, along with the ground truth and predictions output from SM-RN18 and RM-VGG19. The results of eyelid contour, original iris shape, and iris segmentation are also depicted. ICC is used to evaluate the agreement or consistency of measurement values, and its value ranges from -1 to 1. A value close to 1 indicates perfect agreement, while a value close to 0 suggests lack of agreement. The detailed definition of ICC is provided in the supplemental items. When comparing ICC-EOD and ICC-PERCLOS in the regression-based models, the latter has a higher value, indicating that it correctly distinguishes between eye opening and eye closure. Additionally, ICC-PERCLOS has an average value of 0.8245, indicating sufficient agreement [29]. Figure 7 shows the time series distribution plot of the ground truth and prediction of our model based on VGG19 for PERCLOS. It visually demonstrates a high level of agreement between the two. In F-score, Positive is defined as closed eyelid and Negative as open eyelid. This is because the discrimination of closed eyelids is important for PERCLOS, as it represents the proportion of time spent with closed eyelids. Regarding FPS, it is evident that regression-based models achieve higher processing speeds compared to segmentation-based models. This is because segmentation-based models involve multiple steps in handling multidimensional information, whereas regression-based models directly estimate one-dimensional information. Overall, our regression-based models show significantly higher accuracy compared to the segmentation-based models.

5   Conclusions and Future Work

We created a new EOD dataset, taking into consideration the limited availability of the dataset defined by Dinges et al. and the need to directly estimate EOD from low-resolution images near the iris. Our proposed dataset is expected to be useful not only for training models to estimate EOD but also for evaluating vigilance levels. To the best of our knowledge, this is the first study in the field of computer vision that accurately estimated the EOD defined by Dinges et al. Our proposed regression-based models for direct estimation of EOD demonstrated significant performance improvement compared to the segmentation-based models. Furthermore, a high level of agreement is observed when comparing the estimated PERCLOS obtained from the non-contact eye tracker. This demonstrates the effectiveness of vigilance level estimation based solely on time series images. In our future research, we have three considerations: Firstly, we plan to adjust the ratio of open-eye to closed-eye images. This adjustment aims to optimize the balance within the proposed dataset, enhancing the reliability of model training and performance evaluation. Secondly, we plan to apply regression-based models to real driving conditions and validate their accuracy. This step will validate the practical applicability and performance of the proposed dataset and regression-based models, verifying their utility in addressing real-world challenges. Lastly, we plan to utilize the proposed dataset to conduct further investigations of robust regression-based models that take into account time-series data, leveraging techniques such as Long Short-Term Memory [30] and Gated Recurrent Unit [31].

References

1. Dinges, D.F., Mallis, M.M., Maislin, G., Powell, J.W., et al.: Evaluation of techniques for ocular measurement as an index of fatigue and as the basis for alertness management. Technical report (1998)
2. Cohen, D.A., et al.: Uncovering residual effects of chronic sleep loss on human performance. Sci. Transl. Med. 2(14), 14ra3 (2010)
3. National Highway Traffic Safety Administration. Drowsy driving (2018). Accessed 25 June 2023
4. Van Dongen, H.P.A., Maislin, G., Mullington, J.M., Dinges, D.F.: The cumulative cost of additional wakefulness: dose-response effects on neurobehavioral functions and sleep physiology from chronic sleep restriction and total sleep deprivation. Sleep 26(2), 117–126 (2003)
5. Sahayadhas, A., Sundaraj, K., Murugappan, M.: Detecting driver drowsiness based on sensors: a review. Sensors 12(12), 16937–16953 (2012)
6. Drowsiness measures for commercial motor vehicle operations. Accid. Anal. Prev. 126, 146–159 (2019)
7. Wierwille, W.W., Wreggit, S.S., Kirn, C.L., Ellsworth, L.A., Fairbanks, R.J.: Research on vehicle-based driver status/performance monitoring; development, validation, and refinement of algorithms for detection of driver drowsiness. final report. Technical report (1994)
8. Van Dongen, H.P.A., Basner, M., Mullington, J.M., Carlin, M.: Foreword: festschrift in honor of David Dinges, scientist and mentor extraordinaire. SLEEP Adv. (2023)
9. Abe, T.: PERCLOS-based technologies for detecting drowsiness: current evidence and future directions. SLEEP Adv. 4(1) (2023)
10. Soukupova, T., Cech, J.: Eye blink detection using facial landmarks. In: 21st Computer Vision Winter Workshop, Rimske Toplice, Slovenia, p. 2 (2016)

11. Maior, C.B.S., das Chagas Moura, M.J., Santana, J.M.M., Lins, I.D.: Real-time classification for autonomous drowsiness detection using eye aspect ratio. Expert Syst. Appl. **158**, 113505 (2020)
12. Junaedi, S., Akbar, H.: Driver drowsiness detection based on face feature and PERCLOS, vol. 1090, p. 012037. IOP Publishing (2018)
13. Choi, I.-H., Kim, Y.-G.: Head pose and gaze direction tracking for detecting a drowsy driver. In: 2014 International Conference on Big Data and Smart Computing (BIGCOMP), pp. 241–244. IEEE (2014)
14. Zhuang, Q., Kehua, Z., Wang, J., Chen, Q.: Driver fatigue detection method based on eye states with pupil and iris segmentation. IEEE Access **8**, 173440–173449 (2020)
15. Zhao, Q., Jiang, J., Lei, Z., Yi, J.: Detection method of eyes opening and closing ratio for driver's fatigue monitoring. IET Intell. Transp. Syst. **15**(1), 31–42 (2021)
16. Han, W., Yang, Y., Huang, G.-B., Sourina, O., Klanner, F., Denk, C.: Driver drowsiness detection based on novel eye openness recognition method and unsupervised feature learning. In: 2015 IEEE International Conference on Systems, Man, and Cybernetics, pp. 1470–1475. IEEE (2015)
17. Pradhan, T., Bagaria, A.N., Routray, A.: Measurement of PERCLOS using eigen-eyes. In: 2012 4th International Conference on Intelligent Human Computer Interaction (IHCI), pp. 1–4. IEEE (2012)
18. Basner, M., Dinges, D.F.: Maximizing sensitivity of the psychomotor vigilance test (PVT) to sleep loss. Sleep **34**(5), 581–591 (2011)
19. Bazarevsky, V., Kartynnik, Y., Vakunov, A., Raveendran, K., Grundmann, M.: BlazeFace: sub-millisecond neural face detection on mobile GPUs. Comput. Res. Repository (CoRR), abs/1907.05047 (2019)
20. Simonyan, K., Zisserman, A.: Very deep convolutional networks for large-scale image recognition. In: International Conference on Learning Representations (2015)
21. He, K., Zhang, X., Ren, S., Sun, J.: Deep residual learning for image recognition. In: Proceedings of the IEEE Conference on Computer Vision and Pattern Recognition (CVPR), pp. 770–778 (2016)
22. Tan, M., Le, Q.: EfficientNet: rethinking model scaling for convolutional neural networks. In: Proceedings of the 36th International Conference on Machine Learning, vol. 97, pp. 6105–6114. PMLR (2019)
23. Liu, Z., et al.: Swin transformer: hierarchical vision transformer using shifted windows. In: Proceedings of the IEEE/CVF International Conference on Computer Vision (ICCV), pp. 10012–10022 (2021)
24. Ronneberger, O., Fischer, P., Brox, T.: U-net: convolutional networks for biomedical image segmentation. In: Navab, N., Hornegger, J., Wells, W.M., Frangi, A.F. (eds.) MICCAI 2015. LNCS, vol. 9351, pp. 234–241. Springer, Cham (2015). https://doi.org/10.1007/978-3-319-24574-4_28
25. Chen, J.-N., Sun, S., He, J., Torr, P.H.S., Yuille, A., Bai, S.: TransMix: attend to mix for vision transformers. In: Proceedings of the IEEE/CVF Conference on Computer Vision and Pattern Recognition (CVPR), pp. 12135–12144 (2022)
26. Deng, J., Dong, W., Socher, R., Li, L.-J., Li, K., Fei-Fei, L.: ImageNet: a large-scale hierarchical image database. In: 2009 IEEE Conference on Computer Vision and Pattern Recognition (CVPR), pp. 248–255. IEEE (2009)
27. Padole, C., Proença, H.: Periocular recognition: analysis of performance degradation factors. In: Proceedings of the Fifth IAPR/IEEE International Conference on Biometrics, ICB 2012, pp. 439–445. IEEE (2012)
28. Kingma, D.P., Ba, J.: Adam: a method for stochastic optimization. arXiv preprint arXiv:1412.6980 (2014)

29. Koo, T.K., Mae, Y.L.: A guideline of selecting and reporting intraclass correlation coefficients for reliability research. J. Chiropr. Med. **15**(2), 155–163 (2016)
30. Hochreiter, S., Schmidhuber, J.: Long short-term memory. Neural Comput. **9**(8), 1735–1780 (1997)
31. Chung, J., Gulcehre, C., Cho, K., Bengio, Y.: Empirical evaluation of gated recurrent neural networks on sequence modeling. arXiv preprint arXiv:1412.3555 (2014)

Proceedings of the First MICCAI Workshop on Lesion Evaluation and Assessment with Follow-up (LEAF 2023)

A Hierarchical Descriptor Framework for On-the-Fly Anatomical Location Matching Between Longitudinal Studies

Halid Ziya Yerebakan$^{(\boxtimes)}$, Yoshihisa Shinagawa, Mahesh Ranganath, Simon Allen-Raffl, and Gerardo Hermosillo Valadez

Siemens Medical Solutions, Malvern, USA
halid.yerebakan@siemens-healthineers.com

Abstract. We propose a method to match anatomical locations between pairs of medical images in longitudinal comparisons. The matching is made possible by computing a descriptor of the query point in a source image based on a hierarchical sparse sampling of image intensities that encode the location information. Then, a hierarchical search operation finds the corresponding point with the most similar descriptor in the target image. This simple yet powerful strategy reduces the computational time of mapping points to a millisecond scale on a single CPU. Thus, radiologists can compare similar anatomical locations in near real-time without requiring extra architectural costs for precomputing or storing deformation fields from registrations. Our algorithm does not require prior training, resampling, segmentation, or affine transformation steps. We have tested our algorithm on the recently published Deep Lesion Tracking dataset annotations. We observed more accurate matching compared to Deep Lesion Tracker while being 24 times faster than the most precise algorithm reported therein. We also investigated the matching accuracy on CT and MR modalities and compared the proposed algorithm's accuracy against ground truth consolidated from multiple radiologists.

1 Introduction

For many medical image findings, such as lesions, it is essential to assess the progress over time. Thus, comparison between different studies on the medical history of patients is often an indispensable step. However, there is no direct correspondence between the coordinate systems across 3D volumes in different time points due to various scanning conditions. Thus, radiologists must manually navigate to the same anatomical locations in each comparison study.

The mainstream approach for aligning coordinate systems across images is registration. Traditional registration algorithms suffer from computational time since every image pair needs to optimize the deformation field on runtime. Deep learning approaches have improved the computational time of iterative deformable registration methods by learning deformation estimation functions from given pair of images [1,7,8,10,13]. However, the learned network would be

J. Woo et al. (Eds.): MICCAI 2023 Workshops, LNCS 14394, pp. 59–68, 2023.
https://doi.org/10.1007/978-3-031-47425-5_6

optimal only for the dataset types that are present in training. Thus, domain shift adaptation and transfer learning approaches are active research areas in deep learning based medical image registration [14,15].

Full registration is unnecessary for many navigational point matching tasks in routine reading [4,17]. Only corresponding points can be found to reduce computational time. Yan et al. and Cai et al. formulated the problem as a tracking problem [4,17]. They developed an unsupervised learning algorithm for embeddings of anatomical locations in medical images. They used coarse-to-fine embedding levels to combine local and global information. Thanks to these embedding descriptors, finding the corresponding location is reduced to a single convolution operation, which could be computed in 0.23 s using GPU. Liu et al. have extended these descriptors to full registration later [12]. The limited availability of GPUs on runtime and limited generalization of deep models beyond trained body regions or modalities remains a challenge for these models. In the literature, there are other unsupervised/self-supervised/handcrafted descriptor approaches that could be used within similar search framework [3,5,9].

Our point matching algorithm is a descriptor search framework similar to this line of work [4,17]. However, unlike deep learning models, our descriptor is sampling based descriptor, which does not need optimization for training and GPU hardware acceleration. Also, unlike the traditional image matching and tracking methods, our feature representation is more efficient to create, it has a large global receptive field, and it is easy to scale for hierarchical search [2,6,11]. Our method is independent of voxel scaling and modality thanks to world coordinates in medical images. Thus, it has a negligible memory footprint in runtime without the need for preprocessing like affine transformation or resampling.

Our algorithm finds 83.6% of points within 10 mm (or radius for small findings) on the public Deep Lesion Tracking dataset[1] while having runtimes below 200 ms per pair without additional hardware. Also, we have a 1.685 mm median distance error on the mixed modality (CT, MR) dataset, which indicates the general applicability of our method. Our algorithm exhibits higher accuracy as compared to the state-of-the-art machine learning methods while being an order of magnitude faster on runtime.

2   Method

To compare specific locations in follow-up studies, we can set up a function that establishes correspondence in pairs of images. This method is more efficient than fully registering images when only a few points are queried. For example, we can compare a given descriptor in the source image location against every voxel descriptor in the target image. However, this process can still be computationally expensive, especially within 3D volumes. To address this, we've implemented a hierarchical approach in the descriptor formulation and the search processes.

---

[1] https://github.com/JimmyCai91/DLT.

2.1   Descriptor Computation

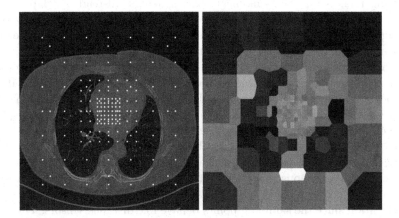

Fig. 1. Descriptors are computed based on fixed sampling offsets for a query location (left). Decoding of the descriptor with nearest neighbor intensities (right).

The central component of any descriptor search approach is designing a good descriptor that produces similar vectors in the same anatomical regions and distinct vectors for different anatomical locations. Distances to neighbor organs are as important as the intensity values at the center to describe the location of the query. Unlike natural images, medical images have accurate spatial dimensions thanks to the world reference frame information included in the image header meta-data, which is the base for medical abnormality assessments. It is especially more stable in longitudinal studies where images are from the same patient. Thus, sampling intensity values with the same spatial offsets have a strong correlation in similar anatomical locations within comparison images.

We first create a sampling model where we define the location offsets in actual mm distances. We prefer more samples in the center and fewer samples in the peripheral regions to reduce descriptor size. This would create a balance between the precision of the location estimation and robustness thanks to the large global field of view. This type of pyramid hierarchy is one of the key ideas in computer vision, validated in many forms for various tasks. In our experiments, we have used 8 mm, 20 mm, 48 mm, and 128 mm distance grids with a grid size of $7 \times 7 \times 7$ in each resolution. As a result, this model creates 1372-dimensional vector descriptors. The maximum value of offsets is 384 mm in this setting, which is sufficient to cover most of the body sizes in medical images. A 2D projection visualization of sampling points is shown in Fig. 1. This sampling model is scaled down by a factor of $1/2$ on each subsequent level of search. In the latest 5th level, these sizes become 0.5 mm, 1.25 mm, 3 mm, and 8 mm in terms of distances which are multiples of typical slice thickness values in CT and MR images. These hyperparameters could be changed according to desired imaging modality. However, we have used the same hyperparameters in all experiments.

After defining the offset model in millimeters, we compute voxel offset according to voxel spacing in the volume. This step will eliminate the requirement of resampling images into the canonical voxel spacings. Instead of adapting the images, we have adapted the offsets of the sampling model accordingly once per image and search level. Thus, the descriptor generation becomes a memory lookup operation of pre-computed offset locations for any given point in the image with almost zero computation and negligible storage, which is much more efficient than any other traditional or deep learning feature extraction. If the offset locations are outside the image volume, they are given the value of 0 for the corresponding dimension. Thus, all descriptors are in the same vector space.

The descriptors are encoded versions of the image since the sampler uses the intensity values directly. Thus, it is possible to reconstruct the image back from the descriptor by using the sampled nearest neighbor intensity values of each voxel location. We demonstrated the center slice of an exemplary reconstructed image from the center point descriptor, as shown in Fig. 1. Our method is sensitive to location since the sampling points behave like distance sensors. Thus, the variance in the visualization is higher than in basic resampling methods. But, this is desirable since translation invariance is harmful for encoding location.

2.2 Similarity

Various similarity measurements are applicable to the proposed approach. However, CT and MR modalities differ from each other in terms of similarity measures. In CT images, intensities are often close to each other due to Hounsfield unit standardization. Thus, Euclidean and cosine similarities are valid choices. We used full vector dimension into cosine similarity which includes the edge information. Intensities and contrasts are variable in the MR modality according to acquisition parameters. In this case, more intensity invariant metric, such as mutual information, is necessary. In our experiments, we obtained better results by combining cosine and mutual information similarities for both modalities.

Mutual information is calculated by taking the joint histogram probability of descriptors $p(x, y)$ of the bin of x and y. The ranges between maximum and minimum intensity values are divided into 16 histogram bins, and the whole histogram is normalized into joint probabilities $p(x, y)$. Then, marginal $p(x)$ and $p(y)$ probabilities could be obtained by adding $p(x, y)$ among rows and columns. Also, sampling offsets outside of the imaging region (which was set to 0) are excluded from mutual information calculation since otherwise, it would distort histogram bins. Finally, the mutual information between two descriptors could be computed as given in the Eq. (1) where K is the number of bins.

$$\sum_{x=1}^{K}\sum_{y=1}^{K} p(x, y) log(p(x, y)/(p(x)p(y))) \tag{1}$$

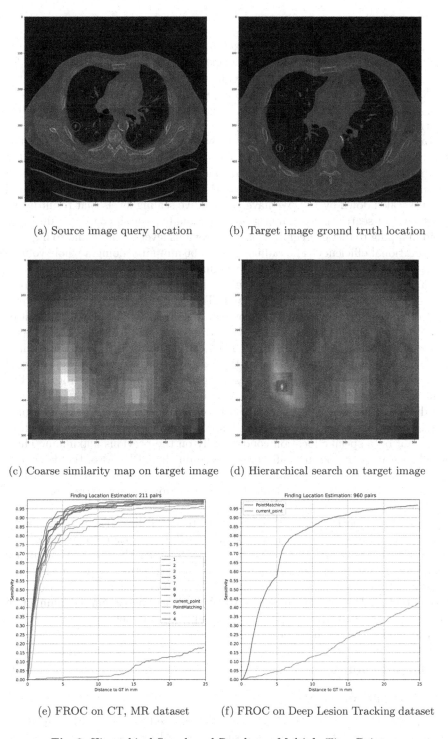

(a) Source image query location

(b) Target image ground truth location

(c) Coarse similarity map on target image

(d) Hierarchical search on target image

(e) FROC on CT, MR dataset

(f) FROC on Deep Lesion Tracking dataset

Fig. 2. Hierarchical Search and Results on Multiple Time Points

2.3 Hierarchical Search

Computing the similarity for every voxel in the target image is computationally expensive. Also, the base sampling model in the original scale is already coarse for descriptor computation which would create similar results on nearby voxels at the top level. Thus, some voxels could be skipped during the search. Based on these facts, we have utilized a coarse-to-fine search strategy to find the corresponding location in the target image.

In the first level, the method starts with a 16 mm equidistant grid. The selected similarity metric is computed for every location in that grid. Then the maximum similarity location is selected to advance the granularity of the search around that location. In the next level, the original sampling model and grid size are scaled down by 1/2. We have applied five scaling levels that result in the finest level of search as the 1 mm grid. Additionally, search space is reduced to avoid mapping to distant regions from the previous level estimate and to improve computational efficiency. The radius is set to 96 mm after doing a whole volume search, and it is reduced to 12 mm in the final level.

In Fig. 2a, there is a lung nodule at the point of interest of the current CT volume as an example of query point. The task is finding the corresponding location in the prior CT volume as shown in Fig. 2b. In the first level, similarities are computed in every location of the 16 mm grid which could be seen as a low-resolution heatmap as in Fig. 2c. Then, until the fifth level, the maximum similarity location is used to continue the search in the next level while reducing the size of the search region. The resulting heatmap is given in Fig. 2d. The similarity in the finest level precisely describes the nodule location. There are two different characteristics as compared to the deep learning-based descriptor search approach [17]. First, the finest similarity is not computed on the whole image but on a specific location conditionally on the previous maximum. Thus, our algorithm is computationally faster, even on the CPU. Also, the descriptor is based on a predefined sampling model, which does not require optimization in training time or any additional computation for feature extraction in the runtime.

Searching in each level is straightforward to parallelize since each similarity calculation is independent with a read-only lookup operation to get candidate descriptors in the target image. Thus, we can compute the different candidate point locations in separate threads. Then, we can select the maximum similarity location after completing all grid points. This approach has massive parallelization potential. However, in practice, CPU hardware has a limited number of threads for parallelization. Thus, we have applied parallelization on the slice level to reduce the overhead of thread creation.

3 Experiments

3.1 Comparison Study

In our first experiment, we compared the proposed method with respect to recently published state-of-the-art results. We utilized Deep Lesion Tracking dataset with testing annotations published by [4]. In our case, however, we did not utilize the training set since training was not necessary. Also, it is worth to note that deep lesion dataset has limited number of slices along z axis which makes it more challenging as compared to regular CT scans.

We have used similar slice sorting steps for loading the image as given in the auxiliary script. Additionally, we have added value 1024 to images to represent them in unsigned integer values due to our imaging environment. The testing set contains 480 × 2 lesion pairs, including both directions from pairs of time points. All images are in the CT modality for this dataset.

Table 1. Deep Lesion Tracking Dataset Results

Method	CPM@10 mm	Average (mm)	Speed(s)
No Registration	12	28.71	–
Affine	48.33	11.2	1.82
VoxelMorph	49.90	10.9	0.46
DEEDS	71.88	7.4	15.3
DLT	78.85	7.0	3.58
PointMatching	**83.6**	**5.94**	**0.149**

We have used the same metrics in our evaluation: Euclidean distance and sensitivity at adaptive distance threshold min(r, 10 mm), where r represents the radius of the finding in comparison as in [4]. Our results are shown in Table 1.

The proposed Point Matching finds closer estimate points with a mean of 5.94 mm in target ground truth compared to other registration or descriptor search methods. We have illustrated the sensitivity at different distance thresholds in an FROC as in Fig. 2f, which represents the cumulative distribution of distances. There is a discontinuity of slope of graph at 5 mm due to the dominant slice thickness of 5 mm. So, if the estimation is one slice off in those cases, the distance would be greater than 5 mm.

The related work reported speed results based on GPU hardware. Our point matching algorithm is faster (149 ms) than all GPU accelerated registration algorithms, even using a single i9-7900x CPU. We have used C++ and OpenMPI for the implementation of the algorithm with 12 threads for parallelization.

3.2 Mixed Modality Dataset

We have evaluated our method additionally on an in-house study dataset containing multi-time point CT and MR modalities. Our dataset contains aortic aneurysms, intracranial aneurysms (ICA), enlarged lymph nodes, kidney lesions, meningioma, and pulmonary nodule pathologies. In this study, the annotations come from multiple annotators. Radiologists were presented with pairs of images along with a description of a predefined finding in the current studies. They were asked to find the corresponding locations in the prior studies.

The measurements are consolidated as ground truth by up to 9 different radiologists by taking the median of their annotations. We have used a series with more than 3 annotators to compare different time points. Overall, 211 pairs of series were selected with this criteria.

We have estimated the corresponding prior locations of the findings with our point matching algorithm compared with expert annotations. We have illustrated the change in sensitivity with different distance thresholds in Fig. 2e. Each annotator is labeled with a number in this figure. Annotators have better localization below the 5 mm. However, due to some annotation disagreement in a few cases, there are two annotators below the automated algorithm in a larger distance range. Notably, our algorithm is very close to an average radiologist annotation robustness at 25 mm.

Table 2. Mixed modality (CT, MR) dataset clinical findings' median errors (mm)

Name	Patients	Pairs	Type	Ours	Expert
Aneurysm	15	44	CT	4.24	2.86
Lung Nodules	15	37	CT	1.14	0.45
Kidney Lesions	15	42	CT	3.08	1.75
ICA	15	33	MR	0.92	0.59
Lymph Nodes	10	27	CT	3.29	2.67
Meningioma	15	28	MR	1.62	1.3
All	85	211	*	1.685	1.11

We have also investigated medians of location estimations of individual pathologies and modalities. The median values of estimations and expert annotations are given in millimeters in Table 2. Lymph nodes and Kidney lesions are more difficult due to less contrast and more variation in abdominal regions. Also, more variation in the center location of findings is present in aortic aneurysms due to larger measurement sizes. Lung nodules are very precise thanks to the reliable chest wall contrast. Similarly, brain MRI studies present good matching performance with the proposed algorithm. Overall algorithm performance is close to the expert annotators with a difference of only 0.6 mm in the medians.

4   Conclusion

We present a simple yet effective method of mapping corresponding locations in a pair of volumetric medical images. Unlike landmarking methods, our method allows arbitrary locations in the source image to be mapped to the target image. Unlike the registration algorithms, it does not map all the points apriori without losing its non-rigid mapping ability. Unlike the deep learning approaches, there is no computation needed to calculate descriptors in the runtime as well as no optimization in training time. Instead, it populates an efficient descriptor with memory lookups in the source image location and finds the corresponding location with the maximum similarity match in the target image with a hierarchical search. Thus, no resampling, initialization, or affine transformation is necessary for the preprocessing. It runs favorably on CPUs while better location estimates than state-of-the-art according to annotations in the public Deep Lesion Benchmark dataset. Additionally, our method works on both CT and MR modalities on different body parts with location estimates comparable to expert annotators.

References

1. Balakrishnan, G., Zhao, A., Sabuncu, M.R., Guttag, J., Dalca, A.V.: VoxelMorph: a learning framework for deformable medical image registration. IEEE Trans. Med. Imaging **38**(8), 1788–1800 (2019)
2. Bay, H., Ess, A., Tuytelaars, T., Van Gool, L.: Speeded-up robust features (SURF). Comput. Vis. Image Underst. **110**(3), 346–359 (2008)
3. Blendowski, M., Nickisch, H., Heinrich, M.P.: How to learn from unlabeled volume data: self-supervised 3D context feature learning. In: Shen, D., et al. (eds.) MICCAI 2019. LNCS, vol. 11769, pp. 649–657. Springer, Cham (2019). https://doi.org/10.1007/978-3-030-32226-7_72
4. Cai, J., et al.: Deep lesion tracker: monitoring lesions in 4D longitudinal imaging studies. In: Proceedings of the IEEE/CVF Conference on Computer Vision and Pattern Recognition, pp. 15159–15169 (2021)
5. Chaitanya, K., Erdil, E., Karani, N., Konukoglu, E.: Contrastive learning of global and local features for medical image segmentation with limited annotations. In: Advances in Neural Information Processing Systems, Pre-proceedings (NeurIPS 2020), vol. 33, pp. 12546–12558 (2020)
6. Grauman, K., Darrell, T.: The pyramid match kernel: discriminative classification with sets of image features. In: Tenth IEEE International Conference on Computer Vision (ICCV 2005), vol. 1, vol. 2, pp. 1458–1465. IEEE (2005)
7. Guo, C.K.: Multi-modal image registration with unsupervised deep learning. Ph.D. thesis, Massachusetts Institute of Technology (2019)
8. Hasenstab, K.A., Tabalon, J., Yuan, N., Retson, T., Hsiao, A.: CNN-based deformable registration facilitates fast and accurate air trapping measurements on inspiratory-expiratory CT. Radiol.: Artif. Intell. e210211 (2021)
9. Heinrich, M.P., et al.: Mind: Modality independent neighbourhood descriptor for multi-modal deformable registration. Med. Image Anal. **16**(7), 1423–1435 (2012)
10. Huang, W., et al.: A coarse-to-fine deformable transformation framework for unsupervised multi-contrast MR image registration with dual consistency constraint. IEEE Trans. Med. Imaging (2021)
11. Karami, E., Prasad, S., Shehata, M.: Image matching using SIFT, SURF, BRIEF and ORB: performance comparison for distorted images. arXiv preprint arXiv:1710.02726 (2017)
12. Liu, F., et al.: SAME: deformable image registration based on self-supervised anatomical embeddings. In: de Bruijne, M., et al. (eds.) MICCAI 2021. LNCS, vol. 12904, pp. 87–97. Springer, Cham (2021). https://doi.org/10.1007/978-3-030-87202-1_9

13. Mok, T.C.W., Chung, A.C.S.: Large deformation diffeomorphic image registration with Laplacian pyramid networks. In: Martel, A.L., et al. (eds.) MICCAI 2020. LNCS, vol. 12263, pp. 211–221. Springer, Cham (2020). https://doi.org/10.1007/978-3-030-59716-0_21
14. Tang, Y., et al.: Self-supervised pre-training of swin transformers for 3D medical image analysis. In: Proceedings of the IEEE/CVF Conference on Computer Vision and Pattern Recognition, pp. 20730–20740 (2022)
15. Varoquaux, G., Cheplygina, V.: Machine learning for medical imaging: methodological failures and recommendations for the future. NPJ Digit. Med. 5(1), 1–8 (2022)
16. Weikert, T., et al.: Reduction in radiologist interpretation time of serial CT and MR imaging findings with deep learning identification of relevant priors, series and finding locations. Acad. Radiol. (2023)
17. Yan, K., et al.: SAM: self-supervised learning of pixel-wise anatomical embeddings in radiological images. IEEE Trans. Med. Imaging 41, 2658–2669 (2022). https://doi.org/10.1109/TMI.2022.3169003

A Two-Species Model for Abnormal Tau Dynamics in Alzheimer's Disease

Zheyu Wen$^{(\boxtimes)}$, Ali Ghafouri, and George Biros

Oden Institute, University of Texas at Austin, 201 E. 24th Street, Austin, TX, USA
{zheyw,ghafouri}@utexas.edu, biros@oden.utexas.edu

Abstract. We construct image-driven, mechanism-based biomarkers for Alzheimer's disease (AD). These markers are parameters and predictions of a biophysical model of misfolded tau propagation, which is calibrated using positron emission tomography (PET) data. An example of such a model is the widely used single-species Fisher-Kolmogorov model (FK). In this article, we reveal a qualitative inconsistency between tau observations and the FK model predictions: FK has a bias towards maintaining the maximum misfolded tau to region of the initial misfolding, which most clinicians and modelers consider it to be the entorhinal cortex (EC). To partially address this EC bias, we introduce a simplified Heterodimer Fisher-Kolmogorov model (HFK) that tracks the dynamics of both abnormal and normal tau. To construct both FK and HFK models, we use a coarse, graph-based representation where nodes represent brain regions and edges represent inter-region connectivity computed using white matter tractography. The model parameters comprise migration, proliferation and clearance rates, which are estimated using a derivative-based optimization algorithm. We compare tau progression predictions between the FK and HFK models and conduct experiments using PET from 45 AD subjects. The HFK model achieved an average of 3.94% less relative fitting error compared to the FK model. Qualitatively, FK model overestimates misfolded tau in EC while HFK does not.

Keywords: Alzheimer tau propagation · Inverse problem · Graph-based representation

1 Introduction

Two prevailing factors in the progression of AD are the progression of misfolding of the amyloid-β and tau protein. Here, we just focus on the misfolded or abnormal tau protein, which is particularly toxic, hindering the proper function of the nervous system and leading to atrophy, necrosis, and ultimately causing death [1,2]. Quantifying the spatio-temporal dynamics of misfolded tau holds the promise of helping understand AD dynamics and generating biomarkers for clinical management. Image-driven biophysical biomarkers have the potential to

Supplementary Information The online version contains supplementary material available at https://doi.org/10.1007/978-3-031-47425-5_7.

help with disease staging and subject stratification [10]. Misfolded tau spreading depends on the initial brain misfolding locations and the rate at which the misfolding amplifies and spreads. Tau aggregates are believed to initiate misfolding in the entorhinal cortex (EC), and primarily invade healthy proteins along neuronal pathways [3,4]. Longitudinal PET scans using F-AV-1451 tracer (tauvid) can image the spread of tau protein. The most commonly used mathematical model for tau progression is the FK model [5,6,15,16]. This model requires the initial state of tau protein and three parameters to describe the migration, proliferation and clearance of tau. However, even qualitatively, the model predicts the highest tau abnormality in regions other than the ones observed in PET scans. This behavior is due to the monotonic property of FK model, which means that the spatial location of the maximum tau does not change and remains the same as the seeding location. This is inconsistent to observed data. We report this inconsistency in Fig. 3 using clinical PET images from Alzheimer's Disease Neuroimaging Initiative (ADNI) [7]. The maximum in the image is not in EC and in some cases it is far from that region.

Contributions: We propose a two-species model, which we term Heterodimer Fisher-Kolmogorov model (HFK) to represent the normal tau (healthy and non-observable) and abnormal tau (observable) progression in AD patients. Our model takes into account the migration, proliferation and clearance of abnormal tau but also its coupling with the normal tau protein. In this context our contributions are the following: (i) We show the monotonic property of FK model both in a synthetic test and clinical results. (ii) We propose the HFK graph model that considers both healthy and unhealthy tau protein. (iii) We propose an inversion algorithm for reconstructing the model parameters. (iv) We test our algorithm on all AD clinical tau PET scans and compare the FK model with the HFK model.

Related Work: FK has been widely studied at different scales in studying protein misfolding in the brain, from molecular level models [11,12] to kinetic equations [9,13,14] and graph models like ours [15–18]. These studies integrated biophysical FK models with MRI and PET data (like us) and relate the initial misfolding location (the seed) and different parameter values to different prion-like diseases, including AD. In AD models, the standard tau seeding location is the EC region. Once biophysical parameters are computed, they are combined with other imaging features for downstream clinical tasks.

There is also work with more complex multi-species AD models [10,19,31] that are similar to our HFK model. In [19], the authors formulate the AD modeling using a two-species framework, and in [10], the authors assume that the healthy tau values are much higher than the abnormal tau and derive the single-species FK model. In all multi-species studies analyze the problem qualitatively and, to our knowledge, they have not fitted these multispecies models to clinical data. Our work aims to provide a first study that does so and compares it with the popular single-species FK model.

2   Methodology

Let $\mathcal{B} \subset \mathbb{R}^3$ be the brain domain and let $\mathbf{x} \in \mathcal{B}$ denote a point. Let $c_a(\mathbf{x}, t)$ denote the abnormal tau, where t represents time from the onset of the disease. To model the spread of abnormal tau in the brain, we first coarsen in space and adopt a graph-based approach that has been widely used in literature [15,16,18]. Specifically, we define a graph $\mathcal{G}$ using a standard parcellation of $\mathcal{B}$. The graph is composed of a set of N vertices, which represents a collection of N regions of interest (ROI) defined in an atlas. Each vertex corresponds to a parcel. The edges between vertices are undirected and their weights $\mathbf{w}$ indicate the white-matter connectivity strength between parcels, from tractography and diffusion tensor imaging. Given the tractography-computed parcel connectivity matrix $\mathbf{D}$ [30], the Laplacian $\mathbf{L}$ is defined by $\mathbf{L} = \mathrm{diag}\left(\sum_{j=1}^{N}[\mathbf{D}(\mathbf{w})]_{ij}\right) - \mathbf{D}(\mathbf{w})$ [20]. We define the set of abnormal tau for all the nodes as $\mathbf{c}_a(t)$ where $c_a^i(t) \in [0, 1]$ represents the abnormal tau at the ith parcel. In order to quantify the level of tau abnormality, we compare the statistical distribution of Tau-PET intensity in gray matter regions with distribution in the cerebellum. To compare these distributions, we employ the Maximum Mean Discrepancy (MMD) metric [24], where we denote μ_i as the MMD score for the ith parcel. Additionally, we normalize the MMD score by defining $c_a^i = 1 - e^{-\mu_i\sigma}$, where σ is a hyperparameter; we select $\sigma = 0.3$ that give the best fit in the inversion. FK and HFK model the tau dynamics at the parcel resolution. They're defined as follows.

Single-species FK Model: The Fisher-Kolmogorov model [5,6,32] is given by

$$\frac{\partial \mathbf{c}_a}{\partial t} = -\kappa \mathbf{L} \mathbf{c}_a + \rho \mathbf{c}_a \odot (\mathbf{1} - \mathbf{c}_a) - \gamma \mathbf{c}_a, \tag{1a}$$

$$\mathbf{c}_a(0) = \mathbf{p}_0. \tag{1b}$$

FK involves three terms: diffusion, reaction and clearance. The diffusion term is defined by $-\kappa \mathbf{L} \mathbf{c}_a$ and $\kappa \in \mathbb{R}^+$ is the diffusion coefficient or migration rate. It captures the spatial spreading. The reaction term is defined by $\rho \mathbf{c}_a \odot (\mathbf{1} - \mathbf{c}_a)$ where $\odot$ is the Hadamard elementwise vector product, and $\rho \in \mathbb{R}^+$ is the proliferation coefficient. Reaction represents growth of abnormal tau within the region. Finally, we define a clearance term as $-\gamma \mathbf{c}_a$ to describe the abnormal protein removal, and $\gamma \in \mathbb{R}^+$ is a clearance coefficient. $\mathbf{p}_0$ is the parametrization of the initial condition $\mathbf{c}_a(0)$. Here, following the current clinical consensus, we fix it at the EC region to be one and zero elsewhere. The time horizon for Eq. (1) is set to one. Using non-dimensional analysis, the change of the time horizon corresponds to just scaling of the model parameters [8]. As we discussed, the FK model is widely used in describing tau propagation but it does not allow the location of maximum tau to change.

Two-species HFK Model: To address this FK limitation, we introduce dynamics for the *normal* tau protein $\mathbf{c}_n$ and we modify the reaction term in

Eq. (1). The HFK model is given by the following ODE system.

$$\frac{\partial \mathbf{c}_a}{\partial t} = -\kappa \mathbf{L} \mathbf{c}_a + \rho \mathbf{c}_a \odot \mathbf{c}_n - \gamma \mathbf{c}_a, \tag{2a}$$

$$\frac{\partial \mathbf{c}_n}{\partial t} = -\rho \mathbf{c}_a \odot \mathbf{c}_n, \tag{2b}$$

$$\mathbf{c}_a(0) = \mathbf{p}_0, \quad \mathbf{c}_n(0) = 1 - \mathbf{p}_0. \tag{2c}$$

Here $\kappa, \rho, \gamma, \mathbf{p}_0$ are defined as in Eq. (1). The time horizon is set to one. Again $\mathbf{p}_0$ is fixed to be one at EC and zero elsewhere. We assume there is no diffusion and clearance for normal tau. Notice that since $\mathbf{c}_n = 0$ at EC at all times, $\mathbf{c}_a$ at EC can only spread and never grow. This minimal change allows the location of maximum tau to temporally change, without introducing any new model parameters.

Parameter Estimation: We aim to estimate the migration κ, proliferation ρ and clearance γ coefficients given the PET data $\mathbf{d}$ (normalized MMD scores). The optimization problem, for the HFK case, is given by

$$\min_{\kappa, \rho, \gamma} J := \frac{1}{2} \|\mathbf{c}_a(1) - \mathbf{d}\|_2^2$$

$$\text{subject to} \begin{cases} \frac{\partial \mathbf{c}_a}{\partial t} = -\kappa \mathbf{L} \mathbf{c}_a + \rho \mathbf{c}_a \odot \mathbf{c}_n - \gamma \mathbf{c}_a, \\ \frac{\partial \mathbf{c}_n}{\partial t} = -\rho \mathbf{c}_a \odot \mathbf{c}_n, \\ \mathbf{c}_a(0) = \mathbf{p}_0, \\ \mathbf{c}_n(0) = 1 - \mathbf{p}_0, \\ \kappa, \ \rho, \ \gamma \geq 0. \end{cases} \tag{3}$$

where $\mathbf{d}$ is the PET subject tau abnormality for all parcels. To solve this constrained optimization problem, we introduce adjoint variables $\mathbf{a}_a$ and $\mathbf{a}_n$ and form the Lagrangian $\mathcal{L}$ [33]. Taking variations w.r.t the adjoints recovers Eq. (2). Taking variations w.r.t to $\mathbf{c}_a$ and $\mathbf{c}_n$ leads to the adjoint equations $\frac{\partial \mathbf{a}_a}{\partial t} = \kappa \mathbf{L}^\mathsf{T} \mathbf{a}_a + \rho \mathbf{c}_n \odot (\mathbf{a}_n - \mathbf{a}_a) + \gamma \mathbf{a}_a$, $\frac{\partial \mathbf{a}_n}{\partial t} = \rho \mathbf{c}_a \odot (\mathbf{a}_n - \mathbf{a}_a)$, $\mathbf{a}_a(1) = \mathbf{d} - \mathbf{c}_a(1)$, $\mathbf{a}_n(1) = \mathbf{0}$. Taking variations w.r.t the model parameters give the gradient equations $\frac{\partial \mathcal{L}}{\partial \kappa} = \int_0^1 \mathbf{a}_a^\mathsf{T}(\mathbf{L}\mathbf{c}_a)dt$, $\frac{\partial \mathcal{L}}{\partial \rho} = \int_0^1 (\mathbf{a}_n - \mathbf{a}_a)^\mathsf{T} \mathbf{c}_a \odot \mathbf{c}_n dt$ and $\frac{\partial \mathcal{L}}{\partial \gamma} = \int_0^1 \mathbf{a}_a^\mathsf{T} \mathbf{c}_a dt$. To evaluate the derivative of J w.r.t the parameters, we first solve Eq. (2) to get $\mathbf{c}_a(t), \mathbf{c}_n(t)$, then we solve the adjoint equations backward in time for $\mathbf{a}_n(t), \mathbf{a}_a(t)$, and finally we plug these values to the gradient.

Numerical Scheme: We use the LSODA ODE solver [26]. The parameters $\kappa, \ \rho, \ \gamma \in [0, \infty]$. We set the initial guess $\kappa = 0, \ \rho = 0, \ \gamma = 0$. The optimization problem is solved using a reduced gradient L-BFGS solver [21]. The optimizer stops when the gradients are below tolerance 1E$-$3. It turns out that the inversion is not sensitive to the initial guess.

3 Results

We evaluate the new model by answering the following two questions:

(Q1) How do the dynamics of the HFK and FK differ?
(Q2) How well can HFK and FK fit clinical scans?

We discuss the first point using synthetic simulations. We provide preliminary results for the second question using all AD scans from ADNI. We evaluate our results both qualitatively and quantitatively.

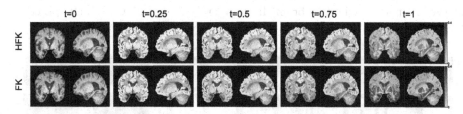

Fig. 1. Spatiotemporal progression of tau using HFK and FK models. Given the same initial tau seed and model parameters for both models, we show the propagation of tau over time (from left to right). The top row are results from HFK model. Results from FK are shown in the bottom row. The EC parcel is highlighted by blue solid contour lines. (Color figure online)

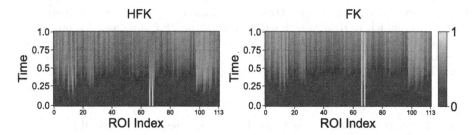

Fig. 2. Average spatio-temporal dynamics of tau propagation for HFK and FK forward model. Given the same initial seed located at the EC parcel, we feed the HFK and FK model with 1000 sets of parameters, and *average* the ODE solution at $t \in [0, T]$ across all parameter sets. X-axis represents parcels in the brain under MUSE template (space information), and Y-axis presents 50 uniformly-spaced time points in $t \in [0, 1]$. The two bright lines correspond to the EC parcels. HFK and FK perform qualitatively differently, as in the majority of cases the maximum misfolding is in the EC region for FK; but not for HFK.

(Q1) Synthetic Simulations: To illustrate the model differences, we generate data using Eq. (1) and Eq. (2) and $\kappa = 4$, $\rho = 5$, $\gamma = 1$. The initial misfolding is placed at the left and right EC parcels. The simulation time horizon is set to one and we sample five time snapshots at $t = 0$, 0.25, 0.5, 0.75, 1. We show the results in Fig. 1. Notice the significant differences in EC $\mathbf{c}_a(t)$ for $t \geq 0.5$.

The FK model maintains the EC to be the maximum whereas HFK does not. Again, at time $t = 1$, EC remains the region with maximum $\mathbf{c}_a$ in FK whereas in HFK other regions have higher $\mathbf{c}_a$. Qualitatively, the HFK dynamics better align with the clinical Tau-PET data.

We repeat these simulations for 1000 sets of parameters, and record the average spatio-temporal dynamics for both models over all sets of parameters. We sample uniformly from $\kappa \in [0, 10]$, $\rho \in [0, 20]$ and $\gamma \in [0, 5]$ for both models. The range of parameters are chosen since the ODE solution from them represent the patterns observed in clinical data. In addition, the inverted parameters lies in these ranges, which makes the choice reasonable. The FK-maximum remains at the EC parcels (the two bright lines in Fig. 1), whereas this is not the case for the HFK model.

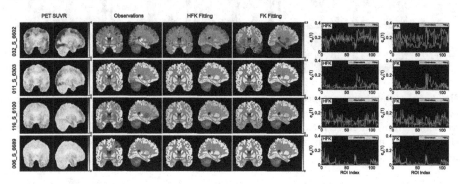

Fig. 3. Model calibration for four AD subjects from ADNI. Each row corresponds to a subject. From left to right in each panel we show the PET abnormal tau, processed regional abnormal tau MMD, the HFK fit, and the FK fit. The 1D curves show the HFK and FK fits as a function of the parcel id (ROI Index). In the 2D images, the EC region is highlighted by a solid contour line.

Table 1. Inversion results for four ADNI subjects using the FK and HFK models. $e_{\mathbf{d},\ell_1}$ and $e_{\mathbf{d},\ell_2}$ (or $\sqrt{2J}/\|\mathbf{d}\|_2$ from Eq. (3)) are relative fitting errors in ℓ_1 and ℓ_2 norms separately. κ, ρ and γ are estimated parameters from each model. For each subject, better fitting with lower errors are in bold.

SubjectId	HFK					FK				
	$e_{\mathbf{d},\ell_2}$	$e_{\mathbf{d},\ell_1}$	κ	ρ	γ	$e_{\mathbf{d},\ell_2}$	$e_{\mathbf{d},\ell_1}$	κ	ρ	γ
032_S_6602	**3.39E−1**	**2.83E−1**	9.86	9.34	3.63	6.78E−1	6.21E−1	4.06	3.68	2.34E−1
011_S_6303	**6.88E−1**	**6.54E−1**	5.58	2.06	1.29E−1	9.10E−1	8.44E−1	2.10	1.94	7.52E−1
116_S_6100	**5.69E−1**	**5.59E−1**	6.72	8.71	4.55	6.31E−1	6.23E−1	5.36	2.93	3.79E−1
006_S_6689	6.96E−1	**6.00E−1**	2.40	1.01	0	**6.94E−1**	6.29E−1	3.10	1.30	2.64E−1

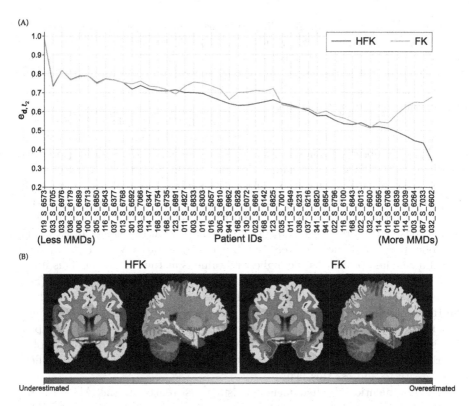

Fig. 4. Evaluation on 45 ADNI AD subjects. (A) ℓ_2 misfit error for FK and HFK (two-subject moving average). The subjects are sorted by total MMD scores (sum over regions). HFK does slightly better but both models struggle especially for subjects with high MMD. (B) Over- and underestimated regions for HFK and FK models. We average the fitting result for each region over all subjects and compare with averaged MMD data. The over- or underestimation for each region is determined by the relative difference between fitting and observation. FK model consistently overestimates the EC region while HFK not

(Q2) Clinical PET Data: We use preprocessed MRI and PET images downloaded from ADNI [7]. Although many subjects have several PET time snapshots available, in this study we only use one of them. (Using more time snapshots is part of ongoing work.) In total, we have 45 AD subjects, 19 of them are female and 26 are male with age mean(std) is 74.95(8.87). The acquisition time spans from 09/07/2017 to 05/17/2022. We follow the preprocessing workflow from [16]. For each subject, affine registration is performed for the T1 image of each subject to healthy brain template using FSL [22]. The subject's image is then parcellated using the MUSE template [23]. PET images are intensity-normalized by the median in the gray matter of cerebellum, which results in Standard Uptake Value Ratio (SUVR). The SUVR values are quite noisy. As discussed above, we define the regional tau abnormality with MMD [24]. As most ADNI patients don't have DTI data, we use 20 Diffusion Tensor Imaging (DTI) scans obtained from the Harvard Aging Brain Study (HABS) [25] to generate 20 connectivity matrices $\mathbf{D}$ using the MRtrix3 software [30]. Throughout all experiments, we consistently utilize the same connectivity matrix, which is obtained by first averaging the connectivity matrices from the 20 DTI images from HABS and then forming the graph Laplacian.

We present our algorithm's performance qualitatively on four clinical scans and quantitatively on all AD subjects from the ADNI dataset. The regional (or per parcel) observed abnormal tau $\mathbf{d}$ is computed by the Tau-PET images described above. We aim to estimate migration, proliferation and clearance coefficients for both models separately. Qualitative evaluations are present in Fig. 3. For each patient, the figure shows its Tau-PET image, parcellated tau MMD data, and inversion results from HFK and FK models. The Tau-PET scans and observations in the first three subjects do not have high tau values in EC. The FK model tries to fit the observed data but it is qualitatively off. Both models do well in the last patient as the highest c_a value is at the EC parcel. This illustrates that HFK is also capable to maintain a high EC tau value if needed. (See supplementary for tau progression videos.) We report the fit errors in Table 1. The HFK model performs slightly better but both models struggle. The results point to the need for a richer parametrization or different models. For example, what if the widely accepted assumption of the EC region being the tau misfolding origination is not correct? Previous studies in the literature have identified the necessity to address this [34].

The aforementioned phenomenon exists consistently in the AD dataset. Figure 4(A) shows the overall performance across all AD patients data. The patients are sorted by their summation of MMD in all regions, lower to higher. In this sense the tau abnormality signal is stronger from left to right. For each subject we report the relative ℓ_2 norm error. HFK achieves 3.94% better relative error in ℓ_2 norm over FK. Furthermore, to visualize the estimation error of FK model on EC region, we present a qualitative evaluation in Fig. 4(B). We average the fitting results for each parcel over patients, and compare with averaged observation MMD data. The under- or overestimation is computed according to the relative difference between regional fitting and regional MMD data. The significant difference lies in EC region between HFK and FK models.

4   Conclusions

We presented HFK, a simple model (in terms of number of free parameters) to describe the abnormal tau propagation in the brain. Our main point is that the commonly used FK model is inconsistent with the observed tau data. Similarly to FK, HFK captures migration, proliferation, and clearance of the abnormal tau in a graph model, but in addition introduces dynamics for the normal tau. The HFK has a *a qualitatively different* behavior and matches the observed data better. We also presented an observation model using MMD and a reconstruction algorithm to estimate migration, proliferation and clearance coefficients of the model based on the observation. We tested the two models on both synthetic and clinical data. From the performance averaged over all AD patients, FK consistently overestimates EC regions. Without increasing the number of model parameters, we improved the model performance. Specifically, when the maximum signal in PET does not lie in EC region, the HFK model outperforms the FK one.

The results however show that both models struggle to fit the data. A possible reason that our assumption of placing the tau abnormality origination at the entorhinal cortex. A potential solution may take initial condition as an additional variable to optimize and apply ℓ_0 or ℓ_1 constraints. Future work includes relaxing this assumption and inverting for the initial condition in Eq. (2), as well as conducting sensitivity studies on the parcellation and tractography algorithms. In the supplementary material, we provide a video demonstrating the fitting results obtained using the exhaustively searched IC. Two other directions in increasing the biophysical model fidelity is coupling to the gray matter atrophy and to amyloid-β dynamics.

References

1. Sintini, I., et al.: Longitudinal tau-pet uptake and atrophy in atypical Alzheimer's disease. NeuroImage: Clin. **23**, 101823 (2019)
2. Bucci, M., Chiotis, K., Nordberg, A.: Alzheimer's disease profiled by fluid and imaging markers: tau pet best predicts cognitive decline. Molecul. Psychiat. **26**(10), 5888–5898 (2021)
3. Braak, H., Del Tredici, K.: The preclinical phase of the pathological process underlying sporadic alzheimer's disease. Brain **138**(10), 2814–2833 (2015)
4. Braak, H., Braak, E.: Neuropathological stageing of Alzheimer-related changes. Acta Neuropathol. **82**(4), 239–259 (1991)
5. Fisher, R.A.: The wave of advance of advantageous genes. Annal. Eugen. **7**(4), 355–369 (1937)
6. Kolmogorov, A.N.: A study of the equation of diffusion with increase in the quantity of matter, and its application to a biological problem. Moscow Univ. Bull. Math. **1**, 1–25 (1937)
7. Petersen, R.C., et al.: Alzheimer's disease neuroimaging initiative (ADNI): clinical characterization. Neurology **74**(3), 201–209 (2010). http://adni.loni.usc.edu/
8. Subramanian, S., Scheufele, K., Mehl, M., Biros, G.: Where did the tumor start? An inverse solver with sparse localization for tumor growth models. Inverse Probl. **36**(4), 045006 (2020)
9. Scheufele, K., Subramanian, S., Biros, G.: Calibration of biophysical models for tau-protein spreading in Alzheimer's disease from pet-MRI. arXiv preprint arXiv: 2007.01236 (2020)
10. Fornari, S., Schäfer, A., Jucker, M., Goriely, A., Kuhl, E.: Prion-like spreading of Alzheimer's disease within the brain's connectome. J. Roy. Soc. Interf. **16**(159), 20190356 (2019)

11. Cohen, F.E., Pan, K.M., Huang, Z., Baldwin, M., Fletterick, R.J., Prusiner, S.B.: Structural clues to prion replication. Science **264**(5158), 530–531 (1994)
12. Jarrett, J.T., Lansbury, P.T., Jr.: Seeding "one-dimensional crystallization" of amyloid: a pathogenic mechanism in Alzheimer's disease and scrapie? Cell **73**(6), 1055–1058 (1993)
13. Bertsch, M., Franchi, B., Marcello, N., Tesi, M.C., Tosin, A.: Alzheimer's disease: a mathematical model for onset and progression. Math. Med. Biol. J. IMA **34**(2), 193–214 (2017)
14. Weickenmeier, J., Kuhl, E., Goriely, A.: Multiphysics of prionlike diseases: progression and atrophy. Phys. Rev. Lett. **121**(15), 158101 (2018)
15. Schäfer, A., Peirlinck, M., Linka, K., Kuhl, E.: Alzheimer's Disease Neuroimaging Initiative (ADNI): Bayesian physics-based modeling of tau propagation in Alzheimer's disease. Front. Physiol. **12**, 702975 (2021)
16. Vogel, J.W., et al.: Spread of pathological tau proteins through communicating neurons in human Alzheimer's disease. Nat. Commun. **11**(1), 2612 (2020)
17. Garbarino, S., Marco, L.: Alzheimer's Disease Neuroimaging Initiative: Investigating hypotheses of neurodegeneration by learning dynamical systems of protein propagation in the brain. Neuroimage **235**, 117980 (2021)
18. Kim, H.R., et al.: Comparison of Amyloid beta and tau spread models in Alzheimer's disease. Cereb. Cortex **29**(10), 4291–4302 (2019)
19. Matthäus, F.: Diffusion versus network models as descriptions for the spread of prion diseases in the brain. J. Theor. Biol. **240**(1), 104–113 (2006)
20. Chung, F.R.: Spectral Graph Theory, Chapter 1. American Mathematical Society (1997)
21. Zhu, C., Byrd, R.H., Lu, P., Nocedal, J.: Algorithm 778: L-BFGS-B: Fortran subroutines for large-scale bound-constrained optimization. ACM Trans. Math. Softw. **23**(4), 550–560 (1997)
22. Smith, S.M., et al.: Advances in functional and structural MR image analysis and implementation as FSL. Neuroimage **23**, S208–S219 (2004)
23. Doshi, J., Erus, G., Ou, Y., Resnick, S.M., Gur, R.C., Gur, R.E.: Alzheimer's Neuroimaging Initiative: MUSE: MUlti-atlas region Segmentation utilizing Ensembles of registration algorithms and parameters, and locally optimal atlas selection. Neuroimage **127**, 186–195 (2016)
24. Gretton, A., Borgwardt, K.M., Rasch, M.J., Schölkopf, B., Smola, A.: A kernel two-sample test. J. Mach. Learn. Res. **13**(1), 723–773 (2012)
25. Dagley, A., et al.: Harvard aging brain study: dataset and accessibility. Neuroimage **144**, 255–258 (2017). https://habs.mgh.harvard.edu/
26. Petzold, L.: Automatic selection of methods for solving stiff and nonstiff systems of ordinary differential equations. SIAM J. Sci. Satist. Comput. **4**(1), 136–148 (1983)
27. Morey, R.D., Romeijn, J.-W., Rouder, J.N.: The philosophy of Bayes factors and the quantification of statistical evidence. J. Math. Psychol. **72**, 6–18 (2016)
28. Spiegelhalter, D.J., Best, N.G., Carlin, B.P., Van Der Linde, A.: Bayesian measures of model complexity and fit. J. Roy. Stat. Soc. Ser. B (Stat. Methodol.) **64**(4), 583–639 (2002)
29. Stoica, P., Selen, Y.: Model-order selection: a review of information criterion rules. IEEE Signal Process. Magaz. **21**(4), 36–47 (2004)
30. Tournier, J.-D., et al.: MRtrix3: a fast, flexible and open software framework for medical image processing and visualisation. Neuroimage **202**, 116–137 (2019)
31. Weickenmeier, J., et al.: A physics-based model explains the prion-like features of neurodegeneration in Alzheimer's disease, Parkinson's disease, and amyotrophic lateral sclerosis. J. Mech. Phys. Solids **124**, 264–281 (2019)

32. Iturria-Medina, Y., et al.: Epidemic spreading model to characterize misfolded proteins propagation in aging and associated neurodegenerative disorders. PLoS Comput. Biol. **10**(11) (2014)
33. Tröltzsch, F.: Optimal control of partial differential equations: theory, methods, and applications. Am. Math. Soc. **112** (2010)
34. Vogel, J.W., et al.: Four distinct trajectories of tau deposition identified in Alzheimer's disease. Nat. Med. **27**(5), 871–881 (2021)

Outlier Robust Disease Classification via Stochastic Confidence Network

Kyungsu Lee[1], Haeyun Lee[2], Georges El Fakhri[3], Jorge Sepulcre[3],
Xiaofeng Liu[3], Fangxu Xing[3], Jae Youn Hwang[1(✉)], and Jonghye Woo[3(✉)]

[1] Department of Electrical Engineering and Computer Science, Daegu Gyeongbuk
Institute of Science and Technology, Daegu 42988, South Korea
jyhwang@dgist.ac.kr
[2] Production Engineering Research Team, Samsung SDI, Yongin 17084, South Korea
[3] Gordon Center for Medical Imaging, Department of Radiology, Massachusetts
General Hospital and Harvard Medical School, Boston, MA 02114, USA

Abstract. Accurate and timely diagnosis and classification of diseases
using medical imaging data are essential for effective treatment planning and prognosis. Yet, the presence of outliers, which are rare and
distinctive data samples, can result in substantial deviations from the
typical distribution of a dataset, particularly due to atypical or uncom-
mon medical conditions. Consequently, outliers can significantly impact
the accuracy of deep learning (DL) models used in medical imaging-
based diagnosis. To counter this, in this work, we propose a novel DL
model, dubbed the Stochastic Confidence Network (SCN), designed to be
robust to outliers. SCN leverages image patches and generates a decoded
latent matrix representing high-level categorical features. By performing
a stochastic comparison of the decoded latent matrix between outliers
and typical samples, SCN eliminates irrelevant patches of outliers and
resamples outliers into a typical distribution, thereby ensuring statistically confident predictions. We evaluated the performance of SCN on two
databases for diagnosing breast tumors with 780 ultrasound images and
Alzheimer's disease with 2,700 3D PET volumes, with outliers present
in both databases. Our experimental results demonstrated the robustness of SCN in classifying outliers, thereby yielding improved diagnostic
performance, compared with state-of-the-art models, by a large margin.
Our findings suggest that SCN can provide precise and outlier-resistant
diagnostic performance in breast cancer and Alzheimer's disease and is
scalable to other medical imaging modalities.

Keywords: PET · Ultrasound · Statistics · Statistical Analysis

1 Introduction

Accurate and timely diagnosis and classification of diseases is essential for effective treatment planning and prognosis. Despite significant advances in deep

Supplementary Information The online version contains supplementary material
available at https://doi.org/10.1007/978-3-031-47425-5_8.

learning (DL), accurate diagnosis and classification of diseases using medical imaging data remain challenging tasks, which can be partially attributed to data quality issues, such as inconsistencies, noise, missing data, outliers, or imbalanced data. In this work, we are particularly interested in developing a DL model for disease classification that is robust to outliers. Outliers in medical images can be caused by various factors, such as noise, acquisition artifacts, non-standard anatomy, inter-patient variability, and extraneous environmental factors during image acquisition. These factors can lead to atypical images, which may not accurately represent the underlying anatomy or pathology being imaged [15, 22, 28]. For example, ultrasound and Positron Emission Tomography (PET) imaging are particularly susceptible to frequent outlier occurrences. This is because saturated pixels can generate atypical images, while low resolution and noisy environments can lead to poor generalization in these imaging techniques [5, 17]. These outliers result in an atypical distribution, characterized by distorted means and abnormal standard deviations, which can hinder the accuracy of DL models, despite their outstanding diagnostic performance [23, 30].

Prior work to deal with outliers in medical imaging data includes outlier detection, resampling, reconstruction, and removal. Early attempts have employed statistical techniques, such as clustering-based [21] and machine learning-based approaches [6] to identify outlier samples in a dataset and the manual removal of these outliers were found to improve diagnostic accuracy [27]. In addition, statistical detection and resampling methods have been extensively utilized to adjust the distribution of a typical dataset, by modifying the outlier samples [16, 18, 28]. Furthermore, reconstructing images to form a typical representation of outlier samples has been shown to enhance the normal structural distribution and predictive accuracy in imaging data [3, 7, 8]. More recently, DL-based approaches have been implemented to remove outlier samples, including intensity-based matching [12], multi-modal approaches [14], and mathematical analysis of DL models [19]. Previous work has shown that using only outlier detection techniques can be inadequate in improving accuracy and can produce suboptimal results.

To address the negative impact of outliers on the performance of DL models, we propose a new DL model, dubbed Stochastic Confidence Network (SCN), that is designed to be robust to outliers in the context of disease classification tasks. The key innovation of SCN is its ability to analyze outlier samples using a stochastic comparison to trained samples and generate confident predictions. Specifically, SCN incorporates image patches into the representation of a decoded latent matrix that encompasses feature-based probability distributions and channel-wise patch weighting. Through statistically automating the rectification of irrelevant patches in outliers, SCN integrates the outlier samples into the normal sample distributions in the training set, thereby improving accuracy. To demonstrate the validity and superiority of our framework, we carry out experiments on breast cancer classification using ultrasound imaging data and Alzheimer's disease classification using PET imaging data.

Our contributions are three-fold:

- We investigate the prevalence of outliers in various medical imaging distributions and present an integrated and stochastic DL-based approach to mitigate the impact of outliers on diagnostic accuracy.
- We propose SCN to enhance robustness against outliers through the automated statistical analysis of outlier samples via novel loss functions based on stochastic principles.
- We apply SCN to classify breast cancer from ultrasound imaging data and Alzheimer's disease from PET imaging data, demonstrating its superior performance over compared methods without handling outliers.

2   Methods

The primary design principle of SCN is to integrate outliers into a typical dataset distribution. To achieve this, the SCN generates an initial decoded latent matrix comprising decoded high-level features and patch-wise weights. Next, the SCN reduces the impact of irrelevant patches based on the weights and produces accurate predictions (Fig. 1).

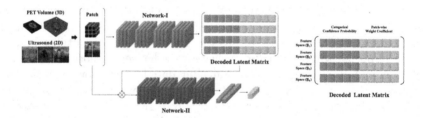

Fig. 1. Left: SCN employs convolution and channel-attention operators (light blue and gray, respectively) and is compatible with any Network-II. **Right:** DLM. (Color figure online)

2.1   Decoded Latent Matrix (DLM)

In the previous work [4], a latent vector was designed to represent the feature space, by encoding the high-dimensional space. The latent vectors, however, are limited in representing high-level features for categorical objects, leading to difficulties in interpretation. As such, in this work, we attempt to represent high-level features by decoding the latent vectors to form a decoded latent matrix (DLM); in this way, this DLM can represent more relevant categorical features.

DLM consists of Categorical Confidence Probability (CCP) and Patch-wise Weight Coefficient (PWC), as illustrated in Fig. 1 (Right). CCP embeds features for each classification category as a distribution. For instance, the first row presents the decoded probability distribution for the "Normal Condition", while

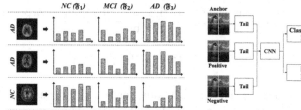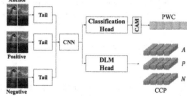

Fig. 2. Left: Decomposition of PET images into CCP of DLM. Samples in the same class exhibit similar distributions. **Right:** Schematic pipeline of Network-I in SCN.

the third row presents the distribution for "Alzheimer's Disease". By leveraging the probability distributions, CCP can effectively capture the distinct features associated with each classification category, thus facilitating accurate and interpretable classification. PWC represents the contribution or weights of input patches in generating CCP and emphasizes important patches in the input image, while reducing the influence of irrelevant patches. Particularly, outliers are data samples that share some similarities with typical samples, but they also possess additional irrelevant features. Thus, by removing irrelevant patches (see Secs. 2.3 and 3.3), typical samples can be distinguished from outliers, resulting in a clearer CCP.

2.2 Stochastic Loss Functions

The fundamental design principle of the DLM is to ensure that two categorically similar samples exhibit statistically similar distributions of CCP. Specifically, samples belonging to the disease group should exhibit statistically similar CCPs, while samples in the normal group should demonstrate distinct CCPs in terms of their stochastic distribution, as illustrated in Fig. 2 (Left). To achieve this, we propose two novel stochastic loss functions for stochastic optimization, including (1) T-test-based optimization for the equivalence of expectations ($\mathbb{E}$) and (2) Levene's test-based optimization for the equivalence of variations (σ^2). Notably, these optimizations focus on the statistical similarity rather than the same elements in terms of Euclidean distance, which can lead to poor representation of high-level features in DLM. Specifically, if two samples are mapped into the same CCP, for instance, $(0, 0, 0, 1)$ for all samples in the disease category, the CCP cannot represent high-level features and is prone to overfitting.

Suppose that X and X^p belong to the same category, while X^n belongs to another category. We denote X, X^p, and X^n as anchor, positive, and negative samples, respectively [24] (Fig. 2; Right). To ensure stochastic similarity, statistical comparisons are utilized with a null hypothesis that the mean and standard deviation values of two CCPs are equal. For X and X^p, the SCN is optimized to produce a small t-statistic, resulting in a significance level greater than 0.05, therefore accepting the null hypothesis. In contrast, SCN is optimized to generate a large t-value for X and X^n, leading to a significance level less than 0.05, hence rejecting the null hypothesis. The statistical loss function, incorporating t-statistic function (t) for X, X^p, and X^n, is given by:

$$\min \left[\mathcal{R}\big(|t(X, X^p)| - t_{c.v.}\big) + \mathcal{R}\big(t_{c.v.} - |t(X, X^n)|\big) \right], \tag{1}$$

where $\mathcal{R}(x) = max(x, 0)$ and $t_{c.v.}$ is a critical value for the significance level of 0.05. Subsequently, let M^θ be the convolution modules with its parameters (θ) in Network-I of the SCN (Fig. 1), and let $\mathfrak{F}_i = [\mathfrak{F}_{i,1}, \mathfrak{F}_{i,2}, ..., \mathfrak{F}_{i,j}]$ ($0 \leq \mathfrak{F}_{i,j} \leq 1$, $j \geq 30$) be the ith CCP for category i (e.g., $\mathfrak{F}_1$ is for NC, $\mathfrak{F}_2$ for MCI, and $\mathfrak{F}_3$ for AD). Here, to approximate the t-distribution into a normal distribution, $j \geq 30$ is constrained. Then, DLM is provided as $M^\theta(X) = [\mathfrak{F}_1(X), \mathfrak{F}_2(X), ..., \mathfrak{F}_c(X)]$, where c is the number of categories. To ensure the statistical similarity in terms of mean values ($\mathbb{E}$), a two-sample t-test is utilized. The t-statistic function for the T-test-based loss function is formulated as follows:

$$t(X_1, X_2) = \Big(\mathbb{E}(\mathfrak{F}(X_1)) - \mathbb{E}(\mathfrak{F}(X_2))\Big)/\sqrt{(V(X_1) + V(X_2))/j}. \tag{2}$$

To ensure statistical similarity between the anchor and positive samples with respect to the equality of variances, we develop a novel loss function based on Levene's test. It is important to note that the statistical relationship between the anchor and negative samples in terms of variance is not of interest. That is, the Levene's test-based loss function only between X and X^p is formulated based on the t-statistics of Levene's test [13]. Furthermore, we employ the triplet loss [24] using the Euclidean distance of CCP to optimize SCN, and we use categorical cross-entropy loss [26] to train Network-II in SCN.

2.3   Resample Outliers

The SCN is also designed to mitigate the impact of irrelevant patches on classification accuracy. To achieve this, the SCN embeds the PWC computed by applying the Grad-CAM of the penultimate layers to input patches and the SoftMax function. The weight ($W_{c,i}$) of ith patch (X_i) on c^{th} feature ($\mathfrak{F}_c$) is formulated as below:

$$W_{c,i} = \exp \frac{\partial \mathfrak{F}_c}{\partial X_i} / \sum_i \exp \frac{\partial \mathfrak{F}_c}{\partial X_i}, \tag{3}$$

where $\exp(x) = e^x$. Subsequently, we use the PWC method to weight the input patches through a Hadamard product, as shown in Fig. 1. This approach attenuates irrelevant patches and allows the model to focus on the relevant patches for categorical features. The PWC confers the advantage of attenuating irrelevant and distinct patches of outliers and incorporating outliers into a typical distribution, despite the presence of outliers in the training and test sets. Furthermore, the PWC method can be used to visualize the weights of each patch for classification, similar to the CAM [31].

Table 1. Left: The number of samples in each category and dataset, including total samples (TS), regular samples (RS), and outlier samples (OS). **Right:** The number of samples for each dataset split configuration, taking into account outlier samples.

USBC	Normal	Benign	Malignant
TS	133	437	210
RS	123	412	195
OS	10	25	15
ADNI	NC	MCI	AD
TS	900	900	900
RS	855	855	855
OS	45	45	45

		Train (70%)		Valid (10%)		Test (20%)	
		RS	OS	RS	OS	RS	OS
USBC	$\tau \not\subset \mathbb{X}_{tr} \cup \mathbb{X}_{te}$	511	-	146	-	73	-
	$\tau \subset \mathbb{X}_{tr} \cup \mathbb{X}_{te}$	511	35	146	5	73	10
	$\tau \subset \mathbb{X}_{te}$	511	-	146	-	73	50
ADNI	$\tau \not\subset \mathbb{X}_{tr} \cup \mathbb{X}_{te}$	1795	-	257	-	513	-
	$\tau \subset \mathbb{X}_{tr} \cup \mathbb{X}_{te}$	1795	95	257	13	513	27
	$\tau \subset \mathbb{X}_{te}$	1795	-	257	-	513	135

3 Experiments

To evaluate the diagnostic performance of SCN for classification tasks, we utilized two publicly available databases: Ultrasound imaging data for Breast Cancer (USBC) [1], which is categorized into normal, benign, and malignant classes, and PET imaging data for Alzheimer's Disease Neuroimaging Initiative (ADNI) [20], which is categorized into normal condition (NC), mild cognitive impairment (MCI), and Alzheimer's disease (AD) classes. In our experiments, we identified outliers by projecting samples with T-SNE and employing the Interquartile Range (IQR) method. Our experimental set-ups comprised three configurations: (i) excluding outliers from both the train and test sets ($\tau \not\subset \mathbb{X}_{tr} \cup \mathbb{X}_{te}$); (ii) including outliers in both the train and test sets ($\tau \subset \mathbb{X}_{tr} \cup \mathbb{X}_{te}$); and (iii) including outliers only in the test set ($\tau \subset \mathbb{X}_{te}$). The detailed numbers of images are illustrated in Table 1.

To evaluate the SCN, we employed different DL models, including CNNs and vision transformers (ViT). Specifically, NFNet [2] and Soup [29] are currently among the top performing NN and ViT models for image classification tasks. MCOD [9] and SMOTE [10] are currently among the best-performing models for outlier-robust classification tasks in the fields of computer vision and medical imaging, respectively. M-Dark [11] and CNN-SVM [25] are currently among the top-performing models for classification tasks based on ultrasound and PET imaging, respectively.

3.1 Ablation Study

To evaluate the best-performing architecture of SCN, we utilized various models as Network-II in SCN. Table 2 presents a comparative analysis of SCN with compared DL models (M), as well as the best-performing SCN. In all scenarios, the use of SCN significantly improved classification accuracy, particularly in the presence of outliers. When the outlier samples were only present in the test set, the DL models exhibited a significant decrease in accuracy, while the SCN demonstrated outlier-robust performance, as reflected in accuracy. The most significant improvement observed in USBC was 5.11% with NFNet, while in contrast, 5.85% in ADNI was achieved with Soup. Additionally, we found that

Table 2. Comparison analysis of SCN with compared DL models. M refers to the baseline model, and M+SCN indicates that M is used as Network-II of SCN. The best-performing models are highlighted in **bold**, and models with strong improvements over the baseline are highlighted as underlined.

	USBC						ADNI					
	$\tau \subset X_{tr} \cup X_{te}$			$\tau \subset X_{te}$			$\tau \subset X_{tr} \cup X_{te}$			$\tau \subset X_{te}$		
	M	M+SCN	Imp.	M	M+SCN	Imp.	M	M+SCN	Improv.	M	M+SCN	Imp.
CNN-SVM	89.38%	91.95%	2.57%	85.74%	89.98%	4.24%	84.74%	87.22%	2.48%	81.03%	86.07%	5.04%
M-Dark	90.27%	**93.36%**	**3.09%**	86.52%	**90.57%**	4.05%	83.32%	86.57%	3.25%	79.85%	84.96%	5.11%
MCOD	87.71%	90.28%	2.57%	84.35%	87.89%	3.54%	84.72%	88.07%	3.35%	80.89%	85.90%	5.01%
NFNet	88.72%	91.71%	2.99%	85.06%	90.17%	5.11%	84.10%	86.93%	2.83%	79.65%	85.02%	5.37%
SMOTE	88.05%	90.47%	2.42%	84.29%	89.37%	5.08%	84.84%	88.33%	3.49%	81.30%	86.24%	4.94%
Soup	89.50%	91.54%	2.04%	85.78%	90.00%	4.22%	84.72%	**88.35%**	**3.63%**	80.53%	**86.38%**	**5.85%**

M-Dark, which is currently the top-performing model for classification tasks based on ultrasound imaging, and Soup, which is currently the state-of-the-art (SotA) ViT model, served as the best-performing baseline for our SCN in the USBC and ADNI databases, respectively. Thus, the SCN with M-Dark and the SCN with Soup provided 93.36% and 86.38% accuracy for USBC and ADNI, respectively. In our analysis, since the number of images in USBC was insufficient to optimally train a ViT, M-Dark showed the best performance for USBC.

Table 3. Ablation study for loss functions. $\mathcal{L}_1$, $\mathcal{L}_2$, and $\mathcal{L}_3$ indicate triplet, T-test, and Levene's Test-based loss functions, respectively.

		M	$M + \mathcal{L}_1$	$M + \mathcal{L}_2$	$M + \mathcal{L}_3$	$M + \mathcal{L}_{1,2}$	$M + \mathcal{L}_{1,3}$	$M + \mathcal{L}_{2,3}$	$M + \mathcal{L}_{1,2,3}$
USBC	$\tau \not\subset X_{tr} \cup X_{te}$	93.15%	93.69%	94.01%	93.77%	94.07%	93.95%	95.82%	**96.12%**
	$\tau \subset X_{tr}$	90.27%	90.39%	92.02%	90.81%	92.15%	91.89%	93.06%	**93.36%**
	$\tau \subset X_{te}$	86.52%	86.75%	87.70%	86.90%	87.78%	87.60%	90.20%	**90.57%**
ADNI	$\tau \not\subset X_{tr} \cup X_{te}$	87.54%	87.63%	88.14%	87.79%	88.18%	88.10%	89.12%	**89.22%**
	$\tau \subset X_{tr}$	84.72%	84.97%	87.35%	85.38%	87.56%	87.20%	88.08%	**88.35%**
	$\tau \subset X_{te}$	80.53%	81.16%	84.97%	82.02%	85.23%	84.54%	85.83%	**86.38%**

In our ablation study (Table 3), we investigated the impact of three loss functions on the USBC and ADNI databases, employing the M-Dark and Soup models as M, respectively. The results indicated that the loss functions significantly enhanced the classification accuracy of both databases, compared with the baseline model (M). Among the three loss functions, the T-test-based loss function ($\mathcal{L}_2$) had the most substantial impact on improving classification accuracy, as evidenced by the performance gains in models ($M + \mathcal{L}_1, M + \mathcal{L}_3$, and $M + \mathcal{L}_2$). This suggests that stochastic similarity, in terms of the same mean values of CCP, can significantly improve the classification accuracy regardless of outliers. Furthermore, the simultaneous utilization of $\mathcal{L}_{2,3}$ resulted in a significant improvement, highlighting the statistical similarity of CCPs as a contributing factor to the improved accuracy.

3.2 Quantitative Analysis

USBC	$\tau \not\subset \mathbb{X}_{tr} \cup \mathbb{X}_{te}$	Accuracy	96.12%(95% CI 95.37%-96.87%)
		Sensitivity	95.03%(95% CI 93.92%-96.13%)
		Specificity	97.21%(95% CI 96.72%-97.71%)
	$\tau \subset \mathbb{X}_{tr}$	Accuracy	93.36%(95% CI 92.81%-93.91%)
		Sensitivity	91.28%(95% CI 90.54%-92.03%)
		Specificity	95.44%(95% CI 95.05%-95.83%)
	$\tau \subset \mathbb{X}_{te}$	Accuracy	90.57%(95% CI 89.62%-91.54%)
		Sensitivity	87.65%(95% CI 86.30%-89.00%)
		Specificity	93.50%(95% CI 92.84%-94.17%)
ADNI	$\tau \not\subset \mathbb{X}_{tr} \cup \mathbb{X}_{te}$	Accuracy	88.70%(95% CI 88.26%-89.13%)
		Sensitivity	84.92%(95% CI 84.38%-85.48%)
		Specificity	92.46%(95% CI 92.06%-92.87%)
	$\tau \subset \mathbb{X}_{tr}$	Accuracy	88.07%(95% CI 87.45%-88.69%)
		Sensitivity	84.09%(95% CI 83.29%-84.89%)
		Specificity	92.05%(95% CI 91.55%-92.54%)
	$\tau \subset \mathbb{X}_{te}$	Accuracy	85.90%(95% CI 84.88%-86.92%)
		Sensitivity	81.20%(95% CI 79.86%-82.55%)
		Specificity	90.60%(95% CI 89.87%-91.34%)

Fig. 3. Left: Comparison analysis of SCN with compared DL models in terms of accuracy and F1-score. **Right:** Detailed evaluation metric values for the best-performing SCN, including 95% confidence intervals (95% CI).

Figure 3 (Left) presents a comparative performance analysis of the SCN against compared DL models, along with a quantitative evaluation of the best-performing SCN for the USBC and the PET database from ADNI. For the USBC and ADNI databases, we used M-Dark and Soup models as the Network-II of SCN, respectively. Our results showed that the best-performing SCN outperformed the compared DL models in terms of diagnostic performance, regardless of outlier samples. This improvement was demonstrated by our quantitative analysis, which showed the impact of outliers on the model's performance. Even when outliers were present in the test set ($\tau \subset \mathbb{X}_{te}$), SCN exhibited outlier-robustness with only a slight decrease in accuracy and F1-score. Specifically, NFNet exhibited a decrease in accuracy by -6.42%, while SCN showed a decrease in accuracy by -2.46% from $\tau \not\subset \mathbb{X}_{tr} \cup \mathbb{X}_{te}$ to $\tau \subset \mathbb{X}_{te}$. Additionally, Fig. 3 (Right) depicts the detailed evaluation metric values, along with a 95% confidence interval.

3.3 Qualitative Analysis

Section 3.1 describes how PWC can be used to visualize attention weights of patches, similar to CAM. Figure 4 visualizes sample illustrations of the attention-map generated by SCN. As the attention weights are assigned to each patch, the resolution of attention maps is determined by the patch size. As demonstrated in Fig. 4 (Left), the SCN primarily focuses on the disease regions of breast cancer. Similarly, as illustrated in Fig. 4 (Right), the SCN highlights the cerebral cortex

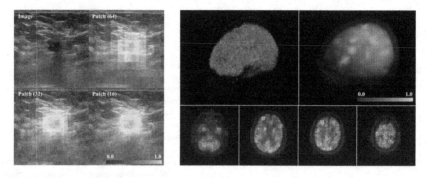

Fig. 4. Left: Sample 2D attention map for the USBC database. **Right:** Sample 3D attention map for the ADNI database, along with its corresponding 2D slices.

region, which plays a crucial role in detecting Alzheimer's disease. Therefore, based on our analysis, our approach offers accurate diagnostic predictions by specifically focusing on regions associated with the disease, thus providing a reasonable and plausible explanation for the diagnosis.

Moreover, the performance and prediction time of the SCN are determined by the patch size, as demonstrated in Fig. 4. A high number of patches (a small size of the window) reduces the ability to recognize contextual information, leading to decreased diagnostic performance. Moreover, an increased number of patches results in more parameters for convolution operators, leading to increased prediction time. However, as demonstrated in Fig. 4, a higher number of patches significantly improves the resolution of the attention-map. Determining the optimal patch size and parameters remains as future work.

4   Conclusion

This work is aimed at developing an outlier-robust DL model for disease classification, termed SCN. SCN extracts high-level categorical features from a decoded latent matrix based on patch-based analysis of vision transformers, and integrates outlier samples into a typical distribution via stochastic embedding with categorical confidence probability and statistical loss functions. By attenuating irrelevant patches of outliers, SCN provides precise diagnostic predictions despite the presence of outliers in medical imaging datasets. SCN outperforms other SotA DL models on two databases of ultrasound images and PET data. SCN has potential applications for multimodal diagnosis using medical imaging data. Future work includes determining the optimal network architecture and parameters.

References

1. Al-Dhabyani, W., Gomaa, M., Khaled, H., Fahmy, A.: Dataset of breast ultrasound images. Data Brief **28**, 104863 (2020)

2. Brock, A., De, S., Smith, S.L., Simonyan, K.: High-performance large-scale image recognition without normalization. In: International Conference on Machine Learning, pp. 1059–1071. PMLR (2021)

3. Chen, X., Pawlowski, N., Rajchl, M., Glocker, B., Konukoglu, E.: Deep generative models in the real-world: an open challenge from medical imaging. arXiv preprint arXiv:1806.05452 (2018)

4. Dosovitskiy, A., et al.: An image is worth 16x16 words: transformers for image recognition at scale. arXiv preprint arXiv:2010.11929 (2020)

5. Fox, P.T., Mintun, M.A., Reiman, E.M., Raichle, M.E.: Enhanced detection of focal brain responses using intersubject averaging and change-distribution analysis of subtracted pet images. J. Cereb. Blood Flow Metab. **8**(5), 642–653 (1988)

6. Grau, V., Mewes, A., Alcaniz, M., Kikinis, R., Warfield, S.K.: Improved watershed transform for medical image segmentation using prior information. IEEE Trans. Med. Imaging **23**(4), 447–458 (2004)

7. Han, C., et al.: MADGAN: unsupervised medical anomaly detection GAN using multiple adjacent brain MRI slice reconstruction. BMC Bioinform. **22**(2), 1–20 (2021)

8. Hu, M., et al.: Reconstruction of a 3D surface from video that is robust to missing data and outliers: application to minimally invasive surgery using stereo and mono endoscopes. Med. Image Anal. **16**(3), 597–611 (2012)

9. Huyan, N., Quan, D., Zhang, X., Liang, X., Chanussot, J., Jiao, L.: Unsupervised outlier detection using memory and contrastive learning. IEEE Trans. Image Process. **31**, 6440–6454 (2022)

10. Ijaz, M.F., Attique, M., Son, Y.: Data-driven cervical cancer prediction model with outlier detection and over-sampling methods. Sensors **20**(10), 2809 (2020)

11. Jabeen, K., et al.: Breast cancer classification from ultrasound images using probability-based optimal deep learning feature fusion. Sensors **22**(3), 807 (2022)

12. Kuklisova-Murgasova, M., Quaghebeur, G., Rutherford, M.A., Hajnal, J.V., Schnabel, J.A.: Reconstruction of fetal brain MRI with intensity matching and complete outlier removal. Med. Image Anal. **16**(8), 1550–1564 (2012)

13. Levene, H.: Robust tests for equality of variances. In: Contributions to Probability and Statistics, pp. 278–292 (1960)

14. Li, W., et al.: Outlier detection and removal improves accuracy of machine learning approach to multispectral burn diagnostic imaging. J. Biomed. Opt. **20**(12), 121305–121305 (2015)

15. Luna, B., Velanova, K., Geier, C.F.: Methodological approaches in developmental neuroimaging studies. Hum. Brain Mapp. **31**(6), 863–871 (2010)

16. Manjon, J.V., et al.: Robust MRI brain tissue parameter estimation by multistage outlier rejection. Magn. Reson. Med. **59**(4), 866–873 (2008)

17. Michailovich, O., Adam, D.: Robust estimation of ultrasound pulses using outlier-resistant de-noising. IEEE Trans. Med. Imaging **22**(3), 368–381 (2003)

18. Morris, D., Nossin-Manor, R., Taylor, M.J., Sled, J.G.: Preterm neonatal diffusion processing using detection and replacement of outliers prior to resampling. Magn. Reson. Med. **66**(1), 92–101 (2011)

19. Oh, G., Lee, J.E., Ye, J.C.: Unpaired MR motion artifact deep learning using outlier-rejecting bootstrap aggregation. IEEE Trans. Med. Imaging **40**(11), 3125–3139 (2021)

20. Petersen, R.C., et al.: Alzheimer's disease neuroimaging initiative (ADNI): clinical characterization. Neurology **74**(3), 201–209 (2010)

21. Prastawa, M., Bullitt, E., Ho, S., Gerig, G.: A brain tumor segmentation framework based on outlier detection. Med. Image Anal. **8**(3), 275–283 (2004)

22. Sairanen, V., Leemans, A., Tax, C.M.: Fast and accurate slicewise outlier detection (SOLID) with informed model estimation for diffusion MRI data. Neuroimage **181**, 331–346 (2018)
23. Sarker, I.H.: Deep learning: a comprehensive overview on techniques, taxonomy, applications and research directions. SN Comput. Sci. **2**(6), 420 (2021)
24. Schroff, F., Kalenichenko, D., Philbin, J.: Facenet: a unified embedding for face recognition and clustering. In: Proceedings of the IEEE Conference on Computer Vision and Pattern Recognition, pp. 815–823 (2015)
25. Sethi, M., Rani, S., Singh, A., Mazón, J.L.V.: A CAD system for Alzheimer's disease classification using neuroimaging MRI 2D slices. Comput. Math. Methods Med. **2022** (2022)
26. Shridhar, K., Laumann, F., Liwicki, M.: A comprehensive guide to bayesian convolutional neural network with variational inference. arXiv preprint arXiv:1901.02731 (2019)
27. Smiti, A.: A critical overview of outlier detection methods. Comput. Sci. Rev. **38**, 100306 (2020)
28. Van Leemput, K., Maes, F., Vandermeulen, D., Colchester, A., Suetens, P.: Automated segmentation of multiple sclerosis lesions by model outlier detection. IEEE Trans. Med. Imaging **20**(8), 677–688 (2001)
29. Wortsman, M., et al.: Model soups: averaging weights of multiple fine-tuned models improves accuracy without increasing inference time. In: International Conference on Machine Learning, pp. 23965–23998. PMLR (2022)
30. Yamashita, R., Nishio, M., Do, R.K.G., Togashi, K.: Convolutional neural networks: an overview and application in radiology. Insights Imaging **9**(4), 611–629 (2018). https://doi.org/10.1007/s13244-018-0639-9
31. Zhou, B., Khosla, A., Lapedriza, A., Oliva, A., Torralba, A.: Learning deep features for discriminative localization. In: Proceedings of the IEEE Conference on Computer Vision and Pattern Recognition, pp. 2921–2929 (2016)

Efficient Registration of Longitudinal Studies for Follow-Up Lesion Assessment by Exploiting Redundancy and Composition of Deformations

Sven Kuckertz[✉], Stefan Heldmann, and Jan Hendrik Moltz

Fraunhofer Institute for Digital Medicine MEVIS, Lübeck/Bremen, Germany
sven.kuckertz@mevis.fraunhofer.de

Abstract. Follow-up assessment of lesions for cancer patients is an important part of radiologists' work. Image registration is a key technology to facilitate this task, as it allows for the automatic establishment of correspondences between previous findings and current observations. However, as the number of examinations increases, more registrations must be computed to allow full correspondence assessment between longitudinal studies. We address the challenge of increased computational time and complexity by identifying and eliminating redundant registration procedures and composing deformations from previously performed registrations, thereby significantly reducing the number of registrations required. We evaluate our proposed methods on a dataset consisting of oncological thoracic follow-up CT scans from 260 patients. By grouping series within a study and identifying reference series, we can reduce the total number of registrations required for a patient by an average factor of 27.5 while maintaining comparable registration quality. Additionally composing deformations further reduces the number of registrations by a factor of 1.86, resulting in an overall average reduction factor of 51.4. Since the number of registrations is directly related to the time required to process the input data, the information is available more quickly and subsequent examinations can be performed sooner. For a single subject, this results in an exemplary reduction of total computation time from 37.4 to 1.3 min.

Keywords: Image registration · Lesion tracking · Follow-up · CT

1 Introduction

Deformable image registration is an important tool in planning and evaluation of cancer treatment. For example, it is used to track lesions over time by establishing correspondences between longitudinal studies [4,6,10]. This allows for rapid and robust localization of lesions found in previous studies, thus simplifying monitoring of treatment success, which is measured mainly by the change in lesion size and amount [2]. Because cancer treatment can be a lengthy process,

J. Woo et al. (Eds.): MICCAI 2023 Workshops, LNCS 14394, pp. 91–99, 2023.
https://doi.org/10.1007/978-3-031-47425-5_9

continuous assessments are required, including the generation of 3D imaging data. Registrations must be performed for each follow-up study to allow full correspondence assessment between longitudinal studies. This leads to the need for more and more computations over time, which slows down data processing, especially as the number and resolution of acquired image data increases [1,9]. In this work, we address the challenge of increased computation time and complexity by determining and eliminating redundant registration procedures and combining previously obtained registration results. We introduce a method based on image properties to identify a reference series of a study that represents a group of images. Furthermore, we compose multiple vector fields rather than computing additional registrations to speed-up processing time. Composing nonparametric deformations is a challenging task, as previously studied and discussed in [7,11]. Here, we combine this method with the exploitation of redundancy for minimal registration effort. We evaluate our approach on a broad dataset and compare it with an extensive registration of all studies and series of a patient.

2   Methods

Image Registration. The aim of deformable image registration is the establishment of dense correspondences between two images, a fixed image $\mathcal{F}$ and a moving image $\mathcal{M}$, with $\mathcal{F}, \mathcal{M} : \mathbb{R}^3 \to \mathbb{R}$ being grayscale images in this work. To achieve this goal, a reasonable deformation vector field $y : \Omega \to \mathbb{R}^3$ is estimated on the field of view $\Omega \subseteq \mathbb{R}^3$ of $\mathcal{F}$ such that the deformed moving image $\mathcal{M}(y(x))$ and $\mathcal{F}(x)$ are similar for $x \in \Omega$. The deformation vector field y is computed by optimizing a suitable cost function, which usually consists of an image similarity measure and a regularization term. The objective function can be formulated as follows

$$\mathcal{J}(\mathcal{F}, \mathcal{M}, y) = \mathcal{D}(\mathcal{F}, \mathcal{M}(y)) + \alpha \mathcal{S}(y), \tag{1}$$

where $\mathcal{D}$ is the so-called distance measure that evaluates the similarity between the fixed image $\mathcal{F}$ and the deformed moving image $\mathcal{M}(y)$. Typical distance measures for images are the sum of squared differences (SSD), mutual information (MI) or normalized cross correlation (NCC). Due to the ill-posedness of the image registration task, an additional regularization term $\mathcal{S}$ is introduced to the objective function. It enforces smoothness of the deformation vector field y, for example by penalizing spatial derivatives or incorporating desired physical properties and is weighted by a factor $\alpha > 0$.

In this work, we follow a three-step registration approach comparable to [6], where in the first step a coarse translational alignment is generated by a brute force grid search. In the second step, a rigid registration is computed using the translational alignment as an initialization, compensating major changes in patient position and anatomy. Then, a deformable registration based on [8] is performed, optimizing the cost function (1) to obtain local and dense correspondences. We choose the normalized gradient fields (NGF) [5] as a distance measure, aiming to align edges in the images. Smoothness is enforced by a curvature regularizer [3]. For both the rigid and deformable registration, a L-BFGS scheme is used to optimize the respective cost function. The deformable registration is implemented with CUDA, speeding-up the calculation due to the parallel computing power of the GPU.

Assume that a patient's imaging data was acquired in n studies (imaging procedures at certain dates), each consisting of m series (multiple consecutive scans or reconstructions). If we want to compute correspondences between all series of each pair of two studies, we need to compute

$$\sum_{i=1}^{n}\sum_{j=i+1}^{n} m^2 = (n-1)m^2 + (n-2)m^2 + \ldots + m^2 = \frac{(n-1)n}{2}m^2 \quad (2)$$

total registrations. For example, for a subject with 3 studies of 6 series each, a total of 108 registrations must be computed (36 between the 1st and 2nd study, 36 between the 1st and 3rd, 36 between the 2nd and 3rd).

Exploiting Redundancy Within a Study. Generally, the imaging procedure during an examination is performed at a specific time in an unchanging environment. In CT scans, for example, the patient is usually scanned once, and the acquired data is reconstructed in several different ways. We can use this fact to reduce the number of registration runs required. To this end, we check whether multiple series of a single study share the same frame of reference UID. This is a standard DICOM tag that indicates whether the images were acquired in the same reference coordinate system. We also check whether the images were acquired within a relatively short period of time ($\epsilon = 1$s). In this way, we ensure that the images show the same content and that they have the same coordinate system. After grouping corresponding series of a study, we identify a reference series by comparing several image properties. The reference series image is characterized by a minimal voxel size and slice thickness while covering most of the image extent of all other series in the group. This ensures that maximum image information is retained during registration and that the field of view of each series is covered by the reference series. By identifying g groups of series for each study, we reduce the number of registrations needed to $\frac{(n-1)n}{2}g^2$ registrations in total, where the number of groups g is mostly significantly smaller than the number of series m. Note that often all series in a study of 3D images can be grouped together ($g = 1$), reducing the number of registrations needed to $\frac{(n-1)n}{2}$. For the example subject with three 6-series studies, the number of registrations to be computed can be reduced from 108 to 3 (one between the 1st and 2nd study, one between the 1st and 3rd, one between the 2nd and 3rd).

Composition of Subsequent Deformations. We use information from previous studies that have already been registered to further reduce the number of registrations to be computed. Therefore, we compose registrations between several consecutive images instead of calculating additional ones. For n studies, where a single study i has one reference series and corresponding image $\mathcal{I}_i$, we compute only the registrations between subsequent images $\mathcal{I}_i$ and $\mathcal{I}_{i+1}$, i.e., $\mathcal{I}_{i+1} \approx \mathcal{I}_i(y_{i+1}^i)$, $i = 1, \ldots, n-1$. We then compose these registrations as follows:

$$\mathcal{I}_{i+k} \approx \mathcal{I}_i \left(y_{i+1}^i \left(\ldots \left(\left(y_{i+k}^{i+k-1} \right) \right) \right) \right) \tag{3}$$

If each study consists of g registration groups, we only need to calculate $\sum_{i=1}^{n-1} g^2 = (n-1)g^2$ total registrations. In the optimal scenario, where the number of groups $g = 1$, this can be further reduced to $n-1$ total number of registrations. For the example subject with three 6-series studies, the number of registrations to be computed can be therefore further reduced to 2 (one between the 1st and 2nd study, one between the 2nd and 3rd).

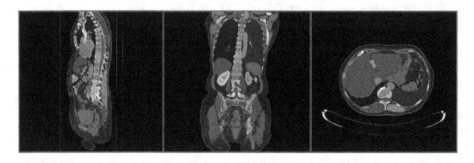

Fig. 1. Exemplary 3D CT image of the dataset used for method verification. Automatically generated structure masks are shown as a coloured overlay.

3   Experiments

Data. We evaluate our methods based on the analysis and registration of oncological thoracic follow-up CT scans. For a total number of 260 patients a baseline study and between 2 and 6 follow-up studies are available, respectively. Overall, 5218 series with 3D CT thorax-abdomen scans, referred by the oncology department at Radboud University Medical Center in Nijmegen, the Netherlands, were acquired in 970 studies from 3 different scanner models. Thus, the data available for each patient consists of an average of 3.7 studies with 5.4 series each. The images of the series may differ e.g. in field of view, orientation, voxel size and slice thickness. Data were anonymized and permission for retrospective analysis was obtained from the ethical review board. For each reference series in a group, the TotalSegmentator segmentation model was used to automatically generate up to 104 major anatomical labels within the entire body [12]. In addition, these anatomical labels were generated for all available images of a selected patient for further in-depth analysis. An example image of the dataset with segmentations is shown in Fig. 1.

Exploiting Redundancy Within a Study. For each patient of the dataset, we analyze each study by extracting DICOM information (frame of reference UID, acquisition time, slice thickness, pixel spacing, spacing between slices) for each included series with a 3D image. With this information, we identify one or more reference series per study and group multiple series. We then analyze how many registrations are required to generate correspondences between all references series of each pair of two studies per patient. This is compared to the standard procedure of registering all combinations of two series from two studies (without grouping).

For the qualitative evaluation of our method, we selected one patient and used each series with a 3D image. We created anatomical labels for all these series and registered all combinations of two series from two studies (without grouping). Using these registrations, we compare (a) the direct registration of two series with (b) the registration of the corresponding reference series. To do this, we deform the corresponding label masks of the (non-reference) series with both registration results and compare the warped masks with the masks of the fixed series/image. To evaluate the mask overlap, we calculate the Dice scores for each anatomical label. Due to the differences in the field of view, only the masks that do not touch the image boundaries are compared and evaluated.

Composition of Subsequent Deformations. Using the composition of deformation vector fields, only registrations between series of consecutive studies need to be computed. Building on the analysis in the previous section, we examine how many registrations are required to generate correspondences between all reference series of each pair of two consecutive studies per patient. This is compared with the standard procedure and the previously introduced exploitation of redundancy by grouping without composition of deformations.

For qualitative evaluation of our method, we identified reference series for each study of each patient and generated anatomical labels for all these series. We registered all consecutive reference series and, in addition, the first (baseline) and last reference series for evaluation. Using these registrations, we compare (a) the direct registration of the first and last reference series with (b) the composition of all registrations of intermediate reference series, resulting in a composed deformation between the first and last series. We therefore deform the corresponding label masks of the first reference series with both registration results and compare the warped masks with the masks of the last reference series/image. To evaluate the mask overlap, we calculate the Dice scores for each anatomical label.

4 Results

Exploiting Redundancy Within a Study. Figure 2 illustrates the total number of registrations required for each proposed method. For the standard method, in which all series of each pair of two studies are registered, between 45 and 810

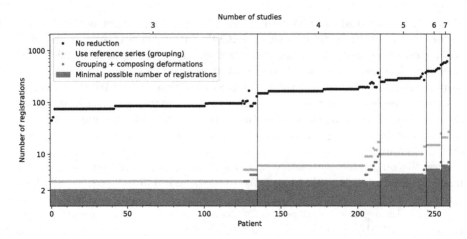

Fig. 2. Comparison of the total number of registrations required to generate all correspondences for each method and patient in the dataset. Patients are grouped by the number of studies; a logarithmic scale is used on the y-axis for a better overview.

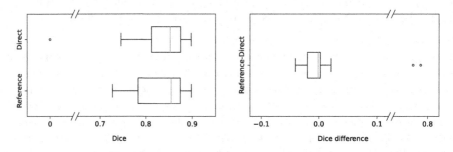

Fig. 3. Comparison of direct image registration between two series and the use of registration of the corresponding reference series for one patient. The left plot shows boxplots of the mean Dice scores of the two methods separately, while the right plot shows their differences. In total, registrations were compared between 159 image pairs.

(average 160.8) registrations per patient are required to generate all correspondences. By taking advantage of redundancy by grouping series, only between 3 and 27 (average 5.9) runs per patient are required, reducing the number of registrations by a factor of 27.5 on average. The minimum factor of reduced registrations is 15, the maximum 35.7.

For the selected patient, 4 studies are available with 5,5,5 and 6 series, respectively. A single reference series was identified for each study, reducing the number of registrations from 165 to 6. Using our GPU-accelerated registration algorithm, this reduces the total computation time from 37.4 to 2.5 min. We compare 159 direct registrations of two series with the registrations of the corresponding reference series, neglecting the 6 direct registrations between two reference series (because there is nothing to compare them with). The results of the analysis are shown in Fig. 3. In 157 of 159 cases, the absolute difference in mean Dice scores is less than 0.05, indicating that there is little difference in registration quality with respect to the overlap of major anatomic structures. The remaining two cases show substantial differences as direct registration yields an undesirable deformation, resulting in an average Dice score of 0. In both cases, the reason is a failed initial alignment step due to differences in the field of view. By registering appropriate reference series, this problem is circumvented by choosing images with a larger field of view as reference.

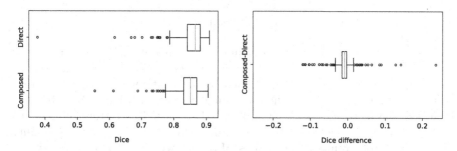

Fig. 4. Comparison of direct image registration between the first and last (reference) series with the composition of all registrations between the intermediate reference series for each patient. The left plot shows boxplots of the mean Dice scores of the two methods separately, while the right plot shows their differences. Two registrations are compared for each of the 260 patients.

Composition of Subsequent Deformations. As shown in Fig. 2, composing consecutive deformations between the reference series of the first (baseline) and the last study requires between 2 and 10 (average 2.9) registrations per patient. This corresponds to an average reduction by a factor of 51.4 compared with the standard procedure and again to a reduction by a factor of 1.86 compared with the use of reference series without composing deformations. For our selected patient, this further reduces the total computation time to just 1.3 min. In Fig. 2, the minimum possible number of registrations for this method is also shown in blue. In some cases, this is not achieved because there may be more than one reference series per study, e.g., due to different frame of reference UIDs.

Qualitative analysis shows that for 239 of 260 patients, the absolute difference in average Dice scores is less than 0.05, again indicating that in most cases there are only minor differences in registration quality with respect to the overlap of major anatomical structures (see Fig. 4). Substantial differences in average Dice scores are mainly due to large deformations caused by different respiratory phases, which is always a challenge for deformable registration algorithms. In addition, image pairs with low Dice scores often have differences in the field of view that show only partial overlap, making the task more difficult.

5   Discussion and Conclusion

In this work, we introduced the concept of assigning comparable series of studies of a patient to a group represented by a reference series, which can reduce the total number of registrations required for a patient by an average factor of 27.5. For an selected subject, this reduces the total computation time from 37.4 to 2.5 min. In addition, we have found that registration accuracy is comparable when using deformations computed on reference series. In some cases, the registration of reference series is even more robust, since the corresponding images can be chosen to cover a larger field of view and have a higher resolution. In summary, our method allows avoiding the computation of redundant registrations between the same reference frame.

Second, we investigated the possibility of further reducing the number of registrations required by composing consecutive deformations between multiple studies, thus eliminating the need to calculate registrations between studies that are further apart. In this way, the total number of registrations can be reduced by an average factor of 51.4. For an selected subject, this further reduces the total computation time from 37.4 to 1.3 min. Analysis of registration quality shows comparable results in most cases. However, when examining difficult corner cases, several challenges emerge that need to be addressed in the future: Differences in the field of view can cause problems for the registration algorithm. These problems are more likely the more registrations are involved in composing multiple deformations. Even one registration with a poor alignment in the chain of composed deformations can yield an erroneous resulting deformation. In addition, it can be difficult to decide which reference series of an intermediate study to use when more than one series group is identified. Finally, composing deformations can lead to undesirable foldings and reduce the smoothness of the resulting deformation.

Registration between multiple studies is a key technology in follow-up CT examination of cancer patients, allowing correspondences to be established between previous findings and current observations. By exploiting redundancy and composing deformations, the number of registrations required to establish complete correspondences between longitudinal studies can be significantly reduced. Because the number of registrations is directly related to the time required to process the input data, the information is available more quickly and subsequent examinations can be performed sooner.

Acknowledgments. We thank Bram van Ginneken and the DIAG group (Radboud UMC, Nijmegen) for making the CT data available within our common "Automation in Medical Imaging" Fraunhofer ICON project.

References

1. Akagi, M., et al.: Deep learning reconstruction improves image quality of abdominal ultra-high-resolution CT. Eur. Radiol. **29**, 6163–6171 (2019)

2. Eisenhauer, E.A., et al.: New response evaluation criteria in solid tumours: revised recist guideline (version 1.1). Eur. J. Can. **45**(2), 228–247 (2009)

3. Fischer, B., Modersitzki, J.: Curvature based image registration. J. Math. Imaging Vis. **18**(1), 81–85 (2003)

4. Folio, L.R., Choi, M.M., Solomon, J.M., Schaub, N.P.: Automated registration, segmentation, and measurement of metastatic melanoma tumors in serial CT scans. Acad. Radiol. **20**(5), 604–613 (2013)

5. Haber, E., Modersitzki, J.: Intensity gradient based registration and fusion of multi-modal images. In: Larsen, R., Nielsen, M., Sporring, J. (eds.) MICCAI 2006. LNCS, vol. 4191, pp. 726–733. Springer, Heidelberg (2006). https://doi.org/10.1007/11866763_89

6. Hering, A., et al.: Whole-body soft-tissue lesion tracking and segmentation in longitudinal CT imaging studies. In: Medical Imaging with Deep Learning, pp. 312–326. PMLR (2021)

7. Kim, B., Kim, D.H., Park, S.H., Kim, J., Lee, J.G., Ye, J.C.: CycleMorph: cycle consistent unsupervised deformable image registration. Med. Image Anal. **71**, 102036 (2021)

8. König, L., Rühaak, J., Derksen, A., Lellmann, J.: A matrix-free approach to parallel and memory-efficient deformable image registration. SIAM J. Sci. Comput. **40**(3), B858–B888 (2018)

9. Moawad, A.W., et al.: Feasibility of automated volumetric assessment of large hepatocellular carcinomas' responses to transarterial chemoembolization. Front. Oncol. **10**, 572 (2020)

10. Tan, M., et al.: A new approach to evaluate drug treatment response of ovarian cancer patients based on deformable image registration. IEEE Trans. Med. Imaging **35**(1), 316–325 (2015)

11. Vercauteren, T., Pennec, X., Perchant, A., Ayache, N.: Diffeomorphic demons: efficient non-parametric image registration. Neuroimage **45**(1), S61–S72 (2009)

12. Wasserthal, J., Meyer, M., Breit, H.C., Cyriac, J., Yang, S., Segeroth, M.: TotalSegmentator: robust segmentation of 104 anatomical structures in CT images. arXiv preprint arXiv:2208.05868 (2022)

Proceedings of the AI for Treatment Response Assessment and predicTion Workshop (AI4Treat 2023)

Graph-Based Multimodal Multi-lesion DLBCL Treatment Response Prediction from PET Images

Oriane Thiery[1]([envelope]) [ID], Mira Rizkallah[1] [ID], Clément Bailly[2,3] [ID],
Caroline Bodet-Milin[2,3] [ID], Emmanuel Itti[4] [ID], René-Olivier Casasnovas[5] [ID],
Steven Le Gouill[3] [ID], Thomas Carlier[2,3] [ID], and Diana Mateus[1] [ID]

[1] Nantes Université, Centrale Nantes, CNRS, LS2N, UMR 6004, Nantes, France
oriane.thiery@ls2n.fr
[2] Nuclear Medicine Department, University Hospital, Nantes, France
[3] Nantes Université, Inserm, CNRS, Université d'Angers, CRCI2NA, Nantes, France
[4] Nuclear Medicine, CHU Henri Mondor, Paris-Est University, Créteil, France
[5] Hematology, CHU Dijon Bourgogne, Dijon, France

Abstract. Diffuse Large B-cell Lymphoma (DLBCL) is a lymphatic cancer involving one or more lymph nodes and extranodal sites. Its diagnostic and follow-up rely on Positron Emission Tomography (PET) and Computed Tomography (CT). After diagnosis, the number of non-responding patients to standard front-line therapy remains significant (30–40%). This work aims to develop a computer-aided approach to identify high-risk patients requiring adapted treatment by efficiently exploiting all the information available for each patient, including both clinical and image data. We propose a method based on recent graph neural networks that combine imaging information from multiple lesions, and a cross-attention module to integrate different data modalities efficiently. The model is trained and evaluated on a private prospective multicentric dataset of 583 patients. Experimental results show that our proposed method outperforms classical supervised methods based on either clinical, imaging or both clinical and imaging data for the 2-year progression-free survival (PFS) classification accuracy.

Keywords: Multimodal data fusion · Graph Neural Networks · Cross-attention · DLBCL · Treatment Response · PET

1 Introduction

Diffuse Large B-cell Lymphoma (DLBCL) is a cancer of the lymphatic system and the most common type of Non-Hodgkin Lymphoma (NHL). Its incidence is regularly growing, accounting for 30–40% of the 77240 new NHL cases in the

---

Supplementary Information The online version contains supplementary material available at https://doi.org/10.1007/978-3-031-47425-5_10.

US in 2020 [15]. The diagnosis and follow-up include analysing clinical biomarkers and the semi-quantitative interpretation of 18F-Fluorodeoxyglucose (FDG)-PET/CT images. To assist such analysis, existing methods in clinical studies focus on clinical data with classical but interpretable methods [9]. In the image analysis domain, the trend is either to use deep learning methods [18] or to focus on automatically extracting quantitative information (radiomics features) from PET images and combining them with machine learning methods [7]. In this context, we aim to develop a computer-aided method to identify high-risk patients at diagnosis, relying on both clinical and imaging information.

We face multiple challenges when designing a risk classification approach from heterogeneous multimodal data. First, the quantity of available data on this disease is often limited. Also, the information in the PET volumes is spread over multiple typically small lesions, making feature extraction difficult. In addition, both image resolution and the number of lesions can vary significantly across patients, hindering generalizability. Finally, the integration of the different modalities is still an open question in the field [3].

In this paper, we rely on recent advances in Graph Attention Networks (GATs) to combine the information from the multiple lesions while handling the variable number of lesions. We further couple the GAT with a cross-attention fusion module to efficiently integrate data from clinical and imaging modalities. The model is trained and evaluated using a private prospective multicentric dataset with 583 patients suffering from DLBCL. Experimental validation results show that our proposed method yields a good 2-year progression-free survival (PFS) classification accuracy while outperforming classical supervised methods based on either clinical, imaging or both clinical and imaging data.

2   Related Work

Recently, there has been a growing interest in developing computer-assisted methods analysing full-body PET images to support diagnosis and treatment decisions of oncological patients. Different approaches have been considered, relying either on a region of interest (ROI) surrounding a single lesion, or on the full image. For example, methods in [1,10] make outcome or prognosis predictions from lesions ROIs. However, images are only part of the patient's information that physicians rely on to determine the best treatment options. Other approaches [14] rely on both clinical data and image features from the most intense focal lesion to predict the PFS of multiple myeloma patients. However, for all these methods, resuming a full-body image to a single ROI may not fully represent the patient's state as it overlooks the information from other lesions and their potentially structured spatial distribution.

Few papers tackle the problem of incorporating both the imaging descriptors and the underlying structure of all the patient lesions [2,8,11]. They rely on graph representations to model this structural information and build a graph neural network (GNN) on top to provide different types of predictions, e.g. of the probability of distant metastasis over time [8], or the PFS [2,11]. Aswathi et al. [2] exploit only imaging descriptors taken from multiple lesions, while [8,11] consider a naive late fusion to incorporate clinical information, i.e. the clinical features are concatenated with imaging descriptors just before the prediction computation at the last fully connected layer. However, given the naive fusion's simplicity, alternative approaches are needed to study the fusion of multiple lesions and heterogenous data modalities.

Beyond PET imaging and cancer risk prediction, there has been an increasing interest in fusing the information from multiple modalities to perform better-informed predictions. As discussed by Baltrušaitis et al. [3], there are multiple ways of fusing multimodal data, e.g. the classical: early, late and hybrid fusion approaches, kernel-based methods, graphical models and some neural networks. However, none is today consensual for dealing with heterogeneous medical data.

Recently, cross-attention modules have been explored to fuse multiple modalities in bio-medical applications. For instance, Mo et al. [12] implemented a cross-attention strategy to fuse the information from two MRI imaging modalities for a segmentation task. Chen et al. [6] computed a cross-attention based on transformers [16] to register two imaging modalities, by considering different modalities for query than for the keys/values. Finally, targeting heterogenous data, Bhalodia et al. [4] used cross-attention for pneumonia localization by computing cosine similarities between images and text embeddings. Beyond the medical domain but relying on graphs, Xie et al. [17] proposed to fuse vectorial and graph data with cross-attention modules for open relation extraction in text analysis.

In this work, we build a multi-lesion graph to capture image and structural properties [2,8,11]. In addition, we take inspiration from [6,17] to propose a cross-attention method between the image lesion graph and clinical data. The proposed model addresses the identification of high-risk patients in DLBCL.

3   Method

Problem Statement. Let a DLBCL clinical exam before treatment be composed of a full-body PET image acquired on a patient, and a set of tabular clinical indicators. Our goal is to perform a PFS 2-year classification, intended to predict whether the disease of a patient will progress within two years after the beginning of the treatment. This indicator helps to identify high-risk patients (more likely to progress). In this context, we propose a learning framework (c.f. Fig. 1), taking as input clinical tabular data and a full-body 3D PET image with 3D segmentation of the lesions, trained to predict a probability of 2-year PFS.

First, we design a *lesion graph* to simultaneously represent the image features of individual lesions and their spatial distribution. Then, a GNN is built on the top of the constructed graph, composed of i) *graph attention* modules that learns a latent representation from multiple lesions; and ii) a *cross-modal* fusion blocks integrating clinical data. A final *prediction* module aggregates the fused information into a classification score.

Lesion Graph Construction. The first step of our framework is the creation of a fully connected graph $\mathcal{G}^{(n)} = \{\mathcal{V}^{(n)}, \mathcal{E}^{(n)}\}$ to group the information from the $L^{(n)}$ lesions present on the PET scan of the nth patient. We construct this

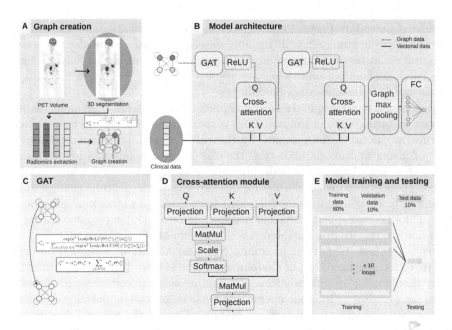

Fig. 1. Method overview: (A) patient-level graph with imaging information from every lesion, (B) model architecture, propagating the information from the multiple nodes (with the GATv2) and fusing it with the clinical data by the cross-attention block, (C) explanation of the GATv2, (D) the cross-attention mechanism, (E) training and testing schemes. The red circles indicate the patient's information provided in the dataset. (Color figure online)

graph as in [2]: each node $v_i^{(n)} \in \mathcal{V}^{(n)}$ corresponds to a single lesion, and is associated with a feature vector $\mathbf{z}_i^{(n)} \in \mathbb{R}^{D_{\text{features}}}$. This vector contains both classical intensity-based and radiomics features[1](c.f Table 1 in Supplementary material). In the following, we denote by $\mathbf{Z}^{(n)} \in \mathbb{R}^{L^{(n)} \times D_{\text{features}}}$ the matrix concatenating all nodes' features $\mathbf{z}_i^{(n)}$, with D_{features} the dimension of the vector including classical and radiomics features.

Edges $e_{ij}^{(n)}$ are drawn between every pair of nodes $v_i^{(n)}$ and $v_j^{(n)}$, including self-loops. Weights $w_{ij}^{(n)}$ are assigned to each edge to favor message passing between closer and more similar lesions. The values of $w_{ij}^{(n)}$ are defined based on the distances between both the feature vectors $\mathbf{z}_i^{(n)}$ and the lesions centroids $\mathbf{p}_i^{(n)}$:

$$w_{ij}^{(n)} = \exp\left(-\frac{||\mathbf{p}_i^{(n)} - \mathbf{p}_j^{(n)}||_2}{\gamma \sigma_1^2}\right) \cdot \exp\left(-\frac{||\mathbf{z}_i^{(n)} - \mathbf{z}_j^{(n)}||_2}{\gamma \sigma_2^2}\right), \qquad (1)$$

---

[1] Here, classical features are quantitative measurements on the segmented lesion describing the intensity distribution of the voxels. Radiomics features instead describe the 3D structure of the lesion, such as shape, or second-order features that reveal the inter-relationship among voxels.

where $||.||_2$ stands for the L2 norm; σ_1, σ_2 denote the population-level standard deviations of the centroid and the feature distances, respectively; and γ is a hyper-parameter tuned to find the best edge weight distribution for our task.

Multi-lesion Representation Learning. To study the relations between the lesions and to pool their information, we define a GNN over our lesion graph. We rely on the GATv2 convolution layer [5] for its capacity to adapt the neighbors' attention weights independently for each node. In our context, the attention scheme of GATv2 implies that the feature vector of each lesion is updated based on information propagated from the most relevant neighboring lesions only. We implement the `torch_geometric` version of this operator, which takes into account edge weights by computing the attention coefficients $\alpha_{i,j}$ as follows:

$$\alpha_{i,j}^{(n)} = \frac{\exp(\mathbf{a}^T \text{LeakyReLU}(\boldsymbol{\Theta}[\mathbf{z}_i^{(n)}||\mathbf{z}_j^{(n)}||w_{ij}^{(n)}]))}{\sum_{k\in\mathcal{N}(i)\cup\{i\}} \exp(\mathbf{a}^T \text{LeakyReLU}(\boldsymbol{\Theta}[\mathbf{z}_i^{(n)}||\mathbf{z}_k^{(n)}||w_{ik}^{(n)}]))}, \tag{2}$$

with $\mathbf{a}$ and $\boldsymbol{\Theta}$ learned parameter matrices, $\cdot||\cdot$ the concatenation operation and $\mathcal{N}(i)$ the neighboring nodes of $v_i^{(n)}$. The features assigned to each lesion (i.e. node in the graph) are updated as:

$$\mathbf{z}_{i_{\text{GAT}}}^{(n)} = \alpha_{i,i}^{(n)}\boldsymbol{\Theta}\mathbf{z}_i^{(n)} + \sum_{j\in\mathcal{N}(i)} \alpha_{i,j}^{(n)}\boldsymbol{\Theta}\mathbf{z}_j^{(n)}. \tag{3}$$

The D_{GAT} dimension of the node's representation $\mathbf{z}_{i_{\text{GAT}}}^{(n)}$ at the output of a GATv2 block is determined by a grid search, as is also the dropout probability applied to this module. Finally, the updated lesion representations are passed through a ReLU activation. The resultant $L^{(n)} \times D_{\text{GAT}}$ feature matrix is a concatenation of the lesions feature vectors: $\mathbf{Z}_{\text{GAT}}^{(n)} = \text{ReLU}([\mathbf{z}_{1_{\text{GAT}}}^{(n)}||\cdots||\mathbf{z}_{L^{(n)}_{\text{GAT}}}^{(n)}]^T)$.

Multimodal Multi-lesion Cross-Attention. We aim now at projecting the updated node features $\mathbf{Z}_{\text{GAT}}^{(n)}$, into a more representative space by integrating the clinical knowledge of the patient n represented by a vector $\mathbf{c}^{(n)} \in \mathbb{R}^{D_{\text{clin}}}$; note that there is a vector $\mathbf{c}^{(n)}$ per patient (and not per lesion). For this purpose, we take advantage of the self-attention module proposed in [16] adapted to the cross-modal case. The module takes as input a query vector $\mathbf{Q}$ and a key/value pair of vectors $\mathbf{K}$ and $\mathbf{V}$ and outputs a weighted sum of the values, where the weight assigned to each value is computed from a compatibility function (i.e. a scalar product) of the query with the corresponding key (normalized by the key dimension d_k). By defining $\mathbf{Q} = \mathbf{Z}_{\text{GAT}}^{(n)}$ and $\mathbf{K} = \mathbf{V} = \mathbf{c}^{(n)}$, the signals assigned to each lesion are updated with the information procured by the clinical data:

$$\mathbf{Z}_{\text{CrossAtt}}^{(n)} = \text{CrossAtt}(\mathbf{Z}_{\text{GAT}}^{(n)}, \mathbf{c}^{(n)}, \mathbf{c}^{(n)})$$

$$= \text{softmax}\left(\frac{\mathbf{Z}_{\text{GAT}}^{(n)}\mathbf{W}^Q(\mathbf{c}^{(n)}\mathbf{W}^K)^T}{\sqrt{d_k}}\right)\mathbf{c}^{(n)}\mathbf{W}^V. \tag{4}$$

We optimize during training the latent representations of $\mathbf{Q}$, $\mathbf{K}$ and $\mathbf{V}$ and the cross attention output via three learnable matrices $\mathbf{W}^Q \in \mathbb{R}^{D_{\mathrm{GAT}} \times D_{\mathrm{clin}}}$, $\mathbf{W}^K \in \mathbb{R}^{1 \times D_{\mathrm{clin}}}$ and $\mathbf{W}^V \in \mathbb{R}^{1 \times D_{\mathrm{GAT}}}$. The result of the cross-attention operation is a matrix $\mathbf{Z}^{(n)}_{\mathrm{CrossAtt}}$ of same size as $\mathbf{Q}$ ($L^{(n)} \times D_{\mathrm{CrossAtt}} = L^{(n)} \times D_{\mathrm{GAT}}$). Intuitively, matrices $\mathbf{W}^Q$ and $\mathbf{W}^K$ project the multi-lesion image data and the clinical vector on to a common space, before computing their compatibility. The softmax output, of size ($L^{(n)} \times D_{\mathrm{clin}}$), provides the attention values that each lesion should give to the entries of the clinical vector. Finally, the attention scores are multiplied with the clinical data vector, lifted to the D_{GAT} dimension by $\mathbf{W}^V$. The updated individual node features correspond to the rows of $\mathbf{Z}^{(n)}_{\mathrm{CrossAtt}}$. The multi-lesion and cross attention modules are repeated for two layers. After the second layer, we end up with $\mathbf{Z}^{(n)}_{\mathrm{CrossAtt}}{}' \in \mathbb{R}^{L^{(n)} \times D_{\mathrm{GAT}}}$.

Prediction. A max pooling on $\mathbf{Z}^{(n)}_{\mathrm{CAtt}}{}'$, across the node dimension, resumes the graph features to a D_{GAT}-dimensional vector, allowing us to handle patients with different numbers of lesions. The pooled vector is given to a linear layer with a sigmoid activation function to make a prediction of the 2-year PFS for a given patient. The learning is controlled by a weighted binary cross-entropy loss function, where weights compensate for the class imbalance (ratio of positive to negative samples $\sim 1 : 5$).

4   Experiments

Dataset. The proposed method was evaluated on the prospective GAINED study (NCT 01659099) [9] which enrolled 670 newly diagnosed and untreated DLBCL patients. In order to perform our binary prediction of the 2-year PFS, we removed the patients who were censored before this time, which left us with 583 samples. Among these patients, 101 were deemed as positive for the PFS because of a progression or a relapse of the disease within two years, while 12 were positive because of death without progression of the disease. In this dataset, are assigned to each patient a PET image at the beginning of the protocol as well as clinical indicators such as age, ECOG scale, Ann Arbor stage or number of extranodal sites (full list is presented in Supp. material). The lesion detection on the PET images is done manually by a clinician and the segmentation is performed using a majority vote between three usual lesion segmentation methods: i) a K-means clustering ($K = 2$), ii) a thresholding that retains only voxels with intensity values larger than 41% of the maximum intensity, and iii) a second thresholding to keep voxels whose normalized SUV (Standard Uptake Value) is more than 2.5. The imaging and clinical features are both standardised by removing the median of the training data and scaling the whole dataset according to the quartile range: $Scaled\ value = \frac{Original\ value - training\ median}{training\ interquartile\ range}$. The distance between the centroid of the lesions (Eq. 1) is standardized in a similar way, but considering the mean and quartiles of the lesions' centroids individually for each patient.

Comparison to Baseline Models. Our model was compared to six other baseline models performing the same task:

- **MLP clinical**: An MLP whose only input is the vector of clinical data of a patient. The model comprises two linear layers with ReLU activations and a 1-dim linear output layer with sigmoid activation. The two intermediate layers have the same dimension, in practice chosen via a grid search.
- **MLP image**: An MLP with the same configuration but taking as input the imaging data. We compute the input image vector as the average of the feature vectors from individual lesions to handle the variable lesion number across patients. For each lesion we extract features as in Sec. 3.
- **MLP clinical+image**: An MLP, with the same configuration as the previous ones, but taking as input the concatenation of both the clinical and imaging data (*i.e.* the input image vector as for the MLP image).
- **MIL image**: A MIL approach taking as input the imaging features from the $L^{(n)}$ lesions of a patient, applies a one-layer MLP followed by a ReLU on each lesion's feature vector, aggregates the results by a maximum operation and projects it linearly (with a sigmoid activation) to get the prediction.
- **GraphConv image**: A GraphConv model [13], taking as input a lesion graph as in Sec. 3, but using a graph convolution aggregation function, see Eq. 5. The model is composed of two GraphConv layers, the first having an output dimension determined by grid search, and the second with an output size of 1. The first layer has a ReLU activation, and the second is followed by a max pooling operation and a sigmoid activation to predict the PFS.

$$\mathbf{z}^{(n)}_{i_{\text{GraphConv}}} = \mathbf{W}_1 \mathbf{z}^{(n)}_i + \mathbf{W}_2\left(\sum_{j \in \mathcal{N}(i)} w^{(n)}_{ij} \mathbf{z}^{(n)}_j \right). \tag{5}$$

Ablation Study. In order to prove the interest of each module in our framework we also do two ablation studies. First, we implement our model with GraphConv layers replacing the GATv2 layers to study the impact of the learned attention weights between the lesions. Then, we replace the cross-attention layers by a simple concatenation $[\mathbf{z}^{(n)}_{i_{GAT}}||\mathbf{c}^{(n)}]$ to verify if the proposed learnable fusion between the two modalities improves the performance of the model. Toward the same goal, we implement a model based on two GATv2 layers with clinical data concatenated to the last linear layer used for the prediction.

Experimental Setup. We strictly divide the 583 patients in three distinct sets of training (80%), validation (10%) and test (10%). Test results are reported for the model with the best validation ROC AUC. To evaluate our model, the split is repeated ten times as follows: a single test set is left out from all the loops, and at each loop the remaining data is randomly split into training and validation sets, while ensuring that the ratio of positive patients is the same in all the sets. Furthermore, to ensure the scores are computed on balanced sets, we repeat the validation and test phases five times: for each run we build a balanced set with all the available positive data and 1/5 of the negative data, randomly sampled from the validation and test sets respectively. The resulting metrics are then averaged to get the final validation or test results. A grid search (c.f. Table 3 in Supp. material) is performed on the learning rate, the hidden channel size and, for the GNN, the parameter γ (used in the lesion graphs construction) to find the model configuration that grants the best validation ROC AUC. Furthermore, in order to validate the statistical significance of our results, we use a t-test to compare the results of our model against the baselines. The whole framework has been coded in Python with `PyTorch` and `torch_geometric` modules.

5   Results

Quantitative Results. We report in Table 1 the results of our comparative study. Our experiments reveal that models based on clinical data perform better than models using imaging data only. Furthermore, for models based on imaging data, considering the lesions individually (as the nodes of a graph or a bag of nodes in the MIL) seems to improve the predictions compared to averaging the feature vectors. Also, using a graph improves over the bag of lesions/MIL approach. Finally, the proposed framework performs significantly better than all the other models (p-value < 0.005), showing it efficiently fuses the information from multiple lesions and from the two considered modalities.

For the **ablation** studies, replacing the cross-attention layers by a simple concatenation results in a big performance drop (test ROC AUC of 0.59 ± 0.06 against 0.72 ± 0.03 initially), as well as doing a late fusion between the modalities (test ROC AUC of 0.54 ± 0.06) , proving the benefit of our multimodal data fusion method. However, replacing the GATv2 layers with GraphConv layers does not significantly affect the performances (test ROC AUC of 0.71 ± 0.04).

The better performance of clinical-based models compared to those based on imaging can be partially explained by the selection of a subset of clinical variables known for being predictive [9]. Another aspect influencing the image-based models is the high complexity of the lesion segmentation task for DLBCL patients given that lesions tend to superpose and have diffuse contours. Nonetheless, we argue that an efficient integration of both kinds of data, and all the lesions, as proposed here, should allow for a better assessment of the patient's state.

Qualitative Results. We also studied the learned attention weights in the cross-attention modules (c.f. figures in Supp. material) in order to better understand where the model focuses when learning to predict the patients' 2-year PFS. Firstly, we observe that the cross-attention weights across patients can behave differently, with either overall constant weights across rows (lesions) and columns (clinical variables), or approximately constant rows, or variations across rows and columns. However, the two cross-attention modules for a patient tend to be similar. Secondly, the contribution of the different clinical features is mostly equilibrated: each clinical feature is given approximately the same amount of attention, which is expected since, as we mentioned before, we rely on known

Table 1. Test ROC AUC of the considered models (best performance in bold), with the p-value comparing the results to those of the cross-attention model.

Model	Clinical data	Image data	AUC	p-value
MLP	x	–	0.66 ± 0.04	0.002
MLP	x	x (average)	0.61 ± 0.04	< 0.001
MLP	–	x (average)	0.47 ± 0.04	< 0.001
MIL	–	x (per lesion)	0.56 ± 0.06	< 0.001
GraphConv	–	x (per lesion)	0.58 ± 0.06	< 0.001
Cross-attention	x	x (per lesion)	$\mathbf{0.72 \pm 0.03}$	–

biomarkers. For some patients, few clinical features stand out. For example, for one patient (Fig. 2 in Supp. material), the model puts a strong attention on his LDH value, which is quite low, and on his aaIPI (age-adjusted International Prognostic Index, which is equal to 1). The prediction for this patient is negative, i.e., no relapse within two years. This seems coherent with the physician's thinking process when trying to asses the condition of a patient, confirming the relevance of the multimodal fusion by the cross-attention module.

6 Conclusion

We address treatment response prediction of DLBCL patients two years after diagnosis. To this end, we propose a new cross-attention graph learning method integrating image information from multiple lesions and clinical tabular data. Experimental validation on a prospective clinical dataset shows that our model can efficiently exploit the complementary information, performing significantly better than all compared baselines. As perspectives, we will consider cost functions adapted to survival analysis for a more fine-grained treatment response estimation in time and a better modelling of censored patients. In addition, studying graphs defined on lesions sub-regions rather than whole lesions [11] could help mitigate the impact of intra/inter-operator segmentation variability, especially for lesions whose delimitation is unclear. Finally, we plan to investigate the generalisation ability of our model to other pathologies.

Acknowledgements. This work has been funded by the AIby4 project (Centrale Nantes-Project ANR-20-THIA-0011), INCa-DGOS-INSERM-ITMO Cancer 18011 (SIRIC ILIAD) with the support from the Pays de la Loire region (GCS IRECAN 220729), the European Regional Development Fund (FEDER), the Pays de la Loire region on the Connect Talent MILCOM programme and Nantes Métropole (Conv. 2017-10470).

References

1. Amyar, A., Ruan, S., Gardin, I., Chatelain, C., Decazes, P., Modzelewski, R.: 3-D RPET-NET: development of a 3-D PET imaging convolutional neural network for radiomics analysis and outcome prediction. IEEE TPRMS **3**(2), 225–231 (2019)
2. Aswathi, A., et al.: Lesion graph neural networks for 2-year progression free survival classification of diffuse large B-cell lymphoma patients. In: IEEE International Symposium on Biomedical Imaging (ISBI) (2023)
3. Baltrušaitis, T., Ahuja, C., Morency, L.P.: Multimodal machine learning: a survey and taxonomy. IEEE TPAMI **41**(2), 423–443 (2019)
4. Bhalodia, R., et al.: Improving pneumonia localization via cross-attention on medical images and reports. In: Med Image Comp and Comp Assisted Interventions (MICCAI) (2021)
5. Brody, S., Alon, U., Yahav, E.: How attentive are graph attention networks? In: International Conference on Learning Representations (2022)
6. Chen, J., Liu, Y., He, Y., Du, Y.: Deformable cross-attention transformer for medical image registration. ArXiv:2303.06179 (2023)
7. Jiang, C., et al.: Optimal PET-based radiomic signature construction based on the cross-combination method for predicting the survival of patients with diffuse large B-cell lymphoma. Eur. J. Nucl. Med. Mol. Imaging **49**(8), 2902–2916 (2022)
8. Kazmierski, M., Haibe-Kains, B.: Lymph node graph neural networks for cancer metastasis prediction, June 2021. http://arxiv.org/abs/2106.01711
9. Le Gouill, S.: Obinutuzumab vs rituximab for advanced DLBCL: a PET-guided and randomized phase 3 study by LYSA. Blood **137**(17), 2307–2320 (2021)
10. Li, H., Boimel, P., et al.: Deep convolutional neural networks for imaging data based survival analysis of rectal cancer. In: IEEE International Symposium on Biomedical Imaging (ISBI) (2019)
11. Lv, W., et al.: Functional-structural sub-region graph convolutional network (FSGCN): application to the prognosis of head and neck cancer with PET/CT imaging. Comput. Methods Programs Biomed. **230**, 107341 (2023)
12. Mo, S., et al.: Mutual information-based graph co-attention networks for multimodal prior-guided magnetic resonance imaging segmentation. IEEE Trans. Circ. Syst. Video Tech. **32**(5), 2512–2526 (2022)
13. Morris, C., et al.: Weisfeiler and Leman go neural: Higher-order graph neural networks. In: Proceedings of the AAAI Conference on Artificial Intelligence, vol. 33, pp. 4602–4609, July 2019
14. Morvan, L., et al.: Leveraging RSF and PET images for prognosis of multiple myeloma at diagnosis. Int. J. Comput. Assist. Radiol. Surg. **15**(1), 129–139 (2019). https://doi.org/10.1007/s11548-019-02015-y
15. Susanibar-Adaniya, S., Barta, S.K.: 2021 update on diffuse large B cell lymphoma: a review of current data and potential applications on risk stratification and management. Am. J. Hematol. **96**(5), 617–629 (2021)
16. Vaswani, A., et al.: Attention is all you need. In: Neural Information Processing Systems (NeurIPS) (2017)
17. Xie, B., Li, Y., Zhao, H., Pan, L., Wang, E.: A cross-attention fusion based graph convolution auto-encoder for open relation extraction. IEEE/ACM TASLP **31**, 476–485 (2023)
18. Yuan, C., et al.: Multimodal deep learning model on interim 18F-FDG PET/CT for predicting primary treatment failure in diffuse large B-cell lymphoma. Eur. Radiol. **33**, 77–88 (2022)

RPTK: The Role of Feature Computation on Prediction Performance

Jonas R. Bohn[1,2,3,4(✉)] ⓘ, Christian M. Heidt[2,5,6], Silvia D. Almeida[1,2,6],
Lisa Kausch[1,7], Michael Götz[8], Marco Nolden[1,2,9], Petros Christopoulos[2,10],
Stephan Rheinheimer[2,5,10], Alan A. Peters[2,5,11,12],
Oyunbileg von Stackelberg[2,5], Hans-Ulrich Kauczor[2,5],
Klaus H. Maier-Hein[1,2,7,9], Claus P. Heußel[2,5,11], and Tobias Norajitra[1,2,9]

[1] Division of Medical Image Computing, German Cancer Research Center (DKFZ),
Heidelberg, Germany
j.bohn@dkfz-heidelberg.de
[2] Translational Lung Research Center (TLRC), Member of the German Center for
Lung Research (DZL), Heidelberg, Germany
[3] Faculty of Biosciences, Heidelberg University, Heidelberg, Germany
[4] National Center for Tumor Diseases (NCT), NCT Heidelberg, A Partnership
between DKFZ and University Medical Center, Heidelberg, Germany
[5] Diagnostic and Interventional Radiology, University Hospital Heidelberg,
Heidelberg, Germany
[6] Medical Faculty, Heidelberg University, Heidelberg, Germany
[7] AI Health Innovation Cluster, German Cancer Research Center (DKFZ),
Heidelberg, Germany
[8] University of Ulm Medical Center, Experimental Radiology, Ulm, Germany
[9] Pattern Analysis and Learning Group, University Hospital Heidelberg, Heidelberg,
Germany
[10] Thoracic Oncology, Thoraxklinik, Heidelberg, Germany
[11] Diagnostic and Interventional Radiology with Nuclear Medicine, Thoraxklinik,
Heidelberg, Germany
[12] Department of Diagnostic, Interventional and Pediatric Radiology, Bern
University Hospital, University of Bern, Bern, Switzerland

Abstract. A rise of radiomics studies and techniques could be observed
over the past few years, which centers around the extraction and analysis
of quantitative features from medical images. Radiomics offers numerous advantages in disease characterization and treatment response prediction. Despite its promise, radiomics faces challenges in standardiz-
ing features and techniques, leading to large variations of approaches
across studies and centers, making it difficult to determine the most
suitable techniques for any given clinical scenario. Additionally, manually constructing optimized radiomics pipelines can be time-consuming.
Recent works (WORC, Autoradiomics) have addressed the aforementioned shortcomings by introducing radiomics-based frameworks for

Supplementary Information The online version contains supplementary material
available at https://doi.org/10.1007/978-3-031-47425-5_11.

automated pipeline optimization. Both approaches comprehensively span the entire radiomics workflow, enabling consistent, comprehensive, and reproducible radiomics analyses. In contrast, finding the ideal solutions for the workflow's feature extractor and feature selection components, has received less attention. To address this, we propose the Radiomics Processing Toolkit (RPTK), which adds comprehensive feature extraction and selection components from PyRadiomics and from the Medical Image Radiomics Processor (MIRP) to the radiomics automation pipeline. To validate our approach and demonstrate benefits from the feature-centered components, we comprehensively compared RPTK with results from WORC and Autoradiomics on six public benchmark data sets. We show that we can achieve higher performance by incorporating the proposed feature processing and selection techniques. Our results provide additional guidance in selecting suitable components for optimized radiomics analyses in clinical use cases such as treatment response prediction.

Keywords: Radiomics · Evaluation · Automated Radiomics Processing · Radiomics Processing Toolkit

1   Introduction

In recent years, there has been a significant increase in the number of published radiomics studies and techniques [5]. Radiomics, a field that focuses on the extraction and analysis of quantitative features from medical images, offers a great number of advantages in disease characterization and treatment response prediction [6]. By utilizing radiomics features, researchers and clinicians can identify patient subgroups likely to respond to specific therapies, enabling tailored treatment plans and reducing unnecessary interventions for non-responders.

While radiomics shows immense promise, it also faces challenges that need to be addressed for successful clinical integration [2,8]. One crucial challenge is the standardization of radiomic features and feature extractor configuration (e.g., size of feature space) to ensure consistency and reproducibility of the underlying data across different studies and institutions. Another major challenge is the lack of standardized techniques (e.g., image processing, feature filtering, and feature selection) and libraries, which altogether leads to large variations in approaches across studies. This makes it difficult to determine which techniques are most suitable for specific clinical scenarios. Additionally, constructing an optimized radiomics pipeline manually can be time-consuming and labor-intensive.

To address these challenges, efforts such as the Image Biomarker Standardization Initiative (IBSI) have defined a total of 162 standardized features for radiomics-based feature extraction which makes radiomics data comparable [11] and enables easier comparison and validation of radiomics studies across different data sets and research groups. Recent achievements have been made in radiomics pipeline creation and validation on the WORC (Workflow for Optimal Radiomics Classification) database [4,5]. Researchers have developed comprehensive pipelines that encompass data preprocessing, feature extraction, using standardized features defined by the IBSI, feature selection, model training, and validation. These pipelines enable consistent and reproducible radiomics analysis across different data sets and research groups. In the realm of radiomics, different libraries with varying levels of standardization offer a range of techniques [8]. However, determining which techniques are truly beneficial in specific application scenarios and finding an optimized radiomics solution can be challenging. To address this, recent advancements have focused on automating the search for optimized solutions, such as the Autoradiomics [9] and the same-named WORC approach [5]. While the concept is promising, Autoradiomics and WORC have their limitations in terms of its library functionalities and missing pipelining aspects on the feature computation.

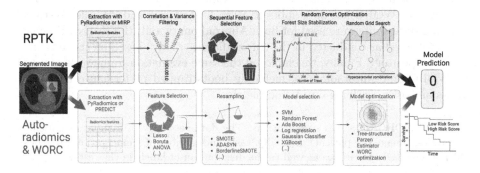

Fig. 1. Overview of our proposed radiomics pipeline (RPTK), in comparison to Autoradiomics [9] and WORC [5]. Our approach differentiates by encompassing feature extraction (PyRadiomics & MIRP) and efficient selection procedures as well as stable two step model optimization (details in Table 2).

To overcome limitations of these pipelines, we propose Radiomics Processing Toolkit (RPTK). We have expanded the Autoradiomics pipeline by incorporating additional feature extraction and selection/filtering functionalities. Specifically, we integrated different radiomics feature extraction tools like PyRadiomics [3], the most widely used feature extraction tool, and the Medical Image Radiomics Processor (MIRP) [10] tool which comprises the whole set of IBSI standardized features and feature filtering/selection methods. In this study we focused on performance comparison between our tool, RPTK and the Autoradiomics and the WORC pipeline (see Fig. 1). Detailed methodological comparison of RPTK to Autoradiomics has been made as Autoradiomics outperforms the WORC pipeline on the majority of data sets in the WORC database. In addition, Autoradiomics enables direct comparison on performance on the same train and test samples and selected features as well as high transparency of all applied models in the pipeline. We compared the performance of our expanded pipeline with the previous approaches of Autoradiomics [9] and WORC [5] on six public benchmark data sets, where we show that better results can be achieved by incorporating the proposed techniques. Our findings can provide additional guidance in selecting suitable components for optimized radiomics analyses in clinical use cases.

2   Material and Methods

This study aims to compare methodological and performance aspects of our tool RPTK (see Fig. 1), and of the Autoradiomics and WORC approaches for radiomics analysis on the WORC benchmark database[1][2]. The WORC database [4,5] provides a large collection of standardized multi-central and well-annotated imaging data, facilitating the development and validation of robust radiomics models. The benchmark database includes six data sets of MR and CT images acquired before treatment or surgery, with different tissue entities, and segmentation/region of interest (ROI) per sample, covering various classification tasks (see Table 1). To promote comparability, we harmonized all methods with respect to data splitting, result reproduction and evaluation wherever possible. Autoradiomics and WORC use data splits of 80 % for training and 20 % for testing. Identical data splits were used for both Autoradiomics and RPTK. Experiments were replicated as conducted in the Autoradiomics study[3] based on the authors' Github repository. Finally, we employed the same evaluation framework as used by WORC and Autoradiomics, including bootstrapped performance measurements and all underlying evaluation metrics.

Table 1. WORC data sets specifications. The data sets vary in number of patients (always one image per patient), modality, task, and number of segmentations/Regions Of Interest (ROI) per image as well as the distribution of labels in the test set.

Data set	Patients	Modality	ROIs	Classification Task	Test Samples per Label
Lipo	115	T1w MR	116	Well-differentiated Liposarcoma (label: 1)/ Lipoma (label: 0)	0=12 1=11
Desmoid	203	T1w MR	203	Desmoid-type fibromatosis (label: 1)/ soft-tissue sarcoma (label: 0)	0=26 1=14
Liver	186	T2w MR	186	Malignant (label: 1)/ benign primary solid liver lesions (label: 0)	0=19 1=19
GIST	246	CT	247	Gastrointestinal stromal tumors (GIST) (label: 1)/ other intra-abdominal tumors (label: 0)	0=25 1=24
CRLM	77	CT	93	Replacement (label: 1)/ desmoplastic histopathological growth patterns in colorectal liver metastases (label: 0)	0=8 1=7
Melanoma	103	CT	169	BRAF mutated gene (label: 1)/ BRAF wild type gene in melanoma lung metastases (label: 0)	0=10 1=9

The architectures of RPTK, Autoradiomics and WORC differ in various places. Differences concern the feature extraction strategy or its configuration (see Table 2 and supplementary Table 3), additional feature processing (normalization & filtering) and feature selection. RPTK employs two pipelines, namely PyRadiomics [3] and MIRP [10], for radiomics feature extraction. Both pipelines

---

[1] The license is comparable to the Creative Commons AttributionNonCommercial-ShareAlike 4.0 (CC BY-NC-SA) license, with the main adjustment that the data cannot be redistributed.

[2] Downloaded on the 17th of March 2023 from: xnat.bmia.nl/data/projects/worc.

[3] Accessed on 15th of May 2023: github.com/pwoznicki/radiomics-benchmark.

are built on standardized IBSI features, but PyRadiomics lacks 34 IBSI features that are included in MIRP. RPTK uses all available image transformations from each feature extraction tool to maximise the feature space. After feature extraction, RPTK performs a z-score normalization and filtering of highly correlated features (searching for surrogate features with Pearson correlation > 0.9), of constant features (features with variation < 0.1 were considered less informative) and of duplicated features. This reduces initial high feature space dimensionality and allows more efficient, faster feature selection. Afterwards, sequential feature selection with a random forest classifier (200 decision trees) was performed to select the 20 most informative features (10 from forward and 10 from backward selection). This differs from the WORC and Autoradiomics feature selection approaches, which rely on feature importance derived from their classifiers and on various other techniques (see Table 2), in contrast to the sequential feature selection adding or removing features in a greedy fashion based on cross validation score [7]. Autoradiomics used three and WORC used six different methods to select best features based on feature importance coming from the model (see Table 2). Number of resulting important features in Autoradiomics vary depending on chosen thresholds.

Table 2. This table compares 7 aspects of the radiomics pipelines of WORC, Autoradiomics and RPTK that affect classifier input, training and performance. (Log Reg: Logistic Regression, SVM: Support Vector Machine, QDA: Quadratic Discriminant Analysis, LDA: Linear Discriminant Analysis, CV: Cross-Validation)

Steps in Pipelines	WORC	Autoradiomics	RPRK
Feature extraction	PyRadiomics (v3.0.1) or PREDICT (v3.1.17)	PyRadiomics (v3.0.1)	PyRadiomics (v3.0.1) & MIRP (v.1.3.0)
Feature selection	Group-wise selection, RELIEF algorithm, LASSO, Log Reg, Random Forest, Principal Component Analysis	Anovar, Boruta, Lasso	Sequential feature selection with Random Forest (sklearn v. 1.2.2)
Models	Random Forest, AdaBoost, Log Reg, SVM, LDA, QDA, XGBoost, Gaussian Classifier	Random Forest, AdaBoost, Log Reg, SVM, XGBoost, Gaussian Classifier	Random Forest (sklearn v. 1.2.2)
Model training	5-Fold CV	5-Fold CV	5-Fold CV
Model optimization	WORC optimization algorithm	Tree-structured Parzen Estimator (optuna)	Random Grid Search CV (sklearn v. 1.2.2)
Selected hyperparameters for random forest	n estimator, max depth, min samples split	n estimator, max depth, max features, min samples leaf, min samples split, bootstrap	n estimator (seperated), max depth, max features, max samples, ccp alpha, criterion
Performance evaluation	AUROC, weighted F1-score, Sensitivity, Specificity	AUROC, F1 score, Sensitivity, Specificity	AUROC, F1 score, Sensitivity, Specificity

For prediction, RPTK used a random forest classifier. A step wise optimization was performed to enable a stable and reproducible model performance. First, the number of estimators (number of decision trees) of the random forest classifier was optimized to find the size of the model which performs most stably from 10 to 700 trees. This was done because unstable performance was inspected for some WORC data sets with smaller numbers of estimators gaining max performance. The model was trained with a 5 fold cross validation to arrive at a stable number of trees (defined as the first point where the gradient of the validation AUROC is 0). Afterwards, hyperparameters were optimized with a seeded RandomizedGridSearchCV from sklearn for 900 iterations [7] (see Table 2 for selected hyperparameters and supplementary Table 2 for used ranges). In contrast, the Autoradiomics pipeline uses four different models for prediction (logistic regression (Log-reg), support vector machines (SVM), random forest (RF), and extreme gradient boosting (XGBoost)) and reports only the best model. These models were optimized using a tree-structured parzen estimator (see Table 2). Finally, results were evaluated on the area under the receiver operating curve (AUROC), F1 score, Specificity, and Sensitivity and calculated on the test set with a 1000 fold bootstrap repetition to extract the 95% confidence interval for performance stability. The classification threshold for the calculation of the F1 score, the Sensitivity, and the Specificity was set to 0.5 for experiments in this study (see supplementary Table 1). Additionally as part of the WORC database, clinicians had performed the respective classification tasks on the Lipo, Desmoid, and Liver data sets (see Table 1). The clinicians had reached a mean AUROC performance of 0.69, 0.84, and 0.85 for the Lipo, Desmoid, and Liver data sets [5].

3   Results

The results of this study are described in Fig. 2 and supplementary Table 1. The performance metrics utilized were derived from the published approaches.

The results obtained from the Autoradiomics study [9] on the WORC data sets were replicated using the exact configurations as provided by the authors. Figure 2 shows box plots of the test AUROC for all WORC data sets, whereas supplementary Table 1 summarizes the results using additional performance metrics as used in the literature. Values in Fig. 2 follow the same bootstrapping evaluation approach used in the WORC and Autoradiomics experiments. Best performing models as selected by Autoradiomcs were: Lipo: Random Forest, Liver: XGBoost, GIST: SVM, CRLM: Logistic Regression, Desmoid: Logistic Regression, Melanoma: SVM. Selected methods for feature selection from Autoradiomics are Lipo: Boruta, Liver: Anova, GIST: Anova, CRLM: Anova, Desmoid: Boruta, Melanoma: Anova. The RPTK pipeline solely relies on trained random forests for all data sets in this study, and always performs a sequential feature selection with an underlying random forest classifier.

The RPTK tool generally performed better than the Autoradiomics and the WORC tool on the mean AUROC and the F1 scores (see supplementary Table 1).

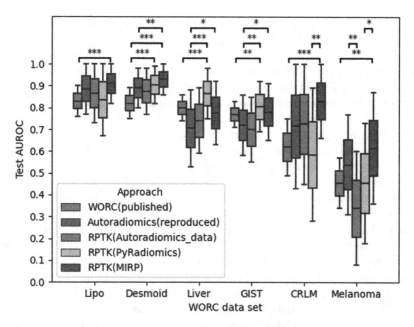

Fig. 2. Comparison of test set performance based on AUROC on the WORC database. The Autoradiomics results come from reproduced experiments, results from the WORC approach have been published [5]. The RPTK approach has been applied on the extracted and selected features from the reproduced Autoradiomics approach. RPTK has also been applied on the WORC database with different feature extractors (PyRadiomics or MIRP). The plot shows the distribution of AUROC scores after bootstrapping. Error bars are related to 2x standard deviation. Significance tested with a t-test (*:p-value=< 0.05, **:p-value=< 0.01, ***:p-value< 0.0001).

Figure 2 shows that RPTK could outperform WORC significantly on all six data sets and Autoradiomics on four of six based on test AUROC. In addition, we could show better performance compared to clinicians (data published in [5]) with a mean AUROC difference of 0.26 on the Lipo data, 0.09 on the Desmoid data, 0.04 on the Liver data, and 0.06 on the GIST data and compared to WORC and Autoradiomics on this data.

4   Discussion

In this study, we were able to demonstrate that configuration of the feature extraction pipeline, increasing feature choice and further feature filtering could lead to better performance of a simple random forest classifier in comparison to automated approaches that apply multiple classifiers and selectors on a reduced choice of features. Comparison in performance is displayed in Fig. 2 and supplementary Table 1. Corresponding p-values of the performance comparison between Autoradiomics and WORC with RPTK show that we were able to significantly gain performance in 50% of the test data sets as compared to the previous best performing Autoradiomics approach (see Fig. 2). Different factors like feature extraction, feature selection as well as model selection and training/optimization could impact the final performance of radiomics pipelines. Selected features for Autoradiomics and RPTK were very different (only one common selected feature in Desmoid and Lipo data set). This indicates that the size of the initial feature space and the selected features have a major impact on capturing information to support the underlying prediction task, and consequently on resulting performance. This can also be seen from the varying performance of RPTK when using PyRadiomics vs MIRP. In order to assess the influence of different classifier choices between Autoradiomics and RPTK, as opposed to influence from selected radiomics features, we trained and optimized the RPTK random forest classifier on the features as extracted and selected by Autoradiomics (Fig. 2, cyan boxplot). RPTK performed constantly worse in mean AUROC on the data from Autoradiomics as compared to using features selected by RPTK. Differences between the Autoradiomics approach and RPTK applied on the data from the Autoradiomics approach show model training/optimization performance influence on the results. These two experiments show highly similar test AUROC values on five of six data sets. Differences in test AUROC were statistically significant only on the Melanoma data set (p-value = 0.009). Applying RPTK with PyRadiomics gained better performance on the same data set which indicates resulting performance differences stemming from the selected feature space. Furthermore, notable improvements in performance were observed specifically in the Liver and GIST data sets when comparing the approaches based on Autoradiomics data and the RPTK approach. Both approaches utilized PyRadiomics for feature extraction but with different configurations. Different degrees of performance variation were observed depending on the underlying data sets. High variations could be observed for the CRLM and the Melanoma data sets were the size of the selected test set is smaller (15, 19) as compared to the other data sets (23–49). The extended feature extractor (MIRP) significantly gained performance on the CRLM and Melanoma data sets (CRLM p-value: 0.005, Melanoma p-value: 0.05) when compared to using PyRadiomics in RPTK. This difference could be caused by missing IBSI features in PyRadiomics and by the different types of applied image transformations (see supplementary Table 3).

Altogether, RPTK has shown that performance can be improved based on the proposed choice of feature-based radiomics components as compared to WORC and Autoradiomics as well as to clinicians on 4 WORC data sets as measured by mean AUROC [4], without loss of performance on other data sets in the WORC database. Limitations of this study concern some aspects found in the data sets. As shown in Table 1, the Melanoma and the CRLM data sets do have several multiple segmentations per sample. The Autoradiomics and the RPTK approach only considered one ROI per sample and ignored the rest. Further limitations may concern heterogeneity of the different image filters as used by PyRadiomics and MIRP for image transformation prior to radiomics feature extraction. Finally, only imaging data was used for the generation of results in this study. Further integration of clinical data may further improve performance of the classifiers, leveraging information not present in underlying images where the WORC approach integrated age and gender. As MRI and CT scans were done before any form of treatment, tasks on these images concern therapeutic biomarker classifications which do have crucial impact on treatment planning and treatment effect prediction [1].

Summarized, we showed drawbacks of published automated radiomics approaches regarding capabilities of extensive and stable features extraction, filtering, and selection. Approaches such as Autoradiomics and WORC made automated radiomics studies easy applicable with a focus on optimizing the machine learning back end in the pipeline. We showed that more extensive feature extraction and feature processing can significantly improve performance by only training and optimizing a random forest model. Future work could include all defined ROIs in the data sets, harmonization of the feature extraction pipelines as well as prepossessing of the manual segmentation's for segmentation errors and feature stability influenced by segmentation errors or different scanner protocols.

References

1. Angus, L., et al.: The BRAF P.V600E mutation status of melanoma lung metastases cannot be discriminated on computed tomography by LIDC criteria nor radiomics using machine learning. J. Personalized Med. **11**(4), 257 (2021). https://doi.org/10.3390/jpm11040257,https://www.mdpi.com/2075-4426/11/4/257

2. Chetan, M.R., Gleeson, F.V.: Radiomics in predicting treatment response in non-small-cell lung cancer: current status, challenges and future perspectives. Eur Radiol **31**(2), 1049–1058 (2021)

3. van Griethuysen, J.J.M., et al.: Computational radiomics system to decode the radiographic phenotype. Cancer Res. **77**(21), e104–e107 (2017)

4. Martijn, P.A.S., et al: The WORC database: MRI and CT scans, segmentations, and clinical labels for 930 patients from six radiomics studies. medRxiv p. 2021.08.19.21262238 (2021). https://doi.org/10.1101/2021.08.19.21262238, https://medrxiv.org/content/early/2021/08/25/2021.08.19.21262238.abstract

5. Martijn, P.A.S., et al: Reproducible radiomics through automated machine learning validated on twelve clinical applications. arXiv pre-print server (2021). arxiv:2108.08618, https://arxiv.org/abs/2108.08618

6. Mu, W., et al.: Non-invasive decision support for NSCLC treatment using pet/CT radiomics. Nat. Commun. **11**(1), 5228 (2020)

7. Pedregosa, F., et al.: Scikit-learn: machine learning in python. J. Mach. Learn. Res. **12**, 2825–2830 (2011) https://WOS:000298103200003

8. van Timmeren, J.E., Cester, D., Tanadini-Lang, S., Alkadhi, H., Baessler, B.: Radiomics in medical imaging-how-to guide and critical reflection. Insights Imaging **11**(1), 91 (2020)

9. Woznicki, P., Laqua, F., Bley, T., Baeßler, B.: Autoradiomics: a framework for reproducible radiomics research. Front. Radiol. **2** (2022). https://doi.org/10.3389/fradi.2022.919133

10. Zwanenburg, A., Leger, S., Agolli, L., Pilz, K., Troost, E.G.C., Richter, C., Lock, S.: Assessing robustness of radiomic features by image perturbation. Sci Rep **9**(1), 614 (2019)
11. Zwanenburg, A., et al.: The image biomarker standardization initiative: standardized quantitative radiomics for high-throughput image-based phenotyping. Radiology **295**(2), 328–338 (2020). https://doi.org/10.1148/radiol.2020191145, www.ncbi.nlm.nih.gov/pubmed/32154773

Proceedings of the Fourth International Workshop on Multiscale Multimodal Medical Imaging (MMMI 2023)

M^2Fusion: Bayesian-Based Multimodal Multi-level Fusion on Colorectal Cancer Microsatellite Instability Prediction

Quan Liu[1,2], Jiawen Yao[1,3], Lisha Yao[4,5], Xin Chen[4], Jingren Zhou[1], Le Lu[1], Ling Zhang[1], Zaiyi Liu[4(✉)], and Yuankai Huo[2]

[1] DAMO Academy, Alibaba Group, Hangzhou, China
[2] Vanderbilt University, Nashville, TN, USA
[3] Hupan Lab, Hangzhou 310023, China
[4] Guangdong Provincial People's Hospital, Guangzhou, China
zyliu@163.com
[5] South China University of Technology, Guangzhou, China

Abstract. Colorectal cancer (CRC) micro-satellite instability (MSI) prediction on histopathology images is a challenging weakly supervised learning task that involves multi-instance learning on gigapixel images. To date, radiology images have proven to have CRC MSI information and efficient patient imaging techniques. Different data modalities integration offers the opportunity to increase the accuracy and robustness of MSI prediction. Despite the progress in representation learning from the whole slide images (WSI) and exploring the potential of making use of radiology data, CRC MSI prediction remains a challenge to fuse the information from multiple data modalities (e.g., pathology WSI and radiology CT image). In this paper, we propose M^2Fusion: a Bayesian-based multimodal multi-level fusion pipeline for CRC MSI. The proposed fusion model M^2Fusion is capable of discovering more novel patterns within and across modalities that are beneficial for predicting MSI than using a single modality alone, as well as other fusion methods. The contribution of the paper is three-fold: (1) M^2Fusion is the first pipeline of multi-level fusion on pathology WSI and 3D radiology CT image for MSI prediction; (2) CT images are the first time integrated into multimodal fusion for CRC MSI prediction; (3) feature-level fusion strategy is evaluated on both Transformer-based and CNN-based method. Our approach is validated on cross-validation of 352 cases and outperforms either feature-level (0.8177 vs. 0.7908) or decision-level fusion strategy (0.8177 vs. 0.7289) on AUC score.

Keywords: Colorectal cancer · Bayesian · Transformer · Pathology

1 Introduction

Microsatellite instability (MSI) in colorectal cancer (CRC) determines whether patients with cancer respond exceptionally well to immunotherapy [18]. Because universal MSI

Q. Liu—Work was done during an internship at Alibaba DAMO Academy.

ⓒ The Author(s), under exclusive license to Springer Nature Switzerland AG 2023
J. Woo et al. (Eds.): MICCAI 2023 Workshops, LNCS 14394, pp. 125–134, 2023.
https://doi.org/10.1007/978-3-031-47425-5_12

testing requires additional complex genetic or immunohistochemical tests, it is not possible for every patient to be tested for MSI in clinical practice. Therefore, a critical need exists for broadly accessible, cost-efficient tools to aid patient selection for testing.

Deep learning-based methods have been successfully applied for automated MSI prediction directly from hematoxylin and eosin (H&E)-stained whole-slide images (WSIs) [12,25]. Kather et al. [12] developed ResNet-based model to predict patients with MSI and MSS tumors. Another work [25] further proposed MSINet and proved the deep learning model exceeded the performance of experienced gastrointestinal pathologists at predicting MSI on WSIs. Despite the vital role of such diagnostic biomarkers [19], patients with similar histology profiles can exhibit diverse outcomes and treatment responses. Novel and more specific biomarkers are needed from a whole spectrum of modalities, ranging from radiology [7,15,24], histology [11,20,21], and genomics [1,13].

Given the large complexity of medical data, there are new trends to integrate complementary information from diverse data sources for multimodal data fusion [3,4,8]. Many models have shown the use of radiology data to consider macroscopic factors could achieve more accurate and objective diagnostic and prognostic biomarkers for various cancer types [5,10,22,26]. However, when integrating radiology images and WSIs for predicting MSI, the large data heterogeneity gap between the two modalities exists and makes the integration very difficult. Specifically, a WSI consists of tens of thousands of patches [2,14,23] while radiology data usually form with 3D shape [9]. How to design an effective fusion strategy and learn important interactions between radiology and pathology images is important but still remains unknown for MSI prediction in CRC.

In this paper, we introduce a new and effective multi-modal fusion pipeline for MSI prediction by combining decision-level fusion and feature-level fusion following Bayesian rules. We also investigated different fusion strategies and found the proposed fusion scheme achieved better results than those methods. The contributions of this paper are: 1) This study generalizes an MSI prediction pipeline in CRC utilizing radiology-guided knowledge. 2) To the best of our knowledge, we are the first to exploit a multi-level fusion strategy for using multi-modal data for MSI prediction. 3) Extensive experimental results suggest the effectiveness of our Bayesian-based multimodal multi-level fusion. It can reduce the gap between pathology and radiology predictions and achieve more robust and accurate fusions than other feature-level or decision-level methods.

2   Method

Problem Statement. In our study, each CRC patient has a 3D CT image, a pathology whole slide image (WSI), and its corresponding label (MSI status). We aim at CRC MSI prediction using both pathology and radiology data. Figure 1 shows the proposed Bayesian-based fusion model. Our fusion model combines three predictions together and can be seen as feature-level and decision-level fusion in a unified framework. It consists of two branches that process each modality (pathology or radiology data) and it introduces a radiology feature-guided pathology fusion model. In the following parts, we will discuss why radiology-guided fusion methods could benefit our final prediction.

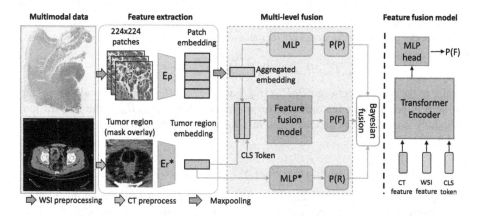

Fig. 1. Our proposed M^2Fusion model. Multimodal data, WSI, and CT images are preprocessed to pathology image patches and CT tumor ROI, respectively. Embeddings are extracted by encoder E_p and E_r. $*$ means the model is well-trained and frozen in pipeline training. $\mathcal{P}_P$ is the pathology uni-model performance $\mathcal{P}(P_{ath})$. P_R is the radiology uni-model performance $\mathcal{P}(R_{ad})$. $\mathcal{P}_F$ is the feature level fusion model probability distribution under pathology and radiology guidance $\mathcal{P}(F_{ea}|P_{ath}R_{ad})$. The final fusion model by P_P, P_R and P_F is $\mathcal{P}(F_{ea}P_{ath}R_{ad})$ in Eq. 4

2.1 Bayesian-Based Multi-modality Fusion Model

Assuming the learnable context from each modality is different, we hypothesize that the fusion between modalities knowledge can enhance the confidence level of the CRC MSI prediction, compared with single modality training. Due to the inherent scale difference between the two modalities (2D gigapixel WSI and 3D CT images), we propose a multimodal fusion strategy, which combines both the decision-level prior and feature-level prior to enhance the interaction between the learnable knowledge from different fields of view.

We first define the predictions from pathology data and from radiology data as events P_{ath} and R_{ad}, respectively. Here, we hypothesize the probabilistic relationship between prediction with Bayes' theorem as follows:

$$\mathcal{P}(P_{ath}R_{ad}) = \mathcal{P}(R_{ad})\mathcal{P}(P_{ath}|R_{ad}) \tag{1}$$

Here $\mathcal{P}(R_{ad})$ is the uni-model performance on radiology data. $\mathcal{P}(P_{ath}|R_{ad})$ denotes the probabilistic prediction on the model well-trained on pathology data with radiology prior. According to Eq. 1, if under the guidance of pre-trained radiology model $\mathcal{P}(R_{ad})$, pathology model $\mathcal{P}(P_{ath}|R_{ad})$ performs better than uni-model on pathology ($\mathcal{P}(P_{ath})$), then modality fusion model should perform better than uni-model ($\mathcal{P}(P_{ath})$ and $\mathcal{P}(R_{ad})$).

$$\mathcal{P}(P_{ath}R_{ad}) \propto \mathcal{P}(P_{ath}|R_{ad}) \tag{2}$$

The Bayes' theorem can be extended to three events: feature level multi-modal fusion model predicts MSI status correct as event F_{ea}. The extended Bayes' theorem is Eq. 3.

$$P(F_{ea}P_{ath}R_{ad}) = P(F_{ea}|P_{ath}R_{ad})P(P_{ath}R_{ad}) \qquad (3)$$

Similar to the relation between $P(P_{ath}|R_{ad})$ and $P(P_{ath}R_{ad})$, Eq. 4. If radiology data can help to get a better feature-level fusion model $P(F_{ea}|P_{ath}R_{ad})$, the final fusion on both the decision-level and feature-level should outperform the decision-level fusion model.

$$P(F_{ea}|P_{ath}R_{ad}) \propto P(F_{ea}|P_{ath}R_{ad}) \qquad (4)$$

Bayes' theorem guarantees that if we want to seek a better final fusion model than decision-level fusion, we have to implement a good feature-level fusion model. Our final model could benefit from both feature-level and decision-level fusion.

2.2   MSI Prediction on Single Modality

Pathology model. Our pathology model is composed of two parts: First, we used the CLAM model [14] to crop the pathology patches from gigapixel WSI. Second, following the previous work [25], the ResNet-18 is used as an encoder to abstract features from pathology patches. We crop the non-overlapping image tiles in size of 224×224 from the WSI foreground. The image patches from all WSI are constructed as a whole pathology patch dataset. The pathology patches label is inherited from the WSI label which it cropped from. The model will predict a patch-level probability of whether the patches belong to MSI or MSS. In the testing phase, the image patches will get the predicted label from the well-trained encoder. The majority vote result of patches from WSI is the patient MSI prediction.

Radiology Model. Based on the 3D radiology CT scans, the tumor region mask of CT volume has been annotated. Two essential slices are cropped from three directions of CT image. One slice is CT tumor region by overlaying the mask on the CT slice. The other slice is the whole CT slice in the direction. The six essential slices (two slices from each direction) are stacked as a six-channel input to build a 2.5D model [17]. The encoder used for MSI prediction is ImageNet pre-trained ResNet-18 (modified input channel to six channels). The original 3-channel pre-trained weights are copied to 4th to 6th channel as initialization.

2.3   Model Prediction Fusion on Multiple Levels

Decision Level Multimodal Fusion. Fig. 2-A shows the decision level fusion. Both models are trained and make the prediction separately. The mean of predicted probability from pathology and radiology is taken as the MSI prediction score for the patient. Based on the well-trained uni-model on pathology images and radiology data, the decision-level multimodal fusion employs the patient-level MSI prediction for the final decision. From the well-trained pathology uni-model, the pathology image W^i

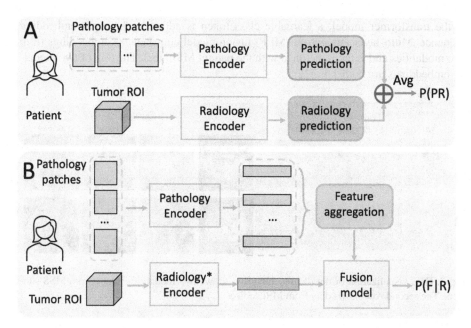

Fig. 2. Baseline experiments on multimodal fusion. A. Decision level multimodal fusion, $\mathcal{P}(P_{ath}R_{ad})$ in Eq. 1. B. Radiology-guided feature-level fusion, probability distribution follows $\mathcal{P}(F_{ea}|R_{ad})$. '*' means the model is well-trained and frozen in pipeline training.

from patient i has predicted MSI probability P_p^i. Similar to pathology prediction, radiology CT scans C^i from patient i can get MSi probability prediction P_r^i. The decision level fused prediction follows $P^i = (P_r^i + P_p^i)/2$.

Feature Level Multi-modal Fusion. Fig. 2-B shows the model fusion on the feature level. The feature embedding abstracted from pathology patches is aggregated as a single feature representing the bag of cropped pathology patches. Each pathology patch is generated as an embedding e^i from patch x^i. The generated embedding $e^i \in \mathbb{R}^{1 \times 512}$ is not representative of the WSI. We first aggregate e^i when $i \in [1, N]$ to a single feature for further feature-level fusion. Referring to the Multi-instance Learning (MIL) methods [16], we use maxing pooling on each channel of embeddings to aggregate the single patches embedding to patient pathology embedding e. The aggregation process follows Eq. 5 where $d \in [0, 511]$ and $e \in \mathbb{R}^{1 \times 512}$.

$$e_d = max_{i=0,...,N} e_d^i \qquad (5)$$

Radiology feature embedding is abstracted from segmented tumor ROI. The feature embeddings from both modalities are fused by feeding into the fusion model. Two major feature-level fusion strategies are investigated in our study, the Transformer-based or MLP-based fusion model. Transformer model [6] takes the aggregated WSI feature embedding and radiology ROI embedding as input. Following the standard approach in the transformer model, a learnable class token is added to the input embedding sequence. Multi-layer Perceptron (MLP) fusion model concatenates embeddings from two modalities and is then finetuned with the patient MSI label. The dim of two modality embeddings are both 1×512.

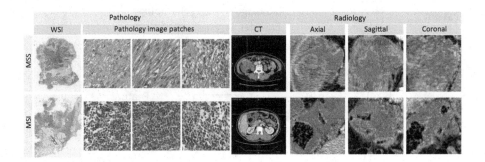

Fig. 3. Data visualization of the dataset. First row shows two modalities image from MSS subjects. The second row shows data from MSI subject.

3   Experiments

3.1   Dataset

We collect an in-house dataset that has the paired pathology WSIs and CT images from 352 patients shown in Fig. 3. The dataset includes 46 MSI patients and 306 MSS patients. The venous phase is used for tumor annotations by a board-certified radiologist with 14 years of specialized experiences. The median imaging spacing is $0.76 \times 0.76 \times 5$ mm^3. The pathology WSI is at a gigapixel level maintained in a pyramid structure. Each level each layer contains a reduced-resolution version of the image from $5\times$, $10\times$, and $40\times$ magnification. The highest level of the pyramid is the full-resolution image which is $40\times$ in 0.25 μm per pixel. The image patches are 448×448 cropped from $40\times$ level and resize to 224×224.

To thoroughly evaluate the dataset performance, we use 5-fold cross-validation in all model evaluations. Since the MSI/MSS ratio is unbalanced, the MSI patients and MSS patients are evenly split into five folds to guarantee a fair MSI/MSS ratio in each fold. For each experiment, three folds of data are used for training, one fold for validation, and the rest one fold for testing. By picking up different folds as testing data, five-set experiments are conducted. The average AUC score is used as the evaluation criterion.

3.2   Experimental Design

In the experiments, we aim at evaluating the proposed Bayesian-based multimodal multi-level fusion model. The experiment parts verify two research questions: (1) whether multimodal fusion provides better performance over the uni-model (rely on single data modality), (2) if our proposed Bayesian-based model $\mathcal{P}(F_{ea}P_{ath}R_{ad})$ achieves the optimal fusion strategy over other fusion models. The ablation study is explored feature aggregation and feature-level fusion strategy.

Pathology Uni-Modal Prediction. The uni-model on pathology data is separated into two steps. First, the WSIs are cropped by the CLAM model into 224×224 patches. The patches use the WSI labels in model training. ImageNet-pretrained ResNet-18 is trained for 100 epochs and the batch size is set to 128. In the testing stage, the average probability of patches from the same WSI is used as patient WSI probability prediction. The final model performance is the average score of 5 testing fold.

Radiology Uni-Modal Prediction. For the Radiology uni-model, we construct the training data by selecting six essential slides based on CT image and annotated tumor region. Only one ROI block is cropped from each CT and constructs the six-channel training data (batch size = 2). ImageNet pre-trained ResNet-18 is employed as the encoder.

Decision Level Fusion Prediction. Different from uni-model training from scratch, decision-level fusion is based on a well-trained uni-model. Based on the 5-fold well-trained model, we feed the test fold data to the corresponding trained model and get the MSI prediction by pathology data. The same process goes for radiology data. The decision-level fused prediction is computed by average MSI probability from two modalities.

Feature-Level Fusion Prediction

Instead of fusing the probability prediction from two modalities, the regular feature level fusion model fuses the embeddings generated from the two modalities' encoders. Both modality encoders are trained from scratch. For the radiology-guided feature level fusion, two modalities of data and a well-trained radiology uni-model are needed. The pathology data is fed into an end-to-end training path. The output of the pathology path is an aggregated feature for pathology WSI. The radiology path is an abstracted feature by pre-trained radiology uni-model from its corresponding training model. For a patient sample, two 1×512 features from pathology and radiology data are fed into fusion model. For the Transformer-based model, we choose ViT-S as our backbone. Our ViT-S model depth is 8, the head number is 12. Multi-layer perception (MLP) hidden feature dimension is 1024. The input matrix is in 3×512. CNN-based feature level fusion concatenates the feature from two modalities into one feature with a length of 1024. An MLP is constructed to map the concatenated feature to the final fusion prediction, which has two fully connected layers when the hidden dimension is 256.

Bayesian-Guided Multi-level Fusion Prediction

For the Bayesian-guided fusion model, we used the same input data as previous fusion experiments: a bag of pathology image patches and radiology CT tumor Region of Interest (ROI). The patient MSI prediction from radiology can be generated by the pre-trained model. The feature abstracted from radiology ROI can be generated from the second last layer's output. The feature and patient-level prediction from pathology follow the same procedure as radiology except the pathology encoder is trainable. The fusion model we used is ViT-S for the Transformer-based model and a two-layer MLP for MLP based fusion model. The average score of the pathology, radiology, and feature fusion MSI probability prediction is used as the final prediction.

4   Result

We conduct experiments on 5-fold cross-validation and model performances are shown in Table 1. Our proposed multi-level multi-modality fusion pipeline is compared with the single-modality model and fusion methods. From the average AUC score across 5-fold experiments, the performance of unimodal relies on pathology image and radiology image are 0.6847 and 0.7348, respectively. The decision-level fusion has an average AUC score of 0.7908 which outperforms unimodal prediction score. The feature-level fusion model shows better performance by using Vision Transformer than MLP. Without radiology guidance, feature-level fusion model (avg AUC: 0.7289) performs better than pathology unimodal but worse than radiology unimodal. The radiology data can guide feature-level fusion model training by getting AUC score of 0.7696 better than 0.7289. Radiology-guided feature-level fusion model shows better performance than feature-level fusion without a guide. By combining the decision-level and feature-level information from two image modalities, our proposed multi-level multi-modality pipeline get the best AUC 0.8177 over the rest of MSI CRC strategies.

Table 1. AUC on MSI prediction

	Fold 1	Fold 2	Fold 3	Fold 4	Fold 5	Average
Patho unimodal[25]	0.6502	0.7282	0.8530	0.8819	0.6500	0.6847
2.5D Radio unimodal	0.5615	0.8333	0.7520	0.7163	0.8158	0.7348
Decision-level fusion	0.6956	0.8313	0.8536	0.8948	0.6785	0.7908
Feature-level fusion	0.619	0.6528	0.7698	0.7083	0.6730	0.7289
Radio-guided feature fusion	0.7218	0.7558	0.7698	0.7678	0.8127	0.7696
M^2**Fusion**	0.8278	0.8055	0.7341	0.8989	0.8222	**0.8177**

An ablation study on exploring the pathology feature aggregation strategy and multimodal feature level fusion backbone is shown in Table 2. The combination of average pooling on pathology feature aggregation and using a Transformer as feature-level fusion backbone has the best AUC performance.

Table 2. Ablation study for pathology feature aggregation and feature-level fusion strategy

Feature aggregation	Feature fusion	Fold 1	Fold 2	Fold 3	Fold 4	Fold 5	Average
Conv	Transformer	0.5423	0.6012	0.7976	0.7540	0.7746	0.6939
Avg	CNN	0.5786	0.7004	0.7202	0.7044	0.7333	0.6874
Conv	CNN	0.6593	0.7321	0.7599	0.6706	0.7047	0.7053
Avg	Transformer	0.7218	0.7758	0.7698	0.7678	0.8127	**0.7696**

5 Conclusion

We proposed a multi-level multi-modality fusion pipeline for colorectal cancer MSI status prediction based on pathology WSIs and CT images. We introduce Bayes' theorem to fuse the information from two image modalities on both the feature level and decision level. The experiment result shows (1) radiology and pathology image fusion (decision level fusion) helps CRC MSI prediction by combining the two modalities' information from the same patient, and (2) radiology-guided feature-level training outperforms the model that directly fuses two modalities' features. Our Bayesian-based fusion on both decision-level and feature-level achieves the best performance.

References

1. Braman, N., Gordon, J.W.H., Goossens, E.T., Willis, C., Stumpe, M.C., Venkataraman, J.: Deep orthogonal fusion: multimodal prognostic biomarker discovery integrating radiology, pathology, genomic, and clinical data. In: de Bruijne, M., et al. (eds.) MICCAI 2021. LNCS, vol. 12905, pp. 667–677. Springer, Cham (2021). https://doi.org/10.1007/978-3-030-87240-3_64
2. Chen, R.J., et al.: Multimodal co-attention transformer for survival prediction in gigapixel whole slide images. In: Proceedings of the IEEE/CVF International Conference on Computer Vision, pp. 4015–4025 (2021)
3. Chen, R.J., et al.: Pan-cancer integrative histology-genomic analysis via multimodal deep learning. Cancer Cell **40**(8), 865–878 (2022)
4. Cui, C. et al.: Survival prediction of brain cancer with incomplete radiology, pathology, genomic, and demographic data. In: Wang, L., Dou, Q., Fletcher, P.T., Speidel, S., Li, S. (eds.) Medical Image Computing and Computer Assisted Intervention - MICCAI 2022. MICCAI 2022. LNCS, vol. 13435, pp. 626–635 Springer, Cham (2022). https://doi.org/10.1007/978-3-031-16443-9_60
5. Dong, D., et al.: Deep learning radiomic nomogram can predict the number of lymph node metastasis in locally advanced gastric cancer: an international multicenter study. Ann. Oncol. **31**(7), 912–920 (2020)
6. Dosovitskiy, A., et al.: An image is worth 16x16 words: transformers for image recognition at scale. arXiv preprint arXiv:2010.11929 (2020)
7. Echle, A., Rindtorff, N.T., Brinker, T.J., Luedde, T., Pearson, A.T., Kather, J.N.: Deep learning in cancer pathology: a new generation of clinical biomarkers. Br. J. Cancer **124**(4), 686–696 (2021)
8. Feng, L., et al.: Development and validation of a radiopathomics model to predict pathological complete response to neoadjuvant chemoradiotherapy in locally advanced rectal cancer: a multicentre observational study. Lancet Digit. Health **4**(1), e8–e17 (2022)
9. Golia Pernicka, J.S., et al.: Radiomics-based prediction of microsatellite instability in colorectal cancer at initial computed tomography evaluation. Abdom. Radiol. **44**(11), 3755–3763 (2019). https://doi.org/10.1007/s00261-019-02117-w
10. He, K., Liu, X., Li, M., Li, X., Yang, H., Zhang, H.: Noninvasive KRAS mutation estimation in colorectal cancer using a deep learning method based on CT imaging. BMC Med. Imaging **20**, 1–9 (2020)
11. Kather, J.N., Calderaro, J.: Development of AI-based pathology biomarkers in gastrointestinal and liver cancer. Nat. Rev. Gastroenterol. Hepatol. **17**(10), 591–592 (2020)
12. Kather, J.N., et al.: Deep learning can predict microsatellite instability directly from histology in gastrointestinal cancer. Nat. Med. **25**(7), 1054–1056 (2019)

13. Lipkova, J., et al.: Artificial intelligence for multimodal data integration in oncology. Cancer Cell **40**(10), 1095–1110 (2022)
14. Lu, M.Y., Williamson, D.F., Chen, T.Y., Chen, R.J., Barbieri, M., Mahmood, F.: Data-efficient and weakly supervised computational pathology on whole-slide images. Nat. Biomed. Eng. **5**(6), 555–570 (2021)
15. Pei, Q., et al.: Pre-treatment CT-based radiomics nomogram for predicting microsatellite instability status in colorectal cancer. Eur. Radiol. **32**, 714–724 (2022)
16. Raju, A., Yao, J., Haq, M.M.H., Jonnagaddala, J., Huang, J.: Graph attention multi-instance learning for accurate colorectal cancer staging. In: Martel, A.L., et al. (eds.) MICCAI 2020. LNCS, vol. 12265, pp. 529–539. Springer, Cham (2020). https://doi.org/10.1007/978-3-030-59722-1_51
17. Roth, H.R., et al.: A New 2.5D representation for lymph node detection using random sets of deep convolutional neural network observations. In: Golland, P., Hata, N., Barillot, C., Hornegger, J., Howe, R. (eds.) MICCAI 2014. LNCS, vol. 8673, pp. 520–527. Springer, Cham (2014). https://doi.org/10.1007/978-3-319-10404-1_65
18. Sahin, I.H., et al.: Immune checkpoint inhibitors for the treatment of MSI-h/MMR-d colorectal cancer and a perspective on resistance mechanisms. Br. J. Cancer **121**(10), 809–818 (2019)
19. Sidaway, P.: MSI-h: a truly agnostic biomarker? Nat. Rev. Clin. Oncol. **17**(2), 68–68 (2020)
20. Ushizima, D., et al.: Deep learning for alzheimer's disease: mapping large-scale histological tau protein for neuroimaging biomarker validation. Neuroimage **248**, 118790 (2022)
21. Wang, C.W., et al.: A weakly supervised deep learning method for guiding ovarian cancer treatment and identifying an effective biomarker. Cancers **14**(7), 1651 (2022)
22. Wang, S., et al.: Predicting EGFR mutation status in lung adenocarcinoma on computed tomography image using deep learning. Eur. Respir. J. **53**(3) (2019)
23. Wei, J.W., Tafe, L.J., Linnik, Y.A., Vaickus, L.J., Tomita, N., Hassanpour, S.: Pathologist-level classification of histologic patterns on resected lung adenocarcinoma slides with deep neural networks. Sci. Rep. **9**(1), 3358 (2019)
24. Wu, J., et al.: The value of single-source dual-energy CT imaging for discriminating microsatellite instability from microsatellite stability human colorectal cancer. Eur. Radiol. **29**, 3782–3790 (2019)
25. Yamashita, R., et al.: Deep learning model for the prediction of microsatellite instability in colorectal cancer: a diagnostic study. Lancet Oncol. **22**(1), 132–141 (2021)
26. Yao, J., et al.: Deep learning for fully automated prediction of overall survival in patients undergoing resection for pancreatic cancer: a retrospective multicenter study. Ann. Surg. **278**(1), e68–e79 (2023)

Query Re-Training for Modality-Gnostic Incomplete Multi-modal Brain Tumor Segmentation

Delin Chen[1,2] , Yansheng Qiu[1,2] , and Zheng Wang[1,2(✉)]

[1] National Engineering Research Center for Multimedia Software, Institute of Artificial Intelligence, School of Computer Science, Wuhan University, Wuhan, China
{chendelin,qiuyansheng,wangzwhu}@whu.edu.cn
[2] Hubei Key Laboratory of Multimedia and Network Communication Engineering, Wuhan, China

Abstract. Although Magnetic Resonance Imaging (MRI) is crucial for segmenting brain tumors, it frequently lacks specific modalities in clinical practice, which limits prediction performance. In current methods, training involves multiple stages, and encoders are different for each modality, which means hybrid modules must be manually designed to incorporate multiple modalities' features, lacking interaction across modalities. To ameliorate this problem, we propose a transformer-based end-to-end model with just one auto-encoder to provide interactive computations in any modality missing condition. Considering that it is challenging for a single model to perceive several missing states, we introduce learnable modality combination queries to assist the transformer decoder in adjusting to the incomplete multi-modal segmentation. Furthermore, to address the suboptimization issue of the Transformer under small datasets, we adopt a re-training mechanism to facilitate convergence to a better local minimum. The extensive experiments on the BraTS2018 and BraTS2020 datasets demonstrate that our method outperforms the current state-of-the-art methods for incomplete multi-modal brain tumor segmentation on average.

Keywords: Query · Re-Training · Incomplete Multi-modal · Brain Tumor Segmentation

1 Introduction

Magnetic resonance image (MRI) segmentation plays an integral role in quantitative brain tumor image analysis, which is designed for different tissues of brain structures and brain tumors with multiple imaging modalities, such as Fluid Attenuation Inversion Recovery (FLAIR), contrast enhanced T1-weighted (T1c), T1-weighted (T1) and T2-weighted (T2). It has been demonstrated that simultaneously combining four modalities could improve multi-modal MRI performance for brain tumor segmentation [8,13,17,23,25]. Nevertheless, missing

J. Woo et al. (Eds.): MICCAI 2023 Workshops, LNCS 14394, pp. 135–146, 2023.
https://doi.org/10.1007/978-3-031-47425-5_13

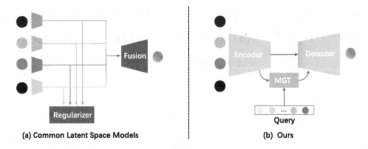

(a) Common Latent Space Models   (b) Ours

Fig. 1. Incomplete Multi-modal Brain Tumor Segmentation Frameworks (colored for residual, ● for missing) - (a) Common Latent Space Models, *i.e.*, RFNet [5] proposes a framework with separate encoders for each modality, a decoder and hierarchical fusion blocks. The four encoders are arranged in a top-to-bottom sequence corresponding to the four different modalities: Flair, T1c, T1, and T2. (b) Our proposed method has a single encoder, a decoder and Modality-Gnostic Transformer (MGT) Modules that learn modality combination queries to solve all conditions effectively.

modalities are prevalent in clinical practice due to data corruption, different scanning protocols, and patient conditions [11,14,15,21] , severely reducing previous segmentation algorithms' performance. Therefore, a robust multi-modal approach is required for flexible, practical clinical applications to address the issue of missing one or more modalities.

Current research on incomplete medical image segmentation [3,5,10,22] primarily considers improving the network's ability to extract features from different modalities by separate encoders and producing discriminative fusion features for segmentation (Fig. 1(a)). Nevertheless, only individual features are learned, and the information across modalities cannot interact, increasing the difficulty of feature fusion [24]. To tackle this problem, we introduce a unified transformer-based encoder that allows direct interaction between different modalities. This approach entails concatenating different modalities and feeding them into the encoder, whereby the design of self-attention allows for the natural interaction of the input. However, unified architectures make it difficult to perceive multiple modalities scenarios and degrade the performance. Fortunately, by exploiting the properties of the attention mechanism, Valanarasu *et al.* [18] propose weather-type learnable embeddings to tackle all adverse weather removal problems in a single encoder-decoder transformer network. Deriving from the random initialization of the learnable embeddings in [18], we codify the modally missing combinations and initialize the learnable embeddings with them, which can provide more informative guidance.

Furthermore, Vision Transformers need a lot of data for training, usually more than what is necessary to standard CNNs [7]. The transformer-based models started with randomly initialized parameters, may easily over-fit a small number of training pairs and make the model be trapped into a poor local minimum. Inspired by [16], adopt a re-training mechanism to facilitate convergence to a better local minimum.

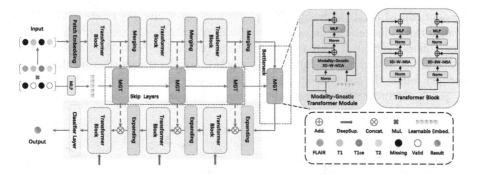

Fig. 2. Illustration of our proposed QuMo architecture. QuMo comprises three primary modules: A transformer encoder to extract hierarchical features, Modality-Gnostic transformer modules and a transformer decoder. A 3D volume concatenated by four different modality volumes multiplied by a modal code is applied to simulate different modalities missing states.

To this end, we propose **QuMo: Qu**ery re-training for **Mo**dality-gnostic incomplete multi-modal brain tumor segmentation to tackle all modality-missing states simultaneously (Fig. 1(b)). Specifically, our contributions are threefold:

- We propose **QuMo: Qu**ery re-training for **Mo**dality-gnostic incomplete multi-modal brain tumor segmentation, an effective solution with only one encoder and one decoder which can provide the direct interaction of different modalities within the network.
- We propose a Modality-Gnostic transformer module with learnable modality combination embeddings as queries to effectively handle all the modality-missing states, making the decoder be aware of different modality combinations. Furthermore, we adopt a query re-training mechanism to facilitate the model convergence to a better local minimum under small datasets.
- Taking advantage of the proposed method, **QuMo** could achieve state-of-the-art performance on the used BraTs2018 and BraTs2020 benchmarks.

2 Method

2.1 Architecture Overview

An overview of QuMo is illustrated in Fig. 2, QuMo contains a transformer-based unified architecture to accept all valid modalities as input simultaneously, which can provide the direct interaction of different modes within the encoder. Following previous methods [1,12,13], we exploit the transformer [19] architecture for explicitly long-range contextual modeling within the input MRI modalities effectively In Vision Transformer (ViT) [7], tokens are required to contain spatial information due to the way they are constructed and the significance of performing self-attention by windowing in ViT has been demonstrated in several recent studies, most notably in Swin Transformer [12]. In particular, the encoder consists of a patch embedding layer and patch merging layers followed by Transformer blocks. The decoder is designed to generate the segmentation mask based on four output feature maps of different resolutions from Modality-Gnostic Transformer modules (MGTs). In implementations, the transformer blocks in the decoder follow the same design as the encoder, and we deviate from the encoder by patch expanding layers and convolutional classifier layers.

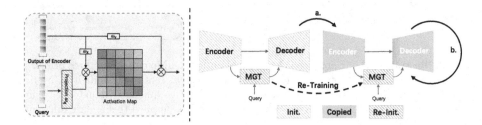

Fig. 3. *Left*: **Configuration of the Modality-Gnostic 3D-W-MCA in the MGTs.** The queries here are learnable embeddings representing the modality combination, while the keys and values are features taken from the output of the transformer encoder. *Right*: **The process of our re-training mechanism.** The parameters of the module with slash color backgrounds are initialized as the original rules, while those with solid background are copied from the former training phase. Noteworthy, only the projection layers in MGTs are re-Initialized.

2.2 Modality-Gnostic Transformer Module

An autoregressive decoder is used in the original transformer decoder [19] to predict the output sequence one element at a time. However, the model's inability to perceive the modal input state makes dynamic handling of different missing modalities difficult. Detection transformer (DETR) [2] uses object queries to decode the box coordinates and class labels to produce the final predictions. Moreover, TransWeather [18] uses weather type queries to decode different restore tasks, predict a task feature vector and use it to restore the clean image. Inspired by them, we define modality combination embeddings as queries to guide the decoder to perceive different modality-missing situations. The queries are learnable embeddings that attend to the feature outputs from the encoder and are learned along with other model parameters during the training phase, illustrated in Fig. 2. Unlike the self-attention transformer block where $\mathbf{Q}$, $\mathbf{K}$, and $\mathbf{V}$ are taken from the same input, in Modality-Gnostic 3D window multi-head cross-attention (W-MCA), $\mathbf{Q}$ is a modality combination learnable embedding. At the same time, $\mathbf{K}$ and $\mathbf{V}$ are tokens from the features taken from the corresponding stage of the transformer encoder after linear mapping, illustrated in Fig. 3. The computation in the MGT can be summarized as:

$$\hat{\mathbf{I}}^l = \text{3D-W-MCA}\left(\text{LN}\left(\mathbf{I}^{l-1}\right), \mathbf{Q}\right) + \mathbf{I}^{l-1}, \mathbf{I}^l = \text{MLP}(\text{LN}(\hat{\mathbf{I}}^l)) + \hat{\mathbf{I}}^l \qquad (1)$$

where $\mathbf{Q}$ denotes the learnable queries, LN refers to Layer Normalization, $\hat{\mathbf{I}}^l$ and $\mathbf{I}^l$ denote the output features of the MCA module and the MLP module for layer l, respectively. The 3D-W-MCA is mathematically described as follows:

$$\mathbf{K}, \mathbf{V} = \omega_{k,v}(\text{LN}\left(\mathbf{I}^{l-1}\right)), \hat{\mathbf{Q}} = \omega_q(\mathbf{Q}), \hat{\mathbf{I}}^l = \text{Softmax}(\frac{\hat{\mathbf{Q}}\mathbf{K}^\top}{\sqrt{d}})\mathbf{V} + \mathbf{I}^{l-1} \quad (2)$$

where $\omega_{k,v}, \omega_q$ are projection functions to produce $\mathbf{K}$, $\mathbf{V}$ and $\hat{\mathbf{Q}}$ respectively, d represents the number of the tokens' channels.

In this paper, the proposed method contains four Modality-Gnostic transformer modules, among which three are at skip-connection layers, and one acts as the bottleneck layer. The output decoded features are fused with the features extracted across the MGTs through skip connections and the bottleneck layer at each stage. At the beginning of the training phase, the learnable embeddings are initialized with modality-code $C = \{C_1, \ldots, C_N\}$, where $C_i \in \{0,1\}$ represents whether the C_i modality is missing or not and N represents the number of modalities. Specifically, we map C through fully connected layers so that the extended query embeddings can perform matrix multiplication operations with $\mathbf{K}$.

2.3   Query Re-Training Strategy

Motivated by the observation that a segmentation model may converge to a better local minimum by equipping the Transformer encoder-decoder with better-initialized parameters [16], we design the query retraining mechanism. After the initial training, we continuously update the encoder and decoder parameters during training, while periodically resetting the MGTs' parameters, specifically the query projection, to encourage improved optimization.

As depicted in Fig. 3, we first randomly initialize the entire model, denoted as process **a**, and terminate training when validation performance stabilizes. To further enhance model performance, we then proceed to continuously train the encoder and decoder after the first initial training while resetting the MGT modules to avoid convergence to sub-optimal local minima, denoted as process **b**. This process is repeated periodically until the best possible performance is achieved.

2.4   Loss Function

The segmentation results are learned under the supervision of the ground truth. Specifically, we supervise the transformer blocks in the decoder in a stage-wise manner. This deep supervision strategy [20] lets the transformer blocks focus on meaningful semantic regions at different scales. The training loss is based on the combination of a weighted cross-entropy loss $\mathcal{L}_{WCE}$ [3] to address the imbalance of different regions and a Dice loss $\mathcal{L}_{DL}$, expressed as:

$$\mathcal{L} = \sum_{i=1}^{N} (\mathcal{L}_{WCE}(\hat{y}_i, y_i) + \mathcal{L}_{DL}(\hat{y}_i, y_i)), \quad (3)$$

where N denotes the number of training data, $\hat{y}_i$ and y_i denote predicted segmentation results and the ground-truth. $\mathcal{L}_{WCE}$ and L_{DL} are formulated as:

$$\mathcal{L}_{WCE} = \sum_{k \in K} \frac{\|-\omega_k \cdot y_k \cdot \log(\hat{y}_k)\|_1}{H \cdot W \cdot Z}, \mathcal{L}_{DL} = 1 - \sum_{k \in K} \frac{2 \cdot \|\hat{y}_k \cap y_k\|_1}{K_{\text{num}} \cdot (\|\hat{y}_k\|_1 + \|y_k\|_1)}, \quad (4)$$

where $\|\cdot\|_1$ denotes the L1 norm, and H, W, Z denote the height, width and slice number of the 3D volumes, respectively. K denotes the set of brain tumor regions, including BG (background), NCR/NET, ED and ET. ω_k is the weight for the region k and $\omega_k = 1 - \frac{\|y_k\|_1}{\sum_{k' \in K} \|y_{k'}\|_1}$. $\cap$ denotes the overlap between predictions and ground-truth masks, and K_{num} denotes the number of regions in K.

3   Experiments

3.1   Implementation Details

Datasets. We evaluate our method on the Multi-modal Brain Tumor Segmentation Challenge 2018 (BraTS2018) dataset and the BraTs2020 dataset. Each subject in the dataset contains four MRI contrasts (FLAIR, T1c, T1, T2), following the challenge, there are three segmentation classes, including whole tumor ("complete"), core tumor ("core") and enhancing tumor ("enhancing"). The ground truth was obtained by expert manual annotation.

Experimental Setup. For the image pre-processing, the MRI images are skull-stripped, co-registered and re-sampled to $1\,\text{mm}^3$ resolution by the data collector. In this work, following [3], we additionally cut out the black background area outside the brain and normalize each MRI modality to zero mean and unit variance in the brain area. During training, input images are randomly cropped to $128 \times 128 \times 128$ and are then augmented with random rotations, intensity shifts and mirror flipping. We train our network with a batch size of 1 in three re-training cycles. Adam optimizer [9] with a cosine scheduler is leveraged to optimize the network with β_1 and β_2 of 0.9 and 0.999 respectively.

3.2   Performance Comparison

To evaluate the performance, we compare our model with four state-of-the-art methods using a commonly used performance metric *Dice* [4], including U-HVED [6], RobustSeg [3], RFNet [5] and mmformer [22], all experiments were conducted employing the same train and test split lists as U-HVED [6] on BRATS2018 and RFNet [5] on BRATS2020 for a fair comparison.

As shown in Table 1 and Fig. 4, our method achieves superior segmentation performance. For example, compared with the previous state-of-the-art method, *i.e.*, RFNet [5], our QuMo improves the average Dice scores by 1.10%, 1.66% and 3.93% in the whole tumor, the tumor core and the enhancing tumor, respectively.

Table 1. Results of state-of-the-art unified models (U-HVED [6], RobustSeg [3], RFNet [5], mmformer [22]) and our method QuMo, on BraTS 2018 dataset. Dice similarity coefficient (DSC) [%] is employed for evaluation with every combination settings of modalities. • and ○ denote available and missing modalities, respectively. The results with <u>underlined</u> denote the second best and with **bold** shows the best performance.

Modalities				Dice (%)															
				Complete					Core					Enhancing					
F	T1	T1c	T2	[6]	[3]	[5]	[22]	Ours	[6]	[3]	[5]	[22]	Ours	[6]	[3]	[5]	[22]	Ours
○	○	○	●	80.90	82.24	<u>85.10</u>	83.90	**86.06**	54.10	57.49	<u>66.95</u>	66.20	**70.53**	30.80	28.97	**44.56**	38.81	<u>42.15</u>
○	○	●	○	62.40	73.31	73.61	<u>74.77</u>	**77.60**	66.70	76.83	<u>80.29</u>	79.92	**81.09**	65.50	67.07	68.10	<u>72.28</u>	**75.55**
○	●	○	○	52.40	70.11	<u>74.79</u>	74.24	**77.51**	37.20	47.90	<u>65.23</u>	62.26	**65.80**	13.70	17.29	<u>34.02</u>	31.34	**40.65**
●	○	○	○	82.10	85.69	85.79	<u>86.00</u>	**89.25**	50.40	53.57	<u>62.57</u>	60.82	**68.28**	24.80	25.69	<u>35.29</u>	33.47	**44.28**
○	○	●	●	82.70	85.19	<u>85.62</u>	85.48	**86.75**	73.70	80.20	82.35	<u>82.46</u>	**83.63**	70.20	69.71	72.53	<u>73.64</u>	**74.97**
○	●	●	○	66.80	77.18	77.53	<u>78.35</u>	**79.36**	69.70	78.72	81.34	<u>81.82</u>	**82.04**	67.00	69.06	73.72	<u>74.81</u>	**76.00**
●	●	○	○	84.30	88.24	<u>88.99</u>	88.26	**90.10**	55.30	60.68	<u>72.22</u>	68.67	**74.19**	24.20	32.13	<u>43.29</u>	35.96	**49.02**
○	●	○	●	82.20	84.78	<u>85.37</u>	85.35	**86.59**	57.20	62.19	<u>71.07</u>	68.51	**73.18**	30.70	32.01	<u>46.06</u>	40.83	**46.37**
●	○	●	○	87.50	88.28	<u>89.28</u>	88.72	**90.37**	59.70	61.16	<u>71.75</u>	67.90	**74.22**	34.60	33.84	<u>47.07</u>	40.20	**48.56**
○	●	●	●	85.50	88.51	<u>89.39</u>	88.61	**89.32**	72.90	80.62	81.56	<u>81.66</u>	**83.28**	70.30	70.30	73.50	<u>74.09</u>	**77.34**
●	●	●	○	86.20	88.73	**89.87**	88.54	<u>89.24</u>	74.20	81.06	82.27	<u>82.63</u>	**83.64**	71.10	70.78	72.78	<u>74.45</u>	**77.46**
●	●	○	●	88.00	88.81	<u>90.00</u>	89.20	**90.51**	61.50	64.38	<u>74.02</u>	70.24	**74.76**	34.10	36.41	<u>45.75</u>	39.67	**52.56**
●	○	●	●	88.60	89.27	**90.36**	89.39	<u>89.69</u>	75.60	80.72	<u>82.56</u>	82.41	**83.41**	71.20	70.88	<u>74.14</u>	74.08	**77.08**
○	●	●	●	83.30	86.01	<u>86.13</u>	85.78	**86.91**	75.30	80.33	<u>82.87</u>	80.33	**83.33**	71.10	70.10	<u>72.84</u>	71.10	**76.53**
●	●	●	●	88.80	89.45	**90.59**	89.45	<u>89.66</u>	76.40	80.86	<u>82.94</u>	80.86	**83.58**	71.70	71.13	<u>72.90</u>	71.70	**77.05**
Average				80.10	84.39	<u>85.49</u>	85.07	**86.59**	64.00	69.78	<u>76.00</u>	74.75	**77.66**	50.00	51.02	<u>58.44</u>	56.95	**62.37**

Moreover, our method outperforms the state-of-the-art methods on the vast majority of fifteen multi-modal combinations, including 11 out of 15 cases for the whole tumor, all cases for the core tumor, 14 out of 15 cases for the enhancing tumor. The quantitative results show that our QuMo brings more significant growth for enhancing tumor region, which are more challenging to segment, particularly improve the Dice scores by 8.99% when only Flair modality exists. We undertake additional validation to verify the efficacy of our model on the Brats2020 dataset. The results illustrated in Table 2 show our method yields superior performance compared to the State-of-the-Art (SOTA).

We conduct a comparison of computational complexity and model size. The result in Table 6 shows that our method is smaller than other algorithms in FLOPs(G) and smaller than transformer-based algorithms mmFormer [22] in model parameters. Visualization results in Fig. 6 illustrate that our method is able to segment brain tumors well in various missing scenarios. For example, QuMo predicts an accurate segmentation map with only the T2 modal image. As the number of modes increases, the performance of the model becomes progressively better, and the performance in some severely missing cases is close to that in the full mode, e.g. T2 and F+T1. These results demonstrate the superiority of our method for incomplete multimodal learning of brain tumor segmentation.

3.3   Ablation Study

In this section, we investigate the MGT module, deep supervision and the re-training strategy, which are the key components of our method. All ablation

Table 2. Results of previous models and our method on BraTS 2020 dataset.

Methods	Dice (%)		
	Comp.	Core	En.
U-HVED [6]	81.24	67.19	48.55
Robust [3]	84.17	73.45	55.49
RFNet [5]	86.98	78.23	61.47
mmFormer [22]	86.49	76.06	63.19
Ours	**87.65**	**78.37**	**63.21**

Table 3. Ablation study of critical components of QuMo.

MGT		D.S.	Init.	Average Dice (%)
Bottle.	Skip.			
✗	✗	✗	–	71.09
✗	✗	✔	–	73.27
✔	✗	✗	Rand	73.62
✔	✗	✔	Rand	75.01
✔	✔	✔	Rand	75.10
✔	✔	✔	Code	**75.54**

Table 4. The number of queries.

Number	Dice (%)			
	Complete	Core	Enhancing	Average
0	85.93	76.24	57.76	73.27
200	85.73	75.90	59.87	73.83
300	86.26	76.42	59.87	74.18
400	86.45	77.61	61.98	75.34
500	86.59	77.66	**62.37**	**75.54**
600	**86.65**	**77.79**	61.43	75.29

Table 5. Number of re-training cycles.

Cycle	Avg. Dice (%)	
	w/o R.T.	Ours
0	72.73	–
1	73.06	73.82
2	72.42	74.04
3	72.57	74.71
4	73.44	**75.54**
5	72.13	75.24

experiments were conducted on the BraTS2018 dataset. We first set up a baseline network ("Baseline") that does not use any MGT modules or deep supervision in our network. Then we add the MGT modules gradually on the Bottleneck Layer and the Skip Connection. We compare the performance of these networks on the Dice score, averaging over the 15 possible situations of input modalities. As shown in Table 3, we evaluate the influence of MGT in the bottleneck layer (Bottle.), skip-connection layers (Skip.), deep supervision (D.S.) and different initialization strategies (Random Initialization and Modal Code Initialization). Specifically, employing a randomly initialized MGT in the bottleneck layer without deep supervision increases the average Dice scores of three tumor regions by 3.92%, compared with "Baseline", which demonstrates the superiority of the introduced queries. Moreover, our method of applying multi-scale MGTs with deep supervision increases the results over the "Baseline" by 4.45%.

As shown in Fig. 5, we also visualized the attention maps corresponding to different queries of our proposed MGTs. The notation Q_n positioned on the left denotes the query's numerical index. Brighter areas represent greater activation values. It is evident from the figure that the sensitivity of the same query varies

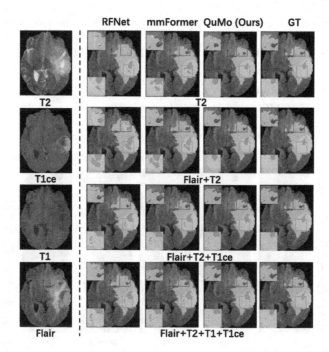

Fig. 4. Qualitative comparison of different models in BraTs2018 dataset.

for different modal combinations, which way would make the decoder aware of the modal combinations.

Moreover, we analyze the impacts of the different numbers of queries. As shown in Table 4, performance increases with the number of queries until the number is around 500, since more queries contain more informative knowledge to perceive different modality-missing states.

Furthermore, we investigate the impact of varying the number of re-training cycles on model performance. Specifically, a comparison was made between a training approach that did not incorporate the re-training strategy but had an equal total epoch count, and a training approach that incorporated the re-training strategy within each cycle, where the model weights for each cycle were initialized using the parameters generated by the preceding re-training cycle. The experimental outcomes are reported in Table 5, which exhibit a noteworthy enhancement in model performance following several re-training cycles. It was observed that a state of equilibrium was attained after four cycles, and therefore, four cycles were selected for the subsequent experiments.

Table 6. Comparison of computational complexity and model size.

Models	FLOPs (G)	Params (MB)
RFNet	830	**8.98**
mmFormer	<u>234</u>	35.34
MFI	2045	30.91
QuMo (Ours)	**233**	<u>24.65</u>

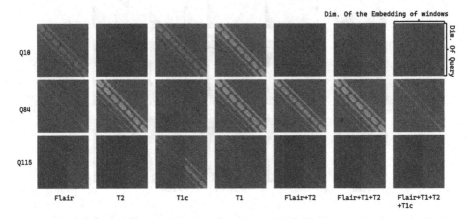

Fig. 5. Visualization of attention maps corresponding to different queries of our proposed MGTs. The notation Q_n positioned on the left denotes the query's numerical index. Brighter areas represent greater activation values. The same query is sensitive to different modal combinations and can be activated by different combinations in multiple degrees, in which way would make the decoder aware of the modal combinations. Furthermore, diagonal activation values, which are higher, indicating that these queries are proficient in acquiring location information, signifying that each part has the maximum response at its corresponding location.

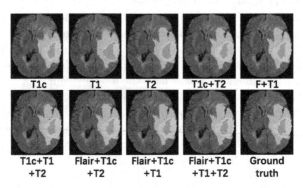

Fig. 6. Visualization of the predicted segmentation results for various modality combinations.

4   Conclusion

In this work, we design a novel incomplete multi-modal brain tumor segmentation method with a unified encoder-decoder architecture, which can provide the direct interaction of different modalities within the network and adopt a re-training mechanism to void convergence to sub-optimal local minima. Specifically, we apply the learnable modality combination embeddings (query) to guide the model to perceive different modality-missing states. Our model outperforms the state-of-the-art approach on the BraTS2018 and BraTS2020 datasets. However, despite the impressive performance of the QuMo, some additional works remain verified. We are particularly interested in QuMo's performance in other multi-modal tasks due to its availability for multi-modal perceptible interactions.

References

1. Cao, H., et al.: Swin-Unet: Unet-like pure transformer for medical image segmentation. In: Karlinsky, L., Michaeli, T., Nishino, K. (eds.) ECCV 2022. LNCS, vol. 13803, pp. 205–218. Springer, Cham (2023). https://doi.org/10.1007/978-3-031-25066-8_9

2. Carion, N., Massa, F., Synnaeve, G., Usunier, N., Kirillov, A., Zagoruyko, S.: End-to-end object detection with transformers. In: Vedaldi, A., Bischof, H., Brox, T., Frahm, J.-M. (eds.) ECCV 2020. LNCS, vol. 12346, pp. 213–229. Springer, End-to-end object detection with transformers (2020). https://doi.org/10.1007/978-3-030-58452-8_13

3. Chen, C., Dou, Q., Jin, Y., Chen, H., Qin, J., Heng, P.-A.: Robust multimodal brain tumor segmentation via feature disentanglement and gated fusion. In: Shen, D., et al. (eds.) MICCAI 2019. LNCS, vol. 11766, pp. 447–456. Springer, Cham (2019). https://doi.org/10.1007/978-3-030-32248-9_50

4. Dice, L.R.: Measures of the amount of ecologic association between species. Ecology **26**(3), 297–302 (1945)

5. Ding, Y., Yu, X., Yang, Y.: RFNet: region-aware fusion network for incomplete multi-modal brain tumor segmentation. In: Proceedings of the IEEE/CVF International Conference on Computer Vision, pp. 3975–3984 (2021)

6. Dorent, R., Joutard, S., Modat, M., Ourselin, S., Vercauteren, T.: Hetero-modal variational encoder-decoder for joint modality completion and segmentation. In: Shen, D., et al. (eds.) MICCAI 2019. LNCS, vol. 11765, pp. 74–82. Springer, Cham (2019). https://doi.org/10.1007/978-3-030-32245-8_9

7. Dosovitskiy, A., et al.: An image is worth 16x16 words: transformers for image recognition at scale (2020). https://doi.org/10.48550/ARXIV.2010.11929. https://arxiv.org/abs/2010.11929

8. Isensee, F., Jaeger, P.F., Kohl, S.A., Petersen, J., Maier-Hein, K.H.: NNU-Net: a self-configuring method for deep learning-based biomedical image segmentation. Nat. Methods **18**(2), 203–211 (2021)

9. Kingma, D.P., Ba, J.: Adam: a method for stochastic optimization. In: Proceedings of the International Conference on Learning Representations (2015)

10. Liu, H., et al.: ModDrop++: a dynamic filter network with intra-subject co-training for multiple sclerosis lesion segmentation with missing modalities (2022). https://doi.org/10.48550/ARXIV.2203.04959. https://arxiv.org/abs/2203.04959

11. Liu, Y., Fan, L., et al.: Incomplete multi-modal representation learning for Alzheimer's disease diagnosis. Med. Image Anal. **69**, 101953 (2021)

12. Liu, Z., Lin, Y., et al.: Swin transformer: hierarchical vision transformer using shifted windows. In: IEEE International Conference on Computer Vision, pp. 10012–10022 (2021)

13. Peiris, H., Hayat, M., Chen, Z., Egan, G., Harandi, M.: A robust volumetric transformer for accurate 3D tumor segmentation. In: Wang, L., Dou, Q., Fletcher, P.T., Speidel, S., Li, S. (eds.) ECCV 2022, Part V. LNCS, vol. 13435, pp. 162–172. Springer, Cham (2022)

14. Qiu, Y., Chen, D., Yao, H., Xu, Y., Wang, Z.: Scratch each other's back: Incomplete multi-modal brain tumor segmentation via category aware group self-support learning. In: Proceedings of the IEEE/CVF International Conference on Computer Vision (2023)

15. Qiu, Y., Zhao, Z., Yao, H., Chen, D., Wang, Z.: Modal-aware visual prompting for incomplete multi-modal brain tumor segmentation. In: Proceedings of the 31th ACM International Conference on Multimedia (2023)

16. Qu, M., et al.: SiRi: a simple selective retraining mechanism for transformer-based visual grounding. In: Avidan, S., Brostow, G., Cissé, M., Farinella, G.M., Hassner, T. (eds.) ECCV 2022, Part XXXV. LNCS, vol. 13695, pp. 546–562. Springer, Cham (2022). https://doi.org/10.1007/978-3-031-19833-5_32

17. Tang, Y., et al.: Self-supervised pre-training of swin transformers for 3d medical image analysis (2021). https://doi.org/10.48550/ARXIV.2111.14791. https://arxiv.org/abs/2111.14791

18. Valanarasu, J.M.J., Yasarla, R., et al.: TransWeather: transformer-based restoration of images degraded by adverse weather conditions. In: IEEE Conference on Computer Vision and Pattern Recognition, pp. 2353–2363 (2022)

19. Vaswani, A., Shazeer, N., et al.: Attention is all you need. In: Proceedings Advances in Neural Information Processing Systems, vol. 30 (2017)

20. Wang, L., Lee, C.Y., et al.: Training deeper convolutional networks with deep supervision. arXiv preprint arXiv:1505.02496 (2015)

21. Wang, S., et al.: LT-Net: label transfer by learning reversible voxel-wise correspondence for one-shot medical image segmentation. In: Proceedings of the IEEE Conference on Computer Vision and Pattern Recognition, pp. 9162–9171 (2020)

22. Zhang, Y., He, N., et al.: mmFormer: multimodal medical transformer for incomplete multimodal learning of brain tumor segmentation. In: Proceedings of the International Conference on Medical Image Computing and Computer-Assisted Intervention, pp. 107–117 (2022)

23. Zhang, Y., et al.: Modality-aware mutual learning for multi-modal medical image segmentation. In: de Bruijne, M., et al. (eds.) MICCAI 2021, Part I. LNCS, vol. 12901, pp. 589–599. Springer, Cham (2021). https://doi.org/10.1007/978-3-030-87193-2_56

24. Zhao, Z., Yang, H., et al.: Modality-adaptive feature interaction for brain tumor segmentation with missing modalities. In: Proceedings of the International Conference on Medical Image Computing and Computer-Assisted Intervention, pp. 183–192 (2022)

25. Zhou, C., Ding, C., Lu, Z., Wang, X., Tao, D.: One-pass multi-task convolutional neural networks for efficient brain tumor segmentation. In: Frangi, A.F., Schnabel, J.A., Davatzikos, C., Alberola-López, C., Fichtinger, G. (eds.) MICCAI 2018, Part III. LNCS, vol. 11072, pp. 637–645. Springer, Cham (2018). https://doi.org/10.1007/978-3-030-00931-1_73

MAD: Modality Agnostic Distance Measure for Image Registration

Vasiliki Sideri-Lampretsa[1,2]([✉]), Veronika A. Zimmer[1], Huaqi Qiu[4],
Georgios Kaissis[1,2,3], and Daniel Rueckert[1,2,4]

[1] Technical University of Munich, Munich, Germany
{vasiliki.sideri-lampretsa,veronika.zimmer,g.kaissis,
daniel.rueckert}@tum.de
[2] Klinkum rechts der Isar, Munich, Germany
[3] Helmholtz Zentrum Munich, Munich, Germany
[4] Department of Computing, Imperial College London, London, UK
huaqi.qiu15@imperial.ac.uk

Abstract. Multi-modal image registration is a crucial pre-processing step in many medical applications. However, it is a challenging task due to the complex intensity relationships between different imaging modalities, which can result in large discrepancy in image appearance. The success of multi-modal image registration, whether it is conventional or learning based, is predicated upon the choice of an appropriate distance (or similarity) measure. Particularly, deep learning registration algorithms lack in accuracy or even fail completely when attempting to register data from an "unseen" modality. In this work, we present Modality Agnostic Distance (MAD), a deep *image distance* measure that utilises random convolutions to learn the inherent geometry of the images while being robust to large appearance changes. Random convolutions are geometry-preserving modules which we use to simulate an infinite number of synthetic modalities alleviating the need for aligned paired data during training. We can therefore train MAD on a mono-modal dataset and successfully apply it to a multi-modal dataset. We demonstrate that not only can MAD affinely register multi-modal images successfully, but it has also a larger capture range than traditional measures such as Mutual Information and Normalised Gradient Fields. Our code is available at: https://github.com/ModalityAgnosticDistance/MAD.

Keywords: Image registration · mutli-modality · distance measure

1 Introduction

Multi-modal image registration is a crucial and challenging application in medical image processing. It generally refers to the process in which two images acquired from different imaging systems, governed by different physics principles, are aligned into the same coordinate space. Fusing the different modalities can result in more informative content. However, this is not a trivial problem due

J. Woo et al. (Eds.): MICCAI 2023 Workshops, LNCS 14394, pp. 147–156, 2023.
https://doi.org/10.1007/978-3-031-47425-5_14

to the highly non-linear relationships between the shapes and the appearance present in different modalities [22].

In order to tackle this challenging issue, several multi-modal image similarity/distance measures have been proposed [6,9,23]. The widely used multi-modal intensity-based measures, Mutual Information (MI) [14,23,26], operates on intensity histograms and is therefore agnostic to the underlying geometry of the image structures. Although MI excels in aligning images that are relatively close in space, it shows limited ability to recover large misalignments without a multi-resolution framework. Other metrics such as Normalised Gradient Fields (NGF), measure the image similarity using edge maps [6,25] while the Modality Independent Neighborhood Descriptor (MIND) measures the image similarity using hand-crafted local descriptors [9,28]. However, these measures make only restrictive assumptions on the intensity relationships between multi-modal images which affect their performance. Apart from the hand-crafted measures, many learning-based distance measures have also been proposed [1,3,7,13,21,25]. Most of these, however, are either used only for mono-modal registration only or require ground truth transformation or pre-aligned paired multi-modal images for training which is very challenging to obtain in a real-world scenario. In this work, we propose Modality Agnostic Distance (MAD), a self-supervised contrast-agnostic geometry-informed deep distance measure that demonstrates a wider capture range than the traditional measures without using a multi-resolution scheme. We overcome the limited assumptions of intensity relations in the intensity-based distance measures by learning geometry-centric relationships with a neural network. This is achieved by using random convolutions to create complex appearance changes, which also enables us to synthesise infinite aligned image pairs of different modalities, alleviating the need for aligned multi-modal paired data in the existing learning-based distance measures. To the best of our knowledge, our work is the first that explores random convolutions as data augmentation in the context of medical imaging and medical image registration. Our contribution can be summarised as follows:

- We introduce learning a general geometry-aware contrast-agnostic deep *image distance* measure for multi-modal registration, formulating an effective self-supervised task that allows the network to assess the *image distance* by grasping the underlying geometry independent of its appearance.
- We propose to use random convolutions to obtain infinite aligned image pairs of different appearances and parametric geometry augmentation to learn a modality-invariant distance measure for image registration.
- We perform a detailed study about the capture range and evaluate the effectiveness of the proposed measure through extensive ablation analysis on two challenging multi-modal registration tasks, namely multi-modal brain registration and Computed Tomography (CT) - Magnetic Resonance (MR) abdominal image registration.

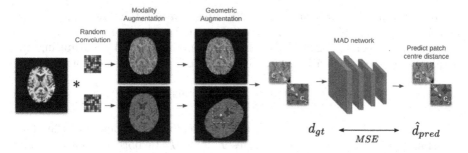

Fig. 1. An overview of our method. We synthesise modalities from a mono-modal dataset using random convolutions (left). Random affine transformations are used as geometric augmentation (middle). Patches are sampled at corresponding locations as input to a CNN to regress the distance between patch centres (right). We compute the MSE between ground truth (d_{gt}) and predicted (d_{gt}) distance.

2   Related Works

Besides the hand-crafted measures described in the introduction, learning-based methods were also proposed to learn an inter-modal loss function [1,3,7,13,21,25]. A recent work, DeepSim [3] proposes to pre-train a feature extractor on an auxiliary segmentation task and then use the semantic features to drive the optimisation of a learning-based registration model. Moreover, Pielawski et al. [18] proposed CoMIR that uses supervised contrastive learning and paired data to learn affine registration on 2D images. Dey et al. [4] proposed a method that involves unsupervised contrastive learning to maximise the mutual information between features. Hoffman et al. [11] proposed a data augmentation pipeline based on labels to simulate synthetic images and assess the image similarity in them. Similar to our work, [21] proposes to learn a metric from patches through a patch-matching classification task. However, the training process relies on aligned paired data which is difficult to acquire for any modality and the model is specifically trained on T1w-T2w images, limiting its generalisability across different domains such as MR-CT.

3   Methods

Problem Formulation. In this paper, we are focusing on affine registration between 3D images. Affine image registration is the task of estimating the best transformation $\mathcal{A} : \Omega_F \to \Omega_M$, between a fixed $F : \Omega_F \subseteq \mathbb{R}^n \to \mathbb{R}$ and a moving image $M : \Omega_M \subseteq \mathbb{R} \to \mathbb{R}^n$ ($n = 3$ in our case). In conventional registration, the transformation parameters μ that parameterise the affine matrix, here denoted by $\mathcal{A}_\mu$, are estimated by solving the following optimisation problem:

$$\mu^* = \arg\min_\mu [\mathcal{D}(F, M(\mathcal{A}_\mu))], \tag{1}$$

where $\mathcal{D}$ is a distance measure which measures how well the images are aligned and $M(\mathcal{A}_\mu)$ is the affinely transformed moving image resampled to Ω_F.

In learning-based registration, this problem is solved by optimising the weights of a neural network instead of the parameters of the transformation:

$$\phi^* = \arg\min_\phi \mathbb{E}[\mathcal{D}(F, M(\mathcal{A}_{g_\phi}))], \tag{2}$$

where $g_\phi(F, M)$ is a neural network that predicts the parameters of the affine transformation which aligns the images F and M. In both conventional and learning-based approaches, selecting an appropriate measure $\mathcal{D}$ is crucial.

Learning Modality-Agnostic Distance Measure. Instead of using an analytically formulated distance measure, we propose to formulate $\mathcal{D}$ as a geometry-aware convolutional neural network that estimates the dissimilarity between images by aggregating the distance between their patches, while remaining contrast agnostic. In other words, we are training the network to estimate the distance between the patch centres sampled from the different images after augmenting using random convolutions. Intuitively, the centre point difference can serve as a similarity indicator, i.e. if the points are close in space that means that the patches should also be close in space and vice versa. The whole process can be schematically outlined in Fig. 1.

Modality Augmentation. In order to reliably achieve multi-modal registration, we would like to devise a dissimilarity measure which is modality-agnostic, removing the need for retraining for every modality pairing. To achieve that, we propose to employ randomly initialised convolutional layers as data augmentation [29]. These layers have the desirable trait that they maintain the underlying geometry of the images, only transforming the local intensity and texture.

Our first task is to extend the formulation presented in [29] to 3D. Convolution is a linear operator, as a result the intensities are linearly mapped to the range $[0, 255]$. This is rather unrealistic as we are often dealing with modality pairs with non-linear intensity relationships. Therefore, we introduce non-linearity in the intensity mapping by performing clamping, taking the absolute value of the result of the random convolutions and passing it through a leaky ReLU with a variable negative slope. This simulates more sophisticated intensity relationships between the augmented domains. The geometric-preserving augmentation enforces identical structure, but different appearance enabling us to generate infinite pairs of aligned modalities only from one mono-modal image, removing the need for paired and pre-aligned multi-modal data.

Geometric Augmentation. Let $F = \text{RandConv}(I)$, $M = \text{RandConv}(I)$ be the fixed and moving image volumes which are the same image mapped to different augmented modalities via random convolutions. To train the learned distance metric, we synthetically transform the moving image to generate controlled geometric misalignment. Following the notation suggested by [16], we sample a random rotation, translation, scaling and shearing parameter from a range of possible configurations and we construct an affine matrix $\mathcal{A}$. Formally, we can write the affine matrix $\mathcal{A}(\mathbf{t}, \mathbf{r}, \mathbf{s}, \mathbf{h})$ where $\mathbf{t}, \mathbf{r}, \mathbf{s}, \mathbf{h} \in \mathbb{R}^3$ are the translation, rotation, scaling and shearing parameters. The affine matrix $\mathcal{A}$ can be composed by a set of geometric transformation matrices: $A = \mathcal{T} \cdot \mathcal{R} \cdot \mathcal{S} \cdot \mathcal{H}$, where $\mathcal{T}$, $\mathcal{R}$, $\mathcal{S}$ and $\mathcal{H}$ denote the translation, rotation, scaling and shearing transformation matrices parameterised by the corresponding geometric transformation parameters.

Finally, we sample N patches of the same size at the same locations in the fixed and transformed moving image resulting in N patch pairs that differ both in appearance and geometry. We are denoting the patches that are sampled from the fixed image by P_F and the patches that are sampled from the moving image by P_M. Since we synthetically transform the moving image with a known affine transformation relative to the fixed, we can also obtain the ground truth deformation field which effectively denote the distance between the patch centres.

MAD. To construct an alignment distance measure from the patches, we employ a convolutional neural network (ResNet [8]) f_θ which is trained to determine the Euclidean distance between the centres of a patch pair from their appearances. The distance measure between the images can be thus calculated by aggregating the distances between all patches:

$$\mathcal{D}_{MAD}(F, M) = \frac{1}{N} \sum_{i=1}^{N} f_\theta(P_F^i, P_M^i), \tag{3}$$

where θ are the network parameters, N is the number of patches, $P_F^i : \Omega_F^P \subset \Omega_F \subseteq \mathbb{R}^3 \to \mathbb{R}^3$ and $P_M^i : \Omega_M^P \subset \Omega_M \subseteq \mathbb{R}^3 \to \mathbb{R}^3$ are patches of the same size sampled at the same location from the fixed and moving image respectively.

We are supervising the training of the patch distance CNN using the patches we generated from the modality and geometric augmentations. Concretely, we optimise the network using a loss function which calculates the Mean Square Error (MSE) between the ground truth and predicted centre point distances:

$$\theta^* = \arg \min_\theta \mathbb{E}[(d_{gt} - \hat{d}_{pred})^2] \tag{4}$$

where θ^* denotes the optimal network parameters, $\hat{d}_{pred}$ denotes the patch distances predicted by the network and d_{gt} denotes the ground truth distances derived from the known affine transformation $\mathcal{A}(\mathbf{t}, \mathbf{r}, \mathbf{s}, \mathbf{h})$ that we sampled.

Intuitively, by presenting the network with a large number of augmented modality pairs with varying intensity relationships, we encourage it to focus on evaluating the difference between image shapes according to their inherent geometric transformations, while placing less emphasis on image appearance. Given that our distance measure is differentiable by construction, it can be optimised using gradient-based optimisation techniques and used as a cost function in both conventional or learning-based registration algorithms.

4 Experiments and Discussion

Datasets. We are evaluating the effectiveness of the proposed measure using three datasets: the Cambridge Centre for Ageing and Neuroscience project

(CamCAN) [20,24], the Retrospective Image Registration Evaluation Project (R.I.R.E.) [27] and the arguably challenging MR-CT dataset of Learn2Reg [10]. We normalise all the brain images to a common MNI space using affine registration, ensuring an isotropic spatial resolution with a voxel size of $1\,mm^3$. We perform skull-stripping using ROBEX [12] and bias-field correction using the N4 algorithm in SimpleITK [15]. For the pre-processing of the CT images in R.I.R.E, we use the steps proposed in [17]. We utilise the 310 3D T1w brain images of the CamCAN project to train MAD (80% training - 20% validation) and we test it on 6 subjects of R.I.R.E. that have uncorrupted T1w, T2w, PD MR and CT brain images. Regarding the abdominal images, we use the 90 unpaired, affinely aligned MR and CT scans for training (80% training - 20% validation) and the 16 paired scans for evaluation. All the images have isotropic spatial resolution with a voxel size of $2\,mm^3$.

Evaluation. We compare MAD to two widely used image similarity measures: NMI introduced by [23], NGF [6] and ClassLoss (CL) which is a learning-based measure based on patch classification [21] and most relevant to our work. We start with images from different modalities that are affinely aligned in space. Then, we transform them with a synthetic affine transformation. The intuition behind this is that by controlling the applied transformation parameters we can evaluate the measures' performance quantitatively. I.e. as we know the synthetic transformation that we are trying to recover, we can also know the ground truth deformation field. As a result, we can evaluate the accuracy of the registration by calculating the Mean Average Error (MAE) and its standard deviation (std) in mm between the ground truth deformations and the predicted ones. We also test if the differences in the reported errors between competing methods are statistically significant ($p < 0.05$) with a t-test [5]. Lastly, we calculate the effect size es considering it small when $es \leq 0.3$, moderate when $0.3 \leq es \leq 0.5$ and strong when $es \leq 0.5$ [2]. We incorporate the baselines and the proposed measure with image registration implemented with Airlab, a conventional registration framework introduced in [19].

4.1 Experiment 1: Loss Landscapes

Setup. We generate the measure landscapes to inspect and compare the convexity and the capture range by translating a CT image relative to a T1w image from the R.I.R.E. dataset. The translations $\mathbf{t} = [t_x, t_y, t_z]$ are in the range of $[-60, 60]\,mm$ with a step size of 10mm and the resulting image distances are normalised for better comparison.

Results. Figure 2 demonstrates that despite NMI, NGF and MAD landscapes being smooth with minima at 0, MAD leads to the largest capture range (further validated by registration results in Table 1) compared to NGF and NMI. This could be explained by the fact that MAD network is trained on complex appearance patches and therefore it is able to capture the underlying geometry better than NGF that is operating on edge maps. NMI is known to perform poorly for large misalignment without the usage of a multi-resolution scheme, showing weak gradients towards the optimal alignment when the translations are large.

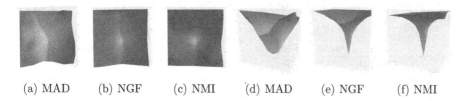

(a) MAD   (b) NGF   (c) NMI   (d) MAD   (e) NGF   (f) NMI

Fig. 2. The loss 2D landscapes for translation in the range of $[-60, 60]$mm. MAD (MAD) [a, d], Normalised Gradient Fields (NGF) [b, e] and Normalised Mutual Information (NMI) [c, f]

4.2   Experiment 2: Recover Random Transformations

Setup. We assess the performance of our *image distance* measure in recovering synthetic affine transformations. We repeat the experiment 100 times for all test subjects and we compute the MAE between the ground truth and the predicted deformation fields. We evaluated the performance on a small and a large range of transformations (Table 1 right) in order to examine the capacity of MAD to restore synthetic transformations without requiring a multi-resolution approach. For the large transformations, we employ a multi-resolution scheme for both NGF and NMI, given the small capture range these measures exhibit in Sect. 4.1.

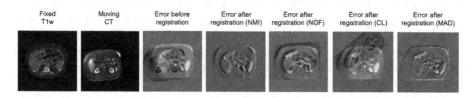

Fig. 3. Qualitative registration results for the MR-CT abdominal dataset using the different measures.

Results. Table 1 shows that, for smaller ranges, MAD is superior to the state-of-the-art learned CL measure and on par with the conventional metrics for all datasets. This is unsurprising given that NGF and NMI are effective at recovering small misalignments, as we observe in Fig. 2. The conclusion of the comparison changes for the large misalignment case, where MAD demonstrates significantly superior performance in all cases, even when NMI and NGF are used in a multi-resolution scheme (Fig. 3). Furthermore, we observe that recovering the larger

Table 1. Registration performance measured using the Mean Absolute Error (mean(std)) in mm between the ground truth and the predicted deformation fields for small and large affine misalignment (left). Grey boxes indicate significance compared to MAD with a $p < 0.05$ and effect sizes small, moderate (*) and strong (**). Affine parameter ranges: Translation (T.), Rotation (R.), Scaling (Sc.), Shearing (Sh.) (right).

	Small misalignment setting				Parameter ranges	
	T1w-PD	T1w-CT	T1w-T2w	CT-MR	Small	
NMI	4.79(3.22)	**4.15(4.32)**	**4.07(3.51)**	7.65(6.28)	T.	$[-30, 30]$mm
NGF	4.92(3.81)	5.38(5.26)	4.89(3.76)	8.81(4.29)	R.	$[-25, 25]°$
CL	5.32(5.11)	5.46(4.38)	4.75(4.71)	9.63(9.51)	Sc.	$[90, 110]\%$
MAD	**4.56(3.8)**	4.27(4.17)	4.15(4.12)	**7.06(2.07)**	Sh.	$[90, 110]\%$
	Large misalignment setting					
	T1w-PD	T1w-CT	T1w-T2w	CT-MR	Large	
NMI	17.79(14.41)	20.21(12.32)*	15.63(15.78)	22.93(19.72)*	T.	$\pm[30, 60]$mm
NGF	23.86(12.74)*	29.98(22.64)**	27.88(25.15)*	25.87(21.56)*	R.	$\pm[25, 45]°$
CL	63.24(48.28)**	67.13(41.79)**	55.84(49.36)**	94.12(83.52)**	Sc.	$[90, 110]\%$
MAD	**13.34(7.59)**	**17.09(9.03)**	**13.21(7.64)**	**20.47(15.63)**	Sh.	$[90, 110]\%$

Table 2. Ablation study that demonstrates the performance of each structural element: number of patches, patch size and the utility of data augmentation.

# Patches			Patch Size			Rand. Conv.	
10	100	300	16	32	64	yes	no
4.44(2.61)	4.22(2.68)	3.69(2.33)	4.39(3.09)	3.96(2.00)	3.69(2.33)	3.69(2.33)	5.07(2.64)

transformations results in larger errors for all image distance measures. This could be caused by the optimisation not converging or converging in a local minimum. This issue is particularly severe for the learned CL measure which demonstrates very large errors, potentially due to the fact that the classification categorical signal is not able to quantify how large the patch mismatch is. Qualitative results can be found in the Supplementary material.

4.3   Experiment 3: Ablation Study

To demonstrate the performance of the design choices, namely the random convolution modality augmentation, patch size and the number of patches sampled, we perform a series of ablation experiments on T1w-CT of R.I.R.E. dataset. The results are demonstrated in Table 2. It can be seen that MAD with random convolution modality augmentation showed a lower registration error (3.69 mm) than MAD without random convolution (5.07 mm). We also found that a higher number of patches leads to better performance as expected. Finally, we demonstrate the method is rather robust to the choice of patch size, with slightly better results from using larger patch sizes.

5   Conclusion

In this work, we design a learned contrast-agnostic geometry-focused learning-based dissimilarity measure for multi-modal image registration. Using the elegant concept of random convolutions as modality augmentation and synthetic geometry augmentation, we are able to address the challenge of learning an image distance measure for multi-modal registration without the need for aligned paired multi-modal data. We carefully study the loss landscape, the capture range and registration accuracy quantitatively in two multi-modal registration scenarios. Evaluation results demonstrate that the proposed framework outperforms established multi-modal dissimilarity measures, especially for large deformation estimation. In future works, we plan to plug the proposed measure in a deep learning registration framework, perform more tests on other multi-modal applications and adapt the framework for multi-modal deformable registration.

References

1. Cheng, X., Zhang, L., Zheng, Y.: Deep similarity learning for multimodal medical images. Comput. Meth. Biomech. Biomed. Eng. Imaging Vis. **6**, 248–252 (2015)
2. Cohen, J.: Statistical Power Analysis for the Behavioral Sciences. The SAGE Encyclopedia of Research Design, Thousand Oaks (1969)
3. Czolbe, S., Krause, O., Feragen, A.: DeepSim: semantic similarity metrics for learned image registration. ArXiv abs/2011.05735 (2020)
4. Dey, N., Schlemper, J., Salehi, S.S.M., Zhou, B., Gerig, G., Sofka, M.: ContraReg: contrastive learning of multi-modality unsupervised deformable image registration. In: Wang, L., Dou, Q., Fletcher, P.T., Speidel, S., Li, S. (eds.) MICCAI 2022. LNCS, vol. 13436, pp. 66–77. Springer, Cham (2022). https://doi.org/10.1007/978-3-031-16446-0_7
5. Bradley, E., Trevor, H.: Computer Age Statistical Inference: Algorithms, Evidence, and Data Science. Cambridge University Press, New York (2016)
6. Haber, E., Modersitzki, J.: Intensity gradient based registration and fusion of multi-modal images. In: Larsen, R., Nielsen, M., Sporring, J. (eds.) MICCAI 2006. LNCS, vol. 4191, pp. 726–733. Springer, Heidelberg (2006). https://doi.org/10.1007/11866763_89
7. Haskins, G., et al.: Learning deep similarity metric for 3D MR-TRUS image registration. Int. J. Comput. Assist. Radiol. Surg. **14**, 417–425 (2018)
8. He, K., Zhang, X., Ren, S., Sun, J.: Deep residual learning for image recognition. In: Proceedings of the IEEE Conference on Computer Vision and Pattern Recognition, pp. 770–778 (2016)
9. Heinrich, M., et al.: Mind: modality independent neighbourhood descriptor for multi-modal deformable registration. Med. Image Anal. **16**(7), 1423–35 (2012)
10. Hering, A., et al.: Learn2Reg: comprehensive multi-task medical image registration challenge, dataset and evaluation in the era of deep learning. IEEE Trans. Med. Imaging **42**, 697–712 (2021)
11. Hoffmann, M., Billot, B., Greve, D.N., Iglesias, J.E., Fischl, B.R., Dalca, A.V.: SynthMorph: learning contrast-invariant registration without acquired images. IEEE Trans. Med. Imaging **41**, 543–558 (2020)

12. Iglesias, J., Liu, C., Thompson, P., Tu, Z.: Robust brain extraction across datasets and comparison with publicly available methods. IEEE Trans. Med. Imaging 30(9), 1617–1634 (2011)

13. Lee, D., Hofmann, M., Steinke, F., Altun, Y., Cahill, N., Schölkopf, B.: Learning similarity measure for multi-modal 3D image registration. In: 2009 IEEE Conference on Computer Vision and Pattern Recognition, pp. 186–193 (2009)

14. Loeckx, D., Slagmolen, P., Maes, F., Vandermeulen, D., Suetens, P.: Nonrigid image registration using conditional mutual information. IEEE Trans. Med. Imaging 29, 19–29 (2010)

15. Lowekamp, B., Chen, D., Ibáñez, L., Blezek, D.: The design of simpleiTK. Front. Neuroinform. 7, 45 (2013)

16. Mok, T., Chung, A.: Affine medical image registration with coarse-to-fine vision transformer. In: 2022 IEEE/CVF Conference on Computer Vision and Pattern Recognition (CVPR), pp. 20803–20812 (2022)

17. Muschelli, J., Ullman, N., Mould, W., Vespa, P., Hanley, D., Crainiceanu, C.: Validated automatic brain extraction of head CT images. Neuroimage 114, 379–385 (2015)

18. Pielawski, N., et al.: CoMIR: contrastive multimodal image representation for registration. ArXiv abs/2006.06325 (2020)

19. Sandkühler, R., Jud, C., Andermatt, S., Cattin, P.: AirLab: autograd image registration laboratory. ArXiv (2018)

20. Shafto, M., et al.: The Cambridge centre for ageing and neuroscience (Cam-CAN) study protocol: a cross-sectional, lifespan, multidisciplinary examination of healthy cognitive ageing. BMC Neurol. 14, 1–25 (2014)

21. Simonovsky, M., Gutiérrez-Becker, B., Mateus, D., Navab, N., Komodakis, N.: A deep metric for multimodal registration. In: International Conference on Medical Image Computing and Computer-Assisted Intervention (2016)

22. Sotiras, A., Davatzikos, C., Paragios, N.: Deformable medical image registration: a survey. IEEE Trans. Med. Imaging 32, 1153–1190 (2013)

23. Studholme, C., Hill, D., Hawkes, D.: An overlap invariant entropy measure of 3d medical image alignment. Pattern Recogn. 32, 71–86 (1999)

24. Taylor, J., et al.: The Cambridge centre for ageing and neuroscience (Cam-CAN) data repository: structural and functional MRI, MEG, and cognitive data from a cross-sectional adult lifespan sample. Neuroimage 144, 262–269 (2017)

25. Wachinger, C., Navab, N.: Entropy and Laplacian images: structural representations for multi-modal registration. Med. Image Anal. 16(1), 1–17 (2012)

26. Wells, W., Viola, P., Atsumi, H., Nakajima, S., Kikinis, R.: Multi-modal volume registration by maximization of mutual information. Med. Image Anal. 1(1), 35–51 (1996)

27. West, J., et al.: Comparison and evaluation of retrospective intermodality image registration techniques. In: Medical Imaging (1996)

28. Woo, J., Stone, M., Prince, J.: Multimodal registration via mutual information incorporating geometric and spatial context. IEEE Trans. Image Process. 24, 757–769 (2015)

29. Xu, Z., Liu, D., Yang, J., Niethammer, M.: Robust and generalizable visual representation learning via random convolutions. ICLR (2021)

Multimodal Context-Aware Detection of Glioma Biomarkers Using MRI and WSI

Tomé Albuquerque[1,2,3]([✉]), Mei Ling Fang[1]([✉]), Benedikt Wiestler[4,5],
Claire Delbridge[1,6], Maria João M. Vasconcelos[7], Jaime S. Cardoso[2,3],
and Peter Schüffler[1]

[1] Institute of General and Surgical Pathology, TUM, 81675 Munich, Germany
[2] INESC TEC, 4200-465 Porto, Portugal
tome.m.albuquerque@inestec.pt
[3] FEUP, University of Porto, 4200-465 Porto, Portugal
[4] Department of Neuroradiology, MRI, TUM, 81675 Munich, Germany
[5] TranslaTUM, TU Munich, 81675 Munich, Germany
[6] Department of Neuropathology, MRI, TUM, 81675 Munich, Germany
[7] Fraunhofer Portugal AICOS, 4200-135 Porto, Portugal

Abstract. The most malignant tumors of the central nervous system are adult-type diffuse gliomas. Historically, glioma subtype classification has been based on morphological features. However, since 2016, WHO recognizes that molecular evaluation is critical for subtyping. Among molecular markers, the mutation status of IDH1 and the codeletion of 1p/19q are crucial for the precise diagnosis of these malignancies. In pathology laboratories, however, manual screening for those markers is time-consuming and susceptible to error. To overcome these limitations, we propose a novel multimodal biomarker classification method that integrates image features derived from brain magnetic resonance imaging and histopathological exams. The proposed model consists of two branches, the first branch takes as input a multi-scale Hematoxylin and Eosin whole slide image, and the second branch uses the pre-segmented region of interest from the magnetic resonance imaging. Both branches are based on convolutional neural networks. After passing the exams by the two embedding branches, the output feature vectors are concatenated, and a multi-layer perceptron is used to classify the glioma biomarkers as a multi-class problem. In this work, several fusion strategies were studied, including a cascade model with mid-fusion; a mid-fusion model, a late fusion model, and a mid-context fusion model. The models were tested using a publicly available data set from The Cancer Genome Atlas. Our cross-validated classification models achieved an area under the curve of 0.874, 0.863, and 0.815 for the proposed multimodal, magnetic resonance imaging, and Hematoxylin and Eosin stain slide images respectively, indicating our multimodal model outperforms its unimodal counterparts and the state-of-the-art glioma biomarker classification methods.

Supplementary Information The online version contains supplementary material available at https://doi.org/10.1007/978-3-031-47425-5_15.

Keywords: Biomarker Detection · Multimodal Learning · Deep Learning · Glioma Classification · Weakly Supervised Learning

1   Introduction

Adult-type diffuse gliomas are the most common malignant tumors that grow in the human brain [20]. Diffuse tumors spread into healthy tissues, making it difficult to determine precisely a clear boundary between healthy and cancerous tissues. In addition, gliomas are highly infiltrative and resistant to immunotherapy, rendering them largely incurable. Despite advances in our understanding of gliomas, survival greatly depends on the subtype of tumors present. Therefore, classification and grading of gliomas have significant implications on prognostic and treatment planning [22]. In the past, the classification of diffuse gliomas has been based on morphological features, and, more recently, molecular markers have become increasingly important in the diagnosis process. Since 2016, the World Health Organization (WHO) expanded its definition of grading adult-type diffuse gliomas by solidifying the centrality of molecular biomarkers and reducing the dependency on phenotypic features. The subtyping under the update varies greatly on isocitrate dehydrogenase 1 (IDH1) mutation status and the 1p/19q codeletion status [19].

The current diagnostic workflow to detect adult-type diffuse gliomas includes Magnetic Resonance Imaging (MRI) and tissue acquisition (histology) [10] (Fig. 1). Usually, several complimentary 3D modalities, such as native T1, T1 with contrast agent (T1ce), T2, and Fluid Attenuation Inversion Recovery (FLAIR), are acquired through brain MRI to enable an initial phenotypic inspection. Then a biopsy, which remains the gold standard for diagnosis, is taken and routinely assessed by molecular analysis in order to differentiate diffuse gliomas [11]. Nevertheless, the genotypic analysis of molecular markers to confirm the histological tumor typing and grading is time-consuming, subjective, and expensive. With the advance of deep learning techniques and the rising computing capability, patterns that are indifferent to human eyes can be recognized by deep neural networks in a relatively short period. Considering the digital data derived from MRI and pathological slides in the form of whole slide images (WSI), it is now possible to apply deep learning to combine both modalities to predict the molecular markers and further subtype gliomas [2].

Since the update of the WHO protocol, intensive research has been conducted on biomarker classification and glioma grading. In recent years, several researchers tried to detect IDH1 and 1p/19q biomarkers from MRI or WSI [6,16,21]. However, most of the works only make a binary classification between IDH1-mutant and IDH1-wildtype or 1p/19q codeleted and non-codeleted. Figure 2 shows the most recent and relevant methods found in the literature for glioma biomarker detection.

In [23], the authors proposed a multi-modal tumor segmentation network that uses four MRI sequences, then combined with pathology images for tumor subtype classification based on biomarkers. Unlike [23], our proposed model is

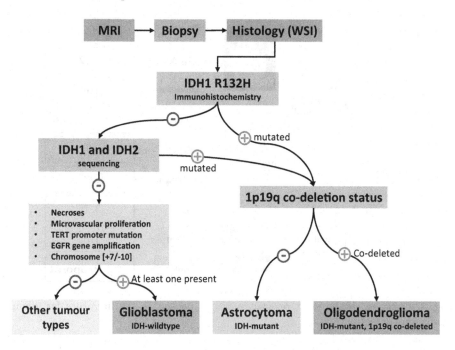

Fig. 1. Simplified overview of the classification pathway for the majority of adult-type diffuse gliomas based on WHO (2021) classification of CNS tumors.

not focused on tumour subtype classification but on detecting the biomarkers. Also, we use public data and do cross-validation in contrast to [23]. Histopathology and MRI both assess the tumor phenotype, albeit on a vastly different scale (MRI: millimeter, microscopy: micrometer). Also, MRI captures the phenotype of the entire tumor. Thus, these methods promise to provide complimentary information on the tumor phenotype, and consequently the tumor genotype. However, given challenges in fusing these modalities (or their latent representations), exploring this synergy remains understudied to-date.

In this work, we propose a joint analysis of unimodal models using MRI and WSI against multiple multimodal models by combining both exams (MRI and WSI) for brain tumor biomarkers classification (IDH1 and 1p/19q) following the 2021 WHO criteria. This problem is tackled as a multiclass problem and it can be divided into three different targets: (class 0) IDH1-wildtype (glioblastoma and diffuse astrocytic glioma with molecular features of glioblastoma), (class 1) IDH1-mutant and 1p/19q codeletion (oligodendroglioma), and (class 2) IDH1-mutant (lower grade astrocytoma) (Table 1). Specifically, the main contributions of this work are: (i) the proposal of new fusion models including a context-aware model and (ii) the presentation of the important role of combing MRI with WSI for detecting IDH mutation and 1p/19q codeletion status for better glioma stratification. The code to reproduce this work is publicly available[1].

---

[1] https://github.com/tomealbuquerque/multimodal-glioma-biomarkers-detection.

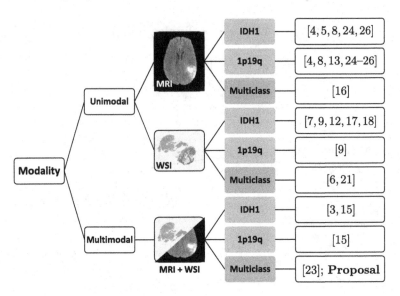

Fig. 2. Overview of the most relevant methods present in the literature for glioma biomarkers detection.

2   Proposed Methodology

This study is divided into two different approaches: unimodal and multimodal. In the unimodal part, which serves as the basis for comparison with the multimodal part, different models were tested for each modality (MRI and WSI). Regarding MRI, two different approaches were investigated, with the original ($255 \times 255 \times 255$ pixels (px)) MRI exams and also the segmented ROI blocks ($96 \times 96 \times 96$ px). Both methods were tested with all four MRI exams (T1, T1ce, T2, and FLAIR) with and without (standalone) combinations to determine the best method, using DenseNet121 as the backbone for the classification of the biomarkers. For WSI, we incorporated a weakly supervised deep learning model based on multiple instance learning (MIL), using only the reported diagnosis as a label per slide. Using ResNet34, in a binary classification problem for the training process of the embedder/encoder, the top 10 tiles per slide were selected based on the output score. Then, a multilayer perceptron model (MLP) was trained to aggregate the 10 tiles for the multiclass classification problem. Three different methods for relevant tiles selection were tested: top tiles containing the biomarkers based on the confidence score from the embedder (Top tiles), top tiles per class (Mix tiles) also based on the confidence score from the embedder, and the expected value ($E[X]$) per tile, to select the most relevant ones (Expected tiles), defined as:

$$E[X] = \sum_{k=1}^{K} x_k \times p(x_k) \tag{1}$$

where $x_1, x_2, ..., x_K$ are the possible outcomes of the tile X, $p(x_1), p(x_2), ..., p(x_K)$ are their corresponding probabilities, and K is the number of classes. For the multimodal part, four different models combining MRI with WSI were tested and proposed as represented in Fig. 3. The different multimodal methods reutilize the same backbone as previously described in the unimodal models for MRI and WSI respectively. However, the final model layers are modified to integrate the feature vectors from both modalities. The proposed multimodal fusion models are the following:

(a) **Cascade with fusion model** - Figure 3(a) - This model is a two-stage classifier where the decision for 1p19q codeletion arises from the MRI branch. Moreover, a feature vector (penultimate linear layer) from the MRI branch is concatenated in the WSI branch through a middle fusion approach to regularize the training process for the IDH1 mutation classifier.

(b) **Mid fusion model** - Figure 3(b) - A mid-fusion approach is tested in this model using the same backbone from MRI and WSI unimodal branches. The last layer for classification was discarded and the two penultimate linear layers were saved as feature vectors from both modalities. The embedder weights were frozen and just the new MLP was trained.

(c) **Late fusion model** - Figure 3(c) - This model follows the same approach as the Mid fusion model, however, instead of concatenating the MRI feature vector in the middle layers of the MLP, they are concatenated in the late layers. Followed by a dilatation layer to learn more complex representations and finalize with a linear layer for the multi-class classification.

(d) **Mid context fusion model** - Figure 3(d) - Based on the Mid context fusion model, an extra branch is added with larger tiles centered on the original tiles to give more context to the model concerning the surrounding areas. This model is based on the base routine of a pathologist who looks at a higher level at the microscope to have more information concerning the ROI. Thus, an extra embedder is trained using 2048×2048 tiles.

3   Experimental Details

3.1   Dataset

The dataset used in this work was obtained from The Cancer Genome Atlas (TCGA), a publicly available database[2]. It includes 3D MRI images ($255 \times 255 \times 255$ px) from four modalities: T1, T1ce, T2, and FLAIR with segmentation blocks ($96 \times 96 \times 96$ px), digital pathology slides with hematoxylin and eosin staining (H&E), and clinical data (age and gender) from 187 patients. Table 1 summarises the target encoding and frequency of samples per class.

3.2   Data Pre-processing

To preserve the class ratios, the dataset was partitioned into five distinct folds using stratified cross-validation. The results are the average and standard deviation of these 5 folds. For the Pathology deep learning embedder it was necessary

---

[2] https://www.cancerimagingarchive.net/.

162   T. Albuquerque et al.

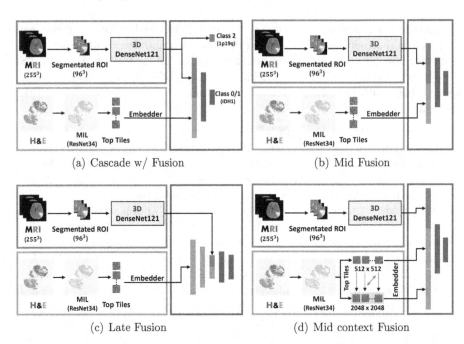

(a) Cascade w/ Fusion   (b) Mid Fusion

(c) Late Fusion   (d) Mid context Fusion

Fig. 3. Schematic representation of the models proposed in this study: (a) Cascade w/ Fusion (b) Mid Fusion (c) Late Fusion (d) Mid context Fusion.

to extract tiles with 512 × 512 px and 2048 × 2048 px dimensions from all WSI. Only tiles with more than 60% of tissue are used. Normalization was also performed to scale the pixel values to 0-1, which speeds up the training process and also helps the network in regularization. Data augmentation was used to cope with the limited amount of data. Each pathology image is subjected to a series of random transformations during training, including HEDJitter (random perturbation in the HED color space of the image), random elastic transformations, random color affine, random Gaussian blur, and also random image rotations. MR images (FLAIR, T1c, T1, T2) were preprocessed using the publicly available BraTS Toolkit [14]. For tumor segmentation (to define the 96 × 96 × 96 center crops around tumor), the SIMPLE fusion approach implemented in BraTS

Table 1. Summary of TCGA dataset with targets encoding and frequency of samples per class.

class	Biomarker		Frequency
	IDH1 mutation	1p/19q codeletion	
0	-	-	102
1	●	-	58
2	●	●	27

Toolkit was applied to a set of candidate segmentations from the best-performing BraTS segmentations. Since multi-channel augmentations for MRI images take more time and slow down the training process, only random image rotations were employed for MRI images.

3.3 Training Details

For the Pathology deep learning embedder, a grid search was first performed to find the best combination of hyperparameters, varying the image size (224×224, 552×552), batch size (128,256,384,512) and training epochs (25,50,100). For the MIL models, the best parameters found for the fine-tuned model were an image size of 552×552, a batch size of 384, and 50 training epochs. These hyperparameters were chosen with respect to the test subset of the first fold. ADAM was used in both modalities as the optimizer and started with a learning rate of 10^{-4} for all models. Cross-entropy (CE) was used as loss function. All the experiments are implemented using the PyTorch framework and the training process was conducted on a single Nvidia Tesla A100 (80GB) GPU.

3.4 Evaluation Metrics

Four different metrics were used to assess the performance of the models: accuracy (ACC), mean average error (MAE), F-score (F1), and the area under the curve (AUC). Accuracy is the most popular metric in classification problems [1] and can be defined as the proportion of cases correctly classified. Despite of being the most popular metric, it presents some drawbacks such as it masks the issue of class imbalance. Thus, to make a suitable measure of the models performance it were used other metrics. MAE is calculated by dividing the sum of absolute errors by the sample size. Therefore, the further the predicted class is from the actual class, the more significant the error becomes. F1 is the weighted harmonic mean of the precision and recall by giving equal weight to precision and recall. An overall measure of performance across all potential classification thresholds is provided by AUC, which can be understood as the probability that a random positive example will be ranked higher than a random negative example in the model. Auc presents two important advantages: is scale-invariant and also classification-threshold-invariant.

4 Results and Discussion

The average performance for the 5-folds of the three different modalities unimodal-WSI, unimodal-MRI, and Multimodal (WSI+MRI) are presented in Table 2. The unimodal-WSI MIL results include three different aggregation methods of the 10 relevant tiles (top tiles for biomarkers, mix tiles, and also expected tiles). For unimodal-MRI all four MRI exams (T1, T1ce, T2, and FLAIR) were tested with combinations and without combinations (standalone), and the best models are presented in Table 2 for T1ce and also T1ce with FLAIR.

The best models are shown in bold. Looking across the different unimodal models, regarding MRI, the best model was obtained using the pre-segmented blocks instead of the original MRI exam. The T1ce and also T1ce with FLAIR showed to be the best combination of MRI modalities when compared with T1 and T2. Concerning WSI, the best model was obtained using 10 expected tiles. This aggregation method will therefore be used for the multimodal models. Comparing the results of unimodal vs multimodal models, it is possible to infer that multimodal models surpass the unimodal counterparts in all metrics. Mid context Fusion model using T1ce and FLAIR in the MRI branch achieved the best results in two metrics with an ACC of 83.4% and an MAE of 0.224. Mid fusion model using also T1ce and FLAIR remains very competitive in several metrics and surpassed mid context fusion model in AUC, with 0.874. Comparing the ACC of the best-proposed model with the state-of-the-art [23], it is clear that the proposed model is above the state-of-the-art results with an ACC of 88.1% against 84.9% for the best fold. Figure 4 shows the receiver operating characteristic (ROC) plot for the 3 best models based on the AUC metric, by comparing unimodal vs multimodal approaches. The previously mentioned ROC plot, emphasizes the use of multimodal approaches, showing a higher curve for the multimodal mid fusion model. The confusion matrices for all models are in the Supplementary Tables S1-S5.

Table 2. Results for all modalities (5-fold cross validation, CE loss) - TCGA dataset.

Modality	Model	Acc (%)	MAE	F1 (%)	AUC
		\multicolumn{4}{c}{**Evaluation Metrics**}			
Seg. orig.	T1ce	65.818 ± 5.430	0.449 ± 0.112	60.260 ± 8.158	0.662 ± 0.048
	T1ce + FLAIR	68.478 ± 4.542	0.385 ± 0.066	63.770 ± 7.090	0.713 ± 0.038
	T1ce	80.214 ± 3.609	0.283 ± 0.048	75.570 ± 6.545	0.863 ± 0.015
	T1ce + FLAIR	73.244 ± 2.717	0.385 ± 0.081	64.290 ± 9.381	0.840 ± 0.037
MIL	Top tiles	73.243 ± 5.963	0.321 ± 0.084	70.649 ± 6.822	0.808 ± 0.101
	Mix tiles	73.243 ± 5.963	0.321 ± 0.084	70.649 ± 6.822	0.808 ± 0.101
	Expected tiles	74.851 ± 3.754	0.310 ± 0.054	71.518 ± 3.462	0.815 ± 0.088
T1ce	Cascade w/ Fusion	77.568 ± 6.269	0.288 ± 0.088	77.970 ± 6.221	0.833 ± 0.068
	Mid Fusion	80.199 ± 2.239	0.262 ± 0.039	78.129 ± 4.765	0.839 ± 0.059
	Late Fusion	79.147 ± 1.942	0.251 ± 0.034	76.337 ± 3.660	0.842 ± 0.058
	Mid Context Fusion	80.740 ± 5.482	0.246 ± 0.074	80.034 ± 5.524	0.866 ± 0.056
T1ce+F	Cascade w/ Fusion	81.707 ± 10.190	0.237 ± 0.144	**82.304 ± 9.814**	0.860 ± 0.068
	Mid Fusion	82.319 ± 3.791	0.246 ± 0.068	81.893 ± 3.627	**0.874 ± 0.061**
	Late Fusion	80.725 ± 3.216	0.251 ± 0.043	78.221 ± 5.039	0.849 ± 0.056
	Mid context Fusion	**83.414 ± 4.658**	**0.224 ± 0.071**	82.094 ± 5.083	0.858 ± 0.041

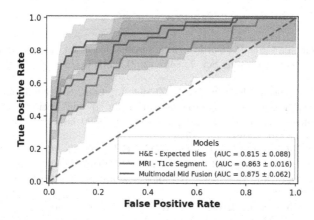

Fig. 4. ROC plot of the 5-folds cross-validation results for the best model per modality.

5 Conclusions

This work introduced and proposed novel multimodal deep learning methods for glioma biomarkers detection. The multimodal networks achieved the best results in several metrics, highlighting the favorable performance gains of using multimodal deep learning methods to tackle this problem. The most effective MRI modalities for the identification of both biomarkers were T1ce and FLAIR. Our proposed multimodal mid context fusion model proved to be very competitive against the other models, however, more experiments varying the size of context tiles should be performed for a better understanding of the extra context information impact. This work is a step toward more efficient use of MRI and histopathological data together and is particularly valuable in encouraging future research to lower the hurdles for point-of-care facilities without rapid access to a molecular genetics laboratory. For further work, we aim to validate the models with external data, however, for complete reproducibility, we used publicly available data and also turn public our code. By combining WSI and MRI into a unified latent space, multimodal solutions may improve the diagnosis with the addition of more training data.

Acknowledgments. The results shown here are in whole based upon data generated by the TCGA Research Network: https://www.cancer.gov/tcga. This work is co-financed by Component 5 - Capitalization and Business Innovation of core funding for Technology and Innovation Centres (CTI), integrated in the Resilience Dimension of the Recovery and Resilience Plan within the scope of the Recovery and Resilience Mechanism (MRR) of the European Union (EU), framed in the Next Generation EU, for the period 2021–2026. Tomé Albuquerque was supported by Ph.D. grant 2021.05102.BD provided by FCT.

References

1. Albuquerque, T., Cruz, R., Cardoso, J.S.: Ordinal losses for classification of cervical cancer risk. PeerJ Comput. Sci. **7**, e457 (2021). https://doi.org/10.7717/peerj-cs. 457
2. Alleman, K., Knecht, E., Huang, J., Zhang, L., Lam, S., DeCuypere, M.: Multimodal deep learning-based prognostication in glioma patients: a systematic review. Cancers **15**(2) (2023). https://doi.org/10.3390/cancers15020545. https://www.mdpi.com/2072-6694/15/2/545
3. Braman, N., Gordon, J.W.H., Goossens, E.T., Willis, C.S., Stumpe, M.C., Venkataraman, J.: Deep orthogonal fusion: multimodal prognostic biomarker discovery integrating radiology, pathology, genomic, and clinical data. arXiv abs/2107.00648 (2021)
4. Choi, K.S., Choi, S.H., Jeong, B.: Prediction of IDH genotype in gliomas with dynamic susceptibility contrast perfusion MR imaging using an explainable recurrent neural network. Neuro-Oncology **21**(9), 1197–1209 (2019). https://doi.org/10.1093/neuonc/noz095
5. Choi, Y.S., et al.: Fully automated hybrid approach to predict the IDH mutation status of gliomas via deep learning and radiomics. Neuro-oncology **23**(2), 304–313 (2020)
6. Chunduru, P., Phillips, J.J., Molinaro, A.M.: Prognostic risk stratification of gliomas using deep learning in digital pathology images. Neuro-Oncol. Adv. **4** (2022)
7. Cui, D., Liu, Y., Liu, G., Liu, L.: A multiple-instance learning-based convolutional neural network model to detect the IDH1 mutation in the histopathology images of glioma tissues. J. Comput. Biol. **27**(8), 1264–1272 (2020). https://doi.org/10.1089/cmb.2019.0410
8. Decuyper, M., Bonte, S., Deblaere, K., Van Holen, R.: Automated MRI based pipeline for segmentation and prediction of grade, IDH mutation and 1p19q co-deletion in glioma. Comput. Med. Imaging Graph. **88**, 101831 (2021). https://doi.org/10.1016/j.compmedimag.2020.101831. https://www.sciencedirect.com/science/article/pii/S0895611120301269
9. Deluche, E., et al.: CHI3L1, NTRK2, 1p/19q and IDH status predicts prognosis in glioma. Cancers **11**, 544 (2019)
10. Gaillard, F.: Diffuse glioma classification (WHO 5th edition, 2021) (2021). https://doi.org/10.53347/rid-94212
11. Haydar, N., et al.: Role of magnetic resonance imaging (MRI) in grading gliomas comparable with pathology: a cross-sectional study from Syria. Ann. Med. Surg. **82**, 104679 (2022). https://doi.org/10.1016/j.amsu.2022.104679. https://www.sciencedirect.com/science/article/pii/S204908012201439X
12. Jiang, S., Zanazzi, G.J., Hassanpour, S.: Predicting prognosis and IDH mutation status for patients with lower-grade gliomas using whole slide images. Sci. Rep. **11**, 16849 (2021)
13. Kim, D., et al.: Prediction of 1P/19Q codeletion in diffuse glioma patients using pre-operative multiparametric magnetic resonance imaging. Front. Comput. Neurosci. **13** (2019). https://doi.org/10.3389/fncom.2019.00052. https://www.frontiersin.org/articles/10.3389/fncom.2019.00052
14. Kofler, F., et al.: Brats toolkit: translating brats brain tumor segmentation algorithms into clinical and scientific practice. Front. Neurosci. **14** (2020). https://doi.org/10.3389/fnins.2020.00125. https://www.frontiersin.org/articles/10.3389/fnins.2020.00125

15. Lee, M.K., Park, J.E., Jo, Y.S., Park, S.Y., Kim, S.J., Kim, H.S.: Advanced imaging parameters improve the prediction of diffuse lower-grade gliomas subtype, IDH mutant with no 1p19q codeletion: added value to the T2/flair mismatch sign. Eur. Radiol. **30**, 844–854 (2019)
16. Li, Y., et al.: Radiomics-based method for predicting the glioma subtype as defined by tumor grade, IDH mutation, and 1p/19q codeletion. Cancers **14**, 1778 (2022)
17. Liechty, B., et al.: Machine learning can aid in prediction of IDH mutation from H&E-stained histology slides in infiltrating gliomas. Sci. Rep. **12**, 22623 (2022)
18. Liu, S., et al.: Isocitrate dehydrogenase (IDH) status prediction in histopathology images of gliomas using deep learning. Sci. Rep. **10**, 7733 (2020). https://doi.org/10.1038/s41598-020-64588-y
19. Louis, D., et al.: The 2021 who classification of tumors of the central nervous system: a summary. Neuro-Oncol. **23**, 1231–1251 (2021). https://doi.org/10.1093/neuonc/noab106
20. Ostrom, Q.T., et al.: CBTRUS statistical report: primary brain and other central nervous system tumors diagnosed in the United States in 2012–2016. Neuro-Oncol. **21**(Suppl._5), v1–v100 (2019). https://doi.org/10.1093/neuonc/noz150
21. Rathore, S., Niazi, T., Iftikhar, A., Chaddad, A.: Glioma grading via analysis of digital pathology images using machine learning. Cancers **12**, 578 (2020). https://doi.org/10.3390/cancers12030578
22. Whitfield, B.T., Huse, J.T.: Classification of adult-type diffuse gliomas: impact of the world health organization 2021 update. Brain Pathol. **32**, e13062 (2022)
23. Xue, Y., et al.: Brain tumor classification with tumor segmentations and a dual path residual convolutional neural network from MRI and pathology images. In: Crimi, A., Bakas, S. (eds.) BrainLes 2019. LNCS, vol. 11993, pp. 360–367. Springer, Cham (2020). https://doi.org/10.1007/978-3-030-46643-5_36
24. Yan, J., et al.: Predicting 1p/19q co-deletion status from magnetic resonance imaging using deep learning in adult-type diffuse lower-grade gliomas: a discovery and validation study. Lab. Invest. **102**, 154–159 (2022). https://doi.org/10.1038/s41374-021-00692-5
25. Yang, X., Lin, Y., Xing, Z., She, D., Su, Y., Cao, D.: Predicting 1p/19q codeletion status using diffusion-, susceptibility-, perfusion-weighted, and conventional MRI in IDH-mutant lower-grade gliomas. Acta Radiol. **62**, 1657–1665 (2020)
26. Zhou, H., et al.: Machine learning reveals multimodal MRI patterns predictive of isocitrate dehydrogenase and 1p/19q status in diffuse low- and high-grade gliomas. J. Neurooncol. **142**(2), 299–307 (2019). https://doi.org/10.1007/s11060-019-03096-0

Modality Cycles with Masked Conditional Diffusion for Unsupervised Anomaly Segmentation in MRI

Ziyun Liang[1]([✉]), Harry Anthony[1], Felix Wagner[1],
and Konstantinos Kamnitsas[1,2,3]

[1] Department of Engineering Science, University of Oxford, Oxford, UK
`ziyun.liang@eng.ox.ac.uk`
[2] Department of Computing, Imperial College London, London, UK
[3] School of Computer Science, University of Birmingham, Birmingham, UK

Abstract. Unsupervised anomaly segmentation aims to detect patterns that are distinct from any patterns processed during training, commonly called abnormal or out-of-distribution patterns, without providing any associated manual segmentations. Since anomalies during deployment can lead to model failure, detecting the anomaly can enhance the reliability of models, which is valuable in high-risk domains like medical imaging. This paper introduces Masked Modality Cycles with Conditional Diffusion (MMCCD), a method that enables segmentation of anomalies across diverse patterns in multimodal MRI. The method is based on two fundamental ideas. First, we propose the use of cyclic modality translation as a mechanism for enabling abnormality detection. Image-translation models learn tissue-specific modality mappings, which are characteristic of tissue physiology. Thus, these learned mappings fail to translate tissues or image patterns that have never been encountered during training, and the error enables their segmentation. Furthermore, we combine image translation with a masked conditional diffusion model, which attempts to 'imagine' what tissue exists under a masked area, further exposing unknown patterns as the generative model fails to recreate them. We evaluate our method on a proxy task by training on healthy-looking slices of BraTS2021 multi-modality MRIs and testing on slices with tumors. We show that our method compares favorably to previous unsupervised approaches based on image reconstruction and denoising with autoencoders and diffusion models. Code is available at: https://github.com/ZiyunLiang/MMCCD.

Keywords: Unsupervised Anomaly Detection and Segmentation ·
Denoising Diffusion Probabilistic Models · Multi-modality

1 Introduction

Performance of deep learning-based image analysis models after deployment can degrade if the model encounters images with 'anomalous' patterns, unlike

---

H. Anthony and F. Wagner—Equal contribution.

ⓒ The Author(s), under exclusive license to Springer Nature Switzerland AG 2023
J. Woo et al. (Eds.): MICCAI 2023 Workshops, LNCS 14394, pp. 168–181, 2023.
https://doi.org/10.1007/978-3-031-47425-5_16

any patterns processed during training. This is detrimental in high-risk applications such as pathology diagnosis where reliability is paramount. An approach attempting to alleviate this is by training a model to identify all possible abnormalities in a *supervised* manner, using methods such as outlier exposure [10,16,22,23]. However, these methods are often impractical due to the high cost associated with data collection and labeling, in conjunction with the diversity of abnormal patterns that can occur during deployment. This diversity is enormous and impractical to cover with a labeled database or to model it explicitly for data synthesis, as it includes any irregularity that can be encountered in real-world deployment, such as irregular physical compositions, discrepancies caused by different acquisition scanners, image artifacts like blurring and distortion and more. Thus, it is advantageous to develop approaches that can address the wide range of abnormalities encountered in real-world scenarios in an *unsupervised* manner. Unsupervised anomaly segmentation works by training a model to learn the patterns exhibited in the training data. Consequently, any image patterns encountered after deployment that deviate from the patterns seen during training will be identified as *anomalies*. In this paper, we delve into unsupervised anomaly segmentation with a focus on multi-modal MRI.

Related Work: Reconstruction-based methods are commonly employed for unsupervised anomaly segmentation. During training, the model is trained to model the distribution of training data. During deployment, the anomalous regions that have never been seen during training will be hard to reconstruct, leading to high reconstruction errors that enable the segmentation of anomalies. This approach employs AutoEncoders (AE), such as for anomaly segmentation in brain CT [18] and MRI [1,5], as well as Variational AutoEncoders (VAE) for brain CT [13] and MRI [5,25]. AE/VAEs have attracted significant interest, though their theoretical properties may be suboptimal for anomaly segmentation, because the encoding and decoding functions they model are not guaranteed to be tissue-specific but may be generic, and consequently they may generalize to unknown patterns. Because of this, they often reconstruct anomalous areas with fidelity which leads to false negatives in anomaly segmentation [24]. Moreover, AE/VAEs often face challenges reconstructing complex known patterns, leading to false positives [19]. Generative Adversarial Networks (GANs) [9] and Adversarially-trained AEs have also been investigated for anomaly segmentation, such as for Optical Coherence Tomography [20] and brain MRI [5] respectively. However, adversarial methods are known for unstable training and unreliable results.

A related and complementary approach is adding noise to the input image and training a model to denoise it, then reconstructing the input such that it follows the training distribution. At test time, when the model processes an unknown pattern, it attempts to 'remove' the anomalous pattern to reconstruct the input so that it follows the training distribution, enabling anomaly segmentation. This has been performed using Denoising AutoEncoders (DAE) [7,12]. It has been shown, however, that choice of magnitude and type of noise largely defines the performance [12]. The challenge lies in determining the optimal noise, which is likely to be specific to the type of anomalies. Since we often lack prior knowledge of the anomalies that might be encountered after model deployment, configuring the noise accordingly becomes a practical challenge. A related compelling approach is Denoising Diffusion Probabilistic Models (DDPM) [11], which iteratively reconstruct an image by reversing the diffusion process. [14] and [6] employed *unconditional* diffusion models by adding Gaussian noise to the input and denoising it, based on the assumption the noise will cover the anomaly and it will not be reconstructed. At the same time, both of them added masks to cover the anomaly. These unconditional Diffusion methods relate to DAE, as they also denoise and reconstruct the input image, but differ in that noise is added during test time and not only during training.

Contributions: This paper introduces a novel unsupervised anomaly segmentation method for tasks where multi-modal data are available during training, such as multi-modal MRI. The method is based on two components. First, we propose the use of cyclic-translation between modalities as a mechanism for enabling anomaly segmentation. An image translation model learns the mapping between tissue appearance in different modalities, which is characteristic of tissue physiology. As this mapping is tissue-specific, the model fails to translate anomalous patterns (e.g. unknown tissues) encountered during testing, and the error enables their segmentation. This differs from reconstruction- and denoising-based approaches, where the learned functions are not necessarily tissue-specific and may generalize to unseen patterns, leading to suboptimal anomaly segmentation. Furthermore, by employing cyclic-translation with two models, mapping back to the original modality, we enable inference on uni-modal data at test time (Fig. 1). Additionally, we combine image-translation with a Conditional Diffusion model. By using input masking, this conditional generative model performs image translation while re-creating masked image regions such that they follow the training distribution, thus removing anomalous patterns, which facilitates their segmentation via higher translation error. We term this method Masked Multi-modality Cyclic Conditional Diffusion (MMCCD). In comparison to previous works using *unconditional* Diffusion models with masking [6,14], our work uses *conditional* Diffusion, different masking strategy, and shows the approach is complementary to image-translation. We evaluate our method on tumor segmentation using multi-modal brain MRIs of BraTS'21 [2,3], a proxy task often used in related literature. We train our model on healthy-looking MRI slices and treat tumors as anomalies for segmentation during testing. We demonstrate that simple Cyclic-Translation with basic Unet outperforms reconstruction and denoising-based methods, including a state-of-the-art Diffusion-based method. We also show that MMCCD, combining cyclic-translation with masked image generation, improves results further and outperforms all compared methods.

2   Multi-modal Cycles with Masked Conditional Diffusion

Primer on Multi-modal MR: MRI (Magnetic Resonance Imaging) is acquired by exciting tissue hydrogen nuclei with Radio Frequency (RF) energy,

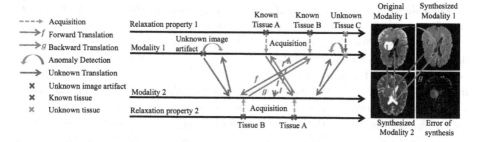

Fig. 1. Illustration of the multi-modal cyclic translation. MRI acquisition assigns different image intensities to different tissues. The cyclic translation model, shown as forward f and backward g translation respectively, learns the mappings between the two modalities for tissues within the training data. The mapping is specific to tissue physiology. Consequently, if unknown patterns are processed after deployment, the model will make random translations, leading to errors in the cyclic translation that indicate the presence of an anomaly. The right panel demonstrates how known tissues and anomalies are cyclically translated.

followed by relaxation of the nuclei. While nuclei relax and return to their low-energy state, a RF signal is emitted. The signal is measured and displayed with the shades of gray that form an MR image. Nuclei of different tissues have different relaxation properties when excited by the same RF pulse. Consequently, the RF signal they emit during relaxation also differs, creating the contrast between shades of gray depicting each tissue in an MRI. However, certain tissues may demonstrate similar relaxation properties when excited with a certain RF pulse, thus the corresponding MRI may not show the contrast between them. Therefore, different MRI modalities are obtained by measuring the relaxation properties of tissues when excited by different RF pulses. As a result, in multi-modal MRI, a tissue is considered visually separable from any other when it exhibits a unique combination of relaxation properties under different excitation signals, i.e. a unique combination of intensities in different modalities.

Cyclic Modality Translation for Anomaly Segmentation: We assume the space of two MRI modalities for simplicity, $\mathcal{X}$ and $\mathcal{Y}$. When a model f is trained to translate an image from one modality to another, $f : \mathcal{X} \rightarrow \mathcal{Y}$, it learns how the response to different RF pulses changes for a specific tissue, which is a unique, distinct characteristic of the tissue. Based on the insight that the modality-translation function is highly complex and has a unique form for different tissue types, we propose using modality-translation for anomaly segmentation. This idea is based on the assumption that in the presence of an anomalous image pattern, such as an 'unknown' tissue type never seen during training, or an out-of-distribution image artifact, the network will fail to translate its appearance to another modality, as it will not have learned the unique and multi-modal 'signature' of this anomalous pattern. Consequently, a disparity will be observed between the synthetic image (created by translation) and the real appearance of the tissue in that modality, marking it as an abnormality.

We assume training data consist of N pairs of images from two modalities, denoted as $D_{tr} = \{\mathbf{x}^i, \mathbf{y}^i\}_{i=1}^N$, where $\mathbf{x} \in \mathcal{X}$ and $\mathbf{y} \in \mathcal{Y}$. A mapping $f: \mathcal{X} \rightarrow \mathcal{Y}$ is learned with a translation network f. We denote as $\overline{\mathbf{y}} = f(\mathbf{x})$ the synthetic image in $\mathcal{Y}$ predicted by the translation network. Using the training image pairs D_{tr}, we train a model to learn the mappings between modalities.

During testing, the model processes unknown data $D_{te} = \{\mathbf{x}^i\}_{i=1}^N$. The model may be required to process images with anomalous patterns. Such patterns can be unknown tissue types or image artifacts never seen during training (Fig. 1). Our goal is to detect any such anomalous parts of input images and obtain a segmentation mask that separates them from 'normal' parts of input images, i.e. patterns that have been encountered during training.

We first perform the learned translation $f: \mathcal{X} \rightarrow \mathcal{Y}$, obtaining $\overline{\mathbf{y}} = f(\mathbf{x})$ for a test sample $\mathbf{x} \in D_{te}$. If we had the real image $\mathbf{y} \in \mathcal{Y}$, we could separate an anomaly by computing the translation error $\mathbf{a}$, which is the L2 distance between the translated image $\overline{\mathbf{y}}$ and $\mathbf{y}$: $\mathbf{a} = \|\mathbf{y} - \overline{\mathbf{y}}\|_2 > h$, where h denotes the threshold for detecting the anomaly. As we assume $\mathbf{y} \in \mathcal{Y}$ is not available during training, we separately train another network $g: \mathcal{Y} \rightarrow \mathcal{X}$ to translate images from modality $\mathcal{Y}$ back to modality $\mathcal{X}$ as $\overline{\mathbf{x}} = g(\overline{\mathbf{y}}) = g(f(\mathbf{x}))$. In this way, a cyclic translation is performed and only images from a single modality $D_{te} = \{\mathbf{x}^i\}_{i=1}^N$ are required for inference/testing. The networks will translate a test image x from modality $\mathcal{X}$ to $\mathcal{Y}$, then back to $\mathcal{X}$ without requiring testing images from modality $\mathcal{Y}$:

$$\overline{\mathbf{x}} = g(f(\mathbf{x})) \tag{1}$$

Then the anomaly is detected by computing the translation error:

$$\mathbf{a} = \|\mathbf{x} - \overline{\mathbf{x}}\|_2 > h \tag{2}$$

The cyclic translation with the two models f and g is illustrated in Fig. 1. Our goal is to detect any anomalous pattern in input image $\mathbf{x} \in \mathcal{X}$ from the cyclic translation error $\mathbf{a}$. It is worth noting at this point that this cyclic mapping process can be modeled by any existing translation network like basic UNet [15].

Conditional Masked Diffusion Models: In a given input modality $\mathcal{X}$, it is possible that an unknown pattern encountered at test time, such as a tissue never seen during training, may exhibit an appearance that is not very distinctive in comparison to another 'known' tissues. This may occur, for instance, when the input modality is not sensitive to an unknown encountered pathology, thus not highlighting it. In this case, the anomaly may be translated similar to a 'known' tissue and back to the original modality with relatively low translation error, leading to suboptimal segmentation. In the experimental section, we later provide an example for this case (Fig. 4).

To alleviate this issue, a conditional generative model f is employed to learn the translation $\mathcal{X} \rightarrow \mathcal{Y}$. We use conditional Denoising Diffusion Probabilistic Models (DDPMs) [11] due to their capability of high-fidelity image generation.

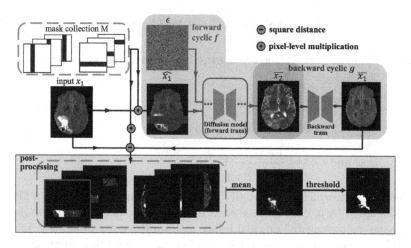

Fig. 2. The inference pipeline of our algorithm MMCCD. Image $\mathbf{x} \in \mathcal{X}$ is the input to the model. It is masked with $\mathbf{m_r}$ to $\hat{\mathbf{x}}_\mathbf{r}$ and is the condition to the forward process, which is a conditional diffusion model. The forward process translates $\mathbf{x}$ to $\overline{\mathbf{y}}$ from modality $\mathcal{Y}$. For backward translation, a UNet translates $\overline{\mathbf{y}}$ back to $\overline{\mathbf{x}}$. Finally, the anomaly is detected from the cyclic-translation error $\| \mathbf{x} - \overline{\mathbf{x}} \|_2$. We average the results from iterations using different masks and use a threshold h to segment the anomaly.

Basic diffusion models are unconditional and generate random in-distribution images. In recent works, various conditioning mechanisms have been proposed to guide the generation [8,17]. We use the input modality image as the condition for DDPM to realize translation, as described below. Furthermore, we iteratively mask different areas of the condition image $x \in \mathcal{X}$ with strong Gaussian noise and perform in-painting of the masked area (Fig. 2). The model re-fills masked areas with generated in-distribution patterns, i.e. types of tissue encountered during training, that are consistent with the surrounding unmasked area. This aims to align the translated image $\overline{y}$ to the training distribution $\mathcal{Y}$. The assumption is that in-painting by DDPM will recreate normal tissues but not recreate the unknown patterns as the model does not model them, thus enlarging the translation error of the anomalous patterns, facilitating their segmentation. We start by introducing the conditioned diffusion model used for translation, then we introduce the masked generation process.

Diffusion models have the *forward* stage and the *reverse* stage. In the *forward* stage, denoted by q, the target image for the translation process $\mathbf{y_0}$ is perturbed by gradually adding Gaussian noise via a fixed Markov chain over T iterations. The noisy image is denoted as $\mathbf{y_t}$ at iteration t. This Markov chain is defined by $q(\mathbf{y_{1:T}} \mid \mathbf{y_0}) = \prod\limits_{t=1}^{T} q(\mathbf{y_t} \mid \mathbf{y_{t-1}})$. Each step of the diffusion model can be denoted as $q(\mathbf{y_t} \mid \mathbf{y_{t-1}}) = \mathcal{N}(\mathbf{y_t} \mid \sqrt{\alpha_t}\mathbf{y_{t-1}}, (1 - \alpha_t)\mathbf{I})$, in which $0 < \alpha_t < 1$ follows a fixed schedule that determines the variance of each step's noise. Importantly, we can characterize the distribution of $\mathbf{y_t}$ as

$$q(\mathbf{y_t} \mid \mathbf{y_0}) = \mathcal{N}(\mathbf{y_t} \mid \sqrt{\overline{\alpha}_t}\mathbf{y_0}, (1 - \overline{\alpha}_t)\mathbf{I}), \tag{3}$$

where $\overline{\alpha}_t = \prod_{t=1}^{t} \alpha_i$. Furthermore, using the Bayes' theorem, we can calculate

$$q(\mathbf{y_{t-1}} \mid \mathbf{y_t}, \mathbf{y_0}) = \mathcal{N}(\mathbf{y_{t-1}} \mid \mu_t, \sigma^2 \mathbf{I}),$$

$$\text{in which} \quad \mu_t = \frac{\sqrt{\overline{\alpha}_{t-1}}\beta_t}{1 - \overline{\alpha}_t}\mathbf{y_0} + \frac{\sqrt{\alpha_t}(1 - \overline{\alpha}_{t-1})}{1 - \overline{\alpha}_t}\mathbf{y_t}, \tag{4}$$

$$\text{and} \quad \sigma^2 = \frac{1 - \overline{\alpha}_{t-1}}{1 - \overline{\alpha}_t}(1 - \alpha_t).$$

The *reverse* step, which is essentially the generative modeling, is also a Markov process denoted by p. This process aims to reverse the forward diffusion process step-by-step to recover the original image y_0 from the noisy image $\mathbf{y_T}$. In order to do this, the conditional generative model, given as condition an image $\mathbf{x}$ from modality $\mathcal{X}$, is optimized to approximate the posterior $q(\mathbf{y_{t-1}} \mid \mathbf{y_t})$ with

$$p_\theta(\mathbf{y_{t-1}} \mid \mathbf{y_t}, \mathbf{x}) = \mathcal{N}(\mathbf{y_{t-1}} \mid \mu_\theta(\mathbf{y_t}, \mathbf{x}, t), \sum_\theta(\mathbf{y_t}, \mathbf{x}, t)). \tag{5}$$

Note that in our setting, we have the image-level condition x_0 to guide the translation process. In this distribution, the variance $\sum_\theta(\mathbf{y_t}, \mathbf{x}, t)$ is fixed by the α_t schedule defined during the forward process. The input of the model is $\mathbf{y_t}$, whose marginal distribution is compatible with Eq. 3: $\tilde{\mathbf{y}}_t = \sqrt{\overline{\alpha}}\mathbf{y_0} + (1 - \overline{\alpha}_t)\epsilon$, where $\epsilon \sim \mathcal{N}(0, I)$. While we want to reverse q, the distribution becomes tractable when conditioned on $\mathbf{y_0}$ as in Eq. 4. We parameterize the model to predict $\mu_\theta(\mathbf{y_t}, \mathbf{x}, t)$ by predicting the original image $\mathbf{y_0}$. Therefore, the training objective of our diffusion model f is:

$$L_f = \|f(\mathbf{y_t}, \mathbf{x}, \alpha_t) - \mathbf{y_0}\|_2 \tag{6}$$

Furthermore, to perform cyclic translation, we also train a deterministic translation model g to translate the image from modality $\mathcal{Y}$ back to modality $\mathcal{X}$.

$$L_g = \|g(\mathbf{y_0}) - \mathbf{x}\|_2 \tag{7}$$

Furthermore, we iteratively apply a set of masks to the condition image and use the generative model to recreate them according to the training data distribution. By applying a mask, the model can in-paint simultaneously with translation. During in-painting, we utilize the strong generative ability of the diffusion model to generate in-distribution patterns under the mask, i.e. types of tissue encountered during training, with the guidance of the surrounding unmasked area. Unknown, anomalous patterns are less likely to be recreated as the DDPM is not modeling them during training. Therefore the translation error after the cyclic process will be higher between the generated parts of the image and the real image when in-painting areas of anomalous patterns, than when in-painting 'normal' (known) tissue types. Given a condition image $\mathbf{x}$ from the input modality, and a mask $\mathbf{m_r}$ where pixels with value 1 indicate the area to be masked and 0 for the unmasked area, the diffusion model becomes:

$$\hat{\mathbf{x}}_{\mathbf{r}} = (1 - \mathbf{m_r}) \odot \mathbf{x} + \mathbf{m_r} \odot \epsilon \tag{8}$$

where $\epsilon \sim \mathcal{N}(0, I)$, covering the masked area with white noise. During training, the mask is randomly positioned within the image. The training loss for the masked diffusion then becomes:

$$L_f = \|f(\mathbf{y_t}, \hat{\mathbf{x}}_{\mathbf{r}}, \alpha_t) - \mathbf{y_0}\|_2 \tag{9}$$

During testing, since we want to detect the abnormality in the whole image, we design a collection of masks, recorded as $\mathbf{M} = \{\mathbf{m_1}, \mathbf{m_2}, ..., \mathbf{m_R}\}$, where R equals the total mask number. For each mask, the diffusion model f performs the reverse steps $t = T, ... 1$ using masked condition $\hat{x}_r$ (Eq. 8) to translate the condition $\hat{x}_r$ to corresponding $\overline{y}_0$ while in-painting masked areas. Then the output prediction $\overline{y}_0$ is given as input to backward translation model g and is translated back to the original modality space $\mathcal{X}$ deterministically, without masking. The final abnormality is detected by:

$$\mathbf{a} = \frac{1}{\sum_{r=1}^{R} \mathbf{m_r}} \sum_{r=1}^{R} \mathbf{m_r} \| g(f(\mathbf{x}, \mathbf{m_r})) - \mathbf{x} \|_2 > h \tag{10}$$

where the sums and division are performed voxel-wise, and f denotes the complete diffusion process with T diffusion step. The prediction from model $f(\mathbf{x}, \mathbf{m_r})$ is the input to g. The threshold for detecting anomalies is given by h. The pipeline for training and testing is shown in Algorithm 1 and Algorithm 2 respectively.

Algorithm 1: Training	**Algorithm 2:** Testing
Data: $(\mathbf{x}, \mathbf{y}) \sim \{\mathbf{x^i}, \mathbf{y^i}\}_{i=1}^{N}$	**Data:** $\mathbf{x} \sim \{\mathbf{x^i}\}_{i=1}^{N}$
1 $\mathbf{m}_r \in \{\mathbf{m_1}, \mathbf{m_2}, ..., \mathbf{m_n}\}$;	1 $\mathbf{y_T} \sim \mathcal{N}(0, I), \mathbf{x_T} \sim \mathcal{N}(0, I)$;
2 $\epsilon_1, \epsilon_2, \epsilon_3, \epsilon_4 \in \mathcal{N}(0, 1)$;	2 **for** $\mathbf{m}_r \in \{\mathbf{m_1}, \mathbf{m_2}, ..., \mathbf{m_n}\}$ **do**
3 $\alpha_t \sim p(\alpha)$;	3 $\quad \epsilon_1 \in \mathcal{N}(0, 1)$;
4 $\hat{\mathbf{y}}_{\mathbf{r}} = (1 - \mathbf{m_r}) \odot \mathbf{y} + \mathbf{m_r} \odot \epsilon_1$;	4 $\quad \hat{\mathbf{x}}_{\mathbf{r}} = (1 - \mathbf{m_r}) \odot \mathbf{x} + \mathbf{m_r} \odot \epsilon_1$;
5 $\hat{\mathbf{x}}_{\mathbf{r}} = (1 - \mathbf{m_r}) \odot \mathbf{x} + \mathbf{m_r} \odot \epsilon_2$;	5 $\quad$ **for** $t = T, ..., 1$ **do**
6 $\tilde{\mathbf{x}}_t = \sqrt{\overline{\alpha}_t}\mathbf{x} + (1 - \overline{\alpha}_t)\epsilon_3$;	6 $\quad\quad \epsilon \sim \mathcal{N}(0, I)$ if $t > 1$, else
7 $\tilde{\mathbf{y}}_t = \sqrt{\overline{\alpha}_t}\mathbf{y} + (1 - \overline{\alpha}_t)\epsilon_4$;	$\quad\quad \epsilon = 0$;
8 Gradient descent on:	7 $\quad\quad \overline{\mathbf{y}}_{\mathbf{t-1, r}} =$
$\quad L_f = \|f(\mathbf{y_t}, \hat{\mathbf{x}}_{\mathbf{r}}, \alpha_t) - \mathbf{y}\|_2$;	$\quad\quad \frac{\sqrt{\overline{\alpha}_{t-1}}\beta_t}{1 - \overline{\alpha}_t} f(\hat{\mathbf{x}}_{\mathbf{r}}, \overline{\mathbf{y}_{\mathbf{t,r}}}, \alpha_t) +$
9 $L_g = \|g(\mathbf{y}) - \mathbf{x}\|_2$;	$\quad\quad \frac{\sqrt{\alpha_t}(1 - \overline{\alpha}_{t-1})}{1 - \overline{\alpha}_t} \overline{\mathbf{y}}_{\mathbf{t,r}} + \sqrt{1 - \alpha_t}\epsilon$
	8 $\quad$ **end**
	9 $\quad \overline{\mathbf{x}}_{\mathbf{r}} = g(\overline{\mathbf{y}}_{\mathbf{r}})$;
	10 **end**
	11 $\mathbf{a} = \frac{1}{\sum_{r=1}^{n} \mathbf{m_r}} \sum_{r=1}^{n} \mathbf{m_r} \odot$
	$\quad\quad \|\overline{\mathbf{x}}_{\mathbf{r}} - \mathbf{x}\|_2 > h$;

3   Experiments

Dataset: For evaluation, as commonly done in literature for unsupervised anomaly segmentation, we evaluate our method on the proxy task of learning normal brain tissues during training and attempt to segment brain pathologies in an unsupervised manner at test time. To conduct the evaluation, we use the BraTS2021 dataset [2,3]. 80% of the images are used for training, 10% for validation, and 10% for testing. We used FLAIR, T1, and T2 in our various experiments. We normalized each image by subtracting the mean and dividing by the standard deviation of the brain intensities between the 2% and 98% percentiles for T1, T2, and 2%–90% for FLAIR which presents more extreme hyper-intensities. We evaluate our method using 2D models, as commonly done in previous works to simplify experimentation. For this purpose, from every 3D image, we extract slices 70 to 90, that mostly capture the central part of the brain. For model training, from the slices extracted from the training subjects, we only use those that do not contain any tumors. For validation and testing of all compared methods, from each validation and test subject, we use the slice that contains the largest tumor area out of the 20 central slices.

Model Configuration: The diffusion model, Cyclic UNet, and MMCCD use the same UNet as in [8] for a fair comparison. The image condition is given by concatenating $\mathbf{x}$ as an input channel with $\mathbf{y_t}$ as in [17]. Adam optimizer is used and the learning rate is set to $1e - 4$. The model is trained with a batch size of 32. To accelerate the sampling process of the diffusion model, the method of DDIM [21] is used that speeds up sampling tenfold. Input slices are resampled to 128×128 pixels to be compatible with this UNet architecture. For MMCCD, the mask's size is 16×128 pixels. To ensure complete coverage of the brain, we gradually move the mask with a stride of 2, obtaining one $\mathbf{m_r}$ (Eq. 10) for each valid position, along with the corresponding prediction. This is repeated for horizontal and vertical masks. All hyper-parameters for our method and compared baselines were found on the validation set.

Evaluation: We compare a variety of unsupervised abnormality segmentation methods. We assess as baselines an AE and DAE [12], VAE [4], and DDPM [14]. In the first setting, as common in previous works, we compare methods for unsupervised segmentation of tumors in the FLAIR modality. We train the aforementioned models on normal-looking FLAIR slices. We then test them on FLAIR slices from the test set that includes tumor. To show the potential of cyclic modality translation for unsupervised anomaly segmentation, we assess a Cyclic UNet, where f and g are two UNets trained separately. In this setting, the two UNets are trained on normal-looking slices where $\mathcal{X}$ is FLAIR and $\mathcal{Y}$ is T2 modality. We emphasize that the real FLAIR and T2 images are only needed during training, whereas the model only needs FLAIR during testing, making Cyclic UNet comparable with the aforementioned baselines at test time. Similarly, to assess the added effect of masking, we train MMCCD similarly to Cyclic UNet. We show performance on the test set in Table 1. Performance is evaluated using Dice coefficient (DICE), area under the curve (AUC), Jaccard index (Jac), precision (Prec), recall (Rec), and average symmetric surface distance (ASSD).

AE and VAE baselines show what a basic reconstruction model can achieve. DAE further improves the abnormality segmentation performance by introducing Gaussian noise. It is likely that more complex noise may improve results, but the type of optimal noise may be dependent on the specific studied task of anomaly segmentation. Since the effect of noise is not studied in this work, we only include the results using Gaussian noise. This also facilitates fair comparison with the DDPM model, which also uses Gaussian noise for distorting the image, similar to [14]. DDPM outperforms the AE, VAE, and DAE baselines. We did not include GAN-based approaches as the DDPM-based model is reported to outperform GAN-based approaches in other works [12,14] and it is notoriously challenging to train adequately. The high performance of Cyclic UNet is evidence that relying on the mapping between modalities is a very promising mechanism for unsupervised anomaly segmentation. The simplest Cyclic UNet, without any noise or masking, significantly outperforms methods relying on reconstructing (i.e. approximate the identity function) in most metrics with AE and VAE, or denoising with DAE and DDPM. Combining the cyclic translation with a diffusion model and masking further improves performance, achieving the best results in almost all metrics (Fig. 3). Finally, we note that masking can be viewed as a type of noise, and thus we speculate that the proposed cyclic-translation mechanism could be combined effectively with other types of noise and not just the proposed masking mechanism, but such investigation is left for future work.

Table 1. Performance for unsupervised anomaly segmentation of tumors with FLAIR as input modality $\mathcal{X}$. Cyclic UNet and MMCCD translate FLAIR ($\mathcal{X}$) to T2 ($\mathcal{Y}$) and back. Best results are shown in bold.

	DICE	AUC	Jac	Prec	Rec	ASSD
AE [4]	0.2249	0.4621	0.1513	0.2190	0.2636	3.5936
VAE [4]	0.2640	0.4739	0.1910	0.2717	0.2837	**3.513**
DAE [12]	0.4619	0.9298	0.3291	0.4346	0.5477	7.5508
DDPM [14]	0.5662	0.9267	0.4172	0.5958	0.5949	6.5021
Cyclic UNet	0.5810	0.9409	0.4470	**0.6545**	0.5823	6.3487
MMCCD	**0.6092**	**0.9409**	**0.4682**	0.6505	**0.6336**	6.1171

We further evaluate the methods using different MRI modalities for $\mathcal{X}$ and $\mathcal{Y}$, as shown in Table 2. In these experiments, input modality $\mathcal{X}$ refers to the modality in which we aim to segment the anomalous patterns. Modality $\mathcal{Y}$ serves as the target for translation by Cyclic Unet and MMCCD. We compare with DAE, as it is the auto-encoder model found most promising in experiments of Table 1, and DDPM for comparing with the state-of-the-art diffusion-based method. For DAE and DDPM, only the first modality is used for both training and testing. For Cyclic UNet and MMCCD, which include the cyclic translation process,

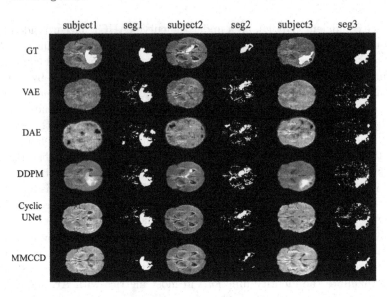

Fig. 3. The visualization results for different methods on three examples from FLAIR modality. Each row from top to bottom: ground-truth of the image/ segmentation label, VAE [4], DAE [12], DDPM [14], Cyclic UNet, and MMCCD.

we include settings on FL-T2-FL, FL-T1-FL, T2-FL-T2, T2-T1-T2, T1-T2-T1, and T1-FL-T1. During testing, Cyclic UNet and MMCCD are tested using only inputs of modality $\mathcal{X}$. Table 2 reports results using DICE. These experiments show that for all methods, as expected, the visibility and distinctiveness of tumors in input $\mathcal{X}$ largely affects segmentation quality. Using FLAIR as input yields the highest scores because tumors in FLAIR exhibit a distinctive intensity response, deviating significantly from the normal tissue. Using T1 as input results in the lowest performance because only part of the tumor is visible in this modality.

Table 2. Performance for different combination of $\mathcal{X}$ and $\mathcal{Y}$ modalities of BraTS. DICE is reported. (FL is FLAIR)

| Input modality ($\mathcal{X}$) | FL | FL | T2 | T2 | T1 | T1 |
Translated modality ($\mathcal{Y}$)	T2	T1	FL	T1	T2	FL
DAE [12]	0.4619	0.4619	0.2803	0.2803	0.2325	0.2325
DDPM [14]	0.5662	0.5662	0.4633	0.4633	0.2865	0.2865
Cyclic UNet	0.5810	0.5732	0.4819	0.4036	0.3262	0.3906
MMCCD	**0.6092**	**0.6090**	**0.4873**	**0.4993**	**0.3337**	**0.4239**

As Table 2 shows, Cyclic UNet outperforms compared methods in most settings, supporting that cyclic translation is a promising approach regardless the modality of the data. One exception arises in the T2-T1-T2 setting, and we attribute this to the similar response to the RF signal in T1 from tumor tissues and non-tumor tissues, as shown in Fig. 4. In this example, the tumor area is erroneously detected as a ventricle and was recreated after cyclic translation, leading to low cyclic-translation error under the tumor area. In this setting, MMCCD that integrates masking and diffusion models exhibits an improvement of 9.57% over Cyclic UNet, and outperforms all methods, highlighting the complementary effectiveness of generative in-painting with modality-cycles.

When input modality $\mathcal{X}$ is T1, the tumor's intensity falls within the range of normal tissue, and it's easy for the network to reconstruct the tumor well instead of perceiving it as unknown, making it challenging to detect anomalies. In this setting, the Cyclic UNet shows noticeable improvements, with 3.97% improvement on T1-T2-T1 setting and a 10.41% on T1-FL-T1, demonstrating Cyclic UNet's ability to effectively capture the subtle differences between tissues.

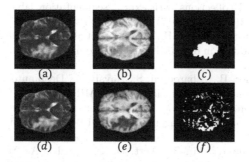

Fig. 4. Example failure case of cyclic translation T2-T1-T2 with Cyclic Unet, because anomaly exhibits similar appearance to normal tissues in the input modality. (a) input modality T2, (b) target modality T1, (c) tumor ground-truth, (d) cyclic translation result $\bar{x}$, (e) forward translation result $\bar{y}$, (f) predicted anomaly.

4   Conclusion

This paper proposed the use of cyclic translation between modalities as a mechanism for unsupervised abnormality segmentation for multimodal MRI. Our experiments showed that translating between modalities with a Cyclic UNet outperforms reconstruction-based approaches with autoencoders and state-of-the-art denoising-based approaches with diffusion models. We further extend the approach using a masked conditional diffusion model to incorporate in-painting into the translation process. We show that the resulting MMCCD model outperforms all compared approaches for unsupervised segmentation of tumors in brain MRI. The method requires multi-modal data for training, but only one modality at inference time. These results demonstrate the potential of multi-modal translation as a mechanism for facilitating unsupervised anomaly segmentation.

Acknowledgements. ZL and HA are supported by scholarships provided by the EPSRC Doctoral Training Partnerships programme [EP/W524311/1]. FW is supported by the EPSRC Centre for Doctoral Training in Health Data Science (EP/S02428X/1), by the Anglo-Austrian Society, and by the Reuben Foundation. The authors also acknowledge the use of the University of Oxford Advanced Research Computing (ARC) facility in carrying out this work (http://dx.doi.org/10.5281/zenodo.22558).

References

1. Atlason, H.E., Love, A., Sigurdsson, S., Gudnason, V., et al.: Unsupervised brain lesion segmentation from MRI using a convolutional autoencoder. In: Medical Imaging 2019: Image Processing, vol. 10949, pp. 372–378. SPIE (2019)
2. Baid, U., Ghodasara, S., Mohan, S., Bilello, M., et al.: The RSNA-ASNR-MICCAI brats 2021 benchmark on brain tumor segmentation and radiogenomic classification. arXiv preprint arXiv:2107.02314 (2021)
3. Bakas, S., Akbari, H., Sotiras, A., Bilello, M., et al.: Advancing the cancer genome atlas glioma MRI collections with expert segmentation labels and radiomic features. Sci. Data **4**(1), 1–13 (2017)
4. Baur, C., Denner, S., Wiestler, B., Navab, N., et al.: Autoencoders for unsupervised anomaly segmentation in brain MR images: a comparative study. Med. Image Anal. **69**, 101952 (2021)
5. Baur, C., Wiestler, B., Albarqouni, S., Navab, N.: Deep autoencoding models for unsupervised anomaly segmentation in brain MR images. In: Crimi, A., Bakas, S., Kuijf, H., Keyvan, F., Reyes, M., van Walsum, T. (eds.) BrainLes 2018. LNCS, vol. 11383, pp. 161–169. Springer, Cham (2019). https://doi.org/10.1007/978-3-030-11723-8_16
6. Bercea, C.I., Neumayr, M., Rueckert, D., Schnabel, J.A.: Mask, stitch, and resample: enhancing robustness and generalizability in anomaly detection through automatic diffusion models. arXiv preprint arXiv:2305.19643 (2023)
7. Chen, X., Pawlowski, N., Rajchl, M., Glocker, B., et al.: Deep generative models in the real-world: an open challenge from medical imaging. arXiv preprint arXiv:1806.05452 (2018)
8. Dhariwal, P., Nichol, A.: Diffusion models beat GANs on image synthesis. Adv. Neural. Inf. Process. Syst. **34**, 8780–8794 (2021)
9. Goodfellow, I., Pouget-Abadie, J., Mirza, M., Xu, B., et al.: Generative adversarial networks. Commun. ACM **63**(11), 139–144 (2020)
10. Hendrycks, D., Mazeika, M., Dietterich, T.: Deep anomaly detection with outlier exposure. In: International Conference on Learning Representations (2018)
11. Ho, J., Jain, A., Abbeel, P.: Denoising diffusion probabilistic models. Adv. Neural. Inf. Process. Syst. **33**, 6840–6851 (2020)
12. Kascenas, A., Pugeault, N., O'Neil, A.Q.: Denoising autoencoders for unsupervised anomaly detection in brain MRI. In: International Conference on Medical Imaging with Deep Learning, pp. 653–664. PMLR (2022)
13. Pawlowski, N., Lee, M.C., Rajchl, M., McDonagh, S., et al.: Unsupervised lesion detection in brain CT using Bayesian convolutional autoencoders (2018)
14. Pinaya, W.H., Graham, M.S., Gray, R., Da Costa, P.F., et al.: Fast unsupervised brain anomaly detection and segmentation with diffusion models. In: Wang, L., Dou, Q., Fletcher, P.T., Speidel, S., Li, S. (eds.) MICCAI 2022. LNCS, vol. 13438, pp. 705–714. Springer, Cham (2022). https://doi.org/10.1007/978-3-031-16452-1_67

15. Ronneberger, O., Fischer, P., Brox, T.: U-Net: convolutional networks for biomedical image segmentation. In: Navab, N., Hornegger, J., Wells, W.M., Frangi, A.F. (eds.) MICCAI 2015. LNCS, vol. 9351, pp. 234–241. Springer, Cham (2015). https://doi.org/10.1007/978-3-319-24574-4_28
16. Roy, A.G., Ren, J., Azizi, S., Loh, A., et al.: Does your dermatology classifier know what it doesn't know? Detecting the long-tail of unseen conditions. Med. Image Anal. **75**, 102274 (2022)
17. Saharia, C., Ho, J., Chan, W., Salimans, T., et al.: Image super-resolution via iterative refinement. IEEE Trans. Pattern Anal. Mach. Intell. **45**(4), 4713–4726 (2022)
18. Sato, D., Hanaoka, S., Nomura, Y., Takenaga, T., et al.: A primitive study on unsupervised anomaly detection with an autoencoder in emergency head CT volumes. In: Medical Imaging 2018: Computer-Aided Diagnosis, vol. 10575, pp. 388–393. SPIE (2018)
19. Saxena, D., Cao, J.: Generative adversarial networks (GANs) challenges, solutions, and future directions. ACM Comput. Surv. (CSUR) **54**(3), 1–42 (2021)
20. Schlegl, T., Seeböck, P., Waldstein, S.M., Langs, G., et al.: f-AnoGAN: fast unsupervised anomaly detection with generative adversarial networks. Med. Image Anal. **54**, 30–44 (2019)
21. Song, J., Meng, C., Ermon, S.: Denoising diffusion implicit models. arXiv preprint arXiv:2010.02502 (2020)
22. Tan, J., Hou, B., Batten, J., Qiu, H., et al.: Detecting outliers with foreign patch interpolation. Mach. Learn. Biomed. Imaging **1**, 1–27 (2022)
23. Tan, Z., Chen, D., Chu, Q., Chai, M., et al.: Efficient semantic image synthesis via class-adaptive normalization. IEEE Trans. Pattern Anal. Mach. Intell. **44**(9), 4852–4866 (2021)
24. Yan, X., Zhang, H., Xu, X., Hu, X., et al.: Learning semantic context from normal samples for unsupervised anomaly detection. In: Proceedings of the AAAI Conference on Artificial Intelligence, vol. 35, pp. 3110–3118 (2021)
25. Zimmerer, D., Isensee, F., Petersen, J., Kohl, S., Maier-Hein, K.: Unsupervised anomaly localization using variational auto-encoders. In: Shen, D., et al. (eds.) MICCAI 2019. LNCS, vol. 11767, pp. 289–297. Springer, Cham (2019). https://doi.org/10.1007/978-3-030-32251-9_32

BreastRegNet: A Deep Learning Framework for Registration of Breast Faxitron and Histopathology Images

Negar Golestani[1]($\boxtimes$) (iD), Aihui Wang[2], Gregory R. Bean[2] (iD), and Mirabela Rusu[1,3,4]($\boxtimes$) (iD)

[1] Department of Radiology, Stanford University, Stanford, CA, USA
{negaar,mirabela.rusu}@stanford.edu
[2] Department of Pathology, Stanford University, Stanford, CA, USA
[3] Department of Urology, Stanford University, Stanford, CA, USA
[4] Department of Biomedical Data Science, Stanford University, Stanford, CA, USA

Abstract. A standard treatment protocol for breast cancer entails administering neoadjuvant therapy followed by surgical removal of the tumor and surrounding tissue. Pathologists typically rely on cabinet X-ray radiographs, known as Faxitron, to examine the excised breast tissue and diagnose the extent of residual disease. However, accurately determining the location, size, and focality of residual cancer can be challenging, and incorrect assessments can lead to clinical consequences. The utilization of automated methods can improve the histopathology process, allowing pathologists to choose regions for sampling more effectively and precisely. Despite the recognized necessity, there are currently no such methods available. Training such automated detection models require accurate ground truth labels on ex-vivo radiology images, which can be acquired through registering Faxitron and histopathology images and mapping the extent of cancer from histopathology to x-ray images. This study introduces a deep learning-based image registration approach trained on mono-modal synthetic image pairs. The models were trained using data from 50 women who received neoadjuvant chemotherapy and underwent surgery. The results demonstrate that our method is faster and yields significantly lower average landmark error (2.1 ± 1.96 mm) over the state-of-the-art iterative (4.43 ± 4.1 mm) and deep learning (4.02 ± 3.15 mm) approaches. Improved performance of our approach in integrating radiology and pathology information facilitates generating large datasets, which allows training models for more accurate breast cancer detection.

Supported by the Department of Radiology at Stanford University, Philips Healthcare, Stanford Cancer Imaging Training Program (T32 CA009695), and National Cancer Institute (R37CA260346). The content is solely the responsibility of the authors and does not necessarily represent the official views of the National Institutes of Health.

J. Woo et al. (Eds.): MICCAI 2023 Workshops, LNCS 14394, pp. 182–192, 2023.
https://doi.org/10.1007/978-3-031-47425-5_17

1   Introduction

Breast cancer is a prevalent and fatal disease, and it ranks as the most frequently diagnosed cancer among women in several nations, including the United States [1]. The diagnostic process usually involves mammography, breast ultrasound, and biopsy, with treatment options dependent on diagnosis results. One standard treatment approach for breast cancers meeting certain clinicopathologic criteria involves neoadjuvant therapy followed by surgery [2]. After surgery, pathologists analyze excised tissue specimens to obtain information on tumor size, grade, stage, and margin status of residual cancer, which is crucial in determining further treatment options. Pathology processing includes imaging gross sections using cabinet x-ray radiographs (Faxitron), with only a select few representative sections being further processed for histology. Pathologists manually select these representative samples based on gross examination and Faxitron radiographs, but it is an estimation and subject to error.

Accurate identification of the tumor site and extent of the disease is a challenging task that can lead to delays in the pathology process and require additional follow-up if the initial estimation is inaccurate [3]. The automated identification of residual tumors or tumor bed on excised tissue radiographs can significantly improve the pathology workflow and diagnostic accuracy, ultimately leading to faster turnaround for results and improved prognosticating of patient outcomes. However, no automated methods currently exist to differentiate residual tumors from reactive stromal changes on Faxitron radiographs. To address this limitation, the registration of Faxitron and histopathology images represents a critical step towards accurately mapping the extent of cancer from histopathology images onto their corresponding Faxitron radiographs of ex-vivo tissue. However, aligning the two images poses three major challenges: variations in cancer appearance across different modalities, imprecise correspondence due to a rough estimate of sampled tissue within the Faxitron image, and differences in image format and content, with Faxitron images displaying a projection of the entire gross slice or macrosection in the x-ray, whereas pathology images are $5\mu m$ sections at various depths through the tissue block, leading to potential inaccuracies in registration.

Multi-modal image registration can be achieved using traditional iterative or deep learning approaches. Iterative methods minimize a cost function through optimization techniques, but they can be computationally demanding and may easily be trapped in local optima, resulting in incorrect alignments [4–8]. In contrast, deep learning-based image registration trains neural networks to align moving images with fixed images, which eliminates the need for an iterative optimization process and can directly align input images, thereby speeding up the registration process [9–16]. Although deep learning has been successful in medical image registration, many studies have relied on supervised approaches that require large labeled datasets [17,18]. However, our Faxitron-Histopathology dataset lacks ground-truth registered images, making it unsuitable for supervised methods. Unsupervised techniques can address the limited training data issue, but they mainly focus on mono-modal registration, with limited studies on multi-modal registration [17].

We introduce the breast registration network (BreastRegNet), a deep learning approach for affine registration of breast Faxitron and histopathology images. To avoid the need for ground truth alignment, we employ weakly supervised strategies during training and integrate unsupervised intensity, segmentation, and regularization terms in our loss function. We train the network on synthetic mono-modal data and their tissue segmentation masks to overcome the limitations of multi-modal similarity measures, which are unsuitable for this problem due to the uncorrelated intensities of Faxitron and histopathology images. During training, the standard distribution distance measure incorporated as the regularizer loss term trains the network to extract input image representations with minimized distribution distance. It enables the network to accurately process multi-modal data at the inference stage without requiring tissue segmentations, as it has learned to solve image registration problems regardless of the image modalities. The main contributions of our study are summarized as follows:

- Introduction of the first deep-learning approach designed to register breast Faxitron-histopathology images.
- Implementation of a weakly supervised network that tackles two main challenges in registering multi-modal data: absence of ground-truth training data and limitations of multi-modal similarity metrics.
- Utilization of domain confusion loss as the regularization term to enable joint optimization of image features for registration and domain invariance.

2   Methods

2.1   Data Description and Analysis

This study, approved by the institutional review board, includes data from 50 women participants who received neoadjuvant chemotherapy and subsequently underwent surgical excision. Tissue samples were processed according to standard protocols, with macrosection distances varying based on the specimen size (~3 mm for lumpectomies and up to ~1 cm for mastectomies). A Faxitron radiograph with a pixel size of 3440×3440 was obtained for each patient to provide an ex-vivo view of the macrosections of resected and sectioned tissue. Depending on the specimen size, histological examination was conducted on either the entire excision or specific sections. Therefore, digital hematoxylin and eosin (H&E) images with a pixel size of 4600×6000 were acquired for the tissue segments with their approximate location annotated as labeled box regions of interest (Box-ROIs) on the corresponding Faxitron image by the pathologists.

The histopathology and Faxitron images corresponding to each tissue segment were extracted and processed. The resulting dataset consisted of 1093 pairs of histopathology and Faxitron images. A breast subspecialty pathologist evaluated the histopathology images using clinical reports and re-reviewed all cases to annotate the extent of residual cancer or tumor bed in cases of complete pathologic response. Tissue masks on both images were automatically extracted and manually verified. Furthermore, matching landmarks were manually annotated based on visual similarities by an expert image analyst with two years of experience reviewing Faxitron and histopathology images of the breast.

2.2   Registration Network

Our proposed network for registering Faxitron and histopathology images of the breast is shown in Fig. 1. In this work, we considered the Faxitron and histopathology images as the fixed and moving images, respectively, and resampled them to 224×224 pixels before feeding them into the network. The registration network consists of two separate feature extraction networks, each tailored for one of the image types (i.e., Faxitron or histopathology), to capture the discriminative features of the input images. We employed pre-trained VGG-16 networks, cropped at the fourth block layer, followed by per-feature L2 normalization. These networks, trained on the ImageNet dataset [19], take the moving image $I_m \in \mathbb{R}^{H \times W \times 3}$ and the fixed image $I_f \in \mathbb{R}^{H \times W \times 3}$ as inputs to produce their corresponding feature maps $F_m, F_f \in \mathbb{R}^{H \times W \times d}$. The resulting feature images, with a grid size of $H \times W$ and d-dimensional voxel vectors, are subsequently normalized and provided as input to a correlation layer.

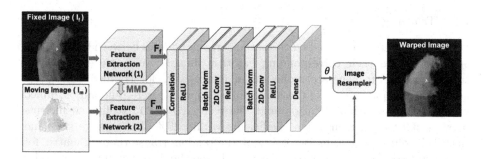

Fig. 1. Overview of the proposed deep learning-based registration network.

This correlation layer integrates the feature images into a single correlation map C_{mf} of the same size and voxel length of $H \times W$, containing all pairwise correlation coefficients between feature vectors [20], as given by:

$$C_{mf}(i,j,k) = \frac{\text{cov}\big[\, F_m(i,j) \cdot F_f(p,q) \,\big]}{\text{std}\big[\, F_m(i,j) \,\big] \, \text{std}\big[\, F_f(p,q) \,\big]} \tag{1}$$

where $k = p + H(q - 1)$, and $F_m(i,j)$ and $F_f(p,q)$ are the feature vectors positioned at (i,j) and (p,q) in the feature maps corresponding to moving and fixed images, respectively. The notation cov[.] indicates covariance, and std[.] denotes standard deviation.

The correlation map obtained is subjected to normalization by applying a rectified linear unit (ReLU) and channel-wise L2 normalization at each spatial location to down-weight ambiguous matches. The normalized correlation map F_{mf} is then passed through two stacked blocks of convolutional layers and a fully connected layer. Each convolutional block consists of a convolutional unit, batch normalization, and ReLU activation designed to reduce the dimensionality of the correlation map. The network outputs a vector of length six representing the affine transformation parameters between the input images.

Instead of using direct estimations as the transformation matrix, we employed the approach proposed in [14], which adds an identity transform to scaled parameters. This technique keeps the initial estimation close to the identity map, thereby improving the stability of the model. The final matrix is defined as $\theta = \alpha\hat{\theta} + \theta_{Id}^{aff}$, where $\hat{\theta}$ is the estimated affine matrix by the network, θ_{Id}^{aff} is the parameter vector for affine identity transform, and the scaling factor α was set to a small constant of 0.1. Using the final transformation matrix, original histopathology images, cancer labels, and landmarks can be mapped to their corresponding Faxitron images. It should be noted that the registration network estimates the transformation parameters using preprocessed and resized Faxitron and histopathology images, while the resampler takes original high-resolution histopathology images and their corresponding data to produce the warped sample.

2.3 Training

Due to the absence of ground truth spatial correspondences between histopathology images and their corresponding Faxitron images, we employed synthetic transformations to generate mono-modal image pairs for training our neural networks. The parameters of the affine transformations were randomly sampled with constraints such as rotation angle between -20 to $20°$, scaling coefficients between 0.9 to 1.1, translation coefficients within 20% of the image size, and shearing coefficients within 5%. We created a random transformation matrix for each histopathology and Faxitron image and used the deformed images as training samples, along with their original image and transformation matrix. The network is trained by minimizing a loss function defined as:

$$\mathcal{L} = L_{int} + L_{seg} + \lambda L_{reg} \tag{2}$$

where L_{int}, L_{seg}, and L_{ref} denote image similarity loss, segmentation loss, and regularization loss, respectively. The hyperparameter $\lambda = 0.01$ controls the contribution of the regularization objective.

We employed the mean squared error (MSE) as an unsupervised measure of intensity loss between the fixed image I_f and the warped images I_w, as the training dataset consisted of synthetic mono-modal samples. Furthermore, we defined the segmentation loss L_{seg} as the Dice loss between the fixed tissue mask M_f and the warped tissue mask M_w. During training, the inclusion of this loss term allows models to learn from tissue masks and eliminates the necessity for masks during inference, resulting in a weakly-supervised approach.

Training a network to estimate transformation parameters using only synthetic mono-modal samples can result in overfitting the model in processing images from the same modality, leading to a suboptimal performance on test data involving multi-modal samples. To address this issue, inspired by domain adaptation approaches [21,22], we utilized the maximum mean discrepancy (MMD) as a regularization loss function to measure the distance between the distributions of fixed and moving features produced by two feature extraction networks. By minimizing the discrepancy between feature representations, the two networks can be trained to generate feature representations that are more similar to each other. It allows us to leverage the neural network trained on mono-modal samples during the training phase to estimate the transformation parameters at inference time when the input samples originate from different modalities and feature representations from distinct domains.

2.4   Evaluation Metrics

We used two metrics to evaluate the alignment accuracy between the moving (histopathology) and corresponding fixed (Faxitron) images. The first metric was the total execution time (ET), which represents the time required for the approach to execute. The second metric used was the mean landmark error (MLE) defined as:

$$MLE = \frac{1}{N} \sum_{i=1}^{N} ||p_i - \phi_\theta(q_i)|| \tag{3}$$

where $\{p_i\}_{i=1}^{N}$ and $\{q_i\}_{i=1}^{N}$ denote the N pairs of landmarks in fixed and moving images. The parameter ϕ_θ represents a transformation parameterized by θ.

2.5   Implementation Details

The models were implemented using PyTorch [23] and trained on an NVIDIA RTX A6000 GPU and an Intel Core i9-10900K CPU (with 16 GB of memory and a 3.70 GHz clock speed). We employed the Adam optimization algorithm [24] with an initial learning rate of 10^{-4}, a learning rate decay of 0.95, a step size of 1, and a batch size of 64 to train the networks. We used 5-fold cross-validation to partition the patient data. For each fold, we trained the model on synthetic data generated from the data of four folds over 50 epochs and then tested it on the clinical data of patients within the remaining fold. The code is available online at: https://github.com/pimed/BreastRegNet.

3   Results

We evaluated the performance of our deep learning model in comparison to existing multi-modal registration techniques, including an iterative approach and a deep learning-based method. The iterative registration method available from SimpleITK [5,6] was implemented as a configurable multi-resolution registration approach trained using normalized mutual information (NMI) loss. Deep learning-based approaches were also employed as baselines for comparative analysis. We utilized the CNNGeometric approach [9], a deep learning network trained on a synthetic dataset with generated affine transformations. The training employed a loss function based on point location differences. Additionally, we implemented ProsRegNet [14], a CNN-based model for MRI-histopathology image registration in prostate cancer. Another baseline approach, C2FViT [25], a coarse-to-fine vision transformer model for affine transformations, was also included.

To ensure consistency and fairness in the evaluation, all models in our study were trained under similar conditions as our proposed BreastRegNet method. The hyperparameters used in each model were based on their original studies. Furthermore, as presented in our model, we parametrized the affine transformations using a weighted sum of an identity transform and the estimated parameter vector for improved stability and robustness.

Figure 2 illustrates the outcomes acquired for the upper and lower regions of a breast tissue segment, corresponding to the superior and inferior halves. The alignment examples generated by our BreastRegNet indicate that the boundaries of breast tissue between the Faxitron and histopathology sections are precisely aligned, demonstrating the efficacy of the method in achieving an accurate global alignment of the tissue. These results suggest that, despite being trained on mono-modal input, our model can process multi-modal data and improve alignment accuracy, as evidenced by the reduction in landmark error. Moreover, the outcomes suggest that iterative registration methods, such as those provided by SimpleITK, may exhibit suboptimal performance in specific scenarios, even inferior to not performing registration. One possible explanation is the inability of the algorithm to handle missing data effectively. For example, when there is a significant mismatch in tissue areas between Faxitron and histopathology images, the SimpleITK iterative registration may attempt to align the histopathology image with the complete tissue in the Faxitron segment without considering shape matching at the boundaries. Such issues can result in poor performance of the method in the alignment of Faxitron and histopathology images.

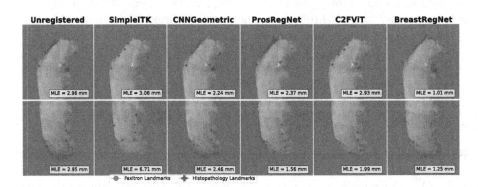

Fig. 2. Overlay of transparent histology onto Faxitron pre-registration and post-registration of two segments with their corresponding landmarks.

Figure 3 presents the MLE results of our registration model compared to other approaches. The findings demonstrate that BreastRegNet outperformed

both iterative and deep learning registration techniques with statistical significance. Moreover, the model performs better when trained in a weakly-supervised
manner that includes segmentation loss compared to its unsupervised counter-
part (US-BreastRegNet). We employed the Mann-Whitney test to evaluate the
statistical significance of the comparison between registration models. Furthermore, the average execution time for the BreastRegNet was 0.07 s, while the
iterative SimpleITK model, CNNGeometric, ProsRegNet, and C2FViT had a
running time of 10.3, 0.32, 0.55, and 0.12 s. In conclusion, our proposed deep
learning approach offers improved alignment of tissue boundaries while being
faster than other registration approaches.

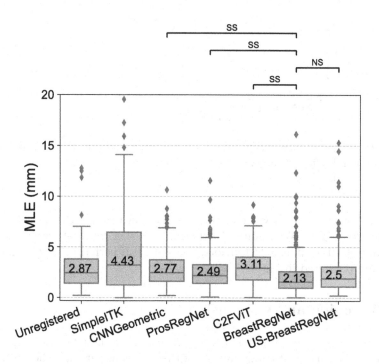

Fig. 3. Mean landmark error comparison before and after registration.
SS: statistically significant (p ≤ 0.01); NS: not significant.

Ablation Study. In our experiments, different pre-trained deep neural networks were utilized as feature extraction networks of the proposed registration
model. Specifically, ResNet101 [26], VGG16 trained on the ImageNet dataset
[19], and ResNet50 trained on the open-access medical image database RadImageNet (RadResNet50) [27] were employed. The performance of these models was
assessed under two scenarios where the layers were either frozen or the final layer
was made trainable. The VGG16 model trained on ImageNet with a trainable
layer demonstrated superior performance among all these deep learning-based
networks. In order to assess the impact of regularization loss, we employed λ

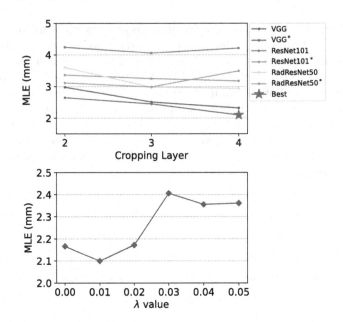

Fig. 4. Performance comparison of feature extraction networks cropped at different layers (top) and different λ values (bottom).
* denotes fine-tuned network.

as a weight factor with a value of zero resulting in training the model without domain adaptation. We conducted experiments using different values of λ and determined that a value of 0.01 yielded the best MLE performance. Comparative results are presented in Fig. 4.

4 Discussion and Conclusion

This paper presents a weakly supervised learning method for the registration of Faxitron and histopathology images of the breast in patients who underwent surgery. The study compares the performance of several methods and demonstrates that the proposed deep learning approach surpasses the existing multimodal registration method, including traditional iterative and deep learning techniques. This pipeline substantially improves landmark error and execution time, overcoming the limitations of conventional methods that are sensitive to initialization parameters and have lengthy computation times. Additionally, our method does not necessitate manual segmentation of tissue during inference. Its rapid image alignment capability makes it a valuable tool for registering Faxitron and histopathology images and producing ground truth data to facilitate the development of models that aid pathologists in tissue processing. In future research, efforts will be made to explore other architectures and test the model on a larger dataset with additional cohorts and multi-reader landmarks to enhance the registration of breast Faxitron and histopathology images, as well as assess its robustness, generalizability, and independence from specific input cohorts.

References

1. American Cancer Society: American cancer society. Eprint https://www.cancer.org/cancer/breast-cancer/about.html (2023). Accessed 07 Feb 2023
2. Britt, K.L., Cuzick, J., Phillips, K.-A.: Key steps for effective breast cancer prevention. Nat. Rev. Can. **20**(8), 417–436 (2020)
3. Lester, S.C.: Manual of Surgical Pathology: Expert Consult-Online and Print. Elsevier Health Sciences (2010)
4. Klein, S., Staring, M., Murphy, K., Viergever, M.A., Pluim, J.P.W.: Elastix: a toolbox for intensity-based medical image registration. IEEE Trans. Med. Imaging **29**(1), 196–205 (2009)
5. Lowekamp, B.C., Chen, D.T., Ibáñez, L., Blezek, D.: The design of simpleitk. Front. Neuroinform. **7**, 45 (2013)
6. Yaniv, Z., Lowekamp, B.C., Johnson, H.J., Beare, R.: Simpleitk image-analysis notebooks: a collaborative environment for education and reproducible research. J. Digit. Imaging **31**(3), 290–303 (2018)
7. Pluim, J.P.W., Antoine Maintz, J.B., Viergever, M.A.: Mutual-information-based registration of medical images: a survey. IEEE Trans. Med. Iimaging **22**(8), 986–1004 (2003)
8. Shen, D., Davatzikos, C.: Hammer: hierarchical attribute matching mechanism for elastic registration. IEEE Trans. Med. Imaging **21**(11), 1421–1439 (2002)
9. Rocco, I., Arandjelovic, R., Sivic, J.: Convolutional neural network architecture for geometric matching. In: Proceedings of the IEEE Conference on Computer vision and Pattern Recognition, pp. 6148–6157 (2017)
10. Balakrishnan, G., Zhao, A., Sabuncu, M.R., Guttag, J., Dalca, A.V.: Voxelmorph: a learning framework for deformable medical image registration. IEEE Trans. Med. Imaging **38**(8), 1788–1800 (2019)
11. De-Vos, B.D., Berendsen, F.F., Viergever, M.A., Sokooti, H., Staring, M., Išgum, I.: A deep learning framework for unsupervised affine and deformable image registration. Med. Image Anal. **52**, 128–143 (2019)
12. Jiang, X., Ma, J., Xiao, G., Shao, Z., Guo, X.: A review of multimodal image matching: methods and applications. Inf. Fusion **73**, 22–71 (2021)
13. Rahate, A., Walambe, R., Ramanna, S., Kotecha, K.: Multimodal co-learning: challenges, applications with datasets, recent advances and future directions. Inf. Fusion **81**, 203–239 (2022)
14. Shao, W., et al.: Prosregnet: a deep learning framework for registration of MRI and histopathology images of the prostate. Med. Image Anal. **68**, 101919 (2021)
15. Zhou, T., Ruan, S., Canu, S.: A review: deep learning for medical image segmentation using multi-modality fusion. Array **3**, 100004 (2019)
16. Theodoros Georgiou, Yu., Liu, W.C., Lew, M.: A survey of traditional and deep learning-based feature descriptors for high dimensional data in computer vision. Int. J. Multimedia Inf. Retrieval **9**(3), 135–170 (2020)
17. Fu, Y., Lei, Y., Wang, T., Curran, W.J., Liu, T., Yang, X.: Deep learning in medical image registration: a review. Phys. Med. Biol. **65**(20), 20TR01 (2020)
18. Haskins, G., Kruger, U., Yan, P.: Deep learning in medical image registration: a survey. Mach. Vis. Appl. **31**(1), 1–18 (2020)

19. Deng, J., Dong, W., Socher, R., Li, L.-J., Li, K., Fei-Fei, L.: Imagenet: a large-scale hierarchical image database. In: 2009 IEEE Conference on Computer Vision and Pattern Recognition, pp. 248–255. IEEE (2009)

20. Kavitha, K., Thirumala Rao, B.: Evaluation of distance measures for feature based image registration using alexnet. arXiv preprint arXiv:1907.12921 (2019)

21. Tzeng, E., Hoffman, J., Zhang, N., Saenko, K., Darrell, T.: Deep domain confusion: Maximizing for domain invariance. arXiv preprint arXiv:1412.3474 (2014)

22. Wang, M., Deng, W.: Deep visual domain adaptation: a survey. Neurocomputing **312**, 135–153 (2018)

23. Paszke, A., et al.: Pytorch: an imperative style, high-performance deep learning library. In: Advances in Neural Information Processing Systems, vol. 32 (2019)

24. Kingma, D.P., Ba, J.: Adam: a method for stochastic optimization. arXiv preprint arXiv:1412.6980 (2014)

25. Mok, T.C.W., Chung, A.: Affine medical image registration with coarse-to-fine vision transformer. In: Proceedings of the IEEE/CVF Conference on Computer Vision and Pattern Recognition, pp. 20835–20844 (2022)

26. He, K., Zhang, X., Ren, S., Sun, J.: Deep residual learning for image recognition. In: Proceedings of the IEEE Conference on Computer Vision and Pattern Recognition, pp. 770–778 (2016)

27. Mei, X., et al.: Radimagenet: an open radiologic deep learning research dataset for effective transfer learning. Radiol. Artif. Intell. **4**(5), e210315 (2022)

Osteoarthritis Diagnosis Integrating Whole Joint Radiomics and Clinical Features for Robust Learning Models Using Biological Privileged Information

Najla Al Turkestani[1,2]([✉]), Lingrui Cai[3], Lucia Cevidanes[1], Jonas Bianchi[4],
Winston Zhang[3], Marcela Gurgel[1], Maxime Gillot[1], Baptiste Baquero[1],
and Reza Soroushmehr[3]

[1] Department of Orthodontics and Pediatric Dentistry, University of Michigan, 1011 North
University Avenue, Ann Arbor, MI 48109, USA
alnajla@umich.edu
[2] Department of Restorative and Aesthetic Dentistry, Faculty of Dentistry, King Abdulaziz
University, Jeddah 22252, Saudi Arabia
[3] Department of Computational Medicine and Bioinformatics, University of Michigan, 100
Washtenaw Avenue, Ann Arbor, MI 48109, USA
[4] Department of Orthodontics, University of the Pacific, Arthur A. Dugoni School of Dentistry,
155 5th Street, San Francisco, CA 94103, USA

Abstract. This paper proposes a machine learning model using privileged information (LUPI) and normalized mutual information feature selection method (NMIFS) to build a robust and accurate framework to diagnose patients with Temporomandibular Joint Osteoarthritis (TMJ OA). To build such a model, we employ clinical, quantitative imaging and additional biological markers as privileged information. We show that clinical features play a leading role in the TMJ OA diagnosis and quantitative imaging features, extracted from cone-beam computerized tomography (CBCT) scans, improve the model performance. As the proposed LUPI model employs biological data in the training phase (which boosted the model performance), this data is unnecessary for the testing stage, indicating the model can be widely used even when only clinical and imaging data are collected. The model was validated using 5-fold stratified cross-validation with hyperparameter tuning to avoid the bias of data splitting. Our method achieved an AUC, specificity and precision of 0.81, 0.79 and 0.77, respectively.

Keywords: Temporomandibular joint · Osteoarthritis · Machine learning ·
Feature selection · Learning using privileged information

N. Al Turkestani and L. Cai—Contributed equally to this work.

© The Author(s), under exclusive license to Springer Nature Switzerland AG 2023
J. Woo et al. (Eds.): MICCAI 2023 Workshops, LNCS 14394, pp. 193–204, 2023.
https://doi.org/10.1007/978-3-031-47425-5_18

1 Introduction

Osteoarthritis (OA) of the temporomandibular joint (TMJ) is a chronic, degenerative disease that affects articular cartilage, synovial tissue and osseous structures of the condyle, articular eminence and articular fossa [1]. It causes chronic pain, jaw dysfunction, deterioration of the quality of life and, in advanced stages, necessitates joint replacement [2]. Current diagnosis of TMJ OA occurs primarily at moderate-severe stage of the disease, following the protocols of the diagnostic criteria for temporomandibular disorders (DC/TMD). Although various therapeutic measures can relieve disease symptoms at these stages, to date, no treatment modality can cure or reverse degenerative changes within the joint tissues [3]. Hence, identification of diagnostic biomarkers that reflect early pathological changes of the joint is crucial for prevention of the irreversible sequelae of the disease.

Animal studies indicated that microstructural change of the subchondral bone was essential for the initiation and progression of OA [4]. However, no robust tools were available to assess these changes, in humans, at early stages of the disease. More recently, advancement of image processing/analysis and high-performance computing techniques allowed extracting quantitative imaging features, i.e., radiomics, which reflect subtle changes within the examined tissues [5]. Along with radiomics, the level of biochemical markers in saliva or blood samples could reflect incipient pathological changes and improve diagnosis, severity assessment and risk of progression of osteoarthritis [6]. The potential of radiomics and biochemical markers has been elucidated in early detection of various diseases, including knee OA; nevertheless, their value in TMJ OA diagnosis has been scarcely investigated [4]. Our preliminary studies [7], showed a significant difference in radiomics at the condyles' subchondral bone in TMJ OA and control subjects. We also found a correlation between the resorptive/anabolic changes of the condyles and the level of several biological markers in TMJ OA subjects [8]. As it is unlikely that a single biomarker would drive or identify a complex disease such as osteoarthritis [9], we hypothesize that clinical symptoms, subchondral bone radiomics and biological markers are optimal integrative indicators of TMJ health status.

Analysis of large and complex datasets derived from different sources yields better understanding of the disease. However, detection of unknown patterns in big data requires the use of high-end computing solutions and advanced analytical approaches such as machine-learning algorithms. Although prediction models can analyze a large amount of data, incorporating less variables into the model reduces computing resources' consumption and prevents model overfitting [10]. Therefore, using a dimensionality reduction technique to identify the optimal subset of the original features is crucial for accurate construction of prediction models. Another challenge for developing a predictive model for TMJ OA diagnosis is inclusion of the biochemical markers. This is due to the restricted specimens' collection, cost and limitations of protein expression measurement systems [11].

In this study, we address the need for comprehensive quantitative phenotyping of OA in the whole jaw joint. We employ a machine learning paradigm called learning using privileged information (LUPI) and train it with clinical, quantitative imaging and additional biological features as privileged information to classify TMJ OA patients. We also adopt feature selection method to remove redundant and irrelevant features from the feature space. Furthermore, we utilize features occurrence and Shapely additive explanations method to interpret the model predictions.

2 Methods

2.1 Dataset

Our dataset consisted of 46 early-stage TMJ OA patients and 46 age and gender-matched healthy controls recruited at the University of Michigan School of Dentistry. All the diagnoses were confirmed by a TMD and orofacial pain specialist based on the DC/TMD. The clinical, biological and radiographic data described below were collected from TMJ OA and control subjects with informed consent and following the guidelines of the Institutional Review Board HUM00113199.

2.1.1 Clinical Data

Clinical dataset entailed three features obtained from diagnostic tests assessed by the same investigator: 1) headaches in the last month, 2) muscle soreness in the last month, 3) vertical range of unassisted jaw opening without pain (mouth opening).

2.1.2 Biological Data

Association of proteins expression with arthritis initiation and progression was investigated in a previous study [12]. In this project, using customized protein microarrays (RayBiotech, Inc. Norcross, GA), the expression level of 13 proteins was measured in the participants' saliva and serum samples. The analyzed proteins included: Angiogenin, BDNF, CXCL16, ENA-78, MMP-3, MMP-7, OPG, PAI-1, TGFb1, TIMP-1, TRANCE, VE-Cadherin and VEGF. As the protein expression of MMP3 was not detected in the saliva, it was excluded from subsequent analysis.

2.1.3 Radiological Data

Using the 3D Accuitomo machine (J. Morita MFG. CORP Tokyo, Japan), cone-beam computed tomography (CBCT) scans were performed for each subject. Radiomics analysis was centered on the lateral region of the articular fossa, articular eminence and condyle, a site where greater OA bone degeneration occurs. Radiomic features were extracted using BoneTexture module in 3D-slicer software v.4.11 (www.3Dslicer.org). We measured 23 texture features: 5 bone morphometry features, 8 Gy Level Co-occurrence Matrix (GLCM) and 10 Grey-Level Run Length Matrix (GLRLM) features. ClusterShade and HaralickCorrelation measurements were highly variable among all participants, therefore, they were not included in the following analysis.

Joint space measurement was evaluated using 3D condylar-to-fossa distances at the anterior, anterolateral, medial, superior and posterior regions.

2.2 Statistical and Machine Learning Approaches

In this section, we describe methods utilized for building a robust TMJOA diagnosis model (Fig. 1). These methods include: 1) cross-validation and grid search, 2) feature selection and 3) learning using privileged information.

2.2.1 Cross-Validation and Grid Search

Cross-validation is an effective approach to model hyperparameter optimization and model selection that attempts to overcome the overfitting issue. The dataset was split into 80% for training and 20% holdout for testing. The 5fold cross-validation with the same portion of data split was nested inside the 80% train dataset, and grid search was performed in each fold of data for hyperparameters tuning. The best combination of hyperparameters was picked based on the mean and standard deviation of F1 scores over the 5-fold cross-validation. The overall procedure was repeated 10 times with 10 random seeds to avoid sampling bias from data partitioning. The final evaluation scores reported in this study are the mean ± standard deviation of the holdout test set performance across all 10 repetitions.

2.2.2 Feature Selection

Feature selection is a common dimensional reduction technique for building a machine learning model. Increasing the number of features often results in decreasing the prediction error. However, it increases the risk of model overfitting particularly with small datasets. Here, we customized a feature selection method that takes the advantages of privileged variables and mutual information to improve the performance of the classifier.

Normalized mutual information feature selection (NMIFS) method and its modified version called called NMIFS+ was used to measure the relevance and redundancy of features with the primary objective of high accuracy with the least possible time complexity. NMIFS+ extends the NMIFS algorithm with the LUPI framework, which could take full account of the privilege features along with standard features and make feature selection from those two sets separately [13]. The NMIFS+ was applied to all the LUPI models in this study and, correspondingly, the NMIFS on non-LUPI models.

2.2.3 LUPI Framework

The idea of learning using privileged information (LUPI) was first proposed as capturing the essence of teacher-student-based learning by Vapnik and Vashist. In contrast to the existing machine learning paradigm, where the model learns and makes predictions with fixed information, the LUPI paradigm considers several specific forms of privileged information, just like a teacher who provides additional information, which can include comments, explanations, and logic to students and thus increases the learning efficiency.

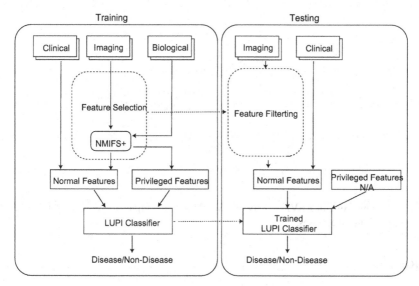

Fig. 1. Diagram of training and testing process

In the classical binary classification model, we were given training pairs $(x_1,y_1),...,(x_l,y_l)$, where $x_i \in X$, $y_i \in \{-1,1\}$, $i = 1,...,l$, and each pair is independently generated by some underlying distribution P_{XY}, which is unknown. The model is trained to find among a given set of functions $f(x,\alpha), \alpha \in \wedge$, the function $y = f(x,\alpha)$ that minimizes the probability of incorrect classifications over the unknown distribution P_{XY}.

In the LUPI framework, we were given training triplets $(x_1,x *_1,y_1),...,(x_l,x *_l,y_l)$, $x_i \in X, x *_i \in X *, y_i \in \{-1,1\}$, $i = 1,...,l$, which is slightly different from the classical one. Each triplet is independently generated by some underlying distribution P_{XX*Y}, which is still unknown. The additional privileged information is available only for the training examples, not for the test phase. In this scenario, we can utilize $X *$ to improve learning performance.

There are a few implementations of LUPI models. One of them is based on random vector functional link network (RVFL) that is a randomized version of the functional link neural network. A kernel-based RVFL, called KRVFL+, has been proposed based on the LUPI paradigm [14]. It incorporates efficient ways to use kernel tricks for highly complicated nonlinear feature training and train RVFL networks with privileged information (Fig. 2). The parameters, including weights and biases, from the input layer to the hidden layers are generated randomly from a fixed domain, and only the output weights need to be computed.

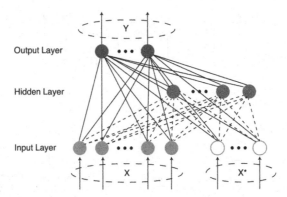

Fig. 2. The architecture of KRVFL+ network. Solid lines are output weights and dash lines stand for random weights and biases.

3   Results

3.1   LUPI and Non-LUPI Models

Figure 3 shows the comparison of the classification performance between LUPI and non-LUPI models. We evaluated the diagnostic potential of imaging features extracted from the articular eminence, articular fossa, condyle, and joint space measurement, as well as clinical features. Only the clinical feature sets provided discriminative models (AUC = 0.723) for TMJ OA diagnosis. By introducing LUPI-based models with additional biological features, LUPI paradigm significantly enhanced the model performance on clinical (AUC = 0.794), joint space measurement (AUC = 0.625), and condyle (AUC = 0.641) datasets.

3.2   Feature Integration Comparison

Table 1 shows the classification performances with different feature integration strategies. Given that clinical features had strong discriminative power for TMJ OA diagnosis, two groups of experiments were conducted to investigate the effect of an enlarged candidate pool for feature selection. Adding more features into the clinical dataset and selecting from combined set improved the model performance markedly, i.e., the models had higher AUC scores. With an AUC = 0.794, the clinical feature model achieved fairly well performance. Selecting features from a pool of condyle radiomic features together with the clinical features increased the AUC score to 0.804. The performance was even higher when feature selection was conducted on all condyle, 3D measurements and clinical datasets, AUC = 0.807. Keeping all clinical criteria and applying feature selection on the remaining dataset resulted in slightly higher AUC values. The AUC scores became 0.808 and 0.809 for the condyle and condyle with additional 3D measurement features models, respectively.

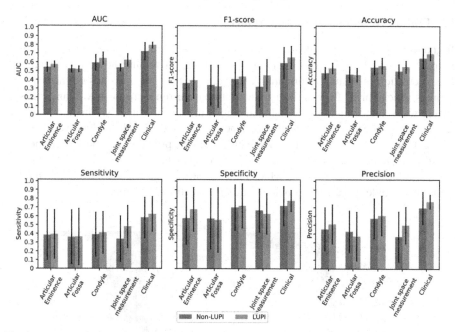

Fig. 3. Comparison of LUPI and non-LUPI models. The non-LUPI models only trained with normal features and RVFL model. The LUPI model trained with KRVFL+ and biological data as privilege information.

Table 1. Comparison of different feature integration methods (in percentage %)

Feature Set	AUC	F1 score	Accuracy	Sensitivity	Specificity	Precision
Cl	79.4 ± 3.4	65.7 ± 12.7	69.9 ± 7.2	62.2.0 ± 19.8	77.6 ± 12.0	76.8 ± 7.8
(Cl + Cd)*	80.4 ± 3.8	67.5 ± 9.4	70.4 ± 5.6	64.4 ± 18.6	76.4 ± 16.0	76.1 ± 9.2
Cl + Cd*	80.8 ± 4.1	64.8 ± 11.6	69.4 ± 6.4	60.2 ± 19.4	78.7 ± 13.5	76.0 ± 9.3
(Cl + Cd JS)*	80.7 ± 3.8	64.2 ± 15.0	69.8 ± 6.9	61.3 ± 22.9	78.2 ± 15.3	75.1 ± 12.2
Cl + Cd JS*	80.9 ± 3.6	66.1 ± 12.2	70.9 ± 6.0	62.7 ± 19.7	79.1 ± 13.6	77.4 ± 9.8

Cl: Clinical; Cd: Condyle; Cd JS: Condyle and 3D Joint Space measurements.
*indicates feature selection by NMIFS+ method.
The feature sets in parentheses have been pooled together for feature selection, otherwise it proceeded on feature set with * separately.
All the models have been trained with KRVFL+ with Biological data as privilege information.

3.3 Feature Occurrence and Importance

To interpret the prediction of our proposed model, we utilized feature occurrence and Shapley values. The NMIFS+ method is a measure of redundancy among features. The calculation of mutual information and redundancy highly depends on the training samples which varied from split to split. Feature occurrence means how many times a feature was selected by NMIFS+ method among the total 50 models. The more times a feature occurs, the more reliable its importance is (Fig. 4A). Shapley values were used to interpret the contribution of individual features into the prediction of the trained model. Contributing features are shown in Fig. 4B according to the order of the mean absolute of Shapley values across all the data, which indicate the average impact of feature on model output magnitude. Figure 4C provides further indication of Shapley values and shows

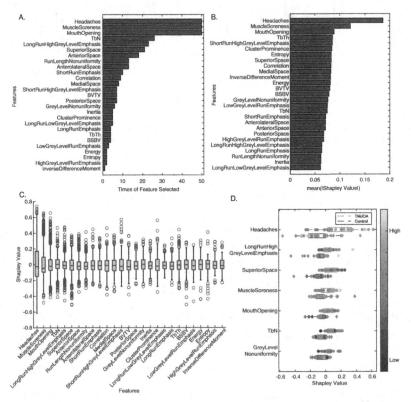

Fig. 4. A. Feature occurrence in 50 trained models using NMIFS method. B. Feature importance measured as the mean absolute Shapley values in 50 models. C. Distribution of Shapley values in each query point in the 50 models. The order of the features shown in the x-axis is based on the feature occurrence. D. Shapley summary plot for one model. The boxplots represent the distribution of TMJOA and control groups (each TMJOA patient is shown as a circle and control as a diamond). The Heatmap color bar shows the value of the feature itself from high to low (yellow to blue). Low number of Shapley value of features reduce the predicted TMJOA diseased probability, a large number of Shapley value increase the probability.

the complexity of feature contribution in models. Each circle represents a feature value of one patient/control, either increases or decreases the prediction (positive value and negative value). Figure 4D combines feature importance with feature effects. Here we picked one model for visualization instead of pulling all 50 models together. Each point in the summary plot is a Shapley value for a feature and a patient/control. The order of the features on the y-axis is based on their importance. The color represents the Shapley value of the features from low to high. We divided the instances into TMJOA diseased group and Control group, displayed in different markers. Higher values of headache, LongRunHighGreyLevelRunEmphasis and muscle soreness increased the probability of assigning TMJ OA diagnosis.

4   Discussion

This study developed an enhanced model for TMJ OA diagnosis, utilizing state-of the art machine learning technology and considering clinical, quantitative imaging markers, and additional biological features used only for training. This is the first study to utilize quantitative imaging markers of the whole joint: condyle, articular space, articular fossa and articular eminence. We employed feature selection to minimize feature sets and improve the model robustness. Furthermore, feature occurrence and Shapley value were assessed to reduce the black-box nature of the machine learning model, as well as improve the domain experts' confidence in the model's prediction. This study findings demonstrate excellent performance of the feature integration methods and LUPI paradigm in predicting TMJ OA status.

The Diagnostic Criteria for Temporomandibular Disorders (DC/TMD) have been the most utilized protocol for TMJ OA diagnosis. However, these criteria are dependent on subjective clinical signs/symptoms and subjective radiological interpretation of imaging features associated with irreversible bone changes [4, 5]. Early treatment and modification of the disease course requires precise diagnosis of TMJ OA at initial stages. In this study, we utilized multi-source data collected from subjects at early stages of TMJ OA. We employed the LUPI paradigm and used biological features of inflammation, neuroception, bone resorption and angiogenesis as privileged information. The LUPI algorithm allowed benefiting from diagnostic information within the existing biological data and eliminated future need for biological samples' collection and analysis. Inclusion of biological data with the LUPI framework boosted our model performance, confirming the need for biological data only for model training. We developed a robust model for TMJ OA diagnosis and validated its performance using extensive evaluation metrics (Fig. 1). Our model demonstrated sensitivity and specificity of 63% and 79%, respectively. These values exceeded the sensitivity and specificity, 58% and 72%, of TMJ OA diagnosis following DC/TMD protocol without imaging. Honda and colleagues [15] reported that the CBCT scan's use improved the sensitivity and specificity for detecting condylar osseous defects to 80% and 90%, sequentially. Nevertheless, CBCT sensitivity is dependent on the defects' size, it is challenging to detect early alterations that are < 2mm. Hence, we extracted objective, quantitative imaging features from the subchondral bones of the condyle, articular fossa and articular eminence. Using the LUPI-based model, we found that only condyle's radiomics could differentiate between healthy and diseased subjects (Table 1). In line with this observation, Massilla and Sivasubramanian [16] reported that patients with early TMJ OA had osteoarthritic bone alterations in their condyles (69.93%) more than articular fossa (10%) and articular eminence (6.6%). Interestingly, we noted that the superior 3D joint space distinguished TMJ OA subjects using LUPI-based models (AUC = .63), denoting the importance of this feature in detecting osteoarthritic changes. Along with radiomics and joint space measurements, we supplemented the model with clinical signs that were measurable in both groups.

Machine learning models are leveraged for clinical predictive modeling, where clinical values are used to predict clinical diagnosis. However, these models do not explain the basis for their prediction. This raise concerns in medical domains and challenge researchers to identify reasons behind the model outcomes [17]. Here, we facilitated the interpretability of our model by reducing the number of candidate features. In general, for a fixed sample size, the error of designed classifier decreases and then increases as the number of features grows. Finding an optimal number of features is crucial in terms of reducing the time to build the learning model and increasing the accuracy in the learning process. For uncorrelated features, the optimal feature size is N-1, where the N is the sample size. As the feature correlation increases, the optimal feature $\sqrt{}$/size becomes proportional to N for highly correlated features. Furthermore, texture features turned out to be highly correlated in Cho's work [18]. Those further proof of the necessity of feature selection.

Using the NMIFS method, we calculated feature occurrence to identify the discriminative features of TMJ OA. Moreover, we calculated Shapley values to demonstrate how each clinical and imaging feature is contributing to the outcome/disease diagnosis in individual patients. Headache, muscle soreness and limited range of vertical mouth opening without pain were among the top features that contributed to the model prediction for TMJ OA. TrabecularNumber, superior 3D joint space and LongRunHighGreyLevelRunEmphasis were the top imaging features selected in the majority of the trained models. Importantly, the amalgamation of different data-sources in this study is essential for comprehensive assessment of individuals' health. In line with our results, Liang and colleagues found significant differences of the TrabecularNumber in subjects with TMJ OA compared to healthy individuals [19]. Our findings corroborate those that indicate radiomics provide an objective assessment of the pathological changes and may overcome the subjectivity of patients-reported symptoms [20]. Zhang et al. [21] validated the importance of detecting TMJ morphological changes using 3D measurements, showing that 2D and 3D TMJ space measurements varied significantly in CBCT scans of healthy individuals. The present study is the first to test whole joint (condylar, articular eminence and articular fossa) radiomics and incorporate 3D joint space measurements into a comprehensive diagnostic tool for TMJ OA.

5   Conclusion

Normalized mutual information feature selection method and LUPI paradigm established a robust model for TMJ OA diagnosis. The identified clinical and quantitative imaging markers can be considered a foundation for reliable detection of TMJ OA pathological alterations and are potential markers for prediction of disease progression in future longitudinal studies.

References

1. Abrahamsson, A.K., Kristensen, M., Arvidsson, L.Z., Kvien, T.K., Larheim, T.A., Haugen, I.K.: Frequency of temporomandibular joint osteoarthritis and related symptoms in a hand osteoarthritis cohort. Osteoarth. Cartilage **25**, 654 (2017). https://doi.org/10.1016/j.joca.2016.12.028

2. Tanaka, E., Detamore, M.S., Mercuri, L.G.: Degenerative disorders of the temporomandibular joint: etiology, diagnosis, and treatment. J. Dental Res. **87**(4), 296–307 (2008). https://doi.org/10.1177/154405910808700406

3. Shi, J., et al.: Association of condylar bone quality with TMJ osteoarthritis. J. Dental Res. **96**(8), 888–894 (2017). https://doi.org/10.1177/0022034517707515

4. Hu, Y., Chen, X., Wang, S., Jing, Y., Su, J.: Subchondral bone microenvironment in osteoarthritis and pain. Bone Res. **9**(1), 1–13 (2021). https://doi.org/10.1038/s41413-021-00147-z

5. Marias, K.: The constantly evolving role of medical image processing in oncology: from traditional medical image processing to imaging biomarkers and radiomics. J. Imaging **7**(8), 124 (2021). https://doi.org/10.3390/jimaging7080124

6. Munjal, A., Bapat, S., Hubbard, D., Hunter, M., Kolhe, R., Fulzele, S.: Advances in molecular biomarker for early diagnosis of osteoarthritis. Biomolecul. Concepts **10**(1), 111–119 (2019). https://doi.org/10.1515/bmc-2019-0014

7. Cevidanes, L., et al.: Quantification of condylar resorption in TMJ osteoarthritis. Oral Surg. Oral Med. Oral Pathol. Oral Radiol. Endodont. **110**(1), 110–117 (2010). https://doi.org/10.1016/j.tripleo.2010.01.008

8. Cevidanes, L.H.S., et al.: 3D osteoarthritic changes in TMJ condylar morphology correlates with specific systemic and local biomarkers of disease. Osteoarth. Cartilage **22**(10), 1657–1667 (2014). https://doi.org/10.1016/j.joca.2014.06.014

9. Al Turkestani, N., et al.: Clinical decision support systems in orthodontics: a narrative review of data science approaches. Orthodont. Craniof. Res. **24**(S2), 26–36 (2021). https://doi.org/10.1111/ocr.12492

10. Aas, K., Jullum, M., Løland, A.: Explaining individual predictions when features are dependent: more accurate approximations to Shapley values. Technical Report arXiv:1903.10464 (February 2020). https://doi.org/10.48550/arXiv.1903.10464

11. Shoukri, B., et al.: Minimally invasive approach for diagnosing TMJ osteoarthritis. J. Dental Res. **98**(10), 1103–1111 (2019). https://doi.org/10.1177/0022034519865187

12. Zhang, W., et al.: Feature selection for privileged modalities in disease classification. In: Multimodal Learning for Clinical Decision Support: 11th International Workshop, ML-CDS 2021, Held in Conjunction with MICCAI 2021, Strasbourg, 1 October 2021, Proceedings, pp. 69–80. Springer, Heidelberg (2021). https://doi.org/10.1007/978-3-030-89847-27

13. Fedorov, A., et al.: 3D slicer as an image computing platform for the quantitative imaging network. Magnet. Resonance Imaging **30**(9), 1323–1341 (2012). https://doi.org/10.1016/j.mri.2012.05.001

14. Estevez, P.A., Tesmer, M., Perez, C.A., Zurada, J.M.: Normalized mutual information feature selection. IEEE Trans. Neural Netw. **20**(2), 189–201 (2009). https://doi.org/10.1109/TNN.2008.2005601

15. Zhang, P.-B., Yang, Z.-X.: A new learning paradigm for random vector functional-link network: RVFL. Neural Netw. Off. J. Int. Neural Netw. Soc. **122**, 94–105 (2020). https://doi.org/10.1016/j.neunet.2019.09.039

16. Honda, K., Larheim, T., Maruhashi, K., Matsumoto, K., Iwai, K.: Osseous abnormalities of the mandibular condyle: diagnostic reliability of cone beam computed tomography compared with helical computed tomography based on an autopsy material. Dentomaxillofac. Radiol. **35**(3), 152–157 (2006)

17. Petch, J., Di, S., Nelson, W.: Opening the black box: the promise and limitations of explainable machine learning in cardiology. Canadian J. Cardiol. (2021)

18. Cho, Y.J., et al.: Computerized texture analysis of pulmonary nodules in pediatric patients with osteosarcoma: differentiation of pulmonary metastases from non-metastatic nodules. PLoS One 14(2), 1–14 (2019). https://doi.org/10.1371/journal.pone.0211969

19. Liang, X., et al.: Evaluation of trabecular structure changes in osteoarthritis of the temporo-mandibular joint with cone beam computed tomography imaging. Oral Surg Oral Med. Oral Pathol. Oral Radiol. 124(3), 315–322 (2017)

20. Patel, V.K., et al.: A practical algorithmic approach to the diagnosis and management of solitary pulmonary nodules: part 1: radiologic characteristics and imaging modalities. Chest 143(3), 825–839 (2013)

21. Zhang, Y., Xu, X., Liu, Z.: Comparison of morphologic parameters of temporomandibular joint for asymptomatic subjects using the two-dimensional and three-dimensional measuring methods. J. Healthc. Eng. (2017)

Graph-Based Counterfactual Causal Inference Modeling for Neuroimaging Analysis

Haixing Dai[1], Mengxuan Hu[1], Qing Li[2,3], Lu Zhang[4], Lin Zhao[1],
Dajiang Zhu[4], Ibai Diez[5], Jorge Sepulcre[5], Fan Zhang[6], Xingyu Gao[7],
Manhua Liu[8], Quanzheng Li[5], Sheng Li[9], Tianming Liu[1], and Xiang Li[5(✉)]

[1] School of Computing, University of Georgia, Athens, USA
[2] State Key Lab of Cognitive Neuroscience and Learning, Beijing Normal University,
Beijing, China
[3] School of Artificial Intelligence, Beijing Normal University, Beijing, China
[4] Department of Computer Science and Engineering, The University of Texas
at Arlington, Arlington, USA
[5] Department of Radiology, Massachusetts General Hospital and Harvard Medical
School, Boston, USA
xli60@mgh.harvard.edu
[6] Department of Radiology, Brigham and Women's Hospital and Harvard Medical
School, Boston, USA
[7] School of Electronic Information and Electrical Engineering,
Shanghai Jiao Tong University, Shanghai, China
[8] The MoE Key Lab of Artificial Intelligence, AI Institute,
Shanghai Jiao Tong University, Shanghai, China
[9] School of Data Science, The University of Virginia, Charlottesville, USA

Abstract. Alzheimer's disease (AD) is a neurodegenerative disorder
that is beginning with amyloidosis, followed by neuronal loss and
deterioration in structure, function, and cognition. The accumulation
of amyloid-β in the brain, measured through 18F-florbetapir (AV45)
positron emission tomography (PET) imaging, has been widely used
for early diagnosis of AD. However, the relationship between amyloid-β
accumulation and AD pathophysiology remains unclear, and causal inference approaches are needed to uncover how amyloid-β levels can impact
AD development. In this paper, we propose a Graph-VCNet for estimating the individual treatment effect with continuous treatment levels
using a graph convolutional neural network. We highlight the potential
of causal inference approaches, including Graph-VCNet, for measuring
the regional causal connections between amyloid-β accumulation and AD
pathophysiology, which may serve as a robust tool for early diagnosis and
tailored care.

Keywords: Causal inference · Amyloid accumulation · Alzehimer's
disease · Counterfactual inference

H. Dai—Contributed equally to this paper.

J. Woo et al. (Eds.): MICCAI 2023 Workshops, LNCS 14394, pp. 205–213, 2023.
https://doi.org/10.1007/978-3-031-47425-5_19

1   Introduction

The differentiation of Alzheimer's disease (AD) from the prodromal stage of AD, which is the mild cognitive impairment (MCI), and normal control (NC) is an important project that interests many researchers making effort on [14,15]. It is commonly recognized through studies that the progression of AD involves a series of gradually intensifying neuropathological occurrences. The process begins with amyloidosis, followed by neuronal loss and subsequent deterioration in the areas of structure, function, and cognition [18]. As a non-invasive method that could measure the accumulation of amyloid in the brain, 18F-florbetapir (AV45) positron emission tomography (PET) imaging has been widely used for early diagnosis of AD [6]. The use of florbetapir-PET imaging to characterize the deposition of amyloid-β has shown to be of significant diagnostic value in identifying the onset of clinical impairment. It has been suggested that brain regions such as the posterior cingulate and lateral temporal cortices are affected more in AD than the NC, with the florbetapir-PET [3].

Some research on florbetapir-PET imaging has revealed that neurodegeneration does not influence the level of amyloid-β accumulation. Instead, amyloid-β pathophysiology is considered a biologically independent process and may play a "catalyst" role in neurodegeneration [10]. There have also been many theories that highlight the amyloid-β pathologies as the main driving forces behind disease progression and cognitive decline. In order to characterize the relationship between the amyloid-β accumulation and AD pathophysiology, the counterfactual causal inference method will be a useful tool to uncover how the patterns of causality or significant changes in regional or temporal amyloid-β levels can impact the development of AD over time.

In recent years, there has been increasing research in counterfactual causal inference to estimate the treatment effect in various domains such as medicine, public health, and marketing, where correlations-based approaches are often inadequate or insufficient for making critical decisions. Especially, estimating the causal effect of continuous treatments is crucial. For example, in precision medicine, a common question is *"What is the ideal medicine dosage to attain the best result?"*. Therefore, an average dose-response function (ADRF) that elucidates the causal relationship between the continuous treatment and the outcome becomes imperative. However, estimating the counterfactual outcome presents a significant challenge in causal effect estimation, which is inherently unobservable as the patient can only receive one treatment among all available treatments. Therefore, a variety of existing work on causal effect estimation focus on counterfactual estimation [8,11,16] under the assumption of binary treatments or continuous treatments (ADRF estimation) [2,9,17,20,26]. Especially, in the context of continuous treatments, the generalized propensity score (GPS), proposed by Hirano and Imbens [9], is a traditional approach to estimate ADRF with counterfactual outcomes. Moreover, as machine learning has gained increasing attention due to its extraordinary ability to solve complex problems, many existing works use machine learning techniques to address the problem. Schwab et al. [20] proposed DRNet to split a continuous treatment into several intervals and built separate prediction heads for them on the latent representation of input. Nie et al. [17] adopted varying coefficient structure to explicitly incorporate continuous treatments as a variable for the parameters of the model, preserving the continuity of ADRF. Other methods, such as GAN [2] and transformer [26], have also been proposed.

In this work, we proposed a novel model, the Graph Varying Coefficient Neural Network (Graph-VCNet), for measuring the regional causal associations between amyloid-β accumulation and AD pathophysiology. Specifically, by comparing our model with the most advanced model, VCNet, we demonstrate that our model achieves better performance in AD classification. Moreover, we adopt K-Means clustering to group the generated average dose-response function (ADRF) curves from each region of interest (ROI) and then map them onto the cortical surface to identify the amyloid-β positive regions.

2   Related Work

2.1   Counterfactual Outcome Estimation

The definition of counterfactual outcome is typically framed using the potential outcome framework [19]. To provide a clear definition, we illustrate with the use of binary treatments, which can be extended to multiple treatments by comparing their potential outcomes. Each individual x_i has two potential outcomes: $Y_i(T = 1)$ and $Y_i(T = 0)$, corresponding to the two possible treatments ($T = 1$ or $T = 0$). Since an individual can only receive one of the two treatments in observational data, only one potential outcome can be observed (observed outcome), while the remaining unobserved outcome is referred to as the counterfactual outcome. Hence, the major challenge in estimating Individual Treatment Effect (ITE) lies in inferring counterfactual outcomes. Once the counterfactual outcomes are obtained, ITE can be calculated as the difference between the two potential outcomes:

$$ITE_i = Y_i(T = 1) - Y_i(T = 0). \tag{1}$$

Many existing approaches have been proposed to estimate the counterfactual outcomes, such as conditional outcome modeling that trains two separate models to predict outcomes for the treatment group and control group and use the predicted value to fill the unobserved counterfactual outcomes. In addition, tree-based and forest-based methods are widely used to estimate ITE [4,7,23]. Additionally, matching methods [16,22], stratification mathods [25], deep representation methods [8,25] have been proposed to address the problem as well.

2.2   Continuous Treatment Effect Estimation

Continuous treatments are of great practical importance in many fields, such as precision medical. Typically, the average dose-response function (ADRF) demonstrates the relationship between the specific continuous treatment and the outcome. Although recent works utilized the representation learning methods for ITE estimation [5,11,21,24], most of the existing works are under the assumption of binary treatments, which cannot be easily extended to continuous treatment due to their unique model design. To address this issue, Schwab et al. [20] extended the TARNet [21] and proposed Dose Response networks (DRNet), which divided the continuous dosage into several equally-sized dosage stratus, and assigned one prediction heads for each strata. To further achieve the continuity of ADRF, Nie et al., [17] proposed a varying-coefficient neural network (VCNet). Instead of the multi-head design, it used a varying coefficient prediction head whose weights are continuous functions of treatment t, which improved the previous methods by preserving a continuous ADRF and enhancing the expressiveness of the model. Hence, in this paper, we adopt it as part of the model to estimate the effect of each Regions of Interest (ROI) for the brain on Alzheimer's disease.

2.3   Traditional Correlation-Based PET Image Analysis Methods

The correlation-based methods on PET images analysis could be used in many clinical applications, such as tumor detection and brain disorder diagnosis. An et al. used canonical correlation analysis-based scheme to estimate a standard-dose PET image from a low-dose one in order to reduce the risk of radiation exposure and preserve image quality [1]. Landau et al. used the traditional corrlation method to compare the retention of the 11-C radiotracer Pittsburgh Compound B and that of two 18-F amyloid radiotracers (florbetapir and flutemetamol) [12]. Zhu et al. used the cannoical representation to consider the correlations relationship between features of PET and other different brain neuroimage modalities [27]. Li et al. used sparse inverse covariance estimation to reveal the relationship between PET and structural magnetic resonance imaging (sMRI) [13].

3   Methodology

3.1   Problem Setting

VCNet is one of the advanced methods for estimating the causal effect with continuous treatments; it can typically generate continuous ADRF and provide promising counterfactual estimation. Hence, in this study, we adopt this model for estimating the causal effect (ADRF) between the amyloid-β level and the probability of gaining AD. Typically, we treat the amyloid-β as treatment T and whether the subject gains AD as the outcome Y.

In our study, we used the Harvard-Oxford Atlas (HOA) to divide the entire brain into 69 regions. Since the brainstem is not a target binding region, we excluded it from our analysis and focused on the other 68 regions. We treated one region as the treatment and used the other regions as covariates (X) to train a separate model for each setting. We iterated this process 68 times to obtain the causal effect and accuracy estimates for each region. To capture more information, we used graph structures of the whole brain denoted as $\mathcal{G} = (\mathcal{V}, \mathcal{E}, \mathcal{X})$,

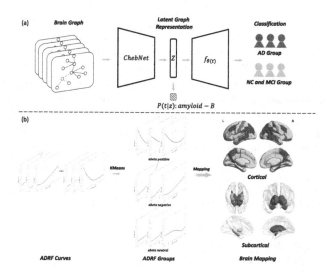

Fig. 1. The framework of Graph-VCNet for AD classification and individual treatment effect estimation. (a) we utilize ChebNet for feature embedding and then integrate treatment in the following dynamic fully connected layer for AD classification task. (b) We employee KMeans cluster algorithm to cluster the individual ADRFs into 3 groups: abeta-positive, abeta-negative and abeta-neutral and mapping these groups on the brain.

where each graph contains 68 nodes representing 68 ROIs, $\mathcal{V}$ represents the node set and $\mathcal{E}$ represents the edge set. Let $X \in R^{N \times F}$ be the input feature matrix, where each row corresponds to a node and each column corresponds to a feature. To estimate the causal effect (ADRF) of one ROI, we removed the corresponding node and all edges related to it and used the rest of the graph as input. Finally, we used the amyloid-B value as the treatment variable (t) for the VCNet analysis. In our work, we follow three fundamental assumptions for identifying ITE with continuous treatments:

Assumption 1 *Stable Unit Treatment Value Assumption (SUTVA): There are no unit interactions, and there is only one version of each treatment, which means that various levels or doses of a specific treatment are considered as separate treatments.*

Assumption 2 *Positivity: Every unit should have non-zero probability of being assigned to every treatment group. Formally, $P(T = t | X = x) \neq 0, \forall t \in \mathcal{T}, \forall x \in X$.*

Assumption 3 *Ignorability: Given covariates x, all potential outcomes $\{Y(T = t)\}_{t \in \mathcal{T}}$ are independent of the treatment assignment, implying that there are no unobserved confounders. Mathematically, $\{Y(T = t)\}_{t \in \mathcal{T}} T | X$.*

3.2 VCNet

VCNet is proposed by Nie et al. [17], which is capable of estimating continuous treatment effect and maintaining the continuity of ADRF simultaneously. A neural network is trained to extract latent representation z from input x. To guarantee z encode useful features, z is used to estimate the conditional density of the corresponding treatment $\mathbb{P}(t|z)$. Then a varying coefficient neural network $f_{\theta(t)}(z)$ is adopted to predict the outcome y, where the network parameters are a function of treatment $f_{\theta(t)}$ instead of fixed parameters. Typically, the B-spline is used to model $\theta(t)$.

$$\theta(t) = [\sum_{l=1}^{L} a_{1,l}\varphi_l^{nn}(t), ..., \sum_{l=1}^{L} a_{d_{\theta(t)},l}\varphi_l^{nn}(t)]^T \in \mathbb{R}^{d(\theta)}, \tag{2}$$

$\varphi_l^{nn}(t)$ denotes the spline basis of the treatment and $a_{1,l}$ are the coefficients to be learned; $d(\theta)$ is the dimension of $\theta(t)$.

3.3 Graph-VCNet

In this paper, to preserve the topological information of PET data. We introduce the Chebyshev neural network (ChebNet) to replace the first two fully connected layers in VCNet. ChebNet uses Chebyshev polynomials to approximate the graph Laplacian filter, which is a commonly used filter in GCNs. Chebyshev polynomials are a sequence of orthogonal polynomials that can be used to approximate any smooth function on a given interval, and can be efficiently computed using recursive formulas. The equation of first ChebNet is as follows:

$$f_{out}(\mathcal{L}, \mathbf{X}) = \sigma \left(\sum_{k=0}^{K-1} \Theta_k T_k(\tilde{\mathcal{L}})\mathbf{X} \right) \tag{3}$$

where $\mathbf{X} \in \mathbb{R}^{N \times F}$ is the input matrix of N nodes, each with F features, $\mathcal{L}$ is the graph Laplacian, and $\tilde{\mathcal{L}}$ is the normalized Laplacian defined as $\tilde{\mathcal{L}} = 2\mathcal{L}/\lambda_{max} - I_N$, where λ_{max} is the largest eigenvalue of $\mathcal{L}$. $T_k(\cdot)$ are Chebyshev polynomials of order k and Θ_k are the learnable filter coefficients for the k-th Chebyshev polynomial. Finally, $\sigma(\cdot)$ is a non-linear activation function such as ReLU or sigmoid that is applied element-wise to the output of the ChebNet. And the binary cross-entropy loss function is utilized to quantify the dissimilarity between the predicted probability of the positive class and its true probability in binary classification tasks.

4 Experiment

4.1 Dataset

In this paper, we evaluated our proposed algorithm on two subsets of ADNI (adni.loni.usc.edu) data, including ADNI-1 and ADNI-2. The subjects were divided into three categories, consisting of AD, NC, and MCI. In this paper, we take AD as the AD group (336 subjects) and NC+MCI as the non-AD group (833 subjects). All florbetapir-PET images were co-registered with each individual's sMRI and subsequently warped to the cohort-specific DARTEL template. We split the dataset into a training set (818 subjects) and a testing set (350 subjects). The proposed model was tested on the testing set to calculate the classification accuracy and generate average dose-response function curves (ADRFs) for each ROI.

4.2   Experiment Setting

In Graph-VCNet, we designate each one of the 68 ROIs as the treatment and use the other ROIs as patient features. The average amyloid-β level serves as the signal for each ROI. We construct the input graph by defining the ROIs as nodes V and the population-wise Pearson's correlation among the ROIs inferred from the training dataset as edges E. We set the learning rate to 1e-4 and β to 0.5. During model training, all networks were trained for 400 epochs.

4.3   Prediction Performance

We compare the classification accuracy between the original VCNet and the proposed Graph-VCNet. The experiment result shows that VCNet model achieves an average accuracy of 83.1%, and the Graph-VCNet model achieves an average accuracy of 84.0%.

5   Conclusion and Discussion

In this paper, we propose a novel model Graph-VCNet, incorporating a graph neural network architecture for estimating the varying coefficients and a targeted regularization approach to improve the model's performance. The capability of this model in making counterfactual causal inferences for the AD progress based on the regional level of Amyloid-β protein has vast potential in patient management, treatment, and drug discovery. Specifically, if the model has demonstrated sufficient robustness and consistency via more validation studies, we can use it to project the personalized AD progression trajectory and inform the patient "what if" the current imaging results would become better/worse. We would also be able to predict the personalized treatment effect of a patient after a medication targeting at the Amyloid-β deposition is administered, as well as the optimal dosage to be used. We envision that the future in imaging-guided diagnosis and prognosis for Alzheimer's disease would be more focused on the discovery of the underlying mechanisms between the imaging target and the disease progression, in which case the proposed counterfactual causal inference modeling would become a more important and effective solution.

References

1. An, L., et al.: Multi-level canonical correlation analysis for standard-dose pet image estimation. IEEE Trans. Image Process. **25**(7), 3303–3315 (2016). https://doi.org/10.1109/TIP.2016.2567072
2. Bica, I., Jordon, J., van der Schaar, M.: Estimating the effects of continuous-valued interventions using generative adversarial networks. Adv. Neural. Inf. Process. Syst. **33**, 16434–16445 (2020)
3. Camus, V., et al.: Using pet with 18f-av-45 (florbetapir) to quantify brain amyloid load in a clinical environment. Eur. J. Nucl. Med. Molecul. Imag. **39**(4), 621–631 (2012)
4. Chipman, H.A., George, E.I., McCulloch, R.E.: Bart: Bayesian additive regression trees. Annal. Appl. Statist. **4**(1), 266–298 (2010)
5. Chu, Z., Rathbun, S.L., Li, S.: Matching in selective and balanced representation space for treatment effects estimation. In: Proceedings of the 29th ACM International Conference on Information and Knowledge Management, pp. 205–214 (2020)
6. Ge, Q., et al.: Tracer-specific reference tissues selection improves detection of 18f-fdg, 18f-florbetapir, and 18f-flortaucipir pet SUVR changes in Alzheimer's disease. Hum. Brain Mapp. **43**(7), 2121–2133 (2022)
7. Hansen, B.B.: The prognostic analogue of the propensity score. Biometrika **95**(2), 481–488 (2008)
8. Hassanpour, N., Greiner, R.: Counterfactual regression with importance sampling weights. In: IJCAI, pp. 5880–5887 (2019)
9. Hirano, K., Imbens, G.W.: The propensity score with continuous treatments. In: Applied Bayesian Modeling and Causal Inference from Incomplete-Data Perspectives, vol. 226164, pp. 73–84 (2004)
10. Jack, C.R., et al.: Rates of β-amyloid accumulation are independent of hippocampal neurodegeneration. Neurology **82**(18), 1605 (2014)
11. Johansson, F., Shalit, U., Sontag, D.: Learning representations for counterfactual inference. In: International Conference on Machine Learning, pp. 3020–3029. PMLR (2016)
12. Landau, S.M., et al.: The Alzheimer's disease neuroimaging initiative: amyloid pet imaging in Alzheimer's disease: a comparison of three radiotracers. Eur. J. Nucl. Med. Mol. Imaging **41**, 1398–1407 (2014)
13. Li, Q., et al.: The Alzheimer's disease neuroimaging initiative: Aberrant connectivity in mild cognitive impairment and Alzheimer disease revealed by multimodal neuroimaging data. Neurodegener. Dis. **18**, 5–18 (2018)
14. Li, Q., et al.: Multi-modal discriminative dictionary learning for Alzheimer's disease and mild cognitive impairment. Comput. Methods Prog. Biomed. **150**, 1–8 (2017)
15. Miller, M.B., et al.: Somatic genomic changes in single Alzheimer's disease neurons. Nature **604** (2022)
16. Morgan, S.L., Winship, C.: Counterfactuals and Causal Inference. Cambridge University Press (2015)
17. Nie, L., Ye, M., Liu, Q., Nicolae, D.: Vcnet and functional targeted regularization for learning causal effects of continuous treatments. arXiv preprint arXiv:2103.07861 (2021)
18. Ossenkoppele, R., et al.: Amyloid and tau pet-positive cognitively unimpaired individuals are at high risk for future cognitive decline. Nat. Med. **28**, 2381–2387 (2022)
19. Rubin, D.B.: Estimating causal effects of treatments in randomized and nonrandomized studies. J. Educ. Psychol. **66**(5), 688 (1974)

20. Schwab, P., Linhardt, L., Bauer, S., Buhmann, J.M., Karlen, W.: Learning counterfactual representations for estimating individual dose-response curves. In: Proceedings of the AAAI Conference on Artificial Intelligence, vol. 34, pp. 5612–5619 (2020)
21. Shalit, U., Johansson, F.D., Sontag, D.: Estimating individual treatment effect: generalization bounds and algorithms. In: International Conference on Machine Learning, pp. 3076–3085. PMLR (2017)
22. Stuart, E.A.: Matching methods for causal inference: a review and a look forward. Statist. Sci. Rev. J. Inst. Math. Statist. **25**(1), 1 (2010)
23. Wager, S., Athey, S.: Estimation and inference of heterogeneous treatment effects using random forests. J. Am. Stat. Assoc. **113**(523), 1228–1242 (2018)
24. Yao, L., Li, S., Li, Y., Huai, M., Gao, J., Zhang, A.: Representation learning for treatment effect estimation from observational data. Adv. Neural Inf. Process. Syst. **31** (2018)
25. Yao, L., et al.: Concept-level model interpretation from the causal aspect. IEEE Trans. Knowl. Data Eng. (2022)
26. Zhang, Y., Zhang, H., Lipton, Z.C., Li, L.E., Xing, E.: Exploring transformer backbones for heterogeneous treatment effect estimation. In: NeurIPS ML Safety Workshop (2022)
27. Zhu, X., Suk, H.-I., Shen, D.: Multi-modality canonical feature selection for Alzheimer's disease diagnosis. In: Golland, P., Hata, N., Barillot, C., Hornegger, J., Howe, R. (eds.) MICCAI 2014. LNCS, vol. 8674, pp. 162–169. Springer, Cham (2014). https://doi.org/10.1007/978-3-319-10470-6_21

Synthesising Brain Iron Maps from Quantitative Magnetic Resonance Images Using Interpretable Generative Adversarial Networks

Lindsay Munroe[1,2(✉)], Maria Deprez[2], Christos Michaelides[1],
Harry G. Parkes[1], Kalotina Geraki[3], Amy H. Herlihy[4], and Po-Wah So[1(✉)]

[1] Department of Neuroimaging, Institute of Psychiatry, Psychology and
Neuroscience, King's College London, London, U.K.
{lindsay.munroe,po-wah.so}@kcl.ac.uk

[2] School of Biomedical Engineering and Imaging Sciences, King's College London,
London, U.K.

[3] Diamond Light Source, Harwell Science and Innovation Campus, Didcot,
Oxfordshire, U.K.

[4] Perspectum Diagnostics, Gemini One, 5520 John Smith Drive, Oxford, U.K.

Abstract. Accurate spatial estimation of brain iron concentration *in-vivo* is vital to elucidate the role of iron in neurodegenerative diseases, among other applications. However, ground truth quantitative iron maps of the brain can only be acquired post-mortem from *ex-vivo* samples. Quantitative magnetic resonance imaging (QMRI) methods are iron-sensitive and hold potential to quantitatively measure brain iron. We hypothesise interpretability methods can identify the most salient QMRI parameter(s) for iron prediction. In this study, a generative adversarial network with spatially adaptive normalisation layers (SPADE) was trained to synthesise maps of brain iron content from QMRI parameters, including those from relaxometry, diffusion and magnetisation transfer MRI. Ground truth maps of iron content were obtained by synchrotron radiation X-ray fluorescence (SRXRF). QMRI and SRXRF datasets were registered, and a distribution-based loss was proposed to address misalignment from multi-modal QMRI-to-SRXRF registration. To enable interpretation, channel attention was incorporated to learn feature importance for QMRI parameters. Attention weights were compared against occlusion and local interpretable model-agnostic explanations. Our model achieved dice scores of 0.97 and 0.95 for grey and white matter, respectively, when comparing tissue boundaries of synthesised vs. MRI images. Examining the contrast in predicted vs. ground truth iron maps, our model achieved 15.2% and 17.8% normalised absolute error for grey and white matter, respectively. All three interpretable methods ranked fractional anisotropy as the most salient, followed by myelin water fraction and magnetisation transfer ratio. The co-location of iron and myelin may explain the finding that myelin-related QMRI parameters are strong predictors of iron.

J. Woo et al. (Eds.): MICCAI 2023 Workshops, LNCS 14394, pp. 214–226, 2023.
https://doi.org/10.1007/978-3-031-47425-5_20

Keywords: Supervised image-to-image translation · Interpretable deep learning · Iron prediction

1 Introduction

Iron is essential for many physiological processes in the brain, such as aerobic respiration and synthesis of myelin and neurotransmitters; however, high brain iron levels may be harmful, and iron is tightly regulated in the body [1]. Dysregulation of brain iron may contribute to neuronal loss via oxidative stress and ferroptosis arising from iron-enhanced detrimental lipid peroxidation [5]. Furthermore, iron dysregulation is thought to play a role in Alzheimer's Disease (AD) pathogenesis [2]. Therefore, iron chelation has been proposed for AD therapy where brain iron levels needs to be monitored non-invasively.

Magnetic resonance imaging (MRI) has been used to image brain iron *in-vivo*. The MRI signal is sensitive to the presence of iron because iron is both paramagnetic and a susceptibility MRI contrast agent, and enhances MRI relaxation rates R1, R2, and R2* [22]. However, MRI does not directly measure iron concentration, but measures the effect of iron on the relaxation rates of surrounding water molecules, which in turn can be modified by other factors, most notably by myelin [21]. There is a need to develop novel methods to learn relationships between various quantitative MRI (QMRI) parameters and ground truth iron measurements, so that QMRI can be leveraged to accurately measure brain iron *in-vivo*.

Generative deep learning (DL) holds great potential for predicting brain iron content from QMRI data. Generative models have been successfully trained to synthesise images across a range of medical imaging applications, including super-resolution [27], domain adaptation [25] and image-to-image translation [26]. The latter involves training a DL model to transform an image from one domain to another domain(s), and may be either supervised or unsupervised, where training data consists of aligned pairs of images or two sets of unrelated images, respectively.

One limitation of DL models is that they are "black boxes", i.e., no logic is provided regarding decision-making. Interpretable deep learning (IDL) methods address this limitation by producing explanations for decisions made by a DL model. IDL methods are either *post-hoc*, when the method reverse engineers an explanation after model training, or *intrinsic*, where interpretable model components are designed prior to model training.

In this study, our aims were to investigate whether brain iron concentration maps can be accurately predicted from QMRI using state-of-the-art supervised image-to-image translation models and to identify the QMRI parameter(s) that are most relevant for iron prediction by incorporating IDL into the above models.

2   Related Work

2.1   Supervised Image-to-Image Translation

Many successful architectures for supervised image-to-image translation are based on the conditional generative adversarial network (cGAN) [15]. Consider the task of translating images from domain A to domain B with a training pair of images denoted as (I^A, I^B). Then a cGAN consists of a discriminator D, conditioned on I^A, that learns to predict whether an image from domain B is real or synthesised; and a generator G that, given I^A and random noise z, learns to synthesise images that fool D. The conditional adversarial loss is defined as (Eq. 1):

$$\mathcal{L}_{adv} = \mathbb{E}_{I^A, I^B}[\log D(I^A, I^B)] + \mathbb{E}_{I^A, z}[\log(1 - D(I^A, G(I^A, z)))] \qquad (1)$$

One such well-established model is Pix2Pix [10], where the loss function is the weighted sum of $\mathcal{L}_{adv}$ and the pixel-wise L1 loss. However, Pix2Pix struggles to generate realistic images at high-resolution and it was later refined to Pix2PixHD [23]. Subsequently, the SPADE model was proposed to address unrealistic texture in images synthesised by both Pix2Pix and Pix2PixHD [17]. SPADE includes spatially adaptive normalisation layers that learn tensors $\gamma(S^A)$ and $\beta(S^A)$ from segmentation masks S^A, which independently modulate each voxel in the activation map. Let a_i with size $B \times C^i \times H^i \times W^i$ be the activation map after batch normalisation of the ith layer of the SPADE generator. Then SPADE learns $\gamma(S^A)$ and $\beta(S^A)$, both of size $C^i \times H^i \times W^i$, using two-layer convolutional networks where the first layer is shared, and then performs the normalisation $\gamma(S^A)a_i + \beta(S^A)$.

2.2   Interpretable Deep Learning

Two popular post-hoc IDL methods are occlusion [28] and local interpretable model-agnostic explanations (LIME) [18], both of which generate feature importance by perturbing input features and measuring the change in model prediction. Occlusion constructs a sensitivity map by sequentially obstructing patches of the input image and computing the change in the model prediction between the original and occluded image. Alternatively, LIME perturbs the input image several times by randomly masking superpixels. A feature vector $v = (v_1, ..., v_n)$ is created for each perturbed image, where $v_i = 0$ if superpixel i was randomly masked and $v_i = 1$ otherwise; the associated label is the model prediction for the perturbed image. A linear model is then trained on weighted feature vectors and labels, and the ith coefficient of the linear model is the feature importance of superpixel i.

On the other hand, attention mechanisms are a popular intrinsic IDL approach, where learnable weights are multiplied with feature maps during training. Attention enables the model to emphasise or ignore different features for the task by increasing or decreasing the weights, respectively. Channel attention learns a weight for each channel of the feature map, i.e. for each filter, to highlight salient filters [9,24].

3 Methods

3.1 Data

Samples: Formalin-fixed samples ($\sim 20 \times 20 \times 5$ mm) were obtained from the mid-temporal gyrus of AD and age- and gender-matched cognitively normal subjects (n = 15/group) from the MRC London Neurodegenerative Diseases Brain Bank and individually immersed in Fomblin (Solvay Solexis, Milan, Italy) for *ex-vivo* quantitative MRI (see below). After MRI, samples were paraffin wax embedded and a 7 μm thick tissue section obtained from the middle of the wax block and mounted on 4mm thick ultralene film (SPEX Sample-Prep, NJ, USA) for synchrotron radiation X-ray fluorescence (SRXRF) elemental iron mapping (see below).

MRI: Quantitative MRI was acquired on a 7 T MRI system (Agilent Technologies Inc., Walnut Creek, CA, USA). Two-dimensional (2D) T1- and T2-relaxometry, and diffusion-weighted (DW) MRI were performed using a spin-echo sequence. For T1, a series of experiments were done with a constant echo time (TE) = 12 ms and varying repetition times (TR). For T2, TR was kept constant at 4000 ms and TE varied. Diffusion-weighted MRI data was performed with diffusion gradients applied in 6-orthogonal directions at a b-value of 1000. 2D-T2* relaxometry and magnetization transfer (MT)-weighted MRI were performed using a gradient echo sequence. T2*-relaxometry was collected with constant TR = 4000 ms and varying TE. For MT-MRI, gradient-echo MRI data was collected with a saturation pulse at "off" resonance and then "on" resonance. All data were collected at 109 μm in-plane resolution with contiguous 0.5 mm thick slices.

Relaxation time (T1, T2 and T2*) maps were calculated by pixel-by-pixel fitting to the equations: $y = M_0[1 - e^{(-TR/T1)}]$, $y = M_0 e^{(-TE/T2)}$ and $y = M_0 e^{(-TE/T2^*)}$, and their reciprocals provided relaxation rate (R1, R2 and R2*) maps. Myelin water fraction (MWF) maps were also estimated with the DECAES package [6] from the gradient echo data used for T2*-relaxometry. The same dataset also provided phase information to estimate quantitative susceptibility maps (QSM) maps using the SEPIA package [11,13,14]. Mean diffusivity (MD) and fractional anisotropy (FA) were computed from the three eigenvalues $\lambda_1, \lambda_2, \lambda_3$ of the diffusion tensor as: $MD = (\lambda_1 + \lambda_2 + \lambda_3)/3$ and $FA = \sqrt{((\lambda_1 - \lambda_2)^2 + (\lambda_2 - \lambda_3)^2 + (\lambda_1 - \lambda_3)^2)/2(\lambda_1^2 + \lambda_2^2 + \lambda_3^2)}$. Magnetisation transfer ratio (MTR) was computed as $100\% \times (S_0 - S_{Sat})/S_0$, where S_0 and S_{Sat} are the signal intensities from the images with a saturation pulse "off" and "on" resonance, respectively.

SRXRF Iron Mapping: Selected regions (including both white and grey matter, $< 10 \times 10$ mm area) of brain tissue sections underwent SRXRF at 100 μm resolution (Beamline I18, Diamond Light Source, Didcot, Oxfordshire, UK) and processed to provide quantitative iron maps as previously described [22].

3.2 Image Registration

Supervised image-to-image translation assumes access to pairs of perfectly aligned images, and thus a pseudo 3D T2-weighted MRI image (moving) was registered to the corresponding 2D SRXRF map (fixed) for each subject. Initially, each slice in the T2-weighted MRI volume was affinely registered to the SRXRF map, and the SRXRF map was initialised into a 3D array at the slice index with the best registration cost. Then, 3D-3D affine registration was performed to further aid alignment of the iron map with the MRI slice. Finally nonlinear B-Spline deformation was applied to allow for any warping during sample handling. The final transform was subsequently applied to all QMRI parameters from the same subject. Registration was implemented in python with the Insight Toolkit (ITK) library. Registration performance was assessed by comparing fixed and moving white matter (WM) and grey matter (GM) masks using the dice coefficient, where all masks were manually annotated.

3.3 Model Architecture

The well-established SPADE was selected as our baseline model [17]. Both variants of the generator that were originally proposed were applied: the first is a decoder that inputs random noise z, whereas the second extends the decoder

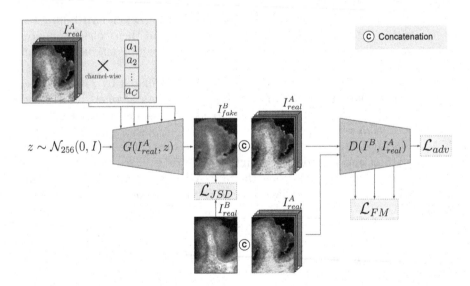

Fig. 1. Model design. Given a training image pair (I_{real}^A, I_{real}^B), the masked MRI I_{real}^A is multiplied channel-wise with attention weights and fed into the SPADE generator G. G learns to synthesise the iron content map $I_{fake}^B = G(I_{real}^A, z)$ to appear realistic in order to fool the discriminator D. Along with the adversarial loss $(\mathcal{L}_{adv})$ and feature matching loss $(\mathcal{L}_{FM})$ of SPADE, we add a loss of Jensen-Shannon divergence $(\mathcal{L}_{JSD})$ between the pixel distributions of I_{real}^B and I_{fake}^B.

to a variational auto-encoder (VAE) so that z is a style vector sampled from the VAE latent space. The input of one-hot masked QMRI images to the spatially adaptive normalisation layers, instead of one-hot segmentation masks, was also investigated. A one-hot masked QMRI image has $C = C_{seq} \times C_{roi}$ channels, where C_{seq} is the number of QMRI parameters ($C_{seq} = 8$) and C_{roi} is the number of brain regions in the mask ($C_{roi} = 3$ for WM, GM and background).

3.4   Model Loss

The feature matching loss proposed in Pix2PixHD [23] was incorporated into the model. Specifically, let $D^i, i = 1, ..., L$ represent the sub-network of discriminator D from the input layer up to and including the ith layer, whose feature map has N^i elements. Then feature matching loss is defined as (Eq. 2):

$$\mathcal{L}_{FM} = \mathbb{E}_{I^A, I^B, z}[\sum_{i=1}^{L} \frac{1}{N^i} \|D^i(I^A, I^B) - D^i(I^A, G(I^A, z))\|_1] \tag{2}$$

Additionally, we proposed a distribution-based loss, since pixel-wise losses were inappropriate for this study, as blurred images were generated due to the misalignment between paired QMRI and SRXRF images. The Jensen-Shannon divergence (JSD) was computed between the ground truth and predicted image, henceforth represented as I^B_{real} and $I^B_{fake} = G(I^A_{real}, z)$, respectively. Assume pixels are gaussian distributed, denoted by $P_{real} \sim \mathcal{N}(\mu_{real}, \sigma_{real})$ and $P_{fake} \sim \mathcal{N}(\mu_{fake}, \sigma_{fake})$. Let $M = \frac{1}{2}(P_{real} + P_{fake}) \sim \mathcal{N}(\mu_M, \sigma_M)$ where $\mu_M = (\mu_{real} + \mu_{fake})/2$ and $\sigma_M = \sqrt{(\sigma_{real}^2 + \sigma_{fake}^2)/4}$. Then JSD loss ($\mathcal{L}_{JSD}$) is defined in terms of Kullback-Leibler divergence (KLD) (Eq. 4):

$$KL(P\|M) = \frac{1}{2} \log \frac{\sigma_M}{\sigma} + \frac{\sigma^2 + (\mu - \mu_M)^2}{2\sigma_M^2} - \frac{1}{2} \tag{3}$$

$$\mathcal{L}_{JSD} = \mathbb{E}_{I^B_{real}, I^B_{fake}}[\frac{1}{2} KL(P_{real}\|M) + \frac{1}{2} KL(P_{fake}\|M)] \tag{4}$$

Means and standard deviations were estimated from the images. We computed $\mathcal{L}_{JSD}$ separately for GM and WM and sum the two losses. The total loss is (Eq. 5):

$$\mathcal{L} = \mathcal{L}_{adv} + \lambda_1 \mathcal{L}_{FM} + \lambda_2 \mathcal{L}_{JSD} \tag{5}$$

3.5   Interpretability

The SPADE architecture was modified to incorporate channel attention, where the attention weights provide a measure of feature importance. To validate the attention weights, we adapted two post-hoc interpretability methods adapted for image-to-image translation, occlusion and LIME.

Channel attention was added to the SPADE architecture to generate feature importance for each QMRI parameter, separately for GM and WM. Specifically, channel attention was incorporated into all SPADE layers in the generator, where learnable weights W of size $1 \times C_{seq}.C_{roi} \times 1 \times 1$ are multiplied with the input of size $B \times C_{seq}.C_{roi} \times H \times W$, prior to feeding through the spatially-adaptive normalisation layer (see Fig. 1). Weights W are constrained to be positive and sum to one.

Occlusion was modified for the image-to-image translation task by considering the change in image similarity between I_{real}^B and I_{fake}^B before and after occluding a brain region for a specific QMRI parameter in I_{real}^A (Algorithm 1). Occlusion weights were averaged across validation images to give feature importance. KLD was used to assess image similarity.

Algorithm 1: Occlusion modified for image-to-image translation

---

    Input   : Validation image-pair from domain A and B, I_{real}^A and I_{real}^B, and
               corresponding segmentations, S^A and S^B.
    Output: Dictionary of feature importance values
1   $featureImportanceDict = \{\}$
2   $I_{fake}^B = \texttt{G}(I_{real}^A, z)$
3   $s = \texttt{imageSimilarity}(I_{fake}^B, I_{real}^B)$
4   **for** p in *parameters* **do**
5   **for** r in $[GM, WM]$ **do**
6          $I_{occ}^A = \texttt{occludeImage}(I_{real}^A, p, r)$
7          $I_{fakeOcc}^B = \texttt{G}(I_{occ}^A, z)$
8          $fi = |s - \texttt{imageSimilarity}(I_{fakeOcc}^B, I_{real}^B)|$
9          $featureImportanceDict[p][r] = fi$
10   **end for**
11 **end for**
12 **return** $featureImportanceDict$

LIME was modified for the image-to-image translation task by setting the label for training the regression model as the image similarity between I^B and the image synthesised from the randomly occluded image from domain A (Algorithm 2). The image similarity metric is the same as for occlusion.

3.6 Performance Metrics

To achieve satisfactory image quality, the synthesised iron maps must fulfil two criteria:

1. **Structural:** the GM and WM boundaries in the synthesised image closely align with the corresponding boundaries in the real QMRI image I_{real}^A
2. **Contrast:** the GM and WM pixel distributions in the synthesised image are similar to the same distributions in the ground truth iron map I_{real}^B

Algorithm 2: LIME modified for image-to-image translation

Input   : Validation image-pair from domain A and B, I_{real}^A and I_{real}^B, and corresponding segmentations, S^A and S^B.

Output: Dictionary of feature importance values

1 $featureImportanceDict = \{\}$
2 $vectors, labels, weights = [], [], []$
3 **for** $i \leftarrow 0$ **to** 30 **do**
4      $I_{occ}^A, v_{occ}^A, w = \texttt{randomOccludeImage}(I_{real}^A, S^A)$
5      $vectors.append(v_{occ}^A)$
6      $weights.append(w)$
7      $I_{fakeOcc}^B = \texttt{G}(I_{occ}^A, z)$
8      $s = \texttt{imageSimilarity}(I_{fakeOcc}^B, I_{real}^B)$
9      $labels.append(s)$
10 **end for**
11 $regressor = Ridge(\alpha = 1)$
12 $regressor.fit(vectors, labels, weights)$
13 $featureImportanceDict[p][r] = \texttt{getCoefficient}(regressor, p, r)$
14 **return** $featureImportanceDict$

We assessed the structural criterion by computing the dice coefficient between synthesised and I_{real}^A region masks, for GM and WM separately. As a baseline, we compared to the performance results for registration as described in Sect. 3.2. For the contrast criterion, we computed the region mean of I_{fake}^B and I_{real}^B — μ_{fake} and μ_{real} respectively — and compute the normalised absolute error (NAE) as $|\mu_{real} - \mu_{fake}|/\mu_{real}$. To further validate the synthetic image contrast, we trained a linear model to predict iron content from normalised, mean MRI parameter values as a baseline measure of performance.

4   Experiments and Results

4.1   Implementation Details

The SPADE generator and discriminator were trained using the two time-scale update rule, where the learning rates were 0.0001 and 0.0004, respectively [8], applying the Adam optimiser with hyperparameters $\beta_1 = 0.5, \beta_2 = 0.999$. Models were trained for 200 epochs using a 6GB Nvidia Quadro P3200 GPU. Instance normalisation and spectral normalisation [16] were applied to all layers of the generator, discriminator, and the VAE encoder.

Extensive data augmentation was applied "on-the-fly" to address the challenge of model overfitting with a small dataset. We randomly sampled 32×32 size patches during training, and also applied random flipping, random rescaling and mixup [29]. Augmentation methods that break the relationship between the MRI and SR-XRF data were avoided such as adding random noise. Furthermore, poor performance was observed on a few samples in the dataset with unusually high iron levels, and counteracted with over-sampling of these rare samples during training. Due to the small sample size, five-fold cross-validation was applied and mean performance across the validation folds was reported. During validation, the synthesised image was reconstructed from overlapping image patches using the approach described by Klages *et al.* [12].

4.2 Analysis of Model Architecture

Performance differences were observed between inputting real images vs. segmentation masks into the SPADE generator. Real inputs slightly worsened alignment of synthesised to ground truth tissue boundaries (Table 1). However, both input types achieve high dice scores $\geq 95\%$ and for WM, the registration baseline performance was surpassed. Therefore, synthesised iron maps attain excellent structural agreement of tissue boundaries with the QMRI data, despite the challenge of misalignment between QMRI and SRXRF iron maps (green arrows in Fig. 2 show this visually).

Conversely, real image input substantially improved accuracy compared to segmentation input with respect to NAE for WM tissue (Table 2). Real input

Table 1. Structural performance. The tissue boundaries of images synthesised by generator G were compared to the boundaries in the MRI input using the dice coefficient. Grey matter (GM) and white matter (WM) boundaries were considered separately.

G	Input	$\mathcal{L}_{FM}$	$\mathcal{L}_{JSD}$	GM Dice↑	WM Dice↑
Baseline: MRI-to-iron registration				*0.97 ± 0.02*	*0.86 ± 0.06*
SPADE	real	✓	✗	0.97 ± 0.01	0.95 ± 0.03
SPADE + VAE	seg	✓	✗	**0.98 ± 0.01**	**0.96 ± 0.02**
SPADE + VAE	real	✓	✗	0.97 ± 0.01	0.95 ± 0.03
SPADE	real	✗	✓	0.97 ± 0.01	0.95 ± 0.03
SPADE	real	✓	✓	0.97 ± 0.01	0.95 ± 0.03

Table 2. Contrast performance. The mean of images predicted by generator G were compared to their corresponding ground truth using normalised absolute error (NAE). Grey matter (GM) and white matter (WM) were considered separately.

G	Input	$\mathcal{L}_{FM}$	$\mathcal{L}_{JSD}$	GM NAE ↓	WM NAE ↓
Baseline: linear model				*18.6% ± 13.9%*	*20.2% ± 14.9%*
SPADE	real	✓	✗	15.3% ± 9.1%	18.7% ± 15.8%
SPADE + VAE	seg	✓	✗	15.1% ± 11.7%	22.5% ± 13.8%
SPADE + VAE	real	✓	✗	**14.8% ± 8.8%**	19.0% ± 15.8%
SPADE	real	✗	✓	15.9% ± 13.7%	21.2% ± 15.2%
SPADE	real	✓	✓	15.2% ± 8.5%	**17.8% ± 15.9%**

into both versions of the SPADE generator also outperformed the baseline linear model in both WM and GM regions. Since the performance of SPADE vs. SPADE + VAE are comparable, we selected SPADE with real input as the best choice of architecture due to possessing fewer parameters (shown in Fig. 1).

4.3   Analysis of Model Loss

The model performance for $\mathcal{L}_{FM}$ only, $\mathcal{L}_{JSD}$ only, and $\lambda_1\mathcal{L}_{FM} + \lambda_2\mathcal{L}_{JSD}$ ($\lambda_1 = 10, \lambda_2 = 1$) were compared, with the latter choice achieving the best performance (Table 2). Visually, the iron maps predicted from the model with only $\mathcal{L}_{FM}$ contained slightly less realistic texture compared to the model with both $\mathcal{L}_{FM}$ and $\mathcal{L}_{JSD}$ (see orange arrows in Fig. 2).

4.4   Analysis of Interpretability

Of the multi-modal quantitative MRI employed for each subject, FA was found to be the most important predictor of iron by all three IDL methods (Fig. 3). Of the three methods, LIME suggested only FA was the most important feature for iron prediction whereas Channel attention proposed MTR and MWF were also important. However, while occlusion suggested MWF was just as important as FA, MTR was relatively unimportant. The traditionally iron-sensitive quantitative MRI measurements, R2, R2* and QSM, appeared to be less important than myelin measures for iron prediction by any of the IDL methods.

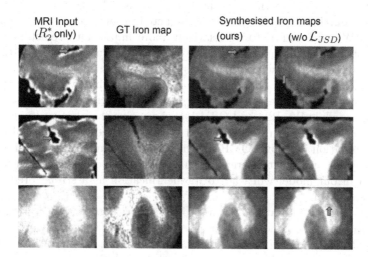

Fig. 2. Qualitative comparison of ground truth (GT) vs. synthesised iron maps. The brain tissue boundaries in the synthesised images closely resemble those in the MRI input (green arrows). The images synthesised without JSD loss ($\mathcal{L}_{JSD}$) contain slightly less realistic texture than images generated from our model with $\mathcal{L}_{JSD}$ (orange arrows). Though only R_2^* quantitative MRI is displayed here, all 8 quantitative MRI parameters were included in the input.

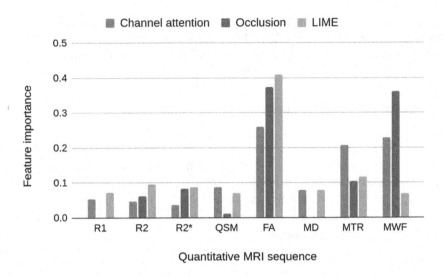

Fig. 3. Interpretability results. All three interpretable deep learning methods were in agreement that fractional anisotropy (FA) is the most important quantitative MRI parameter for predicting iron content.

5   Discussion

In this study, all three of the IDL employed proposed FA as the major predictor of iron. Furthermore, the methods predicted other myelin-sensitive QMRI metrics, MWF and MTR, to be relatively more important predictors of iron compared to the traditional iron-sensitive QMRI measurements, R2, R2* and QSM. Oligodendrocytes whose plasma membranes form myelin, are the highest iron-containing brain cell, and may explain somewhat why the three IDL methods propose myelin-associated MRI measures as strong predictors of iron. Furthermore, while R2, R2* and QSM have been shown to be sensitive to iron, these measurements are in turn impacted by the presence of myelin [7]. Interestingly, χ-separation is a novel QMRI method that discriminates the confounding effect of myelin on iron measurement [20], and we hypothesise inclusion of χ-separation in our model will lead to its identification as a strong predictor of iron concentration.

The main study limitations pertain to the cohort dataset, which is small for DL applications. The cohort dataset size is kept small by limited synchrotron access to obtain ground truth iron maps. In fact, to the best of our knowledge, this is the largest brain dataset acquired with both MRI and quantitative iron maps from the same sample [4]. This demonstrates the difficulties of applying DL to the task of predicting brain iron when ground truth data is required. Another limitation is that supervised image-to-image translation assumes perfectly aligned paired images, however, this is extremely challenging to achieve in practice.

Predicting brain iron maps from QMRI *in-vivo* would greatly benefit research into the role of iron in neurodegeneration, as well as other applications. It is also valuable to identify the most salient QMRI parameters for iron prediction. We trained an interpretable SPADE model on registered QMRI and SRXRF *ex-vivo* data to synthesise brain iron maps. Our results demonstrated that our model is capable of synthesising iron maps that structurally align with QMRI data, whilst having contrast that is broadly consistent with ground truth SRXRF iron maps. Furthermore, QMRI parameters that correlate well with myelin were found to be the most important predictors of brain iron. While our study shows promise in using GANs to predict iron from QMRI data, other state-of-the-art supervised image-to-image translation models, for example diffusion models [19] and vision transformers [3], may be able to better adapt to the limited cohort dataset size often encountered.

References

1. Ashraf, A., Clark, M, So, P.-W.: The aging of iron man. In: Frontiers in Aging Neuroscience **10**, 65 (2018)
2. Ashraf, A., et al.: Iron dyshomeostasis, lipid peroxidation and perturbed expression of cystine/glutamate antiporter in Alzheimer's disease: evidence of ferroptosis. Redox Biol. **32**, 101494 (2020)
3. Dalmaz, O., Yurt, M., Çukur, T.: ResViT: residual vision transformers for multimodal medical image synthesis. IEEE Trans. Med. Imaging **41**(10), 2598–2614 (2022)
4. Barros, A.D., et al.: Matching ex vivo MRI with iron histology: pearls and pitfalls. Front. Neuroan. **13**, 68 (2019)
5. Dixon, S.J., et al.: Ferroptosis: an iron-dependent form of nonapoptotic cell death. Cell **149**(5), 1060–1072 (2012)
6. Doucette, J., Kames, C., Rauscher, A.: DECAES - DEcomposition and component analysis of exponential signals. In: Zeitschrift Fur Medizinische Physik (2020). ISSN: 1876–4436. https://doi.org/10.1016/j.zemedi.2020.04.001
7. Hametner, S., et al.: The influence of brain iron and myelin on magnetic susceptibility and effective transverse relaxation-A biochemical and histological validation study. Neuroimage **179**, 117–133 (2018)
8. Heusel, M., et al.: GANs trained by a two time-scale update rule converge to a local nash equilibrium. In: Advances in Neural Information Processing Systems, vol. 30 (2017)
9. Hu, J., Shen, L., Sun, G.: Squeeze-and-excitation networks. In: Proceedings of the IEEE Conference on Computer Vision and Pattern Recognition, pp. 7132–7141 (2018)
10. Isola, P., et al.: Image-to-image translation with conditional adversarial networks. In: Proceedings of the IEEE Conference on Computer Vision and Pattern Recognition, pp. 1125–1134 (2017)
11. Karsa, A., Shmueli, K.: SEGUE: a speedy region-growing algorithm for unwrapping estimated phase. IEEE Trans. Med. Imaging **38**(6), 1347–1357 (2018)
12. Klages, P., et al.: Patch-based generative adversarial neural network models for head and neck MR-only planning. Med. Phys. **47**(2), 626–642 (2020)

13. Li, W., Bing, W., Liu, C.: Quantitative susceptibility mapping of human brain reflects spatial variation in tissue composition. Neuroimage **55**(4), 1645–1656 (2011)
14. Liu, T., et al.: A novel background field removal method for MRI using projection onto dipole fields. NMR Biomed. **24**(9), 1129–1136 (2011)
15. Mirza, M., Osindero, S.: Conditional generative adversarial nets. arXiv preprint arXiv:1411.1784 (2014)
16. Miyato, T., et al.: Spectral normalization for generative adversarial networks. arXiv preprint arXiv:1802.05957 (2018)
17. Park, T., et al.: Semantic image synthesis with spatially-adaptive normalization. In: Proceedings of the IEEE/CVF Conference on Computer Vision and Pattern Recognition, pp. 2337–2346 (2019)
18. Ribeiro,M.T., Singh, S., Guestrin, C.: Why should i trust you? Explaining the Predictions of Any Classifier. In: Proceedings of the 22nd ACM SIGKDD International Conference on Knowledge Discovery and Data Mining, pp. 1135–1144 (2016)
19. Saharia, C., et al.: Palette: image-to-image diffusion models. In: ACM SIGGRAPH 2022 Conference Proceedings, pp. 1–10 (2022)
20. Shin, H.-G., et al.: χ-separation: magnetic susceptibility source separation toward iron and myelin mapping in the brain. Neuroimage **240**, 118371 (2021)
21. Stüber, C., et al.: Myelin and iron concentration in the human brain: a quantitative study of MRI contrast. Neuroimage **93**, 95–106 (2014)
22. Walker, T., et al.: Dissociation between iron accumulation and ferritin upregulation in the aged substantia NIGRA: attenuation by dietary restriction. Aging (Albany NY) **8**(10), 2488 (2016)
23. Wang, T.-C., et al.: High-resolution image synthesis and semantic manipulation with conditional GANs. In: Proceedings of the IEEE Conference on Computer Vision and Pattern Recognition, pp. 8798–8807 (2018)
24. Woo, S., et al.: CBAM: convolutional block attention module. In: Proceedings of the European Conference on Computer Vision (ECCV), pp. 3–19 (2018)
25. Yan, W., et al.: The domain shift problem of medical image segmentation and vendor-adaptation by Unet-GAN. In: Shen, D., et al. (eds.) MICCAI 2019. LNCS, vol. 11765, pp. 623–631. Springer, Cham (2019). https://doi.org/10.1007/978-3-030-32245-8_69
26. Yang, Q., et al.: MRI cross-modality image-to-image translation. Sci. Rep. **10**(1), 3753 (2020)
27. You, C., et al.: CT super-resolution GAN constrained by the identical, residual, and cycle learning ensemble (GAN-CIRCLE). IEEE Trans. Med. Imaging **39**(1), 188–203 (2019)
28. Zeiler, M.D., Fergus, R.: Visualizing and understanding convolutional networks. In: Fleet, D., Pajdla, T., Schiele, B., Tuytelaars, T. (eds.) ECCV 2014. LNCS, vol. 8689, pp. 818–833. Springer, Cham (2014). https://doi.org/10.1007/978-3-319-10590-1_53
29. Zhang, H., et al.: mixup: beyond empirical risk minimization. arXiv preprint arXiv:1710.09412 (2017)

Identifying Shared Neuroanatomic Architecture Between Cognitive Traits Through Multiscale Morphometric Correlation Analysis

Zixuan Wen[1], Jingxuan Bao[1], Shu Yang[1], Shannon L. Risacher[2],
Andrew J. Saykin[2], Paul M. Thompson[3], Christos Davatzikos[1], Heng Huang[4],
Yize Zhao[5], and Li Shen[1(✉)]

[1] University of Pennsylvania, Philadelphia, PA, USA
li.shen@pennmedicine.upenn.edu
[2] Indiana University, Indianapolis, IN, USA
[3] University of Southern California, Los Angels, CA, USA
[4] University of Maryland, College Park, MD, USA
[5] Yale University, New Haven, CT, USA

Abstract. We introduce an informative metric, called morphometric correlation, as a measure of shared neuroanatomic similarity between two cognitive traits. Traditional estimates of trait correlations can be confounded by factors beyond brain morphology. To exclude these confounding factors, we adopt a Gaussian kernel to measure the morphological similarity between individuals and compare pure neuroanatomic correlations among cognitive traits. In our empirical study, we employ a multiscale strategy. Given a set of cognitive traits, we first perform morphometric correlation analysis for each pair of traits to reveal their shared neuroanatomic correlation at the whole brain (or global) level. After that, we extend our whole brain concept to regional morphometric correlation and estimate shared neuroanatomic similarity between two cognitive traits at the regional (or local) level. Our results demonstrate that morphometric correlation can provide insights into shared neuroanatomic architecture between cognitive traits. Furthermore, we also estimate the morphometricity of each cognitive trait at both global and local levels, which can be used to better understand how neuroanatomic changes influence individuals' cognitive status.

Keywords: Brain image analysis · Morphometricity · Morphometric Correlation · Cognitive Traits · Alzheimer's Disease

---

Z. Wen and J. Bao—These authors contributed equally to this work.
This work was supported in part by the NIH grants U01 AG068057, RF1 AG063481, U01 AG066833, R01 LM013463, P30 AG073105, and R01 AG071470, and the NSF grant IIS 1837964. Data used in this study were obtained from the Alzheimer's Disease Neuroimaging Initiative database (adni.loni.usc.edu), which was funded by NIH U01 AG024904.

J. Woo et al. (Eds.): MICCAI 2023 Workshops, LNCS 14394, pp. 227–240, 2023.
https://doi.org/10.1007/978-3-031-47425-5_21

1 Introduction

To date, magnetic resonance imaging (MRI) scans have been widely used in many anatomical studies of the human brain [12,13,15]. In brain disorder studies, it is an important research topic to identify pathological changes in the brain. Most neurodegenerative diseases, such as Alzheimer's Disease (AD), together with cognitive impairments can be detected through brain atrophy patterns captured by structural MRI (sMRI). Several automated techniques have been developed to assess brain atrophy. Voxel-based morphometry (VBM) [1,20] is one of the widely used techniques that provide biologically plausible results by voxel-wise statistical tests to identify brain anatomy differences between different populations.

Recently, substantial attention has been given to mapping associations between neuroanatomic features and complex behavioral or cognitive traits in the field of brain image analysis [15–17,21]. The concept of "morphometricity" [11] was first proposed to measure the proportion of a trait variance explained by neuroanatomic features in the brain. Grey-matter correlation [3] was introduced to capture the shared morphometricity of two quantitative traits. Both in the morphometricity [11] study and the grey-matter correlation [3] study, the whole brain morphology measurements were used and detailed ROI-level signatures were ignored. Thus, in this work, we propose an informative metric, named "morphometric correlation" and construct the morphological similarity matrix using the Gaussian kernel to measure and reveal the shared neuroanatomic signatures across cognitive traits. Furthermore, we employ a multiscale strategy and extend the concept of morphometricity and morphometric correlation from its original definitions at the whole brain (or global) level to a more focal (or local) level based on a region of interest (ROI).

Our contributions can be summarized as follows.

1. Traditional estimates of correlations between two cognitive traits are confounded by factors beyond the brain morphology. We introduce morphometric correlation, as a measure of shared neuroanatomic similarity between two cognitive traits.
2. We propose a non-linear (Gaussian) kernel to construct the similarity relationship matrix. The Gaussian kernel can better capture nonlinear and multivariate associations between genes and traits [9]. We demonstrate in our empirical study that the proposed Gaussian kernel can capture more neuroanatomic signatures than the traditional linear kernel used in grey-matter correlation [3].
3. The previous studies [2,3,11] only applied region of interest (ROI) analysis on the study of morphometricity. In this work, we perform a multiscale morphometric correlation analysis. Specifically, we extend the whole brain morphometric correlation to the local level and estimate shared neuroanatomic similarity between two cognitive traits at the regional (or local) level.
4. Our empirical study has yielded multiple interesting findings. We have observed that the estimated morphometric correlations are stronger than the

direct phenotypic correlations between most cognitive trait pairs, except for the morphometric correlation between MMSE and ADAS13. The ROI-based morphometric correlation between MMSE and ADAS13 using our multiscale strategy can identify multiple ROIs that capture more shared morphological signatures than the whole brain. At the same time, we also compute the whole brain and ROI-based morphometricity. It suggests cognitive traits MMSE and ADAS13 are most associated with the human brain.

Our study can quantify statistical associations between neuroanatomic features and cognitive phenotypes at the population level. The algorithm we use is computationally efficient in the way that it estimates the (co)variance parameters without cross-validation. Our study provides new insights to investigate the associations between the cognition and brain morphology. Whole brain morphometricity and morphometric correlation are biologically interpretable, and could be used to conduct morphological and cognitive studies in the future. Furthermore, our proposed multiscale strategy can better discover the ROI-level imaging cognition associations and reveal the correlation between two cognitive measurements captured by ROI-level brain morphology.

2   Methods

We summarize our overall experimental pipeline in Fig. 1. The pipeline is designed to identify brain imaging cognition associations at multiple scales: one revealed by the whole brain (global) measurements and the other revealed by the ROI-based (local) measurements. First, we use Statistical Parametric Mapping [1,20] to automatically process sMRI scans and obtain the volumetric summary statistics of each voxel. Voxel-based morphometry (VBM) constitutes a comprehensive measurement of the structural anatomy. Next, we use Gaussian kernel [9] to calculate the pairwise morphological similarity between individuals and obtain a morphological relationship matrix (MRM). First of all, we construct the MRM using all the voxels within the whole brain. After that, we construct the MRM using all the multivariate voxel measures within each ROI. Finally, based on global MRM (or local MRM), we estimate whole brain (or ROI-based) morphometricity and morphometric correlation using the average information restricted maximum likelihood (REML) algorithm. Our simulation experiment demonstrates that applying the Gaussian kernel can be less confounded by factors beyond brain morphology. In the real data experiment, 185,405 voxels are used to analyze the whole-brain morphometricity and morphometric correlation across seven clinical cognitive assessment scores in ADNI [18,19] dataset. Then, we extend our method to explore morphometric patterns at the ROI level instead of the global neuroanatomy by estimating the ROI-based morphometricties and morphometric correlations. Our results demonstrate the promise of our proposed method in offering a unique perspective to reveal the underlying neuroanatomic relationship among cognitive traits.

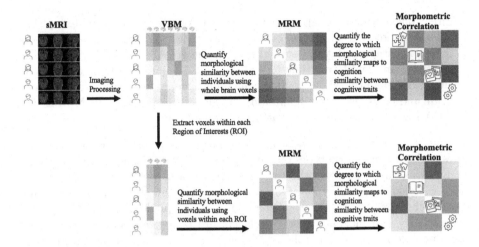

Fig. 1. Morphometric Correlation Analysis Pipeline. Structural MRI scans are processed to obtain voxel-based morphometry (VBM). We first construct a morphological relationship matrix (MRM) using voxels within whole brain. Then, we use this MRM to obtain global morphometricity and morphometric correlation via average information REML algorithm. After that, we construct several morphological relationship matrices using voxels within each ROI. Then, we obtain ROI-based morphometricity and morphometric correlation based on these MRMs

2.1   Bivariate Linear Mixed Effect Model

The morphometricity and morphometric correlation are grounded in the following bivariate linear mixed effect (LME) model [7]:

$$
\begin{aligned}
y_1 &= Xb_1 + a_1 + \varepsilon_1, \\
y_2 &= Xb_2 + a_2 + \varepsilon_2,
\end{aligned}
\tag{1}
$$

where y_i is an $n \times 1$ vector of a quantitative phenotype trait i with n being the number of subjects, b_i is a $s \times 1$ vector of fixed effect, X is an $n \times s$ matrix of confounding variables with s being the number of confounding variables, a_i is an $n \times 1$ vector of random effects with $a_i \sim N(0, A\sigma_{a_i}^2)$ and $\varepsilon_i \sim N(0, I\sigma_{\varepsilon_i}^2)$ is the error term. A is interpreted as the morphological relationship matrix (MRM). MRM quantifies the morphological similarity between two individuals using brain morphology measurements. We use the Gaussian-type similarity metric to accurately measure the similarity from sMRI scan morphometry. The (k, j)-th entry of MRM [9,11] is defined as

$$
A_{kj} = \exp\left(-\sum_l \frac{(z_{kl} - z_{jl})^2}{ms_l^2} \right),
\tag{2}
$$

where z_{kl} is the (k,l)-th elements of imaging measurements matrix Z, refers to the morphometry of l-th voxel of k-th subjects, s_l is the sample standard error of the l-th voxel and m is the number of voxels.

The difference between the morphological relationship matrix and brain relatedness matrix (BRM) used in grey-matter correlation [3] is the method to construct the relationship matrix. Brain relatedness matrix B use linear kernel to quantify the similarities between individuals, which is defined as $B = \frac{1}{m}\widetilde{Z}\widetilde{Z}^T$, where m is the number of measurements, in this case, m is the number of voxels and $\widetilde{Z}$ is a standardized brain imaging measurement matrix.

Formally, the morphometricity of a given trait [11] is the proportion of its phenotypic variation that can be explained by brain morphology, the variation of which is captured by MRM. The morphometricity for trait i can be defined as

$$m_i^2 = \frac{\sigma_{a_i}^2}{\sigma_{a_i}^2 + \sigma_{\varepsilon_i}^2}, \tag{3}$$

where $\sigma_{a_i}^2$ is the phenotypic variance explained by brain morphology, and $\sigma_{a_i}^2 + \sigma_{\varepsilon_i}^2$ is the total phenotypic variance.

Morphometric correlation then measures the degree of brain morphology similarity to which two traits have in common, the correlation of which is captured by MRM. We define the morphometric correlation as

$$r^2 = \frac{\rho}{\sqrt{\sigma_{a_1}^2 \sigma_{a_2}^2}}, \tag{4}$$

where ρ is the covariance between the brain voxels associations with each trait.

We can therefore obtain morphometricity and morphometric correlation by estimating variance and covariance parameters $\theta = (\sigma_{a_1}^2, \sigma_{\varepsilon_1}^2, \sigma_{a_2}^2, \sigma_{\varepsilon_2}^2, \rho)$. The estimators are usually obtained by maximizing a log-likelihood function.

2.2   Efficient Average Information REML Algorithm

The average information restricted maximum likelihood (REML) algorithm has been widely used in estimating variance and covariance parameters [3,8,22]. The average information matrix has been proved [8,23] much more computationally efficient than the observed information matrix [5,10] and Fisher information matrix [5,6]. By assuming bivariate normality of two traits y_1, y_2, the joint distribution of two traits can be written as

$$y = \begin{bmatrix} y_1 \\ y_2 \end{bmatrix} \sim N\left(\begin{bmatrix} X & 0 \\ 0 & X \end{bmatrix} \begin{bmatrix} b_1 \\ b_2 \end{bmatrix}, \mathbf{V}(\theta) \right), \tag{5}$$

The variance matrix $\mathbf{V}(\theta)$ is defined as

$$\mathbf{V}(\theta) = \begin{bmatrix} A\sigma_{a_1}^2 + I\sigma_{\varepsilon_1}^2 & A\rho \\ A\rho & A\sigma_{a_2}^2 + I\sigma_{\varepsilon_2}^2 \end{bmatrix}, \tag{6}$$

where A is the morphological relationship matrix defined in Eq. (2), and I is an $n \times n$ identity matrix. $\sigma_{a_i}^2$ and $\sigma_{\varepsilon_i}^2$ are morphometric variance and residual variance of trait i, respectively, and ρ is the morphometric covariance.

We obtain the estimators by maximizing the restricted log-likelihood function of Eq. (5) (ignoring the constant), $l = -\frac{1}{2}\left(\log|\mathbf{V}(\theta)| + \log|X^T\mathbf{V}(\theta)^{-1}X| + y^TPy\right)$, where $|\cdot|$ refers to the determinant of the matrices. And the matrix P is defined as

$$P = \mathbf{V}(\theta)^{-1} - \mathbf{V}(\theta)^{-1}X(X^T\mathbf{V}(\theta)^{-1}X)^{-1}X^T\mathbf{V}(\theta)^{-1}. \qquad (7)$$

We use restricted maximum likelihood (REML) rather than maximum likelihood (ML) due to the unbiasedness of REML estimation of (co)variance parameters $\hat{\theta}_{\mathrm{REML}} = \mathrm{argmax}_\theta\, l$.

Next, the score function $S(\theta)$ is defined as $S(\theta_i) = \frac{\partial l}{\partial \theta_i} = -\frac{\mathrm{tr}(P\dot{V}_i) - y^TP\dot{V}_iPy}{2}$, where $\mathrm{tr}(\cdot)$ is the trace of the matrix and the (i,j)-th entry of average information matrix [4] is defined as

$$\mathbf{AI}(\theta)_{ij} = \frac{y^TP\dot{V}_iP\dot{V}_jPy}{2}, \qquad (8)$$

where $\dot{V}_i = \frac{\partial \mathbf{V}(\theta)}{\partial \theta_i}$.

The initial guess of parameters is given by arbitrary values. In the first step, we update the parameters using the expected maximization (EM) algorithm, $\theta_i^{(1)} \leftarrow \theta_i^{(0)} + \frac{1}{n}\theta_i^{2(0)}S(\theta_i^{(0)})$. Then, our method switches to the average information REML algorithm, $\theta^{(t+1)} \leftarrow \theta^{(t)} + \mathbf{AI}(\theta^{(t)})^{-1}S(\theta^{(t)})$, updating parameters until the log-likelihood function satisfies the criteria $l^{(t+1)} - l^{(t)} \leq 10^{-4}$. In the iteration process, if any parameters $\sigma_{a_i}^2$ or $\sigma_{\varepsilon_i}^2$ escape from the parameter space, i.e. if $\sigma_{a_i}^2$ or $\sigma_{\varepsilon_i}^2$ is less than 0, it will be set to $10^{-6} \times \sigma_{y_i}^2$. For parameter ρ, if its absolute value $|\rho|$ larger than $\sqrt{\sigma_{a_1}^2\sigma_{a_2}^2}$, it will be set to $\rho = \mathrm{sign}(\mathrm{Cov}\,(y_1, y_2))\sqrt{\sigma_{a_1}^2\sigma_{a_2}^2}$, where $\mathrm{sign}(\cdot)$ is the signum function.

Significance testing of morphometricity estimates m_i^2 can be obtained via the likelihood ratio test (LRT). Under the null hypothesis ($\sigma_{a_i}^2 = 0$), the LRT statistic follows $\frac{1}{2}\chi_0^2 + \frac{1}{2}\chi_1^2$, where χ_1^2 is one degree of freedom χ^2 distribution and χ_0^2 is χ^2 distribution with all probability mass at zero. Similarly, the significance testing for correlation coefficient ρ can also be obtained via LRT.

3   Experimental Results

3.1   Materials

The neuroimaging, demographic, and clinical cognitive assessment data used in the preparation of this article were obtained from the Alzheimer's Disease Neuroimaging Initiative (ADNI) database (http://adni.loni.usc.edu) [18,19]. The ADNI was launched in 2003 as a public-private partnership, led by Principal Investigator Michael W. Weiner, MD. The primary goal of ADNI has been to test whether serial magnetic resonance imaging (MRI), positron emission tomography (PET), other biological markers, and clinical and neuropsychological assessment can be combined to measure the progression of mild cognitive impairment (MCI) and early Alzheimer's disease (AD). Up-to-date information about the ADNI is available at www.adni-info.org.

Structural MRI scans were processed with voxel-based morphometry (VBM) using the Statistical Parametric Mapping (SPM) software tool [1]. All scans were aligned to a T1-weighted template image, segmented into gray matter (GM), white matter (WM), and cerebrospinal fluid (CSF) maps, normalized to the standard Montreal Neurological Institute (MNI) space as $2 \times 2 \times 2$ mm^3 voxels. The GM maps were extracted and smoothed with an 8 mm FWHM kernel, and analyzed in this study. A total of 185,405 non-background voxels, covering cortical, sub-cortical, and cerebellar regions and measuring GM density, were studied in this work as whole brain morphology measurements. Based on the AAL atlas [14], 116 ROI-based morphology measurements are constructed by selecting the voxel-level measurements within each ROI.

Age and gender were used as covariates, following a prior study [11]. Our analysis included seven clinical cognitive assessment scores from the QT-PAD project (http://www.pi4cs.org/qt-pad-challenge). These cognitive scores are Alzheimer's Disease Assessment Scale (ADAS13), Clinical Dementia Rating Sum of Boxes (CDRSB), Rey Auditory Verbal Learning Test (RAVLT.learning), Rey Auditory Verbal Immediate Test (RAVLT.immediate), Rey Auditory Verbal Forgetting Test (RAVLT.forgetting), Mini-Mental State Exam (MMSE), and Functional Activities Questionnaire (FAQ). All subjects with no missing cognitive measures and sMRI measures of the first visit were included in this study. After data preprocessing, there are 1,451 participants ($n = 1,451$) left, including 821 males and 630 females. The average age of participants is 73.9, and the standard deviation of age is 7.1.

3.2   Simulation Results

To show the superior performance of the Gaussian kernel, we also implement the linear kernel for comparison on the simulated data. We first generate 100 pairs of synthetic quantitative traits with joint distribution as shown in Eq. (5). The brain morphometry matrix Z used in the simulation experiment is the left hippocampus voxel-based morphometry. Then the Gaussian kernel MRM A can be obtained by Eq. (2), and the linear kernel BRM B can be obtained by doing the inner product of normalized Z and Z^T. To meet the normality assumption of the model, we first uniformly simulate $\sigma_{a_i}^2$ from $[0, 1]$, then let $\sigma_{\varepsilon_i}^2 = 1 - \sigma_{a_i}^2$, we also uniformly simulate ρ from $[0, 1]$. Then we could obtain ground truth morphometricity and morphometric correlation based on Eq. (3) and Eq. (4) respectively. Next, pair (a_1, a_2) is simulated from bivariate normal distribution

$$\begin{bmatrix} a_1 \\ a_2 \end{bmatrix} \sim N \left(\begin{bmatrix} 0 \\ 0 \end{bmatrix}, \begin{bmatrix} \sigma_{a_1}^2 A & \rho A \\ \rho A & \sigma_{a_2}^2 A \end{bmatrix} \right),$$

ε_i is simulated from normal distribution $N(0, (1 - \sigma_{a_i}^2)I_{n \times n})$, where $I_{n \times n}$ is the n by n identity matrix. The confounding variables we select are age and gender variables. Finally, we have the two traits y_1 and y_2 by Eq. (1). We then estimate the variance and covariance parameters of synthetic quantitative traits using the average information REML algorithm. Once we obtain the estimated $\sigma_{a_i}^2$, $\sigma_{\varepsilon_i}^2$ and ρ, the estimated morphometricity and morphometric correlation can be obtained by Eq. (3) and Eq. (4) respectively.

Figure 2A and Fig. 2B show the comparisons between estimated morphometricities using MRM and BRM [3] respectively. The estimated morphometricity using our method shows better concordance with the synthetic morphometricity, in which the correlation between synthetic and estimated morphometricty is 0.99 (Fig. 2A). The correlation between synthetic and estimated morphometricty using the linear kernel is 0.96 (Fig. 2B), which indicates linear kernel is also reliable in practice. The simulation comparison of morphometricity estimations suggests our method is more accurate than the linear kernel method.

Comparisons of estimated morphometric correlations using different relationship matrices are shown in Fig. 2C (MRM) and Fig. 2D (BRM) [3] respectively. Most of the Gaussian-based estimated morphometric correlations are concordance with the synthetic morphometric correlations (the correlation is 0.95 in Fig. 2C). It indicates that the estimated morphometric correlation is approximately the same as the truth morphometric correlation. However, Fig. 2D reveals the correlation between ground truth and estimated morphometric correlation is only 0.89, which is less accurate. These two figures show that the Gaussian kernel is more reliable and accurate in the morphometric correlation analysis. Estimated morphometric correlation also suggests that morphometric correlation between two traits is not reliable when the morphometricity of either trait is small.

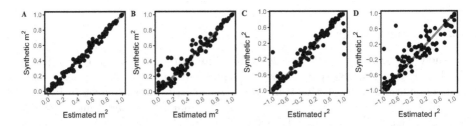

Fig. 2. Comparison of true and estimated morphometricities using different similarity matrix **A.** MRM and **B.** BRM. Comparison of true and estimated morphometric correlation using different similarity matrix **C.** MRM and **D.** BRM.

3.3   Whole Brain Morphometric Correlation and Morphometricity

The traditional phenotypic correlation can be confounded by factors beyond brain morphology. Simulation results indicate that MRM is much more accu-

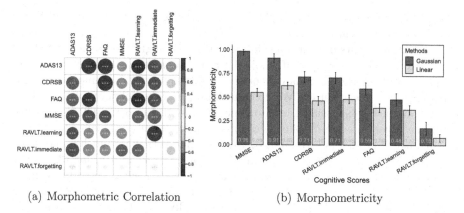

(a) Morphometric Correlation   (b) Morphometricity

Fig. 3. (a) Morphometric correlation among seven cognitive traits. Upper triangle shows the morphometric correlation between two traits, while lower triangle is the phenotypic correlation between pairs of traits. An asterisk indicates significance with $p < 0.05$, two asterisks indicate significance with $p < 0.01$, three asterisks indicates significance with $p < 0.001$. (b) Morphometricity estimations of seven cognitive traits using Gaussian and linear kernel. Error bars indicate SE of the estimates.

rate than BRM when estimating the morphometric correlation. Besides, the grey-matter correlation strategy [3] failed to estimate the brain morphometric correlation between two given cognitive traits in our real experiment. Thus, we present our estimated pairwise morphometric correlations in Fig. 3(a), which reveal the shared neuroanatomic similarity between two cognitive traits. The lower triangle shows the phenotypic correlation between two traits, which is the Pearson correlation between two traits. The upper triangle is our estimated morphometric correlation. The morphometric correlation and phenotypic correlation among seven cognitive traits have the same direction, except for the correlation between MMSE and RAVLT.forgetting. Most of the morphometric correlation and phenotypic correlation are significant ($p < 0.005$). The largest positive morphometric correlation is $\hat{r}^2 = 0.98$, which is presented between ADAS13 and CDRSB, as well as between FAQ and CDRSB. Besides, both the morphometric correlation between ADAS13 and FAQ and the morphometric correlation between RAVLT.learning and RAVLT.immediate are large (with $\hat{r}^2 = 0.97$). They are larger than their underlying phenotypic correlation. The largest negative correlation is founded between FAQ and RAVLT.learning ($\hat{r}^2 = -0.85$), whose corresponding phenotypic correlation is only -0.44.

The morphometric correlation between ADAS13 and MMSE (-0.4) is not as strong as their phenotypic correlation (-0.74). First note that, the negative correlation is reasonable, since the lower scores of MMSE indicating of poorer performance and greater cognitive impairment, while higher scores of ADAS13 reflect poorer performance. Next, this result indicates that the shared brain morphology variants of two traits are able to weaker than their shared phenotypic variants. Finally, we notice that the detailed regional associations can be ignored when using whole brain morphology. This evidence motivates our ROI-based morphometric correlation study.

Simulation results indicate the Gaussian kernel is slightly more accurate than the linear kernel. The results of whole brain morphometricity estimations again demonstrate that the Gaussian kernel can capture more neuroanatomic signatures than the linear kernel. We compare brain morphometricity of seven cognitive traits using Gaussian kernel or linear kernel in Fig. 3(b). These cognitive traits are widely used in measuring cognition impairment and memory loss. The morphometricity results estimated by the Gaussian kernel are much higher than that used by the linear kernel, especially for traits MMSE and ADAS13. All the cognitive traits are statistically significantly associated with whole brain morphology (all the p-value are less than 0.005). The Gaussian-based MRM results reveal that MMSE and ADAS13 are substantially morphometric (with point estimates of 0.98 and 0.91 respectively), suggesting that these two cognitive traits are associated with substantial anatomical signatures. However, morphometricity values of CDRSB, RAVLT.immediate, FAQ, and RAVLT.learning are moderate, all greater than 0.4. Finally, the estimated morphometricity value of RAVLT.forgetting is only 0.18, which indicates only 18% of variation of RAVLT.forgetting traits could be explained by brain morphometry.

In practice, the MMSE score is frequently used for Alzheimer's disease drug studies and the ADAS13 score evaluates memory, reasoning, and language. Our method also reveals that these two traits are associated with substantial anatomical signatures.

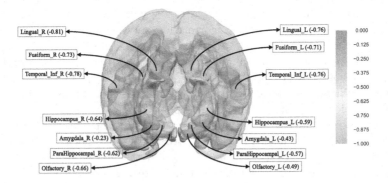

Fig. 4. ROI-based morphometric correlation between ADAS13 and MMSE. The ROIs are those most related to AD.

3.4 Brain ROI-Based Morphometric Correlation and Morphometricity

To reveal ignored morphometric correlations at the regional level, we apply the multiscale strategy by using the voxels within each ROI instead of the whole brain as morphology measurements. Then, we calculate the local (regional) MRM and the variation that could be captured by the local MRM. The extension is important since the spatial association between brain morphology and cognitive traits can not be revealed when using whole brain morphometry. We choose and analyze 14 regions that are most related to AD and reveal the ROI-based morphometric correlation between MMSE and ADAS13. Figure 4 shows the spatial map and values of ROI level morphometric correlation between MMSE and ADAS13. The ROI level morphometric correlation can be larger than that using whole brain morphometry. The shared morphological architectures captured by all AD related regions (except region Amygdala_R) are larger than that captured by the whole brain (−0.40). Especially, regions Lingual_R, Temporal_Inf_R, Temporal_Inf_L, and Lingual_L show the morphometric correlation between two traits are even larger than their phenotypic correlation (−0.74). This finding suggests that some regions are stronger to capture the association between two cognitive traits than the whole brain. Figure 4 also indicates most regions in the right brain can capture more similarity of two traits than regions in the left brain. This evidence is promising and has an important impact on revealing structure changes within ROIs from an evolutionary morphological perspective.

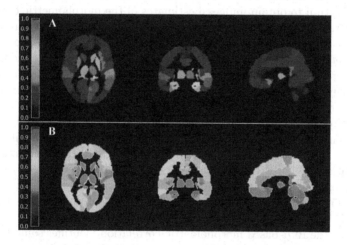

Fig. 5. ROI-based morphometricity of **A.** ADAS13 and **B.** MMSE.

We have shown in Fig. 3(b), MMSE and ADAS13 have substantial neuroanatomic signatures associated with brain morphology. Then, we extend our analysis to the ROI-level morphometricity of ADAS13 and MMSE using multiscale strategy. At this time, we estimate associations between 116 regions and cognitive traits. The regional level morphometricity of these two cognitive traits is shown as spatial morphometricity heatmap in Fig. 5. In contrast to the whole brain morphometricity of ADAS13 cognitive trait (0.91), the top 5 ROIs which are identified as having substantial association with the ADAS13 are Pallidum_R (0.67), Hippocampus_L (0.66), Amygdala_L (0.65),

ParaHippocampal_L (0.61), Hippocampus_R (0.55). For MMSE, the top 5 ROIs are Vermis_1_2 (0.93), Pallidum_R (0.93), Vermis_10 (0.91), Hippocampus_R (0.91), Amygdala_L (0.90). Both ADAS13 and MMSE are highly associated with regions Hippocampus and Amygdala, which suggests our multiscale strategy can provide strong evidence in prioritizing regions that are more related to the given phenotype. Thus, our regional morphometricity strategy bridges the gap that regional information is ignored by whole brain morphometricity.

The spatial morphometricity map also reveals the nonsymmetric distributed morphometricity, suggesting that the variation of cognitive scores captured by ROIs are not equal for left and right regions. The ROI level morphometricity analysis is able to identify relevant neuroimaging biomarkers and to explain brain structure variants related to cognitive variants.

4   Conclusion and Discussions

In this study, we have introduced a novel concept "morphometric correlation" as a measure of the morphological signatures shared by complex traits. To exclude the effect caused by factors other than brain morphology, we have adopted a Gaussian kernel to construct the relationship matrix and average information REML algorithm to obtain unbiased estimates of the morphometric correlation. The estimated morphometric correlation is able to quantify the neuroanatomic aggregate features of pairs of quantitative traits. The superiority of our method has been demonstrated by both simulation results and the applications of estimating morphometric correlations among cognitive traits. We then use a multiscale strategy to extend the concept to the local level by using the voxels within each ROI.

We have observed that the estimated morphometric correlations are stronger than the pure phenotypic correlations between most pairs of cognitive traits. Both the morphometric correlation of ADAS13 and CDRSB and the morphometric correlation of CDRSB and FAQ are significantly high ($\hat{r}^2 = 0.97$, $p < 0.001$). The morphometric correlation of FAQ and RAVLT.learning is significantly low ($\hat{r}^2 = -0.85$, $p < 0.001$). Although the whole brain morphometric correlation between MMSE and ADAS13 is not as strong as the corresponding phenotypic correlations, the ROI-based morphometric correlation identifies some ROIs that capture more shared morphological signatures than the whole brain. The prioritized ROIs may provide new insights for future brain morphology and cognition studies.

We have also estimated the morphometricity of cognitive traits, which is the proportion of the phenotypic variation captured by the brain morphology. In the application to the whole brain morphometricity analysis, our method was able to accurately reveal the variation explained by brain morphology. The cognitive traits MMSE and ADAS13 are substantially morphometric. However, the ROI-based morphometricity of MMSE is moderate, while the ROI-based morphometricity of ADAS13 is modest. The ROI level morphometricity analysis provides important information for understanding brain structural variation related to cognitive variation and can potentially help characterize the progression of AD.

References

1. Ashburner, J., Friston, K.J.: Voxel-based morphometry-the methods. Neuroimage **11**(6), 805–821 (2000)
2. Bao, J., et al.: Identifying imaging genetic associations via regional morphometricity estimation. In: Pacific Symposium on Biocomputing, vol. 27, pp. 97–108 (2022)
3. Couvy-Duchesne, B., et al.: A unified framework for association and prediction from vertex-wise grey-matter structure. Hum. Brain Mapp. **41**(14), 4062–4076 (2020)
4. Gilmour, A.R., Thompson, R., Cullis, B.R.: Average information REML: an efficient algorithm for variance parameter estimation in linear mixed models. Biometrics 1440–1450 (1995)
5. Harville, D.A.: Maximum likelihood approaches to variance component estimation and to related problems. J. Am. Stat. Assoc. **72**(358), 320–338 (1977)
6. Jennrich, R.I., Sampson, P.: Newton-raphson and related algorithms for maximum likelihood variance component estimation. Technometrics **18**(1), 11–17 (1976)
7. Laird, N.M., Ware, J.H.: Random-effects models for longitudinal data. Biometrics 963–974 (1982)
8. Lee, S.H., Van Der Werf, J.H.: An efficient variance component approach implementing an average information REML suitable for combined LD and linkage mapping with a general complex pedigree. Genet. Sel. Evol. **38**(1), 1–19 (2006)
9. Liu, D., Lin, X., Ghosh, D.: Semiparametric regression of multidimensional genetic pathway data: least-squares kernel machines and linear mixed models. Biometrics **63**(4), 1079–1088 (2007)
10. Meyer, K., Smith, S.: Restricted maximum likelihood estimation for animal models using derivatives of the likelihood. Genet. Sel. Evol. **28**(1), 23–49 (1996)
11. Sabuncu, M.R., Ge, T., Holmes, A.J., et al.: Morphometricity as a measure of the neuroanatomical signature of a trait. Proc. Natl. Acad. Sci. **113**(39), E5749–E5756 (2016)
12. Shen, L., et al.: ADNI: identifying neuroimaging and proteomic biomarkers for MCI and AD via the elastic net. Multimodal Brain Image Anal. **7012**, 27–34 (2011)
13. Shen, L., Thompson, P.M.: Brain imaging genomics: integrated analysis and machine learning. Proc. IEEE **108**(1), 125–162 (2020)
14. Tzourio-Mazoyer, N., et al.: Automated anatomical labeling of activations in SPM using a macroscopic anatomical parcellation of the MNI MRI single-subject brain. Neuroimage **15**(1), 273–289 (2002)
15. Wan, J., et al.: Identifying the neuroanatomical basis of cognitive impairment in Alzheimer's disease by correlation- and nonlinearity-aware sparse Bayesian learning. IEEE Trans. Med. Imaging **33**(7), 1475–1487 (2014)
16. Wang, H., Nie, F., Huang, H., Risacher, S., Saykin, A.J., Shen, L.: Identifying ad-sensitive and cognition-relevant imaging biomarkers via joint classification and regression. Med. Image Comput. Comput. Assist. Interv. **14**(Pt 3), 115–23 (2011)
17. Wang, X., et al.: Exploring automated machine learning for cognitive outcome prediction from multimodal brain imaging using streamline. AMIA Jt. Summits Transl. Sci. Proc. **2023**, 544–553 (2023)
18. Weiner, M.W., Veitch, D.P., Aisen, P.S., et al.: The Alzheimer's disease neuroimaging initiative: a review of papers published since its inception. Alzheimers Dement. **9**(5), e111-94 (2013)

19. Weiner, M.W., Veitch, D.P., Aisen, P.S., et al.: Recent publications from the Alzheimer's disease neuroimaging initiative: reviewing progress toward improved AD clinical trials. Alzheimer's Dementia **13**(4), e1–e85 (2017)

20. Wright, I., et al.: A voxel-based method for the statistical analysis of gray and white matter density applied to schizophrenia. Neuroimage **2**(4), 244–252 (1995)

21. Yan, J., et al.: Alzheimer's disease neuroimaging initiative: cortical surface biomarkers for predicting cognitive outcomes using group L2,1 norm. Neurobiol. Aging **36**(Suppl. 1), S185–S193 (2015)

22. Yang, J., Lee, S.H., Goddard, M.E., Visscher, P.M.: GCTA: a tool for genome-wide complex trait analysis. Am. J. Hum. Genet. **88**(1), 76–82 (2011)

23. Zhu, S., Wathen, A.J.: Essential formulae for restricted maximum likelihood and its derivatives associated with the linear mixed models. arXiv preprint arXiv:1805.05188 (2018)

Noisy-Consistent Pseudo Labeling Model for Semi-supervised Skin Lesion Classification

Qi Zhu[2], Sen Li[3], Zhantao Li[1], Xianjun Min[1], and Qian Li[1(✉)]

[1] China Aerospace Science and Industry Group 731 Hospital, Beijing, China
px300@qq.com
[2] College of Computer Science and Information Engineering, Guangxi Normal University, Guilin 541004, Guangxi, China
[3] R&D Department, Yizhun Medical AI Co. Ltd., Beijing, China

Abstract. Automated classification of skin lesions in dermoscopy images has the potential to significantly improve survival rates and reduce the risk of death for skin cancer patients. However, existing supervised learning models heavily depend on well-annotated dermoscopy training data, which is expensive and labor-intensive to obtain. This paper addresses this issue by proposing a semi-supervised framework called Noisy Consistent Pseudo Labeling (NCPL), which only utilizes less annotated images with many unlabeled raw data. The NCPL framework consists of two components: the Noisy-Consistent Sample Learning(NCSL) module to remove low-confidence images, and the Attentive Clustered Feature Integration (ACFI) module, incorporating an uncertainty-aware attention mechanism. Specifically, the NCSL module is introduced to filter and generate reliable pseudo-labels for unlabeled skin images, with excellent capability of removing noisy samples. Additionally, the ACFI module integrates high-dimensional representations of original lesion images in an attentive manner, assisted with the annotated data. By focusing the representative samples and removing noisy images, the NCPL approach performs outstanding experimental results, demonstrating the superiority of the NCPL framework in semi-supervised skin lesion classification task.

Keywords: Skin Lesion Classification · Semi-supervised Learning · Pseudo labeling · Noisy-Consistent Learning · Attentive Feature Clustering

1 Introduction

Skin cancer is one of the most prevalent types of cancer worldwide. In the United States alone, over 9,500 people are diagnosed with skin cancer each day, with approximately 5 million cases of basal cell skin cancer reported annually [1].

Q. Li—Supported by organization x.

J. Woo et al. (Eds.): MICCAI 2023 Workshops, LNCS 14394, pp. 241–252, 2023.
https://doi.org/10.1007/978-3-031-47425-5_22

Timely diagnosis of skin cancer plays a crucial role in improving patient survival rates. Dermoscopy, a technique that allows for the easy acquisition and analysis of skin lesion images, providing sufficient data to train artificial intelligent models [2]. Consequently, the computer-aided diagnosis of skin lesions, particularly melanoma, has become a critical research area in the field of dermoscopy [3,4].

The complexity and challenges associated with human understanding in skin lesion have led to extensive research in automated dermoscopy image diagnosis [5–7]. Most of studies have focused on supervised frameworks, which heavily rely on large amounts of annotated skin images for model training [8–10]. However, this requirement poses significant challenges as it involves extensive labor from highly trained medical professionals, making supervised learning impractical in many clinical scenarios. Consequently, there has been growing interest in semi-supervised approaches to address this issue by using less annotations [11–13].

Although current semi-supervised models have achieved notable performance in skin lesion classification, they suffer from a significant limitation. Specifically, they tend to exhibit poor performance when the unlabeled samples consist of a substantial number of noisy samples [11,14]. Furthermore, their feature learning methods often prioritize entire sample set, often overlooking the different weights that need to be attended for skin images. Due to the various proportion of the pivotal lesion region within a dermoscopy image [15], which is often accompanied by normal skin tissues, the developed models should pay different attention to each image. Therefore, the ability to remove noisy unlabeled samples and focus on crucial data can significantly enhance the diagnostic capability to distinguish inconspicuous skin lesion images with varying characteristics such as contour, color, and tissue appearance.

Motivated by these analyses, it is imperative to explore a novel semi-supervised model for diagnosing skin lesions with fewer costly annotations and utilizing the abundant unlabeled raw skin images. This model should incorporate mechanisms for removing noisy samples and integrating attentive features to extract discriminative information for identifying crucial differences among skin lesions. Hence, this paper proposes a Noisy Consistent Pseudo-Labeling (NCPL) model, aiming to address the challenges in semi-supervised skin lesion classification. To be more specific, the NCPL method incorporates a Noisy-Consistent Sample Learning (NCSL) module to evaluate and eliminate low-confidence images. It takes advantage of the designed uncertainty-aware selection mechanism. Furthermore, the NCPL method introduces an Attentive Clustered Feature Integration (ACFI) module. This module is responsible for generating pairwise attention weights by interpolating between mislabeled and original dermoscopy images, which can reduces the noise caused by incorrect labels in a noisy-consistent manner.

The main **contributions** of this paper are summarized as follows:

(1) This paper introduces an innovative approach for semi-supervised skin lesion classification, called Noisy Consistent Pseudo-Labeling (NCPL). It leverages a smaller set of annotated images along with a larger set of raw data to significantly reduce the burden of expensive annotating work.

(2) We propose a Noisy-Consistent Sample Learning module, which integrates an uncertainty-aware selection strategy into the pseudo-label generation process. This module aims to select high-confidence unlabeled raw skin images and mitigate the impact of noisy samples in the semi-supervised model during the training stage.

(3) An effective Attentive Clustered Feature Integration (ACFI) mechanism is designed to exploit the integrated pairwise attention capability between the noisy and ground-truth datasets. Instead of learning the attention mask with additional layers, the ACFI module assigns attention weights to the interpolated noisy-suppressed samples.

2   Method

2.1   Overview

Aiming at saving the annotating workload, this paper proposes a Noisy-Consistent Pseudo Labeling (NCPL) model for semi-supervised skin lesion classification, consisting the Noisy-Consistent Sample Learning (NCSL) and Attentive Clustered Feature Integration (ACFI), which can resolve the previously mentioned problems in an advanced attentive and noisy-consistent way. The NCSL module plays a crucial role in generating and selecting pseudo labels for the

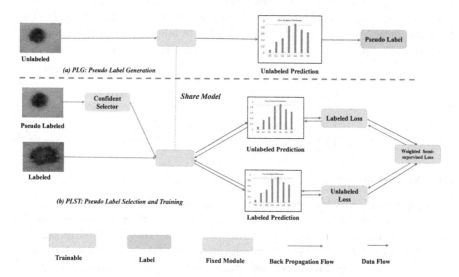

Fig. 1. Illustration of the proposed NCPL framework. (*a*) The Pseudo Label Generation part trains the ACFI model using labeled data to generate a pseudo-labeled set for the training steps. (*b*) The Pseudo Label Selection and Training (PLST) part employs a confident sample selector to choose reliable labeled images, generating pseudo-labels.

unlabeled skin lesion image samples. Its primary objective is to filter out unreliable samples, thus improving the overall confidence in the selected input images. Subsequently, the filtered skin lesion images are utilized to train the ACFI network. This network is specifically designed to enhance the model's ability to resist noise in a focused and attentive manner. The overall framework of our proposed NCPL method is illustrated in Fig. 1. It showcases the integration of the NCSL module and the ACFI network, highlighting their respective roles in addressing the challenges of semi-supervised skin lesion classification.

2.2 Problem Definition

In our NCPL framework, it requires two types of data, $\boldsymbol{X}$ and $\boldsymbol{U}$. Let $\boldsymbol{X} = \{x_i, y_i\}_{i=1}^N$ represent labeled skin images, where x_i and y_i represent the i-th input image and one-hot encoding of its corresponding label, respectively. Specifically, the $y_i = \{y_{ic} \mid c \in [1, 2, \ldots, C], y_{ic} \in \{0,1\}^C\}$. The definition of y_{ic} represents the present or absent of class c for i-th sample, defined by,

$$y_{ic} = \begin{cases} 1, & \text{class c is selected for i-th sample} \\ 0, & \text{class c is not selected for i-th sample} \end{cases} \tag{1}$$

Let $\boldsymbol{U} = \{u_j\}_{j=1}^M$ denote the unlabeled data, where u_j denotes the j-th sample and M represents the number of samples in unlabeled dataset. In our NCPL network, NCSL module generates pseudo labels for unlabeled set $\boldsymbol{U}$, and the filtered annotated data is represented by $\boldsymbol{P} = \{\hat{u}_j, l_j\}_{j=1}^{M_p}$, where l_j is the pseudo label for u_j, and M_p is the number of filtered images after NCSL. Besides, the whole data representation for the union set of labeled and pseudo-annotated unlabeled skin images is $\boldsymbol{C} = \{\hat{x}_i, \hat{y}_i\}_{i=1}^{N+M_p}$, where the $\hat{x}_i$ and $\hat{y}_i$ are defined by,

$$\hat{x}_i = \begin{cases} x_i, & \text{when } i \text{ -th sample is labeled.} \\ \hat{u}_i, & \text{when } i \text{ -th sample is pseudo-labeled.} \end{cases} \tag{2}$$

$$\hat{y}_i = \begin{cases} y_i, & \text{when } i \text{ -th sample is labeled.} \\ l_i, & \text{when } i \text{ -th sample is pseudo-labeled.} \end{cases} \tag{3}$$

2.3 Noisy-Consistent Sample Learning

The proposed Noisy-Consistent Sample Learning (NCSL) module consists of two branches. The first takes unlabeled images as input and produces one-hot encoding pseudo-label predictions. These predictions are then used to generate pseudo labels for $\boldsymbol{P}$. The second branch input both labeled and pseudo-labeled data and generates the final predicted results. To effectively represent the images, an attentive feature learning network called Attentive Clustered Feature Integration (ACFI) is designed in NCSL module. This subsection will discuss the NCSL module, and the ACFI method will be described in subsequent parts.

Pseudo Label Generation. To fully exploit the discriminative information from unlabeled skin images, we firstly train a classification model by the labeled images and generate the pseudo labels for unlabeled data. Given the unlabeled dataset $U = \{u_j\}_{j=1}^{M}$, the purpose of pseudo label generation process is to generate the pseudo-labeled set $P = \{\hat{u}_j, l_j\}_{j=1}^{M_P}$. The learning procedure is implemented with a neural network model f_θ based on our attentive network (ACFI) with trainable parameter θ. As shown in Fig. 1, the pseudo labels are directly generated from the output one-hot predictions by the function f_θ during a few initial training iteration steps. Let p_j, as described in the Eq. (4), denote the output probability representation for j-th sample produced by the neural network f_θ, and p_{jc} represents the probability that j-th sample belongs to c-th class. The pseudo-label generation procedure is described using Eq. (5), where $\max(p_{jc})$ represents the index of maximum predicted probability in p_{jc}.

$$p_j = \{p_{jc} \mid c \in [1, 2, \ldots, C]\} \tag{4}$$

$$l_j = \{c \mid p_{jc} \geqslant \max(p_{jc}), c \in [1, 2, \ldots C]\} \tag{5}$$

Confident Pseudo-labeled Sample Selection. It is inevitable that the generation of pseudo-labels will result in a number of noisy samples with incorrect labels, and removing these noisy pseudo-labeled samples becomes crucial in our network.

We conduct the confident pseudo-labeled sample selection for the unlabeled data U to choose valuable data for the attentive model, which is predicted with high confidence. In detail, The confident sample selector module aims to produce the pseudo-labeled dataset $P = \{u_j, l_j\}_{j=1}^{M_P}$, where M_p denotes the number of samples filtered by the selector. With the output prediction representations from neural network f_θ, the confident sample selection procedure is described in Eq. (6), where the σ represents the threshold for probability score to discriminate high-confidence pseudo-labeled samples. From the implementation level, the confident sample selection module is run periodically to make sure the consistent noisy-aware of the pseudo-labeled set, based on the shared f_θ on both labeled and unlabeled data images.

$$P = \{(x_i, p_i) \mid p_{ic} \geqslant \sigma\} \tag{6}$$

Weighted Semi-supervised Loss. As the pseudo-labeled set $P = \{u_j, l_j\}_{j=1}^{M_P}$ is adaptively generated based on the pseudo label generation and confident psudo-labeled sample section, the unified dataset $C = \{\hat{x}_i, \hat{y}_i\}_{i=1}^{N+M_P}$ is produced by combination of the labeled and pseudo-labeled sets. The neural network model f_θ is continuously trained to update parameters θ, and then the total loss function is calculated in terms of Eq. (7),

$$L_{\text{Total}} = w \cdot L_{\text{Labeled}} + (1 - w) \cdot L_{\text{Pseudo}} \tag{7}$$

where the L_{Labeled} is the classification loss from labeled sample data X, L_{Pseudo} is the calculated from pseudo-labeled set P, and w is the balance weight.

2.4   Attentive Clustered Feature Integration

As described in aforementioned, the Attentive Clustered Feature Integration (ACFI) plays significant role in the NCSL workflow. In detail, given the unified dataset $C = \{\hat{x}_i, \hat{y}_i\}_{i=1}^{N+M_p}$, the ACFI is based on the pairwise cluster mapping and attentive noisy-robust paradigm to learn the attentive representations for skin images. First, the feature representations generated by linear projection, corresponding with labels, are randomly divided into pairwise feature clusters. Subsequently, the representations are integrated with each feature cluster. Moreover, we map the integrated feature vectors in each cluster into the high-dimensional space via a non-linear way, and then a pairwise attentive loss is calculated based on the high-dimensional relationship between the feature vectors in each cluster. Finally, an attentive mixture loss is constructed and implemented following the pairwise attentive weight, which balances the contributions for the original feature representations and the attentive feature integrations. Besides, the overall scheme of ACFI is also elaborated in Fig. 2.

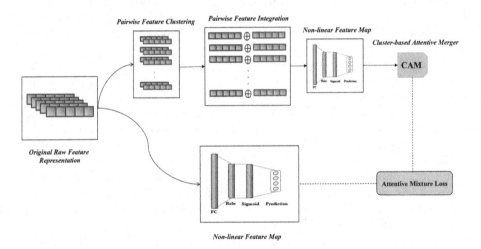

Fig. 2. The proposed Attentive Cluster Feature Integration (ACFI) framework. (*a*) Pairwise feature clustering and integration modules transfer the original features into cluster-based integration space to learn the combined features. (*b*) The components of noisy-consistent attention and attentive mixture loss catch the attention weights from the integration feature representations, combined with original feature representations, enhancing the discriminative ability of noisy-annotated image samples.

Pairwise Feature Clustering. In the ACFI network, the unified dataset $C = \{\hat{x}_i, \hat{y}_i\}_{i=1}^{N+M_p}$ is firstly fed into a pairwise feature clustering step, which can transform C into the a feature space $F = \left\{f_i, \hat{l}_i\right\}_{i=1}^{N+M_p}$, which is achieved by a Resnet backbone network on the input image sample $\hat{x}_i$. Then, the feature vectors in F are randomly divided into multiple pairwise clusters $F_C =$

$\left\{ f^{(i)}, f^{(j)} \mid f^{(i)} \in \boldsymbol{F}, f^{(j)} \in \boldsymbol{F}, f^{(i)} \neq f^{(j)} \right\}$. In each feature cluster, the feature f_i and f_j are projected into high-level linear space following Eq. (8),

$$\begin{cases} M_i = \psi_1\left(f_i\right) \\ M_j = \psi_2(f_j) \end{cases} \tag{8}$$

where the ψ_1 and ψ_2 are two different fully-connected linear projection functions.

Pairwise Feature Integration. After the pairwise feature clustering, we integrate M_i and M_j into a unified vector according to Eq. (9),

$$I_{\langle i,j \rangle} = (M_i \oplus M_j) \tag{9}$$

Specifically, the symbol $\oplus$ represents the sum of two feature vectors. Thus, the individual features in the cluster are integrated into the same feature space.

Attentive Weight Calculation. To represent skin images in an attentive manner, the integrated feature vector $I_{\langle i,j \rangle}$ is then transformed by a non-linearity K, as calculated in Eq. (10),

$$w_{\langle i,j \rangle} = K(I_{\langle i,j \rangle}) \tag{10}$$

Specifically, K is constructed by FC-ReLU-Sigmoid, where FC is a fully-connected layer, ReLU and Sigmoid denote the ReLU and Sigmoid activation functions. As a result of this, the integrated feature vector $I_{\langle i,j \rangle}$ can be mapped into the integrated attentive weight $w_{\langle i,j \rangle}$, which is trying to encourage the model to focus on the discriminative samples rather than noisy ones.

Noisy-Consistent Attention. To remove the negative influence of noisy samples, we propose a noisy-consistent attention mechanism, involving the integration attentive weight $w_{\langle i,j \rangle}$ into the feature learning step by mix up following Eq. (11),

$$\begin{cases} f_{mix\langle i,j \rangle} = w_{\langle i,j \rangle} \cdot f_i + \left(1 - w_{\langle i,j \rangle}\right) \cdot f_j \\ \hat{y}_{mix\langle i,j \rangle} = w_{\langle i,j \rangle} \cdot \hat{y}_i + \left(1 - w_{\langle i,j \rangle}\right) \cdot \hat{y}_j \end{cases} \tag{11}$$

This attention mechanism increases the distinguishing ability between pairwise sample features f_i and f_j. Specifically, the $f_{mix\langle i,j \rangle}$ and $\hat{y}_{mix\langle i,j \rangle}$ are attentive integration feature and label representations in feature space $\boldsymbol{F}$, respectively.

Attentive Integration Loss. To fully train the noisy-consistent attention network, we introduce the attentive integration loss L_{AIL} to optimize the parameters. Besides, the designed L_{AIL} incorporates the mix up loss L_{mix} and individual identification loss L_{ide} to ensure the mixed attentive feature $f_{mix(i,j)})$ and individual feature representations (f_i and f_j) respectively containing discriminative information with consistency to class labels $l_{mix(i,j)}$, $\hat{y}_i$, and $\hat{y}_j$.

Mathematically, the attentive integration loss L_{AIL}, mix up loss L_{mix}, and individual identification loss L_{ide} are defined as follows,

$$L_{AIL} = \eta \cdot L_{mix} + (1 - \eta) \cdot L_{ide} \tag{12}$$

$$L_{mix} = \frac{1}{R} \cdot \sum_{\langle i,j \rangle = \langle 1,1 \rangle}^{R} CE(classifier_1(f_{mix\langle i,j \rangle}), \hat{y}_{mix\langle i,j \rangle}) \qquad (13)$$

$$L_{ide} = \frac{1}{T} \cdot \sum_{i=1}^{T} CE(classifier_2(f_i), \hat{y}_i) \qquad (14)$$

where η in Eq. (12) is the balance weight between L_{mix} and L_{ide}; R and T in Eq. (13) and (14) individually denote the numbers of samples and clusters in each mini-batch training; the $classifier_1$ and $classifier_2$ denotes different classifiers for samples in cluster and original images, respectively. Besides, the CE function is the cross-entropy loss and the classifiers are set as linear transformers.

3   Experiments

3.1   Dataset and Implementation

Dataset. The NCPL model is evaluated on HAM10000 dataset, which is the largest publicly available dataset of skin lesion, consisting of 10,015 dermoscopy images from seven types [16,17]. The dataset was randomly split into a training set of 5,000 images and a testing set of 5,015 images. As semi-supervised scenario, the training set was further divided into labeled and unlabeled subsets of various sizes (500, 1,000, 1,500, 2,000, 2,500), and the remain labels were removed.

Implementation Details. In experiments, we utilize ResNet [18] as the backbone. The weights are initialized with pre-trained Resnet parameters and it uses SGD optimizer in 120 epochs. The batch size is 32 and the initial learning rate is 0.001. All images are resized into 225 × 225, and we apply the random horizontal flipping data augmentation on images. The confident images are annotated and fed into NCPL in each 6 epochs. The experiment is implemented using Pytorch on *RTX 3080 Ti*. Besides, we deploy the **Accuracy, Kappa, F1-score, Recall,** and **Precision** to measure the performance.

3.2   Results

To reveal the effectiveness of NCPL model, we conducted a comparison with several CNN approaches on skin lesion classification task within a semi-supervised framework. The compared results are summarized in Table 1. Specifically, we implemented semi-supervised versions of CNN models, namely AlexNetSemi, GoogleNetSemi, InceptionNetSemi, and VggNetSemi, where pseudo labels were annotated in training stage. The training procedure and experimental settings for these models were kept consistent with our proposed NCPL model.

As shown in Table 1, our NCPL method surpasses all compared methods by achieving an accuracy of 0.839, a kappa coefficient of 0.791, an F1-score of 0.839, a recall of 0.839, and a precision of 0.834 across seven different types of

Table 1. The compared results on semi-supervised skin lesion classification. The best results are highlighted with **bold**

Methods	Accuracy	Kappa	F1-Score	Recall	Precision
GoogleNetSemi	0.812	0.757	0.807	0.809	0.804
AlexNetSemi	0.802	0.728	0.796	0.802	0.794
InceptionNetSemi	0.816	0.744	0.808	0.817	0.804
VggNetSemi	0.806	0.737	0.804	0.807	0.802
FedPerl [19]	0.756	0.742	0.749	0.758	0.750
Our NCPL	**0.839**	**0.791**	**0.839**	**0.839**	**0.834**

skin lesions. Furthermore, Fig. 3 presents the ROC (Receiver Operating Characteristic) curves and box plots, depicting the performance of our NCPL model at different scales of training data. The NCPL model achieves an average AUC value of 0.953 for the seven skin lesion categories, as indicated by the ROC curves. The box plot also highlight the robustness of our proposed NCPL model.

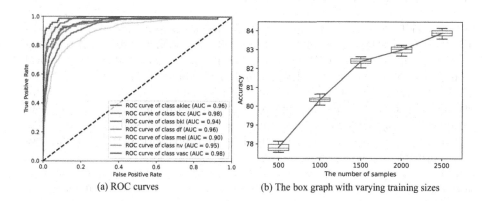

(a) ROC curves   (b) The box graph with varying training sizes

Fig. 3. The ROC curves and box graph with varying training sizes.

Meanwhile, we visualize the T-SNE [20] of the image features from the test set, as shown in Fig. 4. This visualization demonstrates that the features from NCPL model are clearly separated into seven distinct groups, resulting in fewer misdiagnoses. Additionally, Fig. 4 includes the presentation of CAM [21], which allows for a comparison between ResNet and our NCPL model. In Fig. 4 (b), it is evident that our NCPL model accurately attends to the actual lesion region with more precise localization compared to ResNet. This finding further emphasizes that our NCPL model successfully captures the meaningful and relevant regions of attention, served as crucial diagnostic cues for experienced doctors. The above result analysis and visualization show the exceptional ability of NCPL to discriminate between irrelevant background tissues and valuable lesion regions, even in complex and noisy environments.

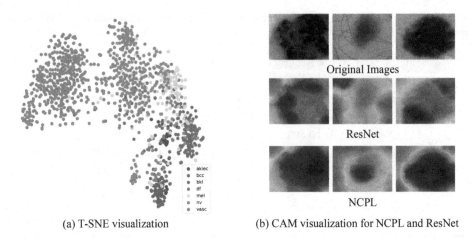

(a) T-SNE visualization   (b) CAM visualization for NCPL and ResNet

Fig. 4. The T-SNE and CAM visualization.

4   Discussion and Conclusion

This paper focuses on semi-supervised skin lesion classification and introduces the Noisy-Consistent Pseudo Labeling (NCPL) model. Compared to existing methods, our proposed NCPL achieves a significant breakthrough in the removal of noisy samples from unlabeled skin samples. This breakthrough is accomplished by incorporating two key components: a more efficient noisy-consistent sample learning module and an attentive clustered feature integration mechanism specifically designed for the semi-supervised skin lesion classification task. This enables us to extract valuable information from unlabeled dermoscopy images while disregarding noisy data.

Moreover, extensive experimental results demonstrate the outstanding performance of our NCPL model in the semi-supervised skin lesion classification task. Our results show that the NCPL model outperformed several other CNN methods. However, it is important to note that the performance of semi-supervised learning models can be highly dependent on the specific dataset and task. Therefore, further research is needed to evaluate the generalizability of our model to other datasets and tasks.

Despite its significant advancements in removing noisy samples from unlabeled skin samples, our proposed approach, NCPL, still has certain limitations. Firstly, it requires a certain amount of labeled data for training. Although NCPL leverages unlabeled data to improve performance, the presence of labeled data is necessary to guide the learning process and provide ground truth information; Secondly, the sample learning of unlabeled data in NCPL introduces an additional computational burden. The process of weighting and incorporating unlabeled data into the learning framework can be time-consuming, especially when dealing with large-scale datasets. This computational overhead may hinder the real-time applicability of NCPL in certain scenarios.

These limitations highlight the trade-off between performance improvement through unlabeled data utilization and the resource constraints associated with labeled data availability and computational complexity. Additionally, while our model showed promising results, there is still room for improvement. For instance, the model could potentially be enhanced by incorporating more sophisticated noise reduction techniques or by using more advanced attention mechanisms. Future research efforts should focus on addressing these limitations to further enhance the practicality and efficiency of the NCPL approach.

References

1. Perez, M., Abisaad, J.A., Rojas, K.D., Marchetti, M.A., Jaimes, N.: Skin cancer: primary, secondary, and tertiary prevention. Part I. J. Am. Acad. Dermatol. **87**(2), 255–268 (2022)
2. Gregoor, A.M.S., et al.: An artificial intelligence based app for skin cancer detection evaluated in a population based setting. NPJ Digital Med. **6**(1), 90 (2023)
3. Yinhao, W., Chen, B., Zeng, A., Pan, D., Wang, R., Zhao, S.: Skin cancer classification with deep learning: a systematic review. Front. Oncol. **12**, 893972 (2022)
4. Zhou, Y., et al.: Multi-site cross-organ calibrated deep learning (MUSCLD): automated diagnosis of non-melanoma skin cancer. Med. Image Anal. **84**, 102702 (2023)
5. Nakai, K., Chen, Y.-W., Han, X.-H.: Enhanced deep bottleneck transformer model for skin lesion classification. Biomed. Signal Process. Control **78**, 103997 (2022)
6. Mishra, S., Zhang, Y., Zhang, L., Zhang, T., Hu, X.S., Chen, D.Z.: Data-driven deep supervision for skin lesion classification. In: Wang, L., Dou, Q., Fletcher, P.T., Speidel, S., Li, S. (eds.) MICCAI 2022. LNCS, vol. 13431, pp. 721–731. Springer, Cham (2022). https://doi.org/10.1007/978-3-031-16431-6_68
7. Wang, L., Zhang, L., Shu, X., Yi, Z.: Intra-class consistency and inter-class discrimination feature learning for automatic skin lesion classification. Med. Image Anal. **85**, 102746 (2023)
8. Lie, J., et al.: Flexible sampling for long-tailed skin lesion classification. In: Wang, L., Dou, Q., Fletcher, P.T., Speidel, S., Li, S. (eds.) MICCAI 2022. LNCS, vol. 13433, pp. 462–471. Springer, Cham (2022). https://doi.org/10.1007/978-3-031-16437-8_44
9. He, X., Tan, E.-L., Bi, H., Zhang, X., Zhao, S., Lei, B.: Fully transformer network for skin lesion analysis. Med. Image Anal. **77**, 102357 (2022)
10. Song, L., Wang, H., Wang, Z.J.: Decoupling multi-task causality for improved skin lesion segmentation and classification. Pattern Recognition **133**, 108995 (2023)
11. Wang, Y., Wang, Y., Cai, J., Lee, T.K., Miao, C., Wang, Z.J.: SSD-KD: a self-supervised diverse knowledge distillation method for lightweight skin lesion classification using dermoscopic images. Med. Image Anal. **84**, 102693 (2023)
12. Zhou, S., et al.: FixMatch-LS: semi-supervised skin lesion classification with label smoothing. Biomed. Signal Process. Control **84**, 104709 (2023)
13. Gao, Z., et al.: A semi-supervised multi-task learning framework for cancer classification with weak annotation in whole-slide images. Med. Image Anal. **83**, 102652 (2023)
14. Zhou, S., et al.: ReFixMatch-LS: reusing pseudo-labels for semi-supervised skin lesion classification. Med. Biol. Eng. Comput. **61**(5), 1033–1045 (2023)
15. Zeng, L., et al.: Advancements in nanoparticle-based treatment approaches for skin cancer therapy. Mol. Can. **22**(1), 10 (2023)

16. Tschandl, P., Rosendahl, C., Kittler, H.: The ham10000 dataset, a large collection of multi-source dermatoscopic images of common pigmented skin lesions. Sci. Data 5(1), 1–9 (2018)
17. Chang, C.H., Wang, W.E., Hsu, F.Y., Chen, R.J., Chang, H.C.: AI HAM 10000 database to assist residents in learning differential diagnosis of skin cancer. In: 2022 IEEE 5th Eurasian Conference on Educational Innovation (ECEI), pp. 1–3. IEEE (2022)
18. He, K., Zhang, X., Ren, S., Sun, J.: Deep residual learning for image recognition. In: Proceedings of the IEEE Conference on Computer Vision and Pattern Recognition, pp. 770–778 (2016)
19. Bdair, T., Navab, N., Albarqouni, S.: FedPerl: semi-supervised peer learning for skin lesion classification. In: de Bruijne, M., et al. (eds.) MICCAI 2021. LNCS, vol. 12903, pp. 336–346. Springer, Cham (2021). https://doi.org/10.1007/978-3-030-87199-4_32
20. Van der Maaten, L., Hinton, G.: Visualizing data using t-SNE. J. Mach. Learni. Res. 9(11), 2579–2605 (2008)
21. Jung, H., Oh, Y.: Towards better explanations of class activation mapping. In: Proceedings of the IEEE/CVF International Conference on Computer Vision, pp. 1336–1344 (2021)

Hessian-Based Similarity Metric for Multimodal Medical Image Registration

Mohammadreza Eskandari[1,2(✉)], Houssem-Eddine Gueziri[2],
and D. Louis Collins[1,2,3]

[1] Department of Biomedical Engineering, McGill University, Montreal QC, Canada
mohammadreza.eskandari@mail.mcgill.ca
[2] McConnell Brain Imaging Center, Montreal Neurological Institute and Hospital,
Montreal, QC, Canada
[3] Department of Neurology and Neurosurgery, McGill University, Montreal, QC,
Canada

Abstract. One of the fundamental elements of both traditional and certain deep learning medical image registration algorithms is measuring the similarity/dissimilarity between two images. In this work, we propose an analytical solution for measuring similarity between two different medical image modalities based on the Hessian of their intensities. First, assuming a functional dependence between the intensities of two perfectly corresponding patches, we investigate how their Hessians relate to each other. Secondly, we suggest a closed-form expression to quantify the deviation from this relationship, given arbitrary pairs of image patches. We propose a geometrical interpretation of the new similarity metric and an efficient implementation for registration. We demonstrate the robustness of the metric to intensity nonuniformities using synthetic bias fields. By integrating the new metric in an affine registration framework, we evaluate its performance for MRI and ultrasound registration in the context of image-guided neurosurgery using target registration error and computation time.

Keywords: Multimodal registration · Similarity metric · Image Hessian

1 Introduction

Aligning images of different modalities is the key to combining functional and anatomical data from multiple sources in image-guided procedures. In this context, quantifying the similarity of images is an important yet challenging task due to different intensity distribution arising from distinct protocols and physical

Supplementary Information The online version contains supplementary material available at https://doi.org/10.1007/978-3-031-47425-5_23.

principles governing each modality. This already-complex problem becomes more complicated in the presence of noise and modality-dependent artifacts. A huge variety of mathematically proven, hand-crafted, and deep learning-based solutions have been proposed for many use cases, each having their own advantages and disadvantages.

One of the earliest successes in multimodal registration was achieved by the introduction of mutual information [12,24]. This measure is very general since it only assumes statistical dependence between the intensities of the images. To improve its performance for certain tasks, several variants have been proposed [11,18,19]. Soon after mutual information, the correlation ratio was introduced [21], with the idea of constraining the relationship between the intensities of the images. The correlation ratio assumes a functional dependence between image intensities and quantifies the compliance of this assumption. There exist some variants of the correlation ratio, however this method did not gain the popularity of mutual information.

Both mutual information and correlation ratio use image intensities directly as the feature space. Another research avenue in multimodal registration has been handcrafting features. Image gradients, local statistical information and local structures such as points, edges, contours, surfaces and volumes, are some commonly used [16]. Many studies have also tried to convert multimodal registration to unimodal registration by simulating one image from the other [1,26] or mapping both images into a third space [25].

More recently, several deep learning methods have been proposed to overcome the challenges of measuring similarity between image pairs of distinct modalities [2,8,22]. The main idea behind these metrics is to use supervised learning to model similarity between registered pairs of patches. As a result, these methods can only perform well on the modalities they have been trained on and generalization to other modalities is highly dependent on data augmentation methods used during training.

One of the well-studied features for image registration and medical image processing in general is image gradient. The gradient can be a good descriptor of a neighborhood; its magnitude and direction describe how the intensities change in a small radius. A popular similarity metric for multimodal registration is the cosine squared of the angle between gradients of two images, which we will refer to as gradient orientation alignment [3]. This method was first intuitively proposed to incorporate local information [7,17]. Later, it was shown that maximizing mutual information on a small patch is equivalent to maximizing gradient orientation alignment [10]. The usefulness of gradient orientation alignment raises the question whether higher order derivatives can be beneficial in quantifying image similarities.

Despite the long-run progress in research on traditional similarity measures and transition to deep learning era, we believe there still exists certain areas to be explored for defining better similarity metrics based on mathematical properties of the images. Our focus is on the Hessian matrix, which contains information regarding the geometry of the image in a neighborhood. One of the most important applications of Hessian matrix in medical image processing is identifying vessel-like structures [5]. This is because a Hessian can approximate a neighborhood with an ellipsoid. Our approach in this paper is similar to that of correlation ratio [21], since we constrain the relation between the two modalities with a functional dependence. We develop the mathematical formulation for using Hessians in measuring image similarity and test the performance of our proposed metric in synthetic and real use cases.

2   Method

2.1   Defining the Hessian-Based Similarity Metric

We define a metric for quantifying pointwise similarity between two medical images of distinct modalities. We refer to the images as the fixed image and the moving image and denote them with $F(\mathbf{x}), M(\mathbf{x}) : \Omega \subset \mathbb{R}^d \rightarrow \mathbb{R}$, respectively, where d is the dimension of the images. We start by deriving the relationship between the Hessians of two aligned patches centered at $\mathbf{x_0}$, assuming a functional dependence between their intensities, i.e., there exists a function $g : \mathbb{R} \rightarrow \mathbb{R}$ that maps the intensities of the fixed patch onto the corresponding intensities of the moving patch. The gradients and the Hessians of the images are represented by ∇F, ∇M, H_F and H_M, respectively. For any $\delta \mathbf{x}$, as long as $\mathbf{x_0} + \delta \mathbf{x}$ lies inside the patch of interest, we can formulate the functional dependence assumption as:

$$M(\mathbf{x_0} + \delta \mathbf{x}) = g(F(\mathbf{x_0} + \delta \mathbf{x})).$$ (1)

Writing the Taylor expansion of both sides up to the second order and equating terms of the same order yields:

$$\nabla M(\mathbf{x_0}) = \frac{dg}{dF} \nabla F(\mathbf{x_0}).$$ (2)

$$H_M(\mathbf{x_0}) = \frac{dg}{dF} H_F(\mathbf{x_0}) + \frac{d^2 g}{dF^2} \nabla F(\mathbf{x_0}) \nabla F^T(\mathbf{x_0}).$$ (3)

Since the mapping between the intensities is not given, the derivatives of g are unknown. We rewrite the above equations by replacing the derivatives of g with scalar variables λ, μ and ν. Note that these equations are valid for any point inside the patch of interest, therefore for convenience of notation, we drop the dependence of the Hessians and the gradients on $\mathbf{x}$.

$$\nabla M = \lambda \nabla F.$$ (4)

$$H_M = \mu H_F + \nu \nabla F \nabla F^T.$$ (5)

These two equations describe how the gradients and the Hessians of two patches relate to each other, subject to a functional dependence between their intensities. The first equation encapsulates d scalar equations and suggests that the gradients of two patches should be aligned or anti-aligned everywhere (depending on the sign of λ). The second equation encapsulates d^2 equations, only $(d^2 + d)/2$ of which are unique due to symmetricity of matrices. It can be inferred from this equation that the Hessian of the moving patch can be decomposed into a linear combination of the Hessian and the gradient outer product of the fixed image. In other words, there exist two scalars, μ and ν, such that they satisfy all encapsulated scalar equations at the same time. We use this equation as the starting point for defining our Hessian-based similarity metric. For arbitrary pairs of patches, there is no functional dependence between their intensities and hence, Eq. 5 will not hold true. To quantify the violation of this equality, we define a normalized quadratic error:

$$E = \frac{||H_M - \mu H_F - \nu \nabla F \nabla F^T||^2}{||H_M||^2}, \tag{6}$$

where $||.||$ denotes the Frobenius norm. To evaluate this error regardless of the unknown scalars, we find μ and ν such that E will be minimized. We denote the optimal solution with $\mu^\star$ and $\nu^\star$ and the optimal value with $E^\star$. To minimize E, we compute its derivatives with respect to μ and ν, equate the derivatives to zero, solve the resulting system of linear equations, obtain $\mu^\star$ and $\nu^\star$ and plug them into equation. $E^\star$ is a measure of dissimilarity and is guaranteed to be bounded by zero and one. We define the Hessian-based similarity metric as $S = 1 - E^\star$. This metric can be represented by a closed-form expression:

$$S = \frac{||\nabla F||^4 tr(H_M^T H_F)^2 + ||H_F||^2 (\nabla F^T H_M \nabla F)^2 - 2tr(H_M^T H_F)(\nabla F^T H_M \nabla F)(\nabla F^T H_F \nabla F)}{||H_M||^2(||\nabla F||^4||H_F||^2 - (\nabla F^T H_F \nabla F)^2)}, \tag{7}$$

where $S = 1$ implies perfect functional dependence between intensities and $S = 0$ implies perfect functional independence. As it was expected from Eq. 5, the metric is assymetric in terms of fixed and moving image. Another way to express this metric is by vectorizing Eq. 5. We can formulate the metric in terms of α, β and γ which denote the angle between $\text{vec}(H_M)$ and $\text{vec}(H_F)$, the angle between $\text{vec}(H_M)$ and $\text{vec}(\nabla F \nabla F^T)$, and the angle between $\text{vec}(H_F)$ and $\text{vec}(\nabla F \nabla F^T)$, respectively.

$$S = \frac{\cos^2 \alpha + \cos^2 \beta - 2 \cos \alpha \cos \beta \cos \gamma}{\sin^2 \gamma}. \tag{8}$$

Additionally, the Hessian-based similarity metric has a clear geometric interpretation. It can be interpreted as the cosine squared of the angle between $\text{vec}(H_M)$ and its projection onto the plane spanned by $\text{vec}(H_F)$ and $\text{vec}(\nabla F \nabla F^T)$. The angles between the vectorized matrices is depicted in Fig. 1. It must be taken into consideration that vectorized Hessian matrices can not be visualized in 3 dimensions and this figure is only intended for providing intuition regarding the defined metric.

We should mention that by following the above steps for Eq. 4 instead of Eq. 5, the resulting similarity metric will be the cosine squared of the angle between the gradients of the two images. The derivation of this metric is included in supplementary material.

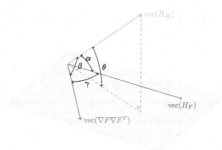

Fig. 1. Geometric interpretation of the Hessian-based similarity metric

In practice, to compute the gradients and the Hessians of the images, we convolve them with first and second order Gaussian derivative kernels. The choice of standard deviation for these Gaussian kernels directly affects the behavior of the similarity metric and enables capturing structures of different scales. The standard deviation should be the same for both images and all components of the Gaussian kernels. By setting the standard deviation to a certain scale, structures of higher scale will not be captured and structures of lower scale will be smoothed out.

2.2   Transforming Hessians

A straightforward strategy for computing the Hessian-based similarity metric during the registration process involves first applying a deformation onto the moving image and then computing its Hessian. Since the cost of computing the Hessian is relatively high, our approach is to compute it only once at the preprocessing stage and to transform it according to each deformation.

Assuming a diffeomorphism $\mathbf{P}(\mathbf{x}) : \mathbb{R}^d \rightarrow \mathbb{R}^d$ that maps $\mathbf{x} = (x_1, ..., x_d)$ from the original image onto $\mathbf{u} = (u_1, ..., u_d)$ from the deformed image, each component of the Hessian in the transformed coordinate can be expressed in terms of the components of the original Hessian and gradient:

$$\frac{\partial^2 M}{\partial u_k \partial u_l} = \sum_{i=1}^{d} \frac{\partial M}{\partial x_i} \frac{\partial^2 x_i}{\partial u_k \partial u_l} + \sum_{i=1}^{d} \sum_{j=1}^{d} \frac{\partial^2 M}{\partial x_i \partial x_j} \frac{\partial x_i}{\partial u_k} \frac{\partial x_j}{\partial u_l}. \tag{9}$$

Partial derivatives of $\mathbf{x}$ with respect to $\mathbf{u}$ are directly computable if the inverse transformation, $\mathbf{P}^{-1}(\mathbf{u})$, is explicitly known. Equation 9 implies that a nonlinear transformation must be C^2 continuous, otherwise the transformed Hessian will be discontinuous. Note that when the transformation is linear, the first term on the right hand of Eq. 9 will vanish and the transformed Hessian can be expressed as $J_{\mathbf{P}}^{-T} H_M J_{\mathbf{P}}^{-1}$, where $J_{\mathbf{P}}$ is the Jacobian matrix of the transformation.

2.3 Implementing the Metric in an Affine Registration Scheme

We present a simple affine registration scheme to test the proposed similarity metric. We start by computing the Hessian of both images and the gradient of the fixed image. We sample N random voxels from the fixed image. The Hessian-based similarity metric is computed over the sampled voxels and their average is used as the similarity score for each deformation. No regularization term is used in this scheme. We use Differential Evolution [23] to find the optimal affine deformation. Affine deformations are defined by a translation vector and three matrices representing rotation, shear, and scaling. Shear and scaling are defined as an upper triangular matrix and a diagonal matrix, respectively. For each affine deformation, its inverse is applied to the location of the sampled voxels to find their corresponding points on the moving image. Hessian of the moving image is linearly interpolated over these points and transformed using the Jacobian of the deformation field. The optimization process terminates as soon as a termination condition is satisfied.

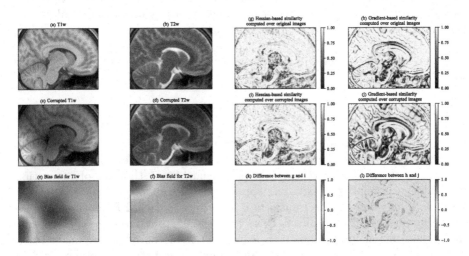

Fig. 2. The effect of intensity nonuniformities on the behavior of the Hessian-based similarity metric and gradient orientation alignment. (a) and (b) show T1w and T2w MNI-ICBM152 templates [14]. (c) and (d) are derived by multiplying (a) and (b) to (e) and (f) as synthetic bias fields, respectively. (g), (h), (i) and (j) show the computed Hessian-based similarity metric and gradient orientation alignment on original and corrupted image pairs. The difference between computed similarity maps are shown in (k) and (l).

3 Experiments

3.1 Robustness to Intensity Nonuniformities

Intensity nonuniformities can degrade the precision of any analysis in medical image computing. Therefore, comping up with a similarity metric that is robust to these low-frequency artefacts is beneficial. To examine qualitatively and visually how robust our metric is to intensity nonuniformities, we compute the metric all over a pair of registered images, before and after applying synthetic bias fields. Figure 2 shows this process for T1w and T2w MNI-ICBM152 templates [14] on the saggital view. As it can be seen, the added artifacts have a negligible effect on the Hessian-based similarity metric; however, their effect on gradient orientation alignment is notable.

3.2   Quantitative Results

We test the registration performance of our method in the context of image-guided neurosurgery for aligning preoperative T1w MR volumes to preresection intraoperative ultrasound volumes of the BITE database [13]. The open-access BITE database contains scans of 14 patients with brain cancer, along with homologous manually annotated landmarks. We reconstruct ultrasound volumes from the ultrasound slices with a voxel size of $0.5 \times 0.5 \times 0.5$ mm using IBIS [4]. We resample MR volumes to the same voxel size. We use provided landmarks to compute mean target registration error (mTRE) as a measure of accuracy.

To run our registration experiments, We set N to 5000 and the standard deviation for computing gaussian derivatives to 1.5 mm. Maximum displacement in each direction and maximum rotation around each axis is set to 10 mm and $5\,^\circ C$, respectively. Maximum shear and scaling in each direction are both set to 5%. For optimization using Differential Evolution we use best/1/bin strategy [15] and set the population size and maximum number of iterations to 24 and 200, respectively. Crossover probability is set to 0.7 and differential weight will be randomly sampled from $(0.5, 1)$ interval. Whenever the standard deviation of population's cost falls below 0.2% of the mean of population's cost, the optimization will terminate.

As a baseline, we implement gradient orientation alignment and run it in the same framework that we have developed. We are choosing this method for two main reasons; first, its effectiveness for MR to ultrasound registration task has been previously demonstrated [3], and second, it follows the same logic as our proposed metric.

The results of the registration process are shown in Table 1 and Fig. 3. CPU time of each method for each case during preprocessing and optimization is reported, too. The preprocessing stage includes parsing images, random sampling, and computing image derivatives. All tests are performed on an Intel® Core™ i7-11370H @ 3.30 GHz CPU.

To further monitor the behavior of each similarity metric, we plot the similarity score vs. mTRE for each deformation that is evaluated during the optimization. Figure 4 shows this scatter plot for case 10 of the BITE database. As it can be seen, both plots have the same general trend; as the similarity metric increases, mTRE decreases. In addition, the points derived from the Hessian-based similarity metric are spread out. This can imply a better capture range for this metric. Scatter plots of all other cases can be found in supplementary material.

Table 1. Mean target registration error (mTRE) and CPU time for registration of preoperative MR to pre-resection ultrasound on BITE database

| case no. | Hessian-based similarity metric | | | Gradient orientation alignment | | |
| | mTRE (mm) | CPU time (s) | | mTRE (mm) | CPU time (s) | |
		preprocess.	optim.		preprocess.	optim.
2	1.78 (0.4–4.5)	30.8	4.9	2.96 (1.1–5.7)	13.1	3.2
3	2.94 (0.7–5.8)	48.8	5.7	2.55 (0.6–6.4)	21.1	3.8
4	1.63 (0.3–4.2)	24.9	7.0	2.29 (0.9–4.5)	10.7	4.3
5	2.18 (0.4–6.6)	33.9	3.0	2.14 (0.3–6.4)	14.5	5.5
6	1.82 (0.4–3.6)	34.0	4.1	1.92 (0.8–3.5)	14.4	3.4
7	2.44 (0.8–5.0)	40.2	5.0	3.17 (1.2–5.9)	17.2	4.0
8	2.71 (0.8–5.1)	37.9	5.5	3.18 (0.5–6.2)	16.2	3.1
9	2.60 (0.5–5.8)	27.2	4.8	2.64 (0.5–6.5)	11.5	4.4
10	1.84 (0.4–3.9)	37.3	5.9	2.28 (0.7–5.7)	16.6	4.0
11	1.59 (0.6–3.2)	32.9	5.6	2.57 (0.3–5.4)	14.2	3.0
12	3.06 (0.7–5.6)	32.0	3.1	2.88 (0.7–6.0)	13.6	3.2
13	3.56 (0.9–6.3)	28.3	4.6	3.99 (1.4–7.6)	12.2	5.7
14	2.73 (0.2–4.8)	35.7	3.0	3.61 (2.0–6.5)	15.6	3.4
mean	2.37	34.15	4.78	2.78	14.68	3.92

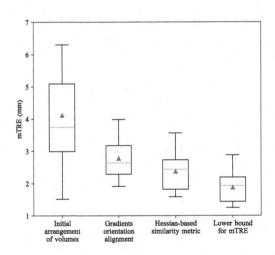

Fig. 3. Box plot of mTRE for registration of preoperative MR to pre-resection ultrasound on BITE database. First box on the left shows mTRE before registering MR to ultrasound. The box on the left shows the minimum mTRE that is achievable using an affine transformation based solely on the landmarks. Orange lines and green triangles represent the median and the mean, respectively. (Color figure online)

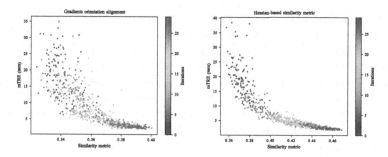

Fig. 4. Scatter plots of mTRE vs. similarity for deformations evaluated during the optimization for one MR-iUS pair. The color of each point shows the iteration in which the deformation was evaluated. We can see that the Hessian-based metric has less variability in optimization.

We carry out a statistical test to determine whether the two metrics demonstrate statistically significant difference in registration accuracy. Our null hypothesis assumes the two methods result in the same distribution for mTRE. Our alternative hypothesis states that the Hessian-based similarity metric results in lower mTRE. Using a paired t-test, we achieve a p-value of 0.0048. Thus, the null hypothesis cannot be accepted, i.e., there is statistically significant improvement in the accuracy when our proposed similarity metric is used.

4 Discussion and Conclusion

In this paper, we introduce a new similarity metric for multimodal medical image registration. Our primary contribution has been deriving a closed form expression for computing the metric. We present geometrical insight into the mechanics of our proposed similarity metric. We address an efficient way for transforming the Hessian matrix to prevent recomputing it after applying deformations. The Hessian-based similarity metric is local, robust to intensity nonuniformities and computable at arbitrary scales. Moreover, the similarity metric is very flexible and can be used in a variety of registration tasks. The metric has shown a significant improvement in registering MR to ultrasound compared to a previously proposed similarity metric. However, this improvement comes at the cost of more computation, both in preprocessing and optimization stages. Since the preprocessing can be completed offline, its duration should not be a major concern. The increase in optimization time does not affect the usability of the method for online use cases.

For comparison, we list the results of some previously proposed methods on the BITE database. CoCoMI [19] and SeSaMI [20] have reported a mean error of 2.35 mm and 2.29 mm, respectively. Both of these methods use variants of mutual information as similarity metric along with cubic BSpline as deformation field. LC^2 [6] method which was originally developoed for US-MR registration based on the physics of ultrasound, has reported a mean error of 2.49 mm using rigid transformation. In another work, through introducing a modality-independent binary descriptor called miLBP [9] for deformable registration, an error of 2.15 mm has been reported. With our Hessian-based similarity metric, the registration error is 2.37 mm, which is very close to that of other publications. It must be noted that unlike our method, other methods usually take advantage of nonlinear transformations, pyramid registration, and computationally-intensive preprocessing steps for outlier suppression or selecting regions with structures. We have acheived high accuracies using our proposed metric only with affine transformations. Therefore, we believe the Hessian-based similarity metric has great potentials for addressing multimodal registration tasks.

As future work, we plan to implement our proposed metric in a deformable registration scheme and test it on a broad range of modality pairs and registration tasks and compare its performance to that of the state-of-the-art methods.

References

1. Arbel, T., et al.: Automatic non-linear MRI-ultrasound registration for the correction of intra-operative brain deformations. Comput. Aided Surg. 9(4), 123–136 (2004). https://doi.org/10.3109/10929080500079248
2. Lee, D., et al.: Learning similarity measure for multi-modal 3D image registration. In: 2009 IEEE Conference on Computer Vision and Pattern Recognition, pp. 186–193. IEEE (2009). https://doi.org/10.1109/CVPR.2009.5206840
3. De Nigris, D., et al.: Multi-modal image registration based on gradient orientations of minimal uncertainty. IEEE Trans. Med. Imag. 31(12), 2343–2354 (2012). https://doi.org/10.1109/TMI.2012.2218116
4. Drouin, S., et al.: IBIS: an OR ready open-source platform for image-guided neurosurgery. Int. J. Comput. Assist. Radiol. Surg. 12(3), 363–378 (2017). https://doi.org/10.1007/s11548-016-1478-0
5. Frangi, A.F., Niessen, W.J., Vincken, K.L., Viergever, M.A.: Multiscale vessel enhancement filtering. In: Wells, W.M., Colchester, A., Delp, S. (eds.) MICCAI 1998. LNCS, vol. 1496, pp. 130–137. Springer, Heidelberg (1998). https://doi.org/10.1007/BFb0056195
6. Fuerst, B., et al.: Automatic ultrasound-MRI registration for neurosurgery using the 2D and 3D LC2 Metric. Med. Image Anal. 18(8), 1312–1319 (2014). https://doi.org/10.1016/j.media.2014.04.008
7. Haber, E., Modersitzki, J.: Beyond mutual information: a simple and robust aternative. In: Bildverarbeitung für die Medizin 2005, pp. 350–354. Springer, Heidelberg (2005). https://doi.org/10.1007/3-540-26431-0_72
8. Haskins, G., et al.: Learning deep similarity metric for 3D MR-TRUS image registration. Int. J. Comput. Assist. Radiol. Surg. 14(3), 417–425 (2019). https://doi.org/10.1007/s11548-018-1875-7
9. Jiang, D., et al.: miLBP: a robust and fast modality-independent 3D LBP for multimodal deformable registration. Int. J. Comput. Assist. Radiol. Surg. 11(6), 997–1005 (2016). https://doi.org/10.1007/s11548-016-1407-2
10. Karacali, B.: Fully elastic multi-modality image registration using mutual information. In: 2004 2nd IEEE International Symposium on Biomedical Imaging: Macro to Nano (IEEE Cat No. 04EX821), pp. 1455–1458 IEEE (2004). https://doi.org/10.1109/ISBI.2004.1398823

11. Loeckx, D., et al.: Nonrigid image registration using conditional mutual information. IEEE Trans. Med. Imag. **29**(1), 19–29 (2010). https://doi.org/10.1109/TMI.2009.2021843
12. Maes, F., et al.: Multimodality image registration by maximization of mutual information. IEEE Trans. Med. Imag. **16**(2), 187–198 (1997). https://doi.org/10.1109/42.563664
13. Mercier, L., et al.: Online database of clinical MR and ultrasound images of brain tumors. Med. Phys. **39**(6Part1), 3253–3261 (2012). https://doi.org/10.1118/1.4709600
14. Manera, A.L., et al.: CerebrA, registration and manual label correction of Mindboggle-101 atlas for MNI-ICBM152 template. Sci. Data **7**(1), 237 (2020). https://doi.org/10.1038/s41597-020-0557-9
15. Mezura-Montes, E., et al.: A comparative study of differential evolution variants for global optimization. In: Proceedings of the 8th Annual Conference on Genetic and Evolutionary Computation, pp. 485–492 ACM, New York (2006). https://doi.org/10.1145/1143997.1144086
16. Oliveira, F.P.M., Tavares, J.M.R.S.: Medical image registration: a review. Comput. Methods Biomechan. Biomed. Eng. **17**(2), 73–93 (2014). https://doi.org/10.1080/10255842.2012.670855
17. Pluim, J.P.W., Maintz, J.B.A., Viergever, M.A.: Image registration by maximization of combined mutual information and gradient information. In: Delp, S.L., DiGoia, A.M., Jaramaz, B. (eds.) MICCAI 2000. LNCS, vol. 1935, pp. 452–461. Springer, Heidelberg (2000). https://doi.org/10.1007/978-3-540-40899-4_46
18. Pradhan, S., Patra, D.: Enhanced mutual information based medical image registration. IET Image Proc. **10**(5), 418–427 (2016). https://doi.org/10.1049/iet-ipr.2015.0346
19. Rivaz, H., et al.: Nonrigid Registration of Ultrasound and MRI Using Contextual Conditioned Mutual Information. IEEE Trans. Med. Imaging **33**(3), 708–725 (2014). https://doi.org/10.1109/TMI.2013.2294630
20. Rivaz, H., et al.: Self-similarity weighted mutual information: a new nonrigid image registration metric. Med. Image Anal. **18**(2), 343–358 (2014). https://doi.org/10.1016/j.media.2013.12.003
21. Roche, A., et al.: The correlation ratio as a new similarity measure for multimodal image registration. In: Medical Image Computing and Computer-Assisted Intervention-MICCAI'98: First International Conference Cambridge, October, pp. 1115–1124 (1998). https://doi.org/10.1007/BFb0056301
22. Simonovsky, M., et al.: Presented at the A Deep Metric for Multimodal Registration (2016). https://doi.org/10.1007/978-3-319-46726-9_2
23. Storn, R., Price, K.: Minimizing the real functions of the ICEC 1996 contest by differential evolution. In: Proceedings of IEEE International Conference on Evolutionary Computation, pp. 842–844. IEEE (1996). https://doi.org/10.1109/ICEC.1996.542711
24. Viola, P., Wells, W.M.: Alignment by maximization of mutual information. Int. J. Comput. Vis. **24**(2), 137–154 (1997). https://doi.org/10.1023/A:1007958904918
25. Wachinger, C., Navab, N.: Entropy and Laplacian images: structural representations for multi-modal registration. Med. Image Anal. **16**(1), 1–17 (2012). https://doi.org/10.1016/j.media.2011.03.001

26. Wein, W., et al.: Automatic CT-ultrasound registration for diagnostic imaging and image-guided intervention. Med. Image Anal. **12**(5), 577–585 (2008). https://doi.org/10.1016/j.media.2008.06.006
27. Xiao, Y., et al.: REtroSpective evaluation of cerebral tumors (RESECT): a clinical database of pre-operative MRI and intra-operative ultrasound in low-grade glioma surgeries. Med. Phys. **44**(7), 3875–3882 (2017). https://doi.org/10.1002/mp.12268

Hybrid Multimodality Fusion with Cross-Domain Knowledge Transfer to Forecast Progression Trajectories in Cognitive Decline

Minhui Yu[1,2], Yunbi Liu[3], Jinjian Wu[4], Andrea Bozoki[5], Shijun Qiu[6], Ling Yue[7], and Mingxia Liu[1(✉)]

[1] Department of Radiology and BRIC, University of North Carolina at Chapel Hill, Chapel Hill, NC 27599, USA
mingxia_liu@med.unc.edu
[2] Joint Department of Biomedical Engineering, University of North Carolina at Chapel Hill and North Carolina State University, Chapel Hill, NC 27599, USA
[3] School of Science and Engineering, The Chinese University of Hong Kong, Shenzhen 518172, China
[4] Department of Acupuncture and Rehabilitation, The Affiliated Hospital of TCM of Guangzhou Medical University, Guangzhou 510130, Guangdong, China
[5] Department of Neurology, University of North Carolina at Chapel Hill, Chapel Hill, NC 27599, USA
[6] Department of Radiology, The First Affiliated Hospital of Guangzhou University of Chinese Medicine, Guangzhou 510000, Guangdong, China
[7] Department of Geriatric Psychiatry, Shanghai Mental Health Center, Shanghai Jiao Tong University School of Medicine, Shanghai 200030, China

Abstract. Magnetic resonance imaging (MRI) and positron emission tomography (PET) are increasingly used to forecast progression trajectories of cognitive decline caused by preclinical and prodromal Alzheimer's disease (AD). Many existing studies have explored the potential of these two distinct modalities with diverse machine and deep learning approaches. But successfully fusing MRI and PET can be complex due to their unique characteristics and missing modalities. To this end, we develop a hybrid multimodality fusion (HMF) framework with cross-domain knowledge transfer for joint MRI and PET representation learning, feature fusion, and cognitive decline progression forecasting. Our HMF consists of three modules: 1) a module to impute missing PET images, 2) a module to extract multimodality features from MRI and PET images, and 3) a module to fuse the extracted multimodality features. To address the issue of small sample sizes, we employ a cross-domain knowledge transfer strategy from the ADNI dataset, which includes 795 subjects, to independent small-scale AD-related cohorts, in order to leverage the rich knowledge present within the ADNI. The proposed HMF is extensively evaluated in three AD-related studies with 272 subjects across multiple disease stages, such as subjective cognitive decline and mild cognitive impairment. Experimental results demonstrate the superiority of our method over several state-of-the-art approaches in forecasting progression trajectories of AD-related cognitive decline.

J. Woo et al. (Eds.): MICCAI 2023 Workshops, LNCS 14394, pp. 265–275, 2023.
https://doi.org/10.1007/978-3-031-47425-5_24

Keywords: Cognitive decline · MRI · PET · Fusion · Transfer learning

1   Introduction

Alzheimer's disease (AD) is a chronic neurodegenerative condition that exhibits progressive cognitive decline over a decade prior to the onset of dementia [1]. The associated cognitive dysfunctions include subjective cognitive decline (SCD) in preclinical AD stage [2–4], and mild cognitive impairment (MCI) in prodromal AD stage [5]. The disease progression trajectory from SCD to MCI even AD represents a neurodegenerative continuum, while only part of individuals with cognitive dysfunctions will eventually convert to the next stage [6,7]. Timely identification of individuals experiencing cognitive decline that are at a heightened risk of progressing towards dementia is important for the successful implementation of interventions and treatments targeting AD-related conditions [8,9].

Structural magnetic resonance imaging (MRI) and positron emission tomography (PET) are two non-invasive imaging techniques that are increasingly used in learning-based investigations of cognitive decline [10–13]. Many existing studies on cognitive decline analysis employ these two complementary modalities via various machine/deep learning techniques, but usually cannot effectively fuse them due to their heterogeneity caused by different inherent characteristics. Several studies concatenate extracted MRI and PET features [14,15] but neglecting their underlying complex association. Some studies model inter-modality association by merging MRI and PET together [16,17], but seldom jointly consider inter- and intra-modality association. In addition, existing research usually has to face missing modality issues, since PET is more difficult to be obtained due to patient dropout or poor image quality compared with MRI. For instance, all subjects in ADNI [18] have available MRI, while only approximately half of them have accessible PET, significantly reducing the quantity of data points.

To this end, we propose a hybrid multimodality fusion (**HMF**) framework to forecast progression trajectories in cognitive decline with MRI and PET. As depicted in Fig. 1, the HMF is composed of 1) a *missing PET imputation* module that performs a subject-wise inspection of the existence of PET data and generates missing ones from corresponding MRIs, 2) a *multimodality feature extraction* module that learns features from the paired MRI and PET data separately using two feature encoders, each constrained by a triplet loss, and 3) a *multimodality fusion* module that performs both inter-modality and intra-modality feature selection and ultimately aids in making categorical predictions. We also utilize a transfer learning approach to enable *cross-domain knowledge transfer* between AD-related datasets. Experimental results on a total of 1,067 subjects from ADNI and two AD-related datasets indicate the superiority of our method over several state-of-the-arts in four different classification tasks.

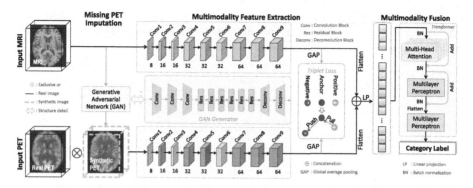

Fig. 1. Illustration of the proposed hybrid multimodality fusion (HMF) framework to forecast progression trajectories in cognitive decline with 1) missing PET imputation via a pre-trained generator based on generative adversarial network, 2) multimodality feature extraction via two parallel feature extractors (*w.r.t.* MRI and PET) constrained by a triplet loss, and 3) multimodality fusion via a transformer for forecasting.

2   Materials and Methodology

2.1   Subjects and Image Preprocessing

We use T1-weighted structural MRI and PET scans of 795 subjects from the public Alzheimer's Disease Neuroimaging Initiative (**ADNI**) [18] as source data for model training, including 436 cognitive normal (CN) (all with MRI, 293 with PET), 359 AD (all with MRI, 240 with PET) subjects. A total of 272 subjects from three datasets, ranging from CN, SCD to MCI along the pre-dementia stages of AD, are used as target data for model evaluation. Specifically, the three validation datasets include: 1) Chinese Longitudinal Aging Study (**CLAS**) with T1-weighted *MRI alone* of 48 stable SCD (sSCD) and 22 progressive SCD (pSCD) subjects defined according to a 7-year follow-up [19], 2) ADNI with *paired MRI and PET* of subjective memory complaints (SMC) subjects, containing 42 stable SMC (sSMC) and 19 progressive SMC (pSMC) subjects that have SMC at baseline and then either stay SMC in a 5-year follow-up or convert to MCI or AD, and 3) a private dataset (called **T2DM**) acquired from the First Affiliated Hospital of Guangzhou University of Chinese Medicine that contains *MRI alone* of 45 subjects of CN, 59 subjects with Type 2 diabetes mellitus (DM), and 37 subjects with diabetes-associated MCI (DM-MCI). In general, SCD and SMC refer to the same disease stage characterized by self-reported memory or cognitive decline with clinically normal results, while the diagnostic criteria differ slightly across different studies. Specifically, SCD is diagnosed based on the criteria defined by Subjective Cognitive Decline Initiative [3], and SMC follows the Cognitive Change Index proposed in an earlier study [20]. The demographic information of the studied subjects is listed in Table 1.

The preprocessing pipeline for T1-weighted MRI scans is consistent across all datasets, which includes skull stripping, intensity normalization, and registration

Table 1. Demographic information of subjects from 3 datasets (*i.e.*, CLAS, ADNI, and T2DM). Age, education, and MMSE are presented with mean and standard deviation. MMSE: mini-mental state examination.

Information	CLAS		ADNI		T2DM			ADNI	
	pSCD	sSCD	pSMC	sSMC	DM-MCI	DM	CN	AD	CN
Subject number	22	48	19	42	37	59	45	359	436
Age (Year)	70.7±6.6	67.4±5.9	73.9±6.0	71.3±5.0	51.5±9.1	45.5±8.1	47.8±8.4	75.3±7.9	74.7±5.9
Gender (Female/Male)	13/9	26/22	9/10	26/16	14/23	28/31	24/21	165/194	222/214
Education (Year)	6.8±4.0	9.8±2.7	16.4±2.7	16.5±2.6	10.2±4.4	12.8±3.1	11.4±3.1	15.2±3.1	16.3±2.7
MMSE	26.6±2.6	28.0±1.9	29.0±s1.4	29.1±1.0	26.9±2.9	28.7±1.3	29.0±1.0	23.2±2.1	29.1±1.1

to MNI space. The PET scans are linearly registered to corresponding MRI scans first. Finally, each scan is cropped to the size of $160 \times 180 \times 160$ (with whole brain preserved).

2.2   Proposed Method

As shown in Fig. 1, the proposed HMF consists of 1) a *missing PET imputation* module, 2) a *multimodality feature extraction* module constrained by triplet loss, and 3) a *multimodality fusion* module for prediction, with details given below.

Missing PET Imputation. To address the missing modality issue, we employ an established generative adversarial network (GAN) [21–23] trained with paired PET and MRI data in ADNI as an image generator, to synthesize missing PET based on existing MRI, for incomplete source and target data. As shown in Fig. 1, the image generator contains 3 convolutional blocks, 6 residual blocks, and 2 deconvolutional blocks. This GAN generator is pre-trained in conjunction with a discriminator by optimizing both an adversarial loss and a reconstruction loss, and its training is independent of the classification task in this work.

Multimodality Feature Extraction. As illustrated in the middle part of Fig. 1, our methodology employs a pair of identical convolutional neural network (CNN) branches, each functioning as a *feature encoder*. These encoders facilitate the extraction of semantic features from both modalities. The upper branch is designed to process 3D MRI scans, while the lower branch handles real or synthetic 3D PET scans. Each encoder comprises 9 convolutional layers, characterized by an incremental filter count, a stride of 1, and a kernel size of 5 for the initial layer, followed by a kernel size of 3 for subsequent layers. Additionally, max-pooling with a size of 2 is applied after the first, third, and sixth convolutional layers. We also integrate an attention block into the middle of each encoder, aiming to highlight discriminative regions voxel-wisely [24]. This attention block divides the activation map into small blocks, performs averaging, and multiplies the result back to the blocks of activation map. The final layer of each CNN produces output from 64 3D kernels, followed by global average pooling.

For an enhanced capacity to distinguish features, we introduce a *triplet constraint* within each of the two encoders. The core concept of triplet loss is to learn features in a manner that, within the latent representation space, samples sharing semantic similarities (*i.e.*, anchor and positive) are mapped to proximate regions, while dissimilar samples (*i.e.*, anchor and negative) are projected to distant regions from each other [25]. This strategic alignment is anticipated to amplify the discriminative efficacy of the model [26,27]. The formulation of the triplet loss is expressed as:

$$L_T(A, P, N) = \max\{||A - P||^2 - ||A - N||^2 + \delta, 0\},\tag{1}$$

where A, P and N denote the l_2 normalized representation of anchor, positive, and negative samples, correspondingly, and δ stands as the designated distance margin. Our application of the triplet loss incorporates a semi-hard negative sample mining technique [25], where the negative samples that fall further than the range of a positive sample but remain in the distance margin of $\delta = 1$ are initially identified to be shifted beyond the distance margin.

Multimodality Fusion. To contextually fuse features of MRI and PET within each modality as well as across both modalities, we employ a transformer block with self-attention technique [28] in our proposed HMF. As depicted in the right of Fig. 1, MRI and PET representations generated by the last layers of two feature extractors are flattened and then concatenated to a feature matrix $\mathbf{X} \in \mathbb{R}^{N_f \times d}$ ($N_f = 128$ and $d = 96$ in this work). This matrix is then linearly projected to feature patches $\mathbf{F}_i \in \mathbb{R}^{N_f \times d_f}$, where $d_f = 64$ is the dimension of each feature in the new feature space. The resulting feature patches defined in $\mathbf{F}_i$ serve as the input of the transformer for feature fusion and abstraction. The transformer block consists of a *multi-head attention* module and two *multilayer perceptron* (MLP) modules, each preceded by batch normalization. In the multi-head attention module, we deploy 4 identical self-attention heads in parallel. Within each of the heads, $\mathbf{F}_i$ enters two encoders and the outputs scan through each other by dot product to generate attention weights $\mathbf{P} \in \mathbb{R}^{N_f \times N_f}$, followed by a softmax to generate the probability map. The probability map are then applied back to N_f encoded features to achieve attention-enhanced features $\mathbf{F}_o \in \mathbb{R}^{N_f \times d_f}$. The above operation of self-attention can be formulated as follows:

$$\mathbf{P}(\mathbf{F}_i) = f_1(\mathbf{F}_i)f_2(\mathbf{F}_i)^\top \quad \mathbf{F}_o(\mathbf{F}_i) = softmax\left(\frac{\mathbf{P}(\mathbf{F}_i)}{\sqrt{d_f}}\right) \cdot f_3(\mathbf{F}_i),\tag{2}$$

where f_1, f_2, and f_3 are three independent encoders of size $N_f \times d_f$. For each MLP module, we stack two dense layers, each followed by a dropout layer, for feature abstraction. There are 128, 64, and 2,048, 1,024 dimensional dense layers in two MLP modules. The dropout rate is set to 0.1 and 0.3 to balance the need for good generalization ability and training efficacy. The output is flattened before entering the last MLP and dropped out again at a rate of 0.3. A skipping operation is applied to the multi-head attention block and the first MLP block.

Hybrid Loss Function. To facilitate progression forecasting of cognitive decline, we employ a binary cross-entropy loss, which is defined as follows:

$$L_C = -\frac{1}{S}\sum_{i=1}^{S} l_i log(p_i) + (1 - l_i)log(1 - p_i),\tag{3}$$

Table 2. Classification results of six methods in task SCD and SMC progression forecasting, presented in average values with standard deviation, with best results in bold.

Method	pSCD vs. sSCD Classification on CLAS					pSMC vs. sSMC Classification on ADNI				
	AUC (%)	ACC (%)	SEN (%)	SPE (%)	F1 (%)	AUC (%)	ACC (%)	SEN (%	SPE (%)	F1 (%)
SVM	65.9*	62.6	70.0	59.2	54.0	53.9*	52.5	52.6	52.4	40.8
XGBoost	60.7*	55.7	59.1	54.2	45.6	56.2*	59.0	57.9	59.5	46.8
RF	63.6±2.2*	59.7±1.4	65.5±2.2	57.1±1.0	50.5±1.7	57.1±0.6*	53.8±1.6	54.7±2.6	53.3±1.2	42.4±2.0
ILF	67.2±5.4*	60.3±3.9	66.4±6.2	57.5±2.8	51.2±4.8	64.9±5.1*	59.0±4.1	63.2±6.7	57.1±3.0	49.0±5.2
FLF	61.1±3.3*	56.3±3.8	60.0±6.0	54.6±2.8	46.3±4.7	74.7±1.9	64.3±3.3	71.6±5.4	61.0±2.4	55.5±4.2
HMF (Ours)	**74.2±2.0**	**63.7±4.2**	**71.8±6.7**	**60.0±3.1**	**55.4±5.2**	**76.2±2.2**	**65.6±2.1**	**73.7±3.3**	**61.9±1.5**	**57.1±2.6**

Table 3. Classification results of six methods in task DM-MCI identification, presented in average values with standard deviation. The best result of each metric is in bold.

Method	DM-MCI vs. CN Classification on T2DM					DM-MCI vs. DM Classification on T2DM				
	AUC (%)	ACC (%)	SEN (%)	SPE (%)	F1 (%)	AUC (%)	ACC (%)	SEN (%	SPE (%)	F1 (%)
SVM	55.6*	53.7	54.1	53.3	51.3	50.7*	53.1	54.1	52.5	47.1
XGBoost	42.6*	46.3	45.9	46.7	43.6	45.8*	44.8	43.2	45.8	37.6
RF	50.1±0.7*	47.3±1.2	47.0±1.3	47.6±1.1	44.6±1.3	48.3±0.3*	46.5±1.6	45.4±2.0	47.1±1.3	39.5±1.8
ILF	51.6±11.7*	52.7±8.0	53.0±8.8	52.4±7.2	50.3±8.4	52.2±7.3*	52.7±5.8	53.5±7.5	52.2±4.7	46.6±6.6
FLF	58.6±3.2*	53.2±1.8	53.5±2.0	52.9±1.7	50.8±1.9	57.9±2.8*	51.5±4.2	51.9±5.5	51.2±3.5	45.2±4.8
HMF (Ours)	**59.1±1.2**	**54.1±2.8**	**54.6±3.2**	**53.8±2.6**	**51.8±3.0**	**61.0±2.5**	**55.2±1.3**	**56.8±1.7**	**54.2±1.1**	**49.4±1.5**

where l_i represents the category label of the subject i, p_i represents the probability score predicted by the proposed model, and S is the number of training samples. With Eq. (1) and Eq. (3), we can formulate the hybrid loss $\mathcal{L}$ as:

$$\mathcal{L} = L_C + \alpha L_T, \tag{4}$$

where α is a hyperparameter of 10^{-3} in our experiments.

Domain Transfer & Implementation. Since the amounts of data in three AD-related target datasets are relatively small, we employ a simple *cross-domain transfer learning* strategy to facilitate knowledge transfer from the large-scale ADNI to these target cohorts. Specifically, we first use paired 3D MRI and PET images of 795 AD+CN subjects from ADNI as source data to train a specific model. Then, this model is directly applied to three target datasets for evaluation. The influence of source data for model training is also investigated in the experiments. We implement the HMF with TensorFlow 2.0 and utilize the Adam optimizer for training. The training batch size is 5, with the input of each mini-batch having at least 2 randomly selected samples per category.

3 Experiment

Experimental Settings. Four tasks are performed in the experiments, including 1) SCD progression forecasting (*i.e.*, pSCD vs. sSCD classification) on CLAS, 2) SMC progression forecasting (*i.e.*, pSMC vs. sSMC classification) on ADNI, 3)

DM-MCI vs. CN classification on T2DM, and 4) DM-MCI vs. DM classification on T2DM. We use five evaluation metrics: area under the ROC curve (AUC), accuracy (ACC), sensitivity (SEN), specificity (SPE), and F1-Score (F1). For the main experiments, we use paired MRI and PET scans of AD and CN subjects from ADNI as source data to train a specific classification model. Then, this model is applied to three target datasets for downstream classification tasks.

Competing Methods. We compare our HMF with five different methods: 1) support vector machine (**SVM**) that inputs 180-dimensional concatenated MRI and PET features, extracted from gray matter volume of 90 regions-of-interests (ROIs) defined by AAL atlas; 2) eXtreme Gradient Boosting (**XGBoost**) with 10 trees, maximum tree depth of 5, learning rate of 0.1, and the same input as SVM; 3) random forest (**RF**) with 1,000 trees, maximum tree depth of 10, with the same input as SVM and XGBoost; 4) image-level fusion (**ILF**) [17] that adds the scans from both modalities voxel-by-voxel, followed by a CNN (with 12 convolutional layers, 4 batch normalization layers and 4 max-pooling layers) for classification; and 5) feature-level fusion (**FLF**) [15] that contains two CNN branches with 5 convolutional layers each and concatenates the produced MRI and PET features for forecasting. To achieve an unbiased comparison, we keep the hyperparameter settings consistent across all deep learning methods to the greatest extent possible and repeat training of each method five times with random parameter initialization to obtain mean and standard deviation results.

Forecasting Results. The results obtained from all methods in SCD and SMC progression forecasting are presented in Table 2, and results of DM-MCI identification are presented in Table 3, where '*' denotes the difference between our HMF and a competing method is statistically significant ($p < 0.05$ via paired t-test). It can be seen from Table 2 and Table 3 that our HMF outperforms the competing methods in four different tasks. For instance, the AUC of HMF (*i.e.*, 74.2%) is 7.0% higher than the second-best ILF (AUC=67.2%) in pSCD vs. sSCD classification. Also, the overall results of all methods in DM-MCI identification are inferior to those in SCD/SMC progression forecasting, possibly due to the complex disease trajectories of subjects in T2DM. Figure 2 shows a probability trajectory of several disease stages *w.r.t.* age, estimated by our HMF. The figure suggests that cognitive decline occurring at an earlier age (*e.g.*, <70 in CLAS) is more likely to remain stable, and cognitive decline presenting at a later age (*e.g.*, >70 in CLAS) is more likely to progress to MCI. This finding aligns with the demographic information presented in Table 1, that progressive SCD/SMC subjects have higher average ages compared to stable subjects.

Ablation Study. We further compare the HMF with its five variants, involving 1) **HMF-T** without triplet loss, 2) **HMF-TF** without transformer, 3) **HMF-P** trained without PET, 4) **HMF-R** trained with real PET and real MRI, and 5) **HMF-S** trained with synthetic PET and real MRI. For a fair comparison,

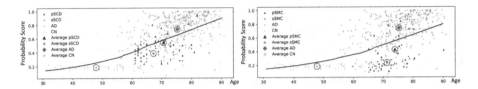

Fig. 2. Fitted trajectory and scattered probability scores for forecasting progression *w.r.t.* age, showing p/sSCD subjects from CLAS (left), p/sSMC subjects from ADNI (right), along with CN subjects from T2DM and AD subjects from ADNI for reference.

Table 4. Classification results of HMF and its five variants in task SCD and SMC progression forecasting, presented in average values with standard deviation.

Method	pSCD vs. sSCD Classification on CLAS					pSMC vs. sSMC Classification on ADNI				
	AUC (%)	ACC (%)	SEN (%)	SPE (%)	F1 (%)	AUC (%)	ACC (%)	SEN (%	SPE (%)	F1 (%)
HMF-T	59.4±6.2*	55.7±4.0	59.1±6.4	54.2±2.9	45.6±5.0	71.5±4.7*	62.3±2.1	68.4±3.3	59.5±1.5	53.1±2.6
HMF-TF	56.9±0.5*	53.4±1.1	55.5±1.8	52.5±0.8	42.8±1.4	70.2±1.5	60.3±1.6	65.3±2.6	58.1±1.2	50.6±2.0
HMF-P	61.1±8.6*	56.9±5.3	60.9±8.4	55.0±3.9	47.0±6.5	68.0±6.2*	59.0±3.6	63.2±5.8	57.1±2.6	49.0±4.5
HMF-R	56.5±6.4*	55.1±4.6	58.2±7.3	53.8±3.3	44.9±5.6	69.1±6.8*	61.6±4.8	67.4±7.7	59.0±3.5	52.2±6.0
HMF-S	57.7±9.7*	54.6±5.0	57.3±7.9	53.3±3.6	44.2±6.1	61.1±10.3*	56.4±7.3	58.9±11.7	55.2±5.3	45.7±9.1
HMF (Ours)	74.2±2.0	63.7±4.2	71.8±6.7	60.0±3.1	55.4±5.2	76.2±2.2	65.6±2.1	73.7±3.3	61.9±1.5	57.1±2.6

these five variants employ a similar network architecture as HMF. The results of SCD and SMC progression forecasting are presented in Table 4, from which we can observe that our HMF outperforms all five variants mostly having statistical significance p <0.05. For instance, HMF yields the AUC of 74.2% in pSCD vs. sSCD classification on CLAS, 17.3% higher than that of HMF-TF. This suggests the effectiveness of our transformer-based multimodality fusion strategy.

Influence of Hyperparameter. We study the influence of hyperparameter α in Eq. (4) by varying its value within $[10^{-6}, 10^1]$, and report the results of HMF in Fig. 3(a)–(d). This figure indicates that our HMF can produce good results when $10^{-4} < \alpha < 10^{-2}$ in four classification tasks on three AD-related datasets. With a very small α (*e.g.*, 10^{-6}), the results of HMF in all four tasks experience a significant decline, suggesting the effectiveness of the triple loss to HMF.

Influence of Source Data. Other than utilizing AD+CN subjects to train the HMF in our main experiments, we also explore the performance of HMF using different source data, including 1) MCI+CN (with 897 MCI and 436 CN), and 2) pMCI+sMCI (with 262 pMCI and 405 sMCI). Figure 3(e)–(f) displays the AUC and ACC results of HMF in four tasks. This figure suggests that our HMF trained on AD+CN leads to the best overall performance, while the use of MCI+CN as the source data yields the least optimal results. This is likely due to the presence of a mix of pMCI and sMCI in MCI, which complicates the data distribution and reduces the discriminative ability of the trained model.

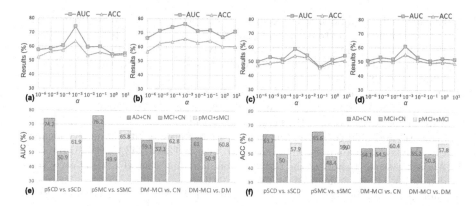

Fig. 3. Result of HMF in (a) pSCD vs. sSCD classification on CLAS, (b) pSMC vs. sSMC classification on ADNI, (c) DM-MCI vs. CN classification on T2DM, and (d) DM-MCI vs. DM classification on T2DM with varying values of α, and four tasks trained with different training domains from ADNI in terms of (e) AUC and (f) ACC.

4 Conclusion

In this work, we present a hybrid multimodality fusion framework that combines structural MRI and PET data, along with cross-domain knowledge transfer, to forecast progression trajectories in AD-related cognitive decline, which includes SCD and MCI. Specifically, HMF contains a missing PET imputation module, a multimodality feature extraction module and a multimodality fusion module. A transfer learning strategy is applied to address the small sample size issue. Experimental results on 795 subjects from a source domain and 272 subjects from three target domains demonstrate the superiority of the proposed HMF over state-of-the-art methods. Considering the prolonged AD development trajectory, it would be interesting to employ baseline multimodality data for longitudinally predicting the specific stage at which a subject will ultimately reach, which will be one of our future works.

Acknowledgements. M. Yu, A. Bozoki, and M. Liu were partly supported by NIH grant AG073297.

References

1. Amieva, H., et al.: Prodromal Alzheimer's disease: Successive emergence of the clinical symptoms. Annals of Neurology: Official Journal of the American Neurological Association and the Child Neurology Society **64**(5), 492–498 (2008)
2. van Harten, A.C., et al.: Subjective cognitive decline and risk of MCI: the mayo clinic study of aging. Neurology **91**(4), e300–e312 (2018)
3. Jessen, F., et al.: A conceptual framework for research on subjective cognitive decline in preclinical Alzheimer's disease. Alzheimer's Dementia **10**(6), 844–852 (2014)

4. Kryscio, R.J., et al.: Self-reported memory complaints: implications from a longitudinal cohort with autopsies. Neurology **83**(15), 1359–1365 (2014)

5. Petersen, R.C., Smith, G.E., Waring, S.C., Ivnik, R.J., Tangalos, E.G., Kokmen, E.: Mild cognitive impairment: clinical characterization and outcome. Arch. Neurol. **56**(3), 303–308 (1999)

6. Dubois, B., et al.: Research criteria for the diagnosis of Alzheimer's disease: revising the NINCDS-ADRDA criteria. Lancet Neurol. **6**(8), 734–746 (2007)

7. Mitchell, A.J., Beaumont, H., Ferguson, D., Yadegarfar, M., Stubbs, B.: Risk of dementia and mild cognitive impairment in older people with subjective memory complaints: Meta-analysis. Acta Psychiatr. Scand. **130**(6), 439–451 (2014)

8. Aisen, P., et al.: Report of the task force on designing clinical trials in early (pre-dementia) AD. Neurology **76**(3), 280–286 (2011)

9. Samanta, M.K., Wilson, B., Santhi, K., Kumar, K.S., Suresh, B.: Alzheimer disease and its management: a review. Am. J .Ther. **13**(6), 516–526 (2006)

10. Grueso, S., Viejo-Sobera, R.: Machine learning methods for predicting progression from mild cognitive impairment to Alzheimer's disease dementia: A systematic review. Alzheimer's Res. Therapy **13**, 1–29 (2021)

11. Hinrichs, C., Singh, V., Xu, G., Johnson, S.C.: Predictive markers for AD in a multi-modality framework: an analysis of MCI progression in the ADNI population. Neuroimage **55**(2), 574–589 (2011)

12. Zhou, T., Thung, K.H., Liu, M., Shi, F., Zhang, C., Shen, D.: Multi-modal latent space inducing ensemble SVM classifier for early dementia diagnosis with neuroimaging data. Med. Image Anal. **60**, 101630 (2020)

13. Pan, Y., Liu, M., Lian, C., Xia, Y., Shen, D.: Spatially-constrained fisher representation for brain disease identification with incomplete multi-modal neuroimages. IEEE Trans. Med. Imaging **39**(9), 2965–2975 (2020)

14. Senanayake, U., Sowmya, A., Dawes, L.: Deep fusion pipeline for mild cognitive impairment diagnosis. In: IEEE 15th International Symposium on Biomedical Imaging (ISBI 2018). IEEE 2018, pp. 1394–1997 (2018)

15. Liu, M., Cheng, D., Wang, K., Wang, Y.: Multi-modality cascaded convolutional neural networks for Alzheimer's disease diagnosis. Neuroinformatics **16**, 295–308 (2018)

16. Dwivedi, S., Goel, T., Tanveer, M., Murugan, R., Sharma, R.: Multimodal fusion-based deep learning network for effective diagnosis of Alzheimer's disease. IEEE Multimedia **29**(2), 45–55 (2022)

17. Song, J., Zheng, J., Li, P., Lu, X., Zhu, G., Shen, P.: An effective multimodal image fusion method using MRI and PET for Alzheimer's disease diagnosis. Front. Digital Jealth **3**, 637386 (2021)

18. Jack Jr, C.R., et al.: The Alzheimer's disease neuroimaging initiative (ADNI): MRI methods. J. Magnetic Resonance Imaging: An Official Journal of the International Society for Magnetic Resonance in Medicine **27**(4), 685–691 (2008)

19. Xiao, S., et al.: The China longitudinal ageing study: overview of the demographic, psychosocial and cognitive data of the Shanghai sample. J. Mental Health **25**(2), 31–136 (2016)

20. Saykin, A., Wishart, H., Rabin, L., Santulli, R., Flashman, L., West, J., McHugh, T., Mamourian, A.: Older adults with cognitive complaints show brain atrophy similar to that of amnestic MCI. Neurology **67**(5), 834–842 (2006)

21. Goodfellow, I., et al.: Generative adversarial networks. Commun. ACM **63**(11), 139–144 (2020)

22. Liu, Y., Yue, L., Xiao, S., Yang, W., Shen, D., Liu, M.: Assessing clinical progression from subjective cognitive decline to mild cognitive impairment with incomplete multi-modal neuroimages. Med. Image Anal. **75**, 102266 (2022)
23. Pan, Y., Liu, M., Xia, Y., Shen, D.: Disease-image-specific learning for diagnosis-oriented neuroimage synthesis with incomplete multi-modality data. IEEE Trans. Pattern Anal. Mach. Intell. **44**(10), 6839–6853 (2021)
24. Yu, M., Guan, H., Fang, Y., Yue, L., Liu, M.: Domain-prior-induced structural MRI adaptation for clinical progression prediction of subjective cognitive decline. In: International Conference on Medical Image Computing and Computer-Assisted Intervention, pp. 24–33. Springer (2022)
25. Schroff, F., Kalenichenko, D., Philbin, J.: FaceNet: A unified embedding for face recognition and clustering. In: Proceedings of the IEEE Conference on Computer Vision and Pattern Recognition, pp. 815–823 (2015)
26. Mensink, T., Verbeek, J., Perronnin, F., Csurka, G.: Metric learning for large scale image classification: generalizing to new classes at near-zero cost. In: Fitzgibbon, A., Lazebnik, S., Perona, P., Sato, Y., Schmid, C. (eds.) ECCV 2012. LNCS, vol. 7573, pp. 488–501. Springer, Heidelberg (2012). https://doi.org/10.1007/978-3-642-33709-3_35
27. Hoffer, E., Ailon, N.: Deep metric learning using triplet network. In: Feragen, A., Pelillo, M., Loog, M. (eds.) SIMBAD 2015. LNCS, vol. 9370, pp. 84–92. Springer, Cham (2015). https://doi.org/10.1007/978-3-319-24261-3_7
28. Vaswani, A., et al.: Attention is all you need. Advances in Neural Information Processing Systems 30 (2017)

MuST: Multimodal Spatiotemporal Graph-Transformer for Hospital Readmission Prediction

Yan Miao and Lequan Yu[✉]

The University of Hong Kong, Hong Kong SAR, China
ymiao7@connect.hku.hk, lqyu@hku.hk

Abstract. Hospital readmission prediction is considered an essential approach to decreasing readmission rates, which is a key factor in assessing the quality and efficacy of a healthcare system. Previous studies have extensively utilized three primary modalities, namely electronic health records (EHR), medical images, and clinical notes, to predict hospital readmissions. However, the majority of these studies did not integrate information from all three modalities or utilize the spatiotemporal relationships present in the dataset. This study introduces a novel model called the Multimodal Spatiotemporal Graph-Transformer (MuST) for predicting hospital readmissions. By employing Graph Convolution Networks and temporal transformers, we can effectively capture spatial and temporal dependencies in EHR and chest radiographs. We then propose a fusion transformer to combine the spatiotemporal features from the two modalities mentioned above with the features from clinical notes extracted by a pre-trained, domain-specific transformer. We assess the effectiveness of our methods using the latest publicly available dataset, MIMIC-IV. The experimental results indicate that the inclusion of multimodal features in MuST improves its performance in comparison to unimodal methods. Furthermore, our proposed pipeline outperforms the current leading methods in the prediction of hospital readmissions.

Keywords: Hospital readmission prediction · Multimodal fusion · Graph neural network · Transformer

1 Introduction

Hospital readmission prediction is considered a crucial aspect of clinical decision-making. It refers to predicting the occurrence of a patient who has been discharged from a medical facility and is subsequently admitted to either the same institution or a different one within a designated timeframe, typically ranging from 30 to 90 days, subsequent to their prior visit [30]. The concept of a revisit typically denotes an instance where a patient's previous in-patient visit was either insufficient or ineffective in addressing their medical needs [30]. As a result, decreasing avoidable hospital readmissions has become a top priority for healthcare systems.

J. Woo et al. (Eds.): MICCAI 2023 Workshops, LNCS 14394, pp. 276–285, 2023.
https://doi.org/10.1007/978-3-031-47425-5_25

The advancement of deep-learning approaches has significantly contributed to the research on hospital readmission prediction in recent years [2,11,25,26, 29,31]. Existing studies have approached the problem from various perspectives. [2,25,29] extracted temporal relationships in longitudinal electronic health records (EHR) clinical data using CNN-, RNN-, and LSTM-based frameworks. Some works utilized clinical notes for hospital readmission prediction as they offer a more comprehensive understanding of the patient compared to structured features [11]. For instance, ClinicalBERT [11] is a variant of bidirectional encoder representations from transformers (BERT) [5] model that is specifically pre-trained on clinical notes from the MIMIC-III dataset [14] and finetuned for the purpose of predicting 30-day hospital readmission. Meanwhile, several studies have attempted to predict readmission by aggregating the diverse perspectives of information provided by different data modalities within the hospitalization records of patients. Zhang et al. [31] proposed a multimodal CNN-based approach that combined structured EHR and unstructured clinical notes to predict hospital readmission. Recently, a novel pipeline called the multimodal, spatiotemporal graph neural network (MM-STGNN) [26] has been proposed to handle the task. It fused longitudinal chest radiographs and EHR of patients, and employed a graph-based approach to capture patient similarity. The pipeline's multimodal and spatiotemporal features resulted in better performance than traditional baselines like gradient-boosting and LSTM. However, the prior research works have a common limitation: they failed to integrate all the valuable EHR, medical imaging, and textual data modalities for better hospital readmission prediction. Moreover, the late-stage multimodal fusion strategy in MM-STGNN is insufficient to model the fine-grained interaction of different modalities, as it only extracts a global representation for each modality.

The Transformer architecture [28], an attention-based deep sequence model, has gained significant attention in the deep learning community due to its exceptional performance across various tasks [5,17,20,23], where most of them either worked under a unimodal [5,20] (i.e., either text or imaging) or visual-language scenario [17,23]. Recently, a few studies [6,19,22] have discovered that the integration of multimodal data using transformers enhanced task performance, providing a more effective approach to modeling dependencies between different modalities. A transformer model treats each modality as a distinct input sequence and utilizes the attention mechanism to selectively attend to parts of the input sequences based on their relevance to the original task. This enables the model to capture intricate relationships between modalities and produce accurate predictions. Previous studies have also explored the utilization of transformers in the context of AI in healthcare [11,18,24]. However, there are limited works to explore how to use transformers to integrate multimodal medical data, and we have yet to find any existing research that integrates multimodal features using transformers for the hospital readmission prediction task.

In this study, we introduce a novel Multimodal Spatialtemporal Graph-Transformer framework (i.e.MuST), which integrates three modalities - EHR, medical image, and clinical note - to collectively predict 30-day all-cause hospital

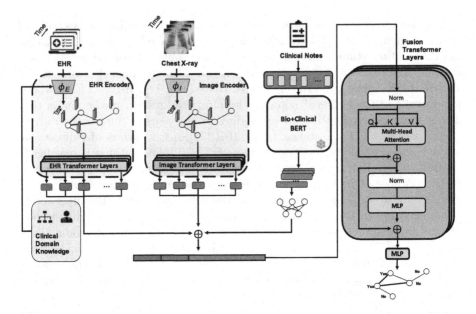

Fig. 1. Overview of the proposed MuST framework. The longitudinal EHR and chest radiographs undergo a spatiotemporal pipeline (i.e., **ST-Transformer**) consisting of a feature extractor, a relationship graph (each node represents a patient), and a temporal transformer. The clinical notes are processed by a BioClinical BERT so as to extract meaningful representations. The resulting features from these pipelines for each modality are then concatenated and aggregated by a fusion transformer to generate hospital readmission predictions for each admission record.

readmission. Specifically, we construct a graph to capture the spatial dependencies between hospital admissions for EHR and imaging modalities and then adopt the pre-trained BioClinical BERT [3] to extract meaningful representations from the clinical notes. We further incorporate the temporal relationships of the EHR and medical images by processing the spatial features of each modality with two distinct temporal transformers. Finally, a fusion transformer is employed to integrate the spatiotemporal features of the EHR and images with the informative representations of clinical notes. Extensive experiments were conducted on the publicly available MIMIC-IV [1,7], MIMIC-CXR-JPG [7,13], and MIMIC-IV-Note [7,15] datasets to validate the effectiveness and superiority of our proposed framework.

2   Methodology

Figure 1 depicts our proposed MuST framework. First, we employ clinical domain knowledge (i.e., ϕ_E in Fig. 1) derived from the hierarchical structure of medical codes [26,27] and clinical expertise [26] to preprocess the input EHR. In parallel, we extract visual representations from the chest radiographs using DenseNet121

[10] (i.e., ϕ_I in Fig. 1). To exploit the spatial and temporal relationships within EHR and images, we create a relationship graph and feed the resulting data into a temporal transformer. Each clinical note file is segmented into several chunks, which are then processed using BioClinical BERT [3] to extract a sequence of representations. A fusion transformer model is adopted to aggregate information across three different modalities and pass the output to a multi-layer perceptron to obtain predictions of future readmission for each admission record.

2.1 Problem Formulation

Hospital admissions can be treated as a sequence of visit records consisting of information from multiple modalities, such as patient EHR, medical images, and clinical note. For the visit record of the m-th patient X_m, it can be represented as $X_m = [x_{m,1}, x_{m,2}, ..., x_{m,t}, ..., x_{m,T_m}]$, where T_m is the total number of visits for this patient in the given dataset, $t \in \{1, 2, .., T_m\}$. $x_{m,t}$ can be further denoted as $x_{m,t} = \{e^o_{m,t}, i^o_{m,t}, n^o_{m,t}\}$, where $e^o_{m,t} \in E^o_m$, $i^o_{m,t} \in I^o_m$, $n^o_{m,t} \in N^o_m$, E^o_m, I^o_m, and N^o_m are the original EHR, chest radiograph, and clinical note data for the m-th patient, respectively. Given the previous visits $[x_{m,1}, x_{m,2}, ..., x_{m,(t-1)}]$ of a discharged patient, the objective for hospital readmission prediction task is to predict whether the patient will be admitted again to the hospital within certain time span (e.g., 30 days in our case).

2.2 Feature Extraction for Single Modality

Graph Construction for Hospital Admissions. For the MIMIC-IV dataset as our original EHR input E^o, we choose to include demographics (age, gender, ethnicity), comorbidities (i.e., ICD-10 codes), lab tests, and medications. We follow the EHR preprocessing procedures [26,27] to incorporate clinical domain knowledge (ϕ_E) consisting of both the hierarchical structure of medical codes and the clinical expertise. Meanwhile, we utilize a pre-trained DenseNet121 model (ϕ_I) [9,10,12] to perform image preprocessing on chest radiographs I^o from MIMIC-CXR-JPG dataset. These can be represented as:

$$V_E = \phi_E(E^o), \quad V_I = \phi_I(I^o),$$

where the resulting $V_E \in \mathbb{R}^{a \times l_{ehr} \times d}$ and $V_I \in \mathbb{R}^{a \times l_{img} \times d}$ are the node features for EHR and imaging modalities. a is the total number of admissions, l is the sequence length, and d is the hidden dimension.

The edges of a graph depicting hospital admissions represent the degree of similarity between the features of medical notes for each modality. Patients with similar demographics and medical records may exhibit similarities in disease prognosis, diagnosis, and readmission probability. Therefore, the adjacency matrix $\mathcal{A} \in \mathbb{R}^{a \times a}$ can be represented as:

$$\mathcal{A}_{ij} = \begin{cases} exp\{-\frac{dist(v_i, v_j)^2}{\sigma^2}\}, & \text{if } \mathcal{A}_{ij} \geq \delta, \\ 0, & \text{otherwise.} \end{cases}$$

where $v_i, v_j \in V_E$ or V_I; δ is designed to filter out the weak connections; $dist(v_i, v_j)$ is the distance/similarity between v_i and v_j. A graph representation for hospital admissions can then be denoted as $\mathcal{G}_E = \{V_E, \mathcal{A}\}$ for EHR and $\mathcal{G}_I = \{V_I, \mathcal{A}\}$ for chest radiograph.

Finally, to enable message passing for the graph representation of each modality, we adopt GraphSAGE [8]:

$$\mathcal{G}_E^{\mathcal{S}} = \sigma(GraphSAGE(\mathcal{G}_E)), \quad \mathcal{G}_I^{\mathcal{S}} = \sigma(GraphSAGE(\mathcal{G}_I)),$$

where $\mathcal{S}$ stands for "spatial"; σ represents the activation function.

Temporal Representation Learning. To capture the temporal dependency between each node feature, we propose to employ a temporal transformer ($\mathbf{T}_{temp}$) model. Each temporal transformer layer can be represented as

$$e_{l+1}^{\mathcal{ST}} = \mathbf{T}_{temp}(e_l^{\mathcal{ST}}; \theta_E), \quad i_{l+1}^{\mathcal{ST}} = \mathbf{T}_{temp}(i_l^{\mathcal{ST}}; \theta_I),$$

where $\mathcal{ST}$ stands for "spatiotemporal"; θ_E and θ_I are model parameters that are different for each modality. Note that $e_0^{\mathcal{ST}} = V_E$ and $i_0^{\mathcal{ST}} = V_I$. We extract the final output representations of the CLS token [5], $E^{\mathcal{ST}} = e_{L,cls}^{\mathcal{ST}}$ and $I^{\mathcal{ST}} = i_{L,cls}^{\mathcal{ST}}$, as the outputs of the overall ST-$Transformers$.

Feature Embedding for Clinical Notes. Clinical notes offer a comprehensive overview of the patient in comparison to structured features [11]. They encompass a wide range of information, including symptoms, diagnostic rationales, radiology findings, daily routines, and patient background [11]. We include unstructured clinical information to our pipeline by utilizing MIMIC-IV-Note dataset, N^o. BioClinical BERT [3] is a variant of BERT [5] model that has been pre-trained on clinical text to learn the domain-specific knowledge. We would like to use it for extracting meaningful features from the clinical notes in MIMIC-IV-Note to boost our model performance. However, according to [5,11], the maximum sequence length supported by the model is set to 512. To efficiently handle the extensive note files, it is necessary to divide them into chunks, process each chunk individually using BioClinical BERT (ϕ_N), and subsequently extract the CLS token from each processed chunk as a representation [5]:

$$N^{\mathcal{B}} = W_d[\phi_N^{CLS}(N_1^o), \phi_N^{CLS}(N_2^o), ..., \phi_N^{CLS}(N_c^o)],$$

where c is the total number of chunks. To account for potential variations in the number of chunks, we ensure that the list of chunk representations is padded to accommodate the maximum number of chunks, which is $C = 25$. $\mathcal{B}$ stands for "BERT", $N^{\mathcal{B}} \in \mathbb{R}^{a \times C \times d}$. W_d is a projection matrix that converts the hidden dimension to d, aligning it with the dimensions of the other two modalities to facilitate subsequent fusion.

2.3   Multimodal Fusion

The final step of our pipeline involves combining the spatiotemporal features $E^{\mathcal{ST}}$ and $I^{\mathcal{ST}}$ for EHR and chest radiograph with the clinical note representations $N^{\mathcal{B}}$. We propose to employ a fusion transformer model ($\mathbf{T}_{fusion}$) for the purpose of aggregating information across all three modalities. Let

$$\mathbf{Z} = E^{\mathcal{ST}} \oplus I^{\mathcal{ST}} \oplus N^{\mathcal{B}},$$

where $\oplus$ is the sign for concatenation and $\mathbf{Z} \in \mathbb{R}^{a \times (l_{ehr} + l_{img} + C) \times d}$. Denote a multimodal transformer layer, $\mathbf{Z}_{l+1} = \mathbf{T}_{fusion}(\mathbf{Z}_l)$ as

$$\mathbf{y}_l = \text{MSA}(\text{LN}(\mathbf{Z}_l)) + \mathbf{Z}_l, \quad \mathbf{Z}_{l+1} = \text{MLP}(\text{LN}(\mathbf{y}_l)) + \mathbf{y}_l,$$

where LN is Layer Normalization, MLP is Multilayer Perceptron, and MSA is Multi-Headed Self-Attention. Let $E^{\mathcal{ST}}_{l,norm}$, $I^{\mathcal{ST}}_{l,norm}$, and $N^{\mathcal{B}}_{l,norm}$ denote the representations of EHR, chest radiographs, and clinical notes at layer l after LN operation, respectively. Then $\text{MSA}(\mathbf{Z}_{l,norm}))$ can be represented as

$$\text{MSA}(\mathbf{Z}_{l,norm})) = \text{Attention}(\mathbf{W}^Q \mathbf{Z}_{l,norm}, \mathbf{W}^K \mathbf{Z}_{l,norm}, \mathbf{W}^V \mathbf{Z}_{l,norm}),$$

$$= (\bigoplus_{j=1}^{J} \mathbf{H}_j) W_o,$$

where

$$\mathbf{H}_j = softmax(\frac{(\mathbf{Z}_{l,norm} W_j^Q)(\mathbf{Z}_{l,norm} W_j^K)^{\intercal}}{\sqrt{d_K}} \mathbf{Z}_{l,norm} W_j^V),$$

$$\mathbf{Z}_{l,norm} = E^{\mathcal{ST}}_{l,norm} \oplus I^{\mathcal{ST}}_{l,norm} \oplus N^{\mathcal{ST}}_{l,norm},$$

$\mathbf{W}^Q$, $\mathbf{W}^K$, $\mathbf{W}^V$, and W_o are projection matrices. The MSA mechanism enables the fusion transformer model to automatically identify and assign greater weight to the most influential modality, thereby enhancing the final prediction.

Finally, we obtain an output representation that is of the same dimension as $\mathbf{Z}$. We perform $Max()$ operation to the second dimension and pass the output to an MLP to generate the final hospital readmission predictions. The objective function is set to be the binary cross entropy $\mathcal{L}_{bce}$.

3   Experiments

Datasets and Evaluation Metrics. We assess the efficacy of the proposed MuST framework on the MIMIC dataset, which is a combination of three datasets: Medical Information Mart for Intensive Care IV (MIMIC-IV) v1.0 [1,7] dataset for EHR, MIMIC-CXR-JPG v2.0.0 [7,13] dataset for chest radiographs, and MIMIC-IV-Note [7,15] dataset for clinical notes. The samples in the three datasets have a unique ID to link together. The following provides a more detailed description of the datasets.

- **MIMIC-IV dataset.** MIMIC-IV is a collaborative effort between Beth Israel Deaconess Medical Center (BIDMC) and Massachusetts Institute of Technology (MIT). The study included 431,231 hospital admissions from 180,733 distinct patients.

Table 1. Comparisons with past research. Following [26], confidence intervals (CI) were calculated using the Delong method [4]. The best results are highlighted in bold. The subscript "coatt" stands for the case where an extra co-attention mechanism is added prior to fusion. Subscripts "mean", "last", and "max" stand for different operations to pool the temporal features. *: our approach.

Model	Modality	MIMIC-IV	
		AUC (%) [95% CI]	ACC (%)
STGNN	Image	71.86 [69.37 74.34]	74.46
STGNN	EHR	78.32 [75.89 80.75]	85.32
MM-STGNN$_{coatt}$	EHR+Image	76.74 [74.19 79.28]	85.29
MM-STGNN$_{mean}$	EHR+Image	79.15 [76.82 81.48]	85.63
MM-STGNN$_{last}$	EHR+Image	79.31 [76.91 81.71]	85.87
MM-STGNN$_{max}$	EHR+Image	79.46 [77.11 81.81]	85.31
ST-Transformer*	Image	72.07 [69.59 74.54]	74.35
ST-Transformer*	EHR	78.42 [75.97 80.87]	85.01
CN-Transformer*	Text	83.06 [80.67 85.45]	91.75
MuST*	EHR+Image+Text	**85.81 [83.66 87.97]**	**92.37**

- **MIMIC-CXR-JPG dataset.** MIMIC-CXR dataset comprises 227,835 imaging studies conducted on 64,588 patients who sought treatment at the BIDMC Emergency Department from 2011 to 2016. The dataset contains 377,110 images.
- **MIMIC-IV-Note dataset.** MIMIC-IV-Note dataset consists of 331,794 deidentified discharge summaries from 145,915 patients who were admitted to the hospital and emergency department at BIDMC.

In our study, we first follow the criteria adopted in [26] for subsetting the MIMIC-IV and MIMIC-CXR-JPG datasets. Since the clinical notes are also incorporated into the proposed pipeline, we obtain the intersection of admissions from the previous subset and the MIMIC-IV-Note dataset. The resulting dataset consists of 13,763 hospital admissions, with a distribution of 8,772 for training, 2,777 for testing, and 2,214 for validation. It includes a total of 82,465 chest radiographs and 82,465 clinical notes from 11,041 different patients. Among these patients, 2,379 admissions involved readmission within 30 days of discharge.

Experimental Setup. Experiments were conducted using the Adam optimizer [16] in PyTorch [21] on a workstation with eight NVIDIA GeForce RTX 3090 (24 GB) GPUs. The final hyperparameters for our proposed MuST model were as follows: (a) learning rate was 0.001; (b) dropout was 0.1; (c) number of epochs was 300; (d) maximum sequence length for both EHR and chest radiographs was 9; (e) number of layers for two temporal transformers and a fusion transformer was 1. The accuracy (ACC) and area under the curve (AUC) are used as the evaluation metrics.

Table 2. Ablation analysis. Best results are highlighted in bold.

Model	Modality	MIMIC-IV	
		AUC (%) [95% CI]	ACC (%)
ST-Transformer + MLP	EHR+Image	78.88 [76.46 81.29]	86.48
ST-Transformer + MLP	EHR+Image+Text	83.83 [81.50 86.17]	92.22
MuST (w/o clinical notes)	EHR+Image	79.87 [77.52 82.23]	85.87
MuST (w/o temporal layers)	EHR+Image+Text	84.23 [81.90 86.56]	91.93
MuST	EHR+Image+Text	**85.81 [83.66 87.97]**	**92.37**

Comparison with Previous Methods. We compare our proposed MuST framework with the previous methods STGNN and MM-STGNN [26] for 30-day all-cause hospital readmission prediction task performed on the MIMIC-IV dataset in Table 1. Our model demonstrates satisfactory performance in both AUC and ACC for predicting hospital readmission. With a single CN-Transformer (ClinicalNote-Transformer, which is constructed by passing the clinical note features extracted by BioClinical BERT to a transformer), we outperform MM-STGNN by almost 4% on AUC and 6% on ACC. The integration of EHR, medical imaging, and textual data results in an overall performance of 85.81% AUC and 92.37% ACC. In conclusion, our model greatly benefits from its multimodal nature and outperforms the previous state-of-the-art.

Ablation Analysis. We further conduct an ablation study and demonstrate the results in Table 2. We test the effect of: (1) temporal layers (4th&5th rows); (2) fusion layers (2nd&5th rows); (3) textual data (1st&2nd and 3rd&5th rows). Refer to Fig. 1 for the definition of the ST-Transformer. The ablation analysis results show that all of the components in MuST contribute to the performance of the model to a certain extent. Obviously, losing the text data significantly decreases the model's performance. Furthermore, for the MuST model specifically, fusion transformer layers have a greater impact on the final predictions than temporal transformer layers.

4   Conclusion

This paper introduces MuST, a framework that efficiently utilizes the multimodal and spatiotemporal properties of clinical data for hospital readmission prediction. We extract the representations from different data modalities with tailored network architectures and then adopt a generic fusion transformer model to aggregate information across three different modalities and pass the output to a multi-layer perceptron to obtain predictions of future readmission for each admission record. Extensive experiments on the MIMIC-IV dataset show that our proposed framework is both effective and efficient, with promising results. For future studies, we may evaluate our model on more internal and external datasets to validate the generalizability of the pipeline and also investigate other fusion approaches to improve the efficiency of our framework.

Acknowledgments. The work described in this paper was partially supported by grants from the National Natural Science Foundation of China (No. 62201483), the Research Grants Council of the Hong Kong Special Administrative Region, China (T45-401/22-N) and HKU seed fund for basic research (202111159073).

References

1. MIMIC-IV, a freely accessible electronic health record dataset. Scientific Data **10**(1), 1 (2023). https://doi.org/10.1038/s41597-022-01899-x
2. Allam, A., Nagy, M., Thoma, G., Krauthammer, M.: Neural networks versus Logistic regression for 30 days all-cause readmission prediction. Sci. Rep. **9**, 9277 (2019). https://doi.org/10.1038/s41598-019-45685-z
3. Alsentzer, E., et al.: Publicly available clinical bert embeddings. arXiv preprint arXiv:1904.03323 (2019)
4. DeLong, E.R., DeLong, D.M., Clarke-Pearson, D.L.: Comparing the areas under two or more correlated receiver operating characteristic curves: a nonparametric approach. Biometrics, pp. 837–845 (1988)
5. Devlin, J., Chang, M.W., Lee, K., Toutanova, K.: Bert: Pre-training of deep bidirectional transformers for language understanding. arXiv preprint arXiv:1810.04805 (2018)
6. Gabeur, V., Sun, C., Alahari, K., Schmid, C.: Multi-modal transformer for video retrieval. In: Vedaldi, A., Bischof, H., Brox, T., Frahm, J.-M. (eds.) ECCV 2020. LNCS, vol. 12349, pp. 214–229. Springer, Cham (2020). https://doi.org/10.1007/978-3-030-58548-8_13
7. Goldberger, A., et al.: PhysioBank, PhysioToolkit, and PhysioNet: components of a new research resource for complex physiologic signals. Circulation **101**, E215-20 (2000). https://doi.org/10.1161/01.CIR.101.23.e215
8. Hamilton, W., Ying, Z., Leskovec, J.: Inductive representation learning on large graphs. Advances in neural information processing systems 30 (2017)
9. He, K., Fan, H., Wu, Y., Xie, S., Girshick, R.: Momentum contrast for unsupervised visual representation learning. In: Proceedings of the IEEE/CVF Conference on Computer Vision and Pattern Recognition, pp. 9729–9738 (2020)
10. Huang, G., Liu, Z., Van Der Maaten, L., Weinberger, K.Q.: Densely connected convolutional networks. In: Proceedings of the IEEE Conference on Computer Vision and Pattern Recognition, pp. 4700–4708 (2017)
11. Huang, K., Altosaar, J., Ranganath, R.: Clinicalbert: Modeling clinical notes and predicting hospital readmission. arXiv preprint arXiv:1904.05342 (2019)
12. Irvin, J., et al.: Chexpert: a large chest radiograph dataset with uncertainty labels and expert comparison. In: Proceedings of the AAAI Conference on Artificial Intelligence, vol. 33, pp. 590–597 (2019)
13. Johnson, A.E., et al.: Mimic-cxr-jpg, a large publicly available database of labeled chest radiographs. arXiv preprint arXiv:1901.07042 (2019)
14. Johnson, A.E., et al.: Mimic-iii, a freely accessible critical care database. Sci. Data **3**(1), 1–9 (2016)
15. Johnson, A., P.T.H.S.C.L.A.M.R.: Mimic-iv-note: Deidentified free-text clinical notes (version 2.2). PhysioNet (2023). https://doi.org/10.13026/1n74-ne17
16. Kingma, D.P., Ba, J.: Adam: a method for stochastic optimization. arXiv preprint arXiv:1412.6980 (2014)

17. Li, L.H., Yatskar, M., Yin, D., Hsieh, C.J., Chang, K.W.: Visualbert: A simple and performant baseline for vision and language. arXiv preprint arXiv:1908.03557 (2019)

18. Li, Y., et al.: Behrt: transformer for electronic health records. Sci. Rep. **10**(1), 7155 (2020)

19. Nagrani, A., Yang, S., Arnab, A., Jansen, A., Schmid, C., Sun, C.: Attention bottlenecks for multimodal fusion. Adv. Neural. Inf. Process. Syst. **34**, 14200–14213 (2021)

20. Parmar, N., Vaswani, A., Uszkoreit, J., Kaiser, L., Shazeer, N., Ku, A., Tran, D.: Image transformer. In: International Conference on Machine Learning, pp. 4055–4064. PMLR (2018)

21. Paszke, A., et al.: Pytorch: an imperative style, high-performance deep learning library. Advances in neural information processing systems 32 (2019)

22. Prakash, A., Chitta, K., Geiger, A.: Multi-modal fusion transformer for end-to-end autonomous driving. In: Proceedings of the IEEE/CVF Conference on Computer Vision and Pattern Recognition, pp. 7077–7087 (2021)

23. Ramesh, A., et al.: Zero-shot text-to-image generation. In: International Conference on Machine Learning, pp. 8821–8831. PMLR (2021)

24. Rao, S., et al.: Targeted-behrt: deep learning for observational causal inference on longitudinal electronic health records. IEEE Trans. Neural Networks Learn. Syst. (2022)

25. Reddy, B., Delen, D.: Predicting hospital readmission for lupus patients: an RNN-LSTM-based deep-learning methodology. Comput. Biol. Med. **101** (2018). https://doi.org/10.1016/j.compbiomed.2018.08.029

26. Tang, S., et al.: Multimodal spatiotemporal graph neural networks for improved prediction of 30-day all-cause hospital readmission. arXiv preprint arXiv:2204.06766 (2022)

27. Tariq, A., et al.: Patient-specific COVID-19 resource utilization prediction using fusion AI model. npj Digital Med. **4** (2021). https://doi.org/10.1038/s41746-021-00461-0

28. Vaswani, A., et al.: Attention is all you need. Advances in neural information processing systems 30 (2017)

29. Wang, H., Cui, Z., Chen, Y., Avidan, M., Abdallah, A.B., Kronzer, A.: Predicting hospital readmission via cost-sensitive deep learning. IEEE/ACM Trans. Comput. Biol. Bioinf. **15**(6), 1968–1978 (2018). https://doi.org/10.1109/TCBB.2018.2827029

30. Wang, S., Zhu, X.: Predictive modeling of hospital readmission: challenges and solutions. IEEE/ACM Trans. Comput. Biol. Bioinf. **19**(5), 2975–2995 (2021)

31. Zhang, D., Yin, C., Zeng, J., Yuan, X., Zhang, P.: Combining structured and unstructured data for predictive models: a deep learning approach. BMC Medical Informatics and Decision Making 20 (2020). https://doi.org/10.1186/s12911-020-01297-6

Groupwise Image Registration with Atlas of Multiple Resolutions Refined at Test Phase

Ziyi He$^{(\boxtimes)}$, Tony C. W. Mok, and Albert C. S. Chung

Department of Computer Science and Engineering,
The Hong Kong University of Science and Technology, Clear Water Bay, Hong Kong
`zheaj@connect.ust.hk`

Abstract. Groupwise image registration (GIR) is a fundamental task that facilitates the simultaneous deformation of a group of subjects towards a specified or implicit center. Existing works mainly focus on either optimization-based methods that provide superb results but consume substantial time, or learning-based methods that are efficient but lack the flexibility to generalize across different domains and scales. To leverage the advantages of both methodologies, we present a robust method, Test-time Atlas adaptation for Groupwise registration (TAG), which generates a high-quality, group-specific atlas for groups of varying resolutions. Our method allows training at the test phase on target groups based on a learning-based GIR framework that bridges the gap between diverse groups. Besides the refinement of atlases at the original resolution, we propose additional modules to extend the scheme to groups of higher or lower resolutions at little cost. The method is evaluated on 3D brain MRI datasets to demonstrate its effectiveness. Evaluations of the registration accuracy and unbiasedness of atlases illustrate that TAG outperforms state-of-the-art benchmarks and maintains flexibility and robustness under a variety of scenarios.

Keywords: Atlas Generation · Test-time Adapation · Multiscale Imaging

1 Introduction

Given a group of medical images, groupwise image registration aims to align them into a common center simultaneously through rigid or non-rigid deformation, which improves the performance of subsequent image analysis tasks like anatomical segmentation and detection [4,26]. In most scenarios, the anticipated atlas is absent from groupwise registration, mandating algorithms for the construction of corresponding unbiased implicit center [1]. Conventional groupwise image registration approaches [14,15,27] construct the atlas by iterative updating registered group subjects using different weighting strategies. The performance of groupwise registration methods is often evaluated by analyzing the registration results and the reliability of the deformation fields [8].

J. Woo et al. (Eds.): MICCAI 2023 Workshops, LNCS 14394, pp. 286–298, 2023.
https://doi.org/10.1007/978-3-031-47425-5_26

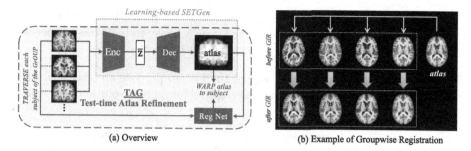

(a) Overview   (b) Example of Groupwise Registration

Fig. 1. (a) The overview of the proposed TAG with test-time atlas refinement on the basis of a learning-based generative model SETGen. (b) An example of groupwise image registration of 4 subjects in the axial view: Row 1 visualizes initial group subjects; Row 2 visualizes the corresponding views of deformed subjects after being registered to the atlas shown at the rightmost of Row 1. The left and right ventricles are delineated in red and yellow. The subjects are significantly aligned after GIR. (Color figure online)

Recent learning-based registration methods use deep neural networks to predict dense displacement fields directly or develop multi-scale architectures to deal with large variations in a coarse-to-fine manner [2,7,19–21]. Fueled by the thriving application of deep learning on image registration and generation, research work tends to utilize deep regression network models to replace the costly numerical optimization [24]. Many groupwise registration methods [5,6,8,25] are proposed to use deep neural architectures to construct the atlas as well as perform pairwise registration. In addition to atlas-based groupwise registration methods, research on performing GIR without an explicit atlas is also active. Some studies have developed graphs [1,10,28] including the tree to hierarchically warp group subjects to the center. Others [11,13] utilize the convolutional neural network to quickly deform subjects to the implicit atlas by evaluating dissimilarity among subjects.

However, both conventional methods and neural network-based atlas construction methods can be time-consuming to optimize. At the same time, learning-based models for medical image analysis usually suffer from limited training datasets, low signal-to-noise ratios in medical images [29], and significant variation in imaging protocol that brings large domain shifts. These challenges negatively impact their ability to generalize across different target groups. To address these issues, we propose a novel learning paradigm for GIR with test-time atlas refinement to fill the vacancy between learning-based and optimization-based methods (Fig. 1). Our contribution can be summarized as follows:

- We present a test-time atlas adaptation scheme TAG built on top of a deep learning-based GIR framework to fine-tune high-quality and unbiased atlases steadily;
- The proposed method can generalize the pre-trained model to groups of different resolutions without onerous re-training. This aspect has been rarely discussed and addressed in previous studies;

– We evaluate existing baseline methods and our method on three scales. Results indicate the proposed method can achieve state-of-the-art performance in registration results and atlas unbiasedness efficiently.

To the best of our knowledge, we are the first to propose an test-time atlas refining method based on a learning-based model for multi-resolution GIR tasks.

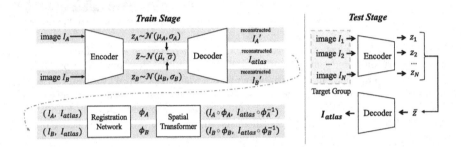

Fig. 2. Overview of SETGen, based on which the proposed method TAG performs test-time atlas refining. The framework utilizes the arithmetic properties of latent vectors of VAEs to decode an atlas from the average latent vector. A siamese training scheme is introduced to encourage the atlas to be close to the common center.

2   Method

In the problem of GIR, given a group of N subjects $\{I_1, I_2, ..., I_N\}$ of the same modality, the goal is to train a robust model with parameters θ to predict the deformation field $\phi_k \in \{\phi_1, ..., \phi_N\}$ for each subject which warps subject images to the unbiased common center. In this work, an explicit atlas T is generated from which all subjects will be registered. Our method **TAG** is developed based on SETGen [12], an atlas generation and groupwise registration framework. We adopt SETGen trained on a training set to iterate the target group and refine the atlas during the test phase. We further add a Higher Resolution Adaptation module before iterating on the target group to extend the scheme to generalize to multiple resolutions.

2.1   Architecture of SETGen

SETGen [12] is a scalable atlas generation and registration framework (shown in Fig. 2) developed from variational autoencoders VAE [16,23]. It utilizes VAE's ability to map inputs into latent space and the arithmetic properties of the latent vector, which is widely discussed and actively explored [3]. The framework's encoder and decoder are responsible for compressing and decompressing information. In the testing stage, the encoder takes group subjects $I_1, ..., I_N$ separately or in parallel to acquire the corresponding sampled latent vectors $z_1, z_2, ..., z_N \sim \mathcal{N}(\mu_i, \sigma_i)$. The average of these latent vectors $\bar{z}$ is computed and fed into the decoder to generate the atlas T of the target group. With this strategy, the framework can be applied to groups of arbitrary size. To improve the quality of the generated atlas that has even registration distances to each subject, SETGen incorporates a siamese scheme that comprises share-weighted encoders and decoders for two parallel inputs and a diffeomorphic registration network in the training phase.

Let the inputs from two sides be I_A and I_B. The atlas I_{atlas} of the two can be decoded from their average latent vector $\bar{z}$. The diffeomorphic registration network takes the I_A, I_B as moving images, and I_{atlas} as the fixed image to predict $\phi_{A \to atlas}$ and $\phi_{B \to atlas}$. Additional loss terms are introduced to encourage the flow field $\phi_{A \to atlas}$ to be opposite to the flow field $\phi_{B \to atlas}$. Besides similarity measurement between the warped atlas and each input, similarity between warped I_A and I_B are added as loss terms to improve the quality of the center image. Mathematically, the framework of siamese-VAE is optimized using the following loss function:

$$\mathcal{L}_{(}I_A, I_B) = \lambda_1 \mathcal{L}_{sim}(I_A, I'_A) + \lambda_1 \mathcal{L}_{sim}(I_B, I'_B)$$
$$+\lambda_2 \mathcal{L}_{KL}(z) + \lambda_3 ||u_A + u_B||^2 + \sum_{i \in \{A,B\}} \mathcal{L}_{sim}(I_{atlas} \circ \phi_i, I_i), \qquad (1)$$

where I'_i refers to the reconstructed image of I_i, u_i indicates spatial displacement for $\phi_{i \to altas} = Id + u_i$. For following deformation fields and spatial displacements, u_i without a direction specified refers to registering the subject to the atlas by default. $\mathcal{L}_{sim}$ refers to mean squared error.

2.2   Test-Time Atlas Generation

Although SETGen is a scalable GIR method, it still has two limitations: (1) it requires large datasets at the training phase, which is rare and costly in the medical imaging area, and target sets are relatively small in many cases; (2) medical images have large inter- and intra-subject variability depending on the setting of imaging machines, which makes the learned model not robust and reliable. We develop a test-time atlas refining method to close the gap between the train and test sets. The overview of the scheme is presented in Fig. 3.

TAG for Sampled Group Subjects. First, we focus on refining the atlas for groups of the original or lower resolution presented in (a) of Fig. 3. Given the target group $G = \{I_1, ..., I_N\}$, we compute the average latent vector $\bar{z}$ from the encoder. Then the decoder will be further trained by the target group. The core is refining the generated atlas to improve the registration accuracy as well as guarantee the unbiasedness of the atlas. However, gathering all of the group subjects like [13] takes up too much GPU space, maintaining a running average $\bar{u}$ and optimizing at each iteration is not stable or realistic for short-term optimization like the adaptation scheme of our method.

Therefore, we present a **one-subject-optimization** strategy. We define one **step** as the forward propagation feeding one group subject to the networks and define one **iteration** as traversing every subject of the group once. The strategy records the gradient of each step and then performs backpropagation and updates the atlas in iterations.

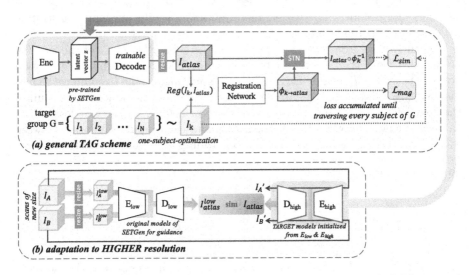

Fig. 3. Overview of the proposed test-time atlas refining method TAG. (a) General scheme for the target group of the same or lower resolution of the training dataset. The atlas is updated by minimizing the magnitude of flow fields from subjects to the atlas and maximizing the similarity between the subjects and the warped atlas. In order not to introduce bias, we update the model after all subjects go through forward propagation. (b) Additional module for groups of higher resolution. We initialize a new pair of encoder-decoder from the pre-trained one for higher resolution subjects and utilize the atlas generated by the original model as a guide for the new model. The new encoder-decoder will be applied in the subsequent general atlas refinement process.

At each step, the atlas generated from the decoder $Dec\ I_{atlas} = Dec(z)$ with one subject I_k out of the target group will be fed to the diffeomorphic registration network to predict the flow field from the subject to the atlas. The method forces the atlas to the group center by utilizing a loss term constraining the magnitude of the displacement field, defined as: $\mathcal{L}_{mag} = ||u_{k \rightarrow Dec(z)}||_2$. In addition, to improve the quality of the atlas, another loss term measuring the dissimilarity between the warped atlas and the subject is added: $\mathcal{L}_{sim} = NCC(I_k, Dec(z) \circ \phi_k^{-1})$, where NCC is local Normalized Cross Correlation. Overall, the goal of test-time atlas optimization is to update the parameters θ of the SETGen framework following:

$$\theta^* = \underset{\theta}{\arg\min}\ \mathbb{E}_{\{I_1,...,I_N\}}[\lambda_1 \mathcal{L}_{mag} + \lambda_2 \mathcal{L}_{sim}].\qquad(2)$$

At each step, the loss function is computed with gradients being accumulated; model parameters will be updated once one iteration is finished, meaning traversing all subjects. This one-subject-optimization mechanism is more GPU efficient than loading all subjects to the model once, as well as leads the atlas to be unbiased.

For target groups of lower resolution, a resizing layer is added after the decoder to resize the generated atlas to the same resolution as the target. At the same time, we also update the registration network on the target and use bi-direction similarity constraints following [7]. The loss function is as follows:

$$\mathcal{L}_{reg} = \gamma_1 \mathcal{L}_{sim}(I_k \circ \phi_k, Dec(z)) + \gamma_1 \mathcal{L}_{sim}(I_k, Dec(z) \circ \phi_k^{-1}) + \gamma_2 ||\nabla u_k||, \quad (3)$$

where we use NCC for $\mathcal{L}_{sim}$. γ_2 aims to smooth the flow field. γ_1 is set to 0.5 and γ_2 is set to 1. λ_1 and λ_2 in Eq. (2) are set to 0.5 and 2.

Generalization to Atlas of Higher Resolution. While collecting high-resolution medical images is difficult and costly due to limitations such as image acquisition time, low irradiation dose, or hardware limits [17], resulting in little presence of high-resolution medical datasets. On the other hand, training a high-resolution version of the model is much more expensive regarding training time and computational resources than training a relatively low-resolution version.

Algorithm 1: Higher resolution atlas refinement

Input: the encoder and decoder of SETGen trained on the relatively low-resolution set, denoted as $\{E_{low}, D_{low}\}$; registration network, denoted as $RegNet$; target group G of higher resolution with $I_i, ..., I_N$

Output: updated I_{atlas} of higher resolution
// stage 1 higher resolution adaptation
1 $\{E_{high}, D_{high}\} \leftarrow \{E_{low}, D_{low}\}$;
2 **for** I_A, I_B in $Dataloader(G)$ **do**
3   I_A^{low}, $I_B^{low} \leftarrow$ Resize(I_A), Resize(I_B) ;
4      $I_{atlas}^{low} \leftarrow D_{low}(Average(E_{low}(I_A^{low}), E_{low}(I_B^{low})))$;
5      $I_A', I_B' \leftarrow D_{high}(E_{high}(I_A)), D_{high}(E_{high}(I_B))$;
6      $I_{atlas} \leftarrow D_{high}(Average(E_{high}(I_A), E_{high}(I_B)))$;
7   Update(E_{high}, D_{high}) using Eq. (4);

    // stage 2 general atlas adaptation
8 **for** i in $num\_of\_iterations$ **do**
9   **for** I_k in G **do**
10         $\phi_k \leftarrow RegNet(I_k \rightarrow I_{atlas})$;
11   Update$(RegNet)$ using Eq. (3) ;
12   accumulate loss and Update(D_{high}) using Eq. (2) ;   .
13   Update(D_{high}) ;

To resolve the dilemma above, we propose to add a higher resolution adaptation module as shown in (b) of Fig. 3 before the general atlas refinement just introduced. The algorithm is given in Algorithm 1.

In **stage 1**, we first initialize the new encoder and decoder for higher resolution from the trained pair. We remove the registration network and keep the Siamese scheme for efficiency, and let the corresponding low-resolution atlas be the extra guidance in the training of high-resolution versions. Specifically, the pre-trained low-resolution model is frozen, and only the new high-resolution model will be updated. For each pair of input images, we impose a similarity loss on the atlas I_{atlas} and its corresponding low-resolution version I_{atlas}^{low}. Therefore, the model is optimized following:

$$\mathcal{L}(I_A, I_B) = \sum_{i \in \{A,B\}} (\mathcal{L}_{sim}(I_i, I_i') + \lambda_1 \mathcal{L}_{KL}(z_i)) + \lambda_2 \mathcal{L}_{sim}(I_{atlas}, I_{atlas}^{low}), \quad (4)$$

I_A, I_B refer to high-resolution subjects, I_i' refers to their corresponding reconstruction image. L_{KL} is used to constrain the distribution of latent vector z. λ_1 is set to 0.002 and λ_2 is set to 200.

In **stage 2**, we apply the newly trained E_{high} and D_{high} to conduct the general atlas refinement by updating the decoder and registration network following Eq. (3) and Eq. (2).

3   Experiments

3.1   Datasets

We have conducted experiments on three groupwise registration tasks with two brain MR datasets to illustrate the effectiveness of the proposed TTA method. OASIS [18] is a public cross-sectional T1-weighted brain MRI dataset consisting of 416 subjects aged from 18 to 96. The scans are preprocessed, including skull stripping, intensity normalization, and affine registration. The dataset is divided into 326, 10, and 80 scans for training, validation, and testing sets. ADNI [22] is a longitudinal study for the early detection and tracking of AD. We used 875 MRI scans from ADNI-3 and preprocess the dataset through standard pipelines, including subcortical structures segmentation using FreeSurfer [9]. The dataset is divided into 715, 80, and 80 scans for train/valid/test sets. For testing groups during the method evaluation, we construct 20 groups of 4 subjects, 10 groups of 8 subjects and 5 groups of 16 subjects out of the test set.

3.2   Baselines

We compared our method with three groupwise image registration baselines ABSORB [14], Deformable Template (abbreviated as Deform) [6], and Aladdin [8]. ABSORB is a conventional standard atlas construction method that clusters subjects by affinity propagation. Deform is a deep neural network model that constructs the atlas deformable given specified conditions forwardly. We used its unconditional implementation as a general GIR method, pretrained the model using the training dataset, and further trained it on each group. Aladdin is the latest atlas-building method with pairwise alignment. We also pretrained Aladdin first and then trained it on each group by initializing the atlas with two variants, denoted as Aladdin-1 and Aladdin-2, in the following comparisons.

3.3   Evaluation Metrics

We evaluate our method from two aspects. First, we applied the widely used Dice Score (DSC) to measure the degree of overlap between warped scans. The final **DSC** was computed by averaging DSC of each pair of subjects. Second, we used two metrics introduced in [6] to measure the unbiasedness, **Centrality** that computes the norm of the mean displacement field $\|\bar{u}\|$ and **AvgDisp** that computes the average displacement size.

3.4   Results of Adaptation with Original Resolution

We list the results of the proposed groupwise registration method with test-time adaptation on the atlas in Table 1. For both OASIS and ADNI, the proposed

Table 1. Quantitative results of refining on the source domain on OASIS and ADNI. **Initial** refers to subjects before GIR. To show the improvement brought by the proposed method, we also added the model SETGen that we performed TTA for comparison. Aladdin-1 refers to using the average scan of the group as the initial atlas, and Aladdin-2 refers to using the atlas generated by SETGen as the initial atlas. ↑: higher is better, ↓: lower is better. Results in **bold** indicate the best outperforms the second best with p-value < 0.05.

Methods	OASIS			ADNI		
	DSC ↑	Centrality ↓	AvgDisp ↓	DSC ↑	Centrality ↓	AvgDisp ↓
Initial	55.11 ± 5.48	–	–	65.46 ± 6.37	–	–
ABOSRB [14]	68.51 ± 1.95	527.6 ± 205	1140 ± 269	75.97 ± 4.45	587.5 ± 178	1160 ± 203
Deform [6]	69.33 ± 2.01	268.6 ± 37.7	880.6 ± 112	76.61 ± 4.85	290.4 ± 28.0	849.5 ± 116
Aladdin [8]-1	67.01 ± 4.29	702.6 ± 375	984.0 ± 325	71.68 ± 6.82	949.0 ± 259	1139 ± 244
Aladdin [8]-2	69.56 ± 1.75	246.1 ± 33.8	842.3 ± 123	76.57 ± 4.49	307.3 ± 61.3	809.8 ± 101
SETGen [12]	69.46 ± 1.76	258.0 ± 33.7	853.6 ± 122	76.56 ± 4.47	301.9 ± 45.0	811.7 ± 98.4
TAG (ours)	**70.15 ± 1.93**	**189.7 ± 24.9**	**755.3 ± 103**	**77.30 ± 4.45**	**220.1 ± 29.2**	**692.4 ± 94.3**

method outperforms baseline methods from all aspects of DSC, Centrality, and AvgDisp. In the test on the OASIS dataset, the proposed method outperforms the second-best method by 0.8%, 22.9% and 10.3% for each metric; the performance of the proposed method remains impressive when applied to the other dataset ADNI, our TAG defeats the second best by 0.9%, 24.2%, and 14.5% for each aspect respectively. The consistent superiority illustrates the robustness of the proposed method TAG. The qualitative comparison can be found in Fig. 4, indicating the high quality of the atlas generated by TAG.

Runtime Analysis. When performing GIR on four subjects, i.e., the group size is 4, ABSORB is the fastest with 64 s, Aladdin takes 136 s, and Deform takes around 960 s, while our TAG takes 168 s; when the group size is 16, ABSORB takes 1190 s, Aladdin takes 810 s, and Deform takes 1480 s, while TAG takes 750 s which comes to be the fastest. It illustrates the trend that TAG acts more effectively when the group size grows.

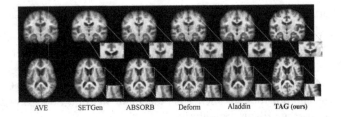

AVE   SETGen   ABSORB   Deform   Aladdin   TAG (ours)

Fig. 4. Qualitative comparison of higher resolution groups in the coronal and axial planes. It is obvious that TAG can generate a delicate and authentic atlas no less than baselines. The atlas generated by TAG is clearer around anatomical borders.

Table 2. Quantitative results of generalizing to high-resolution groups. **SETGen** refers to applying the model trained on low-resolution to high-resolution groups directly. **Aladdin** refers to using the scaled atlas generated by low-resolution SETGen.

Method	DSC ↑	Centrality ↓	AvgDisp ↓
Initial	55.16 ± 6.64	–	–
ABOSRB [14]	71.99 ± 2.52	1263 ± 368	2825 ± 511
Deform [6]	71.97 ± 2.59	575.6 ± 50.3	2086 ± 379
Aladdin [8]	72.05 ± 2.16	689.6 ± 54.5	2041 ± 415
SETGen [12]	71.90 ± 2.22	676.0 ± 31.6	2137 ± 370
TAG (ours)	**72.77 ± 2.20**	**529.0 ± 53.8**	**1781 ± 292**

3.5   Results on Multi-scales Atlas Building

Lower Resolution. As we apply TAG to adapt the trained GIR model SETGen to lower resolution groups of $64 \times 80 \times 64$, we achieve the quantitative result on the test set with 66.15, 96.4 and 309 for DSC, Centrality and AvgDisp respectively, which is significantly superior to the second best Aladdin with 65.3, 119 and 328 respectively.

Higher Resolution. We present the quantitative comparisons of TAG and baselines in Table 2. We have generalized SETGen models trained on MRI scans of $96 \times 112 \times 96$ to $144 \times 160 \times 144$ by Algorithm 1. The proposed method TAG achieves the best performance and outperforms the baselines on each aspect significantly, which illustrates TAG's ability to generalize to high-resolution GIR tasks from a relatively low-resolution version of pre-trained models.

Runtime Analysis. Our method for adaptation on higher resolution atlas generation takes around 22 min, Deform that refines on a trained model takes 25 min, while ABSORB requires 11 min. The training time of SETGen using the low-resolution dataset is around 30 h, while that of the high-resolution dataset is up to 130 h. Given that TTA-based SETGen decreases the remarkable 76% of the training time, it is highly cost-effective to utilize the proposed method to construct high-resolution atlases based on a trained model for low-resolution targets.

3.6   Ablation Study

Loss Terms for General Test-Time Atlas Refinement. In Table 3, we show
the results of the ablation study in the atlas refinement of the source dataset.
First, compared to fine-tuning parameters of SETGen using the target group,
the proposed TAG can achieve significantly higher DSC. Second, it can be found
that DSC remains high without $\mathcal{L}_{mag}$, while the Centrality and AvgDisp increase
significantly, which illustrates the atlas deviates from the implicit center. Last,
removing $\mathcal{L}_{sim}$ would lead the generated image out of the distribution of MRI
images and overfit to the registration network.

Table 3. Ablation study: source domain atlas refinement.

Methods	DSC ↑	Centrality ↓	AvgDisp ↓
fine-tune SETGen	69.87	191.3	677.2
TAG without $\mathcal{L}_{sim}$	63.62	227.7	504.8
TAG without $\mathcal{L}_{mag}$	70.57	292.8	769.9
TAG	**71.05**(+0.6%)	198.5 (−12.8%)	613.8

Two-Stage TAG for Target Groups of Higher Resolution. We propose
a two-stage adaptation to generalize the model trained with the low-resolution
dataset to target groups of high-resolution. We conduct the ablation study of
the necessity of each stage and show the result in Fig. 5. DSC is decreased from
72.5% to 71% if we remove stage 1 and conduct stage 2 alone; If only stage 1 is
applied without stage 2, DSC is 70% compared with 72.5%. Hence, each of the
two stages is pivotal, and the combination of them achieves the best result.

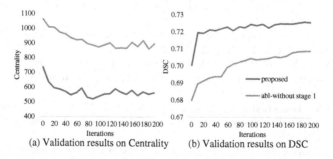

(a) Validation results on Centrality   (b) Validation results on DSC

Fig. 5. Ablation study: generalizing to high-resolution groups. The number of iterations
indicates that of TAG in stage 2. **abl-without stage 1** refers to optimizing the atlas
through the stage 2 general adaptation only.

4 Conclusion

This paper proposes a groupwise image registration method TAG with test-time atlas refinement for multiple resolutions. By training models at the test phase with the target group of subjects in a one-subject-optimization manner, we improve the quality of the atlas and performance of groupwise registration. The auxiliary higher-resolution adaptation module helps generalize the method to targets of higher resolutions. With only one entire training procedure on the dataset, our method can generalize the model to groups of different resolutions using much less computation.

TAG takes advantage of both learning-based and optimization-based methods to achieve a balance of efficiency and effectiveness. Comprehensive experiments on two 3D MRI datasets and three resolutions demonstrate the robustness, flexibility, and effectiveness of our method compared with baselines. We believe that the proposed method can become a paradigm for future research in groupwise image registration.

References

1. Ahmad, S., Fan, J., Dong, P., Cao, X., Yap, P.T., Shen, D.: Deep learning deformation initialization for rapid groupwise registration of inhomogeneous image populations. Front. Neuroinform. **13**, 34 (2019)
2. Balakrishnan, G., Zhao, A., Sabuncu, M.R., Guttag, J., Dalca, A.V.: Voxelmorph: a learning framework for deformable medical image registration. IEEE Trans. Med. Imaging **38**(8), 1788–1800 (2019)
3. Berthelot, D., Raffel, C., Roy, A., Goodfellow, I.: Understanding and improving interpolation in autoencoders via an adversarial regularizer. arXiv preprint arXiv:1807.07543 (2018)
4. Bhatia, K.K., et al.: Groupwise combined segmentation and registration for atlas construction. In: Ayache, N., Ourselin, S., Maeder, A. (eds.) MICCAI 2007. LNCS, vol. 4791, pp. 532–540. Springer, Heidelberg (2007). https://doi.org/10.1007/978-3-540-75757-3_65
5. Che, T., et al.: Deep group-wise registration for multi-spectral images from fundus images. IEEE Access **7**, 27650–27661 (2019)
6. Dalca, A., Rakic, M., Guttag, J., Sabuncu, M.: Learning conditional deformable templates with convolutional networks. In: Advances in Neural Information Processing Systems, vol. 32 (2019)
7. Dalca, A.V., Balakrishnan, G., Guttag, J., Sabuncu, M.R.: Unsupervised learning of probabilistic diffeomorphic registration for images and surfaces. Med. Image Anal. **57**, 226–236 (2019)
8. Ding, Z., Niethammer, M.: Aladdin: joint atlas building and diffeomorphic registration learning with pairwise alignment. In: Proceedings of the IEEE/CVF Conference on Computer Vision and Pattern Recognition, pp. 20784–20793 (2022)
9. Fischl, B.: Freesurfer. Neuroimage **62**(2), 774–781 (2012)
10. Hamm, J., Davatzikos, C., Verma, R.: Efficient large deformation registration via geodesics on a learned manifold of images. In: Yang, G.-Z., Hawkes, D., Rueckert, D., Noble, A., Taylor, C. (eds.) MICCAI 2009. LNCS, vol. 5761, pp. 680–687. Springer, Heidelberg (2009). https://doi.org/10.1007/978-3-642-04268-3_84

11. He, Z., Chung, A.C.S.: Learning-based template synthesis for groupwise image registration. In: Svoboda, D., Burgos, N., Wolterink, J.M., Zhao, C. (eds.) SASHIMI 2021. LNCS, vol. 12965, pp. 55–66. Springer, Cham (2021). https://doi.org/10.1007/978-3-030-87592-3_6

12. He, Z., Chung, A.C.S.: SETgen: scalable and efficient template generation framework for groupwise medical image registration. arXiv preprint arXiv:2211.05622 (2022)

13. He, Z., Chung, A.C.: Unsupervised end-to-end groupwise registration framework without generating templates. In: 2020 IEEE International Conference on Image Processing (ICIP), pp. 375–379. IEEE (2020)

14. Jia, H., Wu, G., Wang, Q., Shen, D.: ABSORB: atlas building by self-organized registration and bundling. Neuroimage 51(3), 1057–1070 (2010)

15. Joshi, S., Davis, B., Jomier, M., Gerig, G.: Unbiased diffeomorphic atlas construction for computational anatomy. Neuroimage 23, S151–S160 (2004)

16. Kingma, D.P., Welling, M.: Auto-encoding variational Bayes. arXiv preprint arXiv:1312.6114 (2013)

17. Li, Y., Sixou, B., Peyrin, F.: A review of the deep learning methods for medical images super resolution problems. IRBM 42(2), 120–133 (2021)

18. Marcus, D.S., Wang, T.H., Parker, J., Csernansky, J.G., Morris, J.C., Buckner, R.L.: Open access series of imaging studies (oasis): cross-sectional MRI data in young, middle aged, nondemented, and demented older adults. J. Cogn. Neurosci. 19(9), 1498–1507 (2007)

19. Mok, T.C.W., Chung, A.C.S.: Large deformation image registration with anatomy-aware Laplacian pyramid networks. In: Shusharina, N., Heinrich, M.P., Huang, R. (eds.) MICCAI 2020. LNCS, vol. 12587, pp. 61–67. Springer, Cham (2021). https://doi.org/10.1007/978-3-030-71827-5_7

20. Mok, T.C.W., Chung, A.C.S.: Conditional deformable image registration with convolutional neural network. In: de Bruijne, M., Cattin, P.C., Cotin, S., Padoy, N., Speidel, S., Zheng, Y., Essert, C. (eds.) MICCAI 2021. LNCS, vol. 12904, pp. 35–45. Springer, Cham (2021). https://doi.org/10.1007/978-3-030-87202-1_4

21. Mok, T.C., Chung, A.: Affine medical image registration with coarse-to-fine vision transformer. In: Proceedings of the IEEE/CVF Conference on Computer Vision and Pattern Recognition, pp. 20835–20844 (2022)

22. Mueller, S.G., et al.: Ways toward an early diagnosis in Alzheimer's disease: the Alzheimer's disease neuroimaging initiative (ADNI). Alzheimer's Dementia 1(1), 55–66 (2005)

23. Rezende, D.J., Mohamed, S., Wierstra, D.: Stochastic backpropagation and approximate inference in deep generative models. In: International Conference on Machine Learning, pp. 1278–1286. PMLR (2014)

24. Shen, Z., Han, X., Xu, Z., Niethammer, M.: Networks for joint affine and non-parametric image registration. In: Proceedings of the IEEE/CVF Conference on Computer Vision and Pattern Recognition, pp. 4224–4233 (2019)

25. Sinclair, M., et al.: Atlas-ISTN: joint segmentation, registration and atlas construction with image-and-spatial transformer networks. Med. Image Anal. 78, 102383 (2022)

26. Tang, Z., Wu, Y., Fan, Y.: Groupwise registration of MR brain images with tumors. Phys. Med. Biol. 62(17), 6853 (2017)

27. Wu, G., Jia, H., Wang, Q., Shen, D.: Sharpmean: groupwise registration guided by sharp mean image and tree-based registration. Neuroimage 56(4), 1968–1981 (2011)

28. Ying, S., Wu, G., Wang, Q., Shen, D.: Hierarchical unbiased graph shrinkage (hugs): a novel groupwise registration for large data set. Neuroimage **84**, 626–638 (2014)
29. Zhu, W., Huang, Y., Xu, D., Qian, Z., Fan, W., Xie, X.: Test-time training for deformable multi-scale image registration. In: 2021 IEEE International Conference on Robotics and Automation (ICRA), pp. 13618–13625. IEEE (2021)

Anatomy-Aware Lymph Node Detection in Chest CT Using Implicit Station Stratification

Ke Yan[1,2]([✉]), Dakai Jin[1], Dazhou Guo[1], Minfeng Xu[1,2], Na Shen[3], Xian-Sheng Hua[1,2], Xianghua Ye[4], and Le Lu[1]

[1] DAMO Academy, Alibaba Group, Hangzhou, China
yanke.yan@alibaba-inc.com
[2] Hupan Lab, Hangzhou 310023, China
[3] Zhongshan Hospital of Fudan University, Shanghai, China
[4] The First Affiliated Hospital Zhejiang University, Hangzhou, China

Abstract. Finding abnormal lymph nodes in radiological images is highly important for various medical tasks such as cancer metastasis staging and radiotherapy planning. Lymph nodes (LNs) are small glands scattered throughout the body. They are grouped or defined to various LN stations according to their anatomical locations. The CT imaging appearance and context of LNs in different stations vary significantly, posing challenges for automated detection, especially for pathological LNs. Motivated by this observation, we propose a novel end-to-end framework to improve LN detection performance by leveraging their station information. We design a multi-head detector and make each head focus on differentiating the LN and non-LN structures of certain stations. Pseudo station labels are generated by an LN station classifier as a form of multi-task learning during training, so we do not need another explicit LN station prediction model during inference. Our algorithm is evaluated on 82 patients with lung cancer and 91 patients with esophageal cancer. The proposed implicit station stratification method improves the detection sensitivity of thoracic lymph nodes from 65.1% to 71.4% and from 80.3% to 85.5% at 2 false positives per patient on the two datasets, respectively, which significantly outperforms various existing state-of-the-art baseline techniques such as nnUNet, nnDetection and LENS.

Keywords: Lymph node detection · Lymph node station · CT

1 Introduction

Lymph nodes play essential roles in the staging and treatment planning of general cancer patients [4,13]. As cancer evolves, tumor cells can spread to lymph nodes and cause them to metastasize and possibly enlarge. Finding all of the abnormal (metastatic) lymph nodes is a crucial task for radiologists and oncologists. Computed tomography (CT) is the primary modality for tumor imaging in the chest [18]. In CT, most lymph nodes can be identified as small, oval-shaped

© The Author(s), under exclusive license to Springer Nature Switzerland AG 2023
J. Woo et al. (Eds.): MICCAI 2023 Workshops, LNCS 14394, pp. 299–310, 2023.
https://doi.org/10.1007/978-3-031-47425-5_27

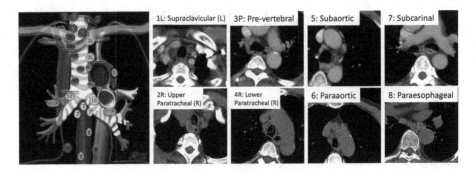

Fig. 1. Lymph node (LN) stations defined for lung cancer staging [5]. The anatomical map on the left is reproduced from [19]. LN examples in some stations are shown on the right in green boxes, either in contrast-enhanced (1st row) or non-contrast (2nd row) images. Note the significant diversity of appearance across stations.

structures with soft-tissue intensity, which are challenging to be differentiated from surrounding soft tissues such as vessels, esophagus, and muscles. Due to its importance and difficulty, automatic lymph node (LN) detection and segmentation has been attracting increasing attentions [2,6,10,14,17,23]. Convolutional neural network (CNN) is becoming the mainstream method in recent years. Oda et al. [14] trained a 3D U-Net using not only LN annotations but also neighboring organs to reduce oversegmentation of LNs. Bouget et al. [2] combined the outputs of 2D U-Net and Mask R-CNN to predict both LNs and neighboring organs. Yan et al. [21] showed that jointly learning multiple datasets improved LN detection accuracy. Zhu et al. [23] divided LNs into two subclasses of tumor-proximal and tumor-distal ones and used a U-Net with two decoder branches to learn the two groups separately. Iuga et al. [10] designed a neural network with multi-scale inputs to fuse information from multiple spatial resolutions.

Different from other types of lesions (e.g., lung nodules) that typically locate in one organ, LNs scatter throughout the body. The anatomical location of a metastatic lymph node is an important indicator to determine the stage of the cancer and even the subsequent treatment recommendations. Taking lung cancer as an example, the International Association for the Study of Lung Cancer (IASLC) defined 14 lymph node stations in the chest based on their relative position with adjacent organs [5], as shown in Fig. 1. We can observe that LNs in different stations are surrounded by varying organs, thus show very diverse contextual layouts. To detect an LN is essentially to distinguish it from surrounding confounding organs and structures, therefore, detecting LNs in different stations may actually be considered as different tasks. Most existing works treat LNs in all stations as one positive class and define other organs as one negative class. We would argue that this representation is suboptimal because the inter-class difference between LNs and non-LNs is sometimes very subtle (e.g., Fig. 1 2R and 8). If we mix the samples from all stations, the model may struggle to learn the coherent imaging feature of LNs and be distracted by their contextual appearance. In this work, we propose to first stratify LNs and non-LNs based on their stations, and then train an LN vs. non-LN classifier for each station group. Figure 3 illustrates our intuition. In addition, the distributions of shape and size of LNs vary in different stations [13,18]. Our stratification strategy could also handle this variation better by separately modeling each station.

In this paper, we instantiate this strategy and propose a station-stratified LN detector. It is based on the widely-used two-stage CNN detection architecture [16,21] with a novel detection branch and a station branch simultaneously. The detection branch contains multiple output heads, each focusing on classifying LN/non-LN in one station group. The station branch predicts a probability vector for each proposal indicating its station group, which in turn is used by the detection branch to compute a weighted loss in training and a final LN likelihood in inference. The group can either be stations or super-stations (by grouping similar stations). A related but different method is [23]. They proposed a segmentation method that groups LNs according to their distance with the tumor, thus the location of tumor needs to be known in prior. We stratify LNs according to the anatomy-related stations and no tumor location is needed. Our method is more widely applicable even for non-cancer patients as a form of screening abnormal LNs by stations implicitly. No extra cost on LN station segmentation is needed in inference. While LN groups in [23] are manually computed and the distance threshold needs to be tuned, ours are predicted by a station branch automatically. Our algorithm employs a 2.5D backbone for better efficiency and accuracy. To convert the predicted 2D boxes to 3D ones, we further design a novel lesion-centric box stacking and merging algorithm.

The proposed framework is extensively evaluated on two datasets of 82 patients with lung cancer and 91 patients with esophageal cancer. A total of 1,380 lymph nodes were annotated in the 14 IASLC stations. By employing the proposed station stratification strategy alone, our LN detection sensitivity is improved from 65.1% to 71.4% and from 80.3% to 85.5% at 2 false positives (FPs) per patient in the two datasets, respectively, outperforming various strong mainstream methods such as nnUNet [9], nnDetection [1], and LENS [21]. To the best of our knowledge, we are the first to demonstrate that the station information can be used to improve LN detection effectively (from recent literature reported). While most prior studies used contrast-enhanced (CE) CTs, we also run our method on 85 more challenging non-contrast (NC) CT scans. Joint learning of CE and NC CT imaging modalities achieves a sensitivity of 83.8% at 2 FPs per patient of NC CT scan, which is an encouraging result for scenarios such as lung nodule screening and radiotherapy planning [23].

2   Method

The framework of our proposed method is illustrated in Fig. 2. It is based on the widely-used two-stage detection framework Faster R-CNN [16]. The input of the network is multiple consecutive axial CT slices. We adopt the 2.5D design in MULAN [22] as backbone. It extracts 2D features for the CT slices and aggregates them to fuse 3D context information, which is important for distinguishing

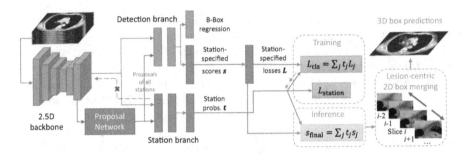

Fig. 2. Framework of our proposed station-stratified LN detector. The blocks in green and orange are our key technical novelties. Red cross mark means gradient stopping. (Color figure online)

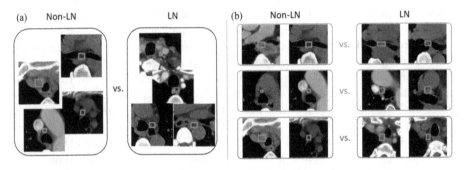

Fig. 3. (a) Existing LN detection algorithms mix samples in different stations and train one classifier. (b) Our method stratifies samples based on stations and learns station-specific classifiers. Samples in each group share similar contextual appearance, so the model can focus on mining the subtle discriminative features to separate LNs/non-LNs.

LNs from other tube-shaped organs such as vessels and esophagus. We empirically find the 2.5D network outperforms pure 3D ones in both convergence speed and accuracy. The fused feature map is fed to a proposal network such as the Fully Convolutional One-Stage detector (FCOS) [20]. It learns to generate 2D LN proposals in all LN stations. We observed that the vast majority of proposals concentrate in LN station areas, but some of them are confounding false positives (FPs) such as vessels, connective tissue, and esophageal tumor inside the station, see examples in the non-LN columns of Fig. 3. This indicates that the proposal network has successfully learned the image context of the LNs, but struggles to differentiate some subtle structures inside the stations.

To solve this problem, we force the network to disambiguate true positive (TPs) and FPs inside the same station to learn more discriminative features. Specifically, we design a novel multi-head detection branch and a station branch as the second stage of the detector. Suppose that there are c stations, the **station branch** predicts a probability vector $\mathbf{t}_i \in \mathbb{R}^c$ to classify the station of each proposal i. It is trained on manually annotated station labels using the cross-entropy loss. The loss is only computed on TP proposals since only TPs have station labels, but the branch can predict station probabilities for both TPs and FPs. Similar to Faster R-CNN [16], the **detection branch** contains a classification layer and a bounding-box regression layer. In our algorithm, we aim to train c LN vs. non-LN classifiers, each corresponding to one station (or station group). Therefore, the classification layer will output a station-specified score vector $\mathbf{s}_i \in \mathbb{R}^c$ for each proposal i. These scores have a common LN/non-LN label y_i, so we can compute a binary cross-entropy loss for each score, forming a station-specified loss vector $\mathbf{L}_i \in \mathbb{R}^c$. Finally, we use the station probabilities $\mathbf{t}_i$ to compute a weighted sum of them:

$$L_{\text{cls}} = \frac{1}{n} \sum_{i=1}^{n} \sum_{j=1}^{c} t_{ij} \left(y_i \log \sigma(s_{ij}) + (1 - y_i)(1 - \log \sigma(s_{ij})) \right), \qquad (1)$$

where n is the number of proposals in a mini-batch, σ is the sigmoid function. During inference, station label is no longer needed because the station branch has learned to predict it. We use the predicted $\mathbf{t}$ to compute a weighted score $s_{i,\text{final}} = \sum_{j=1}^{c} t_{ij} s_{ij}$ for each proposal i.

Ideally, t_{ij} should be 1 if proposal i belongs to station j and 0 otherwise, so only L_{ij} will be counted in L_{cls}, making classifier j receive positive and negative samples in the station j alone. However, some proposals may lie in the intersection area of multiple stations. The predicted station probabilities are also not ideal. Thus, we use a soft-gated loss L_{cls} weighted by $\mathbf{t}$, which is more robust than hard-gating each proposal to only one classifier. The c classifiers are all built upon the feature vector of the final fully-connected (FC) layer in the detection branch, which can be viewed as finding an optimal subspace for each station in the feature space. As shown in Fig. 2, the station branch does not back-propagate gradients to the backbone . We find it yield better detection performance, possibly because it can make the backbone focus on learning features for LN vs. non-LN. In this study, our goal is not improving the station classification accuracy. The mean area-under-ROC-curve (AUC) for station classification is 93.5% in this setting, showing that station classification is a relatively simple task.

The proposed method predicts 2D boxes for each CT slice. It is necessary to merge 2D boxes to 3D ones to describe 3D lesions. LENS [21] proposed a merging algorithm. It starts from the boxes in the first slice, and then merges boxes in the second slice that overlaps with those in the first slice in the axial plane, and repeats until the last slice. This algorithm has a drawback: it starts to generate each 3D box from its first 2D box, which corresponds to the top edge of a lesion that may be inaccurate in detection with a low confidence score. Inspired by the non-maximum suppression (NMS) algorithm, we propose to start generating each 3D box from its 2D box with the highest confidence score, as detailed in Algorithm 1 and Fig. 2. Our experiments show that this lesion-centric merging strategy outperforms the slice-wise scheme in [21].

Algorithm 1. 3D box generation by lesion-centric 2D box merging

---

Input: A list of predicted 2D boxes B_2; Intersection-over-union (IoU) threshold θ.
Output: A list of merged 3D boxes B_3.

1: **while** B_2 is not empty **do**
2:     Take $b \in B_2$ with the highest confidence score. Suppose b is on slice i.
3:     Create a new 2D box list $T = \{b\}$
4:     **for** slices $i + 1, i + 2, \cdots$ **do**
5:         **if** $\exists \tilde{b} \in B_2, \text{IoU}(b, \tilde{b}) > \theta$ **then** $T = T \cup \{\tilde{b}\}, B_2 = B_2 - \tilde{b}$ **else** stop iteration.
6:         **end if**
7:     **end for**
8:     Repeat steps 4–7 for slices $i - 1, i - 2, \cdots$
9:     Compute a 3D box $\hat{b}$ from T, whose x, y, z ranges and confidence score is the maximum of the 2D boxes in T. $B_3 = B_3 \cup \{\hat{b}\}$
10: **end while**

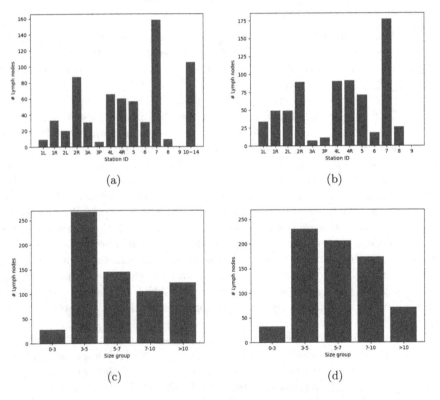

Fig. 4. (a) Station distribution of the lung cancer dataset. (a) Station distribution of the esophageal cancer dataset. (c) Size distribution (in mm) of the lung cancer dataset. (a) Size distribution (in mm) of the esophageal cancer dataset.

3   Experiment

Datasets. Thoracic LNs can be affected by multiple cancer types [18]. In this work, we collected two datasets of different cancer origins. The **lung cancer** dataset includes contrast-enhanced (CE) CTs of 82 patients. 668 LNs were annotated by three board-certified radiation oncologist with more than 10 years of experience. All visible LNs were comprehensively annotated, whose average long and short diameters [4] are 12.3×7.4 mm (min. 1.5 mm, max. 60.6 mm). The **esophageal cancer** dataset contains both CE and non-contrast (NC) CTs of 91 patients. 712 LNs in stations 1–9 with average diameters of 11.0×6.5 mm (min. 2.1 mm, max. 27.0 mm) were annotated by the same group of oncologists. The LNs were annotated on CE CTs in which they were more distinguishable. Then, we registered NC CTs to CE ones for each patient using DEEDS [8], followed by manual verification of the registration quality. In this way, we can train and evaluate our LN detector on NC CTs as well. The masks of LN stations 1–9 were also annotated in this dataset, from which we can infer the station label of each LN. We also trained an LN station segmentation algorithm [7] using these annotations and applied it to the lung cancer dataset to infer their LN stations. Note that LNs in stations 10–14 (pulmonary nodes [5]) exist in the lung cancer dataset but not in the esophageal cancer one. The station segmentation algorithm cannot predict stations 10–14. Hence, when applying it on the lung cancer dataset, we regarded all LNs outside its predicted masks as belonging to stations 10–14. See Fig. 4 for details about distribution of LN stations and sizes in the datasets.

Implementation Details. We implemented our algorithm using PyTorch 1.10 and mmDetection 2.18 [3]. CT images were normalized using a spacing of $0.8 \times 0.8 \times 2$ mm and an intensity window of $[-200, 300]$ Hounsfield unit. Data augmentation included random scaling (0.7–1.4), cropping, rotation ($\pm 15°$), intensity scaling (0.7–1.3), and gamma augmentation (0.7–1.5) [15]. In training, each mini-batch consisted of 4 samples, where each sample included 9 CT slices for 3D feature fusion [22]. The station branch had two 512D FC layers, whereas the detection branch had two 2048D FC layers. We used RAdam [12] to train for 10 epochs and set the base learning rate to 0.0001, and then reduced it by a factor of 10 after the 7th epoch. In each epoch, we used all positive slices (with LN annotations) and randomly sampled 2 times of negative slices (without annotations) [21]. The entire training process took 1.5 h for the esophageal cancer dataset on a Tesla V100 GPU. In the 2D box merging algorithm, we set the IoU threshold θ to 0.7.

Evaluation Metrics. For both datasets, we randomly split the data into 60% training, 15% validation, and 25% testing in the patient level. For the esophageal cancer dataset, we trained a joint model for CE and NC images and show their performance in the test set separately. Following previous lesion detection works [2,11,21,22], we use the free-response receiver operating characteristic (FROC) curve as the evaluation metric and report the sensitivity at different FP levels. When comparing each detected 3D box with the ground-truth 3D

Table 1. Sensitivity (%) at 0.5, 1, 2, and 4 FPs per patient on the lung and esophageal cancer datasets. The number of heads c is varied, where $c = 1$ is the baseline.

	Lung					*Esophageal CE*					*Esophageal NC*				
c	0.5	1	2	4	Avg.	0.5	1	2	4	Avg.	0.5	1	2	4	Avg
1	52	60	65	70	61.9	**66**	70	80	87	75.7	59	68	81	88	73.9
6	**60**	**68**	**71**	**76**	**69.0** $_{7.1\uparrow}$	60	76	**86**	90	**77.8** $_{2.1\uparrow}$	**63**	71	79	**91**	76.1 $_{2.2\uparrow}$
8	56	64	**71**	75	66.3 $_{4.4\uparrow}$	58	72	84	**92**	76.6 $_{0.9\uparrow}$	57	**75**	82	88	75.7 $_{1.8\uparrow}$
14	49	62	68	**76**	63.9 $_{2.0\uparrow}$	63	**78**	83	86	77.3 $_{1.6\uparrow}$	**63**	72	**84**	88	**76.8** $_{2.9\uparrow}$

boxes, if the 3D intersection over detected bounding-box ratio (IoBB) is larger than 0.3, the detected box is counted as hit [21]. According to the RECIST guideline [4], LNs with short axis less than 10 mm are considered normal. However, some studies [18] show that metastatic LNs can be smaller than 10mm. Therefore, we set a smaller size threshold and aim to detect LNs larger than 7 mm during inference. If a ground-truth LN smaller than 7 mm is detected, it is neither counted as a TP nor an FP. In training, we still use all LN annotations.

Quantitative Results. First, we validate our key assumption: stratification of samples based on LN stations improves detection accuracy. Results on the two datasets are displayed in Table 1. $c = 1$ means no stratification; $c = 14$ means the most fine-grained stratification. We also tried to group some stations to super-stations according to radiological literature [5], resulting in $c = 6$ or 8. Note that the lung dataset has one more station label (pulmonary nodes) than the esophageal dataset, so the actual c used for the latter dataset is 1, 5, 7, and 13. In Table 1, station stratification consistently improves accuracy. Increasing c enhances the purity of each group but also reduces the number of samples in each classifier, which is the possible reason why $c = 6$ achieves the most significant improvement in the lung dataset. In the following experiments, we will use $c = 6$. The 6 groups are [5]: supraclavicular (stations 1L, 1R), superior mediastinal (2L, 2R, 3A, 3P, 4L, 4R), aortopulmonary (5, 6), subcarinal (7), inferior mediastinal (8, 9), and pulmonary (10–14) nodes. Detection performance with different size thresholds is shown in Table 2.

Table 2. Comparison of sensitivity (%) at different FPs per patient on each dataset. The performance of lymph nodes with different sizes are reported based on their short axis diameters.

	Lung					*Esophageal CE*					*Esophageal NC*				
Size	0.5	1	2	4	Avg.	0.5	1	2	4	Avg.	0.5	1	2	4	Avg.
All	34	41	51	59	47.1	38	52	59	64	53.4	39	45	52	63	49.9
> 5mm	52	60	63	70	61.1	50	66	73	79	67.1	50	59	67	79	63.6
> 7mm	60	68	71	76	69.0	60	76	86	89	77.8	63	71	79	91	76.1
> 10mm	74	76	79	85	78.7	44	78	83	89	73.6	64	79	93	100	83.9

Table 3. Sensitivity (%) averaged at 0.5, 1, 2, and 4 FPs per patient using different strategies. Sta.: LN station information. LM: Lesion-centric 2D box merging.

Method	Sta	LM	Lung	Eso. CE	Eso. NC	Average
(a) No stratification		✓	61.9	75.7	73.9	70.5
(b) Uniform stratification		✓	62.3	74.0	69.3	68.5
(c) Multi-class	✓	✓	58.1	74.7	72.6	68.5
(d) Hard gating	✓	✓	64.7	**79.9**	73.5	72.7
(e) Slice-wise 2D box merging [21]	✓		65.5	75.0	74.6	71.7
(f) Proposed	✓	✓	**69.0**	77.8	**76.1**	**74.3**

Table 4. Comparison of sensitivity (%) at different FPs per patient on each dataset. nnUNet is a segmentor thus only has one FP point. The number in parenthesis in the last row represents the sensitivity of the proposed method at the FP point of nnUNet.

Method	Lung					Esophageal CE					Esophageal NC					Time
	0.5	1	2	4	Avg.	0.5	1	2	4	Avg.	0.5	1	2	4	Avg.	(s)
nnDetection [1]	47	57	62	70	58.9	43	64	72	75	63.8	59	63	69	72	65.8	86
MULAN [22]	43	57	60	73	58.3	51	63	75	79	67.1	55	68	72	81	68.9	**1.5**
LENS [21]	58	60	67	71	64.1	**64**	**79**	82	84	77.3	60	**74**	79	81	73.5	2.1
Proposed	**60**	**68**	**71**	**76**	**69.0**	60	76	**86**	**89**	**77.8**	**63**	71	79	**91**	**76.1**	**1.5**
nnUNet [9]	71.4@2.8 FPs (vs. **73.0**)					78.9@3.7 FPs (vs. **89.5**)					79.4@3.2 FPs (vs. **89.7**)					53

Next, we evaluate alternative strategies of our algorithm, see Table 3. We trained c station-stratified classifiers. Another possibility is not to stratify samples using stations, but to use all samples to train each classifier and average their prediction during inference. This strategy did not bring improvement in Table 3 row (b), showing the station information is useful and our performance gain is not simply due to increase of parameters and ensemble of predictions. One way to utilize station information is to train a c-way multi-class classifier, instead of the c binary classifiers in our algorithm. In row (c), multi-class classification did not help. It asks the model to distinguish LNs of different stations, but LN detection actually requires the model to distinguish LNs and non-LNs in each station, which is effectively achieved by our strategy. In our algorithm, we use a soft gating strategy to combine classifiers in training and inference by weighted sum. It is better than the hard gating strategy [23] in row (d) which only considers the classifier with the highest station score. In row (e), we show that our lesion-centric 2D box merging outperforms the slice-wise method in [21].

Finally, we compare our algorithm with prior works, see Table 4. nnDetection [1] is a self-configuring 3D detection framework utilizing test time augmentation and model ensemble. MULAN [22] is a 2.5D detection framework which learns lesion detection, classification, and segmentation in a multi-task fashion. LENS [21] is the state of the art for 3D universal lesion detection. It improves lesion detection by jointly learning multiple datasets with a shared backbone and multiple proposal networks and detection heads. We trained it using both lung and esophageal datasets. nnUNet [9] is a strong self-adapting framework that has been widely-used for medical image segmentation. Our proposed method achieves the best accuracy in all datasets with evident margins, while taking only 1.5 s to infer a CT volume. It outperforms LENS even without multi-dataset joint training. More qualitative results are included in Fig. 5.

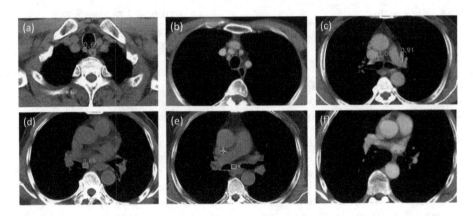

Fig. 5. Exemplar detection results of our algorithm. LNs in different stations and image modalities (CE, NC) are shown. Green, yellow, and red boxes indicate TP, FN, and FPs, respectively, with the confidence score displayed above the box. In (a) and (b), our algorithm can differentiate between LNs and adjacent vessels and esophagus. (e) and (f) are failure cases. In (e), an LN in station 7 has indistinguishable intensity compared with surrounding tissue in an NC image, thus were missed by our algorithm. In (f), the esophagus was mistaken as an LN due to similar intensity and shape. (Color figure online)

4   Conclusion

Lymph nodes (LNs) in different LN stations vary significantly in their contextual appearance. Inspired by this, we propose a lymph node detection algorithm that employs a station branch and a multi-head detection branch to train station-specialized classifiers. Our method is effective and efficient. It also significantly outperforms various leading lesion detection and segmentation methods [1,9,21,22], on two sets of patients with lung or esophageal cancers respectively. Our next step is to extend it to LNs in other body parts beyond thoracic CT scans.

References

1. Baumgartner, M., Jäger, P.F., Isensee, F., Maier-Hein, K.H.: nnDetection: a self-configuring method for medical object detection. In: de Bruijne, M., et al. (eds.) MICCAI 2021. LNCS, vol. 12905, pp. 530–539. Springer, Cham (2021). https://doi.org/10.1007/978-3-030-87240-3_51

2. Bouget, D., Jørgensen, A., Kiss, G., Leira, H.O., Langø, T.: Semantic segmentation and detection of mediastinal lymph nodes and anatomical structures in CT data for lung cancer staging. Int. J. Comput. Ass. Radiol. Surg. 14(6), 977–986 (2019). https://doi.org/10.1007/s11548-019-01948-8

3. Chen, K., et al.: MMDetection: open MMLab detection toolbox and benchmark. arXiv preprint arXiv:1906.07155 (2019)

4. Eisenhauer, E.A., et al.: New response evaluation criteria in solid tumours: revised RECIST guideline (version 1.1). Eur. J. Can. 45(2), 228–247 (2009)

5. El-Sherief, A.H., Lau, C.T., Wu, C.C., Drake, R.L., Abbott, G.F., Rice, T.W.: International association for the study of lung cancer (IASLC) lymph node map: radiologic review with CT illustration. Radiographics 34(6), 1680–1691 (2014)

6. Feulner, J., Kevin Zhou, S., Hammon, M., Hornegger, J., Comaniciu, D.: Lymph node detection and segmentation in chest CT data using discriminative learning and a spatial prior. Med. Image Anal. 17(2), 254–270 (2013)

7. Guo, D., et al.: DeepStationing: thoracic lymph node station parsing in CT scans using anatomical context encoding and key Organ Auto-Search. In: de Bruijne, M., et al. (eds.) MICCAI 2021. LNCS, vol. 12905, pp. 3–12. Springer, Cham (2021). https://doi.org/10.1007/978-3-030-87240-3_1

8. Heinrich, M.P., Jenkinson, M., Brady, S.M., Schnabel, J.A.: Globally optimal deformable registration on a minimum spanning tree using dense displacement sampling. In: Ayache, N., Delingette, H., Golland, P., Mori, K. (eds.) MICCAI 2012. LNCS, vol. 7512, pp. 115–122. Springer, Heidelberg (2012). https://doi.org/10.1007/978-3-642-33454-2_15

9. Isensee, F., Jaeger, P.F., Kohl, S.A., Petersen, J., Maier-Hein, K.H.: nnU-Net: a self-configuring method for deep learning-based biomedical image segmentation. Nat. Methods 18(2), 203–211 (2021)

10. Iuga, A.I., et al.: Automated detection and segmentation of thoracic lymph nodes from CT using 3D foveal fully convolutional neural networks. BMC Med. Imaging 21(1), 69 (2021)

11. Liu, J., et al.: Mediastinal lymph node detection and station mapping on chest CT using spatial priors and random forest. Med. Phys. 43(7), 4362–4374 (2016). https://doi.org/10.1118/1.4954009

12. Liu, L., et al.: On the variance of the adaptive learning rate and beyond. In: ICLR (2020)

13. Mao, Y., Hedgire, S., Harisinghani, M.: Radiologic assessment of lymph nodes in oncologic patients. Curr. Radiol. Rep. 2(2), 1–13 (2014)

14. Oda, H., et al.: Dense volumetric detection and segmentation of mediastinal lymph nodes in chest CT images. In: Mori, K., Petrick, N. (eds.) SPIE, vol. 10575, p. 1. SPIE (2018)

15. Pérez-García, F., Sparks, R., Ourselin, S.: TorchIO: a Python library for efficient loading, preprocessing, augmentation and patch-based sampling of medical images in deep learning. Technical report (2020). https://github.com/fepegar/torchio

16. Ren, S., He, K., Girshick, R., Sun, J.: Faster R-CNN: towards real-time object detection with region proposal networks. In: NIPS, pp. 91–99 (2015). https://doi.org/10.1109/TPAMI.2016.2577031

17. Roth, H.R., et al.: A New 2.5D representation for lymph node detection using random sets of deep convolutional neural network observations. In: Golland, P., Hata, N., Barillot, C., Hornegger, J., Howe, R. (eds.) MICCAI 2014. LNCS, vol. 8673, pp. 520–527. Springer, Cham (2014). https://doi.org/10.1007/978-3-319-10404-1_65

18. Sharma, A., Fidias, P., Hayman, L.A., Loomis, S.L., Taber, K.H., Aquino, S.L.: Patterns of lymphadenopathy in thoracic malignancies. Radiographics **24**(2), 419–434 (2004). https://doi.org/10.1148/rg.242035075

19. Smithuis, R.: Mediastinum Lymph Node Map (2010). https://radiologyassistant.nl/chest/mediastinum/mediastinum-lymph-node-map

20. Tian, Z., Shen, C., Chen, H., He, T.: FCOS: fully convolutional one-stage object detection. In: ICCV (2019)

21. Yan, K., et al.: Learning from multiple datasets with heterogeneous and partial labels for universal lesion detection in CT. IEEE Trans. Med. Imaging **40**, 2759–2770 (2020)

22. Yan, K., et al.: MULAN: multitask universal lesion analysis network for joint lesion detection, tagging, and segmentation. In: Shen, D., et al. (eds.) MICCAI 2019. LNCS, vol. 11769, pp. 194–202. Springer, Cham (2019). https://doi.org/10.1007/978-3-030-32226-7_22

23. Zhu, Z., et al.: Lymph node gross tumor volume detection and segmentation via distance-based gating using 3D CT/PET imaging in radiotherapy. In: Martel, A.L., et al. (eds.) MICCAI 2020. LNCS, vol. 12267, pp. 753–762. Springer, Cham (2020). https://doi.org/10.1007/978-3-030-59728-3_73

Leveraging Contrastive Learning with SimSiam for the Classification of Primary and Secondary Liver Cancers

Ramtin Mojtahedi[1], Mohammad Hamghalam[1,2], William R. Jarnagin[3], Richard K. G. Do[4], and Amber L. Simpson[1,5(✉)]

[1] School of Computing, Queen's University, Kingston, ON, Canada
amber.simpson@queensu.ca
[2] Department of Electrical Engineering, Qazvin Branch, Islamic Azad University, Qazvin, Iran
[3] Hepatopancreatobiliary Service, Department of Surgery, Memorial Sloan Kettering Cancer Center, New York, NY, USA
[4] Department of Radiology, Memorial Sloan Kettering Cancer Center, New York, NY, USA
[5] Department of Biomedical and Molecular Sciences, Queen's University, Kingston, ON, Canada

Abstract. Accurate liver cancer classification is essential, as it substantially influences the selection of effective treatment strategies and impacts patient prognosis. Convolutional neural network (CNN) classifiers typically require extensive labeled datasets for training to attain decent performance. However, the process of obtaining labeled data through manual labeling is time-consuming, potentially biased, and costly when applied to large datasets. This study utilizes the Simple Siamese (SimSiam) contrastive self-supervised learning approach to enhance the classification of liver tumours, especially considering the limited availability of labeled computed tomography (CT) scans of liver cancer. We integrate SimSiam with three baseline CNN-based classifiers - Inception, Xception, and ResNet152 - and pretrain them with two loss functions: mean squared error (MSE) and cosine similarity (COS). Our findings show consistent improvements for three classifiers compared to the baseline models. Specifically, the ResNet152 model exhibits the highest performance among the evaluated networks. With MSE and COS losses, the classification accuracy for ResNet152 improves by 1.27% and 2.53%, respectively. The classification accuracy of the Inception model improves by 3.95% and 5.26%. Similarly, Xception's validation accuracy demonstrates an increase of 2.60% with both loss functions, compared to the baseline models. We validate our pipeline via our multi-resolution in-house abdominal CT scans of primary and secondary liver cancers, including 155 patients with hepatocellular carcinoma, 198 patients with colorectal liver metastases, and 107 patients with intrahepatic cholangiocarcinoma. Source code available at:https://github.com/Ramtin-Mojtahedi/SimSiam-LiverCancer-CL.

© The Author(s), under exclusive license to Springer Nature Switzerland AG 2023
J. Woo et al. (Eds.): MICCAI 2023 Workshops, LNCS 14394, pp. 311–321, 2023.
https://doi.org/10.1007/978-3-031-47425-5_28

312 R. Mojtahedi et al.

Keywords: CT Classification · Liver Tumour Classification · Self-Supervised Learning · Constrastive Learning

1 Introduction

Computed tomography (CT) scans are crucial in managing liver cancer, as they provide essential diagnostic assessments and therapeutic monitoring, improving patient prognosis [1]. CT images facilitate the assessment of factors like tumour size, vascular involvement, and impact on surrounding healthy tissues, which provide pivotal information for treatment planning [2]. Additionally, the early detection of tumour recurrence or metastasis, and the refinement of treatment strategies rely on this information [3]. Therefore, the accurate classification of liver tumours is of utmost importance for guiding treatment decisions and predicting prognosis but also underscores the importance of early diagnosis, particularly considering the significant clinical burden associated with liver cancer [4]. In recent years, the advent of deep learning and convolutional neural networks (CNNs) has led to significant improvements in both the accuracy and efficiency of CT segmentation [9–11] and classification tasks [13]. However, to improve the model's accuracy, overcome overfitting, capture complex and variable features, and address class imbalance, CNN models usually require a large labeled dataset for training [12].

Currently, creating labeled datasets involves the manual segmentation of the liver and liver tumours by radiologists. This process is critical for improving machine learning (ML) algorithms, which have the potential to significantly transform future diagnosis and treatment planning [16]. However, this manual process of creating labeled images is time-consuming and expensive due to the complexity of the liver's anatomy and tumour characteristics. It requires meticulous identification and tracing of boundaries as well as the expertise of radiologists. These operational expenses can burden healthcare institutions. Furthermore, this process is subject to bias due to inter-observer variability and subjective interpretation, both of which can compromise assessment accuracy and standardization [17].

To reduce reliance on labeled data, self-supervised learning (SSL) generates a supervised signal from a corpus of unlabeled data points [18]. Contrastive SSL methods in particular have proven effectiveness in learning input image representations, as they group similar images together and dissimilar images apart in the feature space [24]. Popular SSL techniques include Bootstrap Your Own Latent (BYOL), Simple Contrastive Learning of Visual Representations (SimCLR), Simple Siamese (SimSiam), and Contrastive Predictive Coding (CPC) [25]. BYOL enhances SSL by focusing on different enhanced views of the same data. It employs a target network that predicts and learns from an online network [26]. SimCLR, on the other hand, attempts to reduce the similarity between distinct data samples while amplifying it across various transformations or perspectives of the same data [27]. In contrast, CPC models SSL as a predictive task, learning to predict future input data representations by framing SSL as a contrastive learning problem [28]. SimSiam, introduced by Chen *et al.*, is an SSL strategy that advances conventional methods by creating representations from various transformations of the same image, which boosts the model's resilience to data variations [29]. Through this mechanism, SimSiam could facilitate the extraction of more meaningful and generalized features from images, further improving the model's ability to accurately classify and make it suitable for classifying different types of liver cancer in the limited labeled dataset.

Recent studies in this field have shown promising results. Yasaka *et al.* applied CNN classifier to differentiate between five types of liver masses using dynamic contrast-enhanced CT images. The types of masses included common and rare malignant liver tumours, indeterminate masses, hemangiomas, and cysts. Their results demonstrated that using CNNs in CT images could improve the accuracy and efficiency of classifying liver masses [19]. On the basis of this foundation, Hamm *et al.* expanded the use of CNNs in the diagnosis of liver tumours using multi-phasic magnetic resonance imaging (MRI). They proposed a CNN classifier that was trained to distinguish between six common hepatic lesion types. The successful integration of CNNs with MRI data in this work highlights the adaptability of deep learning techniques and their potential to increase the diagnostic precision of liver cancer classification across multiple imaging modalities [20]. Aligned with these applications, the Inception, Xception, and ResNet152 models stand out among deep learning classifiers in recent years. Inception utilizes factorized convolutions and dimension reductions to optimize computation and accuracy, making it suitable for large-scale applications [21]. To improve feature extraction and classification capabilities, Xception substitutes Inception modules in an inventive way with depthwise separable convolutions [22]. To prevent gradient vanishing or exploding, ResNet152, a more complex variant of the original ResNet, incorporates skip connections [23]. Owing to their unique advantages and proven track records of performance, these models emerge as among the top candidates for classification tasks. Among the few studies that used the these CNN classifiers for liver classification, Nakata *et al.* explored the effectiveness of ensemble CNN models, including Xception, Inception and ResNet152, in classifying ultrasound images of liver tumours [30]. In another similar study, Chen *et al.* proposed a novel CNN network to classify different types of liver cancer histopathological images, and compared its performance with other CNN classifiers, including ResNet variations [4].

In this study, we introduce a robust approach for the classification of liver tumours using advanced CNN classifiers. For the first time in related studies, we deploy an SSL contrastive learning framework using SimSiam, promising to improve liver tumour classification. The summary of the main contributions of this work are:

- Implementing a SimSiam-based SSL approach, in conjunction with Xception, InceptionV3, and ResNet152 classifiers. This is the first study to apply this approach to the classification of cancer tumours in liver CT images.
- Validating the proposed pipeline using our multi-resolution in-house datasets of hepatocellular carcinoma (HCC), intrahepatic cholangiocarcinoma (ICC),

and colorectal liver metastases (CRLM), demonstrating use with various types of liver cancer.

• Evaluating the performance of the models under two different loss functions: cosine similarity (COS) and mean squared error (MSE). This highlights the model's adaptability to different error sensitivities and underscores the influence of loss functions on learning representations, generalization capabilities, and performance metrics.

2   Methods

Figure 1 illustrates our proposed pipeline for classifying three different liver tumour types: HCC, ICC, and CRLM. Liver parenchyma and tumours are annotated by radiologists. We use these annotations to segment tumours from the inside of the liver organ in abdominal CT scans. Subsequently, we generate slices from these segmented tumours for the classification process. In addition, we utilize the SimSiam approach for contrastive pre-training of our classification models to enhance their accuracy.

The SimSiam enabled SSL, allowing the model to discover reliable and generalizable representations before further fine-tuning [31]. SimSiam is chosen in our study for its privileges in computational efficiency, enhanced learning efficacy, and robustness against common learning challenges [29].

We utilize three benchmark classifiers, namely ResNet152, Inception and Xception to categorize images generated from the cropped slices of tumours found in CT scans, both with and without contrastive pretraining. In the baseline approach, there is no contrastive pretraining; instead, we initialize the models using weights from ImageNet during the training process. To further enhance performance, we append three fully connected layers with 7000, 2048, and 3 output nodes respectively to the top of each of the chosen networks, optimizing convergence to the three classes of liver tumours. Additionally, L2 regularization and a rectified linear unit (ReLU) are incorporated into each fully connected layer, serving as the activation function and mitigating the risk of overfitting. A SoftMax layer is then connected to the final fully connected layer, furnishing the final prediction score for each class. We employ a supervised approach to evaluate our non-pretrained (baseline) and pretrained models' capability to classify generated image slices across our multi-resolution in-house triple liver cancer categories.

To evaluate the models' generalizability and capacity to learn different representations, we also conducted experiments in this phase using two different loss functions: MSE and COS. The results obtained from baseline and contrastive loss were then compared to assess the level of improvement in the models' classification performance. The proposed pipeline is shown in Fig. 1.

In the implementation process, the code is developed using TensorFlow, and computations are performed on a CUDA device (NVIDIA A100-40GB). Two datasets, one for training and one for validation, are prepared from the whole dataset with a 70/30% split ratio. The datasets are then batched with a batch

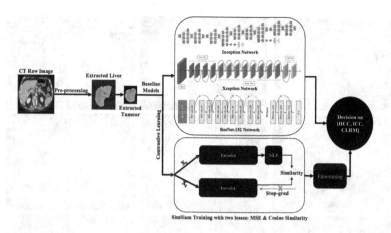

Fig. 1. This pipeline identifies the baselines (Inception, Xception, and ResNet152 models) along with the proposed SimSiam pretraining technique for the classification of HCC, ICC, and CRLM liver tumours. The baseline phase involves training the model without pretraining by contrastive learning. We contrastively pre-train our proposed model using SimSiam, where X_1 and X_2 represent two augmentations of the same image, and then fine-tuned on our multi-resolution in-house datasets.

Table 1. Summary of the employed hyperparameters.

Parameter	Value/Method
Image Size [H×W]	[299×299]
Optimizer	Adam
Learning Rate	0.0001
Learning Rate Decay Factor	Cosine Decay
SimSiam: [Projection Dimension, Latent Dimension]	[1024, 2048]
Batch Size	64
Computational Resource	NVIDIA A100 – 40GB

size of 64 and optimized for performance using prefetching. The model is trained using the Adam optimizer with a cosine decay learning rate schedule, and early stopping is implemented to prevent overfitting. The main hyperparameters are summarized in Table 1.

2.1   Data Description and Preprocessing

Our multi-resolution in-house datasets comprise CT images of the abdomen, collected with precision from patients who were diagnosed with various forms of liver cancer, including HCC involving 155 patients, CRLM with 198 patients, and ICC involving 107 patients. These images were taken prior to surgical resection with a standard imaging protocol for contrast-enhanced CT. The spatial

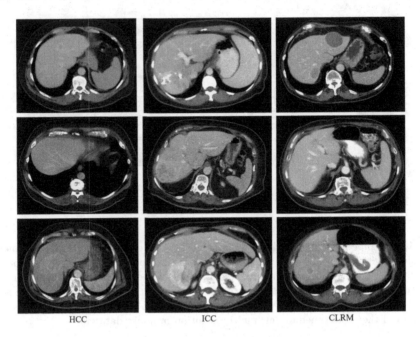

Fig. 2. Sample segmented CT images of HCC, ICC, and CRLM with liver (green) and tumour (yellow) regions in the axial view. (Color figure online)

resolution of these images varied between 0.57 and 0.98 mm for the x- and y-axes, and between 0.8 and 8 mm for the z-axis, which allowed for capturing of detailed information. A certified radiologist validated all the segmentations to ensure the data quality. Examples of three cancer types are shown in Fig. 2.

In the preprocessing step, we start by extracting the largest tumour from the inside of the liver in each image. Subsequently, up to 15 of the largest slices in the axial orientation are extracted from the identified tumour. These images are then normalized from Hounsfield units(HU) using a window width of 350 and levels of 40 [32]. The isolated tumour regions are resized to 299 × 299 pixels and saved as PNG images. Next, these images are used to create TensorFlow training and test datasets. To ensure equal representation of various tumour types, the datasets are oversampled. To improve the model's generalizability and robustness, the training dataset undergoes several data augmentation procedures, introducing randomness and color distortions. These augmentation techniques include random rotation, flipping, and adjustments to brightness and contrast.

2.2   Pre-training Models Using SimSiam

In our SimSiam implementation, we leverage positive pairings, which are different augmented versions of the same image. These augmentations include both geometric and colour jittering transformations. By contrasting these distinct views of the same image, our model is trained to identify invariant features.

This not only simplifies computations but also eliminates the need for maintaining a balance between positive and negative samples. We've also incorporated the stop-gradient mechanism into the model. This step is crucial to prevent the model from learning irrelevant patterns - a common issue seen in most SSL pretraining procedures. The symmetric architecture of our SimSiam implementation ensures equal weight distributions across both pathways. This feature enhances stability and helps generate reliable features.

In terms of the network dimensions, we used a projection dimension of 1024 and a latent dimension of 2048. The projection dimension is responsible for transforming the input data into a lower-dimensional space, which allows for efficient data processing. The latent dimension, on the other hand, plays a crucial role in learning hidden or latent features within the data.

During the pretraining phase for generating pretext models, we integrated two loss functions - COS and MSE. These are used to evaluate the model's adaptability to different error sensitivities. The use of these functions emphasizes the importance of loss functions in learning representations, improving generalization capabilities, and enhancing performance metrics. The pretraining process continues until the loss minimizes. The utilized loss functions are described as follows.

COS Loss. The SimSiam network employs a symmetric negative COS loss function [33]. The mathematical formulation of this loss function is shown in Eq. 1.

$$L = -\frac{z_1^T z_2}{||z_1|| ||z_2||} \tag{1}$$

where L represents the loss, z_1 and z_2 are the output vectors from the two pathways of the SimSiam network, and $||z_1||$ and $||z_2||$ represent the norms of z_1 and z_2, respectively. The caret (^{T}) indicates the transpose of the vector, and the negative sign implies that the network aims to minimize the negative COS, effectively maximizing the similarity between the two vectors. Its objective is to increase the similarity between two differently augmented views of the same image, encapsulated as high-dimensional vectors z_1 and z_2. The COS measures the cosine of the angle between these two vectors, which is a measure of their directional similarity. By minimizing the negative of this value, the objective is to reduce the angle between them, making the vectors directionally similar [34]. This loss function is an essential component of the learning process as it encourages the network to learn feature representations that are invariant to the augmentations, providing a meaningful and robust way to capture the inherent properties of the data [35].

MSE Loss. In conjunction with the COS loss, we used the MSE loss function. It quantifies the average squared deviation between predicted and actual values, penalizing larger discrepancies more due to the squaring operation, and encouraging more precise predictions [36]. This loss can be expressed as Eq. 2.

$$MSE = \frac{1}{d}\sum_{i=1}^{d}(z_{1i} - z_{2i})^2 \tag{2}$$

where d represents the dimension of the embedding space in which the output vectors reside. z_1 and z_2 are the output vectors from the two pathways of the SimSiam network, representing the same image but with different augmentations.

3   Experimental Results and Discussion

We evaluate the effect of loss functions in the SimSiam pretraining approach on various classifiers, as presented in Table 2. We compute accuracy, recall, precision, and F1-score to identify the most accurate classifier in our dataset.

Our results show that when ResNet152 is pre-trained using the COS loss function, it achieves an accuracy of 0.81, an F1-score of 0.77, a precision of 0.77, and a recall of 0.77. These results closely mirror those obtained with the MSE loss. The baseline results for ResNet152 are slightly lower, with accuracy, precision, recall, and F1-Score at 0.79, 0.74, 0.74, and 0.74, respectively.

For the Inception model pre-trained using the COS loss, we observe an accuracy of 0.80, an F1-Score of 0.74, a precision of 0.75, and a recall of 0.74. Using the MSE loss leads to nearly the same performance, with a minor decrease in accuracy to 0.79. Comparatively, the baseline method for Inception yields lower scores across all metrics at 0.72.

Regarding the Xception model, the use of the COS loss function in the self-supervised pretraining process results in an accuracy of 0.79, an F1-Score of 0.73, a precision of 0.75, and a recall of 0.73. Using the MSE loss function produced almost identical results, but with a minor increase in F1-Score and recall to 0.75. Both self-supervised methods outperform the baseline, which exhibited an accuracy of 0.77 and 0.73 for the remaining metrics.

The average results across all three models show that self-supervised pretraining using the COS loss results in an accuracy of 0.80, F1-Score of 0.75, precision of 0.76, and recall of 0.75. These results are similar to those using the MSE loss. As anticipated, the average baseline results are lower, with an accuracy of 0.77, and F1-Score, precision, and recall all at 0.73. The detailed results for all models are shown in Table 2.

Our analysis reveals that the COS loss function performs better than the MSE loss function. Particularly, the Inception model's accuracy improved by roughly 5.26% with the COS loss function and about 3.95% with the MSE loss function. A similar increase is observable in precision, recall, and F1-score. For the Xception model, the accuracy improved by approximately 2.60% over the baseline for both the COS and MSE losses. These loss functions also resulted in enhanced precision, recall, and F1-score. For ResNet152, the most noticeable performance improvement was observed when pretraining with the COS loss

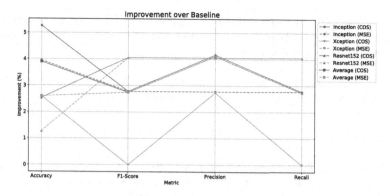

Fig. 3. Summary of the performance improvement across all models and metrics.

Table 2. Comparison of Baseline and Pretrained Classification Results: The terms 'Acc.' and 'Precis.' refer to accuracy and precision, respectively.

Model	Self-supervised Pretrained								Baseline			
	COS				MSE							
	Acc	F1	Precis	Recall	Acc	F1	Precis	Recall	Acc	F1	Precis	Recall
Inception	0.80	0.74	0.75	0.74	0.79	0.74	0.74	0.74	0.76	0.72	0.72	0.72
Xception	0.79	0.73	0.75	0.73	0.79	0.75	0.76	0.75	0.77	0.73	0.73	0.73
ResNet	**0.81**	**0.77**	**0.77**	**0.77**	**0.80**	**0.77**	**0.77**	**0.77**	**0.79**	**0.74**	**0.74**	**0.74**
Average	0.80	0.75	0.76	0.75	0.79	0.75	0.76	0.75	0.77	0.73	0.73	0.73

function, showing an accuracy increase of approximately 2.53%. The MSE-based loss model also improved, with an accuracy increase of about 1.27%.

Across the three models, we observe an accuracy improvement of approximately 3.90% with the COS loss and approximately 2.60% with MSE loss, compared to the baselines. The ResNet152 model pretrained with the COS loss function outperforms the others. The summary of the improvements across all models is shown in Fig. 3.

4 Conclusion

In this study, we utilize the SSL method to enhance liver tumour classification. Implementing this approach on three CNN classifiers - Inception, Xception, and ResNet152, results in an increase in accuracy by roughly 3.90% and 2.60% for the COS and MSE loss functions, respectively. We validate this approach using CT scans from 155 HCC, 198 CRLM, and 107 ICC patients. By pretraining liver cancer CNN-based classifiers with unlabeled data by SSL methods, the problem of labeled data scarcity can be alleviated. From a clinical perspective, our work lays the foundation for enhanced diagnostic precision and informed treatment planning by capitalizing on a significant volume of unlabeled medical imaging data. Therefore, our research presents an opportunity for more accurate disease identification and treatment decisions, underpinning advancements in patient outcomes in the field of oncology.

Acknowledgements. This work was funded by National Institutes of Health and National Cancer Institute grants R01CA233888 and U01CA238444.

References

1. Choi, J.Y., Lee, J.-M., Sirlin, C.B.: CT and MR imaging diagnosis and staging of hepatocellular carcinoma: part I. Development, growth, and spread: key pathologic and imaging aspects. Radiology, **272**, 635–654 (2014)
2. Dar, A.R., McKillop, I., Vickress, J., Lock, M., Yartsev, S.: Prognostic significance of tumour location for liver cancer radiotherapy. Cureus, **10**(12), e3714 (2018)
3. Histed, S.N., Lindenberg, M.L., Mena, E., Turkbey, B., Choyke, P.L., Kurdziel, K.A.: Review of functional/anatomical imaging in oncology. Nucl. Med. Commun. **33**, 349–361 (2012)
4. Chen, C., et al.: Classification of Multi-Differentiated Liver Cancer Pathological Images Based on Deep Learning Attention Mechanism (2022)
5. Types of Liver Cancer: Cholangiocarcinoma, HCC and More. https://www.cancercenter.com/cancer-types/liver-cancer/types. Accessed 08 Mar 2023
6. Chidambaranathan-Reghupaty, S., Fisher, P.B., Sarkar, D.: Hepatocellular carcinoma (HCC): epidemiology, etiology and molecular classification. Adv. Cancer Res. **149**, 1–61 (2021)
7. El-Diwany, R., Pawlik, T.M., Ejaz, A.: Intrahepatic cholangiocarcinoma. Surg. Oncol. Clin. N. Am. **28**, 587–599 (2019)
8. Martin, J., et al.: Colorectal liver metastases: current management and future perspectives. World J. Clin. Oncol. **11**, 761–808 (2020)
9. Hamghalam, M., Do, R., Simpson, A.L.: Attention-Based CT Scan Interpolation for Lesion Segmentation of Colorectal Liver Metastases. Medical Imaging 2023: Biomedical Applications in Molecular, Structural, and Functional Imaging (2023)
10. Mojtahedi, R., Hamghalam, M., Do, R.K., Simpson, A.L.: Towards optimal patch size in vision transformers for Tumour segmentation. In: Multiscale Multimodal Medical Imaging, pp. 110–120 (2022)
11. Mojtahedi, R., Hamghalam, M., Simpson, A.L.: Multi-modal brain Tumour segmentation using transformer with optimal patch size. In: BrainLesion: Glioma, Multiple Sclerosis, Stroke and Traumatic Brain Injuries, pp. 195–204 (2023)
12. Heaton, J.: Ian Goodfellow, Yoshua Bengio, and Aaron Courville: deep learning. Genet. Program Evolvable Mach. **19**, 305–307 (2017)
13. Alzubaidi, L., et al.: Review of deep learning: concepts, CNN architectures, challenges, applications, future directions. J. Big Data, **8**(1), 53 (2021)
14. Villanueva, A.: Hepatocellular carcinoma. N. Engl. J. Med. **380**, 1450–1462 (2019)
15. Rizvi, S., Khan, S.A., Hallemeier, C.L., Kelley, R.K., Gores, G.J.: Cholangiocarcinoma - evolving concepts and therapeutic strategies. Nat. Rev. Clin. Oncol. **15**, 95–111 (2017)
16. Alanazi, A.: Using machine learning for healthcare challenges and opportunities. Inform. Med. Unlocked **30**, 100924 (2022)
17. Solatidehkordi, Z., Zualkernan, I.: Survey on recent trends in medical image classification using semi-supervised learning. Appl. Sci. **12**, 12094 (2022)

18. Reed, C.J., et al.: Self-supervised pretraining improves self-supervised pretraining. In: 2022 IEEE/CVF Winter Conference on Applications of Computer Vision (WACV) (2022)
19. Yasaka, K., Akai, H., Abe, O., Kiryu, S.: Deep learning with convolutional neural network for differentiation of liver masses at dynamic contrast-enhanced CT: a preliminary study. Radiology **286**, 887–896 (2018)
20. Hamm, C.A., et al.: deep learning for liver tumour diagnosis Part I: development of a convolutional neural network classifier for multi-phasic MRI. Eur. Radiol. **29**, 3338–3347 (2019)
21. Szegedy, C., Vanhoucke, V., Ioffe, S., Shlens, J., Wojna, Z.: Rethinking the inception architecture for computer vision. In: 2016 IEEE Conference on Computer Vision and Pattern Recognition (CVPR) (2016)
22. Chollet, F.: Xception: Deep Learning with Depthwise Separable Convolutions. In: 2017 IEEE Conference on Computer Vision and Pattern Recognition (CVPR) (2017)
23. He, K., Zhang, X., Ren, S., Sun, J.: Deep residual learning for image recognition. In: 2016 IEEE Conference on Computer Vision and Pattern Recognition (CVPR) (2016)
24. Huang, S.-C., Pareek, A., Jensen, M., Lungren, M.P., Yeung, S., Chaudhari, A.S.: Self-Supervised Learning for Medical Image Classification: A Systematic Review and Implementation Guidelines. npj Digit. Med. **6**, 74 (2023)
25. Del Pup, F., Atzori, M.: Applications of Self-Supervised Learning to Biomedical Signals: Where Are We Now. (2023)
26. Grill, J.B., et al.: Bootstrap your own latent: a new approach to self-supervised learning. In: NIPS 2020: Proceedings of the 34th International Conference on Neural Information Processing Systems, pp. 21271–21284 (2020)
27. Chen, S., Kornblith, S., Hinton, G.: Simple Contrastive Learning of Visual Representations. arXiv:2002.05709 (2020)
28. Van den Oord, A., Li, Y., Vinyals, O.: Representation Learning with Contrastive Predictive Coding. arXiv:1807.03748 (2018)
29. Chen, X., He, K.: Exploring simple Siamese representation learning. In: 2021 IEEE/CVF Conference on Computer Vision and Pattern Recognition (CVPR) (2021)
30. Nakata, N., Siina, T.: Ensemble Learning of Multiple Models Using Deep Learning for Multiclass Classification of Ultrasound Images of Hepatic Masses (2022)
31. Alam, M.N., et al.: Contrastive Learning-Based Pretraining Improves Representation and Transferability of Diabetic Retinopathy Classification Models (2022)
32. DenOtter, T., Schubert, J.: Hounsfield Unit. https://www.ncbi.nlm.nih.gov/books/NBK547721/. Accessed 06 Mar 2023
33. Li, S., Liu, F., Hao, Z., Jiao, L., Liu, X., Guo, Y.: MinEnt: minimum entropy for self-supervised representation learning. Pattern Recogn. **138**, 109364 (2023)
34. Xia, P., Zhang, L., Li, F.: Learning similarity with cosine similarity ensemble. Inf. Sci. **307**, 39–52 (2015)
35. Jiang, B., Krim, H., Wu, T., Cansever, D.: Refining self-supervised learning in imaging: beyond linear metric. In: 2022 IEEE International Conference on Image Processing (ICIP) (2022)
36. Ermolov, A., Siarohin, A., Sangineto, E., Sebe, N.: Whitening for self-supervised representation learning. In: International Conference on Machine Learning, pp. 3015–3024 (2021)

Proceeding of the Second International Workshop on Resource-Efficient Medical Image Analysis (REMIA 2023)

Operating Critical Machine Learning Models in Resource Constrained Regimes

Raghavendra Selvan[1,2](✉), Julian Schön[1], and Erik B. Dam[1]

[1] Department of Computer Science, University of Copenhagen, Copenhagen,
Denmark
`raghav@di.ku.dk`
[2] Department of Neuroscience, University of Copenhagen, Copenhagen, Denmark

Abstract. The accelerated development of machine learning methods, primarily deep learning, are causal to the recent breakthroughs in medical image analysis and computer aided intervention. The resource consumption of deep learning models in terms of amount of training data, compute and energy costs are known to be massive. These large resource costs can be barriers in deploying these models in clinics, globally. To address this, there are cogent efforts within the machine learning community to introduce notions of resource efficiency. For instance, using quantisation to alleviate memory consumption. While most of these methods are shown to reduce the resource utilisation, they could come at a cost in performance. In this work, we probe into the trade-off between resource consumption and performance, specifically, when dealing with models that are used in critical settings such as in clinics.

Keywords: Resource efficiency · Image Classification · Deep Learning

1 Introduction

Every third person on the planet does not *yet* have universal health coverage according to the estimates from the United Nations [29]. And improving access to universal health coverage is one of the UN Sustainable Development Goals. The use of machine learning (ML) based methods could be instrumental in achieving this objective. Reliable ML in clinical decision support could multiply the capabilities of healthcare professionals by reducing the time spent on several tedious and time-consuming steps. This can free up the precious time and effort of healthcare professionals to cater to the people in need [31].

The deployment of ML in critical settings like clinical environments is, however, currently in a nascent state. In addition to the fundamental challenges related to multi-site/multi-vendor validation, important issues pertaining to fairness, bias and ethics of these methods are still being investigated [23]. The demand for expensive material resources, in terms of computational infrastructure and energy requirements along with the climate impact of ML are also points of concern [24].

© The Author(s), under exclusive license to Springer Nature Switzerland AG 2023
J. Woo et al. (Eds.): MICCAI 2023 Workshops, LNCS 14394, pp. 325–335, 2023.
https://doi.org/10.1007/978-3-031-47425-5_29

In this work, we focus on the question of improving the resource efficiency of developing and deploying deep learning models for resource constrained environments [3,27]. Resource constraints in real world scenarios could be manifested as the need for: low latency (corresponding to urgency), non-specialized hardware (instead of requiring GPU/similar infrastructure) and low-energy requirements (if models are deployed on portable settings). The case for resource efficiency when *deploying* ML models is quite evident due to these aforementioned factors. In this work, we *also* argue that the training resource efficiency is important, as ML systems will be most useful in the clinical settings if they are able to continually learn [4,30]. We validate the usefulness of several methods for improving resource efficiency of deep learning models using detailed experiments. We show that resource efficiency – in terms of reducing compute time, GPU memory usage, energy consumption – can be achieved without degradation in performance for some classes of methods.

2   Methods for Resource Efficiency

In this work we mainly consider reducing the overall memory footprint of deep learning models, which in turn could reduce computation time and the corresponding energy costs. We do not explicitly study the influence of model selection using efficient neural architecture search [28] or model compression using pruning or similar methods [6], as these techniques require additional design choices outside of the normal model development and deployment phases. By focusing on strategies that can be easily incorporated, we also place emphasis on the possible ease of clinical adoption.

Denote a neural network, $f_{\mathbf{W}}(\cdot) : \mathbf{X} \to \mathbf{Y}$ which acts on inputs $\mathbf{X}$ to predict the output $\mathbf{Y}$ and has trainable parameters $\mathbf{W}$. For recent deep neural networks, the number of trainable parameters, $|\mathbf{W}|$, can be quite large [25] in $\mathcal{O}(100M)$.

During training, the weights, $\mathbf{W}$, are updated using some form of a gradient-based update rule. This requires the computation of the gradients of the loss $\mathcal{L}(\cdot)$ with respect to $\mathbf{W}$ at iteration t, $\mathbf{g}_t = \frac{\partial \mathcal{L}}{\partial \mathbf{W}}$. In the case of stateful optimisers that use momentum-based optimisation, such as Adam [16], the first and second order statistics of the gradient over time, $\mathbf{m}_t, \mathbf{v}_t$, respectively, are maintained for improved convergence. Thus, for a neural network with $|\mathbf{W}|$ parameters, at any point during the training there are an additional $\approx 3 \cdot |\mathbf{W}|$ variables stored in memory. Further, the intermediate activations at layer l, $\mathbf{h}_l$ are also stored in memory to efficiently perform backpropagation. Note that all the scalar entries of $\mathbf{W}, \mathbf{g}_t, \mathbf{m}_t, \mathbf{v}_t, \mathbf{h}_l \in \mathbb{R}$. On most computers, these real numbers are discretised into floating point-32 (FP32) format; wherein each variable requires 32 bits.

Resource efficiency in this work is primarily addressed by reducing the precision of these variables by quantisation [13,27]. The implication of using quantised or low-precision variables is that it not only reduces memory footprint but can also reduce the compute cost of matrix multiplications [15] at the expense of loss in precision. Note, however, that the overhead of performing quantisation in some cases might outweigh the gains in computation.

In this work, we investigate a combination of the following three quantisation strategies:

1. **Gradients and intermediate activations**: Drastic quantisation of h_l, g_t have been studied extensively in literature [5,15]. For instance, in [15] the gradients and activations were quantised to 1-bit and still yielded reasonable performance compared to the 32-bit models. However, not all operations are well suited for quantisation. In frameworks like Pytorch [21], the precision of h_l, g_t are automatically cast into 16-bit precision, and recast to 32-bit when necessary. This technique known as `automatic mixed precision` (AMP) can yield considerable reduction of memory costs [18].
2. **Optimiser states**: Until recently, the main focus of quantisation in deep learning has been on compressing g_t, h_l, W. In a recent work in [10], it was shown that the optimiser states, m_t, v_t can use up to 75% of memory. By quantising optimiser states to 8-bits using a dynamic quantisation scheme, this work reduces the memory consumption during model training.
3. **Model weights**: The resolution of the hypothesis space is controlled by the precision of the weights, W. Using lower precision weights for models can reduce their expressive power. This is most evident when a model trained in full precision is then cast into lower precision. In such cases, it is a common strategy to fine tune the quantised model for a few epochs to recover the loss in performance [19]. However, when a model is trained from the outset in low-precision modes, they can achieve similar performances to models with full precision weights [26].

3   Data and Experiments

Nation-wide screening for early detection of cancer is being attempted in many countries. For instance, early breast cancer detection using mammography screening has shown positive impact, both for the subjects and in allocating healthcare resources [8]. To simulate a scenario where ML models are deployed in such screening programs, we use a publicly available mammography screening dataset for the task of recommending follow-up scans. We study the influence of using resource optimised models and their impact on the predictions in the mammography screening.

Datasets: The experiments in this work were primarily performed using a subset of the data available as part of the Radiological Society of North America (RSNA) Mammography Breast Cancer Detection challenge [7][1]. Subjects under the age of 55 yr in the training set were used as the cohort of interest for early detection. This yielded a dataset comprising 3199 unique subjects. As each subject has multiple scans (also from different views), the final dataset consists of 11856 mammography scans. While the dataset provides multiple markers which

---

[1] https://www.kaggle.com/competitions/rsna-breast-cancer-detection/overview. Accessed on 08/03/2023.

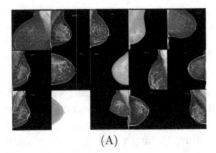 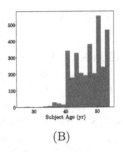

(A)   (B)

Fig. 1. (A): Sample mammography images from the RSNA training set showing the diverse acquisition and anatomical variations. (B): Age distribution of the subjects in the dataset used. Maximum age of 55 yr was used.

could be used as labels, we focus on the BI-RADS[2] score [20]. The dataset provides three grades of the BI-RADS score: 0 if the breast required follow-up, 1 if the breast was rated as negative for cancer, and 2 if the breast was rated as normal. We combine the classes 1 and 2 to make a binary classification task of predicting if a follow-up scan was required or not. This resulted in the following label distribution: [7903, 3953], corresponding to requiring follow-up (class-1) and no follow-up (class-0). The dataset was randomly split into training, validation and test sets based on subject identities. This resulted in a split of [1919,640,640] subjects in the three sets, respectively. In terms of mammography images, the resulting split was [7113,2371,2372] for the training, validation and test sets. Sample images from the dataset and the age distribution of the subjects is shown in Fig. 1. We acknowledge that this classification task is a simplification of the mammography reading done during screening, but depending on the screening setup (e.g. number of readers), even this simple task could supplement the workflow.

Additional experiments on a second dataset for lung nodule detection are also reported for further validation. We use the LIDC-IDRI dataset which consists of 1018 thoracic CT scans and predict the presence or absence of tumours [2]. Further details of the LIDC classification dataset are provided in the Supplementary Material.

Classification Models: To evaluate the impact of resource constraints, different classes of deep learning models are used. Specifically, we use Densenet [14], Efficientnet [28], Vision transformer [11] and Swin Transformer [17]. All models were pretrained on ImageNet and fine tuned on the two datasets[3].

Experimental Design: All the models were trained for a maximum of 50 epochs, with an early stopping patience of 5 epochs using batch size of 32. All the experiments were performed on a desktop workstation with Intel i7 processor, 32GB memory and Nvidia RTX 3090 GPU with 24 GB memory. All experiments

---

[2] BI-RADS:Breast Imaging Reporting & Data System.

[3] Pretrained weights for the models were obtained from https://timm.fast.ai/.

were performed in Pytorch (v1.7.1) [21], and unless otherwise specified using the Adam [16] optimizer with learning rate of 10^{-5}. Measurements of run time, energy and carbon consumption were performed using CarbonTracker [1]. All models were trained three times with different random seeds. The training of models in this work used 25.0 kWh of electricity contributing to 4.7 kg of CO2eq.

Experiments: Resource constraints in real world scenarios could be due to: compute time (corresponding to low latency), specialized hardware (access to GPU infrastructure) and energy consumption (if models are deployed on portable devices). Using these and the test set performance as the axes, we run all the classification models with- and without- any resource optimisation. The three main optimisation techniques we use are related to the methods described in Sect. 2. Firstly, we perform automatic mixed precision training of the models in order to obtain low compute and memory models [18]. This is implemented using the `automatic mixed precision` (AMP) feature in Pytorch. Secondly, we minimize the resource utilisation of the optimizer using an `8-bit optimiser` based on the implementation[4] from [10]. Finally, we also investigate training of a low precision model by casting all the model weights to `half precision` (float-16). We then compare the performance of all the classification models without any explicit resource optimisation and with the combination of the mixed precision training/half-precision models and the 8-bit optimiser. Note that AMP cannot be combined with Half Precision models, as the model itself is in low precision. We use binary accuracy on the test set (P_T), average training time to convergence (T_c), maximum GPU memory required, average inference time on test set (T) and the total energy consumption (E) as the measures to compare the models and different resource efficiency techniques.

Results: Experiments with the various resource optimisation settings and methods for both datasets are reported comprehensively in Table 1. For each method, five settings are reported. We treat the model with no additional resource optimisation as the *baseline*, reported in the first row for each method. For each model, we then report the following settings: [AMP, 8bit optimizer, AMP+ 8bit optimizer, Half precision + 8bit optimiser] yielding five settings for each model. The models are sorted based on the total number of trainable parameters, reported in the third column.

At the outset, it is worth noting that the baseline model performance on the test set of all Densenet and the transformer-based Swin- and Vision- Transformers are comparable (≈ 0.74) in the RSNA mammography dataset.

The use of AMP during training does not degrade the performance of any of the models, while reducing the maximum GPU memory utilised (up to 50% in most cases). The run time, T_c for all the models is also decreased when using AMP.

The use of 8-bit optimiser reduces the GPU memory utilised and the convergence time. The more interesting observation is that in almost all cases (except ViT), it also converges to a better solution, yielding a small perfor-

---

[4] 8-bit optimiser from bitsandbytes.

Table 1. Quantitative comparison of the different classification methods reported over three random initialisations for RSNA and LIDC datasets. The use of 8-bit optimizer (8bit), automatic mixed precision (AMP), and half precision model (Half) are marked. Number of parameters: $|\mathbf{W}|$, mean accuracy with standard deviation over three seeds, average GPU memory required (in GB), average inference time, and average energy consumption of different settings reported when predicting on test set. Models that diverged at least during one of the random initialisations are marked with * in P_T column.

Dataset	Method	$|\mathbf{W}|$(M)	8bit	AMP	Half	P_T	GPU	T_c(s)	T(s)	E(Wh)
RSNA [7]	Densenet [14]	6.9	✗	✗	✗	0.738 ± 0.005	6.6	361.3	2.7	104.2
			✗	✓	✗	0.740 ± 0.005	3.3	296.0	2.7	59.2
			✓	✗	✗	0.743 ± 0.003	6.5	240.0	2.7	58.1
			✓	✗	✓	**0.745 ± 0.004**	**3.2**	**170.3**	**2.1**	34.6
			✓	✓	✗	**0.744 ± 0.006**	3.2	191.3	2.7	42.3
	Swin Trans. [17]	86.9	✗	✗	✗	0.739 ± 0.008	15.3	617.6	7.5	100.1
			✗	✓	✗	0.735 ± 0.006	10.7	497.0	7.5	109.8
			✓	✗	✗	0.739 ± 0.012	14.3	732.3	7.5	86.1
			✓	✗	✓	0.733 ± 0.013	7.5	316.0	4.3	118.5
			✓	✓	✗	0.712 ± 0.01*	9.7	588.6	7.5	95.8
	ViT [11]	116.7	✗	✗	✗	0.728 ± 0.001	5.6	322.3	1.9	52.0
			✗	✓	✗	0.728 ± 0.006	5.6	249.0	1.9	39.8
			✓	✗	✗	0.716 ± 0.009	4.1	497.0	1.9	81.0
			✓	✗	✓	0.690 ± 0.02*	3.5	69.6	1.0	10.7
			✓	✓	✗	0.665 ± 0.02*	4.7	132.6	1.9	21.0
LIDC [2]	Densenet [14]	6.9	✗	✗	✗	0.656 ± 0.005	6.6	674.3	3.4	104.2
			✗	✓	✗	0.655 ± 0.010	3.3	425.7	3.4	59.2
			✓	✗	✗	0.677 ± 0.008	6.5	370.7	3.4	58.1
			✓	✗	✓	0.675 ± 0.007	**3.2**	**234.3**	2.7	34.6
			✓	✓	✗	0.676 ± 0.005	3.2	291.3	2.7	42.3
	Swin Trans. [17]	86.9	✗	✗	✗	0.697 ± 0.018	15.3	678.7	9.6	109.8
			✗	✓	✗	0.696 ± 0.018	10.8	544.0	9.6	86.1
			✓	✗	✗	0.684 ± 0.016	14.4	727.3	9.6	118.5
			✓	✗	✓	**0.704 ± 0.007**	9.9	401.0	5.6	64.1
			✓	✓	✗	0.684 ± 0.020	7.5	615.3	9.6	99.9
	ViT [11]	116.7	✗	✗	✗	0.610 ± 0.041	5.6	231.7	2.4	37.2
			✗	✓	✗	0.608 ± 0.043	5.5	166.3	2.4	25.8
			✓	✗	✗	0.636 ± 0.012	4.3	415.3	2.4	67.1
			✓	✗	✓	0.564 ± 0.072	3.4	123.0	**1.3**	15.2
			✓	✓	✗	0.561 ± 0.076	4.5	99.0	2.4	19.1

mance improvement. This is consistent with the observations reported in [10], where this behaviour is attributed to the elimination of outliers (which otherwise could lead to exploding gradients) during quantisation and dequantisation of the optimiser states.

Setting the model weights to half precision (16-bit instead of 32-bit) immediately gives a reduction in the GPU memory utilisation. In our experiments, however, there were stability issues when the half precision model was trained using

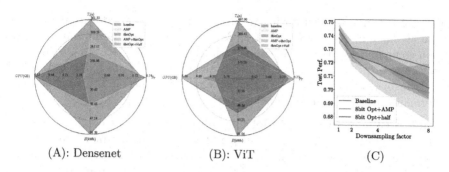

Fig. 2. (A & B): Radar plots showing the mean metrics for performance (P_T, E, GPU, T) reported in Table 1 for the five settings, shown for Densenet [14] and Vision transformer [11]. (C): Influence of different scales of downsampling on the test performance for three configurations of Densenet models on the RSNA dataset. For each, the mean and the standard deviation of the three runs is shown as the curve and the shaded area, respectively.

the standard Adam optimiser. Using the 8-bit optimiser which is quantisation-aware helped convergence [10].

The best performing configuration across all the models for RSNA dataset is the Densenet with 8-bit optimiser either when used with AMP or the half precision model. This is an interesting result showing that these techniques not only reduce resource utilisation but could also improve model convergence.

The observations about the influence of AMP, 8-bit optimiser and half-precision hold within each model category for the LIDC dataset. The best performing configuration across all the models for LIDC dataset is the Swin Transformer with 8-bit optimiser when used with the half precision model.

The performance trends in Table 1 are captured visually in the radar plots presented in Fig. 2-A for Densenet. The mean performance measures of Densenet over the three random initialisations, for the five settings, are shown in different colours. The four axes are used to report four key measures:$[P_T, E, \text{GPU}, T]$. The optimal model would have larger footprint along P_T and smaller values on the other axes. We notice that the baseline model (in blue) spans a larger region over all axes, wheres the half precision model trained with 8-bit optimiser (in red) has smaller span. These trends are also visualised for the Vision transformer model in Fig. 2-B, and for other models in the Supplementary Material.

4   Discussion

Data Quality: One common method to manage the resource constraints during training or inference of deep learning models is the use of reduced quality data. For instance, in image analysis, downsampling of images is a commonly used strategy as this can have a direct impact on the size of the models. Such reduction in data quality are undoubtedly lossy. We illustrate this for the mammography screening task for the Densenet models in Fig. 2-C. We reduce the quality of the images both during training and inference by downsampling the image at different scales: $S = [2, 4, 8]$. We observe a clear performance degradation compared to the models trained with full resolution ($S = 1$). While this might be unsurprising, we argue, in lieu of the results in Table 1 that optimising models instead of degrading data quality can offer a better trade-off between performance and resource efficiency.

Resource Efficiency and Model Complexity: The most common measure of model complexity is the number of parameters. The experiments and results reported in Table 1 reveal slightly surprising trends. The best performing model for the RSNA dataset (Densenet) had the fewest number of parameters (6.9M), and ViT which was the largest model (116.7M) was also the fastest at inference time (<2 s). This is due to the fact that during training the resource overhead for deep learning models is due to factors other than model weights, such as the optimiser states or other derived data like gradients/activation maps as discussed in Sect. 2. We have demonstrated that resource efficiency can also be achieved by optimising these other axes.

Resource Efficiency of Vision Transformers: The use of AMP or 8-bit optimiser settings degrades the performance of both the transformer-based models to some extent in both datasets. This is in contrast to the CNN models, where there is no large performance degradation. One reason for the degradation in performance in transformers when using the 8-bit optimiser could be instability during training. The authors in [10] suggest the use of a `stable embedding` layer when training transformers for NLP tasks. For a fairer comparison with the CNN models, we do not use the stable embedding layer for the two transformer models. Our experiments indicate that CNN models could be less sensitive when compared to transformer-based models in low/mixed precision or quantised settings.

QALY-Like Metrics: Quality Adjusted Life Year (QALY) is a utilitarian index used to estimate the cost-effectiveness of a health treatment; it attempts to arithmetically relate quality and quantity of life [22]. In our experiments, we did not notice degradation in performance for some of the model classes. However, when there is a drop in performance, the tolerance levels in clinical settings would require formulating a Pareto optimisation of performance and resources [9]. It is in this context that a metric similar to QALY could be useful, when balancing resource constraints with critical performance guarantees.

Limitations: This work focused on optimising resource efficiency using only a few of the techniques (mixed precision training, half precision models, 8-bit optimisers). There are several other methods which could further optimise the resource consumption. For instance, formulating model selection that can yield inherently efficient models within neural architecture search (NAS) framework could be a possibility. However, performing NAS in itself is prohibitively expensive [12]. The other main limitation of the work is the gap in validating these methods in actual, resource constrained setting which the authors did not have access to. Testing these resource optimisation measures in diverse settings such as on different edge devices, for instance, could be an interesting direction for future work.

5 Conclusion

Large deep learning models are advancing medical image analysis and will undoubtedly accelerate clinical workflows. For these models to make the most impact, globally, resource efficiency is an important factor. In this work, we have evaluated a subset of resource optimisation methods that can reduce memory consumption, latency, and energy consumption, without any performance degradation (Densenet in RSNA, Swin Trans. in LIDC). In contrast to our initial hypothesis, surprisingly, there is no performance degradation across the board; only systematic ones (like with Transformers which can be handled). This prompts us to recommend these resource optimisation methods to be part of the standard procedures when developing and deploying deep learning methods.

Acknowledgments. The authors would like to thank Christian Igel (UCPH) and Lee Lassen (Ambu A/S) for fruitful discussions, and Pedram Bakhtiarifard (UCPH) for their public repository for making radar plots. RS and JS are partly funded by European Union's HorizonEurope research and innovation programme under grant agreements No. 101070284 and No. 101070408.

References

1. Anthony, L.F.W., Kanding, B., Selvan, R.: Carbontracker: tracking and predicting the carbon footprint of training deep learning models. In: ICML Workshop on Challenges in Deploying and Monitoring Machine Learning Systems (2020). arXiv:2007.03051
2. Armato, S.G., III., et al.: Lung image database consortium: developing a resource for the medical imaging research community. Radiology **232**(3), 739–748 (2004)
3. Bartoldson, B.R., Kailkhura, B., Blalock, D.: Compute-Efficient Deep Learning: Algorithmic Trends and Opportunities. arXiv preprint arXiv:2210.06640 (2022)
4. Baweja, C., Glocker, B., Kamnitsas, K.: Towards continual learning in medical imaging. In: Workshop on Medical Imaging meets NeurIPS (2018). arXiv:1811.02496
5. Chakrabarti, A., Moseley, B.: Backprop with approximate activations for memory-efficient network training. In: Advances in Neural Information Processing Systems, vol. 32 (2019)
6. Cheng, Y., Wang, D., Zhou, P., Zhang, T.: Model compression and acceleration for deep neural networks: the principles, progress, and challenges. IEEE Signal Process. Mag. **35**(1), 126–136 (2018)
7. Carr, C., et al.: RSNA screening mammography breast cancer detection (2022). https://kaggle.com/competitions/rsna-breast-cancer-detection
8. Daysal, N.M., Mullainathan, S., Obermeyer, Z., Sarkar, S.K., Trandafir, M.: An economic approach to machine learning in health policy. University of Copenhagen, Department of Economics Discussion, CEBI Working Paper (24) (2022)

9. Deb, K.: Multi-objective optimisation using evolutionary algorithms: an introduction. In: Wang, L., Ng, A., Deb, K. (eds.) Multi-objective Evolutionary Optimisation for Product Design and Manufacturing, pp. 3–34. Springer, London (2011). https://doi.org/10.1007/978-0-85729-652-8_1

10. Dettmers, T., Lewis, M., Shleifer, S., Zettlemoyer, L.: 8-bit optimizers via blockwise quantization. In: International Conference on Learning Representations (2022). https://openreview.net/forum?id=shpkpVXzo3h

11. Dosovitskiy, A., et al.: An image is worth 16x16 words: transformers for image recognition at scale. In: International Conference on Learning Representations (2020)

12. Elsken, T., Metzen, J.H., Hutter, F.: Neural architecture search: a survey. J. Mach. Learn. Res. 20(1), 1997–2017 (2019)

13. Fiesler, E., Choudry, A., Caulfield, H.J.: Weight discretization paradigm for optical neural networks. In: Optical Interconnections and Networks, vol. 1281, pp. 164–173. SPIE (1990)

14. Huang, G., Liu, Z., Van Der Maaten, L., Weinberger, K.Q.: Densely connected convolutional networks. In: Proceedings of the IEEE Conference on Computer Vision and Pattern Recognition, pp. 4700–4708 (2017)

15. Hubara, I., Courbariaux, M., Soudry, D., El-Yaniv, R., Bengio, Y.: Quantized neural networks: training neural networks with low precision weights and activations. J. Mach. Learn. Res. 18(1), 6869–6898 (2017)

16. Kingma, D., Ba, J.: Adam optimizer, pp. 1–15. arXiv preprint arXiv:1412.6980 (2014)

17. Liu, Z., et al.: Swin transformer: hierarchical vision transformer using shifted windows. In: Proceedings of the IEEE/CVF International Conference on Computer Vision, pp. 10012–10022 (2021)

18. Micikevicius, P., et al.: Mixed precision training. In: International Conference on Learning Representations (2018). https://openreview.net/forum?id=r1gs9JgRZ

19. Nagel, M., Fournarakis, M., Amjad, R.A., Bondarenko, Y., Van Baalen, M., Blankevoort, T.: A white paper on neural network quantization. arXiv preprint arXiv:2106.08295 (2021)

20. Orel, S.G., Kay, N., Reynolds, C., Sullivan, D.C.: BI-RADS categorization as a predictor of malignancy. Radiology 211(3), 845–850 (1999)

21. Paszke, A., et al.: Pytorch: an imperative style, high-performance deep learning library. In: Advances in Neural Information Processing Systems, pp. 8024–8035 (2019)

22. Prieto, L., Sacristán, J.A.: Problems and solutions in calculating quality-adjusted life years (QALYs). Health Qual. Life Outcomes 1, 1–8 (2003)

23. Ricci Lara, M.A., Echeveste, R., Ferrante, E.: Addressing fairness in artificial intelligence for medical imaging. Nat. Commun. 13(1), 4581 (2022)

24. Selvan, R., Bhagwat, N., Wolff Anthony, L.F., Kanding, B., Dam, E.B.: Carbon footprint of selecting and training deep learning models for medical image analysis. In: Wang, L., Dou, Q., Fletcher, P.T., Speidel, S., Li, S. (eds.) MICCAI 2022, Part V. LNCS, vol. 13435, pp. 506–516. Springer, Cham (2022). https://doi.org/10.1007/978-3-031-16443-9_49

25. Sevilla, J., Heim, L., Ho, A., Besiroglu, T., Hobbhahn, M., Villalobos, P.: Compute trends across three eras of machine learning. arXiv preprint arXiv:2202.05924 (2022)

26. Sun, X., et al.: Ultra-low precision 4-bit training of deep neural networks. Adv. Neural. Inf. Process. Syst. 33, 1796–1807 (2020)

27. Sze, V., Chen, Y.H., Yang, T.J., Emer, J.S.: Efficient processing of deep neural networks: a tutorial and survey. Proc. IEEE **105**(12), 2295–2329 (2017)
28. Tan, M., Le, Q.: Efficientnet: rethinking model scaling for convolutional neural networks. In: International Conference on Machine Learning, pp. 6105–6114 (2019)
29. United-Nations: Sustainable development goals report (2022)
30. Vokinger, K.N., Feuerriegel, S., Kesselheim, A.S.: Continual learning in medical devices: FDA's action plan and beyond. Lancet Digit. Health **3**(6), e337–e338 (2021)
31. Yu, K.H., Beam, A.L., Kohane, I.S.: Artificial intelligence in healthcare. Nat. Biomed. Eng. **2**(10), 719–731 (2018)

Data Efficiency of Segment Anything Model for Optic Disc and Cup Segmentation

Fabian Yii[1,2]($\boxtimes$) (iD), Tom MacGillivray[1,2], and Miguel O. Bernabeu[3,4]

[1] Centre for Clinical Brain Sciences, The University of Edinburgh, Edinburgh, UK
fabian.yii@ed.ac.uk
[2] Curle Ophthalmology Laboratory, The University of Edinburgh, Edinburgh, UK
[3] Centre for Medical Informatics, Usher Institute, The University of Edinburgh, Edinburgh, UK
[4] The Bayes Centre, The University of Edinburgh, Edinburgh, UK

Abstract. We investigated the performance of Segment Anything Model (SAM)—the first promptable foundation model for image segmentation—for optic disc (OD) and optic cup (OC) segmentation when fine-tuned on progressively smaller number of fundus images. Three different implementations of SAM with an input prompt were considered: (1) SAM with an OD/OC-centred bounding box (*SAM GT*); (2) SAM with a noise-added (e.g. displacement, size variation) bounding box (*SAM Noise*); and (3) SAM with an automatically predicted (using Faster R-CNN) bounding box (*SAM Auto*). Two popular pre-trained semantic segmentation models, DeepLabV3 with a MobileNetV3-Large backbone and DeepLabV3 with a ResNet-50 backbone were used as baseline models. For OD segmentation, ResNet-50 exhibited comparable if not higher data efficiency (i.e. good performance despite limited training data) than even the most optimal implementation of SAM (*SAM GT*), although SAM was evidently more robust to small training set sizes, e.g. 25, than MobileNetV3-Large and in eyes with more challenging OD morphologies, e.g. significant peri-papillary atrophy. For OC segmentation, however, SAM GT and SAM Noise consistently demonstrated higher data efficiency, particularly in eyes with relatively small cup-to-disc ratio and ill-defined OC margin.

Keywords: Segment Anything Model · Optic Disc · Optic Cup

1 Background

Foundation models are changing the landscape of artificial intelligence [2]. Trained on enormous quantities of data on a scale hitherto unimaginable, these models, with such prominent examples as BERT and GPT-3, are designed to be adaptable/transferrable to a wide range of downstream tasks [2]. In computer vision, the recently introduced Segment Anything Model (SAM) has stirred interest as the first foundation model for image segmentation [9]. SAM was trained on more than 1 billion masks and 11 million

Fabian SL Yii is supported by the Medical Research Council [grant number MR/N013166/1]. This research was conducted in part using data from UK Biobank under project ID 90655.

Supplementary Information The online version contains supplementary material available at https://doi.org/10.1007/978-3-031-47425-5_30.

predominantly non-medical images. This, coupled with its ability to take input prompts including bounding boxes and foreground/background points, gives it tremendous zero-shot capabilities on diverse segmentation tasks involving natural images.

However, several preprints [6, 7, 15, 27] have shown that SAM's zero-shot performance is unsatisfactory when applied to medical imaging modalities including chest X-ray (lungs), MRI (hippocampus), ultrasound (breast tumour and nerve), colonoscopy (polyps) and whole slide imaging (renal tissue), although it performs well on hip X-ray and spleen CT [15]. Furthermore, SAM does not have good zero-shot performance for optic disc (OD), optic cup (OC) and retinal vessel segmentation when applied to fundus photographs [18, 19]. Despite these unfavourable results, simple fine-tuning has been shown to be highly effective in improving SAM's performance to levels comparable to, if not better than, the state-of-the-art medical image segmentation models [14, 25].

The ability to transfer SAM to the medical domain is a promising prospect, not least because its promptable nature allows for a "human in the loop", enabling greater trust to be fostered between clinicians and the system [17]. SAM's prompt engineering may also give it an extra edge over conventional pre-trained models in terms of data efficiency (i.e. robustness to limited training data), since its ability to query prior knowledge from domain experts may enable it to work with more limited or less diverse training data. To the best of our knowledge, though, no work has empirically investigated whether SAM offers any added value in terms of data efficiency in the medical domain. Here, we evaluated SAM's robustness to limited training data, with a specific focus on OD and OC segmentation due to the importance of these features for glaucoma (an eye disease associated with increased cup-to-disc ratio) assessment, not to mention that manual segmentation is labour intensive and annotated data from particular populations at risk of glaucoma, e.g. persons of African [1] and Latin American [23] descent, are extremely scarce.

Our main contributions are: (1) fine-tuning SAM's lightweight mask decoder is a highly effective transfer learning approach, as it yields competitive OD and OC segmentation performance; (2) fine-tuned SAM is *not* necessarily more data efficient than a pre-trained DeepLabV3 model with a ResNet-50 backbone insofar as OD segmentation is concerned, but it is evidently more data efficient when it comes to OC segmentation; and (3) SAM is more robust to challenging OD or OC morphologies.

2 Methods

2.1 Datasets

374 macula-centred colour fundus photographs (2048 × 1536 pixels) from the UK Biobank (UKB) were randomly sampled from a total of 117,175 participants (predominantly White British) who took part in a baseline ophthalmic assessment [5]. An annotator (F.Y) manually segmented the OD in each image using the Image Segmenter app in MATLAB, which allowed regions of interest to be drawn interactively using waypoints. OD margin was defined as the inner margin of the Elschnig's scleral ring per the conventional ophthalmoscopic definition. A random subset (N = 50) of images were re-annotated at least 1 week after the first annotation to assess the intra-rater agreement (Dice score: 96.4%). OC segmentation was not carried out due to time constraints.

Two other publicly available datasets, namely DRISHTI-GS [20] and PAPILA [10], were also used in this work. DRISHTI-GS contains 101 OD-centred colour fundus photographs (2896×1944 pixels) taken from patients at Aravind Eye Hospital in India. Most eyes ($N = 70$) in this dataset have glaucoma. PAPILA, on the other hand, consists of 488 OD-centred colour fundus photographs (2576×1934 pixels) taken from predominantly non-glaucomatous patients ($N = 333$) seen at an ophthalmology department in Spain. Ground-truth OD and OC masks were available from both datasets.

2.2 Experiments

UK Biobank images were first cropped to 1400×1400 pixels to remove the black border around each image, before being resized to 560×560 pixels. Images from DRISHTI-GS and PAPILA were resized to 523×613 pixels and 580×772 pixels, respectively. UK Biobank images were split into 299 training images and 75 test images, whereas 50 and 51 DRISHTI-GS images were used for training and testing per the original train/test split prescribed by the data provider [20]. The first 300 PAPILA images were used as training images, leaving 188 images for testing. In each experiment, different implementations of SAM and two baseline models were fine-tuned and tested using a pre-defined number of training images from one of the 3 datasets above. Training set size was progressively reduced after each experiment, i.e. each time choosing the first N images in the training set, down to a minimum of 25.

Implementations
We considered three different implementations of SAM at inference:

(1) **SAM GT**: SAM with an OD/OC-centred, tight-fitting bounding box manually given as input prompt to simulate the most ideal (noise-free) user scenario.
(2) **SAM Noise**: SAM with noise added to the ground truth bounding box. Noise refers to random addition of up to 10 pixels to each point coordinate of the box, resulting in displacement, size variation and orientation variation.
(3) **SAM Auto**: SAM with an automatically predicted bounding box given as input prompt. The bounding box was predicted using Faster R-CNN (with a ResNet-50-FPN backbone) [11] pre-trained on the COCO dataset [12]. In each experiment, Faster R-CNN was fine-tuned for 10 epochs using a batch size of 10. ADAM optimizer (initial learning rate: 5e-4; weight decay: 1e-2) with a cosine annealing scheduler was used. Data augmentation including random changes of brightness/saturation, horizontal flip and rotation up to $\pm 60°$ was applied on the fly. The model at the last epoch was used at inference. Note that similar training set size was used to fine-tune Faster R-CCN and SAM in each experiment.

Two popular semantic segmentation models, DeepLabV3 [3] with a MobileNetV3-Large backbone and DeepLabV3 with a ResNet-50 backbone (hereafter known as MobileNet and ResNet-50), both pre-trained on the COCO dataset [12], were used as baseline models. The official PyTorch implementations of these models were used in this work. All experiments were conducted using a NVIDIA RTX A5000 24GB GPU.

Training Details

The mask decoder of SAM with the smallest (91M parameters) backbone size (ViT-B image encoder) was fine-tuned due to its lightweight nature. Empirical evidence also indicates that the smallest model is more computationally efficient, as the largest backbone (ViT-H) is slowest at inference and does not have significantly better performance [8]. Noise-added bounding boxes were used as input prompts during training to improve SAM's robustness at inference. Unless otherwise stated, the following training details and hyperparameter settings were consistently applied. Five-fold cross validation was used for hyperparameter tuning and model selection, i.e. model with the lowest validation loss used at inference. Each model was trained for 10 epochs (for each fold) using a batch size of 15, except when fine-tuning ResNet-50 on PAPILA where a batch size of 12 was used (maximum possible size permitted by the GPU memory). ADAM optimizer (initial learning rate: 5e-4; weight decay: 1e-4) was used with a cosine annealing scheduler. Binary cross-entropy loss was used as the loss function, weighting the foreground (OD or OC) pixels by the median ratio of background to foreground pixels due to significant class imbalance. Data augmentation including random changes of brightness/saturation, horizontal flip and rotation up to $\pm 60°$ was applied on the fly.

Evaluation Metrics

Average Precision (AP), commonly used to summarise a precision-recall curve, was adopted as the primary performance metric because it is not contingent upon an arbitrary binary threshold:

$$AP = \sum_n (R_n - R_{n-1})P_n \tag{1}$$

where R_n and P_n denotes recall and precision at the nth threshold. We also computed the Dice score to facilitate comparison with other studies, using 0.95 as the binary threshold (based on the observation that this gave the most clinically accurate binary masks on average):

$$Dice = \frac{2xTP}{(TP + FP) + (TP + FN)} \tag{2}$$

where TP, FP and FN denote true positives, false positives and false negatives. Unless otherwise stated, all results were summarised as mean $\pm$ standard deviation.

3 Results

3.1 OD Segmentation

As shown in Table 1 and Fig. 1, ResNet-50 almost invariably demonstrated higher data efficiency than even the most optimal implementation of SAM, i.e. SAM GT. For example, while the AP achieved by ResNet-50 remained largely unchanged on the UKB test set (around 90%) when the training set size was reduced from 299 to 50, an appreciable reduction in SAM GT's AP, i.e. from 90% to 86%, was observed with a similar reduction in training set size. The AP achieved by ResNet-50 was also

Table 1. Optic disc segmentation: mean test performance (standard deviation in parentheses) of different implementations of SAM and two DeepLabV3 baseline models (one with a MobileNet backbone, B1, and another with a ResNet-50 backbone, B2) across training set sizes (N). Best test performance is highlighted in maroon and bold (note that in the printed version this is only highlighted in bold).

Dataset	N	Average Precision (%)					Dice (%)				
		SAM GT	SAM noise	SAM Auto	B1	B2	SAM GT	SAM noise	SAM Auto	B1	B2
UKB	299	90.2 (3.5)	82.3 (6.0)	88.1 (6.1)	**91.1 (4.1)**	90.0 (4.4)	94.8 (1.9)	90.4 (3.5)	93.6 (3.7)	**95.3 (2.3)**	94.7 (2.5)
	200	89.3 (3.8)	82.1 (6.8)	87.3 (5.5)	89.4 (4.6)	**90.7 (4.2)**	94.3 (2.1)	90.3 (3.9)	93.2 (3.2)	94.4 (2.6)	**95.1 (2.3)**
	100	88.2 (4.3)	80.2 (6.7)	83.9 (11.8)	85.1 (7.5)	**90.0 (4.4)**	93.7 (2.4)	89.1 (4.1)	90.6 (11.4)	91.8 (4.7)	**94.7 (2.5)**
	50	86.2 (4.7)	80.3 (5.9)	84.5 (7.7)	78.4 (15.6)	**89.7 (6.1)**	92.6 (2.7)	89.2 (3.6)	91.5 (4.8)	86.6 (15.6)	**94.5 (3.6)**
	25	82.5 (4.6)	77.1 (7.2)	79.3 (7.4)	68.2 (14.9)	**86.7 (7.7)**	90.6 (2.7)	87.3 (4.3)	88.5 (4.6)	79.9 (15.0)	**92.8 (4.7)**
DRISHTI-GS	50	92.3 (3.3)	91.3 (3.5)	91.4 (4.3)	89.0 (7.0)	**95.3 (2.4)**	95.9 (1.9)	95.3 (2.0)	95.4 (2.5)	93.9 (4.4)	**97.5 (1.3)**
	25	90.9 (9.1)	88.7 (9.3)	88.3 (14.7)	87.0 (5.8)	**93.0 (3.3)**	94.8 (7.5)	93.5 (7.8)	92.5 (14.6)	92.9 (3.4)	**96.3 (1.8)**
PAPILA	300	93.2 (2.4)	89.9 (3.4)	89.8 (3.3)	92.3 (3.6)	**93.1 (3.5)**	**96.4 (1.3)**	94.6 (1.9)	94.6 (1.8)	95.9 (2.0)	**96.4 (1.9)**
	150	92.2 (2.6)	89.1 (3.4)	88.8 (3.6)	90.6 (4.6)	**93.1 (3.2)**	95.8 (1.4)	94.2 (1.9)	94.0 (2.0)	95.0 (2.6)	**96.3 (1.8)**
	50	**91.8 (3.1)**	87.9 (4.2)	87.7 (4.2)	85.0 (11.3)	90.5 (4.7)	**95.7 (1.7)**	93.5 (2.4)	93.4 (2.4)	91.3 (10.5)	94.9 (2.6)
	25	**90.9 (3.3)**	88.0 (3.8)	88.1 (3.9)	76.4 (10.3)	89.9 (5.2)	**95.2 (1.8)**	93.6 (2.1)	93.6 (2.2)	86.2 (7.8)	94.6 (3.0)

noticeably higher than SAM GT, e.g. 93.0% vs 90.9% when the training set size was equal to 25, on the DRISHTI-GS test set. That said, a qualitative assessment of the predicted masks (some examples shown in the top panel of Fig. 2) suggested that SAM was more robust to challenging (also more unusual) OD morphologies, such as when the margin was ill-defined due to significant peripapillary atrophy, which could be seen as irregular pigmentation/brightness in the area adjacent to OD in the presence of high myopia (second image of the UKB image pair in Fig. 2). However, this was contingent upon good bounding box placement, a point best illustrated by the fact that the reduction in SAM Auto's performance when the training set size was decreased (irrespective of dataset) could be attributed to a drastic drop in Faster R-CNN's performance when there was limited training data (Supplementary S1).

3.2 OC Segmentation

SAM GT/Noise consistently yielded superior performance on the DRISHTI-GS test set, with the gain being most evident when the training set size was reduced to 25 (Table 2 and Fig. 2). On the PAPILA test set, SAM (irrespective of implementation type) demonstrated disproportionately better performance than the baseline models. Of note, significant discrepancies in model performance were observed between datasets. On the DRISHTI-GS test set, for instance, where 50 training images would suffice to yield a high AP of 88.1% using SAM GT, a similar level of performance on the PAPILA test set

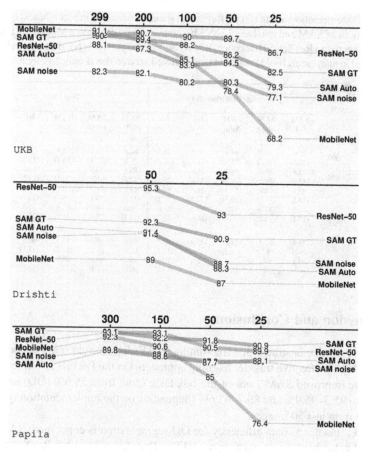

Fig. 1. Optic disc segmentation: mean average precision (%) by training set size and dataset.

was far from evident even with 300 training images (AP equal to 72.8%). In keeping with this, Moris et al. [16] also observed that their best model yielded significantly poorer performance on the PAPILA test set than DRISHTI-GS (more than 20% difference in median Dice score) and other test sets (Fig. 2 in their paper). These discrepancies are attributable to the fact that a higher proportion of eyes in the DRISHTI-GS dataset have a large cup-to-disc ratio (large OC relative to OD) due to glaucoma, giving rise to a "deeper" cup appearance and more defined OC margin. A qualitative assessment of the predicted masks (some examples shown in the bottom panel of Fig. 1) also revealed that small cup-to-disc ratio—commonly found in PAPILA—was generally detrimental to segmentation quality, although SAM (irrespective of implementation type) was more robust to such cases (i.e. PAPILA images) than the baseline models (Fig. 3).

Table 2. OC segmentation: mean test performance (standard deviation in parentheses) of different implementations of SAM and two DeepLabV3 baseline models (one with a MobileNet backbone, B1, and another with a ResNet-50 backbone, B2) across training set sizes (N). Best test performance is highlighted in maroon and bold (note that in the printed version this is only highlighted in bold).

Dataset	N	Average Precision (%)					Dice (%)				
		SAM GT	SAM noise	SAM Auto	B1	B2	SAM GT	SAM noise	SAM Auto	B1	B2
PAPILA	300	72.8 (10.7)	60.4 (18.3)	61.4 (17.9)	56.2 (21.1)	56.2 (22.1)	84.0 (7.3)	74.7 (16.4)	75.7 (15.1)	70.3 (19.0)	69.9 (20.1)
	150	72.8 (13.1)	58.0 (20.0)	58.7 (20.2)	51.0 (24.2)	54.1 (23.8)	83.5 (12.5)	72.5 (19.1)	72.6 (20.7)	64.9 (23.7)	67.8 (22.3)
	50	69.7 (13.3)	57.4 (19.7)	57.3 (19.3)	31.4 (20.5)	40.1 (26.1)	81.5 (12.0)	71.7 (19.7)	72.1 (18.7)	44.8 (23.3)	52.6 (28.8)
	25	60.7 (17.2)	51.9 (21.0)	52.9 (20.6)	22.2 (16.6)	29.6 (20.2)	74.0 (17.2)	66.6 (21.9)	67.5 (21.6)	33.9 (20.0)	42.2 (23.7)
DRISHTI-GS	50	88.1 (5.7)	82.4 (9.1)	78.2 (16.1)	75.9 (15.4)	82.5 (12.1)	93.6 (3.4)	90.3 (5.9)	86.7 (12.2)	85.5 (11.1)	90.1 (7.7)
	25	84.4 (9.7)	82.0 (10.1)	77.1 (16.8)	72.3 (17.0)	79.3 (15.3)	91.2 (6.4)	89.9 (6.4)	85.9 (12.9)	82.7 (13.1)	87.5 (11.5)

4 Discussion and Conclusions

In this work, we demonstrated that fine-tuning SAM's lightweight mask decoder was a simple yet highly effective transfer learning approach. On the DRISHTI-GS test set, for instance, we improved SAM's out-of-the-box Dice score from 55.6% (OD) and 57.1% (OC) [19] to 95.3–95.9% and 86.7–93.6% (depending on the implementation type) after fine-tuning it on just 50 images.

However, insofar as data efficiency for OD segmentation is concerned, SAM offers little added value because an existing model like DeepLabV3 (with a ResNet-50 backbone), coupled with appropriate data augmentation and transfer learning techniques, is already optimised and robust to limited training data. To illustrate, the Dice score achieved by our ResNet-50 model on the benchmark DRISHTI-GS test set using only 50 (97.5%) and 25 (96.3%) training images is comparable to the current state-of-the-art result, i.e. 97.8% [13, 24], and to studies working with significantly more training data. Yu et al. [26], for example, reported a Dice score of 97.4% on the DRISHTI-GS test set by fine-tuning a U-Net pre-trained on more than 600 fundus images (designated for OD segmentation task). Similarly, Sun et al. [21] achieved 97.0% on the same test set using a fine-tuned U-Net pre-trained on 400 fundus images. Moreover, using only 25 images from the PAPILA train set, our ResNet-50 yielded a similar Dice score (94.6%) to that recently reported by Moris et al. (94.5%) [16], who used a combined total of 1169 training images from different datasets. Having said that, our qualitative assessment of the predicted masks indicated that SAM's ability to tap into domain-specific prior knowledge (mask prediction from bounding box), rendered it more robust to images with challenging OD morphologies (ill-defined margin).

For OC segmentation, though, SAM (irrespective of implementation type) is evidently more data efficient than the baseline models across datasets and training set sizes. In addition, SAM GT and SAM Noise (fine-tuned on 50 DRISHTI-GS images)

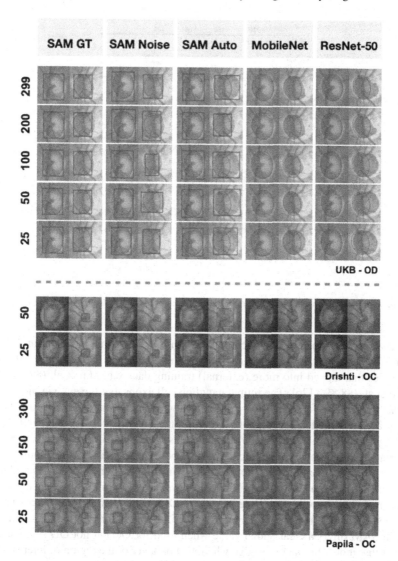

Fig. 2. Top panel (above dotted line) displays some examples of OD segmentation masks (UK Biobank) predicted by different models. The first image in each image pair is more typical, while the second image with significant peri-papillary atrophy (bright area adjacent to OD margin) is more unusual. Bottom panel displays some examples of OC segmentation masks (DRISHTI-GS and PAPILA) predicted by different models. The first image in each DRISHTI-GS image pair with a large cup-to-disc ratio ("deeper" cup and more well-defined margin) is more typical of DRISHTI-GS due to more eyes being glaucomatous. Conversely, most eyes in PAPILA have a normal (small) cup-to-disc ratio, and thus more ill-defined OC margin, as represented by the second image in the PAPILA image pair. Predicted masks are represented by blue overlays; ground truth (OD or OC) margin is circled in red; bounding box (predicted or otherwise) is displayed as appropriate.

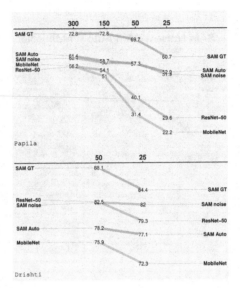

Fig. 3. Optic cup segmentation: mean average precision (%) by training set size and dataset.

yielded superior/comparable Dice score (93.6% and 90.3%) to the state of the art (92.4%) reported by a study that used a larger (internal) training set (70/30 train/test split) [22] and studies that tapped into more (external) training data, e.g. Sun et al. (87.7%) [21] and Yu et al. (88.8%) [26]. The retinal ganglion cell axons exit the eye via the OD and *descend* (as seen en face) into the central pale/whitish excavation that forms the OC [4]. On a colour fundus photograph, therefore, the contrast between OC and its surrounding tissue is intrinsically more attenuated (as some depth information is inevitably lost because of 2D projection) compared to that between OD and its surrounding tissue [4]. As such, the uncertainty in ground truth is invariably higher for OC than that for OD segmentation. For example, in the PAPILA dataset, the intra-observer agreement ranges from 82.7% to 83.4% (Dice score) for OC segmentation, similar to what our fine-tuned SAM GT achieved, compared to 95.5 to 95.8% for OD segmentation. The fact that SAM offers a clear added value when used for OC but not OD segmentation suggests that it only has an extra edge when the boundary of the region of interest is not well defined (also tying in with the observation that SAM is more robust to challenging OD morphologies). Indeed, as discussed earlier, SAM's added value is most evident when applied to PAPILA—where most eyes have a normal (small) cup-to-disc ratio, and therefore (naturally) ill-defined OC margin—which stands in contrast to DRISHTI-GS in which the majority of eyes have a "deeper" and more well-defined OC appearance due to glaucomatous retinal ganglion cell loss.

Taken together, SAM does not offer higher data efficiency when it comes to OD segmentation, although with good bounding box placement it is more robust to challenging (and more unusual) OD morphologies. When it comes to OC segmentation, though, SAM is evidently more data efficient. SAM holds potential as a *clinician-in-the-loop* tool to facilitate accurate OD and OC segmentation in the presence of ill-defined boundaries without necessarily requiring huge amounts of training data.

References

1. Boland, M.V., Quigley, H.A.: Risk factors and open-angle glaucoma: classification and application. J. Glaucoma **16**, 406–418 (2007)
2. Bommasani, R., et al.: On the Opportunities and Risks of Foundation Models. arXiv e-prints arXiv:2108.07258 (2021)
3. Chen, L.-C., Papandreou, G., Schroff, F., Adam, H.: Rethinking Atrous Convolution for Semantic Image Segmentation. arXiv e-prints arXiv:1706.05587 (2017)
4. Cheng, J., Li, Z., Gu, Z., Fu, H., Wong, D.W.K., Liu, J.: Structure-preserving guided retinal image filtering for optic disc analysis. In: Trucco, E., MacGillivray, T., Xu, Y. (eds.) Computational Retinal Image Analysis, pp. 199–221. Academic Press (2019)
5. Chua, S.Y.L., et al.: Cohort profile: design and methods in the eye and vision consortium of UK Biobank. BMJ Open **9**, e025077 (2019)
6. Deng, R., et al.: Segment Anything Model (SAM) for Digital Pathology: Assess Zero-shot Segmentation on Whole Slide Imaging. arXiv e-prints arXiv:2304.04155 (2023)
7. He, S., et al.: Computer-Vision Benchmark Segment-Anything Model (SAM) in Medical Images: Accuracy in 12 Datasets. arXiv e-prints arXiv:2304.09324 (2023)
8. Huang, Y., et al.: Segment Anything Model for Medical Images? arXiv e-prints arXiv:2304.14660 (2023)
9. Kirillov, A., et al.: Segment Anything. arXiv e-prints arXiv:2304.02643 (2023)
10. Kovalyk, O., Morales-Sánchez, J., Verdú-Monedero, R., Sellés-Navarro, I., Palazón-Cabanes, A., Sancho-Gómez, J.L.: PAPILA: dataset with fundus images and clinical data of both eyes of the same patient for glaucoma assessment. Sci. Data **9**, 291 (2022)
11. Li, Y., Xie, S., Chen, X., Dollar, P., He, K., Girshick, R.: Benchmarking Detection Transfer Learning with Vision Transformers. arXiv e-prints arXiv:2111.11429 (2021)
12. Lin, T.-Y., et al.: Microsoft COCO: Common Objects in Context. arXiv e-prints arXiv:1405.0312 (2014)
13. Liu, B., Pan, D., Song, H.: Joint optic disc and cup segmentation based on densely connected depthwise separable convolution deep network. BMC Med. Imaging **21**, 14 (2021)
14. Ma, J., Wang, B.: Segment Anything in Medical Images. arXiv e-prints arXiv:2304.12306 (2023)
15. Mazurowski, M.A., Dong, H., Gu, H., Yang, J., Konz, N., Zhang, Y.: Segment Anything Model for Medical Image Analysis: an Experimental Study. arXiv e-prints arXiv:2304.10517 (2023)
16. Moris, E., et al.: Assessing coarse-to-fine deep learning models for optic disc and cup segmentation in fundus images. pp. 125670R. eprint: arXiv:2209.14383
17. Mosqueira-Rey, E., Hernández-Pereira, E., Alonso-Ríos, D., Bobes-Bascarán, J., Fernández-Leal, Á.: Human-in-the-loop machine learning: a state of the art. Artif. Intell. Rev. **56**, 3005–3054 (2023)
18. Qiu, Z., Hu, Y., Li, H., Liu, J.: Learnable Ophthalmology SAM. arXiv e-prints arXiv:2304.13425 (2023)
19. Shi, P., Qiu, J., Dalike Abaxi, S.M., Wei, H., Lo, F.P.W., Yuan, W.: Generalist Vision Foundation Models for Medical Imaging: A Case Study of Segment Anything Model on Zero-Shot Medical Segmentation. arXiv e-prints arXiv:2304.12637 (2023)
20. Sivaswamy, J., Krishnadas, S.R., Joshi, G.D., Jain, M., Tabish, A.U.S.: Drishti-GS: retinal image dataset for optic nerve head (ONH) segmentation, pp. 53–56 (2014)
21. Sun, J.D., Yao, C., Liu, J., Liu, W., Yu, Z.K.: GNAS-U2Net: a new optic cup and optic disc segmentation architecture with genetic neural architecture search. IEEE Signal Process. Lett. **29**, 697–701 (2022)

22. Tabassum, M., et al.: CDED-Net: joint segmentation of optic disc and optic cup for glaucoma screening. IEEE Access **8**, 102733–102747 (2020)
23. Vajaranant, T.S., Wu, S., Torres, M., Varma, R.: The changing face of primary open-angle glaucoma in the United States: demographic and geographic changes from 2011 to 2050. Am. J. Ophthalmol. **154**, 303-314.e303 (2012)
24. Wei, Z., et al.: RMSDSC-Net: a robust multiscale feature extraction with depthwise separable convolution network for optic disc and cup segmentation. Int. J. Intell. Syst. **37**, 11482–11505 (2022)
25. Wu, J., et al.: Medical SAM Adapter: Adapting Segment Anything Model for Medical Image Segmentation. arXiv e-prints arXiv:2304.12620 (2023)
26. Yu, S., Xiao, D., Frost, S., Kanagasingam, Y.: Robust optic disc and cup segmentation with deep learning for glaucoma detection. Comput. Med. Imaging Graph. **74**, 61–71 (2019)
27. Zhou, T., Zhang, Y., Zhou, Y., Wu, Y., Gong, C.: Can SAM Segment Polyps? arXiv e-prints arXiv:2304.07583 (2023)

Anisotropic Hybrid Networks for Liver Tumor Segmentation with Uncertainty Quantification

Benjamin Lambert[1,2], Pauline Roca[2], Florence Forbes[3], Senan Doyle[2], and Michel Dojat[1(✉)]

[1] Univ. Grenoble Alpes, Inserm, U1216, Grenoble Institut Neurosciences, 38000 Grenoble, France
{benjamin.lambert,michel.dojat}@univ-grenoble-alpes.fr
[2] Pixyl, Research and Development Laboratory, 38000 Grenoble, France
[3] Univ. Grenoble Alpes, Inria, CNRS, Grenoble INP, LJK, 38000 Grenoble, France

Abstract. The burden of liver tumors is important, ranking as the fourth leading cause of cancer mortality. In case of hepatocellular carcinoma (HCC), the delineation of liver and tumor on contrast-enhanced magnetic resonance imaging (CE-MRI) is performed to guide the treatment strategy. As this task is time-consuming, needs high expertise and could be subject to inter-observer variability there is a strong need for automatic tools. However, challenges arise from the lack of available training data, as well as the high variability in terms of image resolution and MRI sequence. In this work, we propose to compare two different pipelines based on anisotropic models to obtain the segmentation of the liver and tumors. The first pipeline corresponds to a baseline multi-class model that performs the simultaneous segmentation of the liver and tumor classes. In the second approach, we train two distinct binary models, one segmenting the liver only and the other the tumors. Our results show that both pipelines exhibit different strengths and weaknesses. Moreover, we propose an uncertainty quantification strategy allowing the identification of potential false positive tumor lesions. Both solutions were submitted to the MICCAI 2023 Atlas challenge regarding liver and tumor segmentation.

Keywords: Hepatocellular carcinoma · Liver · Segmentation · Uncertainty

1 Introduction

Liver cancer is the sixth most common cancer worldwide, the fourth most common cause of cancer-related death and hepatocellular carcinoma (HCC) in particular is the most common type of primary liver cancer in adults. HCC is a cancer with large therapeutic choices depending on the tumor staging. In case

Supplementary Information The online version contains supplementary material available at https://doi.org/10.1007/978-3-031-47425-5_31.

J. Woo et al. (Eds.): MICCAI 2023 Workshops, LNCS 14394, pp. 347–356, 2023.
https://doi.org/10.1007/978-3-031-47425-5_31

of unresectable HCC, transarterial radioembolisation (TARE) is one of the recommended treatments: it consists of the delivering of 20–60 uM-sized yttrium-90 (Y90) microspheres to the tumor arterial supply, causing tumor necrosis through radiation-induced DNA damage and eventual cell death [13]. To calculate dosimetry and plan the intervention, the spatial extent of the tumor needs to be determined [14]. In clinical routine, liver and tumor are delineated using contrast-enhanced magnetic resonance imaging (CE-MRI) with four phases (pre-contrast, arterial, portal venous, delayed phases) allowing to differentiate the tumor from the liver parenchyma. These tasks are time-consuming and required high medical expertise.

In this context, automatic tools could reduce intra- and inter-observer variability and help radiologists to save time. Several studies [1,16] proposed CE-MRI based deep learning methods to segment liver and HCC tumors using private datasets (of 174 and 190 patients respectively). However, open-source MRI datasets are scarce and existing ones [3] do not contain manual annotations, inhibiting the development of automated algorithms. In this context, the "A Tumor and Liver Automatic Segmentation" (ATLAS) challenge has been proposed and relevant datasets provided. The ATLAS's aim is to produce automatic segmentation maps of liver and the tumor(s) using CE-MRI of patients with unresectable HCC based on a small annotated training dataset (60 patients) [12]. This challenge is organised in collaboration with the Medical Image Computing and Computer Assisted Intervention (MICCAI) Workshop on Resource-Efficient Medical Image Analysis (REMIA) which will take place during the MICCAI 2023 edition in Vancouver, Canada. This paper describes our contribution to the challenge, including two different pipelines to segment liver and HCC tumors in CE-MRI. The first pipeline corresponds to a multiclass model that simultaneously segment the liver and tumors. In the second pipeline, we use two different binary models, one focusing on the liver and the other on the tumors. Additionally, we propose to complement the automatic segmentation with the estimation of an uncertainty score for each identified tumor lesion, potentially guiding the reviewing of the result by the user.

2   Materials and Methods

2.1   Dataset

The ATLAS challenge dataset is composed of an open-source training fold (60 subjects), allowing the development of segmentation models, as well as an hidden test set (30 subjects) for evaluation [12]. For each subject, a unique CE-MRI sequence is available, with one of the following phase: arterial, delayed, post-contrast, non-contrast or unknown. A ground truth segmentation mask is associated to each image, containing 3-classes: background, healthy liver and tumor lesions. Training images exhibit variable resolution, ranging from 0.684 mm to 1.4 mm in the XY plane, and from 2 mm to 4.6 mm in the Z-axis (see Fig. 1). To develop our approach, we adopt a 5-fold cross validation scheme. In each fold, 40 subjects are used for training, 8 for validation and 12 for testing. The distribution of data in each fold is resumed in Table 1.

Table 1. Data distribution in each fold. A: arterial, D: delayed, NC: non-contrast, P: portal, U: unkwon

Fold	Training (N = 40)					Validation (N = 8)					Test (N = 12)				
	A	D	NC	P	U	A	D	NC	P	U	A	D	NC	P	U
1	23	6	1	5	5	3	0	1	3	1	7	2	0	2	1
2	24	6	1	4	5	2	1	0	4	1	7	1	1	2	1
3	24	5	1	4	6	2	1	1	4	0	7	2	0	2	1
4	25	5	1	5	4	2	1	1	3	1	6	2	0	2	2
5	24	6	0	6	4	3	1	1	2	1	6	1	1	2	2

2.2 Segmentation Pipelines

In this section, we start by describing the design choices that are common to both pipelines, namely the neural network architecture and loss function. Then, we detail the particularity of both approaches (see Fig. 2 for an illustration).

Joint Design Choices. The first challenge to tackle is the anisotropy of the data, with the Z resolution being up to 4 times that in the plane. Instead of preprocessing the data to obtain a uniform spatial resolution, we instead choose to use a segmentation neural network able to handle the intrinsic anisotropy of the raw data. To this end, our two pipelines revolve around the use of the Anistropic Hybrid U-Net (AHUNet) [8]. This architecture is composed of a pre-trained 2D convolutional encoder ignoring between-slice information, and a 3D convolutional decoder that reconstitutes the 3D context. Second, although not

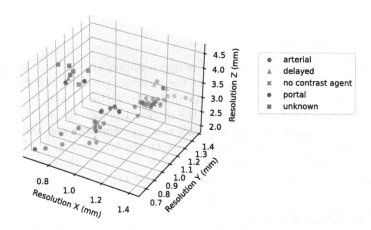

Fig. 1. Distribution of the spatial resolution in the training dataset. Colors indicate the corresponding CE-MRI phase. To facilitate visualization, the plot is generated using jitter.

the scope of the ATLAS challenge, we aim at enhancing the segmentation of the models by an uncertainty quantification module allowing to estimate a confidence score for each tumor lesion. Thus, the calibration of the output probability is of primary importance, which is usually poor with modern networks [5]. To circumvent this limitation, we resort to using the recently proposed Margin-based Label Smoothing loss [9] which has been proposed to improve the calibration of medical image segmentation models.

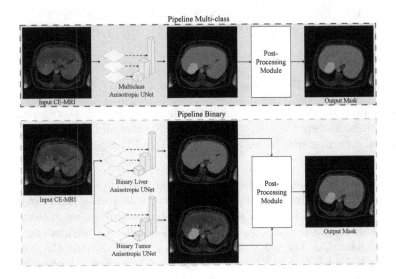

Fig. 2. Illustration of our two proposed pipelines, namely multi-class and binary.

2.3 Pipeline Multi-class

The most direct approach to obtain the segmentation of the liver and tumors is to train a multi-class AHUnet using the 3-classes ground truth masks. We adopt a patch-based approach where the input 3D MRI is divided into patches which are processed independently by the model. To guide the selection of the patches size, we compute bounding-boxes around each liver and tumor lesion in the training dataset using the ground truth masks (see Fig. 3). This study indicates that defining a patch size of $256 \times 256 \times 64$ allows the encompassment of all tumor lesions, while also encompassing most of the livers.

2.4 Dual Binary Pipeline

Motivated by the observation that the segmentation of the liver was a much more easier task than tumor segmentation, we propose an alternative pipeline that disentangles both tasks. To do so, two distinct binary models are trained:

i) a model that segments the *overall* liver (concatenation of the healthy liver class and the tumors) and ii) a model that segments the tumor lesions. From the bounding-box analysis (Fig. 3), we keep the patch size of $256 \times 256 \times 64$ for the binary liver model. However, for the binary tumor model, we use a smaller patch size of $128 \times 128 \times 64$ as it allows to reduce the imbalance between background and tumor voxels, while still encompassing most of the nodules. At inference, the input MRI is processed by each model. The two resulting binary masks are then aggregated to reconstitute the final 3-class segmentation.

2.5 Post-processing Module

Post-processing has been proved as an important step for the automated segmentation of the liver in CT and MRI [4]. We adopt a 3-steps post-processing procedure, which is similar for both pipelines:

Step 1: Only the largest connected component for the liver is kept. A binary morphology *fill holes* operation [15] is performed on the resulting binary mask.

Step 2: Tumor lesions outside the liver are removed. This process differs slightly depending on the pipeline. For the multi-class approach, the binary mask of each identified tumor lesion is dilated. If this dilated mask has no intersection with liver voxels, the lesion is deleted. For the binary-approach, the process is more straightforward, as we simply multiply the liver mask by the tumor mask. As an effect, tumor voxels outside the liver are filtered out.

Step 3: A binary closing morphological operation is applied to the remaining tumor lesions to improve the smoothness of the borders.

2.6 Lesion Uncertainty Quantification

Additionally to the segmentation of the liver and tumors, we propose to add a lesion uncertainty quantification module to our pipelines. This module complements the segmentation with an uncertainty score for each unique nodule. To achieve this, we collect the tumor probabilities $p_{i,tumor}$ ($i \in [1, N]$) for each of the N voxels of the lesion. The *lesion-wise* uncertainty score is then taken as:

$$L_{unc} = 1 - \frac{1}{N} \sum_{i=1}^{N} p_{i,tumor} \tag{1}$$

2.7 Evaluation Protocol

The ATLAS challenge proposes to compare competitors based on 9 metrics: Dice, Surface Dice (SD), Haussdorf Distance (HD) and Average Symmetric Surface Distance (ASD) computed for both the *overall* liver (concatenation of the healthy liver and tumor voxels) and the tumors. Lastly, the Root Mean Square Error (RMSE) on tumor burden is computed, based on the computed volumes for the liver and tumors. To compare each pipeline, we train models on each of

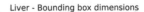

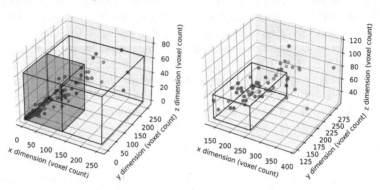

Fig. 3. Dimensions of bounding boxes encompassing the tumor lesions (left) and liver (right) on the Atlas dataset. In overlay we present the selected patch sizes of $256 \times 256 \times 64$ (transparent) and $128 \times 128 \times 64$ (grey).

the 5 folds, and metrics are aggregated over the 5 test folds in a cross-validation scheme. For the final challenge submissions, the models trained on the 5 folds are aggregated in an ensemble for each pipeline separately. Both pipelines (binary and multi-class) are submitted as separate algorithms. Finally, qualitative assessment of the computed tumor uncertainty scores is assessed by monitoring the distribution of uncertainties for True Positives (TP, non-zero intersection with the ground truth tumor mask) and False Positives (FP, null intersection) lesions.

2.8 Ablation Study

To demonstrate the positive impact of using AHUnet over standard 3D segmentation architecture, we reproduced the multi-class pipeline by replacing the AHUnet by a Dynamic Unet 3D (DynUnet) which has been successful in various medical image segmentation challenges [6]. We also run the evaluation procedure without post-processing to demonstrate its gain on performance.

2.9 Implementation Details

Our framework is implemented in Pytorch [10] and experiments are carried on a Nvidia RTX A5000 GPU. AHUnet and DynUnet are implemented using the open-source MONAI library [2]. Models are trained using the ADAM optimizer [7] with a learning rate of $2e-4$ and a batch size of 2, until the loss on validation data stagnates over 30 epochs. During training we use Data Augmentation implemented using the TorchIO library [11] comprising spatial (rotation, flips, affine transforms) as well as intensity (contrast, gamma, bias, noise) augmentations.

3 Results and Discussion

Table 2. Cross-validation performance on the 60 subjects aggregated over the 5 test folds. Mean results are presented along the standard deviation. SD, Surface Dice; HD, Haussdorf Distance; ASD, Average Symmetric Surface Distance; RMSE, Root Mean Square Error

	Post-processing	Multi-class AHUnet		Dual binary AHUnet		DynUnet
		✓	×	✓	×	✓
Liver	ASD ↓	2.06 ± 1.78	3.31 ± 3.53	$\mathbf{1.99 \pm 2.35}$	5.03 ± 5.01	2.57 ± 2.70
	Dice ↑	$\mathbf{0.94 \pm 0.04}$	0.93 ± 0.04	$\mathbf{0.94 \pm 0.06}$	0.92 ± 0.07	0.93 ± 0.06
	HD ($\times 10^1$) ↓	3.22 ± 1.78	11.27 ± 6.03	$\mathbf{2.85 \pm 1.69}$	12.79 ± 6.76	3.60 ± 2.60
	SD ↑	0.82 ± 0.10	0.80 ± 0.11	$\mathbf{0.84 \pm 0.12}$	0.81 ± 0.12	0.81 ± 0.13
Tumor	ASD ($\times 10^1$) ↓	$\mathbf{1.46 \pm 2.5}$	1.62 ± 2.50	1.53 ± 2.31	3.51 ± 4.21	1.90 ± 2.25
	Dice ↑	$\mathbf{0.57 \pm 0.28}$	$\mathbf{0.57 \pm 0.28}$	0.54 ± 0.29	0.49 ± 0.30	0.49 ± 0.29
	HD ($\times 10^1$) ↓	$\mathbf{6.73 \pm 3.84}$	8.87 ± 5.74	7.77 ± 4.13	18.0 ± 7.89	8.49 ± 4.34
	SD ↑	0.40 ± 0.21	0.40 ± 0.21	$\mathbf{0.41 \pm 0.22}$	33.9 ± 0.21	0.33 ± 0.20
	RMSE ($\times 10^{-2}$) ↓	0.73 ± 1.38	0.75 ± 0.01	$\mathbf{0.72 \pm 1.30}$	1.17 ± 2.10	1.04 ± 2.19

Cross-validation performances of each pipeline are presented in Table 2, while Table 3 presents the results on the hidden test dataset. Qualitative assessment of lesion uncertainty is presented in Fig. 4.

Starting with the cross-validation metrics, for both pipelines, the liver is far better segmented than tumors. On the multi-class AHUnet pipeline for example a mean Dice score of 0.94 is reached for liver segmentation whereas for tumor we obtain a value of 0.57. This can be explained by the small volume of tumors as compared to the liver and by the important variability in appearance depending on the contrast phase. Moreover, these results are similar to Bousabarah study [1] that obtained Dice scores per case of 0.91 and 0.48 for liver and tumor segmentation respectively, using a deep-learning method based on the four phases of CE-MRI exams. Our post-processing module enabled an important gain on the 9 metrics for both pipelines. The dual binary pipeline obtain better metrics on the liver than the multi-class one. However, for tumor, the multi-class AHUnet is slightly superior. Finally, the multi-class pipeline relying on the DynUnet (ablation study) is worst than the multi-class AHUnet for all metrics, showing the relevance of using a neural network specifically designed for anisotropic data. To assess if the differences between both proposed pipelines are statistically significant, we perform a significance analysis, presented in Supplementary Materials (SM). Results show that the Liver metrics are significantly better for the Dual binary pipeline than for the multi-class pipeline. On the contrary, the Tumor HD is significantly lower for the multi-class pipeline than for the binary one. Other metrics are not statistically different between both pipelines (Tumor ASD, Dice, HD and RMSE). The performances obtained on the hidden test (Table 3) are similar to those obtained in the cross-validation setting, with even a slight gain for some metrics (e.g. Liver ASD, HD and SD; Tumor SD and RMSE). This can be explained by the fact that the hidden test dataset contains images acquired more recently, and therefore, it can be expected that they have better image quality.

Finally, the qualitative assessment of our lesion uncertainty module (Fig. 4, left) shows that FP lesions tend to be attributed to higher uncertainty scores than TP lesions. The proposed score could thus be used to draw the user's attention to uncertain lesions, which are more likely to be FP. The proposed lesion uncertainty score is highly correlated with the lesion volume (Fig. 4, right), reaching a Spearman correlation coefficient of −0.82, which is intuitive as FP lesions are more frequent for small lesions. To complement this analysis, we provide two examples of the proposed lesion quantification in SM.

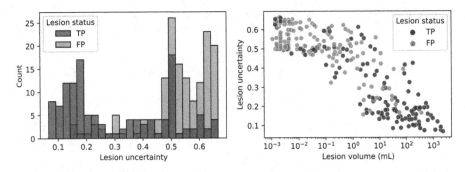

Fig. 4. Qualitative evaluation of the tumor lesion uncertainty obtained with the multi-class pipeline. Left: histogram of uncertainty estimates with respect to the lesion status (True Positive, TP or False Positive, FP). Right: lesion uncertainty with respect to the lesion volume (in log-scale).

Table 3. Performance on the hidden test dataset for both pipelines, as reported in the public leaderboard.

		Multi-class	Dual binary
Liver	ASD ↓	1.7	**1.5**
	Dice ↑	0.95	0.95
	HD ($\times 10^1$)	2.6	**2.5**
	SD ↑	0.95	0.95
Tumor	ASD ($\times 10^1$) ↓	**3.0**	4.0
	Dice ↑	**0.60**	0.59
	HD ($\times 10^1$) ↓	**7.8**	9.3
	SD ↑	57.4	**55.3**
	RMSE ($\times 10^{-2}$) ↓	**0.4**	0.6

4 Conclusion

In this work, we address the problem of segmenting the liver and tumors in CE-MRI. Using the AHUnet architecture as cornerstone, we propose two different pipelines, multi-class and dual binary, demonstrating a gain on tumor and liver segmentation respectively. Additionally, we propose to quantify the uncertainty of identified nodules, which can be used to improve the interpretability of the automated predictions. For the final ATLAS 2023 challenge submissions, both pipelines (binary and multi-class) are submitted as separate algorithms.

References

1. Bousabarah, K., et al.: Automated detection and delineation of hepatocellular carcinoma on multiphasic contrast-enhanced MRI using deep learning. Abdom. Radiol. **46**(1), 216–225 (2021)
2. Cardoso, M.J., et al.: MONAI: an open-source framework for deep learning in healthcare. arXiv preprint arXiv:2211.02701 (2022)
3. Clark, K., et al.: The cancer imaging archive (TCIA): maintaining and operating a public information repository. J. Digit. Imaging **26**, 1045–1057 (2013)
4. Furtado, P.: Loss, post-processing and standard architecture improvements of liver deep learning segmentation from computed tomography and magnetic resonance. Inform. Med. Unlocked **24**, 100585 (2021)
5. Guo, C., Pleiss, G., Sun, Y., Weinberger, K.Q.: On calibration of modern neural networks. In: International Conference on Machine Learning, pp. 1321–1330. PMLR (2017)
6. Isensee, F., et al.: nnU-Net: self-adapting framework for u-net-based medical image segmentation. arXiv preprint arXiv:1809.10486 (2018)
7. Kingma, D.P., Ba, J.: Adam: a method for stochastic optimization. In: 3rd International Conference on Learning Representations, ICLR 2015 (2015)
8. Liu, S., et al.: 3D anisotropic hybrid network: transferring convolutional features from 2D images to 3D anisotropic volumes. In: Frangi, A.F., Schnabel, J.A., Davatzikos, C., Alberola-López, C., Fichtinger, G. (eds.) MICCAI 2018. LNCS, vol. 11071, pp. 851–858. Springer, Cham (2018). https://doi.org/10.1007/978-3-030-00934-2_94
9. Murugesan, B., Liu, B., Galdran, A., Ayed, I.B., Dolz, J.: Calibrating segmentation networks with margin-based label smoothing. Med. Image Anal. **87**, 102826 (2023)
10. Paszke, A., et al.: Pytorch: an imperative style, high-performance deep learning library. In: Advances in Neural Information Processing Systems, vol. 32 (2019)
11. Pérez-García, F., Sparks, R., Ourselin, S.: Torchio: a python library for efficient loading, preprocessing, augmentation and patch-based sampling of medical images in deep learning. Comput. Methods Programs Biomed. **208**, 106236 (2021)
12. Quinton, F., et al.: A tumour and liver automatic segmentation (ATLAS) dataset on contrast-enhanced magnetic resonance imaging for hepatocellular carcinoma. Data **8**(5), 79 (2023)
13. Reig, M., et al.: BCLC strategy for prognosis prediction and treatment recommendation: the 2022 update. J. Hepatol. **76**(3), 681–693 (2022). https://doi.org/10.1016/j.jhep.2021.11.018
14. Smits, M.L., et al.: Radioembolization dosimetry: the road ahead. Cardiovasc. Intervent. Radiol. **38**, 261–269 (2015)

15. Virtanen, P., Gommers, R., Oliphant, T.E., Haberland, M., et al.: SciPy 1.0: fundamental algorithms for scientific computing in python. Nat. Methods **17**, 261–272 (2020)
16. Zheng, R., et al.: Automatic liver tumor segmentation on dynamic contrast enhanced MRI using 4D information: deep learning model based on 3D convolution and convolutional LSTM. IEEE Trans. Med. Imaging **41**(10), 2965–2976 (2022)

PLMVQA: Applying Pseudo Labels for Medical Visual Question Answering with Limited Data

Zheng Yu[1], Yutong Xie[1], Yong Xia[2], and Qi Wu[1(✉)]

[1] The University of Adelaide, Adelaide, Australia
{zheng.yu,qi.wu01}@adelaide.edu.au
[2] Northwestern Polytechnical University, Xi'an, China
yxia@nwpu.edu.cn

Abstract. Different from Visual Question Answering (VQA) in the general domain, Medical VQA is more challenging due to the lack of large-scale labeled datasets. In addition, Medical VQA requires high interpretability when making decisions to answer clinical questions. Thus, it should be clear which visual elements within the medical image such as organs or abnormalities are essential for answering clinical questions. To overcome these challenges, we propose a novel method based on Vision Transformer (ViT), which reformulates Medical VQA as a multi-task learning task. We first construct soft pseudo labels of logits for essential selected visual elements from limited annotation data of the existing Medical VQA dataset. Then, we apply these pseudo labels in our proposed Medical VQA model by predicting the answer and pseudo labels at the same time, which not only improves the performance of the proposed model but also presents better interpretability. Extensive experiments on two Medical VQA datasets demonstrate the effectiveness of our proposed method.

Keywords: Medical Visual Question Answering · Vision Transformer · Pseudo Label · Multi-task Learning

1 Introduction

Medical Visual Question Answering (VQA) has received great attention from the biomedical research community. Given a medical image and a clinical question related to the visual elements in the medical image, the task of Medical VQA is to well understand both the medical image and the clinical question in order to predict the correct answer [1,22,24]. Rather than VQA in the general domain, Medical VQA is much more challenging due to the following reasons: First, Medical VQA lacks large-scale and well-annotated data to effectively train Medical VQA models. Second, Medical VQA requires high interpretability when making decisions to answer clinical questions. Specifically, it should be clear which visual elements within the medical image such as organs or abnormalities are essential and how reliable the visual elements are for answering clinical questions.

J. Woo et al. (Eds.): MICCAI 2023 Workshops, LNCS 14394, pp. 357–367, 2023.
https://doi.org/10.1007/978-3-031-47425-5_32

Previous works normally apply state-of-the-art VQA methods in the medical domain directly, which usually use CNNs to extract medical image features. Due to the lack of large-scale labeled data, the performance of these works can not be guaranteed. To address this problem, methods based on meta-learning [19,26] and multi-modal pre-training [2,10,17] have been proposed recently. However, most of these methods need to collect large amounts of external data such as radiology images or image-caption pairs to pre-train the models, which is not always feasible in the medical area. We notice that existing Medical VQA datasets contain abundant visual elements for answering clinical questions, which have not been fully explored yet.

In this paper, we propose a novel vision-and-language transformer framework called PLMVQA for Medical VQA. PLMVQA is based on Vision Transformer [4] (ViT), which has been proven to have better transfer ability on out-domain tasks and stronger robustness against texture changes compared to CNNs. Thus, it is possible to utilize ViT in Medical VQA tasks to mitigate the lack of large-scale labeled data. In addition, to further improve the interpretability and performance of Medical VQA models, we construct soft pseudo labels of essential visual elements embodied in the limited Medical VQA datasets and apply these pseudo labels for Medical VQA tasks. Specifically, we first refine the Medical VQA dataset and select 17 annotation labels as the pseudo labels of essential visual elements, such as "kidney", "mass" and "nodule" *etc.* Then we use the refined medical images and the corresponding pseudo labels to pre-train a pseudo-label prediction model. We use the pre-trained model to generate soft pseudo-labels from each medical image in the dataset for the Medical VQA task. At last, we reformulate Medical VQA as a multi-task learning paradigm, where pseudo-label prediction and answer prediction are jointly trained.

Extensive experiments on commonly used Medical VQA datasets verify the effectiveness of our proposed PLMVQA. Though without using any external data to pre-train the model, PLMVQA still overcomes the absence of large-scale labeled data and improves the model's performance with better interpretability.

2   Related Work

Medical VQA. Previous works [1,20] often directly utilize classical VQA methods such as SAN [25], MCB [6] and BAN [11] in handling Medical VQA tasks. These methods tend to use CNN networks such as VGGNet [23] and ResNet [8] pre-trained on ImageNet [21] to extract image features. However, due to the lack of large-labeled Medical VQA data and the huge domain gap between general images and medical images, the training for transfer learning in Medical VQA is hard and these methods can hardly work well. To mitigate the lack of labeled Medical VQA data, methods based on meta-learning such as MEVF [19] and CR [26] or based on medical multi-modal pre-training such as MMBERT [10] and MedViLL [17] are proposed. Nevertheless, these methods rely heavily on external medical image data for pre-training, which cost a lot of computation resources. Besides, most of these methods still use CNNs to extract global visual features, which may lack high interpretability.

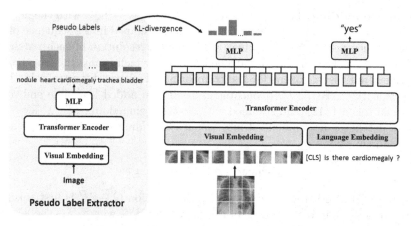

Fig. 1. Overview of our proposed PLMVQA for Medical VQA. The left shows the process of extracting soft pseudo labels of logits for selected visual elements. The right shows the multi-task learning for Medical VQA, where the answer to the question and the pseudo labels are predicted at the same time.

Vision Transformer. Recently, Vision Transformer [4] (ViT) has been proposed and has been proved to have better transfer ability on out-domain tasks and have stronger robustness against texture changes compared to CNNs in [18]. Kim *et al.* [12] first utilize ViT to solve vision-language problems in general domain by pre-training ViT on large-scale image-caption pairs and fine-tuning the model on downstream tasks. These works have shown great potential of ViT's ability of transfer learning and solving vision-language tasks. Thus, we propose a novel vision-language transformer framework based on ViT to solve Medical VQA.

3 Methodology

In this section, we first present the model architecture of PLMVQA. Then, we describe how we construct pseudo labels of essential visual elements from limited data in existing Medical VQA datasets. At last, we provide the details of applying these soft pseudo labels for Medical VQA tasks.

3.1 Model Architecture

The model architecture of PLMVQA is shown in Fig. 1. Taking a medical image and the corresponding clinical question as input, PLMVQA first uses the visual embedding layer and language embedding layer to embed the given image and question. Then, PLMVQA concatenates the multi-modal embeddings and implements interactions between them through multiple transformer layers. At last, the output features of visual tokens and language tokens are pooled and passed through two MLP classifiers respectively for different objectives.

Visual Embedding. The input medical image $I \in \mathbb{R}^{H \times W \times C}$ with the height of H, the width of W, and the channel of C is first reshaped into a sequence of flattened patches $x \in \mathbb{R}^{N \times (P^2 \cdot C)}$, where (P, P) is the resolution of each patch, and $N = HW/P^2$ is the number of flattened patches, which is also the length of the effective input visual tokens for the transformer. Followed by a trainable linear projection $W_v \in \mathbb{R}^{(P^2 \cdot C) \times h}$, concatenated with an added learnable embedding of special token [cls] and summed with position embedding $E_v^{\text{pos}} \in \mathbb{R}^{(N+1) \times h}$, images patches x are embedded into visual embedding $v \in \mathbb{R}^{(N+1) \times h}$, where h is the hidden size:

$$v = \text{CONCAT}[v_{\text{cls}}; x W_v] + E_v^{\text{pos}} \tag{1}$$

Language Embedding. The input clinical question $Q \in \mathbb{R}^D$ is first tokenized by WordPiece [9] into a sequence of tokens $y \in \mathbb{R}^{T \times |V|}$, where D is the length of the original question, T is the length of generated tokens which is also the length of the effective input language tokens for the transformer, $|V|$ is the number of vocabulary. We also added the special token [CLS]. Then, followed by a learnable word embedding matrix $W_q \in \mathbb{R}^{|V| \times h}$, position embedding $E_q^{\text{pos}} \in \mathbb{R}^{(T+1) \times h}$ and Layer Normalization (LN), the language embedding $q \in \mathbb{R}^{(T+1) \times h}$ is generated:

$$q = \text{CONCAT}[q_{\text{cls}}; y W_q] + E_q^{\text{pos}} \tag{2}$$

Cross-Modal Interactions. The type embeddings E_v^{type} and E_q^{type} distinguishing different modalities are firstly added to the visual embedding v and the language embedding q, respectively. These embeddings are concatenated as the joint multi-modal embedding z_0. Next, the input multi-modal embedding z_0 is passed through the transformer encoder, which consists of multiple blocks, each containing a multi-head self-attention (MSA) layer, a MLP layer, layer normalization (LN) and residual connections. At last, the first $(N + 1)$ features of the transformer encoder output are chosen and pooled as the final visual representation f_v, and the rest $(T + 1)$ features are pooled as the final language representation f_q:

$$z_0 = \text{CONCAT}[v + E_v^{\text{type}}; q + E_q^{\text{type}}], \tag{3}$$

$$z_l' = \text{MSA}(\text{LN}(z_{l-1})) + z_{l-1}, \qquad l = 1 \dots L \tag{4}$$

$$z_l = \text{MLP}(\text{LN}(z_l')) + z_l', \qquad l = 1 \dots L \tag{5}$$

$$f_v = \text{POOL}(z_L^{1:(N+1)}), \tag{6}$$

$$f_q = \text{POOL}(z_L^{(N+2):(N+T+2)}) \tag{7}$$

where L is the total number of the transformer blocks which is set as 12. The hidden size h of the transformer is 768 and the number of attention heads is 12. The weights of visual embedding and transformer encoder are initialized from ViT and the weights of language embedding are initialized from BERT.

3.2 Constructing Pseudo Labels from Limited Data

Most existing Medical VQA methods rely heavily on external medical image data to train the models. Nevertheless, annotation data within current Medical VQA datasets has not been fully utilized, especially annotations from SLAKE dataset which contains labels of organs such as "heart" and labels of abnormalities such as "cardiomegaly". These annotations have abundant information that is of great help to answer clinical questions. In other words, these annotations can be served as pseudo labels for Medical VQA. However, not all annotations in the SLAKE are useful for the VQA. Thus, we refine the annotation data according to the label counts in all annotation data within the used Medical VQA datasets. Finally, 193 medical images (187 for training and 7 for validation) from SLAKE dataset are selected to train and validate the pseudo-label prediction model, and 17 classes of pseudo-labels are reserved.

Since a medical image may contain multiple annotation labels, we formalize the pseudo-label prediction as a multi-label classification problem and use the binary cross-entropy loss for optimization. We directly adapt the above-mentioned transformer model to this job, where all language-based components are removed. Specifically, the pooled visual representation f_v of the transformer is passed through an MLP classifier followed by a Sigmoid function to predict scores S_{diag} for each class. Then, the predicted scores S_{diag} can be transformed into a probability distribution P_{diag} using a Softmax operation.

3.3 Applying Pseudo Labels for Medical VQA

First, we use the pre-trained multi-label classification model to extract pseudo labels of each medical image in VQA-RAD and SLAKE datasets. Specifically, we use the pre-trained model to evaluate the given medical image and obtain a probability distribution P_{diag} of refined classes. It is worth mentioning that instead of encoding the distribution into a one-hot hard label, we take this distribution as a soft label that contains morek knowledge on visual elements.

Next, for the task of Medical VQA, we formulate it as a paradigm of multi-task learning, where the output visual representation f_v of the transformer is utilized to learn from soft pseudo labels while the language representation f_q is utilized to answer clinical questions. Specifically, f_v is passed through an MLP classifier followed by softmax to predict probability distribution P'_{diag} over pseudo label classes. The goal is to help the model learn more visual knowledge from generated soft pseudo labels. It is implemented by optimizing the KL-divergence L_{KLD} between P_{diag} and P'_{diag}:

$$L_{KLD} = KLD(P'_{diag}, P_{diag}) \qquad (8)$$

At the same time, f_q is passed through another MLP classifier followed by softmax to predict question answers, and the cross-entropy loss L_{VQA} is used to optimize this process.

At last, we train the model in a multi-task paradigm by optimizing the final loss function L which is defined as follows:

$$L = L_{VQA} + \alpha L_{KLD} \tag{9}$$

where α is a balancing hyper-parameter.

4 Experiments

4.1 Dataset and Evaluation Metric

We employ the most widely-used VQA-RAD dataset [13] and the SLAKE-EN dataset [14] that embodies abundant visual element information to evaluate our proposed method. VQA-RAD consists of 315 images and 3,515 corresponding questions annotated by clinicians. SLAKE-EN is the English subset of bilingual SLAKE dataset, which contains 642 images and 7,033 question-answer pairs. 193 medical images with 17 classes of pseudo labels from SLAKE are selected to train the pseudo-label classification model. The refined 17 classes are shown as follows: `kidney, liver, spleen, mass, nodule, effusion, pneumothorax, cardiomegaly, small bowel, colon, esophagus, trachea, lung, heart, stomach, temporal lobe, bladder`. We use accuracy as evaluation metric.

4.2 Experimental Details

We use PyTorch to implement our models. For all experiments, we use the AdamW optimizer [16] with a learning rate of $5e^{-5}$ and weight decay of 0.01, where the learning rate is warmed up over the first 10% steps of total steps with linear decay. The batch size is 64. The hyper-parameter α is set as 0.5 for performance comparison experiments. For Medical VQA tasks, we train models for 100 epochs. For the pseudo-label classification task, we train the model for 50 epochs. All the experiments are conducted on one NVIDIA 1080Ti GPU.

4.3 Results

We compare our method only with some recent methods on VQA-RAD and SLAKE-EN datasets. Especially, we give the details of whether the reported methods are dedicated models trained for each question type or general models trained for all question types and whether the methods utilize an amount of external medical image data for training.

As shown in Table 1, a great many of methods have been proposed with experiments conducted on the VQA-RAD dataset. While most of these methods rely heavily on external data for training, either pure medical images or medical image-caption pairs. For example, CPRD uses external 20K and CMSA uses 10K radiology images including abdomen CT, brain MRI and chest X-Ray

Table 1. Performance comparison on VQA-RAD test set. PLMVQA represents training without pseudo-label prediction, while PL represents applying pseudo labels, and * represents the same model using a dedicated setting.

Methods	External Data	General Models	Dedicated Models	Accuracy		
				Open	Closed	Overall
MEVF [19]	10K	✓		43.9	75.1	62.6
MMQ [3]	-	✓		53.7	75.8	67.0
MedViLL [17]	90K	✓		59.7	78.2	70.9
MMBERT [10]	80K	✓		**63.1**	77.9	72.0
PubmedCLIP [5]	80K	✓		48.6	78.1	66.5
CPRD [15]	20K	✓		52.5	77.9	67.8
CMSA [7]	10K	✓		56.1	77.3	68.8
PLMVQA	-	✓		59.2	77.9	70.5
PLMVQA-PL	-	✓		60.3	**79.8**	**72.1**
CR [26]	10K		✓	60.0	79.3	71.6
PubmedCLIP* [5]	80K		✓	60.1	80.0	72.1
CPRD* [15]	20K		✓	61.1	80.4	72.7
CMSA* [7]	10K		✓	61.5	**80.9**	73.2
PLMVQA-PL*	-		✓	**62.6**	80.5	**73.4**

images to pre-train visual encoders. MMBERT uses external 80K medical image-caption pairs for multi-modal pre-training. Though our proposed PLMVQA does not utilize external data, it still outperforms other methods with large external data in all settings, no matter whether it is under the general model setting or dedicated model setting. After using pseudo labels, our PLMVQA obtains an overall accuracy of 72.1% with a large improvement of 1.6%, which outperforms all other methods using external data under the general model setting and even keeps competitive with PubmedCLIP dedicated models. When it comes to the dedicated model setting, our PLMVQA achieves an overall accuracy of 73.4%, which still outperforms all other methods. It is worth mentioning that both PLMVQA and MMQ explore visual information only from Medical VQA datasets, but PLMVQA outperforms MMQ with a large margin of 5.1% when applying pseudo labels of important visual elements. Besides, we note that the performance improvement of our dedicated model is not so obvious compared to other methods, which can achieve an average improvement of 5% while ours can only achieve an improvement of about 1.3%. This is maybe because we use the same settings and hyper-parameters in all Medical VQA experiments, either for general models or for dedicated models. In other words, the performance of our dedicated models could be further improved if we use customized setting and hyper-parameters for each dedicated model.

As shown in Table 2, we compare PLMVQA with some recent methods on SLAKE-EN dataset. PLMVQA outperforms other methods with a large margin of at least 1.6% under the general model setting and at least 0.9% under the dedicated model setting. Undoubtedly, these promising results demonstrate the effectiveness of the proposed PLMVQA, though we only utilize limited data from Medical VQA datasets.

Table 2. Performance comparison on SLAKE-EN test set.

Methods	External Data	General Models	Dedicated Models	Accuracy		
				Open	Closed	Overall
PubmedCLIP [5]	80K	✓		76.5	80.4	78.0
CPRD [15]	20K	✓		79.5	83.4	81.1
PLMVQA	-	✓		79.4	85.6	81.8
PLMVQA-PL	-	✓		**79.7**	**87.3**	**82.7**
CR [26]	10K		✓	78.8	82.0	80.0
PubmedCLIP* [5]	80K		✓	78.4	82.5	80.1
CPRD* [15]	20K		✓	**81.2**	83.4	82.1
PLMVQA-PL*	-		✓	80.0	**87.7**	**83.0**

4.4 Ablation Study

As shown in Table 3, to analyze the impact of pseudo labels applied in PLMVQA, we conduct an ablation study on the SLAKE-EN dataset under the general model setting. To adjust the proportion of pseudo-label prediction in the multi-task learning process. We set the balancing hyper-parameter α increasingly from 0 to 1. When α is set to 0.1, even if the proportion of pseudo-label prediction is small, the performance has been improved. When we set α to 0.5, PLMVQA obtains the best performance with a large improvement of 0.9% in overall accuracy. When α increases to 1, though the performance has a slight drop, it still outperforms the model without applying pseudo labels. This result verifies the effectiveness of our proposed methods again. In addition, we note that with the increase of α, the performance continues to promote on closed-type questions with fewer classes while drops on open-type questions with more classes. Besides, the improvement on closed-type questions is larger than that on open-type. This is maybe because our current pseudo labels only have 17 refined classes, which brings performance limitations to the more complicated open-type questions, indicating more diversity and classes should be involved in pseudo labels.

Table 3. Ablation study on the SLAKE-EN dataset.

α	Accuracy		
	Open	Closed	Overall
0	79.4	85.6	81.8
0.1	**79.8**	85.6	82.1
0.5	79.7	87.3	**82.7**
1	78.9	**87.7**	82.4

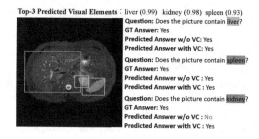

Fig. 2. Qualitative analysis of PLMVQA.

4.5 Qualitative Analysis

As shown in Fig. 2, we provide the qualitative analysis of our proposed method. Given an abdomen MRI image, the pseudo-label prediction model first extracts pseudo labels and we show the top-3 classes of `liver`, `kidney` and `spleen` with high confidence. We note that both PLMVQA with and without applying pseudo labels can locate the prominent organ such as the liver in the given radiology image. However, when the image has multiple organs at the same time, PLMVQA w/o pseudo-labels will neglect the minor organ that appeared such as the kidney. On the contrary, PLMVQA with pseudo-labels can accurately locate both relevant tokens in the question and right organs in the image including the minor one. This result not only demonstrates the effectiveness of our method but also presents our model with high interpretability.

5   Conclusion

In this paper, we proposed a novel Medical VQA framework called PLMVQA, which is based on ViT. By applying pseudo labels of visual elements embodied in limited Medical VQA datasets, even if we do not use any external medical image data to pre-train the model, PLMVQA still achieves better performance on two commonly used Medical VQA datasets with high interpretability compared to other methods relying heavily on large amounts of external data.

References

1. Abacha, A.B., Gayen, S., Lau, J., Rajaraman, S., Demner-Fushman, D.: NLM at imageCLEF 2018 visual question answering in the medical domain. In: CLEF (Working Notes) (2018)
2. Chen, Z., et al.: Multi-modal masked autoencoders for medical vision-and-language pre-training. In: MICCAI. LNCS, vol. 13435, pp. 679–689. Springer, Cham (2022). https://doi.org/10.1007/978-3-031-16443-9_65
3. Do, T., Nguyen, B.X., Tjiputra, E., Tran, M., Tran, Q.D., Nguyen, A.: Multiple meta-model quantifying for medical visual question answering. In: de Bruijne, M., et al. (eds.) MICCAI 2021. LNCS, vol. 12905, pp. 64–74. Springer, Cham (2021). https://doi.org/10.1007/978-3-030-87240-3_7

4. Dosovitskiy, A., et al.: An image is worth 16x16 words: transformers for image recognition at scale. In: ICLR (2021)

5. Eslami, S., de Melo, G., Meinel, C.: Does CLIP benefit visual question answering in the medical domain as much as it does in the general domain? CoRR abs/2112.13906 (2021)

6. Fukui, A., Park, D.H., Yang, D., Rohrbach, A., Darrell, T., Rohrbach, M.: Multimodal compact bilinear pooling for visual question answering and visual grounding. EMNLP abs/1606.01847, pp. 457–468 (2016)

7. Gong, H., Chen, G., Liu, S., Yu, Y., Li, G.: Cross-modal self-attention with multi-task pre-training for medical visual question answering. In: ICMR, pp. 456–460. ACM (2021)

8. He, K., Zhang, X., Ren, S., Sun, J.: Deep residual learning for image recognition. In: CVPR, pp. 770–778 (2016)

9. Johnson, M., et al.: Google's multilingual neural machine translation system: enabling zero-shot translation. Trans. Assoc. Comput. Linguistics 5, 339–351 (2017)

10. Khare, Y., Bagal, V., Mathew, M., Devi, A., Priyakumar, U.D., Jawahar, C.V.: MMBERT: multimodal BERT pretraining for improved medical VQA. In: ISBI, pp. 1033–1036. IEEE (2021)

11. Kim, J., Jun, J., Zhang, B.: Bilinear attention networks. In: Bengio, S., Wallach, H.M., Larochelle, H., Grauman, K., Cesa-Bianchi, N., Garnett, R. (eds.) NIPS, pp. 1571–1581 (2018)

12. Kim, W., Son, B., Kim, I.: ViLT: vision-and-language transformer without convolution or region supervision. In: ICML (2021)

13. Lau, J., Gayen, S., Abacha, A.B., Demner-Fushman, D.: A dataset of clinically generated visual questions and answers about radiology images. Sci. Data 5 (2018)

14. Liu, B., Zhan, L.M., Xu, L., Ma, L., Yang, Y., Wu, X.M.: SLAKE: a semantically-labeled knowledge-enhanced dataset for medical visual question answering. In: 2021 IEEE 18th International Symposium on Biomedical Imaging (ISBI), pp. 1650–1654 (2021)

15. Liu, B., Zhan, L.-M., Wu, X.-M.: Contrastive pre-training and representation distillation for medical visual question answering based on radiology images. In: de Bruijne, M., et al. (eds.) MICCAI 2021. LNCS, vol. 12902, pp. 210–220. Springer, Cham (2021). https://doi.org/10.1007/978-3-030-87196-3_20

16. Loshchilov, I., Hutter, F.: Decoupled weight decay regularization. In: ICLR. OpenReview.net (2019)

17. Moon, J.H., Lee, H., Shin, W., Choi, E.: Multi-modal understanding and generation for medical images and text via vision-language pre-training. CoRR (2021)

18. Naseer, M., Ranasinghe, K., Khan, S.H., Hayat, M., Khan, F.S., Yang, M.: Intriguing properties of vision transformers. CoRR abs/2105.10497 (2021)

19. Nguyen, B.D., Do, T.-T., Nguyen, B.X., Do, T., Tjiputra, E., Tran, Q.D.: Overcoming data limitation in medical visual question answering. In: Shen, D., et al. (eds.) MICCAI 2019. LNCS, vol. 11767, pp. 522–530. Springer, Cham (2019). https://doi.org/10.1007/978-3-030-32251-9_57

20. Peng, Y., Liu, F.: UMass at ImageCLEF medical visual question answering (Med-VQA) 2018 task. In: CLEF (2018)

21. Russakovsky, O., et al.: ImageNet large scale visual recognition challenge. IJCV 115, 211–252 (2015)

22. Shi, L., Liu, F., Rosen, M.P.: Deep multimodal learning for medical visual question answering. In: CLEF (2019)

23. Simonyan, K., Zisserman, A.: Very deep convolutional networks for large-scale image recognition. In: Bengio, Y., LeCun, Y. (eds.) ICLR (2015)
24. Yan, X., Li, L., Xie, C., Xiao, J., Gu, L.: Zhejiang University at ImageCLEF 2019 visual question answering in the medical domain. In: CLEF (2019)
25. Yang, Z., He, X., Gao, J., Deng, L., Smola, A.J.: Stacked attention networks for image question answering. In: CVPR, pp. 21–29 (2016)
26. Zhan, L., Liu, B., Fan, L., Chen, J., Wu, X.: Medical visual question answering via conditional reasoning. In: ACM MM, pp. 2345–2354. ACM (2020)

SAM-U: Multi-box Prompts Triggered Uncertainty Estimation for Reliable SAM in Medical Image

Guoyao Deng[1], Ke Zou[1,3], Kai Ren[2], Meng Wang[3], Xuedong Yuan[2], Sancong Ying[2(✉)], and Huazhu Fu[3]

[1] National Key Laboratory of Fundamental Science on Synthetic Vision, Sichuan University, Sichuan, China
[2] College of Computer Science, Sichuan University, Sichuan, China
yingsancong@scu.edu.cn
[3] Institute of High Performance Computing, Agency for Science, Technology and Research, Singapore, Singapore

Abstract. Recently, Segmenting Anything Model has taken a significant step towards general artificial intelligence. Simultaneously, its reliability and fairness have garnered significant attention, particularly in the field of healthcare. In this study, we propose a multi-box prompt-triggered uncertainty estimation for SAM cues to demonstrate the reliability of segmented lesions or tissues. We estimate the distribution of SAM predictions using Monte Carlo with prior distribution parameters, employing different prompts as a formulation of test-time augmentation. Our experimental results demonstrate that multi-box prompts augmentation enhances SAM performance and provides uncertainty for each pixel. This presents a groundbreaking paradigm for a reliable SAM.

Keywords: Segmenting Anything · reliability · uncertainty estimation · prompt learning

1 Introduction

Large-scale foundation models are increasingly gaining popularity among artificial intelligence researchers. In the realm of natural language processing (NLP), the Generative Pre-trained Transformer (GPT) [1] and ChatGPT, developed by OpenAI, have witnessed rapid growth owing to their exceptional ability to generalize. These models have found applications in diverse domains such as autonomous driving and healthcare. The remarkable generalization capabilities of large models often instill a sense of trust among users; however, their fairness and reliability have also been subject to some degree of scrutiny.

Nowadays, there is a growing wave of enthusiasm surrounding computer vision due to the release of the Segment Anything Model (SAM) [2] by Meta AI. SAM has been trained on a massive SA-1B dataset, which consists of over 11 million images and one billion masks, making it an excellent tool. It excels at

J. Woo et al. (Eds.): MICCAI 2023 Workshops, LNCS 14394, pp. 368–377, 2023.
https://doi.org/10.1007/978-3-031-47425-5_33

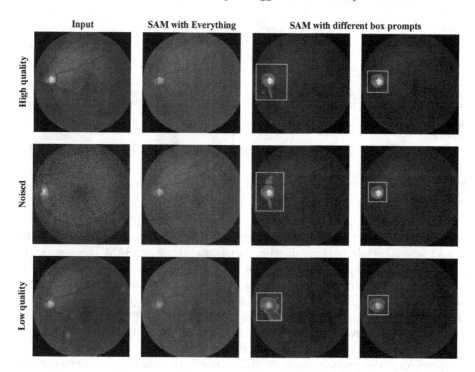

Fig. 1. Prediction results of different quality fundus images in SAM's "everything" and "box" modes.

producing accurate segmentation results from various types of prompts, including foreground/background points, thick boxes or masks, and free-form text. The introduction of SAM has led many researchers to believe that general artificial intelligence has finally arrived. However, some researchers have expressed concerns about the performance of SAM [3–7]. Specifically, they have identified areas such as industrial defect detection [4,5], camouflaged target detection [3–5], and tumor and lesion segmentation [3,6,7] in medical images where further improvements are needed. Additionally, the reliability of SAM still requires further study.

Uncertainty estimation [8] is one of the ways to provide reliability for SAM. Previously, uncertainty estimation has demonstrated its reliability and robustness in several medical segmentation tasks [9,10], including skin lesions and brain tumors [11], among others. The current uncertainty estimation methods can be roughly divided into deterministic-based methods [12,13], Bayesian Neural Network-based methods [14], ensemble-based methods [15], dropout-based methods [8,16,17] and test-time augmentation-based methods [18]. The focus of this paper is to keep the simplicity and retain the original structure of SAM while achieving pixel-level uncertainty estimation.

In Fig. 1, we present the eye disc segmentation results [19] for both high and low-quality fundus images under different conditions. SAM demonstrates better

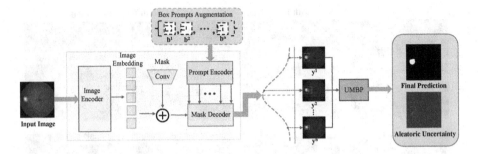

Fig. 2. The overall framework of SAM-U. "U" stands for the ability of uncertainty estimation.

segmentation results for high-quality images, and the inclusion of different conditions leads to certain performance improvements. However, SAM's segmentation results for lower quality images are not satisfactory. Nevertheless, the inclusion of different conditions greatly enhances its performance, particularly with more accurate box prompts. Furthermore, we have observed a phenomenon wherein different levels of box prompts tend to yield diverse results. This observation motivates us to introduce a novel approach, namely multi-box prompts-induced uncertainty estimation, for medical images.

Therefore, the primary focus of this paper is to enhance the segmentation accuracy by employing multiple box prompts. This approach enables us to establish pixel-level reliability through uncertainty estimation. Specifically, we utilize SAM to predict the output distribution using different multi-box prompts. SAM with multi-box prompts generates numerous samples from the predictive distribution. Subsequently, these samples are used to calculate variance, which provide an uncertainty estimation for the medical image segmentation. Our experiments demonstrate that multi-box prompts not only enhances performance on low-quality medical images but also provides uncertainty estimation for them.

2   Method

The overall framework of our proposed method is depicted in Fig. 2. Our main focus is to enhance the reliability and accuracy of SAM in the context of zero-shot learning. To improve the accuracy of SAM, we incorporate multi-box prompts, which enable us to obtain more precise medical image segmentation results from the distribution. Specifically, we estimate the distribution of SAM predictions using Monte Carlo simulation with prior distribution parameters. This approach allows our method to estimate the aleatoric uncertainty by considering multiple forecasts for a single medical image.

2.1   Mask Selection Strategy

Under the "everything" mode, SAM generates multiple binary masks and can pop out several potential objects within an input. For a fair evaluation of interesting regions in a specific segmentation task, we follow the strategy of [4] to select the most appropriate mask based on its ground-truth mask. Formally, given M binary predictions $\{y^i\}_i^M = 1$ and the ground-truth G for an input image, we calculate $Dice$ scores for each pair to generate a set of evaluation scores $\{D^i\}_i^M = 1$. We finally select the mask with the highest $Dice$ score.

2.2 SAM with Multi-box Prompts

Prompts can introduce errors into the model's inferring due to their inherent inaccuracies. In order to reduce the influence of the variance of the prompt. We randomize N box prompts $B = \{b^1, b^2, \cdots, b^N\}$. Each box prompt guides SAM generates different segmentation results. Through this strategy, we obtain the predictions $Y = \{y^1, y^2, \cdots, y^N\}$ of SAM under different prior cues, and combining them can improve the segmentation accuracy of SAM and reduce uncertainty. The combined prediction is computed as:

$$\hat{y} = \frac{1}{N} \sum_{i=1}^{N} f_{SAM}\left(I, b^i\right), \tag{1}$$

where y_C denotes the combined prediction of $image I$.

2.3 Uncertainty Estimation of SAM with Multi-box Prompts

Different box prompts cause variances in SAM's segmentation even if they refer to one object in human's view. Inspired by this, our proposed multi-box prompts algorithm simulates the annotations of multiple clinical experts to generate the final predictions and uncertainty estimations. To quantify the uncertainty triggered by multi-box prompts. Assume N box prompts $B = \{b^1, b^2, \cdots, b^N\}$ that all refers to the ground truth. With N box prompts and input image I, SAM generate a set of predictions $Y = \{y^1, y^2, \cdots, y^N\}$. As shown in Fig. 3, We present an uncertainty estimation procedure for multi-box prompts.

We first describe aleatoric uncertainty from a single given image I by the entropy [20]:

$$U(y^i) = -\int p(y^i|I) \log p(y^i|I) dy, \tag{2}$$

$U(y^i)$ estimates how diverse the prediction y^i for the image I. Where $y^i = \{p_1^i, p_2^i, \cdots, p_K^i\}$ denote the prediction pixels. K denotes the unique values in y^i. Then we run a Monte Carlo simulation using multi-box prompts to obtain a set of predictions. Therefore, the uncertainty distribution is approximated as follows:

$$U(Y|I) \approx \sum_{i=1}^{N} \sum_{j=1}^{K} p_j^i \log p_j^i, \tag{3}$$

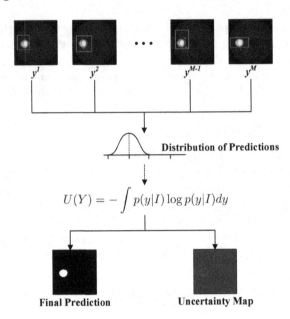

$$U(Y) = -\int p(y|I)\log p(y|I)dy$$

Fig. 3. The uncertainty distribution approximated by Monte Carlo Simulation.

3   Experiments and Results

Two different methods are utilized to perform image degradation to verify the reliability of SAM. In this section, we will describe our evaluation protocols, compare the performance of SAM under different quality datasets, and visualize the qualitative results on fundus image segmentation.

3.1   Data and Implementation Details

All the data are used for evaluation. And our method does not need nay additional training. The N is set to 20 for our experiment. Box prompts are generated based on the area and size of Ground Truth, and the length and width of the box are randomly adjusted to mimic the manually provided box prompt.

3.2   Evaluation Protocols

- **Dataset.** We chose the sub-task of the REFUGE Challenge [21], which does the segmentation of the optic cup and disc in fundus photographs. For simplicity's sake, we consider disc and cup as one category. In order to evaluate the reliability of SAM more objectively, we artificially constructed low-quality data based on high-quality source data by two different methods, which is introducing Gaussian noise with various levels of standard deviations (σ) and the realistic degradation model proposed by *Shen et al.* [22], respectively.

Table 1. Quantitative results of high-quality fundus images in SAM's "everything" and "box" modes. SAM[1], SAM[2] and SAM[3] mean using "everything", "box", and "our" modes, respectively.

Model	Backbone	Dice↑	ECE↓	Sm↑	wFm↑
SAM[1]	ViT-B	0.436	0.050	0.394	0.436
	ViT-L	0.438	0.050	0..394	0.438
	ViT-H	0.441	0.049	0.394	0.441
SAM[2]	ViT-B	0.533	0.016	0.404	0.533
	Difference (Δ)	0.097	-0.034	0.01	0.097
	ViT-L	0.739	0.014	0.408	0.739
	Difference (Δ)	0.301	-0.036	0.014	0.301
	ViT-H	0.691	0.020	0.406	0.691
	Difference (Δ)	0.25	-0.029	0.012	0.25
SAM[3]	ViT-B	0.538	0.016	0.404	0.538
	Difference (Δ)	0.102	-0.034	0.010	0.102
	ViT-L	0.751	0.013	0.408	0.751
	Difference (Δ)	0.313	-0.037	0.014	0.313
	ViT-H	0.718	0.017	0.407	0.718
	Difference (Δ)	0.277	-0.032	0.013	0.277

- **Metrics.** We use four commonly-used metrics for the evaluation: *dice* score (*Dice*), expected calibration error (ECE) [23], structure measure (Sm) [24] and weighted F-measure (wFm) [25].

3.3 Quantitative Evaluation

As shown in Table 1, we present different segmentation results of SAM modes using high-quality medical images. Initially, we compare the segmentation results of SAM in "everything" mode and SAM in "box" mode on normal medical images. It was found that the results using SAM in "box" mode were superior. Moreover, with the introduction of our algorithm, the performance of SAM improved further. Table 2 and Table 3 demonstrate various segmentation results of SAM modes under Gaussian noise and degraded medical images. We compare the results obtained from the aforementioned SAM modes. The performance of SAM in "everything" mode and SAM in "box" mode has declined, whereas the performance of SAM with "multi-box" mode remains at a certain level, with a lower ECE index. Therefore, it can be concluded that the inclusion of multi-box prompts enhances the accuracy and reliability of SAM.

3.4 Qualitative Comparison

As shown in Fig. 4, we first show the uncertainty estimation results under SAM with multi-box mode. As can be seen from it, the periphery of the eye disc is

Table 2. Results on two different situations in which we add Gaussian Noise that $\sigma = 0.05$ and $\sigma = 0.10$.

Model	BackBone	$\sigma = 0.05$				$\sigma = 0.10$			
		Dice	ECE	SM	FM	Dice	ECE	SM	FM
SAM[1]	ViT_B	0.293	0.180	0.552	0.293	0.214	0.318	0.447	0.214
	ViT_L	0.461	0.106	0.667	0.461	0.387	0.266	0.562	0.387
	ViT_H	0.496	0.109	0.680	0.496	0.427	0.171	0.622	0.427
SAM[2]	ViT_B	0.397	0.025	0.621	0.397	0.375	0.030	0.610	0.375
	Difference(Δ)	0.104	-0.155	0.069	0.104	0.161	-0.288	0.163	0.161
	ViT_L	0.700	0.014	0.792	0.700	0.659	0.018	0.761	0.659
	Difference(Δ)	0.239	-0.092	0.125	0.239	0.272	-0.248	0.199	0.272
	ViT_H	0.685	0.017	0.799	0.685	0.665	0.020	0.789	0.665
	Difference(Δ)	0.189	-0.092	0.119	0.189	0.278	-0.246	0.227	0.278
SAM[3]	ViT_B	0.416	0.022	0.633	0.417	0.399	0.025	0.621	0.399
	Difference(Δ)	0.123	-0.158	0.081	0.124	0.185	-0.293	0.174	0.185
	ViT_L	0.726	0.012	0.808	0.726	0.690	0.015	0.779	0.690
	Difference(Δ)	0.265	-0.094	0.141	0.265	0.303	-0.251	0.217	0.303
	ViT_H	0.711	0.014	0.814	0.711	0.710	0.016	0.817	0.710
	Difference(Δ)	0.215	-0.095	0.134	0.215	0.283	-0.155	0.195	0.283

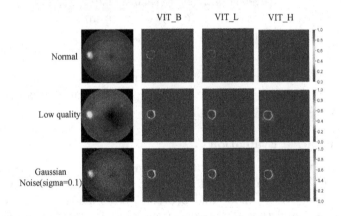

Fig. 4. Uncertainty distributions of the same sample under different states estimated by multi-box prompts.

clearly marked as an area of uncertainty. Furthermore, we compare the results of the segmentation of different modes of SAM under normal and degraded medical images, as shown in Fig. 5. In SAM with "everything" mode, it is difficult to segment the eye disc. Under the box prompt, the eye disc can be segmented under normal conditions, but the results under Gaussian noise and degraded images are not satisfactory. While our method also achieves better segmentation results in degraded images and provides weights for uncertain pixels. This opens a new paradigm for SAM towards robust and reliable medical image segmentation.

Table 3. Results on LQ dataset. The realistic degradation model proposed by *Shen et al.* [22] can generate 7 kinds of low-quality images from '000' to '111' based on the high-quality image. We chose the two that look most different from the original image to the naked eye.

Model	BackBone	"101"				"111"			
		Dice	ECE	SM	FM	Dice	ECE	SM	FM
SAM[1]	ViT_B	0.386	0.222	0.578	0.386	0.396	0.078	0.646	0.396
	ViT_L	0.470	0.130	0.663	0.470	0.465	0.075	0.685	0.465
	ViT_H	0.520	0.126	0.690	0.520	0.505	0.087	0.698	0.505
SAM[2]	ViT_B	0.542	0.019	0.713	0.542	0.541	0.021	0.715	0.541
	Difference(Δ)	0.156	-0.203	0.135	0.156	0.145	-0.057	0.069	0.145
	ViT_L	0.679	0.018	0.773	0.679	0.684	0.020	0.778	0.684
	Difference(Δ)	0.209	-0.012	0.110	0.209	0.219	-0.055	0.093	0.219
	ViT_H	0.596	0.031	0.746	0.596	0.589	0.032	0.742	0.589
	Difference(Δ)	0.076	-0.095	0.056	0.076	0.084	-0.055	0.044	0.084
SAM[3]	ViT_B	0.564	0.016	0.726	0.564	0.566	0.017	0.729	0.566
	Difference(Δ)	0.178	-0.206	0.148	0.178	0.170	-0.061	0.083	0.170
	ViT_L	0.706	0.017	0.793	0.706	0.700	0.018	0.789	0.700
	Difference(Δ)	0.236	-0.113	0.130	0.236	0.235	-0.057	0.104	0.235
	ViT_H	0.628	0.027	0.767	0.628	0.622	0.028	0.763	0.622
	Difference(Δ)	0.108	-0.099	0.077	0.108	0.117	-0.059	0.065	0.117

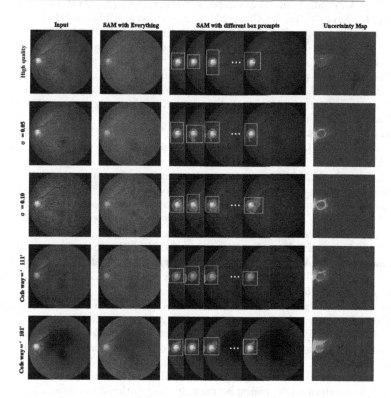

Fig. 5. Qualitative results of different quality fundus images in SAM's "everything" and "box" modes.

4   Discussion and Conclusion

In this paper, we investigated the segmentation performance of SAM on fundus images. The results have shown that the box prompt significantly improves the segmentation, but different box prompts lead to variations in predictions. The main method proposed in this paper, prompt augmentation, can help estimate the variations by aleatoric uncertainty and produce an uncertainty distribution map that highlights challenging areas for segmentation. The uncertainty map not only improves the segmentation process and final results, but also enables the development of more advanced methods for segmenting fundus images. Moreover, the uncertainty map offers valuable guidance in areas where manual annotation is required. The feature of using the uncertainty distribution map for guiding segmentation and improving accuracy is noteworthy. Furthermore, the uncertainty map can help identify possible segmentation errors and support further analysis, providing useful information for clinicians.

References

1. Floridi, L., Chiriatti, M.: GPT-3: its nature, scope, limits, and consequences. Mind. Mach. **30**, 681–694 (2020)
2. Kirillov, A., et al.: Segment anything. arXiv preprint arXiv:2304.02643 (2023)
3. Tang, L., Xiao, H., Li, B.: Can SAM segment anything? When SAM meets camouflaged object detection. arXiv preprint arXiv:2304.04709 (2023)
4. Ji, G.-P., Fan, D.-P., Xu, P., Cheng, M.-M., Zhou, B., Van Gool, L.: SAM struggles in concealed scenes-empirical study on "segment anything". arXiv preprint arXiv:2304.06022 (2023)
5. Ji, W., Li, J., Bi, Q., Li, W., Cheng, L.: Segment anything is not always perfect: an investigation of SAM on different real-world applications. arXiv preprint arXiv:2304.05750 (2023)
6. Sheng, H., Rina, B., Jingpeng, L., Ellen, G.P., Yangming, O.: Accuracy of segment-anything model (SAM) in medical image segmentation tasks. arXiv preprint arXiv:2304.09324 (2023)
7. Roy, S., et al.: SAM.MD: zero-shot medical image segmentation capabilities of the segment anything model. arXiv preprint arXiv:2304.05396 (2023)
8. Gal, Y., Ghahramani, Z.: Dropout as a Bayesian approximation: representing model uncertainty in deep learning. In: International Conference on Machine Learning, pp. 1050–1059. PMLR (2016)
9. Zou, K., Yuan, X., Shen, X., Wang, M., Fu, H.: TBraTS: trusted brain tumor segmentation. In: Wang, L., Dou, Q., Fletcher, P.T., Speidel, S., Li, S. (eds.) MICCAI 2022, vol. 13438, pp. 503–513. Springer, Cham (2022). https://doi.org/10.1007/978-3-031-16452-1_48
10. Zou, K., et al.: EvidenceCap: towards trustworthy medical image segmentation via evidential identity cap. arXiv preprint arXiv:2301.00349 (2023)
11. Li, H., Nan, Y., Del Ser, J., Yang, G.: Region-based evidential deep learning to quantify uncertainty and improve robustness of brain tumor segmentation. Neural Comput. Appl., 1–15 (2022)
12. Van Amersfoort, J., Smith, L., Teh, Y.W., Gal, Y.: Uncertainty estimation using a single deep deterministic neural network. In: International Conference on Machine Learning, pp. 9690–9700. PMLR (2020)

13. Liu, J.Z., Lin, Z., Padhy, S., Tran, D., Bedrax-Weiss, T., Lakshminarayanan, B.: Simple and principled uncertainty estimation with deterministic deep learning via distance awareness. In: Proceedings of the 34th International Conference on Neural Information Processing Systems (2020)

14. Roy, A.G., Conjeti, S., Navab, N., Wachinger, C., Initiative, A.D.N., et al.: Bayesian quickNAT: model uncertainty in deep whole-brain segmentation for structure-wise quality control. Neuroimage **195**, 11–22 (2019)

15. Lakshminarayanan, B., Pritzel, A., Blundell, C.: Simple and scalable predictive uncertainty estimation using deep ensembles. In: Advances in Neural Information Processing Systems, vol. 30 (2017)

16. Kendall, A., Gal, Y.: What uncertainties do we need in Bayesian deep learning for computer vision? In: NIPS (2017)

17. Nair, T., Precup, D., Arnold, D.L., Arbel, T.: Exploring uncertainty measures in deep networks for multiple sclerosis lesion detection and segmentation. Med. Image Anal. **59**, 101557 (2020)

18. Wang, G., Li, W., Ourselin, S., Vercauteren, T.: Automatic brain tumor segmentation using convolutional neural networks with test-time augmentation. In: Crimi, A., Bakas, S., Kuijf, H., Keyvan, F., Reyes, M., van Walsum, T. (eds.) BrainLes 2018. LNCS, vol. 11384, pp. 61–72. Springer, Cham (2019). https://doi.org/10.1007/978-3-030-11726-9_6

19. Fu, H., Cheng, J., Xu, Y., Wong, D.W.K., Liu, J., Cao, X.: Joint optic disc and cup segmentation based on multi-label deep network and polar transformation. IEEE Trans. Med. Imaging **37**(7), 1597–1605 (2018)

20. Bein, B.: Entropy. Best Pract. Res. Clin. Anaesthesiol. **20**(1), 101–109 (2006)

21. Orlando, J.I., et al.: REFUGE Challenge: a unified framework for evaluating automated methods for glaucoma assessment from fundus photographs. Med. Image Anal. **59**, 101570 (2020)

22. Shen, Z., Fu, H., Shen, J., Shao, L.: Modeling and enhancing low-quality retinal fundus images. IEEE Trans. Med. Imaging **40**(3), 996–1006 (2020)

23. Guo, C., Pleiss, G., Sun, Y., Weinberger, K.Q.: On calibration of modern neural networks. In: International Conference on Machine Learning, pp. 1321–1330. PMLR (2017)

24. Fan, D.-P., Cheng, M.-M., Liu, Y., Li, T., Borji, A.: Structure-measure: a new way to evaluate foreground maps. In: Proceedings of the IEEE International Conference on Computer Vision, pp. 4548–4557 (2017)

25. Margolin, R., Zelnik-Manor, L., Tal, A.: How to evaluate foreground maps? In: Proceedings of the IEEE Conference on Computer Vision and Pattern Recognition, pp. 248–255 (2014)

Author Index

J. Woo et al. (Eds.): MICCAI 2023 Workshops, LNCS 14394, pp. 379–381, 2023.
https://doi.org/10.1007/978-3-031-47425-5

Printed in the United States
by Baker & Taylor Publisher Services